American Thought and Writing: The 1890's

Riverside Editions

Under the General Editorship of Gordon N. Ray

American
Thought and Writing:
The 1890's

Edited by

Donald Pizer

Newcomb College, Tulane University

Houghton Mifflin Company   Boston

New York   Atlanta   *Geneva, Ill.*   Dallas   *Palo Alto*

Cover

Left to Right:

Stephen Crane	Courtesy of The George Arents Research Library at Syracuse University
Frank Norris	The Bettmann Archive
Hamlin Garland	The Bettmann Archive
Theodore Dreiser	The Bettmann Archive

Printed in the U.S.A.

Library of Congress Catalog Card Number: 76–177497

ISBN: 0–395–13493–5

Contents

v

PART FIVE: THE CITY

PART SIX: THE SOCIAL CRISIS

Preface

A DECADE IS an arbitrary and artificial historical unit because events and lives are of longer or shorter duration and because ten years as a moment in time has no greater historical significance than nine or eleven years. The *idea* of a decade, however, has a psychological and intellectual reality which can affect the thinking and actions of those living within the period. This responsiveness is especially true of decades at the close of centuries when there is often a sense of both climax and beginning, of death and new life. Moreover, to the historian a decade is a convenient unit of time. It is a period—shorter than a generation but longer than a year—in which he can attempt to describe those threads of relationship and coherence in events and ideas which we call history.

The American 1890's have attracted a number of literary and social historians—among them Thomas Beer, Grant C. Knight, Harold U. Faulkner, and Larzer Ziff. Most writers about the period are substantially in agreement with Harold Faulkner's belief that the 1890's were distinguished less by major social changes than by a full realization of changes which had already occurred—in particular, the change from a predominantly rural, agrarian civilization to an urban, industrial society. The problem presented by this realization was that many of the values and beliefs nurtured by the old ways of life seemed obsolete or inapplicable within the new. At one time literary historians tended to describe the thought of the period as bleakly pessimistic, or "naturalistic," because of the response by many of the younger writers of the decade to this incongruity. It was then only dimly perceived that the challenge of the new did not cause a complete dismissal of the old but, rather, an often unconscious attempt to maintain the viability of traditional values by expressing them within new and radical themes and forms.

Of course, the American 1890's cannot be summarized by any one generalization. Scholars and critics have labored at length to sort out the complex patterns of thought and expression characteristic of this particularly rich decade in the history of the American mind and imagination. All of this writing has been discursive—that is, it is formal history. The present book is an innovation in that it consists almost entirely of material selected from the works of writers of the decade. My own commentary is limited to brief introductions to the various sections of the collection. Nevertheless, my interpretation of the period controls and structures every phase of the book. For instead of arranging the selections chronologically or by author or genre, or confining myself to the best writing by the best authors, I have selected and arranged the material in order to cast light on those aspects of thought and expression which I believe characterize the major issues and preoccupations of the age. By this method I have sought not merely to "illustrate" the age—as in a documentary history—but to reveal through juxtaposition those beliefs (often covertly represented by imagery or by other aspects of rhetoric or form) which constitute the felt response of a writer to the major issues of his time.

A further word about my selections is necessary. Although the bulk of the material was written in the 1890's, I have not held to a strict chronological limitation. Some of William Dean Howells' essays from *Criticism and Fiction* (1891), for example, appeared originally in the late 1880's, and Frank Norris' story "Dying Fires" was written and published in 1902. I have included some items, such as a chapter from Ward McAllister's *Society as I Have Found It*, primarily for their subject matter; but in general I have attempted to combine pertinence and literary quality. Thus, the work of Stephen Crane, Frank Norris, Hamlin Garland, and Theodore Dreiser—the principal new writers of the 1890's—appears frequently, and there is at least one selection from almost every significant literary figure of the decade. Important exceptions are the absence of any work by Henry James and the presence of only one selection by Mark Twain. Both authors produced copiously during the period, but as studies by Robert Falk and Harold Kolb have demonstrated, their writing is best approached in connection with earlier decades.

Finally, some comments about my choice of texts and about documentation. I have for the most part used the text of first book publication, though in some instances the availability of a fuller or more reliable text has led me to choose initial magazine publication or a modern edited text. In my opening note to each selection I cite its earliest appearance (when known) and the text I am reproducing. I also include in this note any information necessary to grasp the general historical context of the selection. I have kept annotation to a minimum, confining myself to information without which the general reader would be adrift. Material omitted from a selection is indicated by asterisks. Since a number of authors included in the collection are represented more than once, I have brought together all biographical notes in the form of a biographical glossary at the close of the book. The reader will also find there a brief chronology of the major social, political, and literary events of the decade and a selected bibliography of writings about the period.

Donald Pizer

Part One

BELIEF

For most educated men of the 1890's, Darwinism was no longer a controversial issue. Evolution was a fact of life, and the Bible and theology were viewed as products of particular historical moments. But though traditional religious faith was moribund, God was far from dead. The most significant writing about belief during the decade often began with a rejection of formal religion and concluded with an affirmation of religious values. Herbert Spencer of course played a major role in encouraging this attitude toward faith. His Synthetic Philosophy was grounded upon evolutionary science, but it also acknowledged both the existence of an "Unknowable" beyond human perception and the evolution of man's psychic nature—or soul —as well as his body. As the essay by John Fiske demonstrates, with Spencer as a guide one could not only reconcile Evolution and Christianity but also use the first to affirm the second.

Lyman Abbott, a clergyman, thus had little difficulty in finding that

1

evolutionary ideas and Christian values were interdependent. And even though John Burroughs and William James explicitly rejected formal Christianity when discussing the supernatural they could, nevertheless, exploit a rhetoric of awe and affirmation which brings them close to traditional faith. Because their ideas were otherwise so diverse, Burroughs and James revealed the major tendency in religious writing of the decade. For while one discovered a God in and above Nature and the other vigorously opposed this concept, both asserted the need for and the efficacy of belief.

For other writers, however, need was more than matched by a sense of quest unfulfilled. The "Light" of E. A. Robinson and the "Blue Battalions" of Stephen Crane are conventional images of a God of knowledge and of militant power, but they appear in a context of doubt and ambiguity rather than of personal victory.

The nineties were thus still an age of belief. But the shift by almost all writers from direct avowal to indirect affirmation through symbol and metaphor (Nature, the Will, the Blue Battalions) suggests that the emotional need for faith had become the principal, if not the only, basis of its survival.

John Fiske
The Doctrine of Evolution:
Its Scope and Purport

IT WAS NOT STRANGE that among the younger men whose opinions were moulded between 1830 and 1840 there should have been one of organizing genius, with a mind inexhaustibly fertile in suggestions, who should undertake to elaborate a general doctrine of evolution, to embrace in one grand coherent system of generalizations all the minor generalizations which workers in different departments of

Given as an address before the Brooklyn Ethical Association, May 31, 1891. Published in A Century of Science and Other Essays (Boston, 1899). Text from The Miscellaneous Writings of John Fiske (Boston, 1902), X, 37–60.

science were establishing. It is this prodigious work of construction that we owe to Herbert Spencer. He is the originator and author of what we know to-day as the doctrine of evolution, the doctrine which undertakes to formulate and put into scientific shape the conception of evolution towards which scientific investigation had so long been tending. In the mind of the general public there seems to be dire confusion with regard to Mr. Spencer and his relations to evolution and to Darwinism. Sometimes, I believe, he is even supposed to be chiefly a follower and expounder of Mr. Darwin! No doubt this is because so many people mix up Darwinism with the doctrine of evolution, and have but the vaguest and haziest notions as to what it is all about. Mr. Darwin's great work was the discovery of natural selection, and the demonstration of its agency in effecting specific changes in plants and animals; and in that work he was completely original. But plants and animals are only a part of the universe, though an important part, and with regard to universal evolution or any universal formula for evolution Darwinism had nothing to say. Such problems were beyond its scope.

The discovery of a universal formula for evolution, and the application of this formula to many diverse groups of phenomena, have been the great work of Mr. Spencer, and in this he has had no predecessor. His wealth of originality is immense, and it is unquestionable. But as the most original thinker must take his start from the general stock of ideas accumulated at his epoch, and more often than not begins by following a clue given him by somebody else, so it was with Mr. Spencer when, about forty years ago, he was working out his doctrine of evolution. The clue was not given by Mr. Darwin. Darwinism was not yet born. Mr. Spencer's theory was worked out in all its parts, and many parts of it had been expounded in various published volumes and essays, before the publication of the "Origin of Species."

The clue which Mr. Spencer followed was given him by the great embryologist, Karl Ernst von Baer, and an adumbration of it may perhaps be traced back through Kaspar Friedrich Wolf to Linnæus. Hints of it may be found, too, in Goethe and in Schelling. The advance from simplicity to complexity in the development of an egg is too obvious to be overlooked by any one, and was remarked upon, I believe, by Harvey; but the analysis of what that advance consists in was a wonderfully suggestive piece of work. Baer's great book was published in 1829, just at the time when so many stimulating ideas were being enunciated, and its significant title was "Entwickelungs-geschichte," or "History of Evolution." It was well known that, so far as the senses can tell us, one ovum is indistinguishable from another, whether it be that of a man, a fish, or a parrot. The ovum is a struc-

tureless bit of organic matter, and, in acquiring structure along with
its growth in volume and mass, it proceeds through a series of differentiations, and the result is a change from homogeneity to heterogeneity. Such was Baer's conclusion, to which scanty justice is done
by such a brief statement. As all know, his work marked an epoch
in the study of embryology; for to mark the successive differentiations
in the embryos of a thousand animals was to write a thousand life
histories upon correct principles.

Here it was that Mr. Spencer started. As a young man, he was
chiefly interested in the study of political government and in history
so far as it helps the study of politics. A philosophical student of
such subjects must naturally seek for a theory of evolution. If I may
cite my own experience, it was largely the absorbing and overmaster-
ing passion for the study of history that first led me to study evolution in order to obtain a correct method. When one has frequent occasion to refer to the political and social *progress* of the human race,
one likes to know what one is talking about. Mr. Spencer needed a
theory of progress. He could see that the civilized part of mankind
has undergone some change from a bestial, unsocial, perpetually
fighting stage of savagery into a partially peaceful and comparatively
humane and social stage, and that we may reasonably hope that the
change in this direction will go on. He could see, too, that along
with this change, there has been a building-up of tribes into nations,
a division of labour, a differentiation of governmental functions, a
series of changes in the relations of the individual to the community.
To see so much as this is to whet one's craving for enlarged resources
wherewith to study human progress. Mr. Spencer had a wide, accurate, and often profound acquaintance with botany, zoölogy, and
allied studies. The question naturally occurred to him, Where do we
find the process of development most completely exemplified from
beginning to end, so that we can follow and exhaustively describe its
consecutive phases? Obviously in the development of the ovum.
There, and only there, do we get the whole process under our eyes
from the first segmentation of the yolk to the death of the matured
individual. In other groups of phenomena we can only see a small
part of what is going on; they are too vast for us, as in astronomy, or
too complicated, as in sociology. Elsewhere our evidences of development are more or less piecemeal and scattered, but in embryology
we do get, at any rate, a connected story.

So Mr. Spencer took up Baer's problem, and carried the solution of
it much further than the great Esthonian naturalist. He showed that
in the development of the ovum the change from homogeneity to
heterogeneity is accompanied by a change from indefiniteness to
definiteness; there are segregations of similarly differentiated units

resulting in the formation of definite organs. He further showed that there is a parallel and equally important change from incoherence to coherence; along with the division of labour among the units there is an organization of labour: at first, among the homogeneous units there is no subordination,—to subtract one would not alter the general aspect; but at last, among the heterogeneous organs there is such subordination and interdependence that to subtract any one is liable to undo the whole process and destroy the organism. In other words, integration is as much a feature of development as differentiation; the change is not simply from a structureless whole into parts, but it is from a structureless whole into an organized whole with a consensus of different functions, and that is what we call an organism. So while Baer said that the evolution of the chick is a change from homogeneity to heterogeneity through successive differentiations, Mr. Spencer said that the evolution of the chick is a continuous change from indefinite incoherent homogeneity to definite coherent heterogeneity through successive differentiations and integrations.

But Mr. Spencer had now done something more than describe exhaustively the evolution of an individual organism. He had got a standard of high and low degrees of organization; and the next thing in order was to apply this standard to the whole hierarchy of animals and plants according to their classified relationships and their succession in geological time. This was done with most brilliant success. From the earliest records in the rocks, the general advance in types of organization has been an advance in definiteness, coherence, and heterogeneity. The method of evolution in the life history of the animal and vegetal kingdoms has been like the method of evolution in the life history of the individual.

To go into the inorganic world with such a formula might seem rash. But as the growth of organization is essentially a particular kind of redistribution of matter and motion, and as redistribution of matter and motion is going on universally in the inorganic world, it is interesting to inquire whether in such simple approaches towards organization as we find, there is any approach towards the characteristics of organic evolution as above described. It was easy for Mr. Spencer to show that the change from a nebula into a planetary system conforms to the definition of evolution in a way that is most striking and suggestive. But in studying the inorganic world Mr. Spencer was led to modify his formula in a way that vastly increased its scope. He came to see that the primary feature of evolution is an integration of matter and concomitant dissipation of motion. According to circumstances, this process may or not be attended with extensive internal rearrangements and development of organization. The continuous internal rearrangement implied in the development of organization is

possible only where there is a medium degree of mobility among the
particles, a plasticity such as is secured only by those peculiar chemical combinations which make up what we call organic matter. In the
inorganic world, where there is an approach to organization there is
an adumbration of the law as realized in the organic world. But in
the former, what strikes us most is the concentration of the mass with
the retention of but little internal mobility; in the latter, what strikes
us most is the wonderful complication of the transformations wrought
by the immense amount of internal mobility retained. These transformations are to us the mark, the distinguishing feature, of life.

Having thus got the nature of the differences between the organic
and inorganic worlds into a series of suggestive formulas, the next
thing to be done was to inquire into the applicability of the law of
evolution to the higher manifestations of vital activity,—in other
words, to psychical and social life. Here it was easy to point out
analogies between the development of society and the development
of an organism. Between a savage state of society and a civilized state,
it is easy to see the contrasts in complexity of life, in division of
labour, in interdependence and coherence of operations and of interests. The difference resembles that between a vertebrate animal and
a worm.

Such analogies are instructive, because at the bottom of the phenomena there is a certain amount of real identity. But Mr. Spencer
did not stop with analogies; he pursued his problem into much deeper
regions. There is one manifest distinction between a society and an
organism. In the organism, the conscious life, the psychical life, is not
in the parts, but in the whole; but in a society, there is no such thing
as corporate consciousness: the psychical life is all in the individual
men and women. The highest development of this psychical life is the
end for which the world exists. The object of social life is the highest
spiritual welfare of the individual members of society. The individual
human soul thus comes to be as much the centre of the Spencerian
world as it was the centre of the world of mediæval theology; and the
history of the evolution of conscious intelligence becomes a theme of
surpassing interest.

This is the part of his subject which Mr. Spencer has handled in
the most masterly manner. Nothing in the literature of psychology is
more remarkable than the long-sustained analysis in which he starts
with complicated acts of quantitative reasoning and revolves them
into their elementary processes, and then goes on to simpler acts of
judgment and perception, and then down to sensation, and so on
resolving and resolving, until he gets down to the simple homogeneous psychical shocks or pulses in the manifold compounding and re-
compounding of which all mental action consists. Then, starting

afresh from that conception of life as the continuous adjustment of inner relations within the organism to outer relations in the environment,—a conception of which he made such brilliant use in his "Principles of Biology,"—he shows how the psychical life gradually becomes specialized in certain classes of adjustments or correspondences, and how the development of psychical life consists in a progressive differentiation and integration of such correspondences. Intellectual life is shown to have arisen by slow gradations, and the special interpretations of reflex action, instinct, memory, reason, emotion, and will are such as to make the "Principles of Psychology" indubitably the most suggestive book upon mental phenomena that was ever written.

Towards the end of the first edition of the "Origin of Species," published in 1859, Mr. Darwin looked forward to a distant future when the conception of gradual development might be applied to the phenomena of intelligence. But the first edition of the "Principles of Psychology," in which this was so successfully done, had already been published four years before,—in 1855,—so that Mr. Darwin in later editions was obliged to modify his statement, and confess that, instead of looking so far forward, he had better have looked about him. I remember hearing Mr. Darwin laugh merrily over this at his own expense.

This extension of the doctrine of evolution to psychical phenomena was what made it a universal doctrine, an account of the way in which the world, as we know it, has been evolved. There is no subject, great or small, that has not come to be affected by the doctrine, and, whether men realize it or not, there is no nook or corner in speculative science where they can get away from the sweep of Mr. Spencer's thought.

This extension of the doctrine to psychical phenomena is by many people misunderstood. The "Principles of Psychology" is a marvel of straightforward and lucid statement; but, from its immense reach and from the abstruseness of the subject, it is not easy reading. It requires a sustained attention such as few people can command, except on subjects with which they are already familiar. Hence few people read it in comparison with the number who have somehow got it into their heads that Mr. Spencer tries to explain mind as evolved out of matter, and is therefore a materialist. How many worthy critics have been heard to object to the doctrine of evolution that you cannot deduce mind from the primeval nebula, unless the germs of mind were present already! But that is just what Mr. Spencer says himself. I have heard him say it more than once, and his books contain many passages of equivalent import. He never misses an opportunity for attacking the doctrine that mind can be explained as evolved from matter. But, in spite of this, a great many people suppose that the gradual evolution of mind *must* mean its evolution out of matter, and are deaf to arguments of which they do not perceive the bearing. Hence Mr. Spencer is so commonly accredited with the doctrine which he so earnestly repudiates.

But there is another reason why people are apt to suppose the doctrine of evolution to be materialistic in its implications. There are able writers who have done good service in illustrating portions of the general doctrine, and are at the same time avowed materialists. One may be a materialist, whatever his scientific theory of things; and to such a person the materialism naturally seems to be a logical consequence from the scientific theory. We have received this evening a communication from Professor Ernst Haeckel, of Jena, in which he lays down five theses regarding the doctrine of evolution:—

1. "The general doctrine appears to be already unassailably founded;

2. "Thereby every supernatural creation is completely excluded;

3. "Transformism and the theory of descent are inseparable constituent parts of the doctrine of evolution;

4. "The necessary consequence of this last conclusion is the descent of man from a series of vertebrates."

So far, very good; we are within the limits of scientific competence, where Professor Haeckel is strong. But now, in his fifth thesis, he enters the region of metaphysics,—the transcendental region, which science has no competent methods of exploring,—and commits himself to a dogmatic assertion:

5. "The beliefs in an 'immortal soul' and in 'a personal God' are therewith" (*i.e.* with the four preceding statements) "completely ununitable (*völlig unvereinbar*)."

Now, if Professor Haeckel had contented himself with asserting that these two beliefs are not susceptible of scientific demonstration; if he had simply said that they are beliefs concerning which a scientific man, in his scientific capacity, ought to refrain from making assertions, because Science knows nothing whatever about the subject, he would have occupied an impregnable position. His fifth thesis would have been as indisputable as his first four. But Professor Haeckel does not stop here. He declares virtually that if an evolutionist is found entertaining the beliefs in a personal God and an immortal soul, nevertheless these beliefs are not philosophically reconcilable with his scientific theory of things, but are mere remnants of an old-fashioned superstition from which he has not succeeded in freeing himself.

Here one must pause to inquire what Professor Haeckel means by "a personal God." If he refers to the Latin conception of a God remote from the world of phenomena, and manifested only through occasional interference,—the conception that has until lately prevailed in the Western world since the time of St. Augustine,—then we may agree with him; the practical effect of the doctrine of evolution is to abolish such a conception. But with regard to the Greek conception entertained by St. Athanasius; the conception of God as immanent in the world of phenomena and manifested in every throb of its mighty rhythmical life; the deity that Richard Hooker, prince of English churchmen, had in mind when he wrote of Natural Law that "her seat is the bosom of God, and her voice the harmony of the world,"—with regard to this conception the practical effect of the doctrine of evolution is not to abolish, but to strengthen and confirm it. For, into whatever province of Nature we carry our researches, the more deeply we penetrate into its laws and methods of action, the more clearly do we see that all provinces of Nature are parts of an organic whole animated by a single principle of life that is infinite and eternal. I have no doubt Professor Haeckel would not only admit this, but would scout any other view as inconsistent with the monism which he professes. But he would say that this infinite and eternal principle of life is not psychical, and therefore cannot be called in any sense "a personal God." In an ultimate analysis, I suspect Professor Haeckel's ubiquitous monistic principle would turn out to be neither more nor less than Dr. Büchner's mechanical force (*Kraft*). On the other hand, I have sought to show—in my little book "The Idea of God"—that the Infinite and Eternal Power that animates the universe must be psychical in its nature, that any attempt to reduce it to mechanical force must end in absurdity, and that the only kind of monism which will stand the test of an ultimate analysis is monotheism. While in the chapter on Anthropomorphic Theism, in my "Cosmic Philosophy," I have taken great pains to point out the difficulties in which (as finite thinkers) we are involved when we try to conceive the Infinite and Eternal Power as psychical in his nature, I have in the chapter on Matter and Spirit, in that same book, taken equal pains to show that we are logically compelled thus to conceive Him.

One's attitude towards such problems is likely to be determined by one's fundamental conception of psychical life. To a materialist the ultimate power is mechanical force, and psychical life is nothing but the temporary and local result of fleeting collocations of material elements in the shape of nervous systems. Into the endless circuit of transformations of molecular motion, says the materialist, there enter certain phases which we call feeling and thoughts; they are part of the circuit; they arise out of motions of material molecules, and disappear by being retransformed into such motions: hence, with the death of the organism in which such motions have been temporarily gath-

ered into a kind of unity, all psychical activity and all personality are
ipso facto abolished. Such is the materialistic doctrine, and such, I
presume, is what Professor Haeckel has in mind when he asserts
that the belief in an immortal soul is incompatible with the doctrine
of evolution. The theory commonly called that of the correlation of
forces, and which might equally well or better be called the theory
of the metamorphosis of motions, is indispensable to the doctrine
of evolution. But for the theory that light, heat, electricity, and nerve-
action are different modes of undulatory motion transformable one
into another, and that similar modes of motion are liberated by the
chemical processes going on within the animal or vegetal organism,
Mr. Spencer's work could never have been done. That theory of
correlation and transformation is now generally accepted, and is
often appealed to by materialists. A century ago Cabanis said that
the brain secretes thought as the liver secretes bile. If he were alive
to-day, he would doubtless smile at this old form of expression as
crude, and would adopt a more subtle phrase; he would say that
"thought is transformed motion."

Against this interpretation I have maintained that the theory of
correlation not only fails to support it, but actually overthrows it. The
arguments may be found in the chapter on Matter and Spirit, in my
"Cosmic Philosophy," published in 1874, and in the essay entitled "A
Crumb for the Modern Symposium," written in 1877, and reprinted
in "Darwinism and Other Essays." Their purport is, that in tracing
the correlation of motions into the organism through the nervous
system and out again, we are bound to get an account of each step
in terms of motion. Unless we can show that every unit of motion that
disappears is transformed into an exact quantitative equivalent, our
theory of correlation breaks down; but when we have shown this we
shall have given a complete account of the whole affair without taking any heed whatever of thought, feeling, or consciousness. In other
words, these psychical activities do not enter into the circuit, but stand
outside of it, as a segment of a circle may stand outside a portion of
an entire circumference with which it is concentric. Motion is never
transformed into thought, but only into some other form of measurable
(in fact, or at any rate in theory, measurable) motion that takes
place in nerve-threads and ganglia. *It is not the thought, but the nerve-
action that accompanies the thought, that is really "transformed motion."* I say that if we are going to verify the theory of correlation,
it must be done (actually or theoretically) by measurement; quantitative equivalence must be proved at every step; and hence we
must not change our unit of measurement; from first to last it must be
a unit of motion: if we change it for a moment, our theory of correlation that moment collapses. I say, therefore, that the theory of cor-

relation and equivalence of forces lends no support whatever to materialism. On the contrary, its manifest implication is that psychical life cannot be a mere product of temporary collocations of matter.

The argument here set forth is my own. When I first used it, I had never met with it anywhere in books or conversation. Whether it has since been employed by other writers I do not know, for during the past fifteen years I have read very few books on such subjects. At all events, it is an argument for which I am ready to bear the full responsibility. Some doubt has recently been expressed whether Mr. Spencer would admit the force of this argument. It has been urged by Mr. S. H. Wilder, in two able papers published in the "New York Daily Tribune," June 13 and July 4, 1890, that the use of this argument marks a radical divergence on my part from Mr. Spencer's own position.

It is true that in several passages of "First Principles" there are statements which either imply or distinctly assert that motion can be transformed into feeling and thought,—*e.g.*: "Those modes of the Unknowable which we call heat, light, chemical affinity, etc., are alike transformable into each other, and into those modes of the Unknowable which we distinguish as sensation, emotion, thought; these, in their turns, being directly or indirectly retransformable into the original shapes;" and again, it is said "to be a necessary deduction from the law of correlation that what exists in consciousness under the form of feeling is transformable into an equivalent of mechanical motion," etc. Now, if this, as literally interpreted, be Mr. Spencer's deliberate opinion, I entirely dissent from it. To speak of quantitative equivalence between a unit of feeling and a unit of motion seems to me to be talking nonsense,—to be combining terms which severally possess a meaning into a phrase which has no meaning. I am therefore inclined to think that the above sentences, literally interpreted, do not really convey Mr. Spencer's opinion. They appear manifestly inconsistent, moreover, with other passages in which he has taken much more pains to explain his position. In the sentence from "First Principles," Mr. Spencer appears to me to mean that the nerve-action, which is the objective concomitant of what is subjectively known as feeling, is transformable into an equivalent of mechanical motion. When he wrote that sentence perhaps he had not shaped the case quite so distinctly in his own mind as he had a few years later, when he made the more elaborate statements in the second edition of the Psychology. Though in these more elaborate statements he does not assert the doctrine I have here maintained, yet they seem consistent with it. When I was finishing the chapter on Matter and Spirit, in my room in London, one afternoon in February, 1874, Mr. Spencer came in, and I read to him nearly the whole chapter, including my argument from correlation above mentioned. He expressed warm approval of the chapter, without making any specific qualifications. In the course of the chapter I had occasion to quote a passage from the Psychology, in which Mr. Spencer twice inadvertently used the phrase "nervous shock" where he meant "psychical shock." As his object was to keep the psychical phenomena and their cerebral concomitants distinct in his argument, this colloquial use of the word "nervous" was liable to puzzle the reader, and give querulous critics a chance to charge Mr. Spencer with the materialistic implications which it was his express purpose to avoid. Accordingly, in my quotation I changed the word "nervous" to "psychical," using brackets and explaining my reasons. On showing all this to Mr. Spencer, he desired me to add in a footnote that he thoroughly approved the emendation.

I mention this incident because our common, every-day speech abounds in expressions that have a materialistic flavour; and sometimes in serious writing an author's sheer intentness upon his main argument may lead him to overlook some familiar form of expression which, when thrown into a precise and formal context, will strike the reader in a very different way from what the author intended. I am inclined to explain in this way the passages in "First Principles" which are perhaps chiefly responsible for the charge of materialism that has so often and so wrongly been brought up against the doctrine of evolution.

As regards the theological implications of the doctrine of evolution, I have never undertaken to speak for Mr. Spencer; on such transcendental subjects it is quite enough if one speaks for one's self. It is told of Diogenes that, on listening one day to a sophistical argument against the possibility of motion, he grimly got up out of his tub and walked across the street. Whether his adversaries were convinced or not, we are not told. Probably not; it is but seldom that adversaries are convinced. So, when Professor Haeckel declares that belief in a "personal God" and an "immortal soul" is incompatible with acceptance of the doctrine of evolution, I can only say, for myself—however much or little the personal experience may be worth—I find that the beliefs in the psychical nature of God and in the immortality of the human soul seem to harmonize infinitely better with my general system of cosmic philosophy than the negation of these beliefs. If Professor Haeckel, or any other writer, prefers a materialistic interpretation, very well. I neither quarrel with him nor seek to convert him; but I do not agree with him. I do not pretend that my opinion on these matters is susceptible of scientific demonstration. Neither is his. I say, then, that his fifth thesis has no business in a series of scientific generalizations about the doctrine of evolution.

Far beyond the limits of what scientific methods, based upon our brief terrestrial experience, can demonstrate, there lies on every side a region with regard to which Science can only suggest questions. As Goethe so profoundly says:—

> Willst du ins Unendliche streiten,
> Geh' nur im Endlichen nach allen Seiten.

It is of surpassing interest that the particular generalization which has been extended into a universal formula of evolution should have been the generalization of the development of an ovum. In enlarging the sphere of life in such wise as to make the whole universe seem actuated by a single principle of life, we are introduced to regions of sublime speculation. The doctrine of evolution, which affects our thought about all things, brings before us with vividness the conception of an ever present God,—not an absentee God who once manufactured a cosmic machine capable of running itself, except for a little jog or poke here and there in the shape of a special providence. The doctrine of evolution destroys the conception of the world as a machine. It makes God our constant refuge and support, and Nature his true revelation; and when all its religious implications shall have been set forth, it will be seen to be the most potent ally that Christianity has ever had in elevating mankind.

Lyman Abbott
Preface, The Evolution of Christianity

WE ARE LIVING in a time of religious ferment. What shall we do? Attempt to keep the new wine in the old bottles? That can only end in destroying the bottles and spilling the wine. Attempt to stop the fermentation? Impossible! And if possible, the only result would be to spoil the wine. No! Put the new wine into new bottles, that both may be preserved. Spiritual experience is always new. It must therefore find a new expression in each age. This book is an attempt to restate

The Evolution of Christianity (Boston, 1892), pp. iii–v. Text from this edition.

the eternal yet ever new truths of the religious life in the terms of modern philosophic thought.

The teachers in the modern church may be divided into three parties: one is endeavoring to defend the faith of the fathers and the forms in which that faith was expressed; one repudiates both the faith and the forms; one holds fast to the faith, but endeavors to restate it in forms more rational and more consistent with modern habits of thought. To confound the second and third of these parties, because they agree in discarding ancient formularies, is a natural but a very radical blunder. The New Theology does not tend toward unfaith; it is, on the contrary, an endeavor to maintain faith by expressing it in terms which are more intelligible and credible. I hope that the reader of these pages will discover that I have not abandoned the historic faith of Christendom to become an evolutionist, but have endeavored to show that the historic faith of Christendom, when stated in the terms of an evolutionary philosophy, is not only preserved, but is so cleansed of pagan thought and feeling, as to be presented in a purer and more powerful form.

Mr. Drummond has contended, not that there is an analogy between natural and spiritual laws, but that the natural and the spiritual belong to one kingdom, so that the natural laws are projected into the spiritual world.[1] It is my endeavor in this volume, in like manner, not to trace an analogy between evolution in the physical realm, and progress in the spiritual realm, but to show that the law of progress is the same in both. In the spiritual, as in the physical, God is the secret and source of life; phenomena, whether material or spiritual, are the manifestation of his presence; but he manifests himself in growth, not in stereotyped and stationary forms; and this growth is from lower to higher, from simpler to more complex forms, according to well defined and invariable laws, and by a force resident in the growing object itself. That unknown force is God—God in nature, God in the church, God in society, and God in the individual soul. The only cognizable difference between evolution in the physical and evolution in the spiritual realms is that nature cannot shut God out, nor hinder his working, nor disregard the laws of its own life; but man can and does. These principles constitute, to borrow a musical phrase, the *motif* of this book.

[1] Henry Drummond's *Natural Law in the Spiritual World* (1883) was a popular reconciliation of evolutionary science and religious belief.

John Burroughs
God and Nature

HALF A CENTURY or more ago a pious Scotch family lately come to
this country moved into the town where I was born. As they were
coming through a deep gorge in the mountains where the scenery
was unusually wild and forbidding, one of the little boys, looking
forth upon the savage and desolate prospect, nestled closer to his
mother and asked with bated breath, "Mither, is there a God here?"
The little boy's question sprang from a feeling which probably most of
us share. The desolate, the terrible, the elemental, the inhuman in
nature, are always more or less a shock to one's notions of the existence of a beneficent Supreme Being. In storms at sea, amid the fury
and wild careening of the elements, or in tempest and darkness upon
the land, when riot and destruction stalk abroad, how faint and far
off seems the notion of the fatherhood of God! The other day in looking over some of Professor Langley's views of the sun, photographic
representations of those immense craters or openings into the solar
furnace into which our little earth would disappear as quickly as a
snowflake into the mouth of a blast furnace, the question of the
little Scotch boy came to me, "Is there a God here?" It is incredible.
The utmost one can do, he cannot begin to conceive of a being adequate to these things. Under the old dispensation, before the advent
of science, when this little world was all, and the sun, moon, and stars
were merely fixtures overhead to give light and warmth, the conception of a being adequate to create and control it all was easier. The
storms were expressive of his displeasure, the heavens were his
throne, and the earth was his footstool. But in the light of modern
astronomy one finds himself looking in vain for the God of his fathers,
the magnified man who ruled the ancient world. In his place we have
an infinite and eternal Power whose expression is the visible universe,
and to whom man is no more and no less than any other creature.

Hence when the man of science says, "There is no God," he only

The Light of Day (Boston, 1900), pp. 163–71. Text from this edition.

gives voice to the feeling of the inadequacy of the old anthropomorphic conception, in the presence of the astounding facts of the universe.

When I look up at the starry heavens at night and reflect upon what it is that I really see there, I am constrained to say, "There is no God." The mind staggers in its attempt to grasp the idea of a being that could do that. It is futile to attempt it. It is not the works of some God that I see there. I am face to face with a power that baffles speech. I see no lineaments of personality, no human traits, but an energy upon whose currents solar systems are but bubbles. In the presence of it man and the race of man are less than motes in the air. I doubt if any mind can expand its conception of God sufficiently to meet the astounding disclosures of modern science. It is easier to say there is no God. The universe is so *un*human, that is, it goes its way with so little thought of man. He is but an incident, not an end. We must adjust our notions to the discovery that things are not shaped to him, but that he is shaped to them. The air was not made for his lungs, but he has lungs because there is air; the light was not created for his eye, but he has eyes because there is light. All the forces of nature are going their own way; man avails himself of them, or catches a ride as best he can. If he keeps his seat he prospers; if he misses his hold and falls he is crushed. Mankind used to think that the dews and rains were sent for their benefit, and the church still encourages this idea by praying for rain in times of drought, but the notion is nearly dissipated. To such a mind as Cardinal Newman the spectacle of the world caused a similar moral shiver and doubt to that which crossed the mind of the little Scotch boy when he looked out upon the wild pass in the mountains. He does not see God there; he says it is like looking into a mirror and not seeing his own face. And the proofs that are drawn from without, from the facts of human society and the course of history, do not warm and enlighten him, do not take away the winter of his unbelief; and the inference he draws is that either there is no God, or else that man is alienated from him,—"the human race is implicated is some terrible aboriginal calamity" (The Fall of Man). But the natural philosopher must discard the theological explanation, and he is left with the other alternative, "There is no God." His piety takes this impious form. His belief is best expressed by a denial; he will be an atheist rather than name the unnamable. Newman finds his God when he looks into his own conscience, and probably this is the only way he is to be found. From this sanctuary the universe, with its suns and systems, and the world, with its horrors and failures, are shut out. We see a God made more or less in our own image; he is human and mindful of us; he is a necessity of thought and of our moral nature. But with the

man of science the visible universe is paramount, and he will probably always ask, "Is there a God here?"

"Howbeit, every nation made gods of their own." Man is, and always has been, a maker of gods. It has been the most serious and
significant occupation of his sojourn in the world. Nearly every race
and people have tried their hand at making a god of some kind around
which their religious aspirations and superstitions could cluster, and
on all occasions they have found the material for their deities near
at hand.

As man arrives at consciousness, he soon recognizes a Power greater
than himself, over which he has no control, and of which he is either
an object of sport or solicitude. This power is what we call Nature,
the nearest and greatest fact of all. This is the mountain out of which.
or some fragment of which, all peoples have carved their gods, giving
them the form and likeness of such ideal as they were capable of.

At first man deifies and worships various objects of visible material
nature. The first god was probably the sun. Nearly all early races have
been sun worshipers. The splendor, the power, the bounty of the
sun, is the most obvious of all the facts of nature. Later, as man
developed and his mind opened, he made himself gods out of invisible
nature. He projected his own ideal into the universe and worshiped
that.

Undoubtedly the most skillful artists in this field, as in so many
others, were the Greeks; their gods were the most beautiful and interesting of all. Apollo stands as a type of grace and power to all succeeding races. Then their lesser divinities,—how charming, how
interesting they all are, the works of master hands.

The old Hebrews were much less as artists, but much greater as
prophets; hence Jehovah, the God of the Hebrew Scriptures, is the
most awful, the most imposing, and the most imminent of all the
gods. How crude, how terrible, how jealous,—a magnified and
heaven-filling despot and king. With a gentle and loving *alter ego* or
deputy, who stands between his stern and awful majesty and guilty
and trembling man, namely, Jesus Christ, he is still the God of
the most enlightened of the human race. With what power and
solemnity he figures in the old Bible; how he filled and shook the
hearts of the old bards and prophets! Open the Scriptures almost
anywhere, and one seems to hear his awful voice, and feel his terrible
tread. It shakes the earth; it fills the heavens; the universe is the
theatre of his love and wrath. What an abysmal depth of conscience
in those old Hebrews; what capacity for remorse, for reverence, for
fear, for terror, for adoration; what a sense of the value of righteousness, and of the dreadfulness of sin! In them we see the unsounded
depths of the religious spirit,—its tidal seas; bitter and estranging, but

sublime. As I have elsewhere said all other sacred books are tame,
are but inland seas, so to speak, compared with this briny deep of
the Hebrew Bible. Little wonder it still sways the hearts and lives
of men. Their imaginations go out upon it. Immensity broods over it.
It is as tender as a tear or as cruel as death. It is a record of the darkest deeds, and luminous with the sublimest devotion and piety. It is
archetypal, elemental. The light of eternity is upon its face. Other
books, other bibles, are as if written in houses or temples or sheltered
groves; here is the solemnity and grandeur of the mountain tops, or
of the great Asiatic plains under the midnight stars. Man is alone with
the Eternal, and with fear and trembling walks and talks with him.

How our fathers read and communed with this book! How much of
the culture of the world has come out of it! The light, the entertainment, the stimulus, which we find in literature, in art, in science, our fathers found in this volume.

The mystery of life deepens when we set up a being, no matter how
large and all powerful, over the universe apart from and independent
of it, and to whom we assign human motives and purposes,—some
sort of economic scheme with reference to it. When a good man
dies with his work half done, how mysterious, we say, that the
master of the vineyard should thus strike down one of his most useful
servants and spare so many worthless and worse than worthless ones.
The universe viewed in the light of anything like human economy
is indeed a puzzle. But this is not the right view. We must get rid of
the great moral governor, or head director. He is a fiction of our
own brains. We must recognize only Nature, the All; call it God if
we will, but divest it of all anthropological conceptions. Nature
we know; we are of it; we are in it. But this paternal Providence above
Nature—events are constantly knocking it down. Here is this vast
congeries of vital forces which we call Nature, regardless of time, because it has all time, regardless of waste because it is the All, regardless of space because it is infinite, regardless of man because man is
a part of it, regardless of life because it is the sum total of life, gain-
ing what it spends, conserving what it destroys, always young, always old, reconciling all contradictions—the sum and synthesis of all
powers and qualities, infinite and incomprehensible. This is all the
God we can know, and this we cannot help but know. We want no
evidence of this God.

> Far or forgot to me is near;
>   Shadow and sunlight are the same;
> The vanished gods to me appear;
>   And one to me are shame and fame.

Men labor to prove the existence of their God, but labor never so much, and you cannot prove the nonexistence of this God. Your proof to the contrary, he is that also.

Such a notion seems to orphan the universe to some souls, but need it be so? This vital Nature out of which we came, out of which father and mother came, out of which all men came, and to which again we all in due time return, why should we fear it or distrust it? It makes our hearts beat and our brains think. When it stops the beating and the thinking, will it not be well also? It looked after us before we were born; it will look after us when we are dead. Every particle of us will be taken care of; the force of every heart-beat is conserved somewhere, somehow. The psychic force or principle of which I am a manifestation will still go on. There is no stoppage and no waste, forever and ever. My consciousness ceases as a flame ceases, but that which made my consciousness does not cease. What comfort is that to the me? Ah, the *me* wants to go on and on. But let the me learn that only Nature goes on and on, that the law which makes the me and unmakes it is alone immortal, and that it is best so. Identity is a thought, a concept of our minds, and not a property of our minds.

The universe is so stupendous, so unspeakable, that we dare not, cannot, name any end or purpose for which it exists. It is because it is. If man exists on other worlds, or if he does not exist, it is all the same. The superior and the inferior planets may run their course and life not appear upon them. It is just like the prodigality, the indifference of Nature. If the conditions are favorable man will appear; if not, not. They are no more there for his sake than yonder river is there for the sake of the fishes, or yonder clay bank for the sake of the brickmakers. Space is no doubt strewn with dead worlds and dead suns as thickly as yonder field with dead boulders, and with worlds upon which only the rudiments of life can ever develop, too hot or too cold. Our own earth must have been millions of years without man, and it will again be millions without him. He is the insect of a summer hour. The scheme of the universe is too big for us to grasp—so big that it is no scheme at all. The infinite—what is that? Is it equal to absolute negation? It is when we have such thoughts that all notions of a God disappear and one says in his heart, "There is no God." Any God we can conceive of is inadequate. The universe is no more a temple than it is a brothel or a library. The Cosmos knows no God—it is *super deus*. In the light of the nebular hypothesis how one wilts! How vain all your striving and ambition. The proudest records of earth must perish like autumn leaves.

William James
Is Life Worth Living?

WHEN MR. MALLOCK'S BOOK with this title appeared some fifteen years ago, the jocose answer that "it depends on the *liver*" had great currency in the newspapers. The answer which I propose to give to-night cannot be jocose. In the words of one of Shakespeare's prologues,—

> I come no more to make you laugh; things now,
> That bear a weighty and a serious brow,
> Sad, high, and working, full of state and woe,—

must be my theme. In the deepest heart of all of us there is a corner in which the ultimate mystery of things works sadly; and I know not what such an association as yours intends, nor what you ask of those whom you invite to address you, unless it be to lead you from the surface-glamour of existence, and for an hour at least to make you heedless to the buzzing and jigging and vibration of small interests and excitements that form the tissue of our ordinary consciousness. Without further explanation or apology, then, I ask you to join me in turning an attention, commonly too unwilling, to the profounder bass-note of life. Let us search the lonely depths for an hour together, and see what answers in the last folds and recesses of things our question may find.

*   *   *

III.

Starting then with nature, we naturally tend, if we have the religious craving, to say with Marcus Aurelius, "O Universe! what thou

Given as an address before the Harvard Young Men's Christian Association, May, 1895. Published in the *International Journal of Ethics*, VI (October, 1895), 1–24. Text from *The Will to Believe, and Other Essays in Popular Philosophy* (New York, 1897), pp. 32, 41–44, 51–62.

wishest I wish." Our sacred books and traditions tell us of one God who made heaven and earth, and, looking on them, saw that they were good. Yet, on more intimate acquaintance, the visible surfaces of heaven and earth refuse to be brought by us into any intelligible unity at all. Every phenomenon that we would praise there exists cheek by jowl with some contrary phenomenon that cancels all its religious effect upon the mind. Beauty and hideousness, love and cruelty, life and death keep house together in indissoluble partnership; and there gradually steals over us, instead of the old warm notion of a man-loving Deity, that of an awful power that neither hates nor loves, but rolls all things together meaninglessly to a common doom. This is an uncanny, a sinister, a nightmare view of life, and its peculiar *unheimlichkeit*, or poisonousness, lies expressly in our holding two things together which cannot possibly agree,—in our clinging, on the one hand, to the demand that there shall be a living spirit of the whole; and, on the other, to the belief that the course of nature must be such a spirit's adequate manifestation and expression. It is in the contradiction between the supposed being of a spirit that encompasses and owns us, and with which we ought to have some communion, and the character of such a spirit as revealed by the visible world's course, that this particular death-in-life paradox and this melancholy-breeding puzzle reside. Carlyle expresses the result in that chapter of his immortal 'Sartor Resartus' entitled 'The Everlasting No.' "I lived," writes poor Teufelsdröckh, "in a continual, indefinite, pining fear; tremulous, pusillanimous, apprehensive of I knew not what: it seemed as if all things in the heavens above and the earth beneath would hurt me; as if the heavens and the earth were but boundless jaws of a devouring monster, wherein I, palpitating, lay waiting to be devoured."

This is the first stage of speculative melancholy. No brute can have this sort of melancholy; no man who is irreligious can become its prey. It is the sick shudder of the frustrated religious demand, and not the mere necessary outcome of animal experience. Teufelsdröckh himself could have made shift to face the general chaos and bedevilment of this world's experiences very well, were he not the victim of an originally unlimited trust and affection towards them. If he might meet them piecemeal, with no suspicion of any whole expressing itself in them, shunning the bitter parts and husbanding the sweet ones, as the occasion served, and as the day was foul or fair, he could have zigzagged toward an easy end, and felt no obligation to make the air vocal with his lamentations. The mood of levity, of 'I don't care,' is for this world's ills a sovereign and practical anæsthetic. But, no! something deep down in Teufelsdröckh and in the rest of us tells us that there *is* a Spirit in things to which we owe allegiance, and for whose sake we must keep up the serious mood. And so the inner fever and discord also are kept up; for nature taken on her visible surface reveals no such Spirit, and beyond the facts of nature we are at the present stage of our inquiry not supposing ourselves to look.

Now, I do not hesitate frankly and sincerely to confess to you that this real and genuine discord seems to me to carry with it the inevitable bankruptcy of natural religion naïvely and simply taken. There were times when Leibnitzes with their heads buried in monstrous wigs could compose Theodicies, and when stall-fed officials of an established church could prove by the valves in the heart and the round ligament of the hip-joint the existence of a "Moral and Intelligent Contriver of the World." But those times are past; and we of the nineteenth century, with our evolutionary theories and our mechanical philosophies, already know nature too impartially and too well to worship unreservedly any God of whose character she can be an adequate expression. Truly, all we know of good and duty proceeds from nature; but none the less so all we know of evil. Visible nature is all plasticity and indifference,—a moral multiverse, as one might call it, and not a moral universe. To such a harlot we owe no allegiance; with her as a whole we can establish no moral communion; and we are free in our dealings with her several parts to obey or destroy, and to follow no law but that of prudence in coming to terms with such of her particular features as will help us to our private ends. If there be a divine Spirit of the universe, nature, such as we know her, cannot possibly be its *ultimate word* to man. Either there is no Spirit revealed in nature, or else it is inadequately revealed there; and (as all the higher religions have assumed) what we call visible nature, or *this* world, must be but a veil and surface-show whose full meaning resides in a supplementary unseen or *other* world.

I cannot help, therefore, accounting it on the whole a gain (though it may seem for certain poetic constitutions a very sad loss) that the naturalistic superstition, the worship of the God of nature, simply taken as such, should have begun to loosen its hold upon the educated mind. In fact, if I am to express my personal opinion unreservedly, I should say (in spite of its sounding blasphemous at first to certain ears) that the initial step towards getting into healthy ultimate relations with the universe is the act of rebellion against the idea that such a God exists.

*　　*　　*

IV.

And now, in turning to what religion may have to say to the question, I come to what is the soul of my discourse. Religion has meant many things in human history; but when from now onward I use the word I mean to use it in the supernaturalist sense, as declaring that the so-called order of nature, which constitutes this world's experience, is only one portion of the total universe, and that there stretches beyond this visible world an unseen world of which we now know nothing positive, but in its relation to which the true significance of our present mundane life consists. A man's religious faith (whatever more special items of doctrine it may involve) means for me essentially his faith in the existence of an unseen order of some kind in which the riddles of the natural order may be found explained. In the more developed religions the natural world has always been regarded as the mere scaffolding or vestibule of a truer, more eternal world, and affirmed to be a sphere of education, trial, or redemption. In these religions, one must in some fashion die to the natural life before one can enter into life eternal. The notion that this physical world of wind and water, where the sun rises and the moon sets, is absolutely and ultimately the divinely aimed-at and established thing, is one which we find only in very early religions, such as that of the most primitive Jews. It is this natural religion (primitive still, in spite of the fact that poets and men of science whose good-will exceeds their perspicacity keep publishing it in new editions tuned to our contemporary ears) that, as I said a while ago, has suffered definitive bankruptcy in the opinion of a circle of persons, among whom I must count myself, and who are growing more numerous every day. For such persons the physical order of nature, taken simply as science knows it, cannot be held to reveal any one harmonious spiritual intent. It is mere *weather*, as Chauncey Wright called it, doing and undoing without end.

Now, I wish to make you feel, if I can in the short remainder of this hour, that we have a right to believe the physical order to be only a partial order; that we have a right to supplement it by an unseen spiritual order which we assume on trust, if only thereby life may seem to us better worth living again. But as such a trust will seem to some of you sadly mystical and execrably unscientific, I must first say a word or two to weaken the veto which you may consider that science opposes to our act.

There is included in human nature an ingrained naturalism and materialism of mind which can only admit facts that are actually tangible. Of this sort of mind the entity called 'science' is the idol. Fond-

ness for the word 'scientist' is one of the notes by which you may
know its votaries; and its short way of killing any opinion that it
disbelieves in is to call it 'unscientific.' It must be granted that there
is no slight excuse for this. Science has made such glorious leaps in
the last three hundred years, and extended our knowledge of nature
so enormously both in general and in detail; men of science, moreover, have as a class displayed such admirable virtues,—that it is no
wonder if the worshippers of science lose their head. In this very
University, accordingly, I have heard more than one teacher say
that all the fundamental conceptions of truth have already been
found by science, and that the future has only the details of the
picture to fill in. But the slightest reflection on the real conditions
will suffice to show how barbaric such notions are. They show such
a lack of scientific imagination, that it is hard to see how one who
is actively advancing any part of science can make a mistake so
crude. Think how many absolutely new scientific conceptions have
arisen in our own generation, how many new problems have been
formulated that were never thought of before, and then cast an
eye upon the brevity of science's career. It began with Galileo, not
three hundred years ago. Four thinkers since Galileo, each informing
his successor of what discoveries his own lifetime had seen achieved,
might have passed the torch of science into our hands as we sit here
in this room. Indeed, for the matter of that, an audience much
smaller than the present one, an audience of some five or six score
people, if each person in it could speak for his own generation, would
carry us away to the black unknown of the human species, to days
without a document or monument to tell their tale. Is it credible that
such a mushroom knowledge, such a growth overnight as this, *can*
represent more than the minutest glimpse of what the universe will
really prove to be when adequately understood? No! our science is
a drop, our ignorance a sea. Whatever else be certain, this at least
is certain,—that the world of our present natural knowledge *is* enveloped in a larger world of *some* sort of whose residual properties
we at present can frame no positive idea.

Agnostic positivism, of course, admits this principle theoretically
in the most cordial terms, but insists that we must not turn it to any
practical use. We have no right, this doctrine tells us, to dream
dreams, or suppose anything about the unseen part of the universe,
merely because to do so may be for what we are pleased to call our
highest interests. We must always wait for sensible evidence for
our beliefs; and where such evidence is inaccessible we must frame
no hypotheses whatever. Of course this is a safe enough position
in abstracto. If a thinker had no stake in the unknown, no vital needs,
to live or languish according to what the unseen world contained, a

philosophic neutrality and refusal to believe either one way or the other would be his wisest cue. But, unfortunately, neutrality is not only inwardly difficult, it is also outwardly unrealizable, where our relations to an alternative are practical and vital. This is because, as the psychologists tell us, belief and doubt are living attitudes, and involve conduct on our part. Our only way, for example, of doubting, or refusing to believe, that a certain thing *is*, is continuing to act as if it were *not*. If, for instance, I refuse to believe that the room is getting cold, I leave the windows open and light no fire just as if it still were warm. If I doubt that you are worthy of my confidence, I keep you uninformed of all my secrets just as if you were *un*worthy of the same. If I doubt the need of insuring my house, I leave it uninsured as much as if I believed there were no need. And so if I must not believe that the world is divine, I can only express that refusal by declining ever to act distinctively as if it were so, which can only mean acting on certain critical occasions as if it were *not* so, or in an irreligious way. There are, you see, inevitable occasions in life when inaction is a kind of action, and must count as action, and when not to be for is to be practically against; and in all such cases strict and consistent neutrality is an unattainable thing.

And, after all, is not this duty of neutrality where only our inner interests would lead us to believe, the most ridiculous of commands? Is it not sheer dogmatic folly to say that our inner interests can have no real connection with the forces that the hidden world may contain? In other cases divinations based on inner interests have proved prophetic enough. Take science itself! Without an imperious inner demand on our part for ideal logical and mathematical harmonies, we should never have attained to proving that such harmonies lie hidden between all the chinks and interstices of the crude natural world. Hardly a law has been established in science, hardly a fact ascertained, which was not first sought after, often with sweat and blood, to gratify an inner need. Whence such needs come from we do not know: we find them in us, and biological psychology so far only classes them with Darwin's 'accidental variations.' But the inner need of believing that this world of nature is a sign of something more spiritual and eternal than itself is just as strong and authoritative in those who feel it, as the inner need of uniform laws of causation ever can be in a professionally scientific head. The toil of many generations has proved the latter need prophetic. Why *may* not the former one be prophetic, too? And if needs of ours outrun the visible universe, why *may* not that be a sign that an invisible universe is there? What, in short, has authority to debar us from trusting our religious demands? Science as such assuredly has no authority, for she can only say what is, not what is not; and the agnostic "thou shalt not believe without coercive sensible evidence" is simply an expression (free to any one to make) of private personal appetite for evidence of a certain peculiar kind.

Now, when I speak of trusting our religious demands, just what do I mean by 'trusting'? Is the word to carry with it license to define in detail an invisible world, and to anathematize and excommunicate those whose trust is different? Certainly not! Our faculties of belief were not primarily given us to make orthodoxies and heresies withal; they were given us to live by. And to trust our religious demands means first of all to live in the light of them, and to act as if the invisible world which they suggest were real. It is a fact of human nature, that men can live and die by the help of a sort of faith that goes without a single dogma or definition. The bare assurance that this natural order is not ultimate but a mere sign or vision, the external staging of a many-storied universe, in which spiritual forces have the last word and are eternal,—this bare assurance is to such men enough to make life seem worth living in spite of every contrary presumption suggested by its circumstances on the natural plane. Destroy this inner assurance, however, vague as it is, and all the light and radiance of existence is extinguished for these persons at a stroke. Often enough the wild-eyed look at life—the suicidal mood—will then set in.

And now the application comes directly home to you and me. Probably to almost every one of us here the most adverse life would seem well worth living, if we only could be *certain* that our bravery and patience with it were terminating and eventuating and bearing fruit somewhere in an unseen spiritual world. But granting we are not certain, does it then follow that a bare trust in such a world is a fool's paradise and lubberland, or rather that it is a living attitude in which we are free to indulge? Well, we are free to trust at our own risks anything that is not impossible, and that can bring analogies to bear in its behalf. That the world of physics is probably not absolute, all the converging multitude of arguments that make in favor of idealism tend to prove; and that our whole physical life may lie soaking in a spiritual atmosphere, a dimension of being that we at present have no organ for apprehending, is vividly suggested to us by the analogy of the life of our domestic animals. Our dogs, for example, are in our human life but not of it. They witness hourly the outward body of events whose inner meaning cannot, by any possible operation, be revealed to their intelligence,—events in which they themselves often play the cardinal part. My terrier bites a teasing boy, for example, and the father demands damages. The dog may be present at every step of the negotiations, and see the money paid, without an inkling of what it all means, without a suspicion that it has anything to do with *him;* and he never *can* know in his natural dog's life. Or take another case which used greatly to impress me in my medical-student days. Consider a poor dog whom they are vivisecting in a laboratory. He lies strapped on a board and shrieking at his executioners, and to his own dark consciousness is literally in a sort of hell. He cannot see a single redeeming ray in the whole business; and yet all these diabolical-seeming events are often controlled by human intentions with which, if his poor benighted mind could only be made to catch a glimpse of them, all that is heroic in him would religiously acquiesce. Healing truth, relief to future sufferings of beast and man, are to be bought by them. It may be genuinely a process of redemption. Lying on his back on the board there he may be performing a function incalculably higher than any that prosperous canine life admits of; and yet, of the whole performance, this function is the one portion that must remain absolutely beyond his ken.

Now turn from this to the life of man. In the dog's life we see the world invisible to him because we live in both worlds. In human life, although we only see our world, and his within it, yet encompassing both these worlds a still wider world may be there, as unseen by us as our world is by him; and to believe in that world *may* be the most essential function that our lives in this world have to perform. But *"may* be! *may* be!" one now hears the positivist contemptuously exclaim; "what use can a scientific life have for maybes?" Well, I reply, the 'scientific' life itself has much to do with maybes, and human life at large has everything to do with them. So far as man stands for anything, and is productive or originative at all, his entire vital function may be said to have to deal with maybes. Not a victory is gained, not a deed of faithfulness or courage is done, except upon a maybe; not a service, not a sally of generosity, not a scientific exploration or experiment or textbook, that may not be a mistake. It is only by risking our persons from one hour to another that we live at all. And often enough our faith beforehand in an uncertified result *is the only thing that makes the result come true.* Suppose, for instance, that you are climbing a mountain, and have worked yourself into a position from which the only escape is by a terrible leap. Have faith that you can successfully make it, and your feet are nerved to its accomplishment. But mistrust yourself, and think of all the sweet things you have heard the scientists say of *maybes,* and you will hesitate so long that, at last, all unstrung and trembling, and launching yourself in a moment of despair, you roll in the abyss. In such a case (and it belongs to an enormous class), the part of wisdom as well as of courage is to *believe what is in the line of your needs,* for only by such belief is the need fulfilled. Refuse to believe, and you shall indeed be right, for you shall irretrievably perish. But believe, and again you shall be right, for you shall save yourself. You make one or the other of two possible universes true by your trust or mistrust,—both universes having been only *maybes,* in this particular, before you contributed your act.

Now, it appears to me that the question whether life is worth living is subject to conditions logically much like these. It does, indeed, depend on you *the liver.* If you surrender to the nightmare view and crown the evil edifice by your own suicide, you have indeed made a picture totally black. Pessimism, completed by your act, is true beyond a doubt, so far as your world goes. Your mistrust of life has removed whatever worth your own enduring existence might have given to it; and now, throughout the whole sphere of possible influence of that existence, the mistrust has proved itself to have had divining power. But suppose, on the other hand, that instead of giving way to the nightmare view you cling to it that this world is not the *ultimatum.* Suppose you find yourself a very well-spring, as Wordsworth says, of—

> Zeal, and the virtue to exist by faith
> As soldiers live by courage; as, by strength
> Of heart, the sailor fights with roaring seas.

Suppose, however thickly evils crowd upon you, that your unconquerable subjectivity proves to be their match, and that you find a more wonderful joy than any passive pleasure can bring in trusting ever in the larger whole. Have you not now made life worth living on these terms? What sort of a thing would life really be, with your qualities ready for a tussle with it, if it only brought fair weather and gave these higher faculties of yours no scope? Please remember that optimism and pessimism are definitions of the world, and that our own reactions on the world, small as they are in bulk, are integral parts of the whole thing, and necessarily help to determine the definition. They may even be the decisive elements in determining the definition. A large mass can have its unstable equilibrium overturned by the addition of a feather's weight; a long phrase may have its sense reversed by the addition of the three letters *n-o-t.* This life *is* worth living, we can say, *since it is what we make it, from the moral point of view;* and we are determined to make it from that point of view, so far as we have anything to do with it, a success.

Now, in this description of faiths that verify themselves I have assumed that our faith in an invisible order is what inspires those efforts and that patience which make this visible order good for moral men. Our faith in the seen world's goodness (goodness now meaning fitness for successful moral and religious life) has verified itself by leaning on our faith in the unseen world. But will our faith in the unseen world similarly verify itself? Who knows?

Once more it is a case of *maybe;* and once more *maybes* are the essence of the situation. I confess that I do not see why the very existence of an invisible world may not in part depend on the personal response which any one of us may make to the religious appeal. God himself, in short, may draw vital strength and increase of very being from our fidelity. For my own part, I do not know what the sweat and blood and tragedy of this life mean, if they mean anything short of this. If this life be not a real fight, in which something is eternally gained for the universe by success, it is no better than a game of private theatricals from which one may withdraw at will. But it *feels* like a real fight,—as if there were something really wild in the universe which we, with all our idealities and faithfulnesses, are needed to redeem; and first of all to redeem our own hearts from atheisms and fears. For such a half-wild, half-saved universe our nature is adapted. The deepest thing in our nature is this *Binnenleben* (as a German doctor lately has called it), this dumb region of the heart in which we dwell alone with our willingnesses and unwillingnesses, our faiths and fears. As through the cracks and crannies of caverns those water exude from the earth's bosom which then form the fountain-heads of springs, so in these crepuscular depths of personality the sources of all our outer deeds and decisions take their rise. Here is our deepest organ of communication with the nature of things; and compared with these concrete movements of our soul all abstract statements and scientific arguments—the veto, for example, which the strict positivist pronounces upon our faith—sound to us like mere chatterings of the teeth. For here possibilities, not finished facts, are the realities with which we have actively to deal; and to quote my friend William Salter, of the Philadelphia Ethical Society, "as the essence of courage is to stake one's life on a possibility, so the essence of faith is to believe that the possibility exists."

These, then, are my last words to you: Be not afraid of life. Believe that life *is* worth living, and your belief will help create the fact. The 'scientific proof' that you are right may not be clear before the day of judgment (or some stage of being which that expression may serve to symbolize) is reached. But the faithful fighters of this hour, or the beings that then and there will represent them, may then turn to the faint-hearted, who here decline to go on, with words like those with which Henry IV greeted the tardy Crillon after a great victory had been gained: "Hang yourself, brave Crillon! we fought at Arques, and you were not there."

Edwin Arlington Robinson
Credo

> *I cannot find my way: there is no star*
> *In all the shrouded heavens anywhere;*
> *And there is not a whisper in the air*
> *Of any living voice but one so far*
> *That I can hear it only as a bar*
> *Of lost, imperial music, played when fair*
> *And angel fingers wove, and unaware,*
> *Dead leaves to garlands where no roses are.*
>
> *No, there is not a glimmer, nor a call,*
> *For one that welcomes, welcomes when he fears,*
> *The black and awful chaos of the night;*
> *For through it all,—above, beyond it all,—*
> *I know the far-sent message of the years,*
> *I feel the coming glory of the Light!*

The Children of the Night (Boston, 1897), p. 65. Text from this edition.

Stephen Crane
The Blue Battalions

> *When a people reach the top of a hill*
> *Then does God lean toward them,*
> *Shortens tongues, lengthens arms.*
> *A vision of their dead comes to the weak.*

Philistine, VII (June, 1898), 9–10. Text from *The Poems of Stephen Crane*, ed. Joseph Katz (New York, 1966), pp. 76–77. Reprinted by permission of Cooper Square Publishers, Inc.

The moon shall not be too old
Before the new battalions rise
    —Blue battalions—
The moon shall not be too old
When the children of change shall fall
Before the new battalions
    —The blue battalions—

Mistakes and virtues will be trampled deep
A church and a thief shall fall together
A sword will come at the bidding of the eyeless,
The God-led, turning only to beckon.
    Swinging a creed like a censer
    At the head of the new battalions
        —Blue battalions—
    March the tools of nature's impulse
    Men born of wrong, men born of right
    Men of the new battalions
        —The blue battalions—

The clang of swords is Thy wisdom
The wounded make gestures like Thy Son's
The feet of mad horses is one part,
—Aye, another is the hand of a mother on the brow of a son.
    Then swift as they charge through a shadow,
    The men of the new battalions
        —Blue battalions—
    God lead them high. God lead them far
    Lead them far, lead them high
    These new battalions
        —The blue battalions—

Part Two

LITERARY CRITICISM

The Centrality of Howells

Hamlin Garland and William Dean Howells

Garland, *Mr. Howells's Latest Novels.* Howells, *Editor's Study.* Eugene Field, *Sharps and Flats.*

Stephen Crane and William Dean Howells

Crane, *Howells Discussed at Avon-by-the-Sea.* Crane, *Fears Realists Must Wait.* Crane to Howells, August 17, 1896. Howells, *Maggie: An Appreciation.* Howells to Cora Crane, July 29, 1900.

Frank Norris and William Dean Howells

Howells, *A Case in Point*

Theodore Dreiser and William Dean Howells

Dreiser, *The Real Howells*

The Critical Debate

William Dean Howells, *Criticism and Fiction*
Hamlin Garland, *Productive Conditions of American Literature*
Stephen Crane, *A Youth in Apparel that Glittered*
Maurice Thompson, *The Ethics of Literary Art*

33

Hamilton Wright Mabie, *The Interpretation of Idealism*
James Lane Allen, *Preface, Summer in Arcady*
Stephen Crane, *Many Red Devils Ran from My Heart*
Frank Norris, *Zola as a Romantic Writer*
Edwin Arlington Robinson, *Zola*
Clarence Darrow, *Realism in Literature and Art*

It was conventional in the 1890's to describe the literary criticism of the decade in terms of a war between realists and romanticists. William Dean Howells and Hamlin Garland were arrayed on one side of the battle line, while Hamilton Wright Mabie, Maurice Thompson, and a host of minor critics and reviewers were on the other. There was indeed much conflict and bitterness in such day-to-day literary business as reviewing, since Howells and Garland warmly greeted writers who dealt with contemporary social life, whereas the "romanticists" or "idealists" viewed those authors with distaste. But the rhetoric of battle and the disagreement over what today would be called "relevancy" disguised the fact that both groups of critics shared certain fundamental assumptions about the nature and purpose of literature.

One way to describe these assumptions is to associate them with a middle-class frame of mind. For Howells and Garland, as well as for Mabie, Thompson, and James Lane Allen, there were aspects of human nature and experience which were never discussed in the home or before mixed company and which therefore had no place in a novel which could enter the home. The middle-class image of the home as a sanctuary was paralled by that of the family as a refuge in which the young were shielded from destructive impulses current in the "outside" world. Of course, the degree of commitment to the belief that literature involves a middle-class author addressing a middle-class reader varied from Thompson's blatant appeal to class prejudice to Howells' pragmatic wisdom, but the belief, nevertheless, underlies most critical writing of the decade and receives its most overt expression in a hostility towards sexual themes in fiction. For example, even though Howells rejected the "ideal grasshopper" and

Mabie appealed for the "ideal" as a complement to the "real," both writers pleaded for a literature of "perspective" or "totality"—that is, for a literature in which the sexual theme was subordinate. The two groups of critics, therefore, found their true antagonist not in each other but in contemporary European fiction, particularly the work of Zola. But Zola was also often the touchstone for those writers who believed that neither the "commonplace" nor the "ideal" adequately represented the "muck" they found in life and in their own hearts. For Stephen Crane, E. A. Robinson, Frank Norris, and Clarence Darrow, violence and passion—especially the violence and passion of sex —were the great "truths" which the writer must attempt to depict. The essential critical debate during the decade, as Norris sensed, was thus not between realists and romanticists but between a bourgeois sensibility which believed in order and progress and a radical sensibility which affirmed that disorder and self-destruction were inseparable from experience. Howells was the key figure in this debate, for his idea of the commonplace not only laid out the ground for much of the critical skirmishing of the decade, but was also a plea for a literature of decorum.

Howells was central to the literary scene of the 1890's in yet another significant way. A man of great personal reserve (Garland once remarked that he could not imagine anyone calling him "Will"), he nevertheless emanated in print and in person a lively interest in what was new and vital in literature. Whether actively supporting young writers such as Garland, Crane, and Norris, or generously giving his time to others such as Theodore Dreiser, Howells was always the "Dean"—wise, genial, paternal. During the early 1890's his presence was both critical and personal—that is, as Garland's 1890 essay reveals, Howells' ideas as well as his character made him the dominant literary figure of the day. But by the end of the decade he had become, as Dreiser depicted him, a fatherly figure whose personality was of greater interest than his critical values.

In almost all his relations with his younger contemporaries, Howells played an ambivalent role. On one hand, as in his association with Crane, he could be both a liberating force and a powerful patron. On the other, it is doubtful whether he fully recognized the meaning of Crane's irony in *Maggie* or of Norris' sexual themes in *McTeague*. But he did sense good writing when he encountered it, and his patronage of the major youthful figures of the 1890's was a noble passage in American literary history.

Hamlin Garland
Mr. Howells's Latest Novels

THERE IS NO MAN in American literature to-day who so challenges discussion as the candid writer of the *Editor's Study*, which has come to be the expression of Americanism in art and literature. Mr. Howells has become an issue in the literary movement of the day, and his utterances from month to month have the effect of dividing the public into two opposing camps. It is no common man whose name can thus become the synonym for a great literary movement; and those who know him the most intimately feel the greatest admiration for him as he pursues his way calmly through the hail of ignoble personalities which opposing critics have ceaselessly rained upon him. He is writing upon conviction, and convictions are not changed by splenetic assaults, especially if these convictions are begotten and sustained by the spirit of a great social movement. The innovator in literature is a sort of Arnold Winkelried; and though he receives the lances of the confronting host, he feels that he has a dauntless band behind him, small though it may be.

Fifteen years ago Mr. Howells was one of the novelists most favorably received by the general careless American public. He wrote charming and graceful stories and essays, and no one thought of assaulting him. He did not stand for progress, did not enunciate definite opinions, and the conservative public considered him delightful for summer reading. He amused the public. Fifteen years is a short time, but it has brought to the author of *A Hazard of New Fortunes* more changes mentally than fall to the lot of most men during an entire lifetime. He has deepened and broadened, gathering

New England Magazine, N. S., II (May, 1890), 243–50. Text from this publication.

Howells' defense of realism in his *Harper's Monthly* "Editor's Study" columns (1886–1892) had brought him under severe attack. Garland had met Howells in the summer of 1887, and the two men remained friends for the remainder of their lives.

sympathy and tenderness, and as a consequence his books have deepened in insight and broadened in humanity. The attention to style, the graceful turn of a phrase are there still, but they are only the scrolls on the column. The first need now is utterance; the form, although not less finished and faithful, has become secondary.

If we attempt to trace out this change in Mr. Howells, we find it beginning in *A Woman's Reason,* where he first grapples with the false and incomplete education of women. This book was in fact a satire, very tender and subtle, and those who have criticised his treatment of women have missed the point entirely, in this and in subsequent books. By showing folly its own image, whether in man or woman, he has labored since the publication of that book for the advancement of men and women alike. He studied American life as few men ever study life, and the results were seen in each new volume.

In each succeeding work his canvas thickened with figures, as his insight grew keener and his range of life broader. *A Modern Instance* came as a magnificent surprise, even to those who knew the writer best, so great was the advance in scope and power. It had a motive, and though the author remained artistically out of sight behind the characters, one felt that a master hand had stated the problem. *A Modern Instance* was a superb book. It had all the grace of humor which his readers had learned to look for, and it had moments of new and surprising force. The characterization is everywhere superb. The handling of Bartley Hubbard is not surpassed in American literature. It was the study of the moral decay of a young and brilliant man. It was a study of a villain in the modern method. The villain of the stage and the conventional novel has given place to the study of a man with weak places in his nature. The villain of the old-time (present-time) stage never existed elsewhere. Bartley Hubbards are everywhere. The subtle moral decay is indicated in little things, insensible declensions, till at last we see the coarse, blatant, fat trickster in the court-room, saying to Halleck, "Say, why don't you marry her yourself?"—and the man's moral death is complete. Yet it came insidiously, merely through taking always the easiest way rather than the right way.

Silas Lapham gave us one of the most characteristic figures in modern American city life. *The Rise of Silas Lapham* is, in fact, the epic of the American business man,—coarse, genial, autocratic, with a contempt for art and literature, and "such nonsense," of indomitable energy, and withal having a sort of inexorable, innate, organic honesty. The treatment of the figures in this book, and the dealing with "vulgar and common people," aroused the first mutterings of discontent, which grew louder as Lemuel Barker fought his way through Boston, from workhouse to the home of Bromfield Cory—that most delightful of cynics.

One of the most striking movements of American social life is the constant stream of young blood from the sparsely settled portions of the country to the towns and cities. The growth of the urban population has been something unparalleled; proportionately very much larger than the growth of the rural population, as the latest census conclusively shows. Not only is this immigration interesting as regards numbers, but as regards quality. For example, Boston, being regarded an educational and literary centre, draws to itself a constantly increasing number of aspirants for literary or artistic preferment, much as New York draws a special class of ambitious business men, and Washington seekers for political place. If, therefore, a novelist were to make his principal character more or less typical of a characteristic class of these seekers, he would make him, according to his proclivities, either an aspirant for wealth, political preferment, or literary recognition; for broadly speaking, these are the distinctive characteristics of these three cities, although they have, of course, many things in common. Thus in the history of Lemuel Barker, quiet and unostentatious as it is, we have a more or less typical case, his life and experiences being representative, in a great measure, of those of thousands of young fortune seekers, students of music, painting, sculpture, journalism, who come and go in Boston and who make up a large and distinctive class. They do not all come with poems to sell, or with the avowed intention of succeeding Mr. Lowell, but they do have a vague, inarticulate desire for a more intellectual life, a broader and more public activity. In *The Minister's Charge* these characters are represented by Lemuel, and by the two young ladies, art students, refined, grave and modest. Berry also has something of the typical about him; and lastly there are the two shop-girls, marvellously delineated, who serve to type the rapidly increasing number of young girls who come from the country to enter shops and offices. When to these figures are added the good-natured, much-afflicted minister and his wife, the glimpses of Miss Vane and Sybil, Bromfield Cory, the tramps at the Chardon-street Home, the horse-car conductors, Lemuel's mother, and the rest, we begin to perceive that the author is reaching out after all types of character and all phases of life. As in *Silas Lapham*, there is a central group of figures accurately outlined, while all around, more and more indistinct, as their connection with the leading figures of the story is slight, are many personages who come for a moment into the half-light, or flit across the background and are gone. In this way is the reader kept aware of the great tides of life rushing up and down the city streets.

The conclusion of this story, with the failure of Lemuel to get rich or famous, is profoundly significant, and profoundly true. Representing the great mass of young adventurers, his failure was as pathetically certain as his struggle was heroic. In the terrible pressure of modern life, boys of the gentleness and moral courage of Lemuel do not often succeed in the worldly way; they drop out of the race, and accept the hard lot of the dumb millions, with a sigh of patience that would be sublime if it were not in a certain way supine.

The most pathetic and moving figure in the book, to one especially who is himself a boy from the country, is the silent, grotesque, and infinitely sorrowful figure of Lemuel's mother. There is a genuine and characteristically American tragedy obscurely set forth in this book; I mean the inevitable and inexorable separation of parent and child, that comes with the entrance of the child upon wider and higher planes of thought and action. The cities are filled with children fighting for standing room, winning here and losing there, and the country is full of homes without sons and daughters to lighten up the gloomy passage of the toil-worn parents on their way to the grave. There they sit, as Lemuel's mother sat, waiting for the weekly letter—all too short in most cases—and dreaming of the success of their children. To many a man in the city the story of Lemuel Barker came with a directness that made the case his own.

Annie Kilburn went deeper into the discussion of social problems than any novel Mr. Howells had previously published, and showed that in his retirement the novelist was moving with his fellows in sympathy with the extraordinary and almost unaccountable rising wave of purely democratic feeling. It was an absorbing and artistic delineation of the changes which a generation has wrought in the life of a New England town—the changes in trade, in social distinctions, and in living, that make the thoughtful man pause and wonder. It was artistic in that the author nowhere forced his opinions upon us, nowhere preached; he simply stated the problem.

All shades of opinion are impartially represented. There are Gerrish and Putney set over against each other as in real life, and Mr. Peck, with his uncompromising honesty, over against the *élite* of South Hatboro', and Annie, with her poor, short-sighted, kindly eyes, externalizing her short-sighted philanthropy; there is J. Milton Northwick, a millionaire tax-dodger, and there is Dr. Morrall, the kindly, laughing physician. All these people have the strongest individuality, expressing themselves with entire freedom, the author simply listening and recording the opinions. The book might have appealed to a wider audience, perhaps, had the author consented to be a little less artistic; that is to say, had he preached in person, his meaning might have been a little more obvious to the careless reader; but the artistic impartiality of the book is, after all, its strong point, its lasting value. The author is content to set the problem before us as it is in life, and let us draw our own conclusions.

That Mr. Howells thus caught and recorded unprecedentedly well a part of the social questioning of our day is not a decline, but an advance in his art. Social regeneration is a living issue—it is in the air, and as a living, present problem is the properest of all subjects for the pen of our greatest novelist. He would have been false to his theories and blind to the world he is depicting had he not taken up the question of progress and poverty, which is alarming and confusing so many minds. It is impossible to go into any town alive to the world without finding Mr. Putney and Mr. Gerrish discussing the question of poverty. It is the theme of every speech; the magazines are full of special articles upon it. The tax-dodger is a reality, the laborers in mills are crying out, orators are going about advocating free trade and free land, the whole of England and America being in a foment. We are living in great days, and the novelist should rightfully be he who has keenest ear, subtlest art of representation, and clearest head. He should teach, but concretely, objectively, not by stopping in the midst of his story to deliver harangues in the manner of the old school. We are no longer children to be fed on pap. Let the novelist give us food—solid bread and meat—and we will chew it for ourselves. This is the aim of such a book as *Annie Kilburn*. The book was full of the most far-reaching questions, and it announced the immense deepening and widening of the author's sympathy. There has been no writing previously in America at once so purposeful and so artistic. It is electric with inquiry. In detail there is an infinite deal of praise to be spoken. The character of poor Putney is one of the most human, sorrowfully humorous and lovable, that Mr. Howells ever sketched. We laugh with him, we admire his keen satirical rapier, which finds the weak spot in the armor of every social pretence at once. His infirmity brings him near to us, and his love for his little crippled son and his helpful, hopeful wife, and his brave struggle against appetite move us almost to tears. A writer never was truer to the dramatic principle than Mr. Howells in this volume, and especially in Putney, Annie, and Gerrish.

The question really discussed in *Annie Kilburn* is set forth by the heroine herself:

> "Even here in America, where I used to think we had the millennium because slavery was abolished, people have more liberty, but they seem just as far off as ever from justice. I think the conditions are all wrong, and that we ought to be *fairer* to people and then we needn't be so *good* to them. I should prefer that. I hate being good to people. I don't like and can't like people who don't interest me. I think I must be very hard-hearted."

The doctor laughed at this.

"Oh, I know," said Annie, "I know the fraudulent reputation I've got for good works."

"Your charity for tramps is the opprobrium of Hatboro'," the doctor consented.

"Oh, I don't mind that. It's easy when people ask you for food or money, but the horrible thing is when they ask you for work. Think of me, who never did anything to earn a cent in my life, being humbly asked by a fellow-creature to let him work for something to eat and drink. It's hideous! It's abominable! At first I used to be flattered by it and try to conjure up something for them to do, and to believe I was helping the deserving poor. Now I give them all money, and tell them they needn't even pretend to work for it. *I* don't work for my money and don't see why they should. . . . I think there is something in the air, the atmosphere, that won't allow you to live in the old way if you've got a grain of conscience or humanity. I don't mean that *I* have. But it seems as if the world couldn't go on as it has been going. . . . I feel that something ought to be done, but I don't know what."

"It would be hard to say," said the doctor.

Around this central idea of distrust of charity and feeling toward justice, the characters are incomparably well grouped. There is Gerrish, who "fixes things himself": "I fix the hours, I fix the wages, and I fix all other conditions, and I say plainly, 'If you don't like them don't come or don't stay,' and I never have any difficulty." Then there is Mrs. Wilmington, once a shop-girl, now the wife of the rich old manufacturer, indolent, amiable, and taking a mild interest in the trials of the shop-girls, from whose drudgery she has escaped through no exertion of her own. And there are the summer residents and gay or haughty or thoughtless Northwicks, or Chapleys, or Brandeths. There, in fact, is Hatboro' and the grand, pathetic, uncompromising figure of Mr. Peck, the minister, filled with a desire to get into genuine helpfulness and near relation again to the poor; preaching "Christ in life," and failing miserably after all, typifying by his death the impotency of the doctrine of "doing good to people," and the stupendousness of the task which faces the reformer who wants justice done to people.

But *Annie Kilburn*, thoughtful as it was, was but a preparatory study to the latest and greatest of the writer's works. In the two-volume novel, *A Hazard of New Fortunes*, Mr. Howells ended all question about his supremacy as an American novelist of life,—if the word novel needs any such addenda. In it he reaches his greatest breadth and his deepest research. He seizes upon the serious social problems now rising in the great cities, their forms, and their develop-

ments. To me the book appears the most impressive and the sanest
study of a city ever made, and it is as much a product of the times
as the electric car. It is the logical sequence of *Annie Kilburn* and
Silas Lapham.

It is interesting to observe the steady growth in the power to handle masses, which the later books show. In his first books Mr. Howells
had only three or four persons, and they had but slight relation to
the outside world—as in *Indian Summer, The Lady of the Aroostook,*
etc. From *A Wedding Journey* to *A Hazard of New Fortunes* is an
immense distance. To those who found *Annie Kilburn* not dramatic
enough, this later book will seem a concession; but the art is the same;
the locality is different—that is all. To go from *Annie Kilburn* to *A
Hazard of New Fortunes* is like leaving the quiet and elm-
shaded village roads of Hatboro', and plunging into actual New York.
The author, leaving his retirement, has joined the vast currents of
human action confluent in our greatest city, a city where the pressure of human life is appalling, where men live two hundred and
ninety thousand to the square mile; where they roar through crevasses
called streets, and sleep in dens called homes. Into the midst of the
splendid, terrible, restless city, our novelist cast himself, and the
result is a marvellous book that is at once a work of art and a profound criticism. It is a section of real life. In it men live and love and
die as in real life. There are strikes, the war called business, and there
are beautiful and devoted souls living lives of charity in the hope of
repairing the havoc caused by the greed of others. It is full of real
individuals, and we comprehend aims, and judge character as in
real life.

It is interesting to put this book over against the old-time studies
of the city, where the houses were askew, doors battered and swinging, blinds squeaking in the blast, trap-doors and cellars full of spooks;
cities filled with caricatures mainly, streams of men with wooden legs
or horrible noses, women too short or too thin, warty, beery—bloodless exaggerations and grotesque peculiarities doing duty as characters, and walking the Rembrandtesque shadows of ram-shackle, perilous, and endless streets; impossible cities filled with impossible
beings, arranged in symmetrical groups of good and bad; the city of
the humorist and the satirist, but not the reality. Here there is no concealing the misery and the crime of life; on the contrary, the blessed
sunlight falls upon the filth and grime of the streets, making the contrast still more hideous and complete. The romantic glooms are
stripped from the haunts of vice and poverty, and the terrible squalor
appalls by its very commonness and nakedness. The reader walks its
streets with the author and studies its life while the sun is shining;
there is no mystery but the mystery of misery and fruitless labor, no

romance beyond the romance of men and women trying to be good and just under conditions which tempt them to be mean and selfish.

As the author's canon of art is to perceive and state as he perceives, and because the question concerning the persistence of poverty in the midst of abounding wealth is everywhere being asked, and social life is full of reformers, therefore in this book of the present we have an elaborate and impartial study of the reform spirit of the day. It will undoubtedly alienate him completely from the ultra conservative class, but it must as certainly win the regard and admiration of all those whose sympathies are broadening with the growing altruism of the age, and deepening with the intellectual perception of the art-value of the infinite drama of our common life.

This book, like *Annie Kilburn*, is artistic in that, while it is filled with the fear and wonder of a great and sympathetic nature when facing the life of the city, it also never preaches. The writer speaks through his characters. It is full of thought that makes the flesh tingle and the breath quicken. There are dramatic episodes treated with perfect freedom from "effectism." It has everywhere the great corrective humor, which forbids exaggeration and fanaticism. Yet it is unswerving in its criticism of things as they are. March and Fulkerson, Miss Vance and Conrad, each utters a characteristic comment upon conditions.

The very heart of the book is the transformation of Jacob Dryfoos from a plain, hard-working farmer to a hard, suspicious possessor of unearned millions, through the discovery of gas-wells under his farm. From that discovery on he becomes a different man. He "caught on," as Fulkerson said. He sells out half of his land, and the other half turns out to be still more valuable. From appropriating a gift of nature he becomes a "financier," with all that that means in these days. He sells his farm in lots to suit purchasers. He moves to New York, and there March studies him, uneasy and unhappy. "He has sharpened, but he has narrowed. He must have undergone a moral deterioration, an atrophy of the generous instincts. His sagacity has turned into suspicion, his caution to meanness, his courage to ferocity, and I'm not very proud when I think such a life and such a man are the ideal and ambition of most Americans."

Dryfoos has a son, Conrad, who has a turn toward the ministry; who is, in fact, a modern reformer—gentle, but firm and persistent. The tragedy of the story comes inevitably from this opposition in the character of father and son, and marks the highest reach of the novelist's art. Nothing can exceed the pathos, the stern yet quiet realism of that great scene, where the two old people stand looking down on the dead boy.

March sums our civilization up in the following fashion:

At my time of life, at every time of life, a man ought to feel that if he will keep on doing his duty he shall not suffer in himself, or in those who are dear to him, except through natural causes. But no man can feel this as things are now, and so we go on, pushing and pulling, climbing and crawling, thrusting aside and trampling under foot, lying, cheating, stealing; and when we get to the end, covered with blood and dirt and sin and shame, and look back over the way we've come to a palace of our own, or the poor-house, which is about the only possession we can claim in common with our brother men, I don't think the retrospect can be pleasing. Conditions make character, and people are greedy and foolish, and wish to have and to shine, because having and shining are held up to them by civilization as the chief good of life. If we felt sure that honest work shared by all would bring food, we'd trust our children with the truth.

This is the central theme, and around it are grouped some of the most penetrating character studies which Mr. Howells has ever made. One has only to recall them—Lindau, the socialist; the Dryfoos family; the irrepressible Fulkerson; Beaton—a remarkable study; Alma Leighton, a modern self-poised, many-sided young woman; the Woodburns, from the reconstructed South. What variety and what distinctiveness! And all around them the infinite drama of the city, tempered and humanized by the author's inexhaustible and sympathetic humor! I confess myself an almost unqualified admirer of this great book; for in the variety and fidelity of its types, the vast social problems involved, its perfect modernness, its freedom from "effectism," its comprehensiveness and its keenness of insight, it certainly stands among the great novels of the world. It shows the author at the very fullness of his powers. His resources are so deep, that we learn he has already turned to the planning of another work of similar import and equal scope. With a technique that is the wonder of his fellow-novelists, and with ever-growing powers, he will undoubtedly yet surpass all previous efforts.

Criticism of Mr. Howells, with previous writers or living writers as criteria, has no value. He can be criticised properly in but one way —by comparison with life. Is he true? is the question to be asked. If he is false to his subject or to himself, then objections are valid. But to say that he is not Scott, or Dickens, or Hugo, or Dumas is certainly true, but it is not criticism. That he is different is a merit and a distinction, not, surely, because Scott and Dickens were not great, but because they no longer represent us. Art, in its progress, refuses to be held accountable to the past. It claims for itself the right to depict in its own way, its own time, just as its predecessors did.

As a critic Mr. Howells may be said to represent the idea of progress in ideals. He stands over against the idea of the statical in art and literature; he is on this point in complete harmony with Ibsen, Valdes, Posnett, and Taine. He emphasizes and exemplifies the sayings of Emerson and Whitman, that "there is more wool and flax in the field"; that there are no bounds to art, that each age should be accountable only to itself, and that the only criterion of the novelist and painter is life and its magnificent reality. This philosophy does not attempt to lessen the true power and beauty of Scott, Dickens, Hugo, Raphael, Valesquez, or Corot, but it declines to take them as models. It gives them due honor for the great work they did in their place and time, and believes that in this day and land they would have been among the radicals. They were all "the radicals" in their day. In short, realism, as voiced by Valdes and Howells, has but one law: "the artist must be true to himself." He should not look to the past for his models, but should write or paint of that which he knows the most about and cares the most about. He should write and paint as nearly as possible as though no other man ever painted or wrote in the world. If this is done, nothing that he paints or writes will be trivial or vulgar, for it is impossible to love a trivial thing. "The greatest poet hardly knows littleness or triviality. If he breathes into anything that was before thought small, it dilates with the grandeur and life of the universe," says Whitman. Valdes, in perhaps the best essay on realism ever published, repeats the thought.

Realism, in truth, is not a theory but a condition of mind upon which a law is founded. The condition is a *genuine love for reality*. Some people seem to have great difficulty in understanding this. The realist does not write of common things so much because he hates romantic things as because he loves actualities,—present, near at hand. Realism has been dragged in the mire, has been taken to mean tanks and fire-engines on the stage, and filth and fury in the novel; but the feeling that underlies the realism of Tolstoi, Valdes, and Howells has nothing in common with this sensationalism. It aims at embodying in art the common landscapes, common figures, and common hopes and loves and ambitions of our common life. It loves normal people, unarranged landscapes, and colors that are not "harmonized." It believes in the physiological rather than the pathological, in the sane and sunny rather than in the abnormal and monstrous; and the justification and the proof of this growing condition of mind are seen in the increasing number of artists of the truth, whose works find favor and reward.

All this Mr. Howells has stood for amid assaults that would have driven another man from the field. Serene and self-poised he has gone on his way, with but a few companions apparently, but in reality with a host at his back. Personal assaults upon him, assaults often from those who cannot and dare not grant to the realist the same privilege the realist grants the conservative, are of no value. The radical, the realist, has no objection to the conservative's adoration of the past, of the heroic, of Scott, of Shakespeare. All he asks is the chance of going on in a humble way of liking modern things, and believing in the present and the future. And he has a suspicion that the case of the conservative is weak in proportion to his vehemence in denouncing the opinions which he persists in calling too baseless and absurd to be worth notice.

If realism is only a passing shadow cast by Mr. Howells and others, its enemies are wasting a deal of valuable time,—it will pass of itself, and the glorious sun of romance will soon illumine the land, and we shall all prefer blue roses to red.

Personally one of the most genial and lovable of men, Mr. Howells is the last person to be taken as a controversialist. His ready laugh and inexhaustible fund of humor make the casual acquaintance wonder if this can be the author of A Hazard of New Fortunes and the target of all the conservative criticisms. But there come moments when the head droops and the strength of the face comes out, and the eyes deepen and darken, till the visitor sees before him one of the greatest personalities in America,—a personality so great that it is content to become the humble percipient and recorder of realities, and so sure of itself as to bow to no criterion but truth.

Mr. Howells carries the sturdy figure and the direct and simple bearing of the man whose boyhood held many a hardship, and who has fought his way to where he is against poverty and discouragement. No man could be more democratic, more approachable, more sympathetic. He has the poet's love for nature, for color, but above all, love for humanity. As one writer has well put it, Mr. Howells "knows how it is himself." This is the quality which makes the author of Annie Kilburn and A Hazard of New Fortunes. It is a quality that is endearing him daily to new circles of readers, who feel that he is stating their case, is voicing their hopes and defeats and longings. The dilettante reader may reject Mr. Howells, but earnest, thinking, suffering men and women find him greater and deeper and truer every day.

As the art which Mr. Howells represents declines to be held accountable to any age, or land, or individual, so it discourages discipleship. It says to the young writer: "Look to nature and to actuality for your model—not to any book, or man, or number of men. Be true to yourself. Write of that of which you know the most and feel the most, and follow faithfully the changes in your feeling. Put yourself down before common realities, common hopes, common men, till their pathos and mystery and significance flood you like a sea, and when the life that is all about you is so rich with drama and poetry, and the vista of human thought and passion so infinite that you are in despair of ever expressing a thousandth part of what you feel, then all idea of discipleship will be at an end. Your whole aim will be to be true to yourself and your infinite teacher, nature, and you will no longer strive to delineate beauty, but truth, and at last truth will be beauty."

The realist of the stamp of Valdes and Howells, so far from being "materialistic," is really a mystic. He reaches at last the mysticism of the philosopher, to whom matter is as mysterious as spirit; of Whitman, who says that "every cubic inch of space is a miracle." "In nature," says Valdes, "there is nothing great or small; nothing is trivial absolutely. All depends upon the mind perceiving; and values are relative in art as in all else." So that to call the work of these realists vulgar or material is to beg the question. To whom are they vulgar or trivial? To say that the modern novel deals largely with the particular is true; that is its distinction. This has been superbly stated by Véron: "We care no longer for gods or heroes, we care for men." And Grant Allen in a recent article has stated the same point, recognizing for the first time the difference between the aims of the real American novelist and all previous fiction.

> The modern American novel is built upon principles all its own, which entirely preclude the possibility of introducing those abrupt changes, sensational episodes, improbable coincidences, which to our contemporary English romance are indispensable ingredients. *It is the real realism, the natural naturalism;* it depends for its effects upon the faithful, almost photographic, delineation of actual life, with its motives, its impulses, its springs of action laid bare to the eye; but with no unnatural straining after the intenser and coarser emotions of blood and fire, no intentional effort to drag in murder, crime, or fierce interludes of passion, without adequate reason. If these things belong by nature to the particular drama as it rises spontaneous in the author's brain, fall into their places they will and may; but the drama certainly won't go out of its own fixed path on purpose to look for them. One has only to glance at the whole past history of literary evolution in order to see that this new conception marks a step in advance—a step along precisely the same lines as all previous advances in the development of the story-telling faculty in humanity at large. For the story starts with the miraculous and the mythical. Gradually, however, as time goes on, the story becomes more human, more definite, more conceivable, more terrestrial. It descends to earth, it condescends to particulars. But still adequacy of motive, consistency of character, accuracy of delineation, are little insisted upon. The critical faculty, as yet but vaguely aroused, can hardly be shocked at all by

the sudden spectacle of the good man becoming bad, or the bad man good, at a stroke of the pen, by impossible conversions and impossible coincidences, by motiveless crimes or unexpected *dénouements*.

Only when the development of literature and art, the incessant change of ideals from age to age, is recognized, as the comparative critic sees it, can full justice be done to the group of young writers now rising in America, who represent this new tendency, and of whom Mr. Howells is the champion and the unquestioned leader.

William Dean Howells
Editor's Study

*   *   *

AT PRESENT WE HAVE only too much to talk about in a book so robust and terribly serious as Mr. Hamlin Garland's volume called *Main-Travelled Roads.* That is what they call the highways in the part of the West that Mr. Garland comes from and writes about; and these stories are full of the bitter and burning dust, the foul and trampled slush of the common avenues of life: the life of the men who hopelessly and cheerlessly make the wealth that enriches the alien and the idler, and impoverishes the producer. If any one is still at a loss to account for that uprising of the farmers in the West, which is the translation of the Peasants' War into modern and republican terms, let him read *Main-Travelled Roads* and he will begin to understand, unless, indeed, Mr. Garland is painting the exceptional rather than the average. The stories are full of those gaunt, grim, sordid, pathetic, ferocious figures, whom our satirists find so easy to caricature as Hayseeds, and whose blind groping for fairer conditions is so grotesque to the newspapers and so menacing to the politicians. They feel that something is wrong, and they know that the wrong is not theirs. The type caught in Mr. Garland's book is not pretty; it is ugly and often ridiculous; but it is heart-breaking in its rude despair. The

"Editor's Study," *Harper's Monthly,* LXXXIII (September, 1891), 639–40. Republished as the Introduction to Garland's *Main-Travelled Roads* (Cambridge and Chicago, 1893). Text from *Harper's Monthly.*

story of a farm mortgage as it is told in the powerful sketch "Under the Lion's Paw" is a lesson in political economy, as well as a tragedy of the darkest cast. "The Return of the Private" is a satire of the keenest edge, as well as a tender and mournful idyl of the unknown soldier who comes back after the war with no blare of welcoming trumpets or flash of streaming flags, but foot-sore, heart-sore, with no stake in the country he has helped to make safe and rich but the poor man's chance to snatch an uncertain subsistence from the furrows he left for the battle-field. "Up the Coulé," however, is the story which most pitilessly of all accuses our vaunted conditions, wherein every man has the chance to rise above his brother and make himself richer than his fellows. It shows us once for all what the risen man may be, and portrays in his good-natured selfishness and indifference that favorite ideal of our system. The successful brother comes back to the old farmstead, prosperous, handsome, well dressed, and full of patronizing sentiment for his boyhood days there, and he cannot understand why his brother, whom hard work and corroding mortgages have eaten all the joy out of, gives him a grudging and surly welcome. It is a tremendous situation, and it is the allegory of the whole world's civilization: the upper dog and the under dog are everywhere, and the under dog nowhere likes it.

But the allegorical effects are not the primary intent of Mr. Garland's work: it is a work of art, first of all, and we think of fine art; though the material will strike many gentilities as coarse and common. In one of the stories, "Among the Corn Rows," there is a good deal of burly, broad-shouldered humor of a fresh and native kind; in "Mrs. Ripley's Trip" is a delicate touch, like that of Miss Wilkins; but Mr. Garland's touches are his own, here and elsewhere. He has a certain harshness and bluntness, an indifference to the more delicate charms of style; and he has still to learn that though the thistle is full of an unrecognized poetry, the rose has a poetry too, that even overpraise cannot spoil. But he has a fine courage to leave a fact with the reader, ungarnished and unvarnished, which is almost the rarest trait in an Anglo-Saxon writer, so infantile and feeble is the custom of our art; and this attains tragical sublimity in the opening sketch, "A Branch Road," where the lover who has quarrelled with his betrothed comes back to find her mismated and miserable, such a farm wife as Mr. Garland has alone dared to draw, and tempts the broken-hearted drudge away from her loveless home. It is all morally wrong, but the author leaves you to say that yourself. He knows that his business was with those two people, their passions and their probabilities. He shows them such as the newspapers know them.

❋   ❋   ❋

Eugene Field
Sharps and Flats

THE CHANCES ARE that to the end of our earthly career we shall keep on regretting that we were not present at that session of the Congress of Authors when Mr. Hamlin Garland and Mrs. Mary Hartwell Catherwood had their famous intellectual wrestling-match. Garland is one of the apostles of realism. Mrs. Catherwood has chosen the better part: she loves the fanciful in fiction; she believes, with us, in fairy godmothers and valorous knights and beautiful princesses who have fallen victims to wicked old witches.

Mr. Garland's heroes sweat and do not wear socks; his heroines eat cold huckleberry pie and are so unfeminine as not to call a cow "he."

Mrs. Catherwood's heroes—and they are the heroes we like—are aggressive, courtly, dashing, picturesque fellows, and her heroines are timid, stanch, beautiful women, and they, too, are our kind of people.

Mr. Garland's *in hoc signo* is a dung-fork or a butter-paddle; Mrs. Catherwood's is a lance or an embroidery-needle. Give us the lance and its companion every time.

Having said this much, it is proper that we should add that we have for Mr. Garland personally the warmest affection, and we admire his work, too, very, very much; it is wonderful photography. Garland is young and impressionable; in an evil hour he fell under the baleful influences of William D. Howells, and—there you are.

If we could contrive to keep Garland away from Howells long enough we'd make a big man of him, for there is a heap of good stuff

"Sharps and Flats," Chicago *Daily Record,* July 27, 1893. Text from *Sharps and Flats,* I (New York, 1900), 47–51.

The "intellectual wrestling-match" occurred on July 14, 1893, at a meeting of the Literary Congress held in conjunction with the World's Columbian Exposition. Garland had read a paper on "Local Color in Fiction," in which he had disparaged the historical romance. Mrs. Catherwood, herself a historical novelist of some note, rose to defend the form, and the "wrestling-match" followed.

in him. Several times we have had him here in Chicago for eight or ten days at a stretch, and when he has associated with us that length of time he really becomes quite civilized and gets imbued with orthodoxy; and then he, too, begins to see fairies and flubduds, and believes in the maidens who have long golden hair and cannot pail the cow; and his heroes are content to perspire instead of sweat, and they exchange their cowhide peg boots for silk hose and mediæval shoon.

But no sooner does Garland reach this point in the way of reform than he gallivants off again down East, and falls into Howells's clutches, and gets pumped full of heresies, and the last condition of that man is worse than the first.

We can well understand how so young and so impressionable a person as Garland is should fall an easy prey to Howells, for we have met Howells, and he is indeed a charming, a most charming gentleman. So conscious were we of the superhuman power of his fascinations that all the time we were with him we kept repeating paternosters lest we, too, should fall a victim to his sugared and persuasive heterodoxy; and even then, after being with them an hour or two, we felt strangely tempted to throw away our collar and necktie and let our victuals drop all over our shirt-front.

The fascination of realism is all the more dangerous because it is so subtle. It is a bacillus undoubtedly, and when you once get it into your system it is liable to break out at any time in a new spot. But Garland is not yet so far gone with the malady but that we can save him if he will only keep away from Howells. In all solemnity we declare it to be our opinion that Howells is the only bad habit Garland has.

So we are glad to hear that there is a prospect of Mr. Garland's making his home here in Chicago, where the ramping prairie winds and the swooping lake breezes contribute to the development of the humane fancy. Verily there will be more joy in Chicago over the one Garland that repenteth than over ninety-and-nine Catherwoods that need no repentance.

Stephen Crane
Howells Discussed at Avon-by-the-Sea

AVON-BY-THE-SEA, Aug. 17 (Special).—At the Seaside Assembly
the morning lecture was delivered by Professor Hamblin [sic] Garland, of Boston, on W. D. Howells, the novelist. He said: "No man
stands for a more vital principle than does Mr. Howells. He stands
for modern-spirit, sympathy and truth. He believes in the progress of
ideals, the relative in art. His definition of idealism cannot be improved upon, 'the truthful treatment of material.' [1] He does not insist
upon any special material, but only that the novelist be true to himself and to things as he sees them. It is absurd to call him photographic. The photograph is false in perspective, in light and shade,
in focus. When a photograph can depict atmosphere and sound, the
comparison will have some meaning, and then it will not be used as a
reproach. Mr. Howells' work has deepened in insight and widened
in sympathy from the first. His canvas has grown large, and has thickened with figures. Between 'Their Wedding Journey' and 'A Hazard
of New Fortunes' there is an immense distance. 'A Modern Instance'
is the greatest, most rigidly artistic novel ever written by an American, and ranks with the great novels of the world. 'A Hazard of New
Fortunes' is the greatest, sanest, truest study of a city in fiction. The

New York *Tribune*, August 18, 1891, p. 5. Republished by Donald Pizer,
"Crane Reports Garland on Howells," *Modern Language Notes*, LXX
(January, 1955), 37–38. Text from *Modern Language Notes*. Reprinted by
permission of Johns Hopkins Press.

A young man of 20, Crane was helping his brother report New Jersey
shore news for the *Tribune*. The Seaside Assembly featured a variety of
prominent speakers on popular subjects. Obviously based on his 1890 essay,
Garland's remarks deeply impressed Crane. The two became friends that
summer, and it was Garland who introduced both Crane and Crane's
Maggie to Howells in early 1893.

[1] A misprint, misquote by Crane, or misuse by Garland of Howells' famous
definition of *realism* (not *idealism*).

test of the value of Mr. Howells' work will come fifty years from now, when his sheaf of novels will form the most accurate, sympathetic and artistic study of American society yet made by an American. Howells is a many-sided man, a humorist of astonishing delicacy and imagination, and he has written of late some powerful poems in a full, free style. He is by all odds the most American and vital of our literary men to-day. He stands for all that is progressive and humanitarian in our fiction, and his following increases each day. His success is very great, and it will last."

Stephen Crane
Fears Realists Must Wait

WILLIAM DEAN HOWELLS leaned his cheek upon the two outstretched fingers of his right hand and gazed thoughtfully at the window—the panes black from the night without, although studded once or twice with little electric stars far up on the west side of the Park. He was looking at something which his memory had just brought to him.

"I have a little scheme," he at last said, slowly. "I saw a young girl out in a little Ohio town once—she was the daughter of the carpet-woman there—that is to say, her mother made ragcarpets and rugs for the villagers. And the girl had the most wonderful instinct in manner and dress. Her people were of the lowest of the low in a way and yet this girl was a lady. It used to completely amaze me—to think how this girl could grow there in that squalor. She was as chic as chic could be, and yet the money spent and the education was nothing —nothing at all. Where she procured her fine taste you could not

New York *Times,* October 28, 1894. Text from this publication.

Although Crane had published *Maggie* and had completed a draft of *The Red Badge of Courage,* he was still a struggling free-lance journalist when Howells granted him this interview, no doubt primarily as an act of generosity. Howells' novels *The Story of a Play* and *Ragged Lady* were not to appear until 1898 and 1899 respectively.

imagine. It was deeply interesting to me—it overturned so many of
my rooted social dogmas. It was the impossible, appearing suddenly.
And then there was another in Cambridge—a wonderful type. I have
come upon them occasionally here and there. I intend to write something of the kind if I can. I have thought of a good title, too, I think
—a name of a flower—'The Ragged Lady.'"

"I suppose this is a long way off," said the other man reflectively.
"I am anxious to hear what you say in 'The Story of a Play.' Do you
raise your voice toward reforming the abuses that are popularly supposed to hide in the manager's office for use upon the struggling artistic playwright and others? Do you recite the manager's divine misapprehension of art?"

"No, I do not," said Mr. Howells.

"Why?" said the other man.

"Well, in the first place, the manager is a man of business. He preserves himself. I suppose he judges not against art, but between art
and act. He looks at art through the crowds."

"I don't like reformatory novels anyhow," said the other man.

"And in the second place," continued Mr. Howells, "it does no good
to go at things hammer and tongs in this obvious way. I believe that
every novel should have an intention. A man should mean something when he writes. Ah, this writing merely to amuse people—why,
it seems to me altogether vulgar. A man may as well blacken his face
and go out and dance on the street for pennies. The author is a sort
of trained bear, if you accept certain standards. If literary men are
to be the public fools, let us at any rate have it clearly understood, so
that those of us who feel differently can take measures. But, on the
other hand, a novel should never preach and berate and storm. It does
no good. As a matter of fact, a book of that kind is ineffably tiresome.
People don't like to have their lives half cudgeled out in that manner,
especially in these days, when a man, likely enough, only reaches for
a book when he wishes to be fanned, so to speak, after the heat of the
daily struggle. When a writer desires to preach in an obvious way he
should announce his intention—let him cry out then that he is in the
pulpit. But it is the business of the novel—"

"Ah!" said the other man.

"It is the business of the novel to picture the daily life in the most
exact terms possible, with an absolute and clear sense of proportion.
That is the important matter—the proportion. As a usual thing, I
think, people have absolutely no sense of proportion. Their noses are
tight against life, you see. They perceive mountains where there are
no mountains, but frequently a great peak appears no larger than a rat
trap. An artist sees a dog down the street—well, his eye instantly relates the dog to its surroundings. The dog is proportioned to the

buildings and the trees. Whereas, many people can conceive of that dog's tail resting upon a hill top."

"You have often said that the novel is a perspective," observed the other man.

"A perspective, certainly. It is a perspective made for the benefit of people who have no true use of their eyes. The novel, in its real meaning, adjusts the proportions. It preserves the balances. It is in this way that lessons are to be taught and reforms to be won. When people are introduced to each other they will see the resemblances, and won't want to fight so badly."

"I suppose that when a man tries to write 'what the people want' —when he tries to reflect the popular desire, it is a bad quarter of an hour for the laws of proportion."

"Do you recall any of the hosts of stories that began in love and ended a little further on? Those stories used to represent life to the people, and I believe they do now to a large class. Life began when the hero saw a certain girl, and it ended abruptly when he married her. Love and courtship was not an incident, a part of life—it was the whole of it. All else was of no value. Men of that religion must have felt very stupid when they were engaged at anything but court-ship. Do you see the false proportion? Do you see the dog with his tail upon the hilltop? Somebody touched the universal heart with the fascinating theme—the relation of man to maid—and, for many years, it was as if no other relation could be recognized in fiction. Here and there an author raised his voice, but not loudly. I like to see the novelists treating some of the other important things of life—the re-lation of mother and son, of husband and wife, in fact all those things that we live in continually. The other can be but fragmentary."

"I suppose there must be two or three new literary people just back of the horizon somewhere," said the other man. "Books upon these lines that you speak of are what might be called unpopular. Do you think them to be a profitable investment?"

"From my point of view it is the right—it is sure to be a profitable investment. After that it is a question of perseverance, courage. A writer of skill cannot be defeated because he remains true to his conscience. It is a long, serious conflict sometimes, but he must win, if he does not falter. Lowell said to me one time: 'After all, the bar-riers are very thin. They are paper. If a man has his conscience and one or two friends who can help him, it becomes very simple at last.' "

"Mr. Howells," said the other man, suddenly, "have you observed a change in the literary pulse of the country within the last four months? Last Winter, for instance, it seemed that realism was about to capture things, but then recently I have thought that I saw coming

a sort of a counter wave, a flood of the other—a reaction, in fact.
Trivial, temporary, perhaps, but a reaction, certainly."

Mr. Howells dropped his hand in a gesture of emphatic assent.
"What you say is true. I have seen it coming. . . . I suppose we shall
have to wait."

Stephen Crane to William Dean Howells, August 17, 1896[1]

[Inscribed in a copy of *The Red Badge of Courage*]

To W. D. HOWELLS this small and belated book as a token of the veneration and gratitude of Stephen Crane for many things he has learned
of the common man and, above all, for a certain re-adjustment of his
point of view victoriously concluded some time in 1892.

Stephen Crane

[1] Misdated August 17, 1895, by Crane.

Stephen Crane: Letters, ed. R. W. Stallman and Lillian Gilkes (New York,
1960), p. 62. Text from this edition. Henry W. and Albert A. Berg Collection, The New York Public Library, Astor, Lenox and Tilden Foundations.
Reprinted by permission of the Berg Collection and Alfred A. Knopf, Inc.

William Dean Howells
Maggie: An Appreciation

I THINK THAT what strikes me most in the story of "Maggie" is that
quality of fatal necessity which dominates Greek tragedy. From the

Stephen Crane, *Maggie: A Child of the Streets* (London, 1896), pp. v–vii.
Text from this edition.

In his preface Howells also refers to Crane's *George's Mother* (1896).

conditions it all had to be, and there were the conditions. I felt this in Mr. Hardy's "Jude," where the principle seems to become conscious in the writer; but there is apparently no consciousness of any such motive in the author of "Maggie." Another effect is that of an ideal of artistic beauty which is as present in the working out of this poor girl's squalid romance as in any classic fable. This will be foolishness, I know, to the many foolish people who cannot discriminate between the material and the treatment in art, and think that beauty is inseparable from daintiness and prettiness, but I do not speak to them. I appeal rather to such as feel themselves akin with every kind of human creature, and find neither high nor low when it is a question of inevitable suffering, or of a soul struggling vainly with an inexorable fate.

My rhetoric scarcely suggests the simple terms the author uses to produce the effect which I am trying to repeat again. They are simple, but always most graphic, especially when it comes to the personalities of the story; the girl herself, with her bewildered wish to be right and good, with her distorted perspective, her clinging and generous affections, her hopeless environments; the horrible old drunken mother, a cyclone of violence and volcano of vulgarity; the mean and selfish lover, dandy, rowdy, with his gross ideals and ambitions; her brother, an Ishmaelite from the cradle, who with his warlike instincts beaten back into cunning, is what the b'hoy of former times has become in our more strenuously policed days. He is, indeed, a wonderful figure in a group which betrays no faltering in the artist's hand. He, with his dull hates, his warped good-will, his cowed ferocity, is almost as fine artistically as Maggie, but he could not have been so hard to do, for all the pathos of her fate is rendered without one maudlin touch. So is that of the simple-minded and devoted and tedious old woman who is George's mother in the book of that name. This is scarcely a study at all, while Maggie is really and fully so. It is the study of a situation merely; a poor inadequate woman, of a commonplace religiosity, whose son goes to the bad. The wonder of it is the courage which deals with persons so absolutely average, and the art which graces them with the beauty of the author's compassion for everything that errs and suffers. Without this feeling the effects of his mastery would be impossible, and if it went further, or put itself into the pitying phrases, it would annul the effects. But it never does this; it is notable how in all respects the author keeps himself well in hand. He is quite honest with his reader. He never shows his characters or his situations in any sort of sentimental glamour; if you will be moved by the sadness of common fates you will feel his intention; but he does not flatter his portraits of people on conditions to take your fancy.

William Dean Howells to Cora Crane, July 29, 1900

Annisquam, Mass.

DEAR MRS. CRANE:/ I would so willingly help you about words for your husband's monument if I were good for anything in that way. But I am not, as I find once more after trying in this case. You know how I valued him who is gone so untimely, and how I prized what he did. I think it was nearly all of it very great work, and if he could have lived what he did would have been nothing to what he could have done.

Hamlin Garland first told me of "Maggie," which your husband then sent me. I was slow in getting at it, and he wrote me a heart-breaking note to the effect that he saw I did not care for his book. On this I read it and found that I did care for it immensely. I asked him to come to me, and he came to tea and stayed far into the evening, talking about his work, and the stress there was on him to put in the profanities which I thought would shock the public from him, and about the semi-savage poor, whose types he had studied in that book. He spoke wisely and kindly about them, and especially about the Tough, who was tough because, as he said, he felt that "Everything was on him." He came several times afterwards, but not at all oftener than I wished, or half so often; and I knew he was holding off from modesty. He never came without leaving behind him some light on the poor, sad life he knew so well in New York, so that I saw it more truly than ever before. He had thought wisely and maturely about it, but he had no plan for it, perhaps not even any hope without a plan. He was the great artist which he was because he was in nowise a sentimentalist. Of course I was struck almost as much by his presence as by his mind, and admired his strange, melancholy beauty,

Stephen Crane: Letters, ed. R. W. Stallman and Lillian Gilkes (New York, 1960), pp. 306–307. Text from this edition. Reprinted by permission of the Butler Library Stephen Crane Collection, Columbia University.

Crane had died in Badenweiler, Germany, on June 5, 1900.

in which there was already the forecast of his early death. His voice charmed me, and the sensitive lips from which it came, with their intelligent and ironical smile, and his mystical, clouded eyes. Inevitably there was the barrier between his youth and my age, that the years make, and I could not reach him where he lived as a young man might. I cannot boast that I understood him fully; a man of power before he comes to its full expression is hard to understand; it is doubtful if he is quite in the secret of himself; but I was always aware of *his* power, and nothing good that he did surprised me. He came to see me last just before he sailed for England the last time, and then he showed the restlessness of the malarial fever that was preying on him; he spoke of having got it in Cuba. But even then, with the sense that we were getting at each other less than ever, I felt his rare quality. I do not think America has produced a more distinctive and vital talent. Yours sincerely,

W. D. Howells

William Dean Howells
A Case in Point

THE QUESTION OF EXPANSION in American fiction lately agitated by a lady novelist of Chicago[1] with more vehemence than power, and more courage than coherence, seems to me again palpitant in the case of a new book by a young writer, which I feel obliged at once to recognise as altogether a remarkable book. Whether we shall abandon the old-fashioned American ideal of a novel as something which may be read by all ages and sexes, for the European notion of it as something fit only for age and experience, and for men rather than women; whether we shall keep to the bounds of the provincial proprieties, or shall include within the imperial territory of our fiction the passions and the motives of the savage world which under-

[1] Howells is referring to an address by Lilian Bell, as reported in the New York *Times* of February 19, 1899.

Literature, N. S. I (March 24, 1899), 241–42. Text from this publication.

lies as well as environs civilisation, are points which this book sums up and puts concretely; and it is for the reader, not for the author, to make answer. There is no denying the force with which he makes the demand, and there is no denying the hypocrisies which the old-fashioned ideal of the novel involved. But society, as we have it, is a tissue of hypocrisies, beginning with the clothes in which we hide our nakedness, and we have to ask ourselves how far we shall part with them at his demand. The hypocrisies are the proprieties, the decencies, the morals; they are by no means altogether bad; they are, perhaps, the beginning of civilisation; but whether they should be the end of it is another affair. That is what we are to consider in entering upon a career of imperial expansion in a region where the Monroe Doctrine was never valid. From the very first Europe invaded and controlled in our literary world. The time may have come at last when we are to invade and control Europe in literature. I do not say that it has come, but if it has we may have to employ European means and methods.

It ought not to be strange that the impulse in this direction should have come from California, where, as I am always affirming rather than proving, a continental American fiction began. I felt, or fancied I felt, the impulse in Mr. Frank Norris' "Moran of the Lady Letty," and now in his "McTeague" I am so sure of it that I am tempted to claim the prophetic instinct of it. In the earlier book there were, at least, indications that forecast to any weather-wise eye a change from the romantic to the realistic temperature, and in the later we have it suddenly, and with the overwhelming effect of a blizzard. It is saying both too much and too little to say that Mr. Norris has built his book on Zolaesque lines, yet Zola is the master of whom he reminds you in a certain epical conception of life. He reminds you of Zola also in the lingering love of the romantic, which indulges itself at the end in an anticlimax worthy of Dickens. He ignores as simply and sublimely as Zola any sort of nature or character beyond or above those of Polk Street in San Francisco, but within the ascertained limits he convinces you, two-thirds of the time, of his absolute truth to them. He does not, of course, go to Zola's lengths, breadths, and depths; but he goes far enough to difference his work from the old-fashioned American novel.

Polite readers of the sort who do not like to meet in fiction people of the sort they never meet in society will not have a good time in "McTeague," for there is really not a society person in the book. They might, indeed, console themselves a little with an elderly pair of lovers on whom Mr. Norris wreaks all the sentimentality he denies himself in the rest of the story; and as readers of that sort do not mind murders as much as vulgarity; they may like to find three of them, not much varying in atrocity. Another sort of readers will not mind the hero's being a massive blond animal, not necessarily bad, though brutal, who has just wit enough to pick up a practical knowledge of dentistry and to follow it as a trade; or the heroine's being a little, pretty, delicate daughter of German-Swiss emigrants, perfectly common in her experiences and ideals, but devotedly industrious, patient, and loyal. In the chemistry of their marriage Mc-Teague becomes a prepotent ruffian, with always a base of bestial innocence; and Trina becomes a pitiless miser without altogether losing her housewifely virtues or ceasing to feel a woman's rapture in giving up everything but her money to the man who maltreats her more and more, and, finally, murders her.

This is rendering in coarse outline the shape of a story realised with a fulness which the outline imparts no sense of. It abounds in touches of character at once fine and free, in little miracles of observation, in vivid insight, in simple and subtle expression. Its strong movement carries with it a multiplicity of detail which never clogs it; the subordinate persons are never shabbed or faked; in the equality of their treatment their dramatic inferiority is lost; their number is great enough to give the feeling of a world revolving round the central figures without distracting the interest from these. Among the minor persons, Maria Macapa, the Mexican chorewoman, whose fable of a treasure of gold turns the head of the Polish Jew Zerkow, is done with rare imaginative force. But all these lesser people are well done; and there are passages throughout the book that live strongly in the memory, as only masterly work can live. The one folly is the insistence on the love-making of those silly elders, which is apparently introduced as an offset to the misery of the other love-making; the anticlimax is McTeague's abandonment in the alkali desert, handcuffed to the dead body of his enemy.

Mr. Norris has, in fact, learned his lesson well, but he has not learned it all. His true picture of life is not true, because it leaves beauty out. Life is squalid and cruel and vile and hateful, but it is noble and tender and pure and lovely, too. By and by he will put these traits in, and then his powerful scene will be a reflection of reality; by and by he will achieve something of the impartial fidelity of the photograph. In the mean time he has done a picture of life which has form, which has texture, which has color, which has what great original power and ardent study of Zola can give, but which lacks the spiritual light and air, the consecration which the larger art of Tolstoy gives. It is a little inhuman, and it is distinctly not for the walls of living-rooms, where the ladies of the family sit and the children go in and out. This may not be a penalty, but it is the inevitable consequence of expansion in fiction.

Theodore Dreiser
The Real Howells

HOWELLS, IT CAN BE TRULY SAID, is greater than his literary volumes make him out to be. If this be considered little enough, then let us say he is even greater than his reputation. Since it is contended that his reputation far outweighs his achievements, let this tribute be taken in full, for he is all that it implies—one of the noblemen of literature.

A striking characteristic of the man is that he understands himself better than any one else, and that he has the courage to write himself down without color or favor. Prof. Boyesen found, when he interviewed him in 1893, that he could "portray himself unconsciously (in conversation) better than I or anybody else could do it for him." His manner is so simple, his wonder at life so fresh and unsatisfied that he appeals to the student and observer as something truly rare —a wholly honest man. He is evidently so honest at heart that he is everywhere at home with himself, and will contribute that quiet, homelike atmosphere to everything and everybody around. He will compel sincerity in you, when you talk with him, not by any suggestion from him, but by the wholesome atmosphere which he exhales, and which steals over all, and makes plain that forms and slight conventionalities are not necessary.

We will not say that he was always thus. One can easily imagine the ideality of his youth when the world seemed young and green. Never insincere, we can believe, but enthusiastic and imaginative. But youth slipped away, the days waned in weariness of work, the mystery of life did not become clearer, and duty come to look more stern. I think that the thought of the final hour is too much with him; that the "watch, for ye know not," rings too much in his ears. He appeals to me as possessing a deeply religious nature unanchored to any religious belief.

Ainslee's, V (March, 1900), 137–42. Text from this publication.

My first sight of him was on a January day in Fifth Avenue. Some one who knew him said, "Here comes Howells," and I saw a stout, thick-set, middle-aged man trudging solemnly forward. He was enveloped in a great fur ulster, and peered, rather ferociously upon the odds and ends of street life that passed. He turned out again and again for this person and that, and I wondered why a stout man with so fierce a mien did not proceed resolutely forward, unswerving for the least or the greatest.

The next time I saw him was for a favor. Some magazine wanted his opinion. A total stranger, I knocked at his door in the apartments overlooking Central Park, and gave no card—only my name. "If he is in he will see you," said the servant, and, sure enough, see me he did, after a few moments. It was with a quiet trudge that he entered the room, and in a glance everything was put at ease. Anybody could talk to him providing the errand was an honest one.

There was none of that "I am a busy man" air. The wrinkles about the eyes were plainly not evidences of natural ferocity, but of kindly age. He even smiled before hearing all my request, motioned me to a chair, and sat down himself. When I had done I arose and suggested that I would not intrude upon his time, but he only shook his head and sat still. Then he propounded some question, for all the world like a kindly bid to conversation, and we were off on an argument in a moment.

How it came around to speculation concerning life and death is almost beyond recall. Andrew Lang had newly re-issued his translations of Greek odes. They deal with the passions and pains of individuals dead thousands of years ago, and I expressed wonder at the long, inexplicable procession of life.

Mr. Howells folded his hands calmly and sat quite silent. Then he said, "Yes, we never know wherefrom or whereto. It seems as if all these ruddy crowds of people are little more than plants wakened by the sun and rain."

"Do you find," I said, "that it is painful to feel life wearing on, slipping away, and change overtaking us all?"

"It is, truly. Life is fine. The morning air is good. When I stroll out of a sunny day it seems too much that it should not stay and endure. It is wistfulness that overtakes us, all the more bitter because so hopeless. Every one suffers from it more or less."

From the flight of time and ever imminent death, the conversation drifted to the crush of modern life and the struggle for existence.

"It is my belief," he said, "that the struggle really does grow more bitter. The great city surprises me. It seems so much a to-do over so little—millions crowding into to obtain subsistence in a region where subsistence is least."

"Where would you have them go?"

"There are more fertile parts of the world. This little island is cold and bleak a great many months of the year. Nothing is grown here. When you come to think, there is no reason why the people of the world should not live in the tropics. The means of subsistence there are greater. Yet here they are scheming and planning, and sometimes dying of starvation."

"You have had no direct experience of this great misery."

"No; but I have observed it. All my experiences have been literary, yet in this field I have seen enough."

"Is it so hard to rise in the literary world?"

"About as difficult as in any other field. There seems to be almost invariably a period of neglect and suffering. Every beginner feels or really finds that the doors are more or less closed against him."

"Your view is rather dispiriting."

"Life seems at times a hopeless tangle. You can only face the conditions bravely and take what befalls."

Other things were talked of, but this struck me at the time as peculiarly characteristic of the work of the man. His sympathies are right, but he is not primarily a deep reasoner. He would not, for instance, choose to follow up his speculations concerning life and attempt to offer some modest theory of improvement. He watches the changeful scene, rejoices or laments over the various and separate instances, but goes no further. He has reached the conclusion that life is difficult and inexplicable without really tracing the various theories by which it is synthetically proved. He is inclined to let the great analysis of things go by the board, sure that it is a mystery and not caring much for the proof.

And yet this attitude which looks so much like pessimism is anything but characteristic of his nature. For all that life with him is a riddle, approaching death a bane, he works and lives gladly. His heart is warm. Since he cannot explain the earthly struggle he chooses to help others make the best of it. Is it a young poet longing, verses in hand, for recognition, Howells will help him. He is not a rich man and must work for his living, yet he will take of his time to read the struggler's material and recommend him according to his merit. The country knows how often he has appeared in print with a liberal commendation of a quite unknown author. He it was who first read Stephen Crane's books and assisted him in New York. It was he who publicly applauded the ghetto story of Abraham Cahan when that beginner was yet unrecognized. He has, time after time, praised so liberally that paragraphers love to speak of him as the "lookout on the watch tower," straining for a first glimpse of approaching genius.

On my first visit, and when we were discussing the difficulties beginners experience, I happened to mention what I considered to be an appropriate instance of a young man in the West who had a fine novel which no publisher seemed to want.

"You consider it good, do you?" he asked.

"Very," I said.

"You might ask him to send it on to me. I should like to read it."

I was rather astonished at the liberal offer, and thanked him for the absent one. It was no idle favor of conversation, either. The book was forwarded, and, true to his word, he read it, doing what he could to make the merit of the work a source of reward for the author. There were several similar instances within a comparatively short period, and I heard of others from time to time until it all became impressively plain—how truly generous and humane is the Dean of American Letters. The great literary philanthropist, I call him.

It is useless to go to the critics for confirmation of this view of the man. Whatever may be said elsewhere, it is better to go to the man's own account of his life and his opinions. What he has put down in "My Literary Passions" rings true as a bell. It is, aside from a record of his likes and dislikes of books, a valuable human document, and in it much of the real Howells can be found, though not so much as in conversation with him. He explains in a style whose chief charm is its evident truth how he began life in an Ohio village and practically educated himself. To any one who knows the man, his account of how he made his father's meagre library his university, how his youthful years were divided between the country schools and the printing office, and how he grew into an understanding of his sphere in life must read wholly true. He endured it all with a cavalier bearing, making the best of the worst, and even to-day shields its memory with words of noble import. When I inquired of him how much time he devoted each day to his literary aims, he answered:

"The length varied with changing conditions. Sometimes I read but little. There were years of work, of the over-work, indeed—which falls to the lot of many, that I should be ashamed to speak of except in accounting for the fact. My father had sold his paper in Hamilton, and had bought an interest in another at Dayton, and at that time we were all straining our utmost to help pay for it."

How strong was that love of literary work that could find a little time to study his favorite author, even though he sat up until midnight waiting for telegraphic news, and arose again at dawn to deliver the papers and toil anew at the case. The history of his early career has a flavor of sentiment and poetry well becoming a genius. How his literary aspirations were stirred by the great authors whom he successively read; how he was perpetually imitating the writings of these—but never willing to own it; how he eventually came to un-

derstand that he must be like himself and no other—all savors of
the youthful dreamer of literary fame. It was of this period that he
wrote: "I had a narrow, little space, under the stairs at home. There
was a desk pushed back against the wall which the irregular ceiling
sloped down to meet, behind it, and at my left was a window, which
gave good light on the writing leaf of my desk. This was my workshop
for six or seven years—and it was not at all a bad one. It seemed, for
a while, so very simple and easy to come home in the middle of the
afternoon when my task at the printing office was done, and sit down
to my books in my little study, which I did not finally leave until the
family were all in bed."

So went the days, with long evenings when, weary with manual
toil, he got out his manuscripts and "sawed and filed and hammered
away at the blessed poems, which were little less than imitations."

The world has not despised these poems for all the author's
modesty. There are things in them which are neither sawed nor hammered nor filed, but rather done out of a sad and tender spirit
weighted down with the mistaken thought of its own inefficiency.

Then came legislative work at the state capitol, more printer's
drudgery, and, finally, for some campaign service, a consulate at
Venice, where he sojourned for four years. This is not a biography,
however, but merely an attempt to get a suggestion, out of the past,
of the present helpful and sincere worker in the cause of humanity.

The most likable trait of this able writer, is his honest, open delight
in being appreciated. The driving force of his youth was this desire
to do fine things and get credit for them. The applause of the world
—what an important thing it seemed. To-day he is wiser, but the heart
is the same.

I said to him: "Have you found that satisfaction in the appreciation of your fellowmen, which in your youth you dreamed it would
give you?"

"Yes," he answered, "truly. It is all that the heart imagines—sweet."

"Worth the toil?"

"Yes. I know of nothing more exquisite than to have labored long
and doubtingly and then to find, for all your fears, your labor com-
mended, your name on many tongues. It is reward enough."

Howells owns to this on every occasion where an expression of opinion is necessary and appropriate, and it makes for greater
dignity in him. One of the most characteristic of these acknowledg-
ments occurs in some paper by him in which he says: "I came into the
hotel office (at Montreal) the evening of a first day's lonely sightsee-
ing, and vainly explored the register for the name of some acquaintance; as I turned from it two smartly dressed young fellows embraced
it, and I heard one of them say, to my great amaze and happiness,

'Hello, here's Howells!' 'Oh,' I broke out upon him, 'I was just looking for some one I knew. I hope you are some one who knows *me!*' 'Only through your contributions to *The Saturday Press*,' said the young fellow, and with these golden words, the precious first personal recognition of my authorship I had ever received from a stranger, and the rich reward of all my literary endeavor, he introduced himself and his friend. I do not know what became of this friend, or where or how he eliminated himself, but we two others were inseparable from that moment. He was a young lawyer from New York, and when I came back from Italy four or five years later, I used to see his sign in Wall street, with a never fulfilled intention of going in to see him. In whatever world he happens now to be, I should like to send him my greetings, and confess to him that my art has never since brought me so sweet a recompense, and nothing a thousandth part so much like Fame, as that outcry of his over the hotel register in Montreal."

Some may think that such open expression of sentiment and pleasure is like hanging one's heart upon one's sleeve for daws to peck at, but more will feel that it is but the creditable exuberance of a heart full of good feelings. He is thus frank in his books, his letters, his conversation. His family get no nearer in many things than those in the world outside who admire his charming qualities. He is the same constantly, a person whose thoughts issue untinged by any corroding wash of show or formality.

What more can be said of a man? He is not rich, and can therefore provide no evidence of his character by his individual disposition of money. His field of endeavor is of that peculiar nature which permits of much and effective masquerading. Many an evil heart is effectively cloaked and hidden from the world by a show of literary talent. We can look only at his individual expression of himself, the hold his nature has taken upon those who know him and the extent and use of his reputation. Fame is a very good collateral in the hands of an able man, and Howells has made good use of his fame.

If Howells, by reason of greater advantages in his youth, had been able to go farther intellectually, if he had had direction along the lines of sociology and philosophy, he might have given the world something most important in that direction. The man has the speculative, philosophic make-up. His sympathies are of a kind that produce able theories for the betterment of mankind. As it is, what he has written, smacks of the social-prophetic.

How true this is the readers of "A Traveler from Altruria" can witness. Therein he sets forth his dream of universal peace and goodwill. He sketches a state of utter degradation from which the brutalized poor rise to the purest altruism.

In a further sense, the socialistic-philosophic turn of his nature is evidenced by his confession of the hold the works of Tolstoi have taken upon him. "He charms me," he said, "by his humanity, his goodness of heart." And in the "Literary Passions" that fine opening to the last chapter confirms this statement, "I come now, though not quite in order of time, to the noblest of all these enthusiasms, namely, my devotion for the writings of Lyof Tolstoi. I should wish to speak of him with his own incomparable truth, yet I do not know how to give a notion of his influence without the effect of exaggeration. As much as one merely human being can help another, I believe that he has helped me; he has not influenced me in aesthetics only, but in ethics, too, so that I can never again see life in the way I saw it before I knew him."

Tolstoi's influence has led him back, as he puts it, "to the only true ideal, away from that false standard of the gentleman to the Man who sought not to be distinguished from other men, but identified with them, to that *Presence* in which the finest gentleman shows his alloy of vanity, and the greatest genius shrinks to the measure of his miserable egotism."

It does not matter whether Howells is the greatest novelist in the world or not, he is a great character. There are many, who find sentiments and feelings so rich, so fair, so delicately drawn, in his work, that it seems as if he had gathered the very moonbeams out of the night to weave a wistful spell over the heart, and it is certain that these perfect parts of his work will live. About the other it does not matter, for the larger part of the work of all authors is more or less less bad, anyhow. What is more important is that he has been an influence for good in American letters—that he has used his strength and popularity in the direction of what he took to be the right. He has helped thousands in more ways than one, and is a sweet and wholesome presence in the world of art. By the side of the egotists in his field, the chasers after fame and the hagglers over money, this man is a towering figure. His greatness is his goodness, his charm his sincerity.

William Dean Howells
Criticism and Fiction

*   *   *

. . . THE TIME IS COMING, I hope, when each new author, each
new artist, will be considered, not in his proportion to any other author
or artist, but in his relation to the human nature, known to us all,
which it is his privilege, his high duty, to interpret. "The true
standard of the artist is in every man's power" already, as Burke says;
Michelangelo's "light of the piazza," the glance of the common eye, is
and always was the best light on a statue; Goethe's "boys and black-
birds" have in all ages been the real connoisseurs of berries; but
hitherto the mass of common men have been afraid to apply their
own simplicity, naturalness, and honesty to the appreciation of the
beautiful. They have always cast about for the instruction of some
one who professed to know better, and who browbeat wholesome
common-sense into the self-distrust that ends in sophistication. They
have fallen generally to the worst of this bad species, and have been
"amused and misled" (how pretty that quaint old use of amuse is!)
"by the false lights" of critical vanity and self-righteousness. They
have been taught to compare what they see and what they read,
not with the things that they have observed and known, but with the
things that some other artist or writer has done. Especially if they
have themselves the artistic impulse in any direction they are taught
to form themselves, not upon life, but upon the masters who became
masters only by forming themselves upon life. The seeds of death
are planted in them, and they can produce only the still-born, the
academic. They are not told to take their work into the public square
and see if it seems true to the chance passer, but to test it by the work
of the very men who refused and decried any other test of their own
work. The young writer who attempts to report the phrase and car-

"Editor's Study," *Harper's Monthly,* LXXVI (December, 1887), 154–55;
LXXII (May, 1886), 973; LXXIV (April, 1887), 825, LXXIX (June, 1889),
151–53. Republished in *Criticism and Fiction* (New York, 1891), pp. 8–17,
95–99, 147–57. Text from *Criticism and Fiction.*

riage of every-day life, who tries to tell just how he has heard men talk and seen them look, is made to feel guilty of something low and unworthy by the stupid people who would like to have him show how Shakespeare's men talked and looked, or Scott's, or Thackeray's, or Balzac's, or Hawthorne's, or Dickens's; he is instructed to idealize his personages, that is, to take the life-likeness out of them, and put the book-likeness into them. He is approached in the spirit of the wretched pedantry into which learning, much or little, always decays when it withdraws itself and stands apart from experience in an attitude of imagined superiority, and which would say with the same confidence to the scientist: "I see that you are looking at a grasshopper there which you have found in the grass, and I suppose you intend to describe it. Now don't waste your time and sin against culture in that way. I've got a grasshopper here, which has been evolved at considerable pains and expense out of the grasshopper in general; in fact, it's a type. It's made up of wire and card-board, very prettily painted in a conventional tint, and it's perfectly indestructible. It isn't very much like a real grasshopper, but it's a great deal nicer, and it's served to represent the notion of a grasshopper ever since man emerged from barbarism. You may say that it's artificial. Well, it is artificial; but then it's ideal too; and what you want to do is to cultivate the ideal. You'll find the books full of my kind of grasshopper, and scarcely a trace of yours in any of them. The thing that you are proposing to do is commonplace; but if you say that it isn't commonplace, for the very reason that it hasn't been done before, you'll have to admit that it's photographic."

As I said, I hope the time is coming when not only the artist, but the common, average man, who always "has the standard of the arts in his power," will have also the courage to apply it, and will reject the ideal grasshopper wherever he finds it, in science, in literature, in art, because it is not "simple, natural, and honest," because it is not like a real grasshopper. But I will own that I think the time is yet far off, and that the people who have been brought up on the ideal grasshopper, the heroic grasshopper, the impassioned grasshopper, the self-devoted, adventureful, good old romantic card-board grasshopper, must die out before the simple, honest, and natural grasshopper can have a fair field. I am in no haste to compass the end of these good people, whom I find in the mean time very amusing. It is delightful to meet one of them, either in print or out of it—some sweet elderly lady or excellent gentleman whose youth was pastured on the literature of thirty or forty years ago—and to witness the confidence with which they preach their favorite authors as all the law and the prophets. They have commonly read little or nothing since, or, if they have, they have judged it by a standard taken from these authors, and never dreamed of judging it by nature; they are destitute of the documents in the case of the later writers; they suppose that Balzac was the beginning of realism, and that Zola is its wicked end; they are quite ignorant, but they are ready to talk you down, if you differ from them, with an assumption of knowledge sufficient for any occasion. The horror, the resentment, with which they receive any question of their literary saints is genuine; you descend at once very far in the moral and social scale, and anything short of offensive personality is too good for you; it is expressed to you that you are one to be avoided, and put down even a little lower than you have naturally fallen.

These worthy persons are not to blame; it is part of their intellectual mission to represent the petrifaction of taste, and to preserve an image of a smaller and cruder and emptier world than we now live in, a world which was feeling its way towards the simple, the natural, the honest, but was a good deal "amused and misled" by lights now no longer mistakable for heavenly luminaries. They belong to a time, just passing away, when certain authors were considered authorities in certain kinds, when they must be accepted entire and not questioned in any particular. Now we are beginning to see and to say that no author is an authority except in those moments when he held his ear close to Nature's lips and caught her very accent. These moments are not continuous with any authors in the past, and they are rare with all. Therefore I am not afraid to say now that the greatest classics are sometimes not at all great, and that we can profit by them only when we hold them, like our meanest contemporaries, to a strict accounting, and verify their work by the standard of the arts which we all have in our power, the simple, the natural, and the honest.

Those good people, those curious and interesting if somewhat musty back-numbers, must always have a hero, an idol of some sort, and it is droll to find Balzac, who suffered from their sort such bitter scorn and hate for his realism while he was alive, now become a fetich in his turn, to be shaken in the faces of those who will not blindly worship him. But it is no new thing in the history of literature: whatever is established is sacred with those who do not think. At the beginning of the century, when romance was making the same fight against effete classicism which realism is making to-day against effete romanticism, the Italian poet Monti declared that "the romantic was the cold grave of the Beautiful," just as the realistic is now supposed to be. The romantic of that day and the real of this are in certain degree the same. Romanticism then sought, as realism seeks now, to widen the bounds of sympathy, to level every barrier against aesthetic freedom, to escape from the paralysis of tradition. It exhausted itself in this impulse; and it remained for realism to assert that fidelity to experience and probability of motive are essential conditions of a great imaginative literature. It is not a new theory, but it has never before universally characterized literary endeavor. When realism becomes false to itself, when it heaps up facts merely, and maps life instead of picturing it, realism will perish too. Every true realist instinctively knows this, and it is perhaps the reason why he is careful of every fact, and feels himself bound to express or to indicate its meaning at the risk of over-moralizing. In life he finds nothing insignificant; all tells for destiny and character; nothing that God has made is contemptible. He cannot look upon human life and declare this thing or that thing unworthy of notice, any more than the scientist can declare a fact of the material world beneath the dignity of his inquiry. He feels in every nerve the equality of things and the unity of men; his soul is exalted, not by vain shows and shadows and ideals, but by realities, in which alone the truth lives. In criticism it is his business to break the images of false gods and misshapen heroes, to take away the poor silly toys that many grown people would still like to play with. He cannot keep terms with Jack the Giant-killer or Puss in Boots, under any name or in any place, even when they reappear as the convict Vautrec, or the Marquis de Montrivaut, or the Sworn Thirteen Noblemen. He must say to himself that Balzac, when he imagined these monsters, was not Balzac, he was Dumas; he was not realistic, he was romantic.

*   *   *

. . . If a novel flatters the passions, and exalts them above the principles, it is poisonous; it may not kill, but it will certainly injure; and this test will alone exclude an entire class of fiction, of which eminent examples will occur to all. Then the whole spawn of so-called unmoral romances, which imagine a world where the sins of sense are unvisited by the penalties following, swift or slow, but inexorably sure, in the real world, are deadly poison: these do kill. The novels that merely tickle our prejudices and lull our judgment, or that coddle our sensibilities or pamper our gross appetite for the marvellous are not so fatal, but they are innutritious, and clog the soul with unwholesome vapors of all kinds. No doubt they too help to weaken the moral fibre, and make their readers indifferent to "plodding perseverance and plain industry," and to "matter-of-fact poverty and commonplace distress."

Without taking them too seriously, it still must be owned that the "gaudy hero and heroine" are to blame for a great deal of harm in the world. That heroine long taught by example, if not precept, that Love, or the passion or fancy she mistook for it, was the chief interest of a life, which is really concerned with a great many other things; that it was lasting in the way she knew it; that it was worthy of every sacrifice, and was altogether a finer thing than prudence, obedience, reason; that love alone was glorious and beautiful, and these were mean and ugly in comparison with it. More lately she has begun to idolize and illustrate Duty, and she is hardly less mischievous in this new role, opposing duty, as she did love, to prudence, obedience, and reason. The stock hero, whom, if we met him, we could not fail to see was a most deplorable person, has undoubtedly imposed himself upon the victims of the fiction habit as admirable. With him, too, love was and is the great affair, whether in its old romantic phase of chivalrous achievement or manifold suffering for love's sake, or its more recent development of the "virile," the bullying, and the brutal, or its still more recent agonies of self-sacrifice, as idle and useless as the moral experiences of the insane asylums. With his vain posturings and his ridiculous splendor he is really a painted barbarian, the prey of his passions and his delusions, full of obsolete ideals, and the motives and ethics of a savage, which the guilty author of his being does his best—or his worst—in spite of his own light and knowledge, to foist upon the reader as something generous and noble. I am not merely bringing this charge against that sort of fiction which is beneath literature and outside of it, "the shoreless lakes of ditch-water," whose miasms fill the air below the empyrean where the great ones sit; but I am accusing the work of some of the most famous, who have, in this instance or in that, sinned against the truth, which can alone exalt and purify men. I do not say that they have constantly done so, or even commonly done so; but that they have done so at all marks them as of the past, to be read with the due historical allowance for their epoch and their conditions. For I believe that, while inferior writers will and must continue to imitate them in their foibles and their errors, no one hereafter will be able to achieve greatness who is false to humanity, either in its facts or its duties. The light of civilization has already broken even upon the novel, and no conscientious man can now set about painting an image of life without perpetual question of the verity of his work, and without feeling bound to distinguish so clearly that no reader of his may be misled, between what is right and what is wrong, what is noble and what is base, what is health and what is perdition, in the actions and the characters he portrays.

*　　*　　*

One of the great newspapers the other day invited the prominent American authors to speak their minds upon a point in the theory and practice of fiction which had already vexed some of them. It was the question of how much or how little the American novel ought to deal with certain facts of life which are not usually talked of before young people, and especially young ladies. Of course the question was not decided, and I forget just how far the balance inclined in favor of a larger freedom in the matter. But it certainly inclined that way; one or two writers of the sex which is somehow supposed to have purity in its keeping (as if purity were a thing that did not practically concern the other sex, preoccupied with serious affairs) gave it a rather vigorous tilt to that side. In view of this fact it would not be the part of prudence to make an effort to dress the balance; and indeed I do not know that I was going to make any such effort. But there are some things to say, around and about the subject, which I should like to have some one else say, and which I may my-self possibly be safe in suggesting.

One of the first of these is the fact, generally lost sight of by those who censure the Anglo-Saxon novel for its prudishness, that it is really not such a prude after all; and that if it is sometimes apparently anx-ious to avoid those experiences of life not spoken of before young peo-ple, this may be an appearance only. Sometimes a novel which has this shuffling air, this effect of truckling to propriety, might defend itself, if it could speak for itself, by saying that such experiences hap-pened not to come within its scheme, and that, so far from maiming or mutilating itself in ignoring them, it was all the more faith-fully representative of the tone of modern life in dealing with love that was chaste, and with passion so honest that it could be openly spoken of before the tenderest society bud at dinner. It might say that the guilty intrigue, the betrayal, the extreme flirtation even, was the exceptional thing in life, and unless the scheme of the story necessarily involved it, that it would be bad art to lug it in, and as bad taste as to introduce such topics in a mixed company. It could say very justly that the novel in our civilization now always ad-dresses a mixed company, and that the vast majority of the company are ladies, and that very many, if not most, of these ladies are young girls. If the novel were written for men and for married women alone, as in continental Europe, it might be altogether different. But the simple fact is that it is not written for them alone among us, and it is a question of writing, under cover of our universal acceptance, things for young girls to read which you would be put out-of-doors for saying to them, or of frankly giving notice of your intention, and so cutting yourself off from the pleasure—and it is a very high and sweet one—of appealing to these vivid, responsive intelligences, which are none the less brilliant and admirable because they are in-nocent.

One day a novelist who liked, after the manner of other men, to repine at his hard fate, complained to his friend, a critic, that he was tired of the restriction he had put upon himself in this regard; for it is a mistake, as can be readily shown, to suppose that others impose it. "See how free those French fellows are!" he rebelled. "Shall we always be shut up to our tradition of decency?"

"Do you think it's much worse than being shut up to their tradition of indecency?" said his friend.

Then that novelist began to reflect, and he remembered how sick the invariable motive of the French novel made him. He perceived finally that, convention for convention, ours was not only more tolerable, but on the whole was truer to life, not only to its complexion, but also to its texture. No one will pretend that there is not vicious love beneath the surface of our society; if he did, the fetid explosions of the divorce trials would refute him; but if he pretended that it was in any just sense characteristic of our society, he could be still more easily refuted. Yet it exists, and it is unquestionably the material of tragedy, the stuff from which intense effects are wrought. The question, after owning this fact, is whether these intense effects are not rather cheap effects. I incline to think they are, and I will try to say why I think so, if I may do so without offence. The material itself, the mere mention of it, has an instant fascination; it arrests, it detains, till the last word is said, and while there is anything to be hinted. This is what makes a love intrigue of some sort all but essential to the popularity of any fiction. Without such an intrigue the intellectual equipment of the author must be of the highest, and then he will succeed only with the highest class of readers. But any author who will deal with a guilty love intrigue holds all readers in his hand, the highest with the lowest, as long as he hints the slightest hope of the smallest potential naughtiness. He need not at all be a great author; he may be a very shabby wretch, if he has but the courage of the trick of that sort of thing. The critics will call him "virile" and "passionate;" decent people will be ashamed to have been limed by him; but the low average will only ask another chance of flocking into his net. If he happens to be an able writer, his really fine and costly work will be unheeded, and the lure to the appetite will be chiefly remembered. There may be other qualities which make reputations for other men, but in his case they will count for nothing. He pays this penalty for his success in that kind; and every one pays some such penalty who deals with some such material. It attaches in like manner to the triumphs of the writers who now almost form a school among us, and who may be said to have established themselves in an easy popularity simply by the study of erotic shivers and fervors. They may find their account in the popularity, or they may not; there is no question of the popularity.

But I do not mean to imply that their case covers the whole
ground. So far as it goes, though, it ought to stop the mouths of those
who complain that fiction is enslaved to propriety among us. It appears that of a certain kind of impropriety it is free to give us all it
will, and more. But this is not what serious men and women writing
fiction mean when they rebel against the limitations of their art in our
civilization. They have no desire to deal with nakedness, as painters
and sculptors freely do in the worship of beauty; or with certain
facts of life, as the stage does, in the service of sensation. But they
ask why, when the conventions of the plastic and histrionic arts liber-
ate their followers to the portrayal of almost any phase of the physical or of the emotional nature, an American novelist may not write a
story on the lines of Anna Karenina or Madame Bovary. Sappho they
put aside, and from Zola's work they avert their eyes. They do not
condemn him or Daudet, necessarily, or accuse their motives; they
leave them out of the question; they do not want to do that kind of
thing. But they do sometimes wish to do another kind, to touch one of
the most serious and sorrowful problems of life in the spirit of Tolstoi
and Flaubert, and they ask why they may not. At one time, they remind us, the Anglo-Saxon novelist did deal with such problems—De
Foe in his spirit, Richardson in his, Goldsmith in his. At what moment did our fiction lose this privilege? In what fatal hour did the
Young Girl arise and seal the lips of Fiction, with a touch of her
finger, to some of the most vital interests of life?

Whether I wished to oppose them in their aspiration for greater
freedom, or whether I wished to encourage them, I should begin to
answer them by saying that the Young Girl had never done anything of the kind. The manners of the novel have been improving
with those of its readers; that is all. Gentlemen no longer swear or
fall drunk under the table, or abduct young ladies and shut them
up in lonely country-houses, or so habitually set about the ruin of
their neighbors' wives, as they once did. Generally, people now call a
spade an agricultural implement; they have not grown decent without having also grown a little squeamish, but they have grown comparatively decent; there is no doubt about that. They require
of a novelist whom they respect unquestionable proof of his seriousness, if he proposes to deal with certain phases of life; they require
a sort of scientific decorum. He can no longer expect to be received
on the ground of entertainment only; he assumes a higher function,
something like that of a physician or a priest, and they expect him
to be bound by laws as sacred as those of such professions; they
hold him solemnly pledged not to betray them or abuse their confidence. If he will accept the conditions, they give him their confidence, and he may then treat to his greater honor, and not at all to

his disadvantage, of such experiences, such relations of men and women as George Eliot treats in Adam Bede, in Daniel Deronda, in Romola, in almost all her books; such as Hawthorne treats in the Scarlet Letter; such as Dickens treats in David Copperfield; such as Thackeray treats in Pendennis, and glances at in every one of his fictions; such as most of the masters of English fiction have at some time treated more or less openly. It is quite false or quite mistaken to suppose that our novels have left untouched these most important realities of life. They have only not made them their stock in trade; they have kept a true perspective in regard to them; they have relegated them in their pictures of life to the space and place they occupy in life itself, as we know it in England and America. They have kept a correct proportion, knowing perfectly well that unless the novel is to be a map, with everything scrupulously laid down in it, a faithful record of life in far the greater extent could be made to the exclusion of guilty love and all its circumstances and consequences.

I justify them in this view not only because I hate what is cheap and meretricious, and hold in peculiar loathing the cant of the critics who require "passion" as something in itself admirable and desirable in a novel, but because I prize fidelity in the historian of feeling and character. Most of these critics who demand "passion" would seem to have no conception of any passion but one. Yet there are several other passions: the passion of grief, the passion of avarice, the passion of pity, the passion of ambition, the passion of hate, the passion of envy, the passion of devotion, the passion of friendship; and all these have a greater part in the drama of life than the passion of love, and infinitely greater than the passion of guilty love. Wittingly or unwittingly, English fiction and American fiction have recognized this truth, not fully, not in the measure of its merits, but in greater degree than most other fiction.

Hamlin Garland
Productive Conditions of
American Literature

AMERICAN LITERATURE must be faithful to American conditions.
Granting the variations in the personal comment of each artist, the
output must be in its general character creative, not imitative. It
should rise out of our conditions as naturally as the corn grows. It
must be distinctly and unmistakably American. This is a fundamental
characteristic of the American realist (or veritist)—there are others
which separate him more or less widely from the romanticist and
idealist. I use the word "veritist" because "realism" has been indis-
criminately applied to everything from a tract on Christian Science
down to a tank drama. I ask indulgence for the word; there is no
other which expresses my meaning in dealing with the new literary
method.

The meaning of the word "realism" varies with the outlook of
every person who uses it. Mr. Howells calls it "the truthful treatment
of material." Véron states it to be the realistic imitation of actual
things. Verestchagin advises the young artist to bring every event
into harmony with the time, place, and light selected. Valdés advises the artist to treat of the thing he loves and it will no longer be
prosaic or dull. My own conception is that realism (or veritism) is the
truthful statement of an individual impression corrected by reference
to the fact.

The difference between the veritist and the romanticist is expressed, first, by choice of subject. The veritist chooses for his subject not the impossible, not even the possible, but always the probable. He does not seek the exceptional, the sensational; he *naturally*

Forum, XVII (August, 1894), 690–98. Text from this publication.

Garland's *Crumbling Idols*, which had appeared in May, 1894, is a more
extended plea for "veritism," a term which Garland had coined and had
begun using in 1890.

finds the probable more interesting than the impossible. Certainly he does not choose it because it pays better, for it does not. The larger portion of the public is composed of grown-up children, and tales of blood and intrigue please them much better than stories of the probable and the wholesome. Mr. Rider Haggard's books sell better than Miss Wilkins's. Thus the poor veritist is too often a martyr to his care for probabilities.

He sees Mr. Marion Crawford and Mr. Conan Doyle winning loud applause and much money by easy-going tales of love and war, the while his unexciting stories of normal human life find only an occasional reader. This is in the nature of things. The new art, the modern statement, must make its way against the traditional. It is like making a new road in the forest. To rouse passion is an easy trick; to produce intellectual emotion is an art. Even to read an original novel requires brains. The veritist chooses a modern theme necessarily. His love of life and his distaste for imitation prevent him from "novelizing" history in the manner of the school of historical novelists, and keeps him from the worn-out themes of the Middle Ages. He feels entirely willing that other men should write "The Iron Mask" and "The Glittering Glaive." To him such work is a waste of time.

The veritist chooses a native story, a near-by theme, and he deals with probable characters. They live,—his men and women; you can find them at home if you call. Having chosen probable characters he does not put them through impossible paces. He does not distort their lives. He respects the characters of his story as if they were personages in life. He cannot shove them about, nor marry them, nor kill them. What they do, they do by their own will or through nature's arrangement. Their very names come by some singular attraction. The veritist cannot name his characters arbitrarily. He cannot call them "Maud St. Ayr" or "Hubert De Montford." They are sometimes named "Maud Jones" or "Percy B. Wilson,"—the corrective influence of fact is shown in the surname. There is more of the whole question in this matter of names than one would think.

The veritist loves his characters not because they do, but because they are; not because they are heroes and heroines, but because they are men and women. The veritist has wearied of gods and heroes; he wants men. He has wearied of maidens who are willowy of form and star-eyed. He has wearied of the constant appeal to the sensual which the tricky novelist knows is organic in every man and woman. He therefore takes an interest in plain women of character. He tells of middle-aged people. He seeks not mere beauty, but beauty and significance. This led Octave Thanet to write of "Whitsun Harp," and Joseph Kirkland of "Zury." They did this, not out of theory, but because they found more to interest, more to depict, in such lives.

A mere love-story has become the most hackneyed theme in the world. Miss Wilkins writes mainly of old people and themes of filial or fraternal love. James Whitcomb Riley puts the same themes in verse. In choosing these, they undoubtedly sacrifice a certain kind of success. The easiest way to succeed in a monetary way is by the delineation of the erotic in the life of youth. Nothing is easier than the excitation of men and women by tales of love and war. It lacks distinction, however, and the veritist finds himself naturally averse to running in such well-worn ruts. He prefers to treat of other affections and interests—as, for example, where Henry James writes the story of a boy-pupil, or Heman Chaplin studies of "Eli."

The veritist sees the individual rather than the type. If the individual chances to be a widely recognized type, well and good—but the individual comes first. Nothing is permitted to overshadow character. The question is not so much, What did they do? as, What did they think? With a background which he loves, and characters which he knows, the veritist begins to write, not in another's way, but in his own way, corrected by reference to life. To allow the fantastic, or the improbable, or the impossible to come in, would destroy the unity of his story. It would be untrue, and would be unjust to his characters, for the action springs from them, and is controlled by them or by social forces around them. The introduction of a sensual or bloody incident into "Silas Lapham" would be monstrous—impossible.

The veritist has wearied of the expected also. He does not contrive to have things come out all right in the end to satisfy some sentimentalist who wants "him" to always marry "her." He cannot provide such endings in opposition to the logic of all that has gone before. If the drift of the action is in a certain direction, it can be changed only by the will of the character or by the working of characters upon social environment.

Neither does he enjoy the fortuitous. The chance thing, the curious coincidence, has small value to the veritist. To him the sunny, the regular, the normal is miraculous. He studies stars, not comets. The spy who is condemned to death is *not* a son of the general, nor a nephew,—not even a son of an old classmate: he is a stranger. This lessens the agony, but raises the novelist's art. In the drama the hero does not rush in at the last moment and bid the villain "stand back." The son and husband who goes off to the war, and whom everybody supposes to be dead, continues to be dead, notwithstanding the need of him at home. The old curmudgeon who holds the mortgage has not the slightest desire to possess the widow—he wants the interest. In this novel the hero does not hear of the heroine's danger; the will stays lost, and the wife marries again, and her step-children get on peaceably with her.

All this because the veritist does not constantly ask himself: "Will this create an effect?" or "Could this happen?"—but asks himself, "*Would* this happen?" He does not say it never happens that the spy looks like the general's classmate, or that the will turns up; he merely knows that it is not probable. In short, life goes on in this novel as under the sun and in the open air. The central figures do not necessarily marry or die at the end of the book—they walk on over the hill. I am quite willing to grant that this is distressing to certain minds, but the writers of such stories are not writing to please or to distress romantically inclined readers, but to satisfy their own ideas of art. That is to say, the veritist forms his novel upon life, not upon some other man's book; not even upon his own caprice, but upon his personal impression of the fact.

It is not true to say that there is no imagination involved. Imagination is generally taken to mean the creation of weird, unnatural, impossible, or pathologic situations. The people who use the word thus are mistaken in their psychology. These are merely the more hackneyed forms of the imagination. Imagination is not a thing possessed only by an occasional morbid writer of sensational fiction. It is a faculty possessed by the bridge-builder, the inventor, the business man, often in far higher degree. To imagine vice and crime and salacious incidents is not to my mind a very high exercise of the imagination. The imagination involved in the writing of truthful novels is just as certainly creative as that used in the "Lone Horseman" or in "Dr. Jekyll and Mr. Hyde." It is a little saner and more wholesome; that is all. That it is not photography or flat reporting can be proved by this fact: the critic cannot distinguish between the entirely fictitious characters of the veritistic novel and the characters drawn from life. The critic is challenged to point out in "A Modern Instance" the characters "photographed" from life.

We are now to consider the objection so often raised that the veritist is a gloomy and depressing writer. The romanticist, notwithstanding his themes of blood and lust and tears, is supposed to be a wholesome and inspiring creature. He can slay men in war, and imprison maidens in donjon keeps, and hound poor peasants to death, and yet be called a joyous and lovely teacher of the splendor and glory of life. Miss Repplier is fond of celebrating such books. Mr. Haggard, Mr. Doyle, Mr. Weyman, and Mr. Crawford act upon this theory. Because the romancer puts his scene afar off and clothes his assassin in scarlet-and-green doublet and in gold-inlaid steel, it is all beautiful and moral and inspiring for our sons and daughters to read! He may reflect for the thousandth time the heartless cruelty and injustice of the Middle Ages; he may perpetuate sordid and lustful views of life; he may celebrate the ideals of feudalism, and repeat

age-worn slanders against women,—and yet be considered excellent
food for American youth! But the man who stands for individuality
and freedom; who puts woman on an equality with man, making
her a human being; who stands for a pure man as well as a
pure woman; who stands for an altruistic and free state where involuntary poverty does not exist; who teaches the danger and degradation
of lust and greed, and who inculcates a love for all who live, teaching justice and equal rights,—this novelist is depressing in his effect upon his readers!

The absurdity involved in this needs no exegesis. It will appear in
the mere statement. As a matter of fact the "romance" dulls thought.
It is a lie that lulls the conscience to sleep. The novel or drama of
life stings, arouses, fires with exultant and awakened humanitarian
religion. To one the reader goes to dream, to sensuously enjoy; from
the other, the reader rises with broader sympathy, with more complete knowledge, better fitted to think and act in the interest of truth
and freedom.

In advocating veritism I am not to be understood as apologizing for
the so-called French realists. In fact they are not realists from my
point of view. They seem to me to be sex-mad. I do not believe they
are true to the men and women who make up the great body of citizens in France. I believe the average man or woman in France is sane
and wholesome. I know this is true in America. They may be rough
and sordid, and grim with a life of toil, but as a rule Americans are
not sex-maniacs. No nation can endure and transact business whose
citizens are as depraved as those set forth by Zola or his feeble imi-
tators here in America. Even were his books true of the French, it
would not justify a vile imitation of them on this side of the ocean.
To imitate a grace is weakness; to imitate a vice is criminal.
Veritism shuts out those novelists who think that only crime is real
and only vice interesting. It does not include dramas which deal with
diseased persons. Zola is a great writer, a terrible satirist: he
is not what I mean by "veritist."

It will be seen that the work of the veritist is most difficult. He sets
himself a most arduous task. His art consists in making others feel his
individual and distinctive comment on the life around him. He cannot
allow mere incident to cover up lack of characterization. He cannot
fly to rape and arson to keep up the interest of his readers. He relies
upon the power and variety and dignity of truth. He has faith in the
physiology rather than in the pathology in human life. It requires
more insight and more creative intelligence to write twenty successful novels—as Mr. Howells has done—without a single crime or
unnatural vice in any of them, than to write a score of romances made
up of murder, adultery, suicide, manslaughter, and all the other in-

dispensable elements of the present-day romance. To write "A New England Nun," or "The Grandissimes," or "The Cliff-Dwellers," requires something better than mechanics and situations. To write "Shore Acres" requires a conscience, a human sympathy, and the power to individualize. To write the ordinary melodrama requires only scissors and the carpenter's hammer.

There is one characteristic which I believe marks the difference between the veritist and all romancers or idealists. The veritist loves actual life; the romancers shrink from it as if from cold water. The veritist loves realities, is moved and exalted by them. He fights greed and depravity face to face. He discerns nobility among his street companions. He laughs with them, not at them. He feels the waves of life beat upon him, and is moved and nerved as if by the dash of ocean spray. He loves the sun and air. He sees the drama of street and market-place. He finds significance and beauty in the things near at hand. He feels no need of "escaping from life."

The romanticist is the opposite of all this, however. As he approaches the idealist, he places great stress on the beautiful. The castle is more interesting than the railway station. He loves subdued lights and retired places. His characters move in a mist of sentiment. He does not enjoy close contact with life. The smell of workmen disgusts him. Business men, and keen, sensible women, alarm him or annoy him. He withdraws into a world of dead people who will keep their distance and nod when he pulls the string. He charters a vessel and goes round the world in search of a motive. When he uses the near-at-hand he distorts and exaggerates it and lights it up with red fire. He lacks repose. He troubles himself much about effect. He organizes ordeals and puts his characters through triumphantly in the face of enormous odds. His story comes out right, finishes, "rounds up," not because it would do so in life, but because it does not do so in life. He treats of people who are not his neighbors, because he does not like common people in real life and of course could not like them better in books. (In this he is essentially aristocratic and lacking in sympathy and insight, from the veritist's point of view.) The brave youth always succeeds; the pure girl secures the approbation of heaven; the immoral are miraculously changed by the power of some good woman. The drunkard keeps his pledge; the villain dies endowing an orphan asylum—all contrary to life as a matter of common observation. This does not disturb the idealist romancer. "It is not true to life," cries the veritist. "No, but it *ought* to be," calmly replies the idealist.

I am not crying out against this. On the contrary I hope it will continue, at least so long as it is a sincere expression of a certain outlook on life. When it is mere effectism I desire to see it fail and die.

These qualifications and descriptions do not all apply to any one writer, but only in part. The romancer is really of all shades and grades. At one extreme he deals in melodrama, at his simplest he approaches the veritist. Often the veritist lapses into the romanticist or idealist momentarily.

It all comes down to a matter of temperament. Certain minds find greater value in realities than others. One mind loves and values the near-at-hand; another finds only the blue distance enchanting. I have no war with any sincere artist, but I despise imitation and effectism. No great art ever rose or ever can rise that is based upon imitation or that sacrifices truth for effect. The romanticist as well as every other artist should ask himself whether he is working to please some cult—some reader. To write in imitation of Zola is as fatal to real utterance as to write in imitation of Scott. Veritism imagines in the image of life. Idealism imagines in the image of some ideal, which is generally of the past. It is not always conventional, not always of the past, but it is apt to be so in form if not in spirit. To create in the image of life is the only road to never-ending art. That means progress, and forever progress. To create in the image of models is to take a road which leads in a circle that never rises but always descends. To create in the image of an ideal, ignoring the earth, is like painting the clouds without landscape.

To recapitulate a little: In the Novel, veritism demands simplicity, genuineness, wholesomeness, perfect truth to the conditions of American life, and unity of effect. It demands significance as well as beauty, and a bold, unshrinking contact with life, but it gives the latitude of personal impression of the fact. It has produced such diverse novelists as Mr. Howells, Mr. James, Miss Wilkins, Miss French ("Octave Thanet"), Mr. Harold Frederic, the late Mr. Joseph Kirkland, Miss Murfree, Mr. Cable, and many more. It is true that some of these writers have their romantic moments; it is true that some of them decline to be classed as veritists. Such things do not disturb the critic. Seeing that their work is based upon truth to certain localities and conditions, and allowing for all extravagances, they certainly represent those localities and conditions with sufficient faithfulness to be classed as veritists.

In Poetry it leads to freedom of form—that is, to a closer approach to the passionate speech of modern men. It leads to disuse of conventional words and phrases and hackneyed themes. It modifies the classic and fixed forms. Whitman stood for one phase of it, Sidney Lanier for another, James Whitcomb Riley for still another. Whitman was a powerful iconoclast and teacher of freedom. Lanier enlarged and modified the ancient forms which Whitman threw away. Riley is striving after the actual emotional utterances of the people.

These poets only prophesy change; they do not complete a cycle: let that be stated again.

In Sculpture, veritism demands freedom from the abstract. It demands a return to the same source from which all true art has sprung —study of actual life. It will lead to the delineation of the habits, amusements, characters of modern life. Whatever the sculptor loves and desires to embody in stone or bronze—that thing is suitable. In this way will original work be done and imitation die out. No great sculpture will come till it comes out of spontaneous effort. The sculptor who chisels a nude figure with the right leg advanced and calls it "Charity," and another similar figure with the left foot advanced and calls it "Faith," is not American, and his work is not art. Better "The Checker-Players" of John Rogers, for that is measurably true— has humor and life in it. The work of a man like Edward Kemys, once a hunter and trapper, now a great sculptor of wild animals, shows the real development. Lanceray's groups in bronze show the marvellous inclusiveness of the word "sculptor," once we are free from conventional adherence to the nude and to the ideal.

In the Drama, veritism demands the abolition of formal plot, of set villains, of asides and soliloquies. It advances the study of human life. It widens the dramatic vocabulary. It relates action on the stage to action in life. It leads to the use of the probable and the wholesome, as in the novel. It discards the abnormal, the exceptional, the diseased, the criminal, in order to deal with the affairs of normal human life, making the drama co-extensive with the novel in the scope of its possible themes. In this connection the dramas of Mr. Herne and Mr. Thomas have significance. Mr. Herne has discarded the soliloquy, the aside, the fixed complication, and the villainous villain. Mr. Thomas, Mr. Matthews, Mr. Fitch, and Mr. Barnard are attempting simple scenes of American life. "Shore Acres" and "In Mizzoura" announce an American drama. They will encourage still more faithful and sympathetic studies of American life.

Finally veritism, as I see it, does not enslave, it sets free. It does not even say, "Idealize life—seek out the beautiful." It places the artist alone before life and says: "You are alone with the fact and your literary conscience. Your product is your own—or should be. It should be your individual comment upon life. Be yourself. Do not cringe or prostrate yourself; above all, do not imitate. As a creative mind, the great masters of the past have nothing for you. There is nothing for you to do but ignore them, as they ignored the masters who came before their time. All that Shakespeare or Goethe knew of humanity, you may know; not through them, not at second or third hand, but through a study of present life—by contact with men and women and with physical nature."

Every creative artist in the past, small or great, created in the image of life as he knew it and loved it. Shakespeare wrote great plays by studying life, not by studying Shakespeare. Were he living to-day he would be writing novels and dramas of living men and women, not imitations of the dramas of feudalism. The only justification for an American writer, painter, or sculptor is that he add something to the literature or other art of the world. To imitate, to shirk, to write for mere gain or to satisfy vanity, will not add a lasting word to any art. The American artist must grow out of American conditions and reflect them without deprecatory shrug or spoken apology. He may not always keep himself on the highest level, but it should be his constant care to be faithful to the fact in the light of his literary conscience. In this way he will at least escape imitation, and he may speak a new word about the soul or catch a new light breaking amid the reeds of the river bank.

Stephen Crane
A Youth in Apparel that Glittered

A youth in apparel that glittered
Went to walk in a grim forest.
There he met an assassin
Attired all in garb of old days;
He, scowling through the thickets,
And dagger poised quivering,
Rushed upon the youth.
"Sir," said this latter,
"I am enchanted, believe me,
To die, thus,
In this medieval fashion,
According to the best legends;
Ah, what joy!"
Then took he the wound, smiling,
And died, content.

The Black Riders and Other Lines (Boston, 1895). Text from The Poems of Stephen Crane, ed. Joseph Katz (New York, 1966), p. 29. Reprinted by permission of Cooper Square Publishers, Inc.

Maurice Thompson
The Ethics of Literary Art

* * *

SPEAKING OF FALSE CRITICS, sturdy and right-minded John Dryden said: "all that is dull, insipid, languishing, and without sinews in a poem they call an imitation of nature." In our day the so-called realists answer to Dryden's description. They boast of holding up a mirror to nature; but they take care to give preference always to ignoble nature. They never hold up their mirror to heroic nature. Have you observed how, as a man becomes a realist, he grows fond of being narrow and of playing with small specialties? Have you thought out the secret force which controls the movements of this so-called realism, and always keeps its votaries sneering at heroic life, while they revel in another sort of life, which fitly to characterize here would be improper? I can tell you what that force is. It is unbelief in ideal standards of human aspiration, and it is impatient scorn of that higher mode of thought which has given the world all the greatest creations of imaginative genius. It is a long cry from Homer and Aeschylus and Shakespeare and Scott to Zola and Ibsen and Tolstoi and Flaubert; but it is exactly measured by the space between a voice which utters the highest note of its time and civilization, and one that utters the lowest. I say that these modern realists utter the cry of our civilization's lowest and most belated element; and they call it the cry of modern science. But science has nothing to do with it. Science never disports itself in the baleful light of mere coarseness; nor does it choose dry or commonplace investigations simply because they are dry and commonplace. In its true sphere science aims to lift us above mysteries. The same may be said of all the great masters of art; they lift us above the mire of degrading things. True, we find coarseness

The Ethics of Literary Art (Hartford, Conn., 1893), pp. 18–23, 29–34. Text from this edition.

amounting to what is foul in all the ancient classics, and even in Chaucer and Shakespeare; but we cannot take shelter behind these to cast forth upon the world our own surplus of filth. The custom of critics is in charity to refer the obscenities of old writers to the moral taste of the time. Shall we credit our own civilization with an appetency for the *Kreützer Sonata*, *Leaves of Grass*, and *Madame Bovary*? Have we moved no farther than this during these centuries of Christianity?

I know absolutely nothing about theology, which is doubtless to be counted in reckoning what I come to, and I frankly say that I could not, to save me, tell the difference between one creed and another; but I have it clearly in mind that Christianity is responsible for our civilization, and is the datum-line to which we must refer in all our measurements. Our enlightenment may be imaginary, the gleam of a myth, but it comes from the Star of Bethlehem.

Every reader is aware that there exists a certain strained relation between art and moral responsibility. The first impulse of a solicitous parent is toward forbidding novels and dramatic literature to his children. The college and the pulpit wrestle with a giant doubt in the matter of approving the current conception of art. We all feel that the contemporary artistic influence is subtly opposed to the ethical verities. We find that in fiction and poetry we are hobnobbing with persons with whom we could not in real life bear a moment's interview. It is not so much the scenes and characters chosen; we might regard these, as in real life, with a deep regret; but the conception of art and its function represented by such a choice of subject and treatment suggests a vicious trend of life.

Matthew Arnold's theory of "sweetness and light" may be a trifle flabby when put to the average test of practical experience; yet to irradiate light and to instill sweetness can never be amiss; this indeed seems to me the only excuse for art. Culture must, however, have its root nourished in a stronger soil than that of mere amiability. Art should stand for more than an expression of good-natured commentary on current life, or of ill-natured caricature of humanity's frailties. "What is realism?" inquired a young woman the other day. Her friend answered, "It's writing what we are too clean to speak, and reading about what we would blush to look at. It is going in books where to go in actual life would disgrace us." Prudery does not appeal to a sound soul, and our strictures on art ought not to be different from our strictures on life. Our associations in art should not be lower than our associations in life. Indeed, to me the main service of imaginative activities is in giving higher experiences than ordinary life can afford. In life we aim at the higher life; in art, why not at the higher life? The most abject prudery is that which makes us ashamed to insist upon cleanness and soundness; the vilest dishonesty suggests that we account for literary villainy on the score of compulsion by "artistic conscience." Evil is the great foe of true happiness; but art must give canvas-room for this dark figure with all its scowls and all its fascinating smiles; it has a mighty value when set over against goodness to the effect that the conception holds fast to the right. But let us not pass the limit of freedom into the domain of license. In life we face the ills and evils of our state; we must do the same in art, and in both life and art there must be moral responsibility. If in writing a book we must not steal the thoughtwork of a fellow, surely in the same pages we must avoid breaking the other nine commandments. Still I have known a man who complained loud and long of the immorality of a publisher who had failed to make accurate copyright reports of sales in the matter of a vilely impure novel. This is the special pleading which in another form demands that the artist clothe himself before painting a naked picture.

*   *   *

Is there a man or a woman in the world who believes that any person ever read a novel or a poem for the stark purpose of moral reform? Do you ever read a novel expecting thereby to wash away some stain from your character? Be honest and answer that in every quest pleasure is your goal. From the notion of heaven down to the wish for a tin whistle your aim is pleasure. You imagine you would enjoy heaven; you feel sure that a tin whistle would delight you. If you buy *Anna Karénina* or *Madame Bovary*, it is for delectation and not for personal purification. Speaking of cant, what cant is worse than that of the artist who entertains you at the table of vice with the avowed purpose of sweetening your life?

It is that wonderful Joubert again who says, "Naturally, the soul repeats to itself all that is beautiful or all that seems so." The writer writes what he likes, the reader reads what is to his taste. Ah, taste! there is the foundation. Can you for a moment credit any man's statement that he reads for delectation and yet against his taste? Perhaps I am a Philistine; at all events I do not hesitate here flatly to charge insincerity. Who could possibly be more hopelessly insincere than the avowedly pure woman who tells you that she has fortified her virtue by reading Ibsen's picture of Hedda Gabler? Woman, you have taken Ibsen's arm and have gone with him into vile company and have been delighted with the novelty of it. The smack of hell is sweet to your lips, as it was to those of new-made Eve. It would be strictly true for such a woman to say, "Yes, I read these novels of impure passion, and there is a strain in my taste which enjoys these pictures of temptation and of evil pleasures. Secretly I like a peep into debauchery;

but then I hold on to my own rectitude." The word "rectitude" as here used means formal rectitude of life's exterior; the intrinsic muscles have responded to a coarse and beastly impulse.

In producing works of art having evil for their source of fascination, and in reading such works, we are tainting the most secret veins of immanent criticism. Civilization inevitably responds to these influences working at the farthest tips of its tenderest roots. Vitiate imagination and you destroy character. No pure woman ever wrote a fiction of illicit love; if she began pure, she ended soiled. Her soul followed her pen. Druggists and physicians have told me that a person who takes to opium-eating will lie, steal, or barter body and soul for a morsel of dried poppy-juice. Never in my life have I known a man or a woman given over to the pleasure of writing or of reading novels based on illicit love who did not habitually lie to avoid the application of personal responsibility.

To the perfectly unbiased observer nothing is clearer than that forbidden fruit is always in demand, and will be as long as human perversity fortifies human animalism. If the author of *Tess of the D'Urbervilles* would say the truth, he would flatly confess that he wrote that brilliantly fascinating, filthy novel, not to make poor young girls cling to virtue, not to prevent rich young men from being villains at heart; but to make a fiction that would appeal to human perversity and delectate human animalism. He reckoned safely; the book sold almost as fast as whisky. It was named by the author "the story of a pure woman." This woman, after being easily led to shame once prior to marriage, fell again during wedlock, and then committed murder and was executed. This is no extreme case; I cite it as typical. Nearly all of the critics were loud in praise of this novel— thousands of good people read it. And to justify themselves both critics and readers claimed for it a high moral influence. What I see wrong in this is that it claims for fiction a power and an exemption not possible to real life. How can association with immoral and debauching people and conditions in our reading differ from our association with them in life? If art is chiefly for delectation, is it not a species of debauchery to indulge in art which takes its fascination from forbidden sources? As I have said, human perversity demands the forbidden. A publisher told me that for a novel to gain the reputation of being written in the highest strain of art and yet on a subject not considered clean was a sure guaranty of success; "and yet," said he, "popular sentiment is strong against such books." Here is the fascination of the unclean—the very fascination which it is the duty of all to avoid and which it is the highest mission of Christian civilization to extinguish. And yet Christian artists demand the right to make commerce of this same evil fascination, and in this demand they are upheld by Christian critics.

In a word, I conclude this part of my argument by propounding a question, Has the immanent meaning of Christian civilization yet showed itself in art? Or, negatively, Is not fine art, and especially literary fine art, still essentially heathen? Is not the most direct and vigorous appeal of current poetry and fiction made to the ancient, elemental, conscienceless substance of humanity? One of two things is certainly true,—the artist is specially exempt from moral responsibility, or he is just as responsible as any other person.

To me it appears that the commercial value of literary filth is really behind every argument in favor of the moral force assumed by authors and critics to be inherent in the dramatic presentation of illicit love. We must admit that novels and poems on this subject are immensely fascinating and that in a cold commercial view they are good property. In the same view whisky and gambling rooms are excellent investments. Gilded dives pay large dividends in the lawful currency. St. Peter's Church has fewer visitors than Monte Carlo. What do you make of this? Is it the true conception of art that the artist may live in honor by the same appeal which enriches the faro-dealer, the saloon-keeper, and the princess of a bagnio? Is the money earned by writing and selling *Tess of the D'Urbervilles* one whit cleaner than that earned by any other play upon the human weakness for unclean things?

*   *   *

Hamilton Wright Mabie
The Interpretation of Idealism

IDEALISM HAS SO OFTEN been associated in recent years with vagueness of thought, slovenly construction, and a weak sentimentalism, that it has been discredited, even among those who had recognised the reality behind it and the great place it must hold in all rich

Books and Culture (New York, 1896), pp. 25–59. Text from this edition.

and noble living. It is the misfortune of what is called Idealism, that, like other spiritual principles, it attracts those who mistake the longings of unintelligent discontent for aspiration, or the changing outlines of vapory fancies for the firm and consistent form and shape of real conceptions deeply realised in the imagination. Idealism has suffered much at the hands of feeble practitioners who have substituted irrational dreams for those far-reaching visions and those penetrating insights which are characteristic of its true use and illustration in the arts. The height of the reaction so vigorously and impressively illustrated in a great group of modern realistic works is due largely to the weakness and extravagance of the idealistic movement. When sentiment is exchanged for its corrupting counterfeit, sentimentalism, and clear and definite thinking gives place to vague and elusive emotions and fancies, reaction is not only inevitable but wholesome; the instinct for sanity in men will always prevent them from becoming mere dreamers and star-gazers.

The true Idealist has his feet firmly planted on reality, and his idealism discloses itself not in a disposition to dream dreams and see visions, but in the largeness of a vision which sees realities in the totality of their relations and not merely in their obvious and superficial relations. It is a great mistake to discern in men nothing more substantial than that movement of hopes and longings which is so often mistaken for aspiration; it is equally a mistake to discern in men nothing more enduring and aspiring than the animal nature; either report, standing by itself, would be fundamentally untrue. Man is an animal; but he is an animal with a soul, and the sane view of him takes both body and soul into account. The defect of a good deal of current Realism lies in its lack of veracity; it is essentially untrue, and it is, therefore, fundamentally unreal. The love of truth, the passion for the fact, the determination to follow life wherever life leads, are noble, artistic instincts, and have borne noble fruit; but what is often called Realism has suffered quite as much as Idealism from weak practitioners, and stands quite as much in need of rectification and restatement.

The essence of Idealism is the application of the imagination to realities; it is not a play of fancy, a golden vision arbitrarily projected upon the clouds and treated as if it had an objective existence. Goethe, who had such a vigorous hold upon the realities of existence, and who had also an artist's horror of mere abstractions, touched the heart of the matter when he defined the Ideal as the completion of the real. In this simple but luminous statement he condensed the faith and practice not only of the greater artists of every age, but of the greater thinkers as well. In the order of life there can be no real break between things as they now exist and things as they will exist in the remotest future; the future cannot contradict the present, nor falsify it; for the future must be the realisation of the full possibilities of the present. The present is related to it as the seed is related to the flower and fruit in which its development culminates. There are vast changes of form and dimension between the seed and the tree hanging ripe with fruit, but there is no contradiction between the germ and its final unfolding.

A rigid Realism, however, sees in the seed nothing but its present hardness, littleness, ugliness; a true and rational Idealism sees all these things, but it sees also not only appearances but potentialities; or, to recall another of Goethe's phrases, it sees the object whole.

To see life clearly and to see it whole is not only to see distinctly the obvious facts of life, but to see these facts in sequence and order; in other words, to explain and interpret them. The power to do this is one of the signs of a great imagination; and, other things being equal, the rank of a work of art may, in the last analysis, be determined by the clearness and veracity with which explanation and interpretation are suggested. Homer is, for this reason, the foremost writer of the Greek race. He is wholly free from any purpose to give ethical instruction; he is absolutely delivered from the temptation to didacticism; and yet he reveals to us the secret of the temperament and genius of his race. And he does this because he sees in his race the potentialities of the seed; the vitality, beauty, fragrance, and growth which lie enfolded in its tiny and unpromising substance. If the reality of a thing is not so much its appearance as the totality of that which is to issue out of it, then nothing can be truly seen without the use of the imagination. All that the Idealist asks is that life shall be seen not only with his eyes but with his imagination. His descriptions are accurate, but they are also vital; they give us the thing not only as it looked standing by itself, but as it appeared in the complete life of which it was a part; he makes us see the physical side of the fact with great distinctness, but he makes us see its spiritual side as well. As a result, there is left in our minds by the intelligent reading of Homer a clear impression of the spiritual, political, and social aptitudes and characteristics of the Greek people of his age,—an impression which no exact report of mere appearances could have conveyed; an impression which is due to the constant play of the poet's imagination upon the facts with which he is dealing.

This is true Idealism; but it is also true Realism. It is not only the fact, but the truth. The fact may be observed, but the truth must be discerned by insight,—it is not within the range of mere observation; and it is this insight, this discernment of realities in their relation to the whole order of things, which characterises true Idealism, and which makes all the greater writers Idealists in the fundamental if not in the technical sense. Tolstoi has often been called a Realist by those who are eager to label everything and everybody succinctly; but Tolstoi is one of the representative Idealists of his time, and his "Master and Man" is one of the most touching and sincere bits of true Idealism which has been given the world for many a day.

There is nothing which needs such constant reinforcement as this faculty of seeing things in their totality; for we are largely at the mercy of the hour unless we invoke the aid of the imagination to set the appearances of the moment in their large relations. To the man who sees things as they rush like a stream before him, there is no order, progression, or intelligent movement in human affairs; but too the student who brings to the study of current events wide and deep knowledge of the great historic movements, these apparently unrelated phenomena disclose the most intimate inter-relations and connections. The most despairing pessimism would be born in the heart of the man who should be fated to see to-day apart from yesterday and to-morrow; a rational and inspiring hope may be born in the soul of the man who sees the day as part of the year and the year as part of the century. The great writers are a refuge from the point of view of the moment, because they set the events of life in a fundamental order, and make us aware of the finer potentialities of our race. They are Idealists in the breadth of their vision and the nobility of the interpretation of events which they offer us.

James Lane Allen
Preface, Summer in Arcady

THIS PREFACE IS a flag of war, here run up and set freely waving on the breastworks of this story. If any timorous stranger, approaching it as an unknown fortress, should hesitate in foot and courage for lack

Summer in Arcady (New York, 1896), pp. vii–xiii. Text from this edition.

Set in rural Kentucky, Allen's novel centers on a love affair in which the youthful pair are drawn together sexually but are able to hold their passions in check until marriage.

of means to discover whether it were more prudent for him to advance or to retire, he will need but to glance up at these colours. They will acquaint him at once with the real nature of the forces entrenched behind; with the spiritual country to which they belong; with the cause they have undertaken to defend. Should the knowledge thus gotten, reveal to him his unexpected nearness to the border-land of a friendly power, he is invited to enter the fort, to study the low earthworks, to inspect the smallish garrison. But if he choose to consider himself confronted by a foe, he is free to depart whither he will, nor shall he be meanly fired upon as he turns his manly back.

Our separate, wholesome, altogether peaceful and rather unambitious world of books, lying far off to itself on this side of the ocean, has of late suffered a twofold invasion from the literature of the mother-country, that has well-nigh swept every living American author away before it. These two armies of invading volumes have had little in common but a port of departure and a port of entry; for while one has reached us as the forces of light—benign and always welcome—the other has spread abroad as the old and evil and ever-hated darkness. To those who understand, there is no need of plainer speech; to all others no need of speech at all. We know them too well—these black, chaotic books of the new fiction—know what unhealthy suggestions they have courted, what exposures of the eternally hidden they have coarsely made, what ideals of personal depravity they have scattered broadcast, what principles of social order they have attacked, what bases of universal decency they have been resolute to undermine. There is hardly a thing of value to the normal portion of the race, in its clean advance toward higher living, that they have not in effect belittled or insulted; there is scarce a thing that the long experience of the race has condemned and tried to cast off from itself as an element of decay, that they have not set upon with approval and recalled to favour.

It is against this downward-moving fiction of manifold disorder that the writer has ventured to advance a protest under cover of a story—a story, he is too well aware, that could not possibly carry with it the weight and measure of an opposing argument, but that should at least contain the taste and quality of healthful repudiation. To this end, and with the use of the weapons put into his hands, he has taken two robust young people in the crimson flush of the earliest summer of life; they are dangerously forefathered; they are carelessly reared; they are temptingly environed; they are alone with one another and with Nature; and Nature, intent on a single aim, directs all her power against their weakness. The writer has thus endeavoured to charge this story with as much peril as may be found in any of the others—even more; he has ventured to lay bare some of the veiled and sacred mysteries of life with no less frankness than they have used, but using, as he hopes, full and far greater reverence; and, nevertheless, from such a situation he has tried to wrest a moral victory for each of the characters, a victory for the old established order of civilized societies, and a victory for those forces of life that hold within themselves the only hope of the perpetuity of the race and the beauty of the world. Such and so far runs the plan and hoped-for mission of his work.

But furthermore: no man has ever sat gravely and sincerely down to study the lights and shadows of our common human destiny, desiring to transfer these in the due proportion of reality to the creations of his art, without sooner or later being driven to perceive that into nearly all the lights falls one dark ray from one great shadow,—the greatest shadow of the world,—its outcast women. This story has been sent very near to the old, old pathway that has always been trodden and is trodden to-day by these, alas! wandering, innumerable ones; and the writer has cast it in that direction with the utmost desire that it might do some good in this way:

If any mother should read this account of the life of a partly irresponsible girl, whose own mother had failed to warn her of the commonest dangers, had neglected to guard and guide her feet to the knowledge that may mean safety, it will haply arouse in her the question whether she herself is giving the needed warnings, throwing forth the proper guard, lending the upward guidance; for how much of the world's chief tragedy lives on and on for the simple lack of these?

If any father should read this story of temptation and struggle in two children, he might perhaps order his own life the better for having had the truth brought home to him, that whenever he weakens the moral fibre of his nature, he may be weakening as well not only the moral fibre of a son, but—what is far more terrible and pitiful in the judgment of the world—the moral fibre of his own daughter, yet unborn; for it is true that the fallen women of the race are in a measure set apart to that awful doom by the inherited immorality of their fathers.

If any girl, alone in the world, having no mother or counsellor of any kind,—alone with her youth, her innocence, her beauty, perhaps her poverty as well and the need of hard work,—not in the country chiefly, but rather in the vast city, in the treacherous town,—if any such poor, undefended child should chance to read this story, she should bear in mind that its main lesson and most solemn warning are addressed to her: the lesson not to trust herself, the warning to trust no other, without reservation—blindly led on by love; or else, sitting lonely in her sorrow on her bed at midnight, she may come to know what her countless sisters have known,—that even the purest love can do wrong, can betray, can be betrayed.

If many a man should read this story—married or unmarried, younger, older—who has resolutely set his feet in the pathway of right, living, there is nothing here to tempt them thence; if they are straying elsewhither, there are some things here that might well follow after him,—if not with the power to recall, at least as a memory to rebuke; for he has found set forth in these pages the case of a boy, who, being greatly wronged by a past beyond his reach and associates beyond his control, nevertheless did struggle upward into something better than he had been,—so winning his happiness in one woman at last, as men must always win it,—by rising to it as something that stands above them, never going down to it as something that waits below.

Stephen Crane
Many Red Devils Ran from My Heart

> Many red devils ran from my heart
> And out upon the page.
> They were so tiny
> The pen could mash them.
> And many struggled in the ink.
> It was strange
> To write in this red muck
> Of things from my heart.

The Black Riders and Other Lines (Boston, 1895). Text from *The Poems of Stephen Crane,* ed. Joseph Katz (New York, 1966), p. 49. Reprinted by permission of Cooper Square Publishers, Inc.

Frank Norris
Zola as a Romantic Writer

IT IS CURIOUS to notice how persistently M. Zola is misunderstood. How strangely he is misinterpreted even by those who conscientiously admire the novels of the "man of the iron pen." For most people Naturalism has a vague meaning. It is a sort of inner circle of realism—a kind of diametric opposite of romanticism, a theory of fiction wherein things are represented "as they really are," inexorably, with the truthfulness of a camera. This idea can be shown to be far from right, that Naturalism, as understood by Zola, is but a form of romanticism after all.

Observe the methods employed by the novelists who profess and call themselves "realists"—Mr. Howells, for instance. Howells's characters live across the street from us, they are "on our block." We know all about them, about their affairs, and the story of their lives. One can go even further. We ourselves are Mr. Howells's characters, so long as we are well behaved and ordinary and bourgeois, so long as we are not adventurous or not rich or not unconventional. If we are otherwise, if things commence to happen to us, if we kill a man or two, or get mixed up in a tragic affair, or do something on a large scale, such as the amassing of enormous wealth or power or fame, Mr. Howells cuts our acquaintance at once. He will none of us if we are out of the usual.

This is the real Realism. It is the smaller details of every-day life, things that are likely to happen between lunch and supper, small passions, restricted emotions, dramas of the reception-room, tragedies of an afternoon call, crises involving cups of tea. Every one will admit there is no romance here. The novel is interesting— which is after all the main point—but it is the commonplace tale of commonplace people made into a novel of far more than common-

San Francisco *Wave*, XV (June 27, 1896), 3. Text from *The Literary Criticism of Frank Norris*, ed. Donald Pizer (Austin, 1966), pp. 71–72. Reprinted by permission of University of Texas Press.

place charm. Mr. Howells is not uninteresting; he is simply not romantic. But that Zola should be quoted as a realist, and as a realist of realists, is a strange perversion.

Reflect a moment upon his choice of subject and character and episode. The Rougon-Macquart live in a world of their own; they are not of our lives any more than are the Don Juans, the Jean Valjeans, the Gil Blases, the Marmions, or the Ivanhoes. We, the bourgeois, the commonplace, the ordinary, have no part nor lot in the *Rougon-Macquart*, in *Lourdes*, or in *Rome*; it is not our world, not because our social position is different, but because we are *ordinary*. To be noted of M. Zola we must leave the rank and the file, either run to the forefront of the marching world, or fall by the roadway; we must separate ourselves; we must become individual, unique. The naturalist takes no note of common people, common in so far as their interests, their lives, and the things that occur in them are common, are ordinary. Terrible things must happen to the characters of the naturalistic tale. They must be twisted from the ordinary, wrenched out from the quiet, uneventful round of every-day life, and flung into the throes of a vast and terrible drama that works itself out in unleashed passions, in blood, and in sudden death. The world of M. Zola is a world of big things; the enormous, the formidable, the terrible, is what counts; no teacup tragedies here. Here Nana holds her monstrous orgies, and dies horribly, her face distorted to a frightful mask; Étienne Lantier, carried away by the strike of coal miners of *Le Voreux*, (the strike that is almost war), is involved in the vast and fearful catastrophe that comes as a climax of the great drama; Claude Lantier, disappointed, disillusioned, acknowledging the futility of his art after a life of effort, hangs himself to his huge easel; Jacques Lantier, haunted by an hereditary insanity, all his natural desires hideously distorted, cuts the throat of the girl he loves, and is ground to pieces under the wheels of his own locomotive; Jean Macquart, soldier and tiller of the fields, is drawn into the war of 1870, passes through the terrible scenes of Sedan and the Siege of Paris only to bayonet to death his truest friend and sworn brother-at-arms in the streets of the burning capital.

Everything is extraordinary, imaginative, grotesque even, with a vague note of terror quivering throughout like the vibration of an ominous and low-pitched diapason. It is all romantic, at times unmistakably so, as in *Le Rêve* or *Rome*, closely resembling the work of the greatest of all modern romanticists, Hugo. We have the same huge dramas, the same enormous scenic effects, the same love of the extraordinary, the vast, the monstrous, and the tragic.

Naturalism is a form of romanticism, not an inner circle of realism.

Where is the realism in the *Rougon-Macquart*? Are such things likely to happen between lunch and supper? That Zola's work is not purely romantic as was Hugo's, lies chiefly in the choice of Milieu. These great, terrible dramas no longer happen among the personnel of a feudal and Renaissance nobility, those who are in the fore-front of the marching world, but among the lower—almost the lowest—classes; those who have been thrust or wrenched from the ranks, who are falling by the roadway. This is not romanticism—this drama of the people, working itself out in blood and ordure. It is not realism. It is a school by itself, unique, somber, powerful beyond words. It is naturalism.

Edwin Arlington Robinson
Zola

> *Because he puts the compromising chart*
> *Of hell before your eyes, you are afraid;*
> *Because he counts the price that you have paid*
> *For innocence, and counts from the start,*
> *You loathe him. But he sees the human heart*
> *Of God meanwhile, and in God's hand has weighed*
> *Your squeamish and emasculate crusade*
> *Against the grim dominion of his art.*
>
> *Never until we conquer the uncouth*
> *Connivings of our shamed indifference*
> *(We call it Christian faith!) are we to scan*
> *The racked and shrieking hideousness of Truth*
> *To find, in hate's polluted self-defence*
> *Throbbing, the pulse, the divine heart of man.*

The Children of the Night (Boston, 1897), p. 44. Text from this edition.

Clarence Darrow
Realism in Literature and Art

MAN IS NATURE'S last and most perfect work, but, however high his development or great his achievements, he is yet a child of the earth and the rude forces that have formed all the life that exists thereon. He cannot separate himself from the environment that gave him birth, and a thousand ties of nature bind him back to the long forgotten past and prove his kinship to all the lower forms of life that have sprung from the great universal mother, Earth.

As there is a common law of being, which controls all living things, from the aimless motions of the mollusk in the sea to the most perfect conduct of the best developed man, so all the activities of human life, from the movements of the savage digging roots, to the work of the greatest artist with his brush, are controlled by universal law, and are good or bad, perfect or imperfect, as they conform to the highest condition nature has imposed.

*   *   *

When the beauty of realism shall be truly known, we shall read the book, or look upon the work of art, and in the light of all we know of life, shall ask our beings whether the picture that the author or the painter creates for us is like the image that is born of the consciousness that moves our soul, and the experiences that have made us know.

Realism worships at the shrine of nature; it does not say that there may not be a sphere in which beings higher than man can live, or that some time an eye may not rest upon a fairer sunset than was ever born behind the clouds and sea, but it knows that through countless ages nature has slowly fitted the brain and eye of man to the earth on which we live and the objects that we see: and the perfect earthly eye must harmonize with the perfect earthly scene.

Arena, IX (December, 1893), 98–113. Republished in *A Persian Pearl and Other Essays* (East Aurora, N.Y., 1899), pp. 107, 113–31, 134–35. Text from *A Persian Pearl*.

To say that realism is coarse and vulgar is to declare against nature and her works, and to assert that the man she made may dream of things higher and grander than nature could unfold. The eye of the great sculptor reveals to him the lines that make the most perfect human form, and he chisels out the marble block until it resembles this image so completely that it almost seems to live. Nature, through ages of experiment and development, has made this almost faultless form. It is perfect because every part is best fitted for the separate work it has to do. The artist knows that he could not improve a single organ if he would, for all the rest of nature must be adjusted to the change. He has the skill to reproduce this shape in lasting stone, and the human brain could not conceive a form more beautiful and fair. Here is a perfect image of the highest work that countless centuries of nature's toil has made, and yet some would seek to beautify and sanctify this work by dressing it in the garb that shifting fashion and changing fancy makes for man.

Only the vulgar superstition of the past ever suggested that the reproduction of human forms in stone was an unholy work. Through long dark centuries religion taught that the flesh was vile and bad, and that the soul of man was imprisoned in a charnel house, unfit for human sight. The early Christians wounded, bruised, and maimed their house of clay; they covered it with skins, which under no circumstances could be removed, and many ancient saints lived and died without ever having looked upon the bodies nature gave. The images of saints and martyrs, which in the name of religion were scattered through Europe, were covered with paint and clothes, and were nearly as hideous as the monks that placed them there. When the condition of Europe and its religious thought are clearly understood, it is not difficult to imagine the reception that greeted the first dawn of modern realistic art. Sculpture and painting deified the material. They told of beauty in the human form which hundreds of years of religious fanaticism had taught was bad and vile. If the flesh was beautiful, what of the monks and priests, who had hidden it from sight, who had kept it covered night and day through all their foolish lives, who maimed and bruised, cut and lacerated, for the glory of the spirit, which they thought was chained within. The church had taught that the death of the flesh was the birth of the soul, and they therefore believed that the artist's resurrection of the flesh was the death of the soul.

This old religious prejudice, born of a misty, superstitious past, has slowly faded from the minds of men, but we find its traces even yet. The origin of the feeling against realistic art has well nigh been forgot, but much of the feeling still remains. No one would now pretend to say that all the body was unholy or unfit for sight, and yet years of custom and inherited belief have made us think that a part is good and the rest is bad: that nature, in her work of building up the human form, has made one part sacred and another vile. It is easy to mistake custom for nature, and inherited prejudice for morality. There is scarcely a single portion of the human body but that some people have thought it holy, and scarcely a single portion but that some have believed it vile. It was not shame that made clothing, but clothing that made shame. If we would eradicate from our beliefs all that inheritance and environment have given, it would be hard for us to guess how much should still remain. Custom has made most things good and most things bad, according to the whim of time and place. To find solid ground we must turn to nature and ask her what it is that conduces to the highest happiness and the longest life.

The realistic artist cannot accept the popular belief, whatever that may be, as to just where the dead line on the human body should be drawn that separates the sacred and profane. There are realists that look at all the beauty and loveliness of the world, and all its maladjustments too, and do not seek to answer the old, old question whether back of this is any all-controlling and designing power; they do not answer, for they cannot know; but they strive to touch the subtle chord that makes their individual lives vibrate in harmony with the great heart of that nature, which they love; and they cannot think but that all parts of life are good, and that while men may differ, nature must know best.

Other realists there are that believe they see in nature the work of a divine maker, who created man in his own image as the last and highest triumph of his skill; that the minutest portion of the universe exists because he wished it thus. To the realist that accepts this all-controlling power, any imputation against a portion of his master's work must reach back to the author that designed it all.

We need not say that the human body might not be better than it is; we need only know that it is the best that man can have, and that its wondrous mechanism has been constructed with infinitely more than human skill; that every portion is adapted for its work, and through the harmony of every part the highest good is reached; and that all is beautiful, for it makes the being best adapted to the earth. Those who denounce realistic art deny that knowledge is power and that wisdom only can make harmony, and they insist instead that there are some things vital to life and happiness that we should not know, but that if we must know these things, we should at all events pretend that we do not. One day the world will learn that all things are good or bad according to the service they perform. One day it ought to learn that the power to create immortality, through infinite succeeding links of human life, is the finest and most terrible that

nature ever gave to man, and that to ignore this power or call it
bad, or fail to realize the great responsibility of this tremendous fact,
is to cry out against the power that gave us life, and commit the greatest human sin, for it may be one that never dies.

The true artist does not find all beauty in the human face or form.
He looks upon the sunset, painting all the clouds with rosy hue, and
his highest wish is to create another scene like this. He never dreams
that he could paint a sunset fairer than the one which lights the fading
world. A fairer sunset would be something else. He sees beauty in
the quiet lake, the grassy field, and running brook; he sees majesty
in the cataract and mountain peak. He knows that he can paint no
streams and mountain peaks more perfect than the ones that nature
made.

The growth of letters has been like the growth of art from the
marvelous and mythical to the natural and true. The tales and legends
of the ancient past were not of common men and common scenes.
These could not impress the undeveloped intellect of long ago. A man
of letters could not deify a serf, or tell the simple story of the poor.
He must write to maintain the status of the world, and please the
prince that gave him food; so he told of kings and queens, of knights
and ladies, of strife and conquest; and the coloring he used was human
blood.

The world has grown accustomed to those ancient tales, to scenes
of blood and war, and novels that would thrill the soul and cause the
hair to stand on end. It has read these tales so long that the true
seems commonplace, and unfit to fill the pages of a book. But all the
time we forget the fact that the story could not charm unless we half
believed it true. The men and women in the tale we learn to love and
hate; we take an interest in their lives; we hope they may succeed or
fail; we must not be told at every page that the people of the book
are men of straw, that no such beings ever lived upon the earth. We
could take no interest in men and women that are myths conjured
up to play their parts, and remind us in every word they speak that,
regardless of the happiness or anguish the author makes them feel,
they are but myths and can know neither joy nor pain.

It may be that the realistic tale is commonplace, but so is life, and
the realistic tale is true. Among the countless millions of the earth it
is only here and there, and now and then, that some soul is born
from out the mighty deep that does not soon return to the great sea
and leave no ripple on the waves.

In the play of life each actor seems important to himself; the world
he knows revolves around him as the central figure of the scene; his
friends rejoice in all the fortune he attains and weep with him in all
his grief. To him the world is bounded by the faces that he knows,

and the scenes in which he lives. He forgets the great surging world outside, and cannot think how small a space he fills in that infinity which bounds his life. He dies, and a few sorrowing friends mourn him for a day, and the world does not know he ever lived or ever died. In the ordinary life nearly all events are commonplace; but a few important days are thinly sprinkled in amongst all of those that intervene between the cradle and the grave. We eat and drink, we work and sleep, and here and there a great joy or sorrow creeps in upon our lives, and leaves a day that stands out against the monotony of all the rest, like the pyramids upon the level plains; but these events are very few and are important only to ourselves, and for the rest we walk with steady pace and slow along the short and narrow path of life, and rely upon the common things alone to occupy our minds and hide from view the marble stone that here and there gleams through the over-hanging trees just where the road leaves off.

The old novel which we used to read and to which the world so fondly clings, had no idea of relation or perspective. It had a hero and a heroine, and sometimes more than one. The revolutions of the planets were less important than their love. War, shipwreck, and conflagration, all conspired to produce the climax of the scene, and the whole world stood still until the lovers' hearts and hands were joined. Wide oceans, burning deserts, arctic seas, impassable jungles, irate fathers, and even designing mothers, were helpless against the decree that fate had made, and when all the barriers were passed and love had triumphed over impossibilities, the tale was done; through the rest of life nothing of interest could occur. Sometimes in the progress of the story, if the complications were too great, a thunderbolt or an earthquake was introduced to destroy the villain and help on the match. Earthquakes sometimes happen, and the realistic novelist might write a tale of a scene like this, but then the love affair would be an incident of the earthquake, and not the earthquake an incident of the love affair.

In real life the affections have played an important part and sometimes great things have been done and suffered in the name of love, but most of the affairs of the human heart have been as natural as the other events of life.

The true love story is generally a simple thing. "Beside a country road, on a sloping hill, lives a farmer, in the house his father owned before. He has a daughter, who skims the milk, and makes the beds, and goes to singing school at night. There are other members of the household, but our tale is no concern of theirs. In the meadow back of the house a woodchuck has dug its hole, and reared a family in its humble home. Across the valley only a mile away, another farmer lives. He has a son, who plows the fields and does the chores and goes to singing school at night. He cannot sing, but attends the school as regularly as if he could. Of course he does not let the girl go home alone, and in the spring, when singing school is out, he visits her on Sunday eve without excuse. If the girl had not lived so near, the boy would have fancied another girl about the same age, who also went to singing school. Back of the second farmer's house is another woodchuck hole and woodchuck home. After a year or two of court-ship the boy and girl are married as their parents were before, and they choose a pretty spot beside the road, and build another house near by, and settle down to common life: and so the world moves on. And a woodchuck on one farm meets a woodchuck on the other, and they choose a quiet place beside a stump, in no one's way, where they think they have a right to be, and dig another hole and make another home." For after all, men and animals are much alike, and nature loves them both and loves them all, and sends them forth to drive the loneliness from off the earth, and then takes them back into her loving breast to sleep.

It may be that there are few great incidents in the realistic take, but each event appeals to life and cannot fail to wake our memories and make us live the past again. The great authors of the natural school—Tolstoi, Hardy, Howells, Daudet, Ibsen, Flaubert, Zola and their kind, have made us think and live. Their words have burnished up our minds and revealed a thousand pictures that hang upon the walls of memory, covered with the dust of years, and hidden from our sight. Sometimes of course we cry with pain at the picture that is thrown before our view, but life consists of emotions, and we cannot truly live unless the depths are stirred. These great masters, it is true, may sometimes shock the over-sensitive with the tales they tell of life, but if the tale is true, why hide it from our sight?

There is nothing more common than the protest against the wicked stories of the realistic school, filled with tales of passion and sin; but he that denies passion denies all the life that exists upon the earth, and cries out against the mother that gave him birth. And he that ignores this truth passes with contempt the greatest fact that nature has impressed upon the world. Those who condemn as sensual the tales of Tolstoi and Daudet still defend the love stories of which our literature is full. Those weak and silly tales that make women fit only to be the playthings of the world, and deny to them a single thought or right except to serve their master, man. These objectors do not contend that tales dealing with the feelings and affections shall not be told, they approve these tales; they simply insist that they shall be false instead of true. The old novel filled the mind of the school girl with a thousand thoughts that had no place in life—with ten thousand pictures she could never see. It taught that some time she should meet a prince in disguise to whom she would freely give her hand and heart. So she went out upon the road to find this prince, and the more disguised he was, the more certain did she feel that he was the prince for whom she sought. The realist paints the passions and affections as they are. Both man and woman can see their beauty and their terror, their true position, and the relation that they bear to all the rest of life. He would not beguile the girl into the belief that her identity should be destroyed and merged for the sake of this feeling, which not once in ten thousand times could realize the promises the novel made; but he would leave her as an individual to make the most she can, and all she can, of life, with all the hope and chance of conquest, which men have taken for themselves. Neither would the realist cry out blindly against these deep passions, which have moved men and women in the past, and which must continue fierce and strong as long as life exists. He is taught by the scientist that the fiercest heat may be transformed to light, and is taught by life that from the strongest passions are sometimes born the sweetest and the purest souls.

In these days of creeds and theories, of preachers in the pulpit and of preachers out, we are told that all novels should have a moral and be written to serve some end. So we have novels on religion, war, marriage, divorce, socialism, theosophy, woman's rights, and other topics without end. It is not enough that the preachers and lecturers shall tell us how to think and act; the novelist must try his hand at preaching too. He starts out with a theory, and every scene and incident must be bent to make it plain that the author believes certain things. The doings of the men and women in the book are secondary to the views the author holds. The theories may be true, but the poor characters that must adjust their lives to these ideal states are sadly wrapped and twisted out of shape. The realist would teach a lesson, too, but he would not violate a single fact for all the theories in the world—for a theory could not be true if it did violence to life. He paints his picture so true and perfect that all men who look upon it know it is a likeness of the world that they have seen; they know that these are men and women and little children that they meet upon the streets; they see the conditions of their lives, and the moral of the picture sinks deep into their minds.

There are so-called scientists that make a theory and then gather facts to prove their theory true; the real scientist patiently and impartially gathers facts, and then forms a theory to explain and harmonize these facts. All life bears a moral, and the true artist must teach a lesson with his every fact. Some contend that the moral teacher must not tell the truth; the realist holds that there can be no moral teaching like the truth. The world has grown tired of preachers

and sermons; to-day it asks for facts. It has grown tired of fairies and
angels, and asks for flesh and blood. It looks on life as it exists, both
its beauty and its horror, its joy and its sorrow; it wishes to see it all;
not the prince and the millionaire alone, but the laborer and the beggar, the master and the slave. We see the beautiful and the ugly,
and with it know what the world is and what it ought to be; and the
true picture, which the author saw and painted, stirs the heart to
holier feelings and to grander thoughts.

It is from the realities of life that the highest idealities are born. The
philosopher may reason with unerring logic, and show us where the
world is wrong. The economist may tell us of the progress and poverty
that go hand in hand; but these are theories, and the abstract cannot
suffer pain. Dickens went out into the streets of the great city and
found poor little Jo sweeping the crossing with his broom. All around
was the luxury and the elegance, which the rich have ever appropriated to themselves; great mansions, fine carriages, beautiful dresses,
but in all the great city of houses and homes, poor little Jo could find
no place to lay his head. His home was in the street, and every time
he halted for a moment in the throng, the policeman touched him
with his club and bade him "move on." At last, ragged, wretched,
almost dead with "moving on," he sank down upon the cold stone
steps of a magnificent building erected for "The Propagation of the
Gospel in Foreign Parts." As we think of wretched, ragged Jo in the
midst of all this luxury and wealth, we see the tens of thousands of
other waifs in the great cities of the world, and we condemn the so-
called civilization of the earth that builds the mansions of the rich
and great upon the rags and miseries of the poor.

The true realist cannot worship at the shrine of power, not prosti-
tute his gifts for gold. With an artist's eye he sees the world exactly
as it is, and tells the story faithful unto life. He feels for every heart
that beats, else he could not paint them as he does. It takes the soul
to warm a statue into life and make living flesh and coursing blood,
and each true picture that he paints or draws makes the world a better place in which to live.

The artists of the realistic school have a sense so fine that they cannot help but catch the inspiration that is filling all the world's best
minds with the hope of greater justice and more equal social life. With
the vision of the seer they feel the coming dawn when true equality shall reign upon the earth; the time when democracy shall no more
be confined to constitutions and to laws, but will be a part of human
life. The greatest artists of the world to-day are telling facts and
painting scenes that cause humanity to stop, and think, and ask why
one should be a master and another be a serf; why a portion of the

world should toil and spin, should wear away its strength and life, that the rest should live in idleness and ease.

The old-time artists thought they served humanity by painting saints and madonnas and angels from the myths they conjured in their brains. They painted war with long lines of soldiers dressed in uniforms, and looking plump and gay; and a battle scene was always drawn from the side of the victorious camp, with the ensign proudly planting his bright colors on the rampart of the foe. One or two were dying, but always in their comrades' arms, and listening to shouts of victory that filled the air, and thinking of the righteous cause for which they fought and died. In the last moments they dreamed of pleasant burial yards at home, and of graves kept green by loving, grateful friends; and a smile of joy shone on their wasted faces that was so sweet, that it seemed a hardship not to die in war. They painted peace as a white winged dove settling down upon a cold and fading earth. Between the two it was plain which choice a boy would make, and thus art served the state and king.

* * *

Not all the world is beautiful, and not all of life is good. The true artist has no right to choose the lovely spots alone and make us think that this is life. He must bring the world before our eyes and make us read and learn. As he loves the true and noble, he must show the false and bad. As he yearns for true equality, he must paint the master and the slave. He must tell the truth, and tell it all, must tell it o'er and o'er again, till the deafest ear will listen and the dullest mind will think. He must not swerve to please the world by painting only pleasant sights and telling only lovely tales. He must think, and paint, and write, and work, until the world shall learn so much and grow so good, that the true will all be beautiful and all the real be ideal.

Part Three

THE WOMAN QUESTION

Mark Twain, *Adam's Diary*
George Ade, *The Fable of the Good Fairy with the Lorgnette,
and Why She Got It Good*
Frank Norris, *The "Fast" Girl*
Mary Wilkins Freeman, *Louisa*
Edith Wharton, *A Journey*
Kate Chopin, *A Respectable Woman*

In his Preface to *The Wings of the Dove* (1902), Henry James
suggested that the American girl was the "heiress of all the ages"—
that her quest for experience and freedom was inseparable from her
nature and breeding. James' novel is set principally in England and
Italy and involves characters of wealth and family. On a more mundane level, the same theme occupied many other writers of the 1890's
and often took the form of polemic essays or Ibsenite stories and plays
which explicitly spelled out their feminist moral. The earnestness of
feminists, as well as such proposals as dress reform, lent themselves
to ridicule and caricature. But there were other, more effective ways
of dismissing the New Woman ideals of equal rights and freedom
both outside and within marriage. For example, Mark Twain, George
Ade, and Frank Norris portrayed feminine characters in the context
of conventional roles that denied them a sense of identity and there-

fore of equality. For Twain, woman was a troublesome but lovable helpmate; for Ade, she was a meddlesome and ignorant do-gooder; for Norris, she may have been "fast" but was so within distinct codes of behavior and propriety.

Role is also a significant theme in short stories by Mary Wilkins Freeman, Edith Wharton, and Kate Chopin. The stories are strikingly different in locale and social milieu, yet each depicts a heroine who rejects a conventional feminine role. Mrs. Freeman's Louisa resists a good match despite the needs of her family and continues to struggle "manfully" in the world. Mrs. Wharton's unnamed heroine rebels inwardly against the role of a wife who sacrifices herself to a weaker husband. And Kate Chopin's Mrs. Baroda may remain respectable but has also discovered a sensual responsiveness outside of marriage. The three heroines thus fail to conform to such conventional stereotypes as those depicted by Twain, Ade, and Norris. They are not lovably inept, clumsily moralistic, or proper even when bold. Rather, they are themselves and are thus both weak and strong, selfish and generous, impetuous and calculating. They are individuals rather than types. Their portrayal in stories of dramatic force by professionally skilled woman authors was as indicative of the direction and strength of the New Woman movement as were the countless articles on the subject in the journals and newspapers of the day.

Mark Twain
Adam's Diary

Monday.—This new creature with the long hair is a good deal in the way. It is always hanging around and following me about. I don't like this; I am not used to company. I wish it would stay with the other

William Dean Howells, Mark Twain, et al., *The Niagara Book* (Buffalo, 1893). Republished in revised form in *Tom Sawyer, Detective* (London, 1897), pp. 141–58. Text from *Tom Sawyer, Detective*. "Extracts from Adam's Diary" in *The $30,000 Bequest and Other Stories* by Mark Twain (Harper & Row). Reprinted by permission.

animals. . . . Cloudy to-day, wind in the east; think we shall have rain. . . . *We?* Where did I get that word? . . . I remember now —the new creature uses it.

Tuesday.—Been looking over the estate. The new creature calls it the 'Garden of Eden'—why, I am sure I do not know. Says it *looks* like the Garden of Eden. That is not a reason, it is mere waywardness and imbecility. I get no chance to name anything myself. The new creature names everything that comes along, before I can get in a protest. And always that same pretext is offered—it *looks* like the thing. There is the dodo, for instance. Says the moment one looks at it one sees at a glance that it 'looks like a dodo.' It will have to keep that name, no doubt. It wearies me to fret about it, and it does no good, anyway. Dodo! It looks no more like a dodo than I do.

Wednesday.—Built me a shelter against the rain, but could not have it to myself in peace. The new creature intruded. When I tried to put it out it shed water out of the holes in the front of its head that it looks with, and wiped it away with the back of its paw, and made a piteous noise such as some of the other animals make when they are in distress. I wish it would not talk; it is always talking. That sounds like a cheap fling at the poor creature, a slur; but I do not mean it so. I have never heard the human voice before, and any new and strange sound intruding itself here upon the solemn hush of these dreaming solitudes offends my ear and seems a false note. And this new sound is so close to me; it is right at my shoulder, right at my ear, first on one side and then on the other, and I am used only to sounds that are more or less remote—sounds that rise upon this brooding vast silence out of far distances—voices of Nature, I take it—moaning of the winds in the woods, the peaceful plash of hidden fountains, the tinkling, faint music that is borne to me in the stillness of the night —from those bright things that glint and sparkle in the sky, I think! My life is not as happy as it was.

Saturday.—The new creature eats too much fruit. We are going to run short, most likely. 'We' again—that is *its* word; mine, too, now, from hearing it so much. Good deal of fog this morning. I do not go out in the fog, myself. The new creature does. It goes out in all weathers, and stumps right in with its muddy feet. And talks. It used to be so pleasant and quiet here.

Sunday.—Pulled through. This day is getting to be more and more trying. It was selected and set apart last November as a day of rest. I already had six of them per week before. This is another of those unaccountable things. There seems to be too much legislation, too much fussing, and fixing, and tidying-up, and not enough of the better-let-well-enough-alone policy. [*Mem.*—Must keep that sort of opinions to myself.] This morning found the new creature trying to clod apples out of that forbidden tree. But it can't hit anything—it throws like—that. I think the apples are safe.

Monday.—The new creature says its name is Eve. That is all right, I have no objections. Says it is to call it by when I want it to come. I said it was superfluous, then. The word evidently raised me in its respect; and indeed it is a large, good word and will bear repetition. It says it is not an It, it is a She. This is probably doubtful; yet it is all one to me; what she is were nothing to me if she would but go by herself and keep quiet.

Saturday.—I escaped last Tuesday night, and travelled two days, and built me another shelter, in a secluded place, and obliterated my tracks as well as I could, but she hunted me out by means of a beast which she has tamed and calls a wolf, and came making that pitiful noise again, and shedding that water out of the places she looks with. I was obliged to return with her, but will presently emigrate again, when occasions offers. She engages herself in many foolish things: among others, trying to study out why the animals that she calls lions and tigers live on grass and flowers, when, as she says, the sort of teeth they wear would indicate that they were intended to eat each other. This is foolish, because to do that would be to kill each other, and that would introduce what, as I understand it, is called 'death'; and death, as I have been told, has not yet entered the world. Which is a pity, on some accounts.

Sunday.—Pulled through.

Monday.—I believe I see what the week is for: it is to give time to rest up from the weariness of Sunday. It seems a good idea, in a region where good ideas are rather conspicuously scarce. [*Mem.*— Must keep this sort of remarks private.] . . . She has been climbing that tree again. Clodded her out of it. She said nobody was looking. Seems to consider that a sufficient justification for chancing any dangerous thing. Told her that. The word justification moved her admiration—and envy, too, I thought. It is a good word.

Thursday.—She told me she was made out of a rib taken from my body. This is at least doubtful, if not more than that. I have not missed any rib. . . . She is in much trouble about the buzzard; says grass does not agree with it; is afraid she can't raise it; thinks it was intended to live on decayed flesh. The buzzard must get along the best it can with what is provided. We cannot overturn the whole scheme to accommodate the buzzard.

Saturday.—She fell in the pond yesterday, when she was looking at herself in it, which she is always doing. She nearly strangled, and said it was most uncomfortable. This made her sorry for the creatures which live in there, which she calls fishes, for she continues to fasten names on to things that don't need them and don't come when they are called by them, which is a matter of no consequence to her, she is such a fool anyway; so she got a lot of them out and brought them in and put them in my bed to keep them warm, but I have noticed them now and then all day and I don't see that they are any happier there than they were before in the water. When night comes I shall throw them outdoors. I won't sleep with them, for I find them clammy and unpleasant to lie among when a person hasn't anything on.

Sunday.—Pulled through.

Tuesday.—She has taken up with a snake, now. The other animals are glad, for she was always experimenting with them and bothering them; and I am glad, because the snake talks; and this enables me to get a rest.

Friday.—She says the snake advises her to try the fruit of that tree, and says the result will be a great and fine and noble education. I told her there would be another result, too—it would introduce death into the world. That was a mistake—it had been better to keep the remark to myself; it only gave her an idea—she could save the sick buzzard, and furnish fresh meat to the despondent lions and tigers. I advised her to keep away from the tree. She said she wouldn't. I foresee trouble. Will emigrate.

Wednesday.—I have had a variegated time. I escaped that night, and rode a horse all night as fast as he could go, hoping to get clear out of the Garden and hide in some other country before the trouble should begin; but it was not to be. About an hour after sun-up, as I was riding through a flowery plain where thousands of animals were grazing, slumbering, or playing with each other, according to their common wont, all of a sudden they broke into a tempest of frightful noises, and in one moment the plain was a frantic commotion as far as the eye could reach, and every beast was destroying its neighbour. I knew what it meant—Eve had eaten that fruit, and death was come into the world. . . . The tigers ate my horse, paying no attention when I ordered them to desist, and they would even have eaten me if I had stayed—which I didn't. . . . I found this place, outside the Garden, and was fairly comfortable for a few days, but she has found me out. In fact, I was not sorry she came, for there are but meagre pickings here, and she brought some of those apples. I was obliged to eat them, I was so hungry. It was against my principles, but I find that principles have no real force except when one is well fed. . . . She came curtained in boughs and bunches of leaves, and when I asked her what she meant by such nonsense, and snatched them away and threw them down, she tittered and blushed. I had never seen a person titter and blush before, and to me it seemed unbecoming and idiotic. She said I would soon know how it was myself. This was correct. Hungry as I was, I laid down the apple half eaten—certainly the best one I ever saw, considering the lateness of the season—and arrayed myself in the discarded boughs and branches, and then spoke to her with some severity and ordered her to go and get some more and not make such a spectacle of herself. She did it, and after this we crept down to where the wild-beast battle had been, and collected some skins, and I made her patch together a couple of suits proper for public occasions. They are uncomfortable, it is true, but stylish, and that is the main point about clothes. . . . I find she is a good deal of a companion. I see I should be lonesome and depressed without her, now that I have lost my property. Another thing; she says it is ordered that we work for our living hereafter. She will be useful. I will superintend.

Ten days later.—She accuses *me* of being partly the cause of our disaster! I like that!

Next year.—We have named it Cain. She caught it while I was up country trapping; caught it in the timber a couple of miles from our dug-out—or it might have been four, she isn't certain which. It resembles us in some ways, and may be a relation. That is what she thinks, but this is an error, in my judgment. The difference in size warrants the conclusion that it is a different and new kind of animal —a fish, perhaps, though when I dumped it in the water to see, it sank, and she plunged in and snatched it out before there was a chance for the experiment to determine the matter. I still think it is a fish, but she is indifferent about what it is, and won't let me have it to try. I do not understand this. The coming of the creature seems to have changed her whole nature and made her unreasonable about experiments. She thinks more of it than she does of any of the other animals, but is not able to explain why. Her mind is disordered— everything shows it. Sometimes she carries this fish in her arms half the night when it complains and wants to get to the water. At such times the water comes out of the places in her face that she looks out of, and she pats the fish on the back and makes soft sounds with her mouth to soothe it, and betrays sorrow and solicitude in a hundred ways. I have never seen her do like this with any other fish, and it troubles me greatly. She used to carry the young tigers around so, and play with them, before we lost our property, but it was only play; she never took on about them like this when their dinner disagreed with them.

Sunday.—She don't work, Sundays, but lies around all tired out with her week's digging and hoeing, and likes to have the fish wallow over her; and she makes fool noises to amuse it, and pretends to chew its paws, and that makes it laugh. I've never seen a fish before that could laugh. This makes me doubt . . . I have come to like Sunday myself. Superintending all the week tires a body so. There ought to be more Sundays. In the old days they were tough, but now they come handy.

Wednesday.—It isn't a fish. I cannot quite make out what it is. It makes curious devilish noises when not satisfied; and when it is, says 'goo-goo.' It is not one of us, for it doesn't walk; it is not a bird, for it doesn't fly; it is not a frog, for it doesn't hop; it is not a snake, for it doesn't crawl; I feel reasonaby sure it is not a fish, though I cannot get a chance to find out whether it can swim or not. It merely wallows around, and mostly on its back, with its feet up. I have not seen any other animal do that before. I said I believed it was an enigma; but she only admired the word without understanding it. In my judgment it is either an enigma or some kind of a bug. If it dies, I will take it apart and examine its works. I never had a thing perplex me so.

Three months later.—The perplexity merely augments instead of diminishing. I sleep but little. It has ceased from lying around, and goes about on its four legs now. Yet it differs from the other four-legged animals, in that its front legs are unusually short, consequently this causes the main part of its person to stick up uncomfortably high in the air, and this is not attractive. It is built much as we are, but its method of travelling shows that it is not of our breed. The short front legs and long hind ones indicate that it is of the kangaroo family, but it is a marked variation of the species, since the true kangaroo hops, whereas this one never does. Still it is a curious and interesting variety, and has not been catalogued before. As I discovered it, I have felt justified in securing the credit of the discovery by attaching my name to it, and hence have called it *Kangaroorum Adamiensis.* . . . It must have been a young one when it came, for it has grown exceedingly since. It must be five times as big now as it was then, and when discontented is able to make from twenty-two to thirty-eight times the noise it made at first. Coercion does not modify this, but has the contrary effect. For this reason I discontinued the system. She reconciles it by persuasion, and by giving it things which she had told it she wouldn't give it before. As observed previously, I was not at home when it first came, and she told me she found it in the woods. It seems odd that it should be the only one, yet it must be so, for I have worn myself out these many weeks trying to find another one to add to my collection, and for this one to play with; for surely then it would be quieter and we could tame it more easily. But I find none, nor any vestige of any; and, strangest of all, no tracks. It has to live on the ground, it cannot help itself; therefore, how does it get about without leaving a track? I have set a dozen traps, but they do no good. I catch all small animals except that one; animals that merely go into the trap out of curiosity, I think, to see what the milk is there for. They never drink it.

Three months later.—The kangaroo still continues to grow, which is very strange and perplexing. I never knew one to be so long getting its growth. It has fur on its head now; not like kangaroo fur, but exactly like our hair except that it is much finer and softer, and instead of being black is red. I am like to lose my mind over the capricious and harassing developments of this unclassifiable zoological freak. If I could catch another one—but that is hopeless; it is a new variety, and the only sample; this is plain. But I caught a true kangaroo and brought it in, thinking that this one, being lonesome, would rather have that for company than no kin at all, or any animal it could feel a nearness to or get sympathy from, in its forlorn condition here among strangers who do not know its ways or habits, or what to do to make it feel that it is among friends; but it was a mistake—it went into such fits at the sight of the kangaroo that I was convinced it had never seen one before. I pity the poor noisy little animal, but there is nothing I can do to make it happy. If I could only tame it—but that is out of the question; the more I try the worse I seem to make it. It grieves me to the heart to see it in its little storms of sorrow and passion. I wanted to let it go, but she wouldn't hear of it. That seemed cruel and hard-hearted, and not like her; and yet she may be right. It might be lonelier than ever; for since I cannot find another one, how could *it?*

Five months later.—It is not a kangaroo. No, for it supports itself by holding to her finger, and thus goes a few steps on its hind legs, and then falls down. It is probably some kind of a bear; and yet it hasn't any tail—as yet—and no fur, except on its head. It still keeps on growing—that is a curious circumstance, for bears get their growth earlier than this. Bears are dangerous—since our catastrophe—and I shall not be satisfied to have this one prowling about the place much longer without a muzzle on. I have offered to get her a kangaroo if she would let this one go, but it did no good—she is determined to run us into all sorts of foolish risks, I think. She was not like this before she lost her mind.

A fortnight later.—I examined its mouth. There is no danger yet; it has only one tooth. It hasn't any tail yet. It makes more noise now than it ever did before—and mainly at night. I have moved out. But I shall go over, mornings, to breakfast, and to see if it has more teeth. If it gets a mouthful of teeth it will be time for it to go, tail or no tail; for a bear does not need a tail in order to be dangerous.

Four months later.—I have been off hunting and fishing a month.

Meantime the bear has learned to paddle around all by itself on its hind legs, and says 'poppa' and 'momma.' It is certainly a new species. This resemblance to words may be purely accidental, of course, and may have no purpose or meaning; but even in that case it is still extraordinary, and is a thing which no other bear can do. This imitation of speech, taken together with general absence of fur and entire absence of tail, sufficiently indicates that this is a new kind of bear. The further study of it will be exceedingly interesting. Meantime I will go off on a far expedition among the forests of the north and make an exhaustive search. There must certainly be another one somewhere, and this one will be less dangerous when it has company of its own species. I will go straightway; but I will muzzle this one first.

Three months later.—It has been a weary, weary hunt, yet I have had no success. In the meantime, without stirring from the home estate, she has caught another one! I never saw such luck. I might have hunted these woods a hundred years, I never would have run across that thing.

Three months later.—I have been comparing the new one with the old one, and it is perfectly plain that they are the same breed. She calls the new one *Abel*. I was going to stuff one of them for my collection, but she is prejudiced against it for some reason or other; so I have relinquished the idea, though I think it is a mistake. It would be an irreparable loss to science if they should get away. The old one is tamer than it was, and can laugh and talk like a parrot, having learned this, no doubt, from being with the parrot so much, and having the imitative faculty in a highly developed degree. I shall be astonished if it turns out to be a new kind of parrot; and yet I ought not to be astonished, for it has already been everything else it could think of, since those first days when it was a fish. The new one is as ugly now as the old one was at first; has the same sulphur-and-raw-meat complexion, and the same singular head without any fur on it.

Ten years later.—They are boys; we found it out long ago. It was their coming in that small, immature shape that fooled us; we were not used to it. There are some girls now. Abel is a good boy, but if Cain had stayed a bear it would have improved him. After all these years, I see that I was mistaken about Eve in the beginning; it is better to live outside the Garden with her than inside it without her. At first I thought she talked too much; but now I should be sorry to have that voice fall silent and pass out of my life. Blessed be the disaster that brought us near together and taught me to know the goodness of her heart and the sweetness of her spirit.

George Ade

The Fable of the Good Fairy
with the Lorgnette,
and Why She Got It Good

ONCE UPON A TIME there was a Broad Girl who had nothing else to do and no Children to look after, so she thought she would be Benevolent.

She had scared all the Red Corpuscles out of the 2 by 4 Midget who rotated about her in a Limited Orbit and was known by Courtesy as her Husband. He was Soft for her, and so she got it Mapped out with Herself that she was a Superior Woman.

She knew that when she switched the Current on to herself she Used up about 6,000 Ohms an hour, and the whole Neighborhood had to put on Blinders.

She had read about nine Subscription Books with Cupid and Dove Tail-Pieces and she believed that she could get away with any Topic that was batted up to her and then slam it over to Second in time to head off the Runner.

Her clothes were full of Pin-Holes where she had been hanging Medals on Herself, and she used to go in a Hand-Ball Court every Day and throw up Bouquets, letting them bounce back and hit Her.

Also, She would square off in front of a Camera every Two Weeks, and the Man was Next, for he always removed the Mole when he was touching up the Negative. In the Photograph the Broad Girl resembled Pauline Hall, but outside of the Photograph, and take it in the Morning when she showed up on the Level, she looked like a Street just before they put on the Asphalt.

But never you Fear, She thought She had Julia Arthur and Mary Mannering Seventeen up and One to play, so far as Good Looks were

Chicago *Record*, July 26, 1899. Republished in *Fables in Slang* (Chicago, 1899), pp. 33–45. Text from *Fables in Slang*.

concerned; and when it came to the Gray Matter—the Cerebrum, the Cerebellum, and the Medulla Oblongata—May Wright Sewall was back of the Flag and Pulled up Lame.

The Down-Trodden Man, whom she had dragged to the Altar, sized Her all right, but he was afraid of his Life. He wasn't Strong enough to push Her in front of a Cable Car, and he didn't have the Nerve to get a Divorce. So he stood for Everything; but in the Summer, when She skated off into the Woods to hear a man with a Black Alpaca Coat lecture to the High Foreheads about the Subverted Ego, he used to go out with a few Friends and tell them his Troubles and weep into his Beer. They would slap him on the Back and tell him she was a Nice Woman; but he knew better.

Annyhow, as Bobby Gaylor used to say, she became restless around the House, with nothing to do except her Husband, so she made up her mind to be Benevolent to beat the Band. She decided that she would allow the Glory of her Presence to burst upon the Poor and the Uncultured. It would be a Big Help to the Poor and Uncultured to see what a Real Razmataz Lady was like.

She didn't Propose to put on Old Clothes, and go and live with Poor People, and be One of Them, and nurse their Sick, as they do in Settlements. Not on Your Previous Existence! She was going to be Benevolent, and be Dead Swell at the Same Time.

Accordingly, she would Lace Herself until she was the shape of a Bass Viol, and put on her Tailor-Made, and the Hat that made her Face seem longer, and then she would Gallop forth to do Things to the Poor. She always carried a 99-cent Lorgnette in one Hand and a Smelling-Bottle in the Other.

"Now," she would say, feeling Behind to make sure that she was all strung up, "Now, to carry Sunshine into the Lowly Places."

As soon as she struck the Plank Walks, and began stalking her prey, the small Children would crawl under the Beds, while Mother would dry her Arms on the Apron, and murmur, "Glory be!" They knew how to stand off the Rent-Man and the Dog-Catcher; but when 235 pounds of Sunshine came wafting up the Street, they felt that they were up against a New Game.

The Benevolent Lady would go into a House numbered 1135A with a Marking Brush, and after she had sized up the front room through the Lorgnette, she would say: "My Good Woman, does your Husband drink?"

"Oh, yes, sir," the grateful Woman would reply. "That is, when he's working. He gets a Dollar Ten."

"And what does he do with all his Money?" the Benevolent Lady would ask.

"I think he plays the Stock Market," would be the Reply.

Then the Benevolent Lady would say: "When the Unfortunate Man comes Home this Evening you tell him that a Kind and Beautiful Lady called and asked him please to stop Drinking, except a Glass of Claret at Dinner, and to be sure and read Eight or Ten Pages from the *Encyclopædia Britannica* each Night before retiring; also tell him to be sure and save his Money. Is that your Child under the Bed?"

"That's little William J."

"How Many have you?"

"Eight or Nine—I forget Which."

"Be sure and dress them in Sanitary Underwear; you can get it for Four Dollars a Suit. Will you be good enough to have the Little Boy come from under the Bed, and spell 'Ibex' for the Sweet Lady?"

"He's afraid of you."

"Kindly explain to him that I take an Interest in him, even though he is the Offspring of an Obscure and Ignorant Workingman, while I am probably the Grandest Thing that ever Swept up the Boulevard. I must go now, but I will Return. Next time I come I hope to hear that your Husband has stopped Drinking and is very Happy. Tell the Small Person under the Bed that if he learns to spell 'Ibex' by the time I call again I will let him look at my Rings. As for you, bear in mind that it is no Disgrace to be Poor; it is simply Inconvenient, that's all."

Having delivered herself of these Helpful Remarks she would Duck, and the Uplifted Mother would put a Nickel in the Can and send Lizzie over to the Dutchman's.

In this manner the Benevolent Lady carried forward the Good Work, and Dazzled the whole Region between O'Hara's Box Factory and the City Dump. It didn't Cost anything, and she derived much Joy from the Knowledge that Hundreds of People were Rubbering at her, and remarking in Choked Whispers: "Say, ain't she the Smooth Article?"

But one day a Scrappy Kid, whose Mother didn't have any Lorgnette or Diamond Ear-Bobs, spotted the Benevolent Lady. The Benevolent Lady had been in the House telling his Mother that it was a Glorious Privilege to wash for a Living.

After the Benevolent Lady went away the Kid's Mother sat down and had a Good Cry, and the Scrappy Kid thought it was up to him. He went out to the Alley and found a Tomato Can that was not working, and he waited.

In a little while the Benevolent Lady came out of a Basement, in which she had been telling a Polish Family to look at her and be Happy. The Scrappy Kid let drive, and the Tomato Can struck the Benevolent Lady between the Shoulder Blades. She squawked and started to run, fell over a Garbage Box, and had to be picked up by a Policeman.

She went Home in a Cab, and told her Husband that the Liquor League had tried to Assassinate her, because she was Reforming so many Drunkards. That settled it with her—she said she wouldn't try to be Benevolent any more—so she joined an Ibsen Club.

The Scrappy Kid grew up to be a Corrupt Alderman, and gave his Mother plenty of Good Clothes, which she was always afraid to wear.

MORAL: *In uplifting, get underneath.*

Frank Norris
The "Fast" Girl

SHE DRESSES in a black, close-fitting bolero jacket of imitation astrachan with enormous leg-of-mutton sleeves of black velvet, a striped silk skirt, and a very broad hat, tilted to one side. Her hair is very blonde, though, somehow, coarse and dry, and a little flat curl of it lies low over her forehead. She is marvelously pretty.

She belongs to a certain class of young girl that is very common in the city. She is what men, amongst each other, call "gay," though that is the worst that can be said of her. She is virtuous, but the very fact that it is necessary to say so is enough to cause the statement to be doubted.

When she was younger and a pupil at the Girls' High School, she had known, and had even been the companion of, girls of good family, but since that time these girls have come to ignore her. Now almost all of her acquaintances are men, and to most of these she has never been introduced. They have managed to get acquainted with her on Kearny Street, at the theaters, at the Mechanics' Fair, and at baseball games. She tells these men that her name is "Ida." She loves to have a "gay time" with them, which, for her, means to drink California champagne, to smoke cigarettes, and to kick at the chandelier. Understand distinctly, however, that she is not "bad," that there is nothing

San Francisco *Wave*, XV (May 9, 1896), 5. Text from *Frank Norris of "The Wave*," ed. Oscar Lewis (San Francisco, 1931), pp. 213–16.

vicious about her. Ida is too clever to be "bad," and is as morbidly careful of appearances and as jealous of her reputation as only fast girls can be.

She lives with her people on Golden Gate Avenue. Her father has a three-fourths interest in a carpet-cleaning "establishment" in the Mission, and her mother gives lessons in hand-painting on china and on velvet.

In the evening, especially if it be a Saturday evening, Ida invents all sorts of excuses to go "down town." You see her then on Kearny or Market streets about the time the theaters open, arm in arm with one or perhaps two other girls who are precisely like her. At this time she is not in the least "loud," either in dress or in conversation, but somehow when she is in the street she cannot raise a finger or open her mouth without attracting attention.

Like "Jonesee," Sunday is her great day. Ida usually spends it "Across the Bay" somewhere. A party is gotten up and there is no "chaperon." Two or three of the men with whom she and her friends have become acquainted during the week arrange the "date." The day's amusement is made to include a lunch at one of the suburban hotels and a long drive in a hired "rig." The party returns home on one of the ferry boats late in the afternoon. By that time they are quite talked out, their good spirits are gone, and they sit in a row, side by side, exchanging monosyllables. Ida's face is red, her hair is loose, and the little blonde curl has lost its crispness. She has taken off her gloves by this time. In one of her bare hands she carries her escort's cane, and in the other a bunch of wilted wild flowers. Sometimes, however, the party returns to the city in a later boat, one that makes the trip after dark. Then everything is changed. The party "pairs off" at once. You will see Ida and her "fellar" sitting in one of the dark corners of the deck. The fellar sits as close as the length of his acquaintance with Ida will justify. He rests his elbow on the rail back of her and, by and by, carelessly lets his forearm drop at full length.

When the Mechanics' Fair opens Ida rarely misses an evening. I remember that I once saw her and the fellar in the art gallery upstairs. Ida's mother, "who gives lessons in hand-painting," had an exhibit there which they were interested to find: a bunch of yellow poppies painted on black velvet and framed in gilt. When they had found it they stood before it some little time hazarding their opinions and then moved on from one picture to another. Ida had the fellar buy a catalogue and made it a duty to find the title of every picture, for she professes to be very fond of hand-painting. She had "taken it up" at one time and abandoned it only because the oil or the turpentine or something had been unhealthy for her.

On this occasion she looked at each picture carefully, her head on one side. "Of course," she explained to the fellar, "I'm no critic, I only know what I like. I like those 'heads,' those ideal heads like that one," and she pointed with her arm outstretched to a picture of the head of a young girl with disheveled brown hair and upturned eyes. The title of the picture was "Faith."

"Yes," said Ida, reflectively, "I like that kind."

Mary Wilkins Freeman
Louisa

"I DON'T SEE what kind of ideas you've got in your head for my part." Mrs. Britton looked sharply at her daughter Louisa, but she got no response.

Louisa sat in one of the kitchen chairs close to the door. She had dropped into it when she first entered. Her hands were all brown and grimy with garden-mould; it clung to the bottom of her old dress and her coarse shoes.

Mrs. Britton, sitting opposite by the window, waited, looking at her. Suddenly Louisa's silence seemed to strike her mother's will with an electric shock; she recoiled, with an angry jerk of her head. "You don't know nothin' about it. You'd like him well enough after you was married to him," said she, as if in answer to an argument.

Louisa's face looked fairly dull; her obstinacy seemed to cast a film over it. Her eyelids were cast down; she leaned her head back against the wall.

"Sit there like a stick if you want to!" cried her mother.

Louisa got up. As she stirred, a faint earthy odor diffused itself through the room. It was like a breath from a ploughed field.

Mrs. Britton's little sallow face contracted more forcibly.

"I s'pose now you're goin' back to your potater patch," said she. "Plantin' potaters out there jest like a man, for all the neighbors to see. Pretty sight, I call it."

A New England Nun, and Other Stories (New York, 1891), pp. 384–406. Text from this edition.

"If they don't like it, they needn't look," returned Louisa. She spoke quite evenly. Her young back was stiff with bending over the potatoes, but she straightened it rigorously. She pulled her old hat farther over her eyes.

There was a shuffling sound outside the door and a fumble at the latch. It opened, and an old man came in, scraping his feet heavily over the threshold. He carried an old basket.

"What you got in that basket, father?" asked Mrs. Britton.

The old man looked at her. His old face had the round outlines and naïve grin of a child.

"Father, what you got in that basket?"

Louisa peered apprehensively into the basket. "Where did you get those potatoes, grandfather?" said she.

"Digged 'em." The old man's grin deepened. He chuckled hoarsely.

"Well, I'll give up if he ain't been an' dug up all them potaters you've been plantin'!" said Mrs. Britton.

"Yes, he has," said Louisa. "Oh, grandfather, didn't you know I'd jest planted those potatoes?"

The old man fastened his bleared blue eyes on her face, and still grinned.

"Didn't you know better, grandfather?" she asked again.

But the old man only chuckled. He was so old that he had come back into the mystery of childhood. His motives were hidden and inscrutable; his amalgamation with the human race was so much weaker.

"Land sakes! don't waste no more time talkin' to him," said Mrs. Britton. "You can't make out whether he knows what he's doin' or not. I've give it up. Father, you jest set them pertaters down, an' you come over here an' set down in the rockin'-chair; you've done about 'nough work to-day."

The old man shook his head with slow mutiny.

"Come right over here."

Louisa pulled at the basket of potatoes. "Let me have 'em, grandfather," said she. "I've got to have 'em."

The old man resisted. His grin disappeared, and he set his mouth. Mrs. Britton got up, with a determined air, and went over to him. She was a sickly, frail-looking woman, but the voice came firm, with deep bass tones, from her little lean throat.

"Now, father," said she, "you jest give her that basket, an' you walk across the room, and you set down in that rockin'-chair."

The old man looked down into her little, pale, wedge-shaped face. His grasp on the basket weakened. Louisa pulled it away, and pushed past out of the door, and the old man followed his daughter sullenly across the room to the rocking-chair.

The Brittons did not have a large potato field; they had only an acre of land in all. Louisa had planted two thirds of her potatoes; now she had to plant them all over again. She had gone to the house for a drink of water; her mother had detained her, and in the meantime the old man had undone her work. She began putting the cut potatoes back in the ground. She was careful and laborious about it. A strong wind, full of moisture, was blowing from the east. The smell of the sea was in it, although this was some miles inland. Louisa's brown calico skirt blew out in it like a sail. It beat her in the face when she raised her head.

"I've got to get these in to-day somehow," she muttered. "It'll rain to-morrow."

She worked as fast as she could, and the afternoon wore on. About five o'clock she happened to glance at the road—the potato field lay beside it—and she saw Jonathan Nye driving past with his gray horse and buggy. She turned her back to the road quickly, and listened until the rattle of the wheels died away. At six o'clock her mother looked out of the kitchen window and called her to supper.

"I'm comin' in a minute," Louisa shouted back. Then she worked faster than ever. At half-past six she went into the house, and the potatoes were all in the ground.

"Why didn't you come when I called you?" asked her mother.

"I had to get the potatoes in."

"I guess you wa'n't bound to get 'em all in to-night. It's kind of discouragin' when you work, an' get supper all ready, to have it stan' an hour, I call it. An' you've worked 'bout long enough for one day out in this damp wind, I should say."

Louisa washed her hands and face at the kitchen sink, and smoothed her hair at the little glass over it. She had wet her hair too, and made it look darker: it was quite a light brown. She brushed it in smooth straight lines back from her temples. Her whole face had a clear bright look from being exposed to the moist wind. She noticed it herself, and gave her head a little conscious turn.

When she sat down to the table her mother looked at her with admiration, which she veiled with disapproval.

"Jest look at your face," said she; "red as a beet. You'll be a pretty-lookin' sight before the summer's out, at this rate."

Louisa thought to herself that the light was not very strong, and the glass must have flattered her. She could not look as well as she had imagined. She spread some butter on her bread very sparsely. There was nothing for supper but some bread and butter and weak tea, though the old man had his dish of Indian-meal porridge. He could not eat much solid food. The porridge was covered with milk and molasses. He bent low over it, and ate large spoonfuls with loud noises. His daughter had tied a towel around his neck as she would have tied a pinafore on a child. She had also spread a towel over the tablecloth in front of him, and she watched him sharply lest he should spill his food.

"I wish I could have somethin' to eat that I could relish the way he does that porridge and molasses," said she. She had scarcely tasted anything. She sipped her weak tea laboriously.

Louisa looked across at her mother's meagre little figure in its neat old dress, at her poor small head bending over the tea-cup, showing the wide parting in the thin hair.

"Why don't you toast your bread, mother?" said she. "I'll toast it for you."

"No, I don't want it. I'd jest as soon have it this way as any. I don't want no bread, nohow. I want somethin' to relish—a herrin', or a little mite of cold meat, or somethin'. I s'pose I could eat as well as anybody if I had as much as some folks have. Mis' Mitchell was sayin' the other day that she didn't believe but what they had butcher's meat up to Mis' Nye's every day in the week. She said Jonathan he went to Wolfsborough and brought home great pieces in a market-basket every week. I guess they have everything."

Louisa was not eating much herself, but now she took another slice of bread with a resolute air. "I guess some folks would be thankful to get this," said she.

"Yes, I s'pose we'd ought to be thankful for enough to keep us alive, anybody takes so much comfort livin'," returned her mother, with a tragic bitterness that sat oddly upon her, as she was so small and feeble. Her face worked and strained under the stress of emotion; her eyes were full of tears; she sipped her tea fiercely.

"There's some sugar," said Louisa. "We might have had a little cake."

The old man caught the word. "Cake?" he mumbled, with pleased inquiry, looking up, and extending his grasping old hand.

"I guess we ain't got no sugar to waste in cake," returned Mrs. Britton. "Eat your porridge, father, an' stop teasin'. There ain't no cake."

After supper Louisa cleared away the dishes; then she put on her shawl and hat.

"Where you goin'?" asked her mother.

"Down to the store."

"What for?"

"The oil's out. There wasn't enough to fill the lamps this mornin'. I ain't had a chance to get it before."

It was nearly dark. The mist was so heavy it was almost rain. Louisa went swiftly down the road with the oil-can. It was a half-mile to the store where the few staples were kept that sufficed the simple folk in this little settlement. She was gone a half-hour. When she returned, she had besides the oil-can a package under her arm. She went into the kitchen and set them down. The old man was asleep in the rocking-chair. She heard voices in the adjoining room. She frowned, and stood still, listening.

"Louisa!" called her mother. Her voice was sweet, and higher pitched than usual. She sounded the *i* in Louisa long.

"What say?"

"Come in here after you've taken your things off."

Louisa knew that Jonathan Nye was in the sitting-room. She flung off her hat and shawl. Her old dress was damp, and had still some earth stains on it; her hair was roughened by the wind, but she would not look again in the glass; she went into the sitting-room just as she was.

"It's Mr. Nye, Louisa," said her mother, with effusion.

"Good-evenin', Mr. Nye," said Louisa.

Jonathan Nye half arose and extended his hand, but she did not notice it. She sat down peremptorily in a chair at the other side of the room. Jonathan had the one rocking-chair; Mrs. Britton's frail little body was poised anxiously on the hard rounded top of the carpet-covered lounge. She looked at Louisa's dress and hair, and her eyes were stony with disapproval, but her lips still smirked, and she kept her voice sweet. She pointed to a glass dish on the table.

"See what Mr. Nye has brought us over, Louisa," said she.

Louisa looked indifferently at the dish.

"It's honey," said her mother; "some of his own bees made it. Don't you want to get a dish an' taste of it? One of them little glass sauce dishes."

"No, I guess not," replied Louisa. "I never cared much about honey. Grandfather'll like it."

The smile vanished momentarily from Mrs. Britton's lips, but she recovered herself. She arose and went across the room to the china closet. Her set of china dishes was on the top shelves, the lower were filled with books and papers. "I've got somethin' to show you, Mr. Nye," said she.

This was scarcely more than a hamlet, but it was incorporated, and had its town books. She brought forth a pile of them, and laid them on the table beside Jonathan Nye. "There," said she, "I thought mebbe you'd like to look at these." She opened one and pointed to the school report. This mother could not display her daughter's accomplishments to attract a suitor, for she had none. Louisa did not own a piano or organ; she could not paint; but she had taught school acceptably for eight years—ever since she was sixteen—and in every one of the town books was testimonial to that effect, intermixed with glowing eulogy. Jonathan Nye looked soberly through the books; he was a slow reader. He was a few years older than Louisa, tall and clumsy, long-featured and long-necked. His face was a deep red with embarrassment, and it contrasted oddly with his stiff dignity of demeanor.

Mrs. Britton drew a chair close to him while he read. "You see, Louisa taught that school for eight year," said she; "an' she'd be teachin' it now if Mr. Mosely's daughter hadn't grown up an' wanted somethin' to do, an' he put her in. He was committee, you know. I dun' know as I'd ought to say so, an' I wouldn't want you to repeat it, but they do say Ida Mosely don't give very good satisfaction, an' I guess she won't have no reports like these in the town books unless her father writes 'em. See this one."

Jonathan Nye pondered over the fulsome testimony to Louisa's capability, general worth, and amiability, while she sat in sulky silence at the farther corner of the room. Once in a while her mother, after a furtive glance at Jonathan, engrossed in a town book, would look at her and gesticulate fiercely for her to come over, but she did not stir. Her eyes were dull and quiet, her mouth closely shut; she looked homely. Louisa was very pretty when pleased and animated, at other times she had a look like a closed flower. One could see no prettiness in her.

Jonathan Nye read all the school reports; then he arose heavily. "They're real good," said he. He glanced at Louisa and tried to smile; his blushes deepened.

"Now don't be in a hurry," said Mrs. Britton.

"I guess I'd better be goin'; mother's alone."

"She won't be afraid; it's jest on the edge of the evenin'."

"I don't know as she will. But I guess I'd better be goin'." He looked hesitatingly at Louisa.

She arose and stood with an indifferent air.

"You'd better set down again," said Mrs. Britton.

"No; I guess I'd better be goin'." Jonathan turned towards Louisa. "Good-evenin'," said he.

"Good-evenin'."

Mrs. Britton followed him to the door. She looked back and beckoned imperiously to Louisa, but she stood still. "Now come again, do," Mrs. Britton said to the departing caller. "Run in any time; we're real lonesome evenin's. Father he sets an' sleeps in his chair, an' Louisa an' me often wish somebody'd drop in; folks round here ain't none too neighborly. Come in any time you happen to feel like it, an' we'll both of us be glad to see you. Tell your mother I'll send home that dish to-morrer, an' we shall have a real feast off that beautiful honey."

When Mrs. Britton had fairly shut the outer door upon Jonathan Nye, she came back into the sitting-room as if her anger had a propelling power like steam upon her body.

"Now, Louisa Britton," said she, "you'd ought to be ashamed of yourself—ashamed of yourself! You've treated him like a—hog!"

"I couldn't help it."

"Couldn't help it! I guess you could treat anybody decent if you tried. I never saw such actions! I guess you needn't be afraid of him. I guess he ain't so set on you that he means to ketch you up an' run off. There's other girls in town full as good as you an' better-lookin'. Why didn't you go an' put on your other dress? Comin' into the room with that old thing on, an' your hair all in a frowse! I guess he won't want to come again."

"I hope he won't," said Louisa, under her breath. She was trembling all over.

"What say?"

"Nothin'."

"I shouldn't think you'd want to say anything, treatin' him that way, when he came over and brought all that beautiful honey! He was all dressed up, too. He had on a real nice coat—cloth jest as fine as it could be, an' it was kinder damp when he come in. Then he dressed all up to come over here this rainy night an' bring this honey." Mrs. Britton snatched the dish of honey and scudded into the kitchen with it. "Sayin' you didn't like honey after he took all that pains to bring it over!" said she. "I'd said I liked it if I'd lied up hill and down." She set the dish in the pantry. "What in creation smells so kinder strong an' smoky in here?" said she, sharply.

"I guess it's the herrin'. I got two or three down to the store."

"I'd like to know what you got herrin' for?"

"I thought maybe you'd relish 'em."

"I don't want no herrin's, now we've got this honey. But I don't know that you've got money to throw away." She shook the old man by the stove into partial wakefulness, and steered him into his little bedroom off the kitchen. She herself slept in one off the sitting-rooms; Louisa's room was up-stairs.

Louisa lighted her candle and went to bed, her mother's scolding voice pursuing her like a wrathful spirit. She cried when she was in bed in the dark, but she soon went to sleep. She was too healthfully tired with her out-door work not to. All her young bones ached with the strain of manual labor as they had ached many a time this last year since she had lost her school.

The Brittons had been and were in sore straits. All they had in the world was this little house with the acre of land. Louisa's meagre school money had bought their food and clothing since her father died. Now it was almost starvation for them. Louisa was struggling to wrest a little sustenance from their stony acre of land, toiling like a European peasant woman, sacrificing her New England dignity. Lately she had herself split up a cord of wood which she had bought of a neighbor, paying for it in instalments with work for his wife.

"Think of a school-teacher goin' into Mis' Mitchell's house to help clean!" said her mother.

She, although she had been of poor, hard-working people all her life, with the humblest surroundings, was a born aristocrat, with that fiercest and most bigoted aristocracy which sometimes arises from independent poverty. She had the feeling of a queen for a princess of the blood about her school-teacher daughter; her working in a neighbor's kitchen was as galling and terrible to her. The projected marriage with Jonathan Nye was like a royal alliance for the good of the state. Jonathan Nye was the only eligible young man in the place; he was the largest land-owner; he had the best house. There were only himself and his mother; after her death the property would all be his. Mrs. Nye was an older woman than Mrs. Britton, who forgot her own frailty in calculating their chances of life.

"Mis' Nye is considerable over seventy," she said often to herself; "an' then Jonathan will have it all."

She saw herself installed in that large white house as reigning dowager. All the obstacle was Louisa's obstinacy, which her mother could not understand. She could see no fault in Jonathan Nye. So far as absolute approval went, she herself was in love with him. There was no more sense, to her mind, in Louisa's refusing him than there would have been in a princess refusing the fairy prince and spoiling the story.

"I'd like to know what you've got against him," she said often to Louisa.

"I ain't got anything against him."

"Why don't you treat him different, then, I want to know?"

"I don't like him." Louisa said "like" shamefacedly, for she meant love, and dared not say it.

"*Like!* Well, I don't know nothin' about such likin's as some pretend to, an' I don't want to. If I see anybody is good an' worthy, I like 'em, an' that's all there is about it."

"I don't—believe that's the way you felt about—father," said Louisa, softly, her young face flushed red.

"Yes, it was. I had some common-sense about it."

And Mrs. Britton believed it. Many hard middle-aged years lay between her and her own love-time, and nothing is so changed by distance as the realities of youth. She believed herself to have been actuated by the same calm reason in marrying young John Britton, who had had fair prospects, which she thought should actuate her daughter in marrying Jonathan Nye.

Louisa got no sympathy from her, but she persisted in her refusal. She worked harder and harder. She did not spare herself in doors or out. As the summer wore on her face grew as sunburnt as a boy's, her hands were hard and brown. When she put on her white dress to go to meeting on a Sunday there was a white ring around her neck where the sun had not touched it. Above it her face and neck showed browner. Her sleeves were rather short, and there were also white rings above her brown wrists.

"You look as if you were turnin' Injun by inches," said her mother.

Louisa, when she sat in the meeting-house, tried slyly to pull her sleeves down to the brown on her wrists; she gave a little twitch to the ruffle around her neck. Then she glanced across, and Jonathan Nye was looking at her. She thrust her hands, in their short-wristed, loose cotton gloves, as far out of the sleeves as she could; her brown wrists showed conspicuously on her white lap. She had never heard of the princess who destroyed her beauty that she might not be forced to wed the man whom she did not love, but she had something of the same feeling, although she did not have it for the sake of any tangible lover. Louisa had never seen anybody whom she would have preferred to Jonathan Nye. There was no other marriageable young man in the place. She had only her dreams, which she had in common with other girls.

That Sunday evening before she went to meeting her mother took some old wide lace out of her bureau drawer. "There," said she, "I'm goin' to sew this in your neck an' sleeves before you put your dress on. It'll cover up a little; it's wider than the ruffle."

"I don't want it in," said Louisa.

"I'd like to know why not? You look like a fright. I was ashamed of you this mornin'."

Louisa thrust her arms into the white dress sleeves peremptorily. Her mother did not speak to her all the way to meeting. After meeting, Jonathan Nye walked home with them, and Louisa kept on the other side of her mother. He went into the house and stayed an hour. Mrs. Britton entertained him, while Louisa sat silent. When he had gone, she looked at her daughter as if she could have used bodily force, but she said nothing. She shot the bolt of the kitchen door noisily. Louisa lighted her candle. The old man's loud breathing sounded from his room; he had been put to bed for safety before they went to meeting; through the open windows sounded the loud murmur of the summer night, as if that, too, slept heavily.

"Good-night, mother," said Louisa, as she went up-stairs; but her mother did not answer.

The next day was very warm. This was an exceptionally hot summer. Louisa went out early; her mother would not ask her where she was going. She did not come home until noon. Her face was burning; her wet dress clung to her arms and shoulders.

"Where have you been?" asked her mother.

"Oh, I've been out in the field."

"What field?"

"Mr. Mitchell's."

"What have you been doin' out there?"

"Rakin' hay."

"Rakin' hay with the men?"

"There wasn't anybody but Mr. Mitchell and Johnny. Don't, mother!"

Mrs. Britton had turned white. She sank into a chair. "I can't stan' it nohow," she moaned. "All the daughter I've got."

"Don't, mother! I ain't done any harm. What harm is it? Why can't I rake hay as well as a man? Lots of women do such things, if nobody round here does. He's goin' to pay me right off, and we need the money. Don't, mother!" Louisa got a tumbler of water. "Here, mother, drink this."

Mrs. Britton pushed it away. Louisa stood looking anxiously at her. Lately her mother had grown thinner than ever; she looked scarcely bigger than a child. Presently she got up and went to the stove.

"Don't try to do anything, mother; let me finish getting dinner," pleaded Louisa. She tried to take the pan of biscuits out of her mother's hands, but she jerked it away.

The old man was sitting on the door-step, huddled up loosely in the sun, like an old dog.

"Come, father," Mrs. Britton called, in a dry voice, "dinner's ready —what there is of it!"

The old man shuffled in, smiling.

There was nothing for dinner but the hot biscuits and tea. The fare was daily becoming more meagre. All Louisa's little hoard of school money was gone, and her earnings were very uncertain and slender. Their chief dependence for food through the summer was their garden, but that had failed them in some respects.

One day the old man had come in radiant, with his shaking hands full of potato blossoms; his old eyes twinkled over them like a mischievous child's. Reproaches were useless; the little potato crop was sadly damaged. Lately, in spite of close watching, he had picked the squash blossoms, piling them in a yellow mass beside the kitchen door. Still, it was nearly time for the pease and beans and beets; they would keep them from starvation while they lasted.

But when they came, and Louisa could pick plenty of green food every morning, there was still a difficulty: Mrs. Britton's appetite and digestion were poor; she could not live upon a green-vegetable diet; and the old man missed his porridge, for the meal was all gone.

One morning in August he cried at the breakfast-table like a baby, because he wanted his porridge, and Mrs. Britton pushed away her own plate with a despairing gesture.

"There ain't no use," said she. "I can't eat no more garden-sauce nohow. I don't blame poor father a mite. You ain't got no feelin' at all."

"I don't know what I can do; I've worked as hard as I can," said Louisa, miserably.

"I know what you can do, and so do you."

"No, I don't, mother," returned Louisa, with alacrity. "He ain't been here for two weeks now, and I saw him with my own eyes yesterday carryin' a dish into the Moselys', and I knew 'twas honey. I think he's after Ida."

"Carryin' honey into the Moselys'? I don't believe it."

"He was; I saw him."

"Well, I don't care if he was. If you're a mind to act decent now, you can bring him round again. He was dead set on you, an' I don't believe he's changed round to that Mosely girl as quick as this."

"You don't want me to ask him to come back here, do you?"

"I want you to act decent. You can go to meetin' tonight, if you're a mind to—I sha'n't go; I ain't got strength 'nough—an' 'twouldn't hurt you none to hang back a little after meetin', and kind of edge round his way. 'Twouldn't take more'n a look."

"Mother!"

"Well, I don't care. 'Twouldn't hurt you none. It's the way more'n one girl does, whether you believe it or not. Men don't do all the courtin'—not by a long shot. 'Twon't hurt you none. You needn't look so scart."

Mrs. Britton's own face was a burning red. She looked angrily away from her daughter's honest, indignant eyes.

"I wouldn't do such a thing as that for a man I liked," said Louisa; "and I certainly sha'n't for a man I don't like."

"Then me an' your grandfather'll starve," said her mother; "that's all there is about it. We can't neither of us stan' it much longer."

"We could—"

"Could what?"

"Put a—little mortgage on the house."

Mrs. Britton faced her daughter. She trembled in every inch of her weak frame. "Put a mortgage on this house, an' by-an'-by not have a roof to cover us! Are you crazy? I tell you what 'tis, Louisa Britton, we may starve, your grandfather an' me, an' you can follow us to the graveyard over there, but there's only one way I'll ever put a mortgage on this house. If you have Jonathan Nye, I'll ask him to take a little one to tide us along an' get your weddin' things."

"Mother, I'll tell you what I'm goin' to do."

"What?"

"I am goin' to ask Uncle Solomon."

"I guess when Solomon Mears does anythin' for us you'll know it. He never forgave your father about that wood lot, an' he's hated the whole of us ever since. When I went to his wife's funeral he never answered when I spoke to him. I guess if you go to him you'll take it out in goin'."

Louisa said nothing more. She began clearing away the breakfast dishes and setting the house to rights. Her mother was actually so weak that she could scarcely stand, and she recognized it. She had settled into the rocking-chair, and leaned her head back. Her face looked pale and sharp against the dark calico cover.

When the house was in order, Louisa stole up-stairs to her own chamber. She put on her clean old blue muslin and her hat, then she went slyly down and out the front way.

It was seven miles to her uncle Solomon Mears's, and she had made up her mind to walk them. She walked quite swiftly until the house windows were out of sight, then she slackened her pace a little. It was one of the fiercest dog-days. A damp heat settled heavily down upon the earth; the sun scalded.

At the foot of the hill Louisa passed a house where one of her girl acquaintances lived. She was going in the gate with a pan of early apples. "Hullo, Louisa," she called.

"Hullo, Vinnie."

"Where you goin'?"

"Oh, I'm goin' a little way."

"Ain't it awful hot? Say, Louisa, do you know Ida Mosely's cuttin' you out?"

"She's welcome."

The other girl, who was larger and stouter than Louisa, with a sallow, unhealthy face, looked at her curiously. "I don't see why you wouldn't have him," said she. "I should have thought you'd jumped at the chance."

"Should you if you didn't like him, I'd like to know?"

"I'd like him if he had such a nice house and as much money as Jonathan Nye," returned the other girl.

She offered Louisa some apples, and she went along the road eating them. She herself had scarcely tasted food that day.

It was about nine o'clock; she had risen early. She calculated how many hours it would take her to walk the seven miles. She walked as fast as she could to hold out. The heat seemed to increase as the sun stood higher. She had walked about three miles when she heard wheels behind her. Presently a team stopped at her side.

"Good-mornin'," said an embarrassed voice.

She looked around. It was Jonathan Nye, with his gray horse and light wagon.

"Good-mornin'," said she.

"Goin' far?"

"A little ways."

"Won't you—ride?"

"No, thank you. I guess I'd rather walk."

Jonathan Nye nodded, made an inarticulate noise in his throat, and drove on. Louisa watched the wagon bowling lightly along. The dust flew back. She took out her handkerchief and wiped her dripping face.

It was about noon when she came in sight of her uncle Solomon Mears's house in Wolfsborough. It stood far back from the road, behind a green expanse of untrodden yard. The blinds on the great square front were all closed; it looked as if everybody were away. Louisa went around to the side door. It stood wide open. There was a thin blue cloud of tobacco smoke issuing from it. Solomon Mears sat there in the large old kitchen smoking his pipe. On the table near him was an empty bowl; he had just eaten his dinner of bread and milk. He got his own dinner, for he had lived alone since his wife died. He looked at Louisa. Evidently he did not recognize her.

"How do you do, Uncle Solomon?" said Louisa.

"Oh, it's John Britton's daughter! How d'ye do?"

He took his pipe out of his mouth long enough to speak, then replaced it. His eyes, sharp under their shaggy brows, were fixed on Louisa; his broad bristling face had a look of stolid rebuff like an ox; his stout figure, in his soiled farmer dress, surged over his chair. He sat full in the doorway. Louisa standing before him, the perspiration trickling over her burning face, set forth her case with a certain dignity. This old man was her mother's nearest relative. He had property and to spare. Should she survive him, it would be hers, unless willed away. She, with her unsophisticated sense of justice, had a feeling that he ought to help her.

The old man listened. When she stopped speaking he took the

pipe out of his mouth slowly, and stared gloomily past her at his hay field, where the grass was now a green stubble.

"I ain't got no money I can spare jest now," said he. "I s'pose you know your father cheated me out of consider'ble once?"

"We don't care so much about money, if you have got something you could spare to—eat. We ain't got anything but garden-stuff."

Solomon Mears still frowned past her at the hay field. Presently he arose slowly and went across the kitchen. Louisa sat down on the door-step and waited. Her uncle was gone quite a while. She, too, stared over at the field, which seemed to undulate like a lake in the hot light.

"Here's some things you can take, if you want 'em," said her uncle, at her back.

She got up quickly. He pointed grimly to the kitchen table. He was a deacon, an orthodox believer; he recognized the claims of the poor, but he gave alms as a soldier might yield up his sword. Benevolence was the result of warfare with his own conscience.

On the table lay a ham, a bag of meal, one of flour, and a basket of eggs.

"I'm afraid I can't carry 'em all," said Louisa.

"Leave what you can't then." Solomon caught up his hat and went out. He muttered something about not spending any more time as he went.

Louisa stood looking at the packages. It was utterly impossible for her to carry them all at once. She heard her uncle shout to some oxen he was turning out of the barn. She took up the bag of meal and the basket of eggs and carried them out to the gate; then she returned, got the flour and ham, and went with them to a point beyond. Then she returned for the meal and eggs, and carried them past the others. In that way she traversed the seven miles home. The heat increased. She had eaten nothing since morning but the apples that her friend had given her. Her head was swimming, but she kept on. Her resolution was as immovable under the power of the sun as a rock. Once in a while she rested for a moment under a tree, but she soon arose and went on. It was like a pilgrimage, and the Mecca at the end of the burning, desert-like road was her own maiden independence.

It was after eight o'clock when she reached home. Her mother stood in the doorway watching for her, straining her eyes in the dusk.

"For goodness sake, Louisa Britton! where have you been?" she began; but Louisa laid the meal and eggs down on the step.

"I've got to go back a little ways," she panted.

When she returned with the flour and ham, she could hardly get

into the house. She laid them on the kitchen table, where her mother
had put the other parcels, and sank into a chair.

"Is this the way you've brought all these things home?" asked her
mother.

Louisa nodded.

"All the way from Uncle Solomon's?"

"Yes."

Her mother went to her and took her hat off. "It's a mercy if you
ain't got a sunstroke," said she, with a sharp tenderness. "I've got
somethin' to tell you. What do you s'pose has happened? Mr. Mosely
has been here, an' he wants you to take the school again when it
opens next week. He says Ida ain't very well, but I guess that ain't
it. They think she's goin' to get somebody. Mis' Mitchell says so.
She's been in. She says he's carryin' things over there the whole
time, but she don't b'lieve there's anything settled yet. She says they
feel so sure of it they're goin' to have Ida give the school up. I told
her I thought Ida would make him a good wife, an' she was easier
suited than some girls. What do you s'pose Mis' Mitchell says? She
says old Mis' Nye told her that there was one thing about it: if Jonathan had you, he wa'n't goin' to have me an' father hitched on to
him; he'd look out for that. I told Mis' Mitchell that I guess there
wa'n't none of us willin' to hitch, you nor anybody else. I hope she'll
tell Mis' Nye. Now I'm a-goin' to turn you out a tumbler of milk—
Mis' Mitchell she brought over a whole pitcherful; says she's got
more'n they can use—they ain't got no pig now—an' then you go an'
lay down on the sittin'-room lounge, an' cool off; an' I'll stir up some
porridge for supper, an' boil some eggs. Father'll be tickled to
death. Go right in there. I'm dreadful afraid you'll be sick. I never
heard of anybody doin' such a thing as you have."

Louisa drank the milk and crept into the sitting-room. It was warm
and close there, so she opened the front door and sat down on the
step. The twilight was deep, but there was a clear yellow glow in
the west. One great star had come out in the midst of it. A dewy coolness was spreading over everything. The air was full of bird calls
and children's voices. Now and then there was a shout of laughter.
Louisa leaned her head against the door-post.

The house was quite near the road. Some one passed—a man
carrying a basket. Louisa glanced at him, and recognized Jonathan
Nye by his gait. He kept on down the road toward the Moselys', and
Louisa turned again from him to her sweet, mysterious, girlish dreams.

Edith Wharton
A Journey

As SHE LAY in her berth, staring at the shadows overhead, the rush of the wheels was in her brain, driving her deeper and deeper into circles of wakeful lucidity. The sleeping-car had sunk into its night-silence. Through the wet window-pane she watched the sudden lights, the long stretches of hurrying blackness. Now and then she turned her head and looked through the opening in the hangings at her husband's curtains across the aisle . . .

She wondered restlessly if he wanted anything and if she could hear him if he called. His voice had grown very weak within the last months and it irritated him when she did not hear. This irritability, this increasing childish petulance seemed to give expression to their imperceptible estrangement. Like two faces looking at one another through a sheet of glass they were close together, almost touching, but they could not hear or feel each other: the conductivity between them was broken. She, at least, had this sense of separation, and she fancied sometimes that she saw it reflected in the look with which he supplemented his failing words. Doubtless the fault was hers. She was too impenetrably healthy to be touched by the irrelevancies of disease. Her self-reproachful tenderness was tinged with the sense of his irrationality: she had a vague feeling that there was a purpose in his helpless tyrannies. The suddenness of the change had found her so unprepared. A year ago their pulses had beat to one robust measure; both had the same prodigal confidence in an exhaustless future. Now their energies no longer kept step: hers still bounded ahead of life, preëmpting unclaimed regions of hope and activity, while his lagged behind, vainly struggling to overtake her.

When they married, she had such arrears of living to make up: her days had been as bare as the white-washed school-room where she forced innutritious facts upon reluctant children. His coming had

The Greater Inclination (New York, 1899), pp. 27–45. Text from this edition.

broken in on the slumber of circumstance, widening the present till
it became the encloser of remotest chances. But imperceptibly the
horizon narrowed. Life had a grudge against her: she was never to
be allowed to spread her wings.

At first the doctors had said that six weeks of mild air would set
him right; but when he came back this assurance was explained as
having of course included a winter in a dry climate. They gave up
their pretty house, storing the wedding presents and new furniture,
and went to Colorado. She had hated it there from the first. Nobody
knew her or cared about her; there was no one to wonder at the
good match she had made, or to envy her the new dresses and the
visiting-cards which were still a surprise to her. And he kept growing
worse. She felt herself beset with difficulties too evasive to be
fought by so direct a temperament. She still loved him, of course;
but he was gradually, undefinably ceasing to be himself. The man
she had married had been strong, active, gently masterful: the male
whose pleasure it is to clear a way through the material obstructions
of life; but now it was she who was the protector, he who must be
shielded from importunities and given his drops or his beef-juice
though the skies were falling. The routine of the sick-room bewildered
her; this punctual administering of medicine seemed as idle as some
uncomprehended religious mummery.

There were moments, indeed, when warm gushes of pity swept
away her instinctive resentment of his condition, when she still found
his old self in his eyes as they groped for each other through the
dense medium of his weakness. But these moments had grown rare.
Sometimes he frightened her: his sunken expressionless face seemed
that of a stranger; his voice was weak and hoarse; his thin-lipped
smile a mere muscular contraction. Her hand avoided his damp soft
skin, which had lost the familiar roughness of health: she caught
herself furtively watching him as she might have watched a strange
animal. It frightened her to feel that this was the man she loved;
there were hours when to tell him what she suffered seemed the one
escape from her fears. But in general she judged herself more leni-
ently, reflecting that she had perhaps been too long alone with him,
and that she would feel differently when they were at home again,
surrounded by her robust and buoyant family. How she had rejoiced
when the doctors at last gave their consent to his going home! She
knew, of course, what the decision meant; they both knew. It meant
that he was to die; but they dressed the truth in hopeful euphuisms,
and at times, in the joy of preparation, she really forgot the purpose
of their journey, and slipped into an eager allusion to next year's
plans.

At last the day of leaving came. She had a dreadful fear that they would never get away; that somehow at the last moment he would fail her; that the doctors held one of their accustomed treacheries in reserve; but nothing happened. They drove to the station, he was installed in a seat with a rug over his knees and a cushion at his back, and she hung out of the window waving unregretful farewells to the acquaintances she had really never liked till then.

The first twenty-four hours had passed off well. He revived a little and it amused him to look out of the window and to observe the humours of the car. The second day he began to grow weary and to chafe under the dispassionate stare of the freckled child with the lump of chewing-gum. She had to explain to the child's mother that her husband was too ill to be disturbed: a statement received by that lady with a resentment visibly supported by the maternal sentiment of the whole car. . . .

That night he slept badly and the next morning his temperature frightened her: she was sure he was growing worse. The day passed slowly, punctuated by the small irritations of travel. Watching his tired face, she traced in its contractions every rattle and jolt of the train, till her own body vibrated with sympathetic fatigue. She felt the others observing him too, and hovered restlessly between him and the line of interrogative eyes. The freckled child hung about him like a fly; offers of candy and picture-books failed to dislodge her: she twisted one leg around the other and watched him imperturbably. The porter, as he passed, lingered with vague proffers of help, probably inspired by philanthropic passengers swelling with the sense that "something ought to be done;" and one nervous man in a skull-cap was audibly concerned as to the possible effect on his wife's health.

The hours dragged on in a dreary inoccupation. Towards dusk she sat down beside him and he laid his hand on hers. The touch startled her. He seemed to be calling her from far off. She looked at him helplessly and his smile went through her like a physical pang.

"Are you very tired?" she asked.

"No, not very."

"We'll be there soon now."

"Yes, very soon."

"This time to-morrow—"

He nodded and they sat silent. When she had put him to bed and crawled into her own berth she tried to cheer herself with the thought that in less than twenty-four hours they would be in New York. Her people would all be at the station to meet her—she pictured their round unanxious faces pressing through the crowd. She only hoped they would not tell him too loudly that he was looking splendidly and would be all right in no time: the subtler sympathies developed by long contact with suffering were making her aware of a certain coarseness of texture in the family sensibilities.

Suddenly she thought she heard him call. She parted the curtains and listened. No, it was only a man snoring at the other end of the car. His snores had a greasy sound, as though they passed through tallow. She lay down and tried to sleep . . . Had she not heard him move? She started up trembling . . . The silence frightened her more than any sound. He might not be able to make her hear—he might be calling her now . . . What made her think of such things? It was merely the familiar tendency of an over-tired mind to fasten itself on the most intolerable chance within the range of its forebodings . . . Putting her head out, she listened; but she could not distinguish his breathing from that of the other pairs of lungs about her. She longed to get up and look at him, but she knew the impulse was a mere vent for her restlessness, and the fear of disturbing him restrained her. . . . The regular movement of his curtain reassured her, she knew not why; she remembered that he had wished her a cheerful good-night; and the sheer inability to endure her fears a moment longer made her put them from her with an effort of her whole sound tired body. She turned on her side and slept.

She sat up stiffly, staring out at the dawn. The train was rushing through a region of bare hillocks huddled against a lifeless sky. It looked like the first day of creation. The air of the car was close, and she pushed up her window to let in the keen wind. Then she looked at her watch: it was seven o'clock, and soon the people about her would be stirring. She slipped into her clothes, smoothed her dishevelled hair and crept to the dressing-room. When she had washed her face and adjusted her dress she felt more hopeful. It was always a struggle for her not to be cheerful in the morning. Her cheeks burned deliciously under the coarse towel and the wet hair about her temples broke into strong upward tendrils. Every inch of her was full of life and elasticity. And in ten hours they would be at home!

She stepped to her husband's berth: it was time for him to take his early glass of milk. The window-shade was down, and in the dusk of the curtained enclosure she could just see that he lay sideways, with his face away from her. She leaned over him and drew up the shade. As she did so she touched one of his hands. It felt cold . . .

She bent closer, laying her hand on his arm and calling him by name. He did not move. She spoke again more loudly; she grasped his shoulder and gently shook it. He lay motionless. She caught hold of his hand again: it slipped from her limply, like a dead thing. A dead thing? . . . Her breath caught. She must see his face. She leaned forward, and hurriedly, shrinkingly, with a sickening reluctance of the flesh, laid her hands on his shoulders and turned him over. His head fell back; his face looked small and smooth; he gazed at her with steady eyes.

She remained motionless for a long time, holding him thus; and they looked at each other. Suddenly she shrank back: the longing to scream, to call out, to fly from him, had almost overpowered her. But a strong hand arrested her. Good God! If it were known that he was dead they would be put off the train at the next station—

In a terrifying flash of remembrance there arose before her a scene she had once witnessed in travelling, when a husband and wife, whose child had died in the train, had been thrust out at some chance station. She saw them standing on the platform with the child's body between them; she had never forgotten the dazed look with which they followed the receding train. And this was what would happen to her. Within the next hour she might find herself on the platform of some strange station, alone with her husband's body. . . . Anything but that! It was too horrible— She quivered like a creature at bay.

As she cowered there, she felt the train moving more slowly. It was coming then—they were approaching a station! She saw again the husband and wife standing on the lonely platform; and with a violent gesture she drew down the shade to hide her husband's face.

Feeling dizzy, she sank down on the edge of the berth, keeping away from his outstretched body, and pulling the curtains close, so that he and she were shut into a kind of sepulchral twilight. She tried to think. At all costs she must conceal the fact that he was dead. But how? Her mind refused to act: she could not plan, combine. She could think of no way but to sit there, clutching the curtains, all day long . . .

She heard the porter making up her bed; people were beginning to move about the car; the dressing-room door was being opened and shut. She tried to rouse herself. At length with a supreme effort she rose to her feet, stepping into the aisle of the car and drawing the curtains tight behind her. She noticed that they still parted slightly with the motion of the car, and finding a pin in her dress she fastened them together. Now she was safe. She looked round and saw the porter. She fancied he was watching her.

"Ain't he awake yet?" he enquired.

"No," she faltered.

"I got his milk all ready when he wants it. You know you told me to have it for him by seven."

She nodded silently and crept into her seat.

At half-past eight the train reached Buffalo. By this time the other passengers were dressed and the berths had been folded back for the day. The porter, moving to and fro under his burden of sheets and pillows, glanced at her as he passed. At length he said: "Ain't he going to get up? You know we're ordered to make up the berths as early as we can."

She turned cold with fear. They were just entering the station.

"Oh, not yet," she stammered. "Not till he's had his milk. Won't you get it, please?"

"All right. Soon as we start again."

When the train moved on he reappeared with the milk. She took it from him and sat vaguely looking at it: her brain moved slowly from one idea to another, as though they were stepping-stones set far apart across a whirling flood. At length she became aware that the porter still hovered expectantly.

"Will I give it to him?" he suggested.

"Oh, no," she cried, rising. "He—he's asleep yet, I think—"

She waited till the porter had passed on; then she unpinned the curtains and slipped behind them. In the semi-obscurity her husband's face stared up at her like a marble mask with agate eyes. The eyes were dreadful. She put out her hand and drew down the lids. Then she remembered the glass of milk in her other hand: what was she to do with it? She thought of raising the window and throwing it out; but to do so she would have to lean across his body and bring her face close to his. She decided to drink the milk.

She returned to her seat with the empty glass and after a while the porter came back to get it.

"When'll I fold up his bed?" he asked.

"Oh, not now—not yet; he's ill—he's very ill. Can't you let him stay as he is? The doctor wants him to lie down as much as possible."

He scratched his head. "Well, if he's *really* sick—"

He took the empty glass and walked away, explaining to the passengers that the party behind the curtains was too sick to get up just yet.

She found herself the centre of sympathetic eyes. A motherly woman with an intimate smile sat down beside her.

"I'm real sorry to hear your husband's sick. I've had a remarkable amount of sickness in my family and maybe I could assist you. Can I take a look at him?"

"Oh, no—no, please! He mustn't be disturbed."

The lady accepted the rebuff indulgently.

"Well, it's just as you say, of course, but you don't look to me as if you'd had much experience in sickness and I'd have been glad to assist you. What do you generally do when your husband's taken this way?"

"I—I let him sleep."

"Too much sleep ain't any too healthful either. Don't you give him any medicine?"

"Y—yes."

"Don't you wake him to take it?"

"Yes."

"When does he take the next dose?"

"Not for—two hours—"

The lady looked disappointed. "Well, if I was you I'd try giving it oftener. That's what I do with my folks."

After that many faces seemed to press upon her. The passengers were on their way to the dining-car, and she was conscious that as they passed down the aisle they glanced curiously at the closed curtains. One lantern-jawed man with prominent eyes stood still and tried to shoot his projecting glance through the division between the folds. The freckled child, returning from breakfast, waylaid the passers with a buttery clutch, saying in a loud whisper, "He's sick;" and once the conductor came by, asking for tickets. She shrank into her corner and looked out of the window at the flying trees and houses, meaningless hieroglyphs of an endlessly unrolled papyrus.

Now and then the train stopped, and the newcomers on entering the car stared in turn at the closed curtains. More and more people seemed to pass—their faces began to blend fantastically with the images surging in her brain . . .

Later in the day a fat man detached himself from the mist of faces. He had a creased stomach and soft pale lips. As he pressed himself into the seat facing her she noticed that he was dressed in black broadcloth, with a soiled white tie.

"Husband's pretty bad this morning, is he?"

"Yes."

"Dear, dear! Now that's terribly distressing, ain't it?" An apostolic smile revealed his gold-filled teeth. "Of course you know there's no sech thing as sickness. Ain't that a lovely thought? Death itself is but a deloosion of our grosser senses. On'y lay yourself open to the influx of the sperrit, submit yourself passively to the action of the divine force, and disease and dissolution will cease to exist for you. If you could indooce your husband to read this little pamphlet—"

The faces about her again grew indistinct. She had a vague recollection of hearing the motherly lady and the parent of the freckled child ardently disputing the relative advantages of trying several medicines at once, or of taking each in turn; the motherly lady maintaining that the competitive system saved time; the other objecting that you couldn't tell which remedy had effected the cure; their voices went on and on, like bell-buoys droning through a fog . . . The porter came up now and then with questions that she did not understand, but that somehow she must have answered since he went away again without repeating them; every two hours the motherly lady reminded her that her husband ought to have his drops; people left the car and others replaced them . . .

Her head was spinning and she tried to steady herself by clutching at her thoughts as they swept by, but they slipped away from her like bushes on the side of a sheer precipice down which she seemed to be falling. Suddenly her mind grew clear again and she found herself vividly picturing what would happen when the train reached New York. She shuddered as it occurred to her that he would be quite cold and that some one might perceive he had been dead since morning.

She thought hurriedly:—"If they see I am not surprised they will suspect something. They will ask questions, and if I tell them the truth they won't believe me—no one would believe me! It will be terrible"—and she kept repeating to herself:—"I must pretend I don't know. I must pretend I don't know. When they open the curtains I must go up to him quite naturally—and then I must scream." . . . She had an idea that the scream would be very hard to do.

Gradually new thoughts crowded upon her, vivid and urgent: she tried to separate and restrain them, but they beset her clamorously, like her school-children at the end of a hot day, when she was too tired to silence them. Her head grew confused, and she felt a sick fear of forgetting her part, of betraying herself by some unguarded word or look.

"I must pretend I don't know," she went on murmuring. The words had lost their significance, but she repeated them mechanically, as though they had been a magic formula, until suddenly she heard herself saying: "I can't remember, I can't remember!"

Her voice sounded very loud, and she looked about her in terror; but no one seemed to notice that she had spoken.

As she glanced down the car her eye caught the curtains of her husband's berth, and she began to examine the monotonous arabesques woven through their heavy folds. The pattern was intricate and difficult to trace; she gazed fixedly at the curtains and as she did so the thick stuff grew transparent and through it she saw her husband's face—his dead face. She struggled to avert her look, but her eyes refused to move and her head seemed to be held in a vice. At last, with an effort that left her weak and shaking, she turned away; but it was of no use; close in front of her, small and smooth, was her husband's face. It seemed to be suspended in the air between her and the false braids of the woman who sat in front of her. With an uncontrollable gesture she stretched out her hand to push the face away, and suddenly she felt the touch of his smooth skin. She repressed a cry and half started from her seat. The woman with the false braids looked around, and feeling that she must justify her movement in some way she rose and lifted her travelling-bag from the opposite seat. She unlocked the bag and looked into it; but the first object her hand met was a small flask of her husband's, thrust there at the last moment, in the haste of departure. She locked the bag and closed her eyes . . . his face was there again, hanging between her eye-balls and lids like a waxen mask against a red curtain . . .

She roused herself with a shiver. Had she fainted or slept? Hours seemed to have elapsed; but it was still broad day, and the people about her were sitting in the same attitudes as before.

A sudden sense of hunger made her aware that she had eaten nothing since morning. The thought of food filled her with disgust, but she dreaded a return of faintness, and remembering that she had some biscuits in her bag she took one out and ate it. The dry crumbs choked her, and she hastily swallowed a little brandy from her husband's flask. The burning sensation in her throat acted as a counter-irritant, momentarily relieving the dull ache of her nerves. Then she felt a gently-stealing warmth, as though a soft air fanned her, and the swarming fears relaxed their clutch, receding through the stillness that enclosed her, a stillness soothing as the spacious quietude of a summer day. She slept.

Through her sleep she felt the impetuous rush of the train. It seemed to be life itself that was sweeping her on with headlong inexorable force—sweeping her into darkness and terror, and the awe of unknown days.— Now all at once everything was still—not a sound, not a pulsation . . . She was dead in her turn, and lay beside him with smooth upstaring face. How quiet it was!—and yet she heard feet coming, the feet of the men who were to carry them away . . . She could feel too—she felt a sudden prolonged vibration, a series of hard shocks, and then another plunge into darkness: the darkness of death this time—a black whirlwind on which they were both spinning like leaves, in wild uncoiling spirals, with millions and millions of the dead . . .

She sprang up in terror. Her sleep must have lasted a long time, for the winter day had paled and the lights had been lit. The car was in confusion, and as she regained her self-possession she saw that the passengers were gathering up their wraps and bags. The woman with the false braids had brought from the dressing-room a sickly ivy-plant in a bottle, and the Christian Scientist was reversing his cuffs. The porter passed down the aisle with his impartial brush. An impersonal figure with a gold-banded cap asked for her husband's

ticket. A voice shouted "Baig-gage *express!*" and she heard the
clicking of metal as the passengers handed over their checks.

Presently her window was blocked by an expanse of sooty wall,
and the train passed into the Harlem tunnel. The journey was over;
in a few minutes she would see her family pushing their joyous way
through the throng at the station. Her heart dilated. The worst terror
was past . . .

"We'd better get him up now, hadn't we?" asked the porter,
touching her arm.

He had her husband's hat in his hand and was meditatively revolving it under his brush.

She looked at the hat and tried to speak; but suddenly the car
grew dark. She flung up her arms, struggling to catch at something,
and fell face downward, striking her head against the dead man's
berth.

Kate Chopin
A Respectable Woman

Mrs. BARODA was a little provoked to learn that her husband expected his friend, Gouvernail, up to spend a week or two on the
plantation.

They had entertained a good deal during the winter; much of the
time had also been passed in New Orleans in various forms of mild
dissipation. She was looking forward to a period of unbroken rest,
now, and undisturbed tête-a-tête with her husband, when he informed her that Gouvernail was coming up to stay a week or two.

This was a man she had heard much of but never seen. He had
been her husband's college friend; was now a journalist, and in no
sense a society man or "a man about town," which were, perhaps,
some of the reasons she had never met him. But she had unconsciously formed an image of him in her mind. She pictured him tall,
slim, cynical; with eye-glasses, and his hands in his pockets; and she

Vogue, III (February 15, 1894). Republished in *A Night in Acadie*
(Chicago, 1897), pp. 389–96. Text from *A Night in Acadie.*

did not like him. Gouvernail was slim enough, but he wasn't very tall
nor very cynical; neither did he wear eye-glasses nor carry his hands
in his pockets. And she rather liked him when he first presented himself.

But why she liked him she could not explain satisfactorily to herself when she partly attempted to do so. She could discover in him
none of those brilliant and promising traits which Gaston, her husband, had often assured her that he possessed. On the contrary, he
sat rather mute and receptive before her chatty eagerness to make
him feel at home and in face of Gaston's frank and wordy hospitality.
His manner was as courteous toward her as the most exacting woman
could require; but he made no direct appeal to her approval or even
esteem.

Once settled at the plantation he seemed to like to sit upon the
wide portico in the shade of one of the big Corinthian pillars, smoking his cigar lazily and listening attentively to Gaston's experience
as a sugar planter.

"This is what I call living," he would utter with deep satisfaction,
as the air that swept across the sugar field caressed him with its
warm and scented velvety touch. It pleased him also to get on familiar
terms with the big dogs that came about him, rubbing themselves
sociably against his legs. He did not care to fish, and displayed no
eagerness to go out and kill grosbecs when Gaston proposed doing
so.

Gouvernail's personality puzzled Mrs. Baroda, but she liked him.
Indeed, he was a lovable, inoffensive fellow. After a few days, when
she could understand him no better than at first, she gave over being
puzzled and remained piqued. In this mood she left her husband and
her guest, for the most part, alone together. Then finding that Gouvernail took no manner of exception to her action, she imposed her
society upon him, accompanying him in his idle strolls to the mill and
walks along the batture. She persistently sought to penetrate the reserve in which he had unconsciously enveloped himself.

"When is he going—your friend?" she one day asked her husband.
"For my part, he tires me frightfully."

"Not for a week yet, dear. I can't understand; he gives you no
trouble."

"No. I should like him better if he did; if he were more like others,
and I had to plan somewhat for his comfort and enjoyment."

Gaston took his wife's pretty face between his hands and looked
tenderly and laughingly into her troubled eyes. They were making a
bit of toilet sociably together in Mrs. Baroda's dressing-room.

"You are full of surprises, ma belle," he said to her. "Even I can never count upon how you are going to act under given conditions." He kissed her and turned to fasten his cravat before the mirror.

"Here you are," he went on, "taking poor Gouvernail seriously and making a commotion over him, the last thing he would desire or expect."

"Commotion!" she hotly resented. "Nonsense! How can you say such a thing? Commotion, indeed! But, you know, you said he was clever."

"So he is. But the poor fellow is run down by overwork now. That's why I asked him here to take a rest."

"You used to say he was a man of ideas," she retorted, unconciliated. "I expected him to be interesting, at least. I'm going to the city in the morning to have my spring gowns fitted. Let me know when Mr. Gouvernail is gone; I shall be at my Aunt Octavie's."

That night she went and sat alone upon a bench that stood beneath a live oak tree at the edge of the gravel walk.

She had never known her thoughts or her intentions to be so confused. She could gather nothing from them but the feeling of a distinct necessity to quit her home in the morning.

Mrs. Baroda heard footsteps crunching the gravel; but could discern in the darkness only the approaching red point of a lighted cigar. She knew it was Gouvernail, for her husband did not smoke. She hoped to remain unnoticed, but her white gown revealed her to him. He threw away his cigar and seated himself upon the bench beside her; without a suspicion that she might object to his presence.

"Your husband told me to bring this to you, Mrs. Baroda," he said, handing her a filmy, white scarf with which she sometimes enveloped her head and shoulders. She accepted the scarf from him with a murmur of thanks, and let it lie in her lap.

He made some commonplace observation upon the baneful effect of the night air at that season. Then as his gaze reached out into the darkness, he murmured, half to himself:

Night of south winds—night of the large few stars!
Still nodding night——

She made no reply to this apostrophe to the night, which indeed, was not addressed to her.

Gouvernail was in no sense a diffident man, for he was not a self-conscious one. His periods of reserve were not constitutional, but the result of moods. Sitting there beside Mrs. Baroda, his silence melted for the time.

He talked freely and intimately in a low, hesitating drawl that was not unpleasant to hear. He talked of the old college days when he and Gaston had been a good deal to each other; of the days of keen and blind ambitions and large intentions. Now there was left with him, at least, a philosophic acquiescence to the existing order—only a desire to be permitted to exist, with now and then a little whiff of genuine life, such as he was breathing now.

Her mind only vaguely grasped what he was saying. Her physical being was for the moment predominant. She was not thinking of his words, only drinking in the tones of his voice. She wanted to reach out her hand in the darkness and touch him with the sensitive tips of her fingers upon the face or the lips. She wanted to draw close to him and whisper against his cheek—she did not care what—as she might have done if she had not been a respectable woman.

The stronger the impulse grew to bring herself near him, the further, in fact, did she draw away from him. As soon as she could do so without an appearance of too great rudeness, she rose and left him there alone.

Before she reached the house, Gouvernail had lighted a fresh cigar and ended his apostrophe to the night.

Mrs. Baroda was greatly tempted that night to tell her husband —who was also her friend—of this folly that had seized her. But she did not yield to the temptation. Beside being a respectable woman she was a very sensible one; and she knew there are some battles in life which a human being must fight alone.

When Gaston arose in the morning, his wife had already departed. She had taken an early morning train to the city. She did not return till Gouvernail was gone from under her roof.

There was some talk of having him back during the summer that followed. That is, Gaston greatly desired it; but this desire yielded to his wife's strenuous opposition.

However, before the year ended, she proposed, wholly from herself, to have Gouvernail visit them again. Her husband was surprised and delighted with the suggestion coming from her.

"I am glad, chère amie, to know that you have finally overcome your dislike for him; truly he did not deserve it."

"Oh," she told him, laughingly, after pressing a long, tender kiss upon his lips, "I have overcome everything! you will see. This time I shall be very nice to him."

Part Four

THE WEST AS THEME AND SYMBOL

The West has been a constant symbol in American life, but in the 1890's its symbolic import took on added resonance. Among the reasons for this greater significance were the supposed closing of the frontier (as announced in the census of 1890), the political revolt by the plains and mountain states in the elections of 1892 and 1896, the immense popularity of the Rooseveltian ethic of Manliness with its Western associations, and the widespread acceptance of the Anglo-Saxon myth of history which portrayed the Westerner as the last survivor of his virile Friesland ancestors. These events and ideas accentuated certain permanent features of an already deeply engrained American myth of the West.

Frederick Jackson Turner played a major role in encouraging this new emphasis on old ideas. His famous "The Significance of the Frontier in American History" (1893) and his later, usually more concise essays made one basic point—that those qualities of life which collectively constitute the American character (strength, courage, equality, individualism, and possessiveness) were derived from our three centuries as a westering people. The appeal of this idea and its ready adaptability to allegory can be seen in Frank Norris' story "Dying Fires." Overbeck, the young writer of the Sierras, is an archetypal Westerner. Untutored and therefore untrammeled, he has the power and insight necessary to shape his experience into a worthwhile novel, *The Vision of Bunt McBride*. But the bulk of Norris' story is devoted to the destruction of Overbeck's literary virility by an effete Eastern culture. And this emphasis suggests a major impulse behind the revitalization of a mythic West in the 1890's: the appeal of the West as an image of freedom and masculinity at a time when there was widespread fear that these values could no longer be nurtured by an industrial, urban society. In the mythic landscape of the 1890's, therefore, the West was a source of "American" virtues, and the East was increasingly a threat to these qualities.

The most important literary representation of American life as a Western experience is the Cowboy or Western story, particularly in the form of a narrative in which a hardened Westerner helps initiate an Easterner into the realities of life. Theodore Roosevelt's anecdotes of "Cowboy Land" are autobiographical in form but nevertheless contain many of the basic characteristics of the Western story: a tall-tale grotesqueness of incident, a jocular tone (reinforced in later writers by the influence of Kipling), and a defense of the morality of the Westerner despite his lawlessness. Owen Wister, who wrote the first "classic" Western novel, *The Virginian* (1902), reshaped this anecdotal core into the formulas of popular fiction. His Specimen Jones is tough, knowledgeable, and not above trickery. Yet Jones adopts the innocent Easterner who would otherwise perish and struggles shrewdly and courageously against their common enemy. To Turner's and Norris' list of Western virtues, Wister adds the most crucial of all—compassion, self-sacrifice, and honor. Out of the rough-and-tumble, vicious, and macabre world of the Arizona desert rode the Christian knight disguised as a Cowboy.

By the 1890's, Wister could draw not only upon the Cowboy as depicted by Roosevelt and other commentators on the West but also upon the stereotypes of the Western story popularized by a generation of dime-novel hack writers. It is not surprising, therefore, that Western stories or poems by such "serious" writers as Stephen Crane, Eugene Field, and Wister himself almost always contained an element of parody and that Jack London could transfer its conventions of plot and character almost unchanged to the Klondike. But whether the setting of the Western is the range, the desert, or the white silence of the North, and whether its style is Crane's blend of parody and symbolic truth or London's forthright earnestness, the mystique of the Western hero remains constant. Even though he suffers or dies, he does so as a "man" because he does so with courage, in freedom, and at one with his companions.

Thus, by the 1890's the symbolic truth of the West was that it was a world in which a man could still be strong, resourceful, and kind. Much like the pastoral in earlier European literature, the West functioned not only as an image of what America had been but of what it should again strive to be. So, Roosevelt could use a Western rhetoric of "manliness" in calling for public participation in politics, and Norris could stretch the Anglo-Saxon "long march" theory of history into a call for international brotherhood. The pervasiveness of this transformation of Western myth into national aspiration is clearly revealed in Finley Peter Dunne's satire of the vogue of Anglo-Saxonism. We are all Anglo-Saxons, Mr. Dooley concludes, though Jews or Frenchmen or Italians, because it is the Angle-Saxon in our national character which helped defeat Spain. In a like sense, we all longed to be Westerners—to be free, manly, tough, and compassionate—as the city and factory closed their walls around us. It is no wonder that the Western in the 1890's took its first major step toward becoming the principal modern American myth.

Frederick Jackson Turner
The Problem of the West

THE PROBLEM OF THE WEST is nothing less than the problem of American development. A glance at the map of the United States reveals the truth. To write of a "Western sectionalism," bounded on the east by the Alleghanies, is, in itself, to proclaim the writer a provincial. What is the West? What has it been in American life? To have the answers to these questions, is to understand the most significant features of the United States of to-day.

The West, at bottom, is a form of society, rather than an area. It is the term applied to the region whose social conditions result from the application of older institutions and ideas to the transforming influences of free land. By this application, a new environment is suddenly entered, freedom of opportunity is opened, the cake of custom is broken, and new activities, new lines of growth, new institutions and new ideals, are brought into existence. The wilderness disappears, the "West" proper passes on to a new frontier, and, in the former area, a new society has emerged from this contact with the backwoods. Gradually this society loses its primitive conditions, and assimilates itself to the type of the older social conditions of the East; but it bears within it enduring and distinguishing survivals of its frontier experience. Decade after decade, West after West, this rebirth of American society has gone on, has left its traces behind it, and has reacted on the East. The history of our political institutions, our democracy, is not a history of imitation, of simple borrowing; it is a history of the evolution and adaptation of organs in response to changed environment, a history of the origin of new political species. In this sense, therefore, the West has been a constructive force of the highest significance in our life. To use the words of that acute and widely informed observer, Mr. Bryce, "The West is the most

Atlantic Monthly, LXXVIII (September, 1896), 289–97. Text from this publication.

In 1896 the West was a problem in the sense that the Populist Party drew most of its strength from the area and was viewed with alarm in the East.

American part of America. . . . What Europe is to Asia, what England is to the rest of Europe, what America is to England, that the Western States and Territories are to the Atlantic States."

The West, as a phase of social organization, began with the Atlantic coast, and passed across the continent. But the colonial tide-water area was in close touch with the Old World, and soon lost its Western aspects. In the middle of the eighteenth century, the newer social conditions appeared along the upper waters of the tributaries of the Atlantic. Here it was that the West took on its distinguishing features, and transmitted frontier traits and ideals to this area in later days. On the coast were the fishermen and skippers, the merchants and planters, with eyes turned toward Europe. Beyond the falls of the rivers were the pioneer farmers, largely of non-English stock, Scotch-Irish and German. They constituted a distinct people, and may be regarded as an expansion of the social and economic life of the middle region into the back country of the South. These frontiersmen were the ancestors of Boone, Andrew Jackson, Calhoun, Clay, and Lincoln. Washington and Jefferson were profoundly affected by these frontier conditions. The forest clearings have been the seed plots of American character.

In the Revolutionary days, the settlers crossed the Alleghanies and put a barrier between them and the coast. They became, to use their phrases, "the men of the Western waters," the heirs of the "Western world." In this era, the backwoodsmen, all along the western slopes of the mountains, with a keen sense of the difference between them and the dwellers on the coast, demanded organization into independent States of the Union. Self-government was their ideal. Said one of their rude, but energetic petitions for statehood: "Some of our fellow-citizens may think we are not able to conduct our affairs and consult our interests; but if our society is rude, much wisdom is not necessary to supply our wants, and a fool can sometimes put on his clothes better than a wise man can do it for him." This forest philosophy is the philosophy of American democracy. But the men of the coast were not ready to admit its implications. They apportioned the state legislatures so that the property-holding minority of the tide-water lands were able to outvote the more populous back counties. A similar system was proposed by federalists in the Constitutional Convention of 1787. Gouverneur Morris, arguing in favor of basing representation on property as well as numbers, declared that "he looked forward, also, to that range of new States which would soon be formed in the West. He thought the rule of representation ought to be so fixed, as to secure to the Atlantic States a prevalence in the national councils." "The new States," said he, "will know less

of the public interest than these; will have an interest in many respects
different; in particular will be little scrupulous of involving the community in wars, the burdens and operations of which would fall
chiefly on the maritime States. Provision ought, therefore, to be made
to prevent the maritime States from being hereafter outvoted by
them." He added that the Western country "would not be able to
furnish men equally enlightened to share in the administration of our
common interests. The busy haunts of men, not the remote wilderness, was the proper school of political talents. If the Western people
get power into their hands, they will ruin the Atlantic interest. The
back members are always most averse to the best measures." Add to
these utterances of Gouverneur Morris the impassioned protest of
Josiah Quincy, of Massachusetts, in the debates in the House of
Representatives, on the admission of Louisiana. Referring to the
discussion over the slave votes and the West in the Constitutional
Convention, he declared, "Suppose, then, that it had been distinctly
foreseen that, in addition to the effect of this weight, the whole population of a world beyond the Mississippi was to be brought into this
and the other branch of the legislature, to form our laws, control our
rights, and decide our destiny. Sir, can it be pretended that the patriots of that day would for one moment have listened to it? . . .
They had not taken degrees at the hospital of idiocy. . . . Why, sir,
I have already heard of six States, and some say there will be, at no
great distance of time, more. I have also heard that the mouth of the
Ohio will be far to the east of the centre of the contemplated empire. . . . You have no authority to throw the rights and property of
this people into 'hotch-pot' with the wild men on the Missouri, nor
with the mixed, though more respectable, race of Anglo-Hispano-
Gallo-Americans who bask on the sands in the mouth of the Mississippi. . . . Do you suppose the people of the Northern and Atlantic States will, or ought to, look on with patience and see Representatives and Senators from the Red River and Missouri, pouring
themselves upon this and the other floor, managing the concerns of a
seaboard fifteen hundred miles, at least, from their residence; and having a preponderancy in councils into which, constitutionally, they
could never have been admitted?"

Like an echo from the fears expressed by the East at the close of
the eighteenth century come the words of an eminent Eastern man
of letters at the end of the nineteenth century, in warning against the
West: "Materialized in their temper; with few ideals of an ennobling
sort; little instructed in the lessons of history; safe from exposure to
the direct calamities and physical horrors of war; with undeveloped
imaginations and sympathies—they form a community unfortunate
and dangerous from the possession of power without a due sense of

its corresponding responsibilities; a community in which the passion for war may easily be excited as the fancied means by which its greatness may be convincingly exhibited, and its ambitions gratified. . . . Some chance spark may fire the prairie."

Here, then, is the problem of the West, as it looked to New England leaders of thought in the beginning and at the end of this century. From the first, it was recognized that a new type was growing up beyond the mountains, and that the time would come when the destiny of the nation would be in Western hands. The divergence of these societies became clear in the struggle over the ratification of the federal constitution. The interior agricultural region, the communities that were in debt and desired paper money, opposed the instrument; but the areas of intercourse and property carried the day.

It is important to understand, therefore, what were some of the ideals of this early Western democracy. How did the frontiersman differ from the man of the coast?

The most obvious fact regarding the man of the Western waters is that he had placed himself under influences destructive to many of the gains of civilization. Remote from the opportunity for systematic education, substituting a log hut in the forest clearing for the social comforts of the town, he suffered hardships and privations, and reverted in many ways to primitive conditions of life. Engaged in a struggle to subdue the forest, working as an individual, and with little specie or capital, his interests were with the debtor class. At each stage of its advance, the West has favored an expansion of the currency. The pioneer had boundless confidence in the future of his own community, and when seasons of financial contraction and depression occurred, he, who had staked his all on confidence in Western development, and had fought the savage for his home, was inclined to reproach the conservative sections and classes. To explain this antagonism requires more than denunciation of dishonesty, ignorance, and boorishness as fundamental Western traits. Legislation in the United States has had to deal with two distinct social conditions. In some portions of the country there was, and is, an aggregation of property, and vested rights are in the foreground: in others, capital is lacking, more primitive conditions prevail, with different economic and social ideals, and the contentment of the average individual is placed in the foreground. That in the conflict between these two ideals an even hand has always been held by the government would be difficult to show.

The separation of the Western man from the seaboard, and his environment, made him in a large degree free from European precedents and forces. He looked at things independently and with small regard or appreciation for the best Old World experience. He had no ideal of a philosophical, eclectic nation, that should advance civilization by "intercourse with foreigners and familiarity with their point of view, and readiness to adopt whatever is best and most suitable in their ideas, manners, and customs." His was rather the ideal of conserving and developing what was original and valuable in this new country. The entrance of old society upon free lands meant to him opportunity for a new type of democracy and new popular ideals. The West was not conservative: buoyant self-confidence and self-assertion were distinguishing traits in its composition. It saw in its growth nothing less than a new order of society and state. In this conception were elements of evil and elements of good.

But the fundamental fact in regard to this new society was its relation to land. Professor Boutmy has said of the United States, "Their one primary and predominant object is to cultivate and settle these prairies, forests, and vast waste lands. The striking and peculiar characteristic of American society is that it is not so much a democracy as a huge commercial company for the discovery, cultivation, and capitalization of its enormous territory. The United States are primarily a commercial society, and only secondarily a nation." Of course, this involves a serious misapprehension. By the very fact of the task here set forth, far-reaching ideals of the state and of society have been evolved in the West, accompanied by loyalty to the nation representative of these ideals. But M. Boutmy's description hits the substantial fact, that the fundamental traits of the man of the interior were due to the free lands of the West. These turned his attention to the great task of subduing them to the purposes of civilization, and to the task of advancing his economic and social status in the new democracy which he was helping to create. Art, literature, refinement, scientific administration, all had to give way to this Titanic labor. Energy, incessant activity, became the lot of this new American. Says a traveler of the time of Andrew Jackson, "America is like a vast workshop, over the door of which is printed in blazing characters, 'No admittance here, except on business.'" The West of our own day reminds Mr. Bryce "of the crowd which Vathek found in the hall of Eblis, each darting hither and thither with swift steps and unquiet mien, driven to and fro by a fire in the heart. Time seems too short for what they have to do, and the result always to come short of their desire."

But free lands and the consciousness of working out their social destiny did more than turn the Westerner to material interests and devote him to a restless existence. They promoted equality among the Western settlers, and reacted as a check on the aristocratic influences of the East. Where everybody could have a farm, almost for taking it, economic equality easily resulted, and this involved political equality. Not without a struggle would the Western man abandon this ideal, and it goes far to explain the unrest in the remote West to-day.

Western democracy included individual liberty, as well as equality. The frontiersman was impatient of restraints. He knew how to preserve order, even in the absence of legal authority. If there were cattle thieves, lynch law was sudden and effective: the regulators of the Carolinas were the predecessors of the claims associations of Iowa and the vigilance committees of California. But the individual was not ready to submit to complex regulations. Population was sparse, there was no multitude of jostling interests, as in older settlements, demanding an elaborate system of personal restraints. Society became atomic. There was a reproduction of the primitive idea of the personality of the law, a crime was more an offense against the victim than a violation of the law of the land. Substantial justice, secured in the most direct way, was the ideal of the backwoodsman. He had little patience with finely drawn distinctions or scruples of method. If the thing was one proper to be done, then the most immediate, rough and ready, effective way was the best way.

It followed from the lack of organized political life, from the atomic conditions of the backwoods society, that the individual was exalted and given free play. The West was another name for opportunity. Here were mines to be seized, fertile valleys to be preëmpted, all the natural resources open to the shrewdest and the boldest. The United States is unique in the extent to which the individual has been given an open field, unchecked by restraints of an old social order, or of scientific administration of government. The self-made man was the Western man's ideal, was the kind of man that all men might become. Out of his wilderness experience, out of the freedom of his opportunities, he fashioned a formula for social regeneration,—the freedom of the individual to seek his own. He did not consider that his conditions were exceptional and temporary.

Under such conditions, leadership easily develops,—a leadership based on the possession of the qualities most serviceable to the young society. In the history of Western settlement, we see each forted village following its local hero. Clay, Jackson, Harrison, Lincoln, were illustrations of this tendency in periods when the Western hero rose to the dignity of national hero.

The Western man believed in the manifest destiny of his country. On his border, and checking his advance, were the Indian, the Spaniard, and the Englishman. He was indignant at Eastern indifference and lack of sympathy with his view of his relations to these peoples; at the short-sightedness of Eastern policy. The closure of the Mississippi by Spain, and the proposal to exchange our claim of freedom of navigating the river, in return for commercial advantages to New England, nearly led to the withdrawal of the West from the Union. It was the Western demands that brought about the purchase of Louisiana, and turned the scale in favor of declaring the War of 1812. Militant qualities were favored by the annual expansion of the settled area in the face of hostile Indians and the stubborn wilderness. The West caught the vision of the nation's continental destiny. Henry Adams, in his History of the United States, makes the American of 1800 exclaim to the foreign visitor, "Look at my wealth! See these solid mountains of salt and iron, of lead, copper, silver, and gold. See these magnificent cities scattered broadcast to the Pacific! See my cornfields rustling and waving in the summer breeze from ocean to ocean, so far that the sun itself is not high enough to mark where the distant mountains bound my golden seas. Look at this continent of mine, fairest of created worlds, as she lies turning up to the sun's never failing caress her broad and exuberant breasts, overflowing with milk for her hundred million children." And the foreigner saw only dreary deserts, tenanted by sparse, ague-stricken pioneers and savages. The cities were log huts and gambling dens. But the frontiersman's dream was prophetic. In spite of his rude, gross nature, this early Western man was an idealist withal. He dreamed dreams and beheld visions. He had faith in man, hope for democracy, belief in America's destiny, unbounded confidence in his ability to make his dreams come true. Said Harriet Martineau in 1834, "I regard the American people as a great embryo poet, now moody, now wild, but bringing out results of absolute good sense: restless and wayward in action, but with deep peace at his heart; exulting that he has caught the true aspect of things past, and the depth of futurity which lies before him, wherein to create something so magnificent as the world has scarcely begun to dream of. There is the strongest hope of a nation that is capable of being possessed with an idea."

It is important to bear this idealism of the West in mind. The very materialism that has been urged against the West was accompanied by ideals of equality, of the exaltation of the common man, of national expansion, that make it a profound mistake to write of the West as though it were engrossed in mere material ends. It has been, and is, preëminently a region of ideals, mistaken or not.

It is obvious that these economic and social conditions were so fundamental in Western life that they might well dominate whatever accessions came to the West by immigration from the coast sections or from Europe. Nevertheless, the West cannot be understood without bearing in mind the fact that it has received the great streams from the North and from the South, and that the Mississippi compelled these currents to intermingle. Here it was that sectionalism first gave way under the pressure of unification. Ultimately the conflicting ideas and institutions of the old sections struggled for dominance in this area under the influence of the forces that made for uniformity, but this is merely another phase of the truth that the West must become unified, that it could not rest in sectional groupings. For precisely this reason the struggle occurred. In the period from the Revolution to the close of the War of 1812, the democracy of the Southern and Middle States contributed the main streams of settlement and social influence to the West. Even in Ohio political power was soon lost by the New England leaders. The democratic spirit of the Middle region left an indelible impress on the West in this its formative period. After the War of 1812, New England, its supremacy in the carrying trade of the world having vanished, became a beehive from which swarms of settlers went out to western New York and the remoter regions. These settlers spread New England ideals of education and character and political institutions, and acted as a leaven of great significance in the Northwest. But it would be a mistake to believe that an unmixed New England influence took possession of the Northwest. These pioneers did not come from the class that conserved the type of New England civilization pure and undefiled. They represented a less contented, less conservative influence. Moreover, by their sojourn in the Middle region, on their westward march, they underwent modification, and when the farther West received them, they suffered a forest-change, indeed. The Westernized New England man was no longer the representative of the section that he left. He was less conservative, less provincial, more adaptable and approachable, less rigorous in his Puritan ideals, less a man of culture, more a man of action.

As might have been expected, therefore, the Western men, in the era of good feeling, had much homogeneity throughout the Mississippi valley, and began to stand as a new national type. Under the lead of Henry Clay they invoked the national government to break down the mountain barrier by internal improvements, and thus to give their crops an outlet to the coast. Under him they appealed to the national government for a protective tariff to create a home market. A group of frontier States entered the Union with democratic provisions respecting the suffrage, and with devotion to the nation that had given them their lands, built their roads and canals, regulated their territorial life, and made them equals in the sisterhood of States. At last these Western forces of aggressive nationalism and democracy took possession of the government in the person of the man who best embodied them, Andrew Jackson. This new democracy that captured the country and destroyed the older ideals of statesmanship came from no theorist's dreams of the German forest. It came, stark and strong and full of life, from the American forest. But the triumph of this Western democracy revealed also the fact that it could rally to its aid the laboring classes of the coast, then just beginning to acquire self-consciousness and organization.

The next phase of Western development revealed forces of division between the northern and southern portions of the West. With the spread of the cotton culture went the slave system and the great plantation. The small farmer in his log cabin, raising varied crops, was displaced by the planter raising cotton. In all except the mountainous areas, the industrial organization of the tidewater took possession of the Southwest, the unity of the back country was broken, and the solid South was formed. In the Northwest this was the era of railroads and canals, opening the region to the increasing stream of Middle State and New England settlement, and strengthening the opposition to slavery. A map showing the location of the men of New England ancestry in the Northwest would represent also the counties in which the Free Soil party cast its heaviest votes. The commercial connections of the Northwest likewise were reversed by the railroad. The result is stated by a writer in De Bow's Review in 1852 in these words:—

"What is New Orleans now? Where are her dreams of greatness and glory? . . . Whilst she slept, an enemy has sowed tares in her most prolific fields. Armed with energy, enterprise, and an indomitable spirit, that enemy, by a system of bold, vigorous, and sustained efforts, has succeeded in reversing the very laws of nature and of nature's God,—rolled back the mighty tide of the Mississippi and its thousand tributary streams, until their mouth, practically and commercially, is more at New York or Boston than at New Orleans."

The West broke asunder, and the great struggle over the social system to be given to the lands beyond the Mississippi followed. In the Civil War the Northwest furnished the national hero,—Lincoln was the very flower of frontier training and ideals,—and it also took into its hands the whole power of the government. Before the war closed, the West could claim the President, Vice-President, Chief Justice, Speaker of the House, Secretary of the Treasury, Postmaster-General, Attorney-General, General of the army, and Admiral of the navy. The leading generals of the war had been furnished by the West. It was the region of action, and in the crisis it took the reins.

The triumph of the nation was followed by a new era of Western development. The national forces projected themselves across the prairies and plains. Railroads, fostered by government loans and land grants, opened the way for settlement and poured a flood of European immigrants and restless pioneers from all sections of the Union into the government lands. The army of the United States pushed back the Indian, rectangular Territories were carved into checkerboard States, creations of the federal government, without a history, without physiographical unity, without particularistic ideas. The later frontiersman leaned on the strong arm of national power.

At the same time the South underwent a revolution. The plantation, based on slavery, gave place to the farm, the gentry to the democratic elements. As in the West, new industries, of mining and of manufacture, sprang up as by magic. The New South, like the New West, was an area of construction, a debtor area, an area of unrest; and it, too, had learned the uses to which federal legislation might be put.

In the mean time the old Northwest (the present States of Ohio, Indiana, Illinois, Michigan, and Wisconsin) has passed through an economic and social transformation. The whole West has furnished an area over which successive waves of economic development have passed. The Indian hunters and traders were followed by the pioneer farmers, engaged in raising unrotated crops; after this came the wave of more settled town life and varied agriculture; the wave of manufacture followed. These stages of development have passed in succession across large parts of the old Northwest. The State of Wisconsin, now much like parts of the State of New York, was at an earlier period like the State of Nebraska of to-day; the granger movement and the greenback party had for a time the ascendency; and in the northern counties of the State, where there is a sparser population, and the country is being settled, its sympathies are still with the debtor class. Thus the old Northwest is a region where the older frontier conditions survive in parts, and where the inherited ways of looking at things are largely to be traced to its frontier days. At the same time it is a region in many ways assimilated to the East. It understands both sections. It is not entirely content with the existing structure of economic society in the sections where wealth has accumulated and corporate organizations are powerful; but neither has it seemed to feel that its interests lie in supporting the programme of the prairies and the South. In the Fifty-third Congress it voted for the income tax, but it rejected free coinage. It is still affected by the ideal of the self-made man, rather than by the ideal of industrial nationalism. It is more American, but less cosmopolitan than the seaboard.

We are now in a position to see clearly some of the factors involved in the Western problem. For nearly three centuries the dominant fact in American life has been expansion. With the settlement of the Pacific coast and the occupation of the free lands, this movement has come to a check. That these energies of expansion will no longer operate would be a rash prediction; and the demands for a vigorous foreign policy, for an interoceanic canal, for a revival of our power upon the seas, and for the extension of American influence to out-lying islands and adjoining countries, are indications that the move-ment will continue. The stronghold of these demands lies west of the Alleghanies.

In the remoter West, the restless, rushing wave of settlement has broken with a shock against the arid plains. The free lands are gone, the continent is crossed, and all this push and energy is turning into channels of agitation. Failures in one area can no longer be made good by taking up land on a new frontier; the conditions of a settled society are being reached with suddenness and with confusion. The West has been built up with borrowed capital, and the question of the stability of gold, as a standard of deferred payments, is eagerly agitated by the debtor West, profoundly dissatisfied with the industrial con-ditions that confront it, and actuated by frontier directness and rigor in its remedies. For the most part, the men who built up the West beyond the Mississippi, and who are now leading the agitation, came as pioneers from the old Northwest, in the days when it was just passing from the stage of a frontier section. For example, Senator Allen of Nebraska, president of the recent national Populist Conven-tion, and a type of the political leaders of his section, was born in Ohio in the middle of the century; went in his youth to Iowa, and not long after the Civil War made his home in Nebraska. As a boy, he saw the buffalo driven out by the settlers; he saw the Indian retreat as the pioneer advanced. His training is that of the old West, in its frontier days. And now the frontier opportunities are gone. Discon-tent is demanding an extension of governmental activity in its behalf. In these demands, it finds itself in touch with the depressed agricul-tural classes and the workingmen of the South and East. The Western problem is no longer a sectional problem; it is a social problem on a national scale. The greater West, extending from the Alleghanies to the Pacific, cannot be regarded as a unit; it requires analysis into regions and classes. But its area, its population, and its material re-sources would give force to its assertion that if there is a sectionalism in the country, the sectionalism is Eastern. The old West, united to the new South, would produce, not a new sectionalism, but a new Americanism. It would not mean sectional disunion, as some have speculated, but it might mean a drastic assertion of national govern-ment and imperial expansion under a popular hero.

This, then, is the real situation: a people composed of heteroge-neous materials, with diverse and conflicting ideals and social in-terests, having passed from the task of filling up the vacant spaces of the continent, is now thrown back upon itself, and is seeking an equi-librium. The diverse elements are being fused into national unity. The forces of reorganization are turbulent and the nation seems like a witches' kettle:

> Double, double, toil and trouble,
> Fire burn and cauldron bubble.

But the far West has its centres of industrial life and culture not unlike those of the East. It has state universities, rivaling in conservative and scientific economic instruction those of any other part of the Union, and its citizens more often visit the East, than do Eastern men the West. As time goes on, its industrial development will bring it more into harmony with the East.

Moreover, the old Northwest holds the balance of power, and is the battlefield on which these issues of American development are to be settled. It has more in common with all regions of the country than has any other region. It understands the East, as the East does not understand the West. The White City[1] which recently rose on the shores of Lake Michigan fitly typified its growing culture as well as its capacity for great achievement. Its complex and representative industrial organization and business ties, its determination to hold fast to what is original and good in its Western experience, and its readiness to learn and receive the results of the experience of other sections and nations, make it an open-minded and safe arbiter of the American destiny. In the long run the centre of the Republic may be trusted to strike a wise balance between the contending ideals. But she does not deceive herself; she knows that the problem of the West means nothing less than the problem of working out original social ideals and social adjustment for the American nation.

[1] A common synonym for the Chicago World's Columbian Exposition of 1893.

Frank Norris
Dying Fires

YOUNG OVERBECK'S FATHER was editor and proprietor of the county paper in Colfax, California, and the son, so soon as his high-school days were over, made his appearance in the office as his father's assistant. So abrupt was the transition that his diploma, which was to hang over the editorial desk, had not yet returned from the framer's, while the first copy that he was called on to edit was his own commencement oration on the philosophy of Dante. He had worn a white piqué cravat and a cutaway coat on the occasion of its delivery, and the county commissioner, who was the guest of honor on the platform, had congratulated him as he handed him his sheepskin. For Overbeck was the youngest and the brightest member of his class.

Colfax was a lively town in those days. The teaming from the valley over into the mining country on the other side of the Indian River was at its height then. Colfax was the headquarters of the business, and the teamsters—after the long pull up from the Indian River Cañon—showed interest in an environment made up chiefly of saloons.

Then there were the mining camps over by Iowa Hill, the Morning Star, the Big Dipper, and further on, up in the Gold Run country, the Little Providence. There was Dutch Flat, full of Mexican-Spanish girls and "breed" girls, where the dance-halls were of equal number with the bars. There was—a little way down the line—Clipper Gap, where the mountain ranches began, and where the mountain cowboy lived up to the traditions of his kind.

And this life, tumultuous, headstrong, vivid in color, vigorous in action, was bound together by the railroad, which not only made a single community out of all that part of the east slope of the Sierras' foothills, but contributed its own life as well—the life of oilers, engineers, switchmen, eating-house waitresses and cashiers, "lady" operators, conductors, and the like.

Of such a little world news-items are evolved—sometimes even

Smart Set, VII (July, 1902), 95–101. Republished in *The Third Circle* (New York, 1909). Text from the *Smart Set*.

scarehead, double-leaded descriptive articles—supplemented by interviews with sheriffs and ante-mortem statements. Good grist for a county paper; good opportunities for an unspoiled, observant, imaginative young fellow at the formative period of his life. Such was the time, such the environment, such the conditions that prevailed when young Overbeck, at the age of twenty-one, sat down to the writing of his first novel.

He completed it in five months, and, though he did not know the fact then, the novel was good. It was not great—far from it, but it was not merely clever. Somehow, by a miracle of good fortune, young Overbeck had got started right at the very beginning. He had not been influenced by a fetich of his choice till his work was a mere replica of some other writer's. He was not literary. He had not much time for books. He lived in the midst of a strenuous, eager life, a little primal even yet; a life of passions that were often elemental in their simplicity and directness. His schooling and his newspaper work— it was he who must find or ferret out the news all along the line, from Penrhyn to Emigrant Gap—had taught him observation without—here was the miracle—dulling the edge of his sensitiveness. He saw, as those few, few people see who live close to life at the beginning of an epoch. He saw into the life and the heart beneath the life; the life and the heart of Bunt McBride, as with eight horses and much abjuration he negotiated a load of steel "stamps" up the sheer leap of the Indian Cañon; he saw into the life and into the heart of Irma Tejada, who kept case for the faro players at Dutch Flat; he saw into the life and heart of Lizzie Toby, the biscuit-shooter in the railway eating-house, and into the life and heart of "Doc" Twitchel, who had degrees from Edinburgh and Leipsic, and who, for obscure reasons, chose to look after the measles, sprains and rheumatisms of the countryside.

And, besides, there were others and still others, whom young Overbeck learned to know to the very heart's heart of them: blacksmiths, traveling pedlers, section-bosses, miners, horse-wranglers, cow-punchers, the stage-drivers, the storekeeper, the hotelkeeper, the ditch-tender, the prospector, the seamstress of the town, the postmistress, the schoolmistress, the poetess. Into the lives of these and the hearts of these young Overbeck saw, and the wonder of that sight so overpowered him that he had no thought and no care for other people's books. And he was only twenty-one! Only twenty-one, and yet he saw clearly into the great, complicated, confused human machine that clashed and jarred around him. Only twenty-one, and yet he read the enigma that men of fifty may alone hope to solve! Once in a great while this thing may happen—in such out of the way places as that country around Colfax in Placer County, California, where no

outside influences have play, where books are few and misprized
and the reading circle a thing unknown. From time to time such men
are born, especially along the line of cleavage where the furthest
skirmish line of civilization thrusts and girds at the wilderness. A
very few find their true profession before the fire is stamped out of
them; of these few, fewer still have the force to make themselves
heard. Of these last the majority die before they attain the faculty
of making their message intelligible. Those that remain are the world's
great men.

At the time when his first little book was on its initial journey to the
Eastern publishing houses, Overbeck was by no means a great man.
The immaturity that was yet his, the lack of knowledge of his tools,
clogged his work and befogged his vision. The smooth running of the
cogs and the far-darting range of vision would come in the course of
the next fifteen years of unrelenting persistence. The ordering and
organizing and controlling of his machine he could, with patience
and by taking thought, accomplish for himself. The original impetus had come straight from the almighty gods. That impetus was
young yet, feeble yet, coming down from so far it was spent by the
time it reached the earth—at Colfax, California. A touch now might
divert it. Judge with what care such a thing should be nursed and
watched; compared with the delicacy with which it unfolds, the
opening of a rosebud is an abrupt explosion. Later on, such insight,
such undeveloped genius may become a tremendous world-power,
a thing to split a nation in twain as the axe cleaves the block. But at
twenty-one, a whisper—and it takes flight; a touch—it withers; the
lifting of a finger—it is gone.

The same destiny that had allowed Overbeck to be born, and that
thus far had watched over his course, must have inspired his choice,
his very first choice, of a publisher, for the manuscript of "The Vision
of Bunt McBride" went straight as a homebound bird to the one man
of all others who could understand the beginnings of genius and
recognize the golden grain of truth in the chaff of unessentials. His
name was Conant, and he accepted the manuscript by telegram.

He did more than this, and one evening Overbeck stood on the
steps of the post-office and opened a letter in his hand, and, looking
up and off, saw the world transfigured. His chance had come. In half
a year of time he had accomplished what other men—other young
writers—strive for throughout the best years of their youth. He had
been called to New York. Conant had offered him a minor place on
his editorial staff.

Overbeck reached the great city a fortnight later, and the cutaway
coat and piqué cravat—unworn since Commencement—served to

fortify his courage at the first interview with the man who was to make him—so he believed—famous.

Ah, the delights, the excitement, the inspiration of that day! Let those judge who have striven toward the Great City through years of deferred hope and heart-sinkings and sacrifice daily renewed. Over-beck's feet were set in those streets whose names had become leg-endary to his imagination. Public buildings and public squares familiar only through the weekly prints defiled before him like a pageant, but friendly for all that, inviting, even. But the vast conglomerate life that roared by his ears, like the systole and diastole of an almighty heart, was for a moment disquieting. Soon the human resemblance faded. It became as a machine, infinitely huge, infinitely formidable. It challenged him with superb condescension.

"I must down you," he muttered, as he made his way toward Co-nant's, "or you will down me." He saw it clearly. There was no other alternative. The young boy in his foolish finery of a Colfax tailor's make, with no weapons but such wits as the gods had given him, was pitted against the leviathan.

There was no friend nearer than his native state on the other fringe of the continent. He was fearfully alone.

But he was twenty-one. The wits that the gods had given him were good, and the fine fire that was within him, the radiant freshness of his nature, stirred and leaped to life at the challenge. Ah, he would win, he would win! And in his exuberance, the first dim conscious-ness of his power came to him. He could win, he had it in him; he began to see that now. That nameless power was his which would enable him to grip this monstrous life by the very throat, and bring it down on its knee before him to listen respectfully to what he had to say.

The interview with Conant was no less exhilarating. It was in the reception-room of the great house that it took place, and while wait-ing for Conant to come in, Overbeck, his heart in his mouth, recog-nized, in the original drawings on the walls, picture after picture, signed by famous illustrators, that he had seen reproduced in Conant's magazine.

Then Conant himself had appeared and shaken the young author's hand a long time, and had talked to him with the utmost kindness of his book, of his plans for the immediate future, of the work he would do in the editorial office and of the next novel he wished him to write.

"We'll only need you here in the mornings," said the editor, "and you can put in your afternoons on your novel. Have you anything in mind as good as 'Bunt McBride'?"

"I have a sort of notion for one," hazarded the young man; and Conant had demanded to hear it.

Stammering, embarrassed, Overbeck outlined it.

"I see, I see!" Conant commented. "Yes, there is a good story in that. Maybe Hastings will want to use it in the monthly. But we'll make a book of it, anyway, if you work it up as well as the McBride story."

And so the young fellow made his first step in New York. The very next day he began his second novel.

In the editorial office, where he spent his mornings reading proof and making up "front matter," he made the acquaintance of a middle-aged lady, named Miss Patten, who asked him to call on her, and later on introduced him into the "set" wherein she herself moved. The set called itself the "New Bohemians," and once a week met at Miss Patten's apartment up-town. In a month's time Overbeck was a fixture in "New Bohemia."

It was made up of minor poets whose opportunity in life was the blank space on a magazine page below the end of an article; of men past their prime, who, because of an occasional story in a second-rate monthly, were considered to have "arrived"; of women who translated novels from the Italian and Hungarian; of decayed dramatists who could advance unimpeachable reasons for the non-production of their plays; of novelists whose books were declined by publishers because of professional jealousy on the part of the "readers," or whose ideas, stolen by false friends, had appeared in books that sold by the hundreds of thousands. In public the New Bohemians were fulsome in the praise of one another's productions. Did a sonnet called, perhaps, "A Cryptogram is Stella's Soul" appear in a current issue, they fell on it with eager eyes, learned it by heart and recited lines of it aloud; the conceit of the lover translating the cipher by the key of love was welcomed with transports of delight.

"Ah, one of the most exquisitely delicate allegories I've ever heard, and so true—so 'in the tone'!"

Did a certain one of the third-rate novelists, reading aloud from his unpublished manuscript, say of his heroine: "It was the native catholicity of his temperament that lent strength and depth to her innate womanliness," the phrase was snapped up on the instant.

"How he understands women!"

"Such *finesse!* More subtle than Henry James."

"Paul Bourget has gone no further," said one of the critics of New Bohemia; "our limitations are determined less by our renunciations than by our sense of proportion in our conception of ethical standards."

The set abased itself. "Wonderful, ah, how pitilessly you fathom our poor human nature!" New Bohemia saw color in word effects. A poet read aloud:

> The stalwart rain!
> Ah, the rush of down-toppling waters;
> The torrent!
> Merge of mist and musky air;
> The current
> Sweeps thwart by blinded sight again.

"Ah!" exclaimed one of the audience, "see, see that bright green flash!"

Thus in public. In private all was different. Walking home with one or another of the set, young Overbeck heard their confidences.

"Keppler is a good fellow right enough, but, my goodness, he can't write verse!"

"That thing of Miss Patten's tonight! Did you ever hear anything so unconvincing, so obvious? Poor old woman!"

"I'm really sorry for Martens; awfully decent sort, but he never should try to write novels."

By rapid degrees young Overbeck caught the lingo of the third-raters. He could talk about "tendencies" and the "influence of reactions." Such and such a writer had a "sense of form," another a "feeling for word effects." He knew all about "tones" and "notes" and "philistinisms." He could tell the difference between an allegory and a simile as far as he could see them. An anti-climax was the one unforgivable sin under heaven. A mixed metaphor made him wince, and a split infinitive hurt him like a blow.

But the great word was "convincing." To say a book was convincing was to give positively the last verdict. To be "unconvincing" was to be shut out from the elect. If the New Bohemians decided that the last popular book was unconvincing, there was no appeal. The book was not to be mentioned in polite conversation.

And the author of "The Vision of Bunt McBride," as yet new to the world as the day he was born, with all his eager ambition and quick sensitiveness, thought that all this was the real thing. He had never so much as seen literary people before. How could he know the difference? He honestly believed that New Bohemia was the true literary force of New York. He wrote home that the association with such people, thinkers, poets, philosophers, was an inspiration; that he had learned more in one week in their company than he had learned in Colfax in a whole year.

Perhaps, too, it was the flattery he received that helped to carry Overbeck off his feet. The New Bohemians made a little lion of him

when "Bunt McBride" reached its modest pinnacle of popularity.
They kotowed to him, and toadied to him, and fagged and tooted for
him, and spoke of his book as a masterpiece. They said he had succeeded where Kipling had ignominiously failed. They said there was
more harmony of prose effects in one chapter of "Bunt McBride"
than in everything that Bret Harte ever wrote. They told him he was a
second Stevenson—only with more refinement.

Then the women of the set, who were of those who did not write,
who called themselves "mere dilettantes," but who "took an interest
in young writers" and liked to influence their lives and works, began
to flutter and buzz around him. They told him that they understood
him; that they understood his temperament; that they could see where
his forte lay; and they undertook his education.

There was in "The Vision of Bunt McBride" a certain sane and
healthy animalism that hurt nobody, and that, no doubt, Overbeck, in
later books, would modify. He had taken life as he found it to make
his book; it was not his fault that the teamsters, biscuit-shooters and
"breed" girls of the foothills were coarse in fibre. In his sincerity he
could not do otherwise in his novel than paint life as he saw it. He
had dealt with it honestly; he did not dab at the edge of the business;
he had sent his fist straight through it.

But the New Bohemians could not abide this.

"Not so much *faroucherie*, you dear young Lochinvar!" they said.
"Art must uplift. 'Look thou not down, but up toward uses of a cup';"
and they supplemented the quotation by lines from Walter Pater,
and read to him from Ruskin and Matthew Arnold.

Ah, the spiritual was the great thing. We were here to make the
world brighter and better for having lived in it. The passions of a
waitress in a railway eating-house—how sordid the subject! Dear
boy, look for the soul, strive to rise to higher planes! Tread upward;
every book should leave a clean taste in the mouth, should tend to
make one happier, should elevate, not debase.

So by degrees Overbeck began to see his future in a different light.
He began to think that he really had succeeded where Kipling had
failed; that he really was Stevenson with more refinement, and that
the one and only thing lacking in his work was soul. He believed
that he must strive for the spiritual, and "let the ape and tiger die."
The originality and unconventionality of his little book he came to regard as crudities.

"Yes," he said one day to Miss Patten and a couple of his friends, "I
have been re-reading my book of late. I can see its limitations—now.
It has a lack of form; the tonality is a little false. It fails somehow to
convince."

Thus the first Winter passed. In the mornings Overbeck assiduously edited copy and made up front matter on the top floor of the Conant building. In the evenings he called on Miss Patten, or some other member of the set. Once a week, up-town, he fed fat on the literary delicatessen that New Bohemia provided. In the meantime, every afternoon, from luncheon-time till dark, he toiled on his second novel, "Renunciations." The environment of "Renunciations" was a far cry from Colfax, California. It was a city-bred story, with no fresher atmosphere than that of bought flowers. Its *dramatis personæ* were all of the leisure class, opera-goers, intriguers, riders of blood horses, certainly more refined than Lizzie Toby, biscuit-shooter, certainly more *spirituelle* than Irma Tejada, case-keeper in Dog Omahone's faro joint, certainly more elegant than Bunt McBride, teamster of the Colfax Iowa Hill Freight Transportation Company.

From time to time, as the novel progressed, he read it to the dilettante women whom he knew best among the New Bohemians. They advised him as to its development, and "influenced" its outcome and dénouement.

"I think you have found your *métier*, dear boy," said one of them, when "Renunciations" was nearly completed. "To portray the concrete—is it not a small achievement, sublimated journalese, nothing more? But to grasp abstractions, to analyze a woman's soul, to evoke the spiritual essence in humanity, as you have done in your ninth chapter of 'Renunciations'—that is the true function of art. *Je vous fais mes compliments.* 'Renunciations' is a *chef-d'œuvre.* Can't you see yourself what a stride you have made, how much broader your outlook has become, how much more catholic, since the days of 'Bunt McBride'?"

To be sure, Overbeck could see it. Ah, he was growing, he was expanding. He was mounting higher planes. He was more—catholic. That, of all words, was the one to express his mood. Catholic, ah, yes, he was catholic!

When "Renunciations" was finished he took the manuscript to Conant and waited a fortnight in an agony of suspense and repressed jubilation for the great man's verdict. He was all the more anxious to hear it because, every now and then, while writing the story, doubts —distressing, perplexing—had intruded. At times and all of a sudden, after days of the steadiest footing, the surest progress, the story —the whole set and trend of the affair—would seem, as it were, to escape from his control. Where once, in "Bunt McBride," he had gripped, he must now grope. What was it? He had been so sure of himself, with all the stimulus of new surroundings, the work in this second novel should have been all the easier. But the doubt would

fade, and for weeks he would plough on, till again, and all unex-
pectedly, he would find himself in an agony of indecision as to the
outcome of some vital pivotal episode of the story. Of two methods of
treatment, both equally plausible, he could not say which was the
true, which the false; and he must needs take, as it were, a leap in
the dark—it was either that or abandoning the story, trusting to
mere luck that he would, somehow, be carried through.

A fortnight after he had delivered the manuscript to Conant he
presented himself in the publisher's office.

"I was just about to send for you," said Conant. "I finished your
story last week."

There was a pause. Overbeck settled himself comfortably in his
chair, but his nails were cutting his palms.

"Hastings has read it, too—and—well, frankly, Overbeck, we were
disappointed."

"Yes?" inquired Overbeck, calmly. "H'm—that's too b-bad."

He could not hear, or at least could not understand, just what the
publisher said next. Then, after a time that seemed immeasurably
long, he caught the words:

"It would not do you a bit of good, my boy, to have us publish it
—it would harm you. There are a good many things I would lie about,
but books are not included. This 'Renunciations' of yours is—is, why,
confound it, Overbeck, it's foolishness."

Overbeck went out and sat on a bench in a square near by, looking vacantly at a fountain as it rose and fell and rose again with an incessant cadenced splashing. Then he took himself home to his hall
bedroom. He had brought the manuscript of his novel with him, and
for a long time he sat at his table listlessly turning the leaves, confused, stupid, all but inert. The end, however, did not come suddenly. A few weeks later "Renunciations" was published, but not
by Conant. It bore the imprint of an obscure firm in Boston. The
covers were of limp dressed leather, olive green, and could be tied
together by thongs, like a portfolio. The sale stopped after five hundred copies had been ordered, and the real critics, those who did not
belong to New Bohemia, hardly so much as noticed the book.

In the Autumn, when the third-raters had come back from their
vacations, the "evenings" at Miss Patten's were resumed, and Overbeck hurried to the very first meeting. He wanted to talk it all over
with them. In his chagrin and cruel disappointment he was hungry
for some word of praise, of condolement. He wanted to be told again,
even though he had begun to suspect many things, that he had succeeded where Kipling had failed, that he was Stevenson with more
refinement.

But the New Bohemians, the same women and fakirs and half-baked minor poets who had "influenced" him and had ruined him, could hardly find time to notice him now. The guest of the evening was a new little lion who had joined the set. A symbolist versifier who wrote over the pseudonym of de la Houssaye, with black, oily hair and long white hands; him the Bohemians thronged about in crowds as before they had thronged about Overbeck. Only once did any one of them pay attention to the latter. This was the woman who had nicknamed him "Young Lochinvar." Yes, she had read "Renunciations," a capital little thing, a little thin in parts, lacking in *finesse*. He must strive for his true medium of expression, his true note. Ah, art was long! Study of the new symbolists would help him. She would beg him to read Monsieur de la Houssaye's "The Monoliths." Such subtlety, such delicious word-chords! It could not fail to inspire him.

Shouldered off, forgotten, the young fellow crept back to his little hall bedroom and sat down to think it over. There in the dark of the night his eyes were opened, and he saw, at last, what these people had done to him; saw the Great Mistake, and that he had wasted his substance.

The golden apples, that had been his for the stretching of the hand, he had flung from him. Tricked, trapped, exploited, he had prostituted the great good thing that had been his by right divine, for the privilege of eating husks with swine. Now was the day of the mighty famine, and the starved and broken heart of him, crying out for help, found only a farrago of empty phrases.

He tried to go back; he did in very fact go back to the mountains and the cañons of the great Sierras. "He arose and went to his father," and, with such sapped and broken strength as New Bohemia had left him, strove to wrest some wreckage from the dying fire.

But the ashes were cold by now. The fire that the gods had allowed him to snatch, because he was humble and pure and clean and brave, had been stamped out beneath the feet of minor and dilettante poets, and now the gods guarded close the brands that yet remained on the altars.

They may not be violated twice, those sacred fires. Once in a lifetime the very young and the pure in heart may see the shine of them and pluck a brand from the altar's edge. But, once possessed, it must be watched with a greater vigilance than even that of the gods, for its light will live only for him who snatched it first. Only for him that shields it, even with his life, from the contact of the world does it burst into a burning and a shining light. Let once the touch of alien fingers disturb it, and there remains only a little heap of bitter ashes.

Theodore Roosevelt
In Cowboy Land

OUT ON THE FRONTIER, and generally among those who spend their lives in, or on the borders of, the wilderness, life is reduced to its elemental conditions. The passions and emotions of these grim hunters of the mountains, and wild rough-riders of the plains, are simpler and stronger than those of people dwelling in more complicated states of society. As soon as the communities become settled and begin to grow with any rapidity, the American instinct for law asserts itself; but in the earlier stages each individual is obliged to be a law to himself and to guard his rights with a strong hand. Of course the transition periods are full of incongruities. Men have not yet adjusted their relations to morality and law with any niceness. They hold strongly by certain rude virtues, and on the other hand they quite fail to recognize even as shortcomings not a few traits that obtain scant mercy in older communities. Many of the desperadoes, the man-killers, and road-agents have good sides to their characters. Often they are people who, in certain stages of civilization, do, or have done, good work, but who, when these stages have passed, find themselves surrounded by conditions which accentuate their worst qualities, and make their best qualities useless. The average desperado, for instance, has, after all, much the same standard of morals that the Norman nobles had in the days of the battle of Hastings, and, ethically and morally, he is decidedly in advance of the vikings, who were the ancestors of these same nobles—and to whom, by the way, he himself could doubtless trace a portion of his blood. If the transition from the wild lawlessness of life in the wilderness or on the border to a higher civilization were stretched out over a term of centuries, he and his descendants would doubtless accommodate themselves by degrees to the changing circumstances. But unfortunately in the far West the transition takes place with marvellous

The Wilderness Hunter (New York, 1893), pp. 412–24. Text from this edition.

Roosevelt deals with the period of the mid-1880's, when he spent much time in the western portion of the Dakota Territory.

abruptness, and at an altogther unheard-of speed, and many a man's nature is unable to change with sufficient rapidity to allow him to harmonize with his environment. In consequence, unless he leaves for still wilder lands, he ends by getting hung instead of founding a family which would revere his name as that of a very capable, although not in all respects a conventionally moral, ancestor.

Most of the men with whom I was intimately thrown during my life on the frontier and in the wilderness were good fellows, hardworking, brave, resolute, and truthful. At times, of course, they were forced of necessity to do deeds which would seem startling to dwellers in cities and in old settled places; and though they waged a very stern and relentless warfare upon evil-doers whose misdeeds had immediate and tangible bad results, they showed a wide toleration of all save the most extreme classes of wrong, and were not given to inquiring too curiously into a strong man's past, or to criticising him over-harshly for a failure to discriminate in finer ethical questions. Moreover, not a few of the men with whom I came in contact —with some of whom my relations were very close and friendly— had at different times led rather tough careers. This fact was accepted by them and by their companions as a fact, and nothing more. There were certain offences, such as rape, the robbery of a friend, or murder under circumstances of cowardice and treachery, which were never forgiven; but the fact that when the country was wild a young fellow had gone on the road—that is, become a highwayman, or had been chief of a gang of desperadoes, horse-thieves, and cattle-killers, was scarcely held to weigh against him, being treated as a regrettable, but certainly not shameful, trait of youth. He was regarded by his neighbors with the same kindly tolerance which respectable mediæval Scotch borderers doubtless extended to their wilder young men who would persist in raiding English cattle even in time of peace.

Of course if these men were asked outright as to their stories they would have refused to tell them or else would have lied about them; but when they had grown to regard a man as a friend and companion they would often recount various incidents of their past lives with perfect frankness, and as they combined in a very curious degree both a decided sense of humor, and a failure to appreciate that there was anything especially remarkable in what they related, their tales were always entertaining.

Early one spring, now nearly ten years ago, I was out hunting some lost horses. They had strayed from the range three months before, and we had in a roundabout way heard that they were ranging near some broken country, where a man named Brophy had a ranch, nearly fifty miles from my own. When I started thither the weather was warm, but the second day out it grew colder and a heavy snow-storm came on. Fortunately I was able to reach the ranch all right, finding there one of the sons of a Little Beaver ranchman, and a young cowpuncher belonging to a Texas outfit, whom I knew very well. After putting my horse into the corral and throwing him down some hay I strode into the low hut, made partly of turf and partly of cottonwood logs, and speedily warmed myself before the fire. We had a good warm supper, of bread, potatoes, fried venison, and tea. My two companions grew very sociable and began to talk freely over their pipes. There were two bunks one above the other. I climbed into the upper, leaving my friends, who occupied the lower, sitting together on a bench recounting different incidents in the careers of themselves and their cronies during the winter that had just passed. Soon one of them asked the other what had become of a certain horse, a noted cutting pony, which I had myself noticed the preceding fall. The question aroused the other to the memory of a wrong which still rankled, and he began (I alter one or two of the proper names):

"Why, that was the pony that got stole. I had been workin' him on rough ground when I was out with the Three Bar outfit and he went tender forward, so I turned him loose by the Lazy B ranch, and when I come back to git him there wasn't anybody at the ranch and I couldn't find him. The sheep-man who lives about two miles west, under Red Clay butte, told me he seen a fellow in a wolfskin coat, ridin' a pinto bronco, with white eyes, leadin' that pony of mine just two days before; and I hunted round till I hit his trail and then I followed to where I'd reckoned he was headin' for—the Short Pine Hills. When I got there a rancher told me he had seen the man pass on towards Cedartown, and sure enough when I struck Cedartown I found he lived there in a 'dobe house, just outside the town. There was a boom on the town and it looked pretty slick. There was two hotels and I went into the first, and I says, 'Where's the justice of the peace?' says I to the bartender.

" 'There ain't no justice of the peace,' says he, 'the justice of the peace got shot.'

" 'Well, where's the constable?' says I.

" 'Why, it was him that shot the justice of the peace!' says he; 'he's skipped the country with a bunch of horses.'

" 'Well, ain't there no officer of the law left in this town?' says I.

" 'Why, of course,' says he, 'there's a probate judge; he is over tendin' bar at the Last Chance Hotel.'

"So I went over to the Last Chance Hotel and I walked in there. 'Mornin',' says I.

" 'Mornin',' says he.

" 'You're the probate judge?' says I.

" 'That's what I am,' says he. 'What do you want?' says he.

" 'I want justice,' says I.

" 'What kind of justice do you want?' says he. 'What's it for?'

" 'It's for stealin' a horse,' says I.

" 'Then by God you'll git it,' says he. 'Who stole the horse?' says he.

" 'It is a man that lives in a 'dobe house, just outside the town there,' says I.

" 'Well, where do you come from yourself?' said he.

" 'From Medory,' said I.

"With that he lost interest and settled kind o' back, and says he, 'There wont no Cedartown jury hang a Cedartown man for stealin' a Medory man's horse,' said he.

" 'Well, what am I to do about my horse?' says I.

" 'Do?' says he; 'well, you know where the man lives, don't you?' says he; 'then sit up outside his house tonight and shoot him when he comes in,' says he, 'and skip out with the horse.'

" 'All right,' says I, 'that is what I'll do,' and I walked off.

"So I went off to his house and I laid down behind some sagebrushes to wait for him. He was not at home, but I could see his wife movin' about inside now and then, and I waited and waited, and it growed darker, and I begun to say to myself, 'Now here you are lyin' out to shoot this man when he comes home; and it's gettin' dark, and you don't know him, and if you do shoot the next man that comes into that house, like as not it won't be the fellow you're after at all, but some perfectly innocent man a-comin' there after the other man's wife!'

"So I up and saddled the bronc' and lit out for home," concluded the narrator with the air of one justly proud of his own self-abnegating virtue.

The "town" where the judge above-mentioned dwelt was one of those squalid, pretentiously named little clusters of makeshift dwellings which on the edge of the wild country spring up with the rapid growth of mushrooms, and are often no longer lived. In their earlier stages these towns are frequently built entirely of canvas, and are subject to grotesque calamities. When the territory purchased from the Sioux, in the Dakotas, a couple of years ago, was thrown open to settlement, there was a furious inrush of men on horseback and in wagons, and various ambitious cities sprang up overnight. The new settlers were all under the influence of that curious craze which causes every true westerner to put unlimited faith in the unknown and untried; many had left all they had in a far better farming country, because they were true to their immemorial belief that, wherever they were, their luck would be better if they went somewhere

else. They were always on the move, and headed for the vague beyond. As miners see visions of all the famous mines of history in
each new camp, so these would-be city founders saw future St. Pauls
and Omahas in every forlorn group of tents pitched by some muddy
stream in a desert of gumbo and sage-brush; and they named both
the towns and the canvas buildings in accordance with their bright
hopes for the morrow, rather than with reference to the mean facts
of the day. One of these towns, which when twenty-four hours old
boasted of six saloons, a "court-house," and an "opera house," was
overwhelmed by early disaster. The third day of its life a whirlwind
came along and took off the opera house and half the saloons; and
the following evening lawless men nearly finished the work of the
elements. The riders of a huge trail-outfit from Texas, to their glad
surprise discovered the town and abandoned themselves to a night of
roaring and lethal carousal. Next morning the city authorities were
lamenting, with oaths of bitter rage, that "them hell-and-twenty Flying A cowpunchers had cut the court-house up into pants." It was
true. The cowboys were in need of chaps, and with an admirable mixture of adventurousness, frugality, and ready adaptability to circumstances, had made substitutes therefor in the shape of canvas overalls, cut from the roof and walls of the shaky temple of justice.

One of my valued friends in the mountains, and one of the best
hunters with whom I ever travelled, was a man who had a peculiarly
light-hearted way of looking at conventional social obligations. Though
in some ways a true backwoods Donatello, he was a man of much
shrewdness and of great courage and resolution. Moreover, he possessed what only a few men do possess, the capacity to tell the truth.
He saw facts as they were, and could tell them as they were, and he
never told an untruth unless for very weighty reasons. He was pre-
eminently a philosopher, of a happy, sceptical turn of mind. He had
no prejudices. He never looked down, as so many hard characters
do, upon a person possessing a different code of ethics. His attitude
was one of broad, genial tolerance. He saw nothing out of the way
in the fact that he had himself been a road-agent, a professional
gambler, and a desperado at different stages of his career. On the
other hand, he did not in the least hold it against any one that he had
always acted within the law. At the time that I knew him he had become a man of some substance, and naturally a staunch upholder of
the existing order of things. But while he never boasted of his past
deeds, he never apologized for them, and evidently would have been
quite as incapable of understanding that they needed an apology as
he would have been incapable of being guilty of mere vulgar boast-
fulness. He did not often allude to his past career at all. When he
did, he recited its incidents perfectly naturally and simply, as events,

without any reference to or regard for their ethical significance. It was this quality which made him at times a specially pleasant companion, and always an agreeable narrator. The point of his story, or what seemed to him the point, was rarely that which struck me. It was the incidental sidelights the story threw upon his own nature and the somewhat lurid surroundings amid which he had moved.

On one occasion when we were out together we killed a bear, and after skinning it, took a bath in a lake. I noticed he had a scar on the side of his foot and asked him how he got it, to which he responded, with indifference:

"Oh, that? Why, a man shootin' at me to make me dance, that was all."

I expressed some curiosity in the matter, and he went on:

"Well, the way of it was this: It was when I was keeping a saloon in New Mexico, and there was a man there by the name of Fowler, and there was a reward on him of three thousand dollars—"

"Put on him by the State?"

"No, put on by his wife," said my friend; "and there was this—"

"Hold on," I interrupted; "put on by his wife did you say?"

"Yes, by his wife. Him and her had been keepin' a faro bank, you see, and they quarrelled about it, so she just put a reward on him, and so—"

"Excuse me," I said, "but do you mean to say that this reward was put on publicly?" to which my friend answered, with an air of gentlemanly boredom at being interrupted to gratify my thirst for irrelevant detail:

"Oh, no, not publicly. She just mentioned it to six or eight intimate personal friends."

"Go on," I responded, somewhat overcome by this instance of the primitive simplicity with which New Mexican matrimonial disputes were managed, and he continued:

"Well, two men come ridin' in to see me to borrow my guns. My guns was Colt's self-cockers. It was a new thing then, and they was the only ones in town. These come to me, and 'Simpson,' says they, 'we want to borrow your guns; we are goin' to kill Fowler.'

"'Hold on for a moment,' said I, 'I am willin' to lend you them guns, but I ain't goin' to know what you'r' goin' to do with them, no sir; but of course you can have the guns.'" Here my friend's face lightened pleasantly, and he continued:

"Well, you may easily believe I felt surprised next day when Fowler came ridin' in, and, says he, 'Simpson, here's your guns!' He had shot them two men! 'Well, Fowler,' says I, 'if I had known them men was after you, I'd never have let them have them guns no-how,' says I. That wasn't true, for I did know it, but there was no cause to tell him that." I murmured my approval of such prudence, and Simpson continued, his eyes gradually brightening with the light of agreeable reminiscence:

"Well, they up and they took Fowler before the justice of the peace. The justice of the peace was a Turk."

"Now, Simpson, what do you mean by that?" I interrupted:

"Well, he come from Turkey," said Simpson, and I again sank back, wondering briefly what particular variety of Mediterranean outcast had drifted down to New Mexico to be made a justice of the peace. Simpson laughed and continued.

"That Fowler was a funny fellow. The Turk, he committed Fowler, and Fowler, he riz up and knocked him down and tromped all over him and made him let him go!"

"That was an appeal to a higher law," I observed. Simpson assented cheerily, and continued:

"Well, that Turk, he got nervous for fear Fowler he was goin' to kill him, and so he comes to me and offers me twenty-five dollars a day to protect him from Fowler; and I went to Fowler, and 'Fowler,' says I, 'that Turk's offered me twenty-five dollars a day to protect him from you. Now, I ain't goin' to get shot for no twenty-five dollars a day, and if you are goin' to kill the Turk, just say so and go and do it; but if you ain't goin' to kill the Turk, there's no reason why I shouldn't earn that twenty-five dollars a day!' and Fowler, says he, 'I ain't goin' to touch the Turk; you just go right ahead and protect him.'"

So Simpson "protected" the Turk from the imaginary danger of Fowler, for about a week, at twenty-five dollars a day. Then one evening he happened to go out and met Fowler, "and," said he, "the moment I saw him I knowed he felt mean, for he begun to shoot at my feet," which certainly did seem to offer presumptive evidence of meanness. Simpson continued:

"I didn't have no gun, so I just had to stand there and take it until something distracted his attention, and I went off home to get my gun and kill him, but I wanted to do it perfectly lawful; so I went up to the mayor (he was playin' poker with one of the judges), and says I to him, 'Mr. Mayor,' says I, 'I am goin' to shoot Fowler. And the mayor he riz out of his chair and he took me by the hand, and says he, 'Mr. Simpson, if you do I will stand by you'; and the judge, he says, 'I'll go on your bond.'"

Fortified by this cordial approval of the executive and judicial branches of the government, Mr. Simpson started on his quest. Meanwhile, however, Fowler had cut up another prominent citizen, and they already had him in jail. The friends of law and order feeling some little distrust as to the permanency of their own zeal for righteousness, thought it best to settle the matter before there was time for cooling, and accordingly, headed by Simpson, the mayor, the judge, the Turk, and other prominent citizens of the town, they broke into the jail and hanged Fowler. The point in the hanging which especially tickled my friend's fancy, as he lingered over the reminiscence, was one that was rather too ghastly to appeal to our own sense of humor. In the Turk's mind there still rankled the memory of Fowler's very unprofessional conduct while figuring before him as a criminal. Said Simpson, with a merry twinkle of the eye: "Do you know that Turk, he was a right funny fellow too after all. Just as the boys were going to string up Fowler, says he, 'Boys, stop; one moment, gentlemen,— Mr. Fowler, good-by,' and he blew a kiss to him!"

❊   ❊   ❊

Eugene Field
At Cheyenne

> *Young Lochinvar came in from the west,*
> *With fringe on his trousers and fur on his vest;*
> *The width of his hat brim could nowhere be beat,*
> *His No. 10 brogans were chock full of feet,*
> *His girdle was horrent with pistols and things,*
> *And he flourished a handful of aces on kings.*
>
> *The fair Mariana sate watching a star,*
> *When who should turn up but the young Lochinvar!*
> *Her pulchritude gave him a pectoral glow,*
> *And he reined up his hoss with stentorian "Whoa!"*
> *Then turned on the maiden a rapturous grin,*
> *And modestly asked if he might n't step in.*
>
> *With presence of mind that was marvellous quite,*
> *The fair Mariana replied that he might;*

Second Book of Verse (New York, 1893), pp. 126–27. Text from this edition.

> So in through the portal rode young Lochinvar,
> Pre-empted the claim, and cleaned out the bar.
> Though the justice allowed he wa'n't wholly to blame,
> He taxed him ten dollars and costs, just the same.

Owen Wister
Specimen Jones

EPHRAIM, THE PROPRIETOR of Twenty Mile, had wasted his day in burying a man. He did not know the man. He had found him, or what the Apaches had left of him, sprawled among some charred sticks just outside the Cañon del Oro. It was a useful discovery in its way, for otherwise Ephraim might have gone on hunting his strayed horses near the cañon, and ended among charred sticks himself. Very likely the Indians were far away by this time, but he returned to Twenty Mile with the man tied to his saddle, and his pony nervously snorting. And now the day was done, and the man lay in the earth, and they had even built a fence round him; for the hole was pretty shallow, and coyotes have a way of smelling this sort of thing a long way off when they are hungry, and the man was not in a coffin. They were always short of coffins in Arizona.

Day was done at Twenty Mile, and the customary activity prevailed inside that flat-roofed cube of mud. Sounds of singing, shooting, dancing, and Mexican tunes on the concertina came out of the windows hand in hand, to widen and die among the hills. A limber, pretty boy, who might be nineteen, was dancing energetically, while a grave old gentleman, with tobacco running down his beard, pointed a pistol at the boy's heels, and shot a hole in the earth now and then to show that the weapon was really loaded. Everybody was quite used to all of this—excepting the boy. He was an Eastern new-comer, passing his first evening at a place of entertainment.

Night in and night out every guest at Twenty Mile was either

Harper's Monthly, LXXXIX (July, 1894), 204–16. Republished in *Red Men and White* (New York, 1896), pp. 36–63. Text from *Red Men and White*.

happy and full of whiskey, or else his friends were making arrangements for his funeral. There was water at Twenty Mile—the only water for twoscore of miles. Consequently it was an important station on the road between the southern country and Old Camp Grant, and the new mines north of the Mescal Range. The stunt, liquor-perfumed adobe cabin lay on the gray floor of the desert like an isolated slab of chocolate. A corral, two desolate stable-sheds, and the slowly turning windmill were all else. Here Ephraim and one or two helpers abode, armed against Indians, and selling whiskey. Variety in their vocation of drinking and killing was brought them by the travellers. These passed and passed through the glaring vacant months—some days only one ragged fortune-hunter, riding a pony; again by twos and threes, with high-loaded burros; and sometimes they came in companies, walking beside their clanking freight-wagons. Some were young, and some were old, and all drank whiskey, and wore knives and guns to keep each other civil. Most of them were bound for the mines, and some of them sometimes returned. No man trusted the next man, and their names, when they had any, would be O'Rafferty, Angus, Schwartzmeyer, José Maria, and Smith. All stopped for one night; some longer, remaining drunk and profitable to Ephraim; now and then one stayed permanently, and had a fence built round him. Whoever came, and whatever befell them, Twenty Mile was chronically hilarious after sundown—a dot of riot in the dumb Arizona night.

On this particular evening they had a tenderfoot. The boy, being new in Arizona, still trusted his neighbor. Such people turned up occasionally. This one had paid for everybody's drink several times, because he felt friendly, and never noticed that nobody ever paid for his. They had played cards with him, stolen his spurs, and now they were making him dance. It was an ancient pastime; yet two or three were glad to stand round and watch it, because it was some time since they had been to the opera. Now the tenderfoot had misunderstood these friends at the beginning, supposing himself to be among good fellows, and they therefore naturally set him down as a fool. But even while dancing you may learn much, and suddenly. The boy, besides being limber, had good tough black hair, and it was not in fear, but with a cold blue eye, that he looked at the old gentleman. The trouble had been that his own revolver had somehow hitched, so he could not pull it from the holster at the necessary moment.

"Tried to draw on me, did yer?" said the old gentleman. "Step higher! Step, now, or I'll crack open yer kneepans, ye robin's egg."

"Thinks he's having a bad time," remarked Ephraim. "Wonder how he'd like to have been that man the Injuns had sport with?"

"Weren't his ear funny?" said one who had helped bury the man.

"Ear?" said Ephraim. "You boys ought to been along when I found him, and seen the way they'd fixed up his mouth." Ephraim explained the details simply, and the listeners shivered. But Ephraim was a humorist. "Wonder how it feels," he continued, "to have—"

Here the boy sickened at his comments and the loud laughter. Yet a few hours earlier these same half-drunken jesters had laid the man to rest with decent humanity. The boy was taking his first dose of Arizona. By no means was everybody looking at his jig. They had seen tenderfeet so often. There was a Mexican game of cards; there was the concertina; and over in the corner sat Specimen Jones, with his back to the company, singing to himself. Nothing had been said or done that entertained him in the least. He had seen everything quite often.

"Higher! skip higher, you elegant calf," remarked the old gentleman to the tenderfoot. "High-yer!" And he placidly fired a fourth shot that scraped the boy's boot at the ankle and threw earth over the clock, so that you could not tell the minute from the hour hand.

" 'Drink to me only with thine eyes,' " sang Specimen Jones, softly. They did not care much for his songs in Arizona. These lyrics were all, or nearly all, that he retained of the days when he was twenty, although he was but twenty-six now.

The boy was cutting pigeon-wings, the concertina played "Matamoras," Jones continued his lyric, when two Mexicans leaped at each other, and the concertina stopped with a quack.

"Quit it!" said Ephraim from behind the bar, covering the two with his weapon. "I don't want any greasers scrapping round here tonight. We've just got cleaned up."

It had been cards, but the Mexicans made peace, to the regret of Specimen Jones. He had looked round with some hopes of a crisis, and now for the first time he noticed the boy.

"Blamed if he ain't neat," he said. But interest faded from his eye, and he turned again to the wall. " 'Lieb Vaterland magst ruhig sein,' " he melodiously observed. His repertory was wide and refined. When he sang he was always grammatical.

"Ye kin stop, kid," said the old gentleman, not unkindly, and he shoved his pistol into his belt.

The boy ceased. He had been thinking matters over. Being lithe and strong, he was not tired nor much out of breath, but he was trembling with the plan and the prospect he had laid out for himself. "Set 'em up," he said to Ephraim. "Set 'em up again all round."

His voice caused Specimen Jones to turn and look once more, while the old gentleman, still benevolent, said, "Yer langwidge means pleasanter than it sounds, kid." He glanced at the boy's holster, and knew he need not keep a very sharp watch as to that. Its owner had bungled over it once already. All the old gentleman did was to place himself next the boy on the off side from the holster; any move the tenderfoot's hand might make for it would be green and unskilful, and easily anticipated. The company lined up along the bar, and the bottle slid from glass to glass. The boy and his tormentor stood together in the middle of the line, and the tormentor, always with half a thought for the holster, handled his drink on the wet counter, waiting till all should be filled and ready to swallow simultaneously, as befits good manners.

"Well, my regards," he said, seeing the boy raise his glass; and as the old gentleman's arm lifted in unison, exposing his waist, the boy reached down a lightning hand, caught the old gentleman's own pistol, and jammed it in his face.

"Now you'll dance," said he.

"Whoop!" exclaimed Specimen Jones, delighted. "*Blamed* if he ain't neat!" And Jones's handsome face lighted keenly.

"Hold on!" the boy sang out, for the amazed old gentleman was mechanically drinking his whiskey out of sheer fright. The rest had forgotten their drinks. "Not one swallow," the boy continued. "No, you'll not put it down either. You'll keep hold of it, and you'll dance all round this place. Around and around. And don't you spill any. And I'll be thinking what you'll do after that."

Specimen Jones eyed the boy with growing esteem. "Why, he ain't bigger than a pint of cider," said he.

"Prance away!" commanded the tenderfoot, and fired a shot between the old gentleman's not widely straddled legs.

"You hev the floor, Mr. Adams," Jones observed, respectfully, at the old gentleman's agile leap. "I'll let no man here interrupt you." So the capering began, and the company stood back to make room. "I've saw juicy things in this Territory," continued Specimen Jones, aloud, to himself, "but this combination fills my bill."

He shook his head sagely, following the black-haired boy with his eye. That youth was steering Mr. Adams round the room with the pistol, proud as a ring-master. Yet not altogether. He was only nineteen, and though his heart beat stoutly, it was beating alone in a strange country. He had come straight to this from hunting squirrels along the Susquehanna, with his mother keeping supper warm for him in the stone farm-house among the trees. He had read books in which hardy heroes saw life, and always triumphed with precision on the last page, but he remembered no receipt for this particular situation. Being good game American blood, he did not think now about the Susquehanna, but he did long with all his might to know what he ought to do next to prove himself a man. His buoyant rage, being glutted with the old gentleman's fervent skipping, had cooled, and a stress of reaction was falling hard on his brave young nerves. He imagined everybody against him. He had no notion that there was another American wanderer there, whose reserved and whimsical nature he had touched to the heart.

The fickle audience was with him, of course, for the moment, since he was upper dog and it was a good show; but one in that room was distinctly against him. The old gentleman was dancing with an ugly eye; he had glanced down to see just where his knife hung at his side, and he had made some calculations. He had fired four shots; the boy had fired one. "Four and one hez always made five," the old gentleman told himself with much secret pleasure, and pretended that he was going to stop his double-shuffle. It was an excellent trap, and the boy fell straight into it. He squandered his last precious bullet on the spittoon near which Mr. Adams happened to be at the moment, and the next moment Mr. Adams had him by the throat. They swayed and gulped for breath, rutting the earth with sharp heels; they rolled to the floor and floundered with legs tight tangled, the boy blindly striking at Mr. Adams with the pistol-butt, and the audience drawing closer to lose nothing, when the bright knife flashed suddenly. It poised, and flew across the room, harmless, for a foot had driven into Mr. Adams's arm, and he felt a cold ring grooving his temple. It was the smooth, chilly muzzle of Specimen Jones's six-shooter.

"That's enough," said Jones. "More than enough."

Mr. Adams, being mature in judgment, rose instantly, like a good old sheep, and put his knife back obedient to orders. But in the brain of the overstrained, bewildered boy universal destruction was whirling. With a face stricken lean with ferocity, he staggered to his feet, plucking at his obstinate holster, and glaring for a foe. His eye fell first on his deliverer, leaning easily against the bar watching him, while the more and more curious audience scattered, and held themselves ready to murder the boy if he should point his pistol their way. He was dragging at it clumsily, and at last it came. Specimen Jones sprang like a cat, and held the barrel vertical and gripped the boy's wrist.

"Go easy, son," said he. "I know how you're feelin'."

The boy had been wrenching to get a shot at Jones, and now the quietness of the man's voice reached his brain, and he looked at Specimen Jones. He felt a potent brotherhood in the eyes that were considering him, and he began to fear he had been a fool. There was his dwarf Eastern revolver, slack in his inefficient fist, and the singular person still holding its barrel and tapping one derisive finger over the end, careless of the risk to his first joint.

"Why, you little —— ——," said Specimen Jones, caressingly,

to the hypnotized youth, "if you was to pop that squirt off at me, I'd turn you up and spank y'u. Set 'em up, Ephraim."

But the commercial Ephraim hesitated, and Jones remembered. His last cent was gone. It was his third day at Ephraim's. He had stopped, having a little money, on his way to Tucson, where a friend had a job for him, and was waiting. He was far too experienced a character ever to sell his horse or his saddle on these occasions, and go on drinking. He looked as if he might, but he never did; and this was what disappointed business men like Ephraim in Specimen Jones.

But now, here was this tenderfoot he had undertaken to see through, and Ephraim reminding him that he had no more of the wherewithal. "Why, so I haven't," he said, with a short laugh, and his face flushed. "I guess," he continued, hastily, "this is worth a dollar or two." He drew a chain up from below his flannel shirt-collar and over his head. He drew it a little slowly. It had not been taken off for a number of years—not, indeed, since it had been placed there originally. "It ain't brass," he added, lightly, and strewed it along the counter without looking at it. Ephraim did look at it, and, being satisfied, began to uncork a new bottle, while the punctual audience came up for its drink.

"Won't you please let me treat?" said the boy, unsteadily. "I ain't likely to meet you again, sir." Reaction was giving him trouble inside.

"Where are you bound, kid?"

"Oh, just a ways up the country," answered the boy, keeping a grip on his voice.

"Well, you *may* get there. Where did you pick up that—that thing? Your pistol, I mean."

"It's a present from a friend," replied the tenderfoot, with dignity.

"Farewell gift, wasn't it, kid? Yes; I thought so. Now I'd hate to get an affair like that from a friend. It would start me wondering if he liked me as well as I'd always thought he did. Put up that money, kid. You're drinking with me. Say, what's yer name?"

"Cumnor—J. Cumnor."

"Well, J. Cumnor, I'm glad to know y'u. Ephraim, let me make you acquainted with Mr. Cumnor. Mr. Adams, if you're rested from your quadrille, you can shake hands with my friend. Step around, you Miguels and Serapios and Cristobals, whatever y'u claim your names are. This is Mr. J. Cumnor."

The Mexicans did not understand either the letter or the spirit of these American words, but they drank their drink, and the concertina resumed its acrid melody. The boy had taken himself off without being noticed.

"Say, Spec," said Ephraim to Jones, "I'm no hog. Here's yer chain. You'll be along again."

"Keep it till I'm along again," said the owner.

"Just as you say, Spec," answered Ephraim, smoothly, and he hung the pledge over an advertisement chromo of a nude cream-colored lady with bright straw hair holding out a bottle of somebody's champagne. Specimen Jones sang no more songs, but smoked, and leaned in silence on the bar. The company were talking of bed, and Ephraim plunged his glasses into a bucket to clean them for the morrow.

"Know anything about that kid?" inquired Jones, abruptly.

Ephraim shook his head as he washed.

"Travelling alone, ain't he?"

Ephraim nodded.

"Where did y'u say y'u found that fellow layin' the Injuns got?"

"Mile this side the cañon. 'Mong them sand-humps."

"How long had he been there, do y'u figure?"

"Three days, anyway."

Jones watched Ephraim finish his cleansing. "Your clock needs wiping," he remarked. "A man might suppose it was nine, to see that thing the way the dirt hides the hands. Look again in half an hour and it'll say three. That's the kind of clock gives a man the jams. Sends him crazy."

"Well, that ain't a bad thing to be in this country," said Ephraim, rubbing the glass case and restoring identity to the hands. "If that man had been crazy he'd been livin' right now. Injuns'll never touch lunatics."

"That band have passed here and gone north," Jones said. "I saw a smoke among the foot-hills as I come along day before yesterday. I guess they're aiming to cross the Santa Catalina. Most likely they're that band from round the San Carlos that were reported as raiding down in Sonora."

"I seen well enough," said Ephraim, "when I found him that they wasn't going to trouble us any, or they'd have been around by then."

He was quite right, but Specimen Jones was thinking of something else. He went out to the corral, feeling disturbed and doubtful. He saw the tall white freight-wagon of the Mexicans, looming and silent, and a little way off the new fence where the man lay. An odd sound startled him, though he knew it was no Indians at this hour, and he looked down into a little dry ditch. It was the boy, hidden away flat on his stomach among the stones, sobbing.

"Oh, snakes!" whispered Specimen Jones, and stepped back. The Latin races embrace and weep, and all goes well; but among Saxons tears are a horrid event. Jones never knew what to do when it was a woman, but this was truly disgusting. He was well seasoned by the frontier, had tried a little of everything: town and country, ranches, saloons, stage-driving, marriage occasionally, and latterly mines. He had sundry claims staked out, and always carried pieces of stone in his pockets, discoursing upon their mineral-bearing capacity, which was apt to be very slight. That is why he was called Specimen Jones. He had exhausted all the important sensations, and did not care much for anything any more. Perfect health and strength kept him from discovering that he was a saddened, drifting man. He wished to kick the boy for his baby performance, and yet he stepped carefully away from the ditch so the boy should not suspect his presence. He found himself standing still, looking at the dim, broken desert.

"Why, hell," complained Specimen Jones, "he played the little man to start with. He did so. He scared that old horse-thief, Adams, just about dead. Then he went to kill me, that kep' him from bein' buried early to-morrow. I've been wild that way myself, and wantin' to shoot up the whole outfit." Jones looked at the place where his middle finger used to be, before a certain evening in Tombstone. "But I never—" He glanced towards the ditch, perplexed. "What's that mean? Why in the world does he git to cryin' for *now*, do you suppose?" Jones took to singing without knowing it. " 'Ye shepherds, tell me, have you seen my Flora pass this way?' " he murmured. Then a thought struck him. "Hello, kid!" he called out. There was no answer. "Of course," said Jones. "Now he's ashamed to hev me see him come out of there." He walked with elaborate slowness round the corral and behind a shed. "Hello, you kid!" he called again.

"I was thinking of going to sleep," said the boy, appearing quite suddenly. "I—I'm not used to riding all day. I'll get used to it, you know," he hastened to add.

" 'Ha-ve you seen my Flo'— Say, kid, where y'u bound, anyway?"

"San Carlos."

"San Carlos? Oh. Ah. 'Flo-ra pass this way?' "

"Is it far, sir?"

"Awful far, sometimes. It's always liable to be far through the Arivaypa Cañon."

"I didn't expect to make it between meals," remarked Cumnor.

"No. Sure. What made you come this route?"

"A man told me."

"A man? Oh. Well, it *is* kind o' difficult, I admit, for an Arizonan not to lie to a stranger. But I think I'd have told you to go by Tres Alamos and Point of Mountain. It's the road the man that told you would choose himself every time. Do you like Injuns, kid?"

Cumnor snapped eagerly.

"Of course y'u do. And you've never saw one in the whole minute-and-a-half you've been alive. I know all about it."

"I'm not afraid," said the boy.

"Not afraid? Of course y'u ain't. What's your idea in going to Carlos? Got town lots there?"

"No," said the literal youth, to the huge internal diversion of Jones. "There's a man there I used to know back home. He's in the cavalry. What sort of a town is it for sport?" asked Cumnor, in a gay Lothario tone.

"*Town?*" Specimen Jones caught hold of the top rail of the corral. "*Sport?* Now I'll tell y'u what sort of a town it is. There ain't no streets. There ain't no houses. There ain't any land and water in the usual meaning of them words. There's Mount Turnbull. It's pretty near a usual mountain, but y'u don't want to go there. The Creator didn't make San Carlos. It's a heap older than Him. When He got around to it after slickin' up Paradise and them fruit-trees, He just left it to be as He found it, as a sample of the way they done business before He come along. He 'ain't done any work around that spot at all, He 'ain't. Mix up a barrel of sand and ashes and thorns, and jam scorpions and rattlesnakes along in, and dump the outfit on stones, and heat yer stones red-hot, and set the United States army loose over the place chasin' Apaches, and you've got San Carlos."

Cumnor was silent for a moment. "I don't care," he said. "I want to chase Apaches."

"Did you see that man Ephraim found by the cañon?" Jones inquired.

"Didn't get here in time."

"Well, there was a hole in his chest made by an arrow. But there's no harm in that if you die at wunst. That chap didn't, y'u see. You heard Ephraim tell about it. They'd done a number of things to the man before he could die. Roastin' was only one of 'em. Now your road takes you through the mountains where these Injuns hev gone. Kid, come along to Tucson with me," urged Jones, suddenly.

Again Cumnor was silent. "Is my road different from other people's?" he said, finally.

"Not to Grant, it ain't. These Mexicans are hauling freight to Grant. But what's the matter with your coming to Tucson with me?"

"I started to go to San Carlos, and I'm going," said Cumnor.

"You're a poor chuckle-headed fool!" burst out Jones, in a rage. "And y'u can go, for all I care—you and your Christmas-tree pistol. Like as not you won't find your cavalry friend at San Carlos. They've killed a lot of them soldiers huntin' Injuns this season. Good-night."

Specimen Jones was gone. Cumnor walked to his blanket-roll, where his saddle was slung under the shed. The various doings of the evening had bruised his nerves. He spread his blankets among the dry cattle-dung, and sat down, taking off a few clothes slowly. He lumped his coat and overalls under his head for a pillow, and, putting the despised pistol alongside, lay between the blankets. No object showed in the night but the tall freight-wagon. The tenderfoot thought he had made altogether a fool of himself upon the first trial trip of his manhood, alone on the open sea of Arizona. No man, not even Jones now, was his friend. A stranger, who could have had nothing against him but his inexperience, had taken the trouble to direct him on the wrong road. He did not mind definite enemies. He had punched the heads of those in Pennsylvania, and would not object to shooting them here; but this impersonal, surrounding hostility of the unknown was new and bitter: the cruel, assassinating, cowardly Southwest, where prospered those jail-birds whom the vigilantes had driven from California. He thought of the nameless human carcass that lay near, buried that day, and of the jokes about its mutilations. Cumnor was not an innocent boy, either in principles or in practice, but this laughter about a dead body had burned into his young, unhardened soul. He lay watching with hot, dogged eyes the brilliant stars. A passing wind turned the windmill, which creaked a forlorn minute, and ceased. He must have gone to sleep and slept soundly, for the next he knew it was the cold air of dawn that made him open his eyes. A numb silence lay over all things, and the tenderfoot had that moment of curiosity as to where he was now which comes to those who have journeyed for many days. The Mexicans had already departed with their freight-wagon. It was not entirely light, and the embers where these early starters had cooked their breakfast lay glowing in the sand across the road. The boy remembered seeing a wagon where now he saw only chill, distant peaks, and while he lay quiet and warm, shunning full consciousness, there was a stir in the cabin, and at Ephraim's voice reality broke upon his drowsiness, and he recollected Arizona and the keen stress of shifting for himself. He noted the gray paling round the grave. Indians? He would catch up with the Mexicans, and travel in their company to Grant. Freighters made but fifteen miles in the day, and he could start after breakfast and be with them before they stopped to noon. Six men need not worry about Apaches, Cumnor thought. The voice of Specimen Jones came from the cabin, and sounds of lighting the stove, and the growling conversation of men getting up. Cumnor, lying in his blankets, tried to overhear what Jones was saying, for no better reason than that this was the only man he had met lately who had seemed to care whether he were alive or dead. There was the clink of Ephraim's whiskey-bottles, and the cheerful tones of old Mr. Adams, saying, "It's better 'n brushin' yer teeth"; and then further clinking, and an inquiry from Specimen Jones.

"Whose spurs?" said he.

"Mine." This from Mr. Adams.

"How long have they been yourn?"

"Since I got 'em, I guess."

"Well, you've enjoyed them spurs long enough." The voice of Specimen Jones now altered in quality. "And you'll give 'em back to that kid."

Muttering followed that the boy could not catch. "You'll give 'em back," repeated Jones. "I seen y'u lift 'em from under that chair when I was in the corner."

"That's straight, Mr. Adams," said Ephraim. "I noticed it myself, though I had no objections, of course. But Mr. Jones has pointed out—"

"Since when have you growed so honest, Jones?" cackled Mr. Adams, seeing that he must lose his little booty. "And why didn't you raise yer objections when you seen me do it?"

"I didn't know the kid," Jones explained. "And if it don't strike you that game blood deserves respect, why it does strike me."

Hearing this, the tenderfoot, outside in his shed, thought better of mankind and life in general, arose from his nest, and began preening himself. He had all the correct trappings for the frontier, and his toilet in the shed gave him pleasure. The sun came up, and with a stroke struck the world to crystal. The near sand-hills went into rose, the crabbed yucca and the mesquite turned transparent, with lances and pale films of green, like drapery graciously veiling the desert's face, and distant violet peaks and edges framed the vast enchantment beneath the liquid exhalations of the sky. The smell of bacon and coffee from open windows filled the heart with bravery and yearning, and Ephraim, putting his head round the corner, called to Cumnor that he had better come in and eat. Jones, already at table, gave him the briefest nod; but the spurs were there, replaced as Cumnor had left them under a chair in the corner. In Arizona they do not say much at any meal, and at breakfast nothing at all; and as Cumnor swallowed and meditated, he noticed the cream-colored lady and the chain, and he made up his mind he should assert his identity with regard to that business, though how and when was not clear to him. He was in no great haste to take up his journey. The society of the Mexicans whom he must sooner or later overtake did not tempt him. When breakfast was done he idled in the cabin, like the other guests, while Ephraim and his assistant busied about the premises. But the morning grew on, and the guests, after a season of smoking and tilted silence against the wall, shook themselves and their effects together, saddled, and were lost among the waste thorny hills. Twenty Mile became hot and torpid. Jones lay on three consecutive chairs, occasionally singing, and old Mr. Adams had not gone away either, but watched him, with more tobacco running down his beard.

"Well," said Cumnor, "I'll be going."

"Nobody's stopping y'u," remarked Jones.

"You're going to Tucson?" the boy said, with the chain problem still unsolved in his mind. "Good-bye, Mr. Jones. I hope I'll—we'll—"

"That'll do," said Jones; and the tenderfoot, thrown back by this severity, went to get his saddle-horse and his burro.

Presently Jones remarked to Mr. Adams that he wondered what Ephraim was doing, and went out. The old gentleman was left alone in the room, and he swiftly noticed that the belt and pistol of Specimen Jones were left alone with him. The accoutrement lay by the chair its owner had been lounging in. It is an easy thing to remove cartridges from the chambers of a revolver, and replace the weapon in its holster so that everything looks quite natural. The old gentleman was entertained with the notion that somewhere in Tucson Specimen Jones might have a surprise, and he did not take a minute to prepare this, drop the belt as it lay before, and saunter innocently out of the saloon. Ephraim and Jones were criticising the tenderfoot's property as he packed his burro.

"Do y'u make it a rule to travel with ice-cream?" Jones was inquiring.

"They're for water," Cumnor said. "They told me at Tucson I'd need to carry water for three days on some trails."

It was two good-sized milk-cans that he had, and they bounced about on the little burro's pack, giving him as much amazement as a jackass can feel. Jones and Ephraim were hilarious.

"Don't go without your spurs, Mr. Cumnor," said the voice of old Mr. Adams, as he approached the group. His tone was particularly civil.

The tenderfoot had, indeed, forgotten his spurs, and he ran back to get them. The cream-colored lady still had the chain hanging upon her, and Cumnor's problem was suddenly solved. He put the chain in his pocket, and laid the price of one round of drinks for last night's company on the shelf below the chromo. He returned with his spurs on, and went to his saddle that lay beside that of Specimen Jones under the shed. After a moment he came with his saddle to where the men stood talking by his pony, slung it on, and tightened the cinches; but the chain was now in the saddle-bag of Specimen Jones, mixed up with some tobacco, stale bread, a box of matches, and a hunk of fat bacon. The men at Twenty Mile said good-day to the tenderfoot, with monosyllables and indifference, and watched him depart into the heated desert. Wishing for a last look at Jones, he turned once, and saw the three standing, and the chocolate brick of the cabin, and the windmill white and idle in the sun.

"He'll be gutted by night," remarked Mr. Adams.

"I ain't buryin' him, then," said Ephraim.

"Nor I," said Specimen Jones. "Well, it's time I was getting to Tucson."

He went to the saloon, strapped on his pistol, saddled, and rode away. Ephraim and Mr. Adams returned to the cabin; and here is the final conclusion they came to after three hours of discussion as to who took the chain and who had it just then:

Ephraim. Jones, he hadn't no cash.

Mr. Adams. The kid, he hadn't no sense.

Ephraim. The kid, he lent the cash to Jones.

Mr. Adams. Jones, he goes off with his chain.

Both. What damn fools everybody is, anyway!

And they went to dinner. But Mr. Adams did not mention his relations with Jones's pistol. Let it be said, in extenuation of that performance, that Mr. Adams supposed Jones was going to Tucson, where he said he was going, and where a job and a salary were awaiting him. In Tucson an unloaded pistol in the holster of so handy a man on the drop as was Specimen would keep people civil, because they would not know, any more than the owner, that it was unloaded; and the mere possession of it would be sufficient in nine chances out of ten—though it was undoubtedly for the tenth that Mr. Adams had a sneaking hope. But Specimen Jones was not going to Tucson. A contention in his mind as to whether he would do what was good for himself, or what was good for another, had kept him sullen ever since he got up. Now it was settled, and Jones in serene humor again. Of course he had started on the Tucson road, for the benefit of Ephraim and Mr. Adams.

The tenderfoot rode along. The Arizona sun beat down upon the deadly silence, and the world was no longer of crystal, but a mesa, dull and gray and hot. The pony's hoofs grated in the gravel, and after a time the road dived down and up among lumpy hills of stone and cactus, always nearer the fierce glaring Sierra Santa Catalina. It dipped so abruptly in and out of the shallow sudden ravines that, on coming up from one of these into sight of the country again, the tenderfoot's heart jumped at the close apparition of another rider quickly bearing in upon him from gullies where he had been moving unseen. But it was only Specimen Jones.

"Hello!" said he, joining Cumnor. "Hot, ain't it?"

"Where are you going?" inquired Cumnor.

"Up here a ways." And Jones jerked his finger generally towards the Sierra, where they were heading.

"Thought you had a job in Tucson."

"That's what I have."

Specimen Jones had no more to say, and they rode for a while, their ponies' hoofs always grating in the gravel, and the milk-cans lightly clanking on the burro's pack. The bunched blades of the yuccas bristled steel-stiff, and as far as you could see it was a gray waste of mounds and ridges sharp and blunt, up to the forbidding boundary walls of the Tortilita one way and the Santa Catalina the other. Cumnor wondered if Jones had found the chain. Jones was capable of not finding it for several weeks, or of finding it at once and saying nothing.

"You'll excuse my meddling with your business?" the boy hazarded.

Jones looked inquiring.

"Something's wrong with your saddle-pocket."

Specimen saw nothing apparently wrong with it, but perceiving Cumnor was grinning, unbuckled the pouch. He looked at the boy rapidly, and looked away again, and as he rode, still in silence, he put the chain back round his neck below the flannel shirt-collar.

"Say, kid," he remarked, after some time, "what does J stand for?"

"J? Oh, my name! Jock."

"Well, Jock, will y'u explain to me as a friend how y'u ever come to be such a fool as to leave yer home—wherever and whatever it was—in exchange for this here God-forsaken and iniquitous hole?"

"If you'll explain to me," said the boy, greatly heartened, "how you come to be ridin' in the company of a fool, instead of goin' to your job at Tucson."

The explanation was furnished before Specimen Jones had framed his reply. A burning freight-wagon and five dismembered human stumps lay in the road. This was what had happened to the Miguels and Serapios and the concertina. Jones and Cumnor, in their dodging and struggles to exclude all expressions of growing mutual esteem from their speech, had forgotten their journey, and a sudden bend among the rocks where the road had now brought them revealed the blood and fire staring them in the face. The plundered wagon was three parts empty; its splintered, blazing boards slid down as they burned into the fiery heap on the ground; packages of soda and groceries and medicines slid with them, bursting into chemical spots of green and crimson flame; a wheel crushed in and sank, spilling more packages that flickered and hissed; the garbage of combat and murder littered the earth, and in the air hung an odor that Cumnor knew, though he had never smelled it before. Morsels of dropped booty up among the rocks showed where the Indians had gone, and one horse remained, groaning, with an accidental arrow in his belly.

"We'll just kill him," said Jones; and his pistol snapped idly, and snapped again, as his eye caught a motion—a something—two hundred yards up among the bowlders on the hill. He whirled round. The enemy was behind them also. There was no retreat. "Yourn's no good!" yelled Jones, fiercely, for Cumnor was getting out his little, foolish revolver. "Oh, what a trick to play on a man! Drop off yer horse, kid; drop, and do like me. Shootin's no good here, even if I was loaded. *They* shot, and look at them now. God bless them ice-cream freezers of yourn, kid! Did y'u ever see a crazy man? If you 'ain't, *make it up as y'u go along!*"

More objects moved up among the bowlders. Specimen Jones ripped off the burro's pack, and the milk-cans rolled on the ground. The burro began grazing quietly, with now and then a step towards new patches of grass. The horses stood where their riders had left them, their reins over their heads, hanging and dragging. From two hundred yards on the hill the ambushed Apaches showed, their dark, scattered figures appearing cautiously one by one, watching with suspicion. Specimen Jones seized up one milk-can, and Cumnor obediently did the same.

"You kin dance, kid, and I kin sing, and we'll go to it," said Jones. He rambled in a wavering loop, and diving eccentrically at Cumnor, clashed the milk-cans together. " 'Es schallt ein Ruf wie Donnerhall,' " he bawled, beginning the song of "Die Wacht am Rhein." "Why don't you dance?" he shouted, sternly. The boy saw the terrible earnestness of his face, and, clashing his milk-cans in turn, he shuffled a sort of jig. The two went over the sand in loops, toe and heel; the donkey continued his quiet grazing, and the flames rose hot and yellow from the freight-wagon. And all the while the stately German hymn pealed among the rocks, and the Apaches crept down nearer the bowing, scraping men. The sun shone bright, and their bodies poured with sweat. Jones flung off his shirt; his damp, matted hair was half in ridges and half glued to his forehead, and the delicate gold chain swung and struck his broad, naked breast. The Apaches drew nearer again, their bows and arrows held uncertainly. They came down the hill, fifteen or twenty, taking a long time, and stopping every few yards. The milk-cans clashed, and Jones thought he felt the boy's strokes weakening. "Die Wacht am Rhein" was finished, and now it was " 'Ha-ve you seen my Flora pass this way?' " "Y'u mustn't play out, kid," said Jones, very gently. "Indeed y'u mustn't;" and he at once resumed his song. The silent Apaches had now reached the bottom of the hill. They stood some twenty yards away, and Cumnor had a good chance to see his first Indians. He saw them move, and the color and slim shape of their bodies, their thin arms, and their long, black hair. It went through his mind that if he had no more clothes on than that, dancing would come easier. His boots were growing heavy to lift, and his overalls seemed to wrap his sinews in wet, strangling thongs. He wondered how long he had been keeping this up. The legs of the Apaches were free, with light moccasins only half-way to the thigh, slenderly held up by strings from the waist. Cumnor envied their unencumbered steps as he saw them again walk nearer to where he was dancing. It was long since he had eaten, and he noticed a singing dulness in his brain, and became frightened at his thoughts, which were running and melting into one fixed idea. This idea was to take off his boots, and offer to trade them for a pair of moccasins. It terrified him—this endless, molten rush of thoughts; he could see them coming in different shapes from different places in his head, but they all joined immediately, and always formed the same fixed idea. He ground his teeth to master this encroaching inebriation of his will and judgment. He clashed his can more loudly to wake him to reality, which he still could recognize and appreciate. For a time he found it a good plan to listen to what Specimen Jones was singing, and tell himself the name of the song, if he knew it. At present it was "Yankee Doodle," to which Jones was fitting words of his own. These ran, "Now I'm going to try a bluff, And mind you do what I do"; and then again, over and over. Cumnor waited for the word "bluff"; for it was hard and heavy, and fell into his thoughts, and stopped them for a moment. The dance was so long now he had forgotten about that. A numbness had been spreading through his legs, and he was glad to feel a sharp pain in the sole of his foot. It was a piece of gravel that had somehow worked its way in, and was rubbing through the skin into the flesh. "That's good," he said, aloud. The pebble was eating the numbness away, and Cumnor drove it hard against the raw spot, and relished the tonic of its burning friction. The Apaches had drawn into a circle. Standing at some interval apart, they entirely surrounded the arena. Shrewd, half convinced, and yet with awe, they watched the dancers, who clashed their cans slowly now in rhythm to Jones's hoarse, parched singing. He was quite master of himself, and led the jig round the still blazing wreck of the wagon, and circled in figures of eight between the corpses of the Mexicans, clashing the milk-cans above each one. Then, knowing his strength was coming to an end, he approached an Indian whose splendid fillet and trappings denoted him of consequence; and Jones was near shouting with relief when the Indian shrank backward. Suddenly he saw Cumnor let his can drop, and without stopping to see why, he caught it up, and, slowly rattling both, approached each Indian in turn with tortuous steps. The circle that had never uttered a sound till now receded, chanting almost in a whisper some exorcising song which the man with the fillet had begun. They gathered round him, retreating always, and the strain, with its rapid muttered words, rose and fell softly among them. Jones had supposed the boy was overcome by faintness, and looked to see where he lay. But it was not faintness. Cumnor, with his boots off, came by and walked after the Indians in a trance. They saw him, and quickened their pace, often turning to be sure he was not overtaking them. He called to them unintelligibly, stumbling up the sharp hill, and pointing to the boots. Finally he sat down. They continued ascending the mountain, herding close round the man with the feathers, until the rocks and the filmy tangles screened them from sight; and like a wind that hums uncertainly in grass, their chanting died away.

The sun was half behind the western range when Jones next moved. He called, and, getting no answer, he crawled painfully to where the boy lay on the hill. Cumnor was sleeping heavily; his head was hot, and he moaned. So Jones crawled down, and fetched blankets and the canteen of water. He spread the blankets over the boy, wet a handkerchief and laid it on his forehead; then he lay down himself.

The earth was again magically smitten to crystal. Again the sharp cactus and the sand turned beautiful, and violet floated among the mountains, and rose-colored orange in the sky above them.

"Jock," said Specimen at length.

The boy opened his eyes.

"Your foot is awful, Jock. Can y'u eat?"

"Not with my foot."

"Ah, God bless y'u, Jock! Y'u ain't turrible sick. But *can* y'u eat?"

Cumnor shook his head.

"Eatin's what y'u need, though. Well, here." Specimen poured a judicious mixture of whiskey and water down the boy's throat, and wrapped the awful foot in his own flannel shirt. "They'll fix y'u over to Grant. It's maybe twelve miles through the cañon. It ain't a town any more than Carlos is, but the soldiers'll be good to us. As soon as night comes you and me must somehow git out of this."

Somehow they did, Jones walking and leading his horse and the imperturbable little burro, and also holding Cumnor in the saddle. And when Cumnor was getting well in the military hospital at Grant, he listened to Jones recounting to all that chose to hear how useful a weapon an ice-cream freezer can be, and how if you'll only chase Apaches in your stocking feet they are sure to run away. And then Jones and Cumnor both enlisted; and I suppose Jones's friend is still expecting him in Tucson.

Stephen Crane
A Man and Some Others

I

DARK MESQUIT SPREAD from horizon to horizon. There was no house or horseman from which a mind could evolve a city or a crowd. The world was declared to be a desert and unpeopled. Sometimes, however, on days when no heat-mist arose, a blue shape, dim, of the substance of a specter's veil, appeared in the southwest, and a pondering sheep-herder might remember that there were mountains.

In the silence of these plains the sudden and childish banging of a tin pan could have made an iron-nerved man leap into the air. The sky was ever flawless; the manoeuvering of clouds was an unknown pageant; but at times a sheep-herder could see, miles away, the long, white streamers of dust rising from the feet of another's flock, and the interest became intense.

Bill was arduously cooking his dinner, bending over the fire, and toiling like a blacksmith. A movement, a flash of strange color, perhaps, off in the bushes, caused him suddenly to turn his head. Presently he arose, and, shading his eyes with his hand, stood motionless and gazing. He perceived at last a Mexican sheep-herder winding through the brush toward his camp.

"Hello!" shouted Bill.

The Mexican made no answer, but came steadily forward until he was within some twenty yards. There he paused, and, folding his arms, drew himself up in the manner affected by the villain in the play. His serape muffled the lower part of his face, and his great sombrero shaded his brow. Being unexpected and also silent, he had something of the quality of an apparition; moreover, it was clearly his intention to be mystic and sinister.

The American's pipe, sticking carelessly in the corner of his mouth, was twisted until the wrong side was uppermost, and he held his frying-pan poised in the air. He surveyed with evident surprise this apparition in the mesquit. "Hello, José!" he said; "what's the matter?"

Century, LIII (February, 1897), 601–607. Text from this publication.

The Mexican spoke with the solemnity of funeral tollings: "Beel, you mus' geet off range. We want you geet off range. We no like. Un'erstan'? We no like."

"What you talking about?" said Bill. "No like what?"

"We no like you here. Un'erstan'? Too mooch. You mus' geet out. We no like. Un'erstan'?"

"Understand? No; I don't know what the blazes you're gittin' at." Bill's eyes wavered in bewilderment, and his jaw fell. "I must git out? I must git off the range? What you givin' us?"

The Mexican unfolded his serape with his small yellow hand. Upon his face was then to be seen a smile that was gently, almost caressingly murderous. "Beel," he said, "git out!"

Bill's arm dropped until the frying-pan was at his knee. Finally he turned again toward the fire. "Go on, you dog-gone little yaller rat!" he said over his shoulder. "You fellers can't chase me off this range. I got as much right here as anybody."

"Beel," answered the other in a vibrant tone, thrusting his head forward and moving one foot, "you geet out or we keel you."

"Who will?" said Bill.

"I—and the others." The Mexican tapped his breast gracefully.

Bill reflected for a time, and then he said: "You ain't got no manner of license to warn me off'n this range, and I won't move a rod. Understand? I've got rights, and I suppose if I don't see 'em through, no one is likely to give me a good hand and help me lick you fellers, since I'm the only white man in half a day's ride. Now, look; if you fellers try to rush this camp, I'm goin' to plug about fifty per cent. of the gentlemen present, sure. I'm goin' in for trouble, an' I 'll git a lot of you. 'Nuther thing: if I was a fine valuable caballero like you, I'd stay in the rear till the shootin' was done, because I'm goin' to make a particular p'int of shootin' you through the chest." He grinned affably, and made a gesture of dismissal.

As for the Mexican, he waved his hands in a consummate expression of indifference. "Oh, all right," he said. Then, in a tone of deep menace and glee, he added: "We will keel you eef you no geet. They have decide'."

"They have, have they?" said Bill. "Well, you tell them to go to the devil!"

II.

Bill had been a mine-owner in Wyoming, a great man, an aristocrat, one who possessed unlimited credit in the saloons down the gulch. He had the social weight that could interrupt a lynching or advise a bad man of the particular merits of a remote geographical point. However, the fates exploded the toy balloon with which they had amused Bill, and on the evening of the same day he was a professional gambler with ill fortune dealing him unspeakable irritation in the shape of three big cards whenever another fellow stood pat. It is well here to inform the world that Bill considered his calamities of life all dwarfs in comparison with the excitement of one particular evening, when three kings came to him with criminal regularity against a man who always filled a straight. Later he became a cowboy, more weirdly abandoned than if he had never been an aristocrat. By this time all that remained of his former splendor was his pride, or his vanity, which was one thing which need not have remained. He killed the foreman of the ranch over an inconsequent matter as to which of them was a liar, and the midnight train carried him eastward. He became a brakeman on the Union Pacific, and really gained high honors in the hobo war that for many years has devastated the beautiful railroads of our country. A creature of ill fortune himself, he practised all the ordinary cruelties upon these other creatures of ill fortune. He was of so fierce a mien that tramps usually surrendered at once whatever coin or tobacco they had in their possession; and if afterward he kicked them from the train, it was only because this was a recognized treachery of the war upon the hoboes. In a famous battle fought in Nebraska in 1879, he would have achieved a lasting distinction if it had not been for a deserter from the United States army. He was at the head of a heroic and sweeping charge, which really broke the power of the hoboes in that county for three months; he had already worsted four tramps with his own coupling-stick, when a stone thrown by the ex-third baseman of F. Troop's nine laid him flat on the prairie, and later enforced a stay in the hospital in Omaha. After his recovery he engaged with other railroads, and shuffled cars in countless yards. An order to strike came upon him in Michigan, and afterward the vengeance of the railroad pursued him until he assumed a name. This mask is like the darkness in which the burglar chooses to move. It destroys many of the healthy fears. It is a small thing, but it eats that which we call our conscience. The conductor of No. 419 stood in the caboose within two feet of Bill's nose, and called him a liar. Bill requested him to use a milder term. He had not bored the foreman of Tin Can Ranch with any such request, but had killed him with expedition. The conductor seemed to insist, and so Bill let the matter drop.

He became the bouncer of a saloon on the Bowery in New York. Here most of his fights were as successful as had been his brushes with the hoboes in the West. He gained the complete admiration of the four clean bartenders who stood behind the great and glittering bar. He was an honored man. He nearly killed Bad Hennessy, who, as a matter of fact, had more reputation than ability, and his fame moved up the Bowery and down the Bowery.

But let a man adopt fighting as his business, and the thought grows constantly within him that it is his business to fight. These phrases became mixed in Bill's mind precisely as they are here mixed; and let a man get this idea in his mind, and defeat begins to move toward him over the unknown ways of circumstances. One summer night three sailors from the U. S. S. *Seattle* sat in the saloon drinking and attending to other people's affairs in an amiable fashion. Bill was a proud man since he had thrashed so many citizens, and it suddenly occurred to him that the loud talk of the sailors was very offensive. So he swaggered upon their attention, and warned them that the saloon was the flowery abode of peace and gentle silence. They glanced at him in surprise, and without a moment's pause consigned him to a worse place than any stoker of them knew. Whereupon he flung one of them through the side door before the others could prevent it. On the sidewalk there was a short struggle, with many hoarse epithets in the air, and then Bill slid into the saloon again. A frown of false rage was upon his brow, and he strutted like a savage king. He took a long yellow night-stick from behind the lunch-counter, and started importantly toward the main doors to see that the incensed seamen did not again enter.

The ways of sailormen are without speech, and, together in the street, the three sailors exchanged no word, but they moved at once. Landsmen would have required three years of discussion to gain such unanimity. In silence, and immediately, they seized a long piece of scantling that lay handily. With one forward to guide the battering-ram, and with two behind him to furnish the power, they made a beautiful curve, and came down like the Assyrians on the front door of that saloon.

Mystic and still mystic are the laws of fate. Bill, with his kingly frown and his long night-stick, appeared at precisely that moment in the doorway. He stood like a statue of victory; his pride was at its zenith; and in the same second this atrocious piece of scantling punched him in the bulwarks of his stomach, and he vanished like a mist. Opinions differed as to where the end of the scantling landed him, but it was ultimately clear that it landed him in southwestern Texas, where he became a sheep-herder.

The sailors charged three times upon the plate-glass front of the saloon, and when they had finished, it looked as if it had been the victim of a rural fire company's success in saving it from the flames. As the proprietor of the place surveyed the ruins, he remarked that Bill was a very zealous guardian of property. As the ambulance surgeon surveyed Bill, he remarked that the wound was really an excavation.

III.

As his Mexican friend tripped blithely away, Bill turned with a thoughtful face to his frying-pan and his fire. After dinner he drew his revolver from its scarred old holster, and examined every part of it. It was the revolver that had dealt death to the foreman, and it had also been in free fights in which it had dealt death to several or none. Bill loved it because its allegiance was more than that of man, horse, or dog. It questioned neither social nor moral position; it obeyed alike the saint and the assassin. It was the claw of the eagle, the tooth of the lion, the poison of the snake; and when he swept it from its holster, this minion smote where he listed, even to the battering of a far penny. Wherefore it was his dearest possession, and was not to be exchanged in southwestern Texas for a handful of rubies, nor even the shame and homage of the conductor of No. 419.

During the afternoon he moved through his monotony of work and leisure with the same air of deep meditation. The smoke of his supper-time fire was curling across the shadowy sea of mesquit when the instinct of the plainsman warned him that the stillness, the desolation, was again invaded. He saw a motionless horseman in black outline against the pallid sky. The silhouette displayed serape and sombrero, and even the Mexican spurs as large as pies. When this black figure began to move toward the camp, Bill's hand dropped to his revolver.

The horseman approached until Bill was enabled to see pronounced American features, and a skin too red to grow on a Mexican face. Bill released his grip on his revolver.

"Hello!" called the horseman.

"Hello!" answered Bill.

The horseman cantered forward. "Good evening," he said, as he again drew rein.

"Good evenin'," answered Bill, without committing himself by too much courtesy.

For a moment the two men scanned each other in a way that is not ill-mannered on the plains, where one is in danger of meeting horse-thieves or tourists.

Bill saw a type which did not belong in the mesquit. The young fellow had invested in some Mexican trappings of an expensive kind. Bill's eyes searched the outfit for some sign of craft, but there was none. Even with his local regalia, it was clear that the young

man was of a far, black Northern city. He had discarded the enormous
stirrups of his Mexican saddle; he used the small English stirrup, and
his feet were thrust forward until the steel tightly gripped his ankles.
As Bill's eyes traveled over the stranger, they lighted suddenly upon
the stirrups and the thrust feet, and immediately he smiled in a
friendly way. No dark purpose could dwell in the innocent heart of
a man who rose thus on the plains.

As for the stranger, he saw a tattered individual with a tangle of
hair and beard, and with a complexion turned brick-color from the
sun and whisky. He saw a pair of eyes that at first looked at him as
the wolf looks at the wolf, and then became childlike, almost timid,
in their glance. Here was evidently a man who had often stormed
the iron walls of the city of success, and who now sometimes valued
himself as the rabbit values his prowess.

The stranger smiled genially, and sprang from his horse. "Well,
sir, I suppose you will let me camp here with you to-night?"

"Eh?" said Bill.

"I suppose you will let me camp here with you to-night?"

Bill for a time seemed too astonished for words. "Well,"—he answered, scowling in inhospitable annoyance—"well, I don't believe
this here is a good place to camp to-night, mister."

The stranger turned quickly from his saddle-girth.

"What?" he said in surprise. "You don't want me here? You don't
want me to camp here?"

Bill's feet scuffled awkwardly, and he looked steadily at a cactus-
plant. "Well, you see, mister," he said, "I'd like your company well
enough, but—you see, some of these here greasers are goin' to chase
me off the range to-night; and while I might like a man's company all
right, I couldn't let him in for no such game when he ain't got nothin'
to do with the trouble."

"Going to chase you off the range?" cried the stranger.

"Well, they said they were goin' to do it," said Bill.

"And—great heavens! will they kill you, do you think?"

"Don't know. Can't tell till afterwards. You see, they take some
feller that's alone like me, and then they rush his camp when he ain't
quite ready for 'em, and ginerally plug 'im with a sawed-off shot-gun
load before he has a chance to git at 'em. They lay around and wait
for their chance, and it comes soon enough. Of course a feller alone
like me has got to let up watching some time. Maybe they ketch 'im
asleep. Maybe the feller gits tired waiting, and goes out in broad day,
and kills two or three just to make the whole crowd pile on him and
settle the thing. I heard of a case like that once. It's awful hard on a
man's mind—to git a gang after him."

"And so they're going to rush your camp to-night?" cried the stranger. "How do you know? Who told you?"

"Feller come and told me."

"And what are you going to do? Fight?"

"Don't see nothin' else to do," answered Bill, gloomily, still staring at the cactus-plant.

There was a silence. Finally the stranger burst out in an amazed cry. "Well, I never heard of such a thing in my life! How many of them are there?"

"Eight," answered Bill. "And now look-a-here; you ain't got no manner of business foolin' around here just now, and you might better lope off before dark. I don't ask no help in this here row. I know your happening along here just now don't give me no call on you, and you better hit the trail."

"Well, why in the name of wonder don't you go get the sheriff?" cried the stranger.

"Oh, h———!" said Bill.

IV.

Long, smoldering clouds spread in the western sky, and to the east silver mists lay on the purple gloom of the wilderness.

Finally, when the great moon climbed the heavens and cast its ghastly radiance upon the bushes, it made a new and more brilliant crimson of the camp-fire, where the flames capered merrily through its mesquit branches, filling the silence with the fire chorus, an ancient melody which surely bears a message of the inconsequence of individual tragedy—a message that is in the boom of the sea, the sliver of the wind through the grass-blades, the silken clash of hemlock boughs.

No figures moved in the rosy space of the camp, and the search of the moonbeams failed to disclose a living thing in the bushes. There was no owl-faced clock to chant the weariness of the long silence that brooded upon the plain.

The dew gave the darkness under the mesquit a velvet quality that made air seem nearer to water, and no eye could have seen through it the black things that moved like monster lizards toward the camp. The branches, the leaves, that are fain to cry out when death approaches in the wilds, were frustrated by these mystic bodies gliding with the finesse of the escaping serpent. They crept forward to the last point where assuredly no frantic attempt of the fire could discover them, and there they paused to locate the prey. A romance relates the tale of the black cell hidden deep in the earth, where, upon entering, one sees only the little eyes of snakes fixing him in menaces. If a man could have approached a certain spot in the bushes, he would not have found it romantically necessary to have his hair rise. There would have been a sufficient expression of horror in the feeling of the death-hand at the nape of his neck and in his rubber knee-joints.

Two of these bodies finally moved toward each other until for each there grew out of the darkness a face placidly smiling with tender dreams of assassination. "The fool is asleep by the fire, God be praised!" The lips of the other widened in a grin of affectionate appreciation of the fool and his plight. There was some signaling in the gloom, and then began a series of subtle rustlings, interjected often with pauses, during which no sound arose but the sound of faint breathing.

A bush stood like a rock in the stream of firelight, sending its long shadow backward. With painful caution the little company traveled along this shadow, and finally arrived at the rear of the bush. Through its branches they surveyed for a moment of comfortable satisfaction a form in a gray blanket extended on the ground near the fire. The smile of joyful anticipation fled quickly, to give place to a quiet air of business. Two men lifted shot-guns with much of the barrels gone; and sighting these weapons through the branches, pulled trigger together.

The noise of the explosions roared over the lonely mesquit as if these guns wished to inform the entire world; and as the gray smoke fled, the dodging company back of the bush saw the blanketed form twitching. Whereupon they burst out in chorus in a laugh, and arose as merry as a lot of banqueters. They gleefully gestured congratulations, and strode bravely into the light of the fire.

Then suddenly a new laugh rang from some unknown spot in the darkness. It was a fearsome laugh of ridicule, hatred, ferocity. It might have been demoniac. It smote them motionless in their gleeful prowl, as the stern voice from the sky smites the legendary malefactor. They might have been a weird group in wax, the light of the dying fire on their yellow faces, and shining athwart their eyes turned toward the darkness whence might come the unknown and the terrible.

The thing in the gray blanket no longer twitched; but if the knives in their hands had been thrust toward it, each knife was now drawn back, and its owner's elbow was thrown upward, as if he expected death from the clouds.

This laugh had so chained their reason that for a moment they had no wit to flee. They were prisoners to their terror. Then suddenly the belated decision arrived, and with bubbling cries they turned to run; but at that instant there was a long flash of red in the darkness, and with the report one of the men shouted a bitter shout, spun once, and tumbled headlong. The thick bushes failed to impede the rout of the others.

The silence returned to the wilderness. The tired flames faintly illumined the blanketed thing and the flung corse of the marauder, and sang the fire chorus, the ancient melody which bears the message of the inconsequence of human tragedy.

V.

"Now you are worse off than ever," said the young man, dry-voiced and awed.

"No, I ain't," said Bill, rebelliously. "I'm one ahead."

After reflection, the stranger remarked, "Well, there's seven more."

They were cautiously and slowly approaching the camp. The sun was flaring its first warming rays over the gray wilderness. Upreared twigs, prominent branches, shone with golden light, while the shadows under the mesquit were heavily blue.

Suddenly the stranger uttered a frightened cry. He had arrived at a point whence he had, through openings in the thicket, a clear view of a dead face.

"Gosh!" said Bill, who at the next instant had seen the thing; "I thought at first it was that there José. That would have been queer, after what I told 'im yesterday."

They continued their way, the stranger wincing in his walk, and Bill exhibiting considerable curiosity.

The yellow beams of the new sun were touching the grim hues of the dead Mexican's face, and creating there an inhuman effect, which made his countenance more like a mask of dulled brass. One hand, grown curiously thinner, had been flung out regardlessly to a cactus bush.

Bill walked forward and stood looking respectfully at the body. "I know that feller; his name is Miguel. He—"

The stranger's nerves might have been in that condition when there is no backbone to the body, only a long groove. "Good heavens!" he exclaimed, much agitated; "don't speak that way!"

"What way?" said Bill. "I only said his name was Miguel."

After a pause the stranger said:

"Oh, I know; but—" He waved his hand. "Lower your voice, or something. I don't know. This part of the business rattles me, don't you see?"

"Oh, all right," replied Bill, bowing to the other's mysterious mood. But in a moment he burst out violently and loud in the most extraordinary profanity, the oaths winging from him as the sparks go from the funnel.

He had been examining the contents of the bundled gray blanket, and he had brought forth, among other things, his frying-pan. It was now only a rim with a handle; the Mexican volley had centered upon it. A Mexican shot-gun of the abbreviated description is ordinarily loaded with flat-irons, stove-lids, lead pipe, old horseshoes, sections of chain, window weights, railroad sleepers and spikes, dumb-bells, and any other junk which may be at hand. When one of these loads encounters a man vitally, it is likely to make an impression upon him, and a cooking-utensil may be supposed to subside before such an assault of curiosities.

Bill held high his desecrated frying-pan, turning it this way and that way. He swore until he happened to note the absence of the stranger. A moment later he saw him leading his horse from the bushes. In silence and sullenly the young man went about saddling the animal. Bill said, "Well, goin' to pull out?"

The stranger's hands fumbled uncertainly at the throat-latch. Once he exclaimed irritably, blaming the buckle for the trembling of his fingers. Once he turned to look at the dead face with the light of the morning sun upon it. At last he cried, "Oh, I know the whole thing was all square enough—couldn't be squarer—but—somehow or other, that man there takes the heart out of me." He turned his troubled face for another look. "He seems to be all the time calling me a—he makes me feel like a murderer."

"But," said Bill, puzzling, "you didn't shoot him, mister; I shot him."

"I know; but I feel that way, somehow. I can't get rid of it."

Bill considered for a time; then he said diffidently, "Mister, you're a' eddycated man, ain't you?"

"What?"

"You're what they call a'—a' eddycated man, ain't you?"

The young man, perplexed, evidently had a question upon his lips, when there was a roar of guns, bright flashes, and in the air such hooting and whistling as would come from a swift flock of steam-boilers. The stranger's horse gave a mighty, convulsive spring, snorting wildly in its sudden anguish, fell upon its knees, scrambled afoot again, and was away in the uncanny death run known to men who have seen the finish of brave horses.

"This comes from discussin' things," cried Bill, angrily.

He had thrown himself flat on the ground facing the thicket whence had come the firing. He could see the smoke winding over the bush-tops. He lifted his revolver, and the weapon came slowly up from the ground and poised like the glittering crest of a snake. Somewhere on his face there was a kind of smile, cynical, wicked, deadly, of a ferocity which at the same time had brought a deep flush to his face, and had caused two upright lines to glow in his eyes.

"Hello, José!" he called, amiable for satire's sake. "Got your old blunderbusses loaded up again yet?"

The stillness had returned to the plain. The sun's brilliant rays swept over the sea of mesquit, painting the far mists of the west with faint rosy light, and high in the air some great bird fled toward the south.

"You come out here," called Bill, again addressing the landscape, "and I'll give you some shootin' lessons. That ain't the way to shoot." Receiving no reply, he began to invent epithets and yell them at the thicket. He was something of a master of insult, and, moreover, he dived into his memory to bring forth imprecations tarnished with age, unused since fluent Bowery days. The occupation amused him, and sometimes he laughed so that it was uncomfortable for his chest to be against the ground.

Finally the stranger, prostrate near him, said wearily, "Oh, they've gone."

"Don't you believe it," replied Bill, sobering swiftly. "They're there yet—every man of 'em."

"How do you know?"

"Because I do. They won't shake us so soon. Don't put your head up, or they'll get you, sure."

Bill's eyes, meanwhile, had not wavered from their scrutiny of the thicket in front. "They're there, all right; don't you forget it. Now you listen." So he called out: "José! Ojo, José! Speak up, *hombre!* I want have talk. Speak up, you yaller cuss, you!"

Whereupon a mocking voice from off in the bushes said, "Señor?"

"There," said Bill to his ally; "didn't I tell you? The whole batch." Again he lifted his voice. "José—look—ain't you gittin' kinder tired? You better go home, you fellers, and git some rest."

The answer was a sudden furious chatter of Spanish, eloquent with hatred, calling down upon Bill all the calamities which life holds. It was as if some one had suddenly enraged a cageful of wildcats. The spirits of all the revenges which they had imagined were loosened at this time, and filled the air.

"They're in a holler," said Bill, chuckling, "or there'd be shootin'."

Presently he began to grow angry. His hidden enemies called him nine kinds of coward, a man who could fight only in the dark, a baby who would run from the shadows of such noble Mexican gentlemen, a dog that sneaked. They described the affair of the previous night, and informed him of the base advantage he had taken of their friend. In fact, they in all sincerity endowed him with every quality which

he no less earnestly believed them to possess. One could have seen
the phrases bite him as he lay there on the ground fingering his
revolver.

VI.

It is sometimes taught that men do the furious and desperate thing
from an emotion that is as even and placid as the thoughts of a village
clergyman on Sunday afternoon. Usually, however, it is to be believed
that a panther is at the time born in the heart, and that the subject
does not resemble a man picking mulberries.

"B' G——!" said Bill, speaking as from a throat filled with dust,
"I'll go after 'em in a minute."

"Don't you budge an inch!" cried the stranger, sternly. "Don't you
budge!"

"Well," said Bill, glaring at the bushes—"well—"

"Put your head down!" suddenly screamed the stranger, in white
alarm. As the guns roared, Bill uttered a loud grunt, and for a moment leaned panting on his elbow, while his arm shook like a twig.
Then he upreared like a great and bloody spirit of vengeance, his
face lighted with the blaze of his last passion. The Mexicans came
swiftly and in silence.

The lightning action of the next few moments was of the fabric
of dreams to the stranger. The muscular struggle may not be real to
the drowning man. His mind may be fixed on the far, straight shadows back of the stars, and the terror of them. And so the fight, and his
part in it, had to the stranger only the quality of a picture half
drawn. The rush of feet, the spatter of shots, the cries, the swollen
faces seen like masks on the smoke, resembled a happening of the
night.

And yet afterward certain lines, forms, lived out so strongly from
the incoherence that they were always in his memory.

He killed a man, and the thought went swiftly by him, like the
feather on the gale, that it was easy to kill a man.

Moreover, he suddenly felt for Bill, this grimy sheep-herder, some
deep form of idolatry. Bill was dying, and the dignity of last defeat,
the superiority of him who stands in his grave, was in the pose of the
lost sheep-herder.

The stranger sat on the ground idly mopping the sweat and powder-
stain from his brow. He wore the gentle idiot smile of an aged beggar
as he watched three Mexicans limping and staggering in the distance.
He noted at this time that one who still possessed a serape had from

it none of the grandeur of the cloaked Spaniard, but that against the
sky the silhouette resembled a cornucopia of childhood's Christmas.

They turned to look at him, and he lifted his weary arm to menace
them with his revolver. They stood for a moment banded together,
and hooted curses at him.

Finally he arose, and, walking some paces, stooped to loosen Bill's
gray hands from a throat. Swaying as if slightly drunk, he stood looking down into the still face.

Struck suddenly with a thought, he went about with dulled eyes
on the ground, until he plucked his gaudy blanket from where it lay
dirty from trampling feet. He dusted it carefully, and then returned
and laid it over Bill's form. There he again stood motionless, his mouth
just agape and the same stupid glance in his eyes, when all at once
he made a gesture of fright and looked wildly about him.

He had almost reached the thicket when he stopped, smitten with
alarm. A body contorted, with one arm stiff in the air, lay in his path.
Slowly and warily he moved around it, and in a moment the bushes,
nodding and whispering, their leaf-faces turned toward the scene
behind him, swung and swung again into stillness and the peace of
the wilderness.

Jack London
The White Silence

"CARMEN WON'T LAST more than a couple of days." Mason spat
out a chunk of ice and surveyed the poor animal ruefully, then put
her foot in his mouth and proceeded to bite out the ice which clustered cruelly between the toes.

"I never saw a dog with a highfalutin' name that ever was worth

Overland Monthly, Ser. 2, XXXIII (February, 1899), 138–42. Republished
in *The Son of the Wolf: Tales of the Far North* (Boston, 1900), pp. 1–20.
Text from *The Son of the Wolf*.

The Malemute Kid appears in many of London's early Klondike stories.

a rap," he said, as he concluded his task and shoved her aside. "They just fade away and die under the responsibility. Did he ever see one go wrong with a sensible name like Cassiar, Siwash, or Husky? No, sir! Take a look at Shookum here, he's"—

Snap! The lean brute flashed up, the white teeth just missing Mason's throat.

"Ye will, will ye?" A shrewd clout behind the ear with the butt of the dogwhip stretched the animal in the snow, quivering softly, a yellow slaver dripping from its fangs.

"As I was saying, just look at Shookum, here—he's got the spirit. Bet ye he eats Carmen before the week's out."

"I'll bank another proposition against that," replied Malemute Kid, reversing the frozen bread placed before the fire to thaw. "We'll eat Shookum before the trip is over. What d' ye say, Ruth?"

The Indian woman settled the coffee with a piece of ice, glanced from Malemute Kid to her husband, then at the dogs, but vouchsafed no reply. It was such a palpable truism that none was necessary. Two hundred miles of unbroken trail in prospect, with a scant six days' grub for themselves and none for the dogs, could admit no other alternative. The two men and the woman grouped about the fire and began their meagre meal. The dogs lay in their harnesses, for it was a midday halt, and watched each mouthful enviously.

"No more lunches after to-day," said Malemute Kid. "And we've got to keep a close eye on the dogs,—they're getting vicious. They'd just as soon pull a fellow down as not, if they get a chance."

"And I was president of an Epworth once, and taught in the Sunday school." Having irrelevantly delivered himself of this, Mason fell into a dreamy contemplation of his steaming moccasins, but was aroused by Ruth filling his cup. "Thank God, we've got slathers of tea! I've seen it growing, down in Tennessee. What wouldn't I give for a hot corn pone just now! Never mind, Ruth; you won't starve much longer, nor wear moccasins either."

The woman threw off her gloom at this, and in her eyes welled up a great love for her white lord,—the first white man she had ever seen,—the first man whom she had known to treat a woman as something better than a mere animal or beast of burden.

"Yes, Ruth," continued her husband, having recourse to the macaronic jargon in which it was alone possible for them to understand each other; "wait till we clean up and pull for the Outside. We'll take the White Man's canoe and go to the Salt Water. Yes, bad water, rough water,—great mountains dance up and down all the time. And so big, so far, so far away,—you travel ten sleep, twenty sleep, forty sleep" (he graphically enumerated the days on his fingers), "all the time water, bad water. Then you come to great village, plenty

people, just the same mosquitoes next summer. Wigwams oh, so high,
—ten, twenty pines. Hi-yu skookum!"

He paused impotently, cast an appealing glance at Malemute Kid,
then laboriously placed the twenty pines, end on end, by sign language. Malemute Kid smiled with cheery cynicism; but Ruth's eyes
were wide with wonder, and with pleasure; for she half believed he
was joking, and such condescension pleased her poor woman's heart.

"And then you step into a—a box, and pouf! up you go." He
tossed his empty cup in the air by way of illustration, and as he deftly
caught it, cried: "And biff! down you come. Oh, great medicine-men!
You go Fort Yukon, I go Arctic City,—twenty-five sleep,—big string,
all the time,—I catch him string,—I say, 'Hello, Ruth! How are ye?'
—and you say, 'Is that my good husband?' —and I say 'Yes,' —and
you say, 'No can bake good bread, no more soda,'—then I say, 'Look
in cache, under flour; good-by.' You look and catch plenty soda. All
the time you Fort Yukon, me Arctic City. Hi-yu medicine-man!"

Ruth smiled so ingenuously at the fairy story, that both men burst
into laughter. A row among the dogs cut short the wonders of the
Outside, and by the time the snarling combatants were separated,
she had lashed the sleds and all was ready for the trail.

"Mush! Baldy! Hi! Mush on!" Mason worked his whip smartly, and
as the dogs whined low in the traces, broke out the sled with the gee-
pole. Ruth followed with the second team, leaving Malemute Kid,
who had helped her start, to bring up the rear. Strong man, brute that
he was, capable of felling an ox at a blow, he could not bear to beat
the poor animals, but humored them as a dog-driver rarely does,—
nay, almost wept with them in their misery.

"Come, mush on there, you poor sore-footed brutes!" he murmured,
after several ineffectual attempts to start the load. But his patience
was at last rewarded, and though whimpering with pain, they hastened to join their fellows.

No more conversation; the toil of the trail will not permit such extravagance. And of all deadening labors, that of the Northland trail
is the worst. Happy is the man who can weather a day's travel at
the price of silence, and that on a beaten track.

And of all heart-breaking labors, that of breaking trail is the worst.
At every step the great webbed shoe sinks till the snow is level with
the knee. Then up, straight up, the deviation of a fraction of an inch
being a certain precursor of disaster, the snowshoe must be lifted till
the surface is cleared; then forward, down, and the other foot is
raised perpendicularly for the matter of half a yard. He who tries
this for the first time, if haply he avoids bringing his shoes in dangerous propinquity and measures not his length on the treacherous

footing, will give up exhausted at the end of a hundred yards; he who can keep out of the way of the dogs for a whole day may well crawl into his sleeping-bag with a clear conscience and a pride which passeth all understanding; and he who travels twenty sleeps on the Long Trail is a man whom the gods may envy.

The afternoon wore on, and with the awe, born of the White Silence, the voiceless travelers bent to their work. Nature has many tricks wherewith she convinces man of his finity,—the ceaseless flow of the tides, the fury of the storm, the shock of the earthquake, the long roll of heaven's artillery,—but the most tremendous, the most stupefying of all, is the passive phase of the White Silence. All movement ceases, the sky clears, the heavens are as brass; the slightest whisper seems sacrilege, and man becomes timid, affrighted at the sound of his own voice. Sole speck of life journeying across the ghostly wastes of a dead world, he trembles at his audacity, realizes that his is a maggot's life, nothing more. Strange thoughts arise unsummoned, and the mystery of all things strives for utterance. And the fear of death, of God, of the universe, comes over him,—the hope of the Resurrection and the Life, the yearning for immortality, the vain striving of the imprisoned essence,—it is then, if ever, man walks alone with God.

So wore the day away. The river took a great bend, and Mason headed his team for the cut-off across the narrow neck of land. But the dogs balked at the high bank. Again and again, though Ruth and Malemute Kid were shoving on the sled, they slipped back. Then came the concerted effort. The miserable creatures, weak from hunger, exerted their last strength. Up—up—the sled poised on the top of the bank; but the leader swung the string of dogs behind him to the right, fouling Mason's snowshoes. The result was grievous. Mason was whipped off his feet; one of the dogs fell in the traces; and the sled toppled back, dragging everything to the bottom again.

Slash! the whip fell among the dogs savagely, especially upon the one which had fallen.

"Don't, Mason," entreated Malemute Kid; "the poor devil's on its last legs. Wait and we'll put my team on."

Mason deliberately withheld the whip till the last word had fallen, then out flashed the long lash, completely curling about the offending creature's body. Carmen—for it was Carmen—cowered in the snow, cried piteously, then rolled over on her side.

It was a tragic moment, a pitiful incident of the trail,—a dying dog, two comrades in anger. Ruth glanced solicitously from man to man. But Malemute Kid restrained himself, though there was a world of reproach in his eyes, and bending over the dog, cut the traces. No word was spoken. The teams were double-spanned and the difficulty overcome; the sleds were under way again, the dying dog dragging herself along in the rear. As long as an animal can travel, it is not shot, and this last chance is accorded it,—the crawling into camp, if it can, in the hope of a moose being killed.

Already penitent for his angry action, but too stubborn to make amends, Mason toiled on at the head of the cavalcade, little dreaming that danger hovered in the air. The timber clustered thick in the sheltered bottom, and through this they threaded their way. Fifty feet or more from the trail towered a lofty pine. For generations it had stood there, and for generations destiny had had this one end in view,—perhaps the same had been decreed of Mason.

He stooped to fasten the loosened thong of his moccasin. The sleds came to a halt and the dogs lay down in the snow without a whimper. The stillness was weird; not a breath rustled the frost-encrusted forest; the cold and silence of outer space had chilled the heart and smote the trembling lips of nature. A sigh pulsed through the air,— they did not seem to actually hear it, but rather felt it, like the premonition of movement in a motionless void. Then the great tree, burdened with its weight of years and snow, played its last part in the tragedy of life. He heard the warning crash and attempted to spring up, but almost erect, caught the blow squarely on the shoulder.

The sudden danger, the quick death,—how often had Malemute Kid faced it! The pine needles were still quivering as he gave his commands and sprang into action. Nor did the Indian girl faint or raise her voice in idle wailing, as might many of her white sisters. At his order, she threw her weight on the end of a quickly extemporized handspike, easing the pressure and listening to her husband's groans, while Malemute Kid attacked the tree with his axe. The steel rang merrily as it bit into the frozen trunk, each stroke being accompanied by a forced, audible respiration, the "Huh!" "Huh!" of the woodsman.

At last the Kid laid the pitiable thing that was once a man in the snow. But worse than his comrade's pain was the dumb anguish in the woman's face, the blended look of hopeful, hopeless query. Little was said; those of the Northland are early taught the futility of words and the inestimable value of deeds. With the temperature at sixty-five below zero, a man cannot lie many minutes in the snow and live. So the sled-lashings were cut, and the sufferer, rolled in furs, laid on a couch of boughs. Before him roared a fire, built of the very wood which wrought the mishap. Behind and partially over him was stretched the primitive fly,—a piece of canvas, which caught the radiating heat and threw it back and down upon him,—a trick which men may know who study physics at the fount.

And men who have shared their bed with death know when the

call is sounded. Mason was terribly crushed. The most cursory examination revealed it. His right arm, leg, and back, were broken; his limbs were paralyzed from the hips; and the likelihood of internal injuries was large. An occasional moan was his only sign of life.

No hope; nothing to be done. The pitiless night crept slowly by, —Ruth's portion, the despairing stoicism of her race, and Malemute Kid adding new lines to his face of bronze. In fact, Mason suffered least of all, for he spent his time in Eastern Tennessee, in the Great Smoky Mountains, living over the scenes of his childhood. And most pathetic was the melody of his long-forgotten Southern vernacular, as he raved of swimming-holes and coon-hunts and watermelon raids. It was as Greek to Ruth, but the Kid understood and felt,—felt as only one can feel who has been shut out for years from all that civilization means.

Morning brought consciousness to the stricken man, and Malemute Kid bent closer to catch his whispers.

"You remember when we foregathered on the Tanana, four years come next ice-run? I didn't care so much for her then. It was more like she was pretty, and there was a smack of excitement about it, I think. But d'ye know, I've come to think a heap of her. She's been a good wife to me, always at my shoulder in the pinch. And when it comes to trading, you know there isn't her equal. D'ye recollect the time she shot the Moosehorn Rapids to pull you and me off that rock, the bullets whipping the water like hailstones?—and the time of the famine at Nuklukyeto?—or when she raced the ice-run to bring the news? Yes, she's been a good wife to me, better 'n that other one. Didn't know I'd been there? Never told you, eh? Well, I tried it once, down in the States. That's why I'm here. Been raised together, too. I came away to give her a chance for divorce. She got it.

"But that's got nothing to do with Ruth. I had thought of cleaning up and pulling for the Outside next year,—her and I,—but it's too late. Don't send her back to her people, Kid. It's beastly hard for a woman to go back. Think of it!—nearly four years on our bacon and beans and flour and dried fruit, and then to go back to her fish and cariboo. It's not good for her to have tried our ways, to come to know they're better 'n her people's, and then return to them. Take care of her, Kid,—why don't you,—but no, you always fought shy of them, —and you never told me why you came to this country. Be kind to her, and send her back to the States as soon as you can. But fix it so as she can come back,—liable to get homesick, you know.

"And the youngster—it's drawn us closer, Kid. I only hope it is a boy. Think of it!—flesh of my flesh, Kid. He mustn't stop in this country. And if it's a girl, why she can't. Sell my furs; they'll fetch at least five thousand, and I've got as much more with the company. And handle my interests with yours. I think that bench claim will show up. See that he gets a good schooling; and Kid, above all, don't let him come back. This country was not made for white men.

"I'm a gone man, Kid. Three or four sleeps at the best. You've got to go on. You must go on! Remember, it's my wife, it's my boy,—O God! I hope it's a boy! You can't stay by me,—and I charge you, a dying man, to pull on."

"Give me three days," pleaded Malemute Kid. "You may change for the better; something may turn up."

"No."

"Just three days."

"You must pull on."

"Two days."

"It's my wife and my boy, Kid. You would not ask it."

"One day."

"No, no! I charge"—

"Only one day. We can shave it through on the grub, and I might knock over a moose."

"No,—all right; one day, but not a minute more. And Kid, don't— don't leave me to face it alone. Just a shot, one pull on the trigger. You understand. Think of it! Think of it! Flesh of my flesh, and I'll never live to see him!

"Send Ruth here. I want to say good-by and tell her that she must think of the boy and not wait till I'm dead. She might refuse to go with you if I didn't. Good-by, old man; good-by.

"Kid! I say—a—sink a hole above the pup, next to the slide. I panned out forty cents on my shovel there.

"And Kid!" he stooped lower to catch the last faint words, the dying man's surrender of his pride. "I'm sorry—for—you know— Carmen."

Leaving the girl crying softly over her man, Malemute Kid slipped into his *parka* and snowshoes, tucked his rifle under his arm, and crept away into the forest. He was no tyro in the stern sorrows of the North-land, but never had he faced so stiff a problem as this. In the abstract, it was a plain, mathematical proposition,—three possible lives as against one doomed one. But now he hesitated. For five years, shoulder to shoulder, on the rivers and trails, in the camps and mines, facing death by field and flood and famine, had they knitted the bonds of their comradeship. So close was the tie, that he had often been conscious of a vague jealousy of Ruth, from the first time she had come between. And now it must be severed by his own hand.

Though he prayed for a moose, just one moose, all game seemed to have deserted the land, and nightfall found the exhausted man crawling into camp, light-handed, heavy-hearted. An uproar from the dogs and shrill cries from Ruth hastened him.

Bursting into the camp, he saw the girl in the midst of the snarling pack, laying about her with an axe. The dogs had broken the iron rule of their masters and were rushing the grub. He joined the issue with his rifle reversed, and the hoary game of natural selection was played out with all the ruthlessness of its primeval environment. Rifle and axe went up and down, hit or missed with monotonous regularity; lithe bodies flashed, with wild eyes and dripping fangs; and man and beast fought for supremacy to the bitterest conclusion. Then the beaten brutes crept to the edge of the firelight, licking their wounds, voicing their misery to the stars.

The whole stock of dried salmon had been devoured, and perhaps five pounds of flour remained to tide them over two hundred miles of wilderness. Ruth returned to her husband, while Malemute Kid cut up the warm body of one of the dogs, the skull of which had been crushed by the axe. Every portion was carefully put away, save the hide and offal, which were cast to his fellows of the moment before.

Morning brought fresh trouble. The animals were turning on each other. Carmen, who still clung to her slender thread of life, was downed by the pack. The lash fell among them unheeded. They cringed and cried under the blows, but refused to scatter till the last wretched bit had disappeared,—bones, hide, hair, everything.

Malemute Kid went about his work, listening to Mason, who was back in Tennessee, delivering tangled discourses and wild exhortations to his brethren of other days.

Taking advantage of neighboring pines, he worked rapidly, and Ruth watched him make a cache similar to those sometimes used by hunters to preserve their meat from the wolverines and dogs. One after the other, he bent the tops of two small pines toward each other and nearly to the ground, making them fast with thongs of moosehide. Then he beat the dogs into submission and harnessed them to two of the sleds, loading the same with everything but the furs which enveloped Mason. These he wrapped and lashed tightly about him, fastening either end of the robes to the bent pines. A single stroke of his hunting-knife would release them and send the body high in the air.

Ruth had received her husband's last wishes and made no struggle. Poor girl, she had learned the lesson of obedience well. From a child, she had bowed, and seen all women bow, to the lords of creation, and it did not seem in the nature of things for woman to resist. The Kid permitted her one outburst of grief, as she kissed her husband,

—her own people had no such custom,—then led her to the foremost sled and helped her into her snowshoes. Blindly, instinctively, she took the gee-pole and whip, and "mushed" the dogs out on the trail. Then he returned to Mason, who had fallen into a coma; and long after she was out of sight, crouched by the fire, waiting, hoping, praying for his comrade to die.

It is not pleasant to be alone with painful thoughts in the White Silence. The silence of gloom is merciful, shrouding one as with protection and breathing a thousand intangible sympathies; but the bright White Silence, clear and cold, under steely skies, is pitiless.

An hour passed,—two hours,—but the man would not die. At high noon, the sun, without raising its rim above the southern horizon, threw a suggestion of fire athwart the heavens, then quickly drew it back. Malemute Kid roused and dragged himself to his comrade's side. He cast one glance about him. The White Silence seemed to sneer, and a great fear came upon him. There was a sharp report; Mason swung into his aerial sepulchre; and Malemute Kid lashed the dogs into a wild gallop as he fled across the snow.

Theodore Roosevelt
The Manly Virtues and Practical Politics

SOMETIMES, in addressing men who sincerely desire the betterment of our public affairs, but who have not taken active part in directing them, I feel tempted to tell them that there are two gospels which should be preached to every reformer. The first is the gospel of morality; the second is the gospel of efficiency.

To decent, upright citizens it is hardly necessary to preach the doctrine of morality as applied to the affairs of public life. It is an even graver offence to sin against the commonwealth than to sin against an individual. The man who debauches our public life, whether by malversation of funds in office, by the actual bribery of voters or of legislators, or by the corrupt use of the offices as spoils wherewith to reward the unworthy and the vicious for their nox-

Forum, XVII (July, 1894), 551–57. Text from this publication.

ious and interested activity in the baser walks of political life,—this man is a greater foe to our well-being as a nation than is even the defaulting cashier of a bank, or the betrayer of a private trust. No amount of intelligence and no amount of energy will save a nation which is not honest, and no government can ever be a permanent success if administered in accordance with base ideals. The first requisite in the citizen who wishes to share the work of our public life, whether he wishes himself to hold office or merely to do his plain duty as an American by taking part in the management of our political machinery, is that he shall act disinterestedly and with a sincere purpose to serve the whole commonwealth.

But disinterestedness and honesty and unselfish desire to do what is right are not enough in themselves. A man must not only be disinterested, but he must be efficient. If he goes into politics he must go into practical politics, in order to make his influence felt. Practical politics must not be construed to mean dirty politics. On the contrary, in the long run the politics of fraud and treachery and foulness is unpractical politics, and the most practical of all politicians is the politician who is clean and decent and upright. But a man who goes into the actual battles of the political world must prepare himself much as he would for the struggle in any other branch of our life. He must be prepared to meet men of far lower ideas than his own, and to face things, not as he would wish them, but as they are. He must not lose his own high ideal, and yet he must face the fact that the majority of the men with whom he must work have lower ideals. He must stand firmly for what he believes; and yet he must realize that political action, to be effective, must be the joint action of many men, and that he must sacrifice somewhat of his own opinions to those of his associates if he ever hopes to see his desires take practical shape.

The prime thing that every man who takes an interest in politics should remember is that he must act, and not merely criticise the actions of others. It is not the man who sits by his fireside reading his evening paper, and saying how bad our politics and politicians are, who will ever do anything to save us; it is the man who goes out into the rough hurly-burly of the caucus, the primary, and the political meeting, and there faces his fellows on equal terms. The real service is rendered, not by the critic who stands aloof from the contest, but by the man who enters into it and bears his part as a man should, undeterred by the blood and the sweat. It is a pleasant but a dangerous thing to associate merely with cultivated, refined men of high ideals and sincere purpose to do right, and to think that one has done all one's duty by discussing politics with such associates. It is a good thing to meet men of this stamp; indeed it is a necessary thing, for we thereby brighten our ideals, and keep in touch with the people who are unselfish in their purposes; but if we associate with such men exclusively we can accomplish nothing. The actual battle must be fought out on other and less pleasant fields. The actual advance must be made in the field of practical politics among the men who represent or guide or control the mass of the voters, the men who are sometimes rough and coarse, who sometimes have lower ideals than they should, but who are capable, masterful, and efficient. It is only by mingling on equal terms with such men, by showing them that one is able to give and to receive heavy punishment without flinching, and that one can master the details of political management as well as they can, that it is possible for a man to establish a standing that will be useful to him in fighting for a great reform. Every man who wishes well to his country is in honor bound to take an active part in political life. If he does his duty and takes that active part he will be sure occasionally to commit mistakes and to be guilty of shortcomings. For these mistakes and shortcomings he will receive the unmeasured denunciation of the critics who commit neither because they never do anything but criticise. Nevertheless he will have the satisfaction of knowing that the salvation of the country ultimately lies, not in the hands of his critics, but in the hands of those who, however imperfectly, actually do the work of the nation. I would not for one moment be understood as objecting to criticism or failing to appreciate its importance. We need fearless criticism of our public men and public parties; we need unsparing condemnation of all persons and all principles that count for evil in our public life: but it behooves every man to remember that the work of the critic, important though it is, is of altogether secondary importance, and that, in the end, progress is accomplished by the man who does the things, and not by the man who talks about how they ought or ought not to be done.

Therefore the man who wishes to do good in his community must go into active political life. If he is a Republican, let him join his local Republican association; if a Democrat, the Democratic association; if an Independent, then let him put himself in touch with those who think as he does. In any event let him make himself an active force and make his influence felt. Whether he works within or without party lines he can surely find plenty of men who are desirous of good government, and who, if they act together, become at once a power on the side of righteousness. Of course, in a government like ours, a man can accomplish anything only by acting in combination with others, and equally, of course, a number of people can act together only by each sacrificing certain of his beliefs or prejudices. That man is indeed unfortunate who cannot in any given district find some people with whom he can conscientiously act. He may find that he can do best by acting within a party organization; he may find that he can do best by acting, at least for certain purposes, or at certain times, outside of party organizations, in an independent body of some kind; but with some association he must act if he wishes to exert any real influence.

One thing to be always remembered is that neither independence on the one hand nor party fealty on the other can ever be accepted as an excuse for failure to do active work in politics. The party man who offers his allegiance to party as an excuse for blindly following his party, right or wrong, and who fails to try to make that party in any way better, commits a crime against the country; and a crime quite as serious is committed by the independent who makes his independence an excuse for easy self-indulgence, and who thinks that when he says he belongs to neither party he is excused from the duty of taking part in the practical work of party organizations. The party man is bound to do his full share in party management. He is bound to attend the caucuses and the primaries, to see that only good men are put up, and to exert his influence as strenuously against the foes of good government within his party, as, through his party machinery, he does against those who are without the party. In the same way the independent, if he cannot take part in the regular organizations, is bound to do just as much active constructive work (not merely the work of criticism) outside; he is bound to try to get up an organization of his own and to try to make that organization felt in some effective manner. Whatever course the man who wishes to do his duty by his country takes in reference to parties or to independence of parties, he is bound to try to put himself in touch with men who think as he does, and to help make their joint influence felt in behalf of the powers that go for decency and good government.

Yet another thing to be remembered by the man who wishes to make his influence felt for good in our politics is that he must act purely as an American. If he is not deeply imbued with the American spirit he cannot succeed. Any organization which tries to work along the line of caste or creed, which fails to treat all American citizens on their merits as men, will fail, and will deserve to fail. Where our political life is healthy, there is and can be no room for any movement organized to help or to antagonize men because they do or do not profess a certain religion, or because they were or were not born here or abroad. We have a right to ask that those with whom we associate, and those for whom we vote, shall be themselves good Americans in heart and spirit, unhampered by adherence to foreign ideals, and acting without regard to the national and religious prejudices of European countries; but if they really are good Americans in spirit and thought and purpose, that is all that we have any right to consider in regard to them. In the same way there must be no discrimination for or against any man because of his social standing. On the one side, there is nothing to be made out of a political organization which draws an exclusive social line, and on the other it must be remembered that it is just as un-American to vote against a man because he is rich as to vote against him because he is poor. The one man has just as much right as the other to claim to be treated purely on his merits as a man. In short, to do good work in politics, the men who organize must organize wholly without regard to whether their associates were born here or abroad, whether they are Protestants or Catholics, Jews or Gentiles, whether they are bankers or butchers, professors or day-laborers. All that can rightly be asked of one's political associates is that they shall be honest men, good Americans, and substantially in accord as regards their political ideas.

Another thing that must not be forgotten by the man desirous of doing good political work is the need of the rougher, manlier virtues, and above all the virtue of personal courage, physical as well as moral. If we wish to do good work for our country we must be unselfish, disinterested, sincerely desirous of the well-being of the commonwealth, and capable of devoted adherence to a lofty ideal; but in addition we must be vigorous in mind and body, able to hold our own in rough conflict with our fellows, able to suffer punishment without flinching, and, at need, to repay it in kind with full interest. A peaceful and commercial civilization is always in danger of suffering the loss of the virile fighting qualities without which no nation, however cultured, however refined, however thrifty and prosperous, can ever amount to anything. Every citizen should be taught, both in public and in private life, that while he must avoid brawling and quarrelling, it is his duty to stand up for his rights. He must realize that the only man who is more contemptible than the blusterer and bully is the coward. No man is worth much to the commonwealth if he is not capable of feeling righteous wrath and just indignation, if he is not stirred to hot anger by misdoing, and is not impelled to see justice meted out to the wrongdoers. No man is worth much anywhere if he does not possess both moral and physical courage. A politician who really serves his country well, and deserves his country's gratitude, must usually possess some of the hardy virtues which we admire in the soldier who serves his country well in the field.

An ardent young reformer is very apt to try to begin by reforming too much. He needs always to keep in mind that he has got to serve as a sergeant before he assumes the duties of commander-in-chief. It is right for him from the beginning to take a great interest in national, State, and municipal affairs, and to try to make himself felt in them if the occasion arises; but the best work must be done by the citizen working in his own ward or district. Let him associate himself with the men who think as he does, and who, like him, are sincerely devoted to the public good. Then let them try to make themselves felt in the choice of alderman, of councilman, of assemblyman. The politicians will be prompt to recognize their power, and the people will recognize it too, after a while. Let them organize and work, undaunted by any temporary defeat. If they fail at first, and if they fail again, let them merely make up their minds to redouble their efforts, and perhaps alter their methods; but let them keep on working.

It is sheer unmanliness and cowardice to shrink from the contest because at first there is failure, or because the work is difficult or repulsive. No man who is worth his salt has any right to abandon the effort to better our politics merely because he does not find it pleasant, merely because it entails associations which to him happen to be disagreeable. Let him keep right on, taking the buffets he gets good-humoredly, and repaying them with heartiness when the chance arises. Let him make up his mind that he will have to face the violent opposition of the spoils politician, and also, too often, the unfair and ungenerous criticism of those who ought to know better. Let him be careful not to show himself so thin-skinned as to mind either; let him fight his way forward, paying only so much regard to both as is necessary to enable him to win in spite of them. He may not, and indeed probably will not, accomplish nearly as much as he would like to, or as he thinks he ought to: but he will certainly accomplish something; and if he can feel that he has helped to elevate the type of representative sent to the municipal, the State, or the national legislature, from his district, or to elevate the standard of duty among the public officials in his own ward, he has a right to be profoundly satisfied with what he has accomplished.

Finally, there is one other matter which the man who tries to wake his fellows to higher political action would do well to ponder. It is a good thing to appeal to citizens to work for good government because it will better their estate materially, but it is a far better thing to appeal to them to work for good government because it is right in itself to do so. Doubtless, if we can have clean, honest politics, we shall be better off in material matters. A thoroughly pure, upright, and capable administration of the affairs of New York city would result in a very appreciable increase of comfort to each citizen. We should have better systems of transportation; we should have cleaner streets, better sewers, and the like. But it is sometimes difficult to show the individual citizen that he will be individually better off in his business and in his home affairs for taking part in politics. I do not think it is worth while to show that this will be the case. The citizen should be appealed to primarily on the ground that it is his plain duty, if he wishes to deserve the name of freeman, to do his full share in the hard and difficult work of self-government. He must do his share unless he is willing to prove himself unfit for free institutions, fit only to live under a government where he will be plundered and bullied because he deserves to be plundered and bullied, on account of his selfish timidity and short-sightedness. A clean and decent government is sure in the end to benefit all our citizens in the material circumstances of their lives; but each citizen should be appealed to, to take part in bettering our politics, not for the sake of any possible improvement it may bring to his affairs, but on the ground that it is his plain duty to do so, and that this is a duty which it is cowardly and dishonorable in him to shirk.

To sum up, then, the men who wish to work for decent politics must work practically, and yet must not swerve from their devotion to a high ideal. They must actually do things, and not merely confine themselves to criticising those who do them. They must work disinterestedly, and appeal to the disinterested element in others, although they must also do work which will result in the material betterment of the community. They must act as Americans through and through, in spirit and hope and purpose, and, while being disinterested, unselfish, and gentle in their dealings with others, they must also show that they possess the essential manly virtues of energy, of resolution, and of indomitable personal courage.

Frank Norris
The Frontier Gone at Last

SUDDENLY WE HAVE FOUND that there is no longer any Frontier. Until the day when the first United States marine landed in China we had always imagined that out yonder somewhere in the West was the borderland where civilization disintegrated and merged into the un-

World's Work, III (February, 1902), 1728–31. Text from *The Literary Criticism of Frank Norris,* ed. Donald Pizer (Austin, 1964), pp. 111–17. Reprinted by permission of University of Texas Press.

tamed.[1] Our skirmish-line was there, our posts that scouted and scrim-maged with the wilderness, a thousand miles in advance of the steady march of civilization.

And the Frontier has become so much an integral part of our conception of things that it will be long before we shall all understand that it is gone. We liked the Frontier; it was romance, the place of the poetry of the Great March, the firing-line where there was action and fighting, and where men held each other's lives in the crook of the forefinger. Those who had gone out came back with tremendous tales, and those that stayed behind made up other and even more tremendous tales.

When we—we Anglo-Saxons—busked ourselves for the first stage of the march, we began from that little historic reach of ground in the midst of the Friesland swamps, and we set our faces Westward, feeling no doubt the push of the Slav behind us. Then the Frontier was Britain and the sober peacefulness of land where are the ordered, cultivated English farmyards of today was the Wild West of the Frisians of that century; and for the little children of the Frisian peat cottages, Hengist was the Apache Kid and Horsa Deadwood Dick—freebooters, law-defiers, slayers-of-men, epic heroes, blood brothers if you please to Boone and Bowie.

Then for centuries we halted and the van closed up with the firing-line, and we filled all England and all Europe with our clamor because for a while we seemed to have gone as far Westward as it was possible; and the checked energy of the race reacted upon itself, rebounded as it were, and back we went to the Eastward again—crusading, girding at the Mahommedan, conquering his cities, breaking into his fortresses with mangonel, siege engine and catapult—just as the boy shut indoors finds his scope circumscribed and fills the whole place with the racket of his activity.

But always, if you will recall it, we had a curious feeling that we had not reached the ultimate West even yet, and there was still a Frontier. Always that strange sixth sense turned our heads toward the sunset; and all through the Middle Ages we were peeking and prying at the Western horizon, trying to reach it, to run it down, and the queer tales about Vineland and that storm-driven Viking's ship would not down.

And then at last a naked savage on the shores of a little island in what is now our West Indies, looking Eastward one morning, saw the caravels, and on that day the Frontier was rediscovered, and promptly

[1] The United States had sent a detachment of marines to Peking during the Boxer Rebellion of mid-1900 to protect our legation.

a hundred thousand of the more hardy rushed to the skirmish-line
and went at the Wilderness as only the Anglo-Saxon can.

And then the skirmish-line decided that it would declare itself independent of the main army behind and form an advance column of
its own, a separate army corps, and no sooner was this done than again
the scouts went forward, went Westward, pushing the Frontier
ahead of them, scrimmaging with the wilderness, blazing the way. At
last they forced the Frontier over the Sierra Nevadas down to the
edge of the Pacific. And here it would have been supposed that the
Great March would have halted again as it did before the Atlantic,
that here at last the Frontier ended.

But on the first of May, eighteen hundred and ninety-eight, a gun
was fired in the Bay of Manila, still further Westward, and in response
the skirmish-line crossed the Pacific, still pushing the Frontier before
it. Then came a cry for help from Legation Street in Peking and as the
first boat bearing its contingent of American marines took ground on
the Asian shore, the Frontier—at last after so many centuries, after so
many marches, after so much fighting, so much spilled blood, so much
spent treasure, dwindled down and vanished; for the Anglo-Saxon in
his course of empire had circled the globe and brought the new civilization to the old civilization, had reached the starting point of history,
the place from which the migrations began. So soon as the marines
landed there was no longer any West, and the equation of the horizon, the problem of the centuries for the Anglo-Saxon was solved.

So, lament it though we may, the Frontier is gone, an idiosyncrasy
that has been with us for thousands of years, the one peculiar
picturesqueness of our life is no more. We may keep alive for many
years yet the idea of a Wild West, but the hired cowboys and paid
rough riders of Mr. William Cody are more like "the real thing" than
can be found today in Arizona, New Mexico or Idaho. Only the imitation cowboys, the college-bred fellows who "go out on a ranch"
carry the revolver or wear the poncho. The Frontier has become conscious of itself, acts the part for the Eastern visitor; and this self-consciousness is a sign, surer than all others, of the decadence of a
type, the passing of an epoch. The Apache Kid and Deadwood Dick
have gone to join Hengist and Horsa and the heroes of the *Magnus-
son Saga*.

But observe. What happened in the Middle Ages when for awhile
we could find no Western Frontier? The race impulse was irresistible.
March we must, conquer we must, and checked in the Westward
course of empire we turned Eastward and expended the resistless
energy that by blood was ours in conquering the Old World behind
us.

Today we are the same race, with the same impulse, the same power and, because there is no longer a Frontier to absorb our overplus of energy, because there is no longer a wilderness to conquer and because we still must march, still must conquer, we remember the old days when our ancestors before us found the outlet for their activity checked and, rebounding, turned their faces Eastward, and went down to invade the Old World. So we. No sooner have we found that our path to the Westward has ended than, reacting Eastward, we are at the Old World again, marching against it, invading it, devoting our overplus of energy to its subjugation.

But though we are the same race, with the same impulses, the same blood-instincts as the old Frisian marsh people, we are now come into a changed time and the great word of our century is no longer War but Trade.

But though we are the same race, with the same impulses, the same blood-instincts as the old Frisian marsh people, we are now come into a changed time and the great word of our century is no longer War but Trade.

Or if you choose it is only a different word for the same race-characteristic. The desire for conquest—say what you will—was as big in the breast of the most fervid of the Crusaders as it is this very day in the most peacefully-disposed of American manufacturers. Had the Lion-Hearted Richard lived today he would have become a "leading representative of the Amalgamated Steel Companies," and doubt not for one moment that he would have underbid his Manchester rivals in the matter of bridge girders. Had Mr. Andrew Carnegie been alive at the time of the preachings of Peter the Hermit he would have raised a company of *gens d'armes* sooner than all of his brothers-in-arms, would have equipped his men better and more effectively, would have been first on the ground before Jerusalem, would have built the most ingenious siege engine and have hurled the first cask of Greek-fire over the walls.

Competition and conquest are words easily interchangeable, and the whole spirit of our present commercial crusade to the Eastward betrays itself in the fact that we cannot speak of it but in terms borrowed from the glossary of the warrior. It is a commercial "invasion," a trade "war," a "threatened attack" on the part of America; business is "captured," opportunities are "seized," certain industries are "killed," certain former monopolies are "wrested away." Seven hundred years ago a certain Count Baldwin, a great leader in the attack of the Anglo-Saxon Crusaders upon the Old World, built himself a siege engine which would help him enter the beleaguered city of Jerusalem. Jerusalem is beleaguered again today, and the hosts of the Anglo-Saxon commercial crusaders are knocking at the gates. And now a company named for another Baldwin—and for all we know a descendant of the count—leaders of the invaders of the Old World, advance upon the city, and, to help in the assault, build an engine—only now the engine is no longer called a mangonel, but a locomotive.

The difference is hardly of kind and scarcely of degree. It is a mere matter of names, and the ghost of Saladin watching the present engagement might easily fancy the old days back again.

So perhaps we have not lost the Frontier, after all. A new phrase, reversing that of Berkeley's, is appropriate to the effect that "Eastward the course of commerce takes its way," and we must look for the lost battle-line not toward the sunset, but toward the East. And so rapid has been the retrograde movement that we must go far to find it, that scattered firing-line, where the little skirmishes are heralding the approach of the Great March. We must already go further afield than England. The main body, even to the reserves, are intrenched there long since, and even continental Europe is to the rear of the skirmishers.

Along about Suez we begin to catch up with them where they are deepening the great canal, and we can assure ourselves that we are fairly abreast of the most distant line of scouts only when we come to Khiva, to Samarcand, to Bokhara and the Trans-Baikal country.

Just now one hears much of the "American commercial invasion of England." But adjust the field glasses and look beyond Britain and search for the blaze that the scouts have left on the telegraph poles and mile posts of Hungary, Turkey, Turkey in Asia, Persia, Baluchistan, India and Siam. You'll find the blaze distinct and the road, though rough hewn, is easy to follow. Prophecy and presumption be far from us, but it would be against all precedent that the Grand March should rest forever upon its arms and its laurels along the Thames, the Mersey and the Clyde, while its pioneers and Frontiersmen are making roads for it to the Eastward.

Is it too huge a conception, too inordinate an idea to say that the American conquest of England is but an incident of the Greater Invasion, an affair of outposts preparatory to the real manoeuver that shall embrace Europe, Asia, the whole of the Old World? Why not? And the blaze is ahead of us, and every now and then from far off there in the countries that are under the rising sun we catch the faint sounds of the skirmishing of our outposts. One of two things invariably happens under such circumstances as these: either the outposts fall back upon the main body or the main body moves up to the support of its outposts. One does not think that the outposts will fall back.

And so goes the great movement, Westward, then Eastward, forward and then back The motion of the natural forces, the elemental energies, somehow appear to be thus alternative—action first, then reaction. The tides ebb and flow again, the seasons have their slow vibrations, touching extremes at periodic intervals. Not impossibly, in the larger view, is the analogy applicable to the movements of the races. First Westward with the great migrations, now Eastward with the course of commerce, moving in a colossal arc measured only by the hemispheres, as though upon the equator a giant dial hand oscillated, in gradual divisions through the centuries, now marking off the Westward progress, now traveling proportionately to the reaction toward the East.

Races must follow their destiny blindly, but is it not possible that we can find in this great destiny of ours something a little better than mere battle and conquest, something a little more generous than mere trading and underbidding? Inevitably with constant change of environment comes the larger view, the more tolerant spirit, and every race movement, from the first step beyond the Friesland swamp to the adjustment of the first American theodolite on the Himalayan watershed, is an unconscious lesson in patriotism. Just now we cannot get beyond the self-laudatory mood, but is it not possible to hope that, as the progress develops, a new patriotism, one that shall include all peoples, may prevail? The past would indicate that this is a goal toward which we trend.

In the end let us take the larger view, ignoring the Frieslanders, the Anglo-Saxons, the Americans. Let us look at the peoples as a people and observe how inevitably as they answer the great Westward impulse the true patriotism develops. If we can see that it is so with all of them we can assume that it must be so with us, and may know that mere victory in battle as we march Westward, or mere supremacy in trade as we react to the East is not after all the great achievement of the races but patriotism. Not our selfish present-day conception of the word, but a new patriotism, whose meaning is now the secret of the coming centuries.

Consider then the beginnings of patriotism. At the very first, the seed of the future nation was the regard of family; the ties of common birth held men together and the first feeling of patriotism was the love of family. But the family grows, develops by lateral branches, expands and becomes the clan. Patriotism is the devotion to the clan, and the clansmen will fight and die for its supremacy.

Then comes the time when the clans, tired of the roving life of herders, halt a moment and settle down in a chosen spot; the tent becoming permanent evolves the dwellinghouse, and the encampment of the clan becomes at last a city. Patriotism now is civic pride, the clan absorbed into a multitude of clans is forgotten; men speak of themselves as Athenians not as Greeks, as Romans not as Italians. It is the age of cities.

The city extends its adjoining grazing fields, they include outlying towns, other cities, and finally the State comes into being. Patriotism no longer confines itself to the walls of the city, but is enlarged to encompass the entire province. Men are Hanoverians or Wurtemburgers not Germans; Scots or Welsh not English; are even Carolinians or Alabamans rather than Americans.

But the States are federated, pronounced boundaries fade, State makes common cause with State and at last the nation is born. Patriotism at once is a national affair, a far larger, broader, truer sentiment than that first huddling about the hearthstone of the family. The word "brother" may be applied to men unseen and unknown, and a countryman is one of many millions.

We have reached this stage at the present, but if all signs are true, if all precedent may be followed, if all augury may be relied on and the tree grow as we see the twig is bent, the progress will not stop here.

By war to the Westward the family fought its way upward to the dignity of the nation, by reaction Eastward the nation may in patriotic effect merge with other nations, and others and still others, peacefully, the bitterness of trade competition may be lost, the business of the nations seen as a friendly *quid pro quo*, give and take arrangement, guided by a generous reciprocity. Every century the boundaries are widening, patriotism widens with the expansion, and our countrymen are those of different race, even different nations.

Will it not go on, this epic of civilization, this destiny of the races, until at last and at the ultimate end of all, we who now arrogantly boast ourselves as Americans, supreme in conquest, whether of battle-ship or of bridge-building, may realize that the true patriotism is the brotherhood of man and know that the whole world is our nation and simple humanity our countrymen?

Finley Peter Dunne
On the Anglo-Saxon

"WELL," said Mr. Dooley, "I see be th' pa-apers that th' snow-white pigeon iv peace have tied up th' dogs iv war. It's all over now. All we've got to do is to arrest th' pathrites an' make th' reconcenthradios pay th' stamp tax, an' be r-ready f'r to take a punch at Germany or France or Rooshia or anny counthry on th' face iv th' globe.

"An' I'm glad iv it. This war, Hinnissy, has been a gr-reat sthrain on me. To think iv th' suffrin' I've endured! F'r weeks I lay awake at nights fearin' that th' Spanish ar-rmadillo'd lave the Cape Verde Islands, where it wasn't, an' take th' thrain out here, an' hur-rl death an' desthruction into me little store. Day by day th' pitiless exthries come out an' beat down on me. Ye hear iv Teddy Rosenfelt plungin' into ambus-cades an' Sicrity iv Wars; but d'ye hear iv Martin Dooley, th' man behind th' guns, four thousan' miles behind thim, an' willin' to be further? They ar-re no bokays f'r me. I'm what Hogan calls wan iv th' mute, ingloryous heroes iv th' war; an' not so dam mute, ayther. Some day, Hinnissy, justice'll be done me, an' th' likes iv me; an', whin th' story iv a gr-reat battle is written, they'll print th' kilt, th' wounded, th' missin', an' th' seryously disturbed. An' thim that have bore thimsilves well an' bravely an' paid th' taxes an' faced th' deadly newspa-apers without flinchin' 'll be advanced six pints an' given a chanst to tur-rn jack f'r th' game.

"But me wurruk ain't over jus' because Mack has inded th' war an' Teddy Rosenfelt is comin' home to bite th' Sicrety iv War. You an' me, Hinnissy, has got to bring on this here Anglo-Saxon 'lieance. An Anglo-Saxon, Hinnissy, is a German that's forgot who was his parents. They're a lot iv thim in this counthry. There must be as manny as two in Boston: they'se wan up in Maine, an' another lives at Bogg's Ferry in New York State, an' dhrives a milk wagon. Mack is an Anglo-

Mr. Dooley in Peace and in War (Boston, 1898), pp. 53–57. Text from this edition.

Mr. Dooley is the proprietor of a bar on "Archey Road" in Chicago. One of his frequent patrons and listeners is Mr. Hennessy. "Mack" is McKinley.

Saxon. His folks come fr'm th' County Armagh, an' their naytional Anglo-Saxon hymn is 'O'Donnell Aboo.' Teddy Rosenfelt is another Anglo-Saxon. An' I'm an Anglo-Saxon. I'm wan iv th' hottest Anglo-Saxons that iver come out iv Anglo-Saxony. Th' name iv Dooley has been th' proudest Anglo-Saxon name in th' County Roscommon f'r many years.

"Schwartzmeister is an Anglo-Saxon, but he doesn't know it, an' won't till some wan tells him. Pether Bowbeen down be th' Frinch church is formin' th' Circle Francaize Anglo-Saxon club, an' me ol' frind Dominigo that used to boss th' Ar-rchey R-road wagon whin Callaghan had th' sthreet conthract will march at th' head iv th' Dago Anglo-Saxons whin th' time comes. There ar-re twinty thousan' Rooshian Jews at a quarther a vote in th' Sivinth Ward; an', ar-rmed with rag hooks, they'd be a tur-r-ble thing f'r anny inimy iv th' Anglo-Saxon 'lieance to face. Th' Bohemians an' Pole Anglo-Saxons may be a little slow in wakin' up to what th' pa-apers calls our common hurt-age, but ye may be sure they'll be all r-right whin they're called on. We've got together an Anglo-Saxon 'lieance in this wa-ard, an' we're goin' to ilict Sarsfield O'Brien prisidint, Hugh O'Neill Darsey vice-prisidint, Robert Immitt Clancy sicrety, an' Wolfe Tone Malone three-asurer. O'Brien'll be a good wan to have. He was in the Fenian r-raid, an' his father carrid a pike in forty-eight. An' he's in th' Clan. Be-sides, he has a sthrong pull with th' Ancient Ordher iv Anglo-Saxon Hi-bernyans.

"I tell ye, whin th' Clan an' th' Sons iv Sweden an' th' Banana Club an' th' Circle Francaize an' th' Pollacky Benivolent Society an' th' Rooshian Sons of Dinnymite an' th' Benny Brith an' th' Coffee Clutch that Schwartzmeister r-runs an' th' Tur-rnd'ye-mind an' th' Holland society an' th' Afro-Americans an' th' other Anglo-Saxons begin f'r to raise their Anglo-Saxon battle-cry, it'll be all day with th' eight or nine people in th' wurruld that has th' misfortune iv not bein' brought up Anglo-Saxons."

"They'se goin' to be a debate on th' 'lieance at th' ninety-eight picnic at Ogden's gr-rove," said Mr. Hennessy.

"P'r'aps," said Mr. Dooley, sweetly, "ye might like to borry th' loan iv an ice-pick."

Part Five

THE CITY

Jacob Riis, *How the Other Half Lives*
William Dean Howells, *An East-Side Ramble*
Benjamin Orange Flower, *A Pilgrimage and a Vision*
Stephen Crane, *An Experiment in Misery*
Frank Norris, *A Hotel Bedroom*
Stephen Crane, *The Men in the Storm*
Theodore Dreiser, *Curious Shifts of the Poor*

By the 1890's the city had become a paradigm of the American social dilemma. Swollen by European and rural immigration and governed corruptly or inadequately, the great cities of the Eastern seaboard and the Midwest were painful reminders that a country which boasted of its Christian and democratic ideals did not necessarily practice them. The image of two Englands—the rich and the poor—used by Disraeli in the 1840's was adapted by Jacob Riis in *How the Other Half Lives*. The "Other Half" of America's greatest city lived poorly indeed, as Riis' widely read book documented, and the gap between ideal and reality which he and other writers publicized raised the inevitable question: What to Do?

William Dean Howells, Benjamin Orange Flower, and many other men of good will attempted to answer this question. Though their replies differed in tone and literary skill, they displayed many similarities in theme and form. Typically, the author described slum life within the framework of a visit by an outsider, a device which permitted explicit and implicit comparisons of the two worlds of the city, the rich and the poor. The visitor was shocked by the realities of slum life, but he found that the slum dwellers themselves were not to blame for the conditions of their lives. They were for the most part "good people" whose degradation was a result of their surroundings. Personal charity, therefore, was not a solution to their ills. Rather, Christ's principles were to serve as the basis for shaping a new environment and a new society. Thus, the visit often concluded with an account of a third world, that of the ideal city of the future—though this programmatic conclusion varied from Howells' vague reference to "public control" to Flower's full-blown vision of a Utopia of human brotherhood.

Stephen Crane's "An Experiment in Misery" is partly within this form, but the sketch also represents a significant departure from its central ethic. Although the Bowery visitor is an outsider, he not only observes but also shares. His first-hand experience of Bowery life leads him not to a plea for reform but to a recognition of the unbridgeable chasm between the two divisions of the city. The "sternly high" buildings of downtown New York are "emblematic" of the distance between the derelicts of City Hall Park and the successful businessmen who hurry through the Park on their way to work.

Crane's ability to distinguish between observed reality and moral suasion also characterizes Frank Norris' and Theodore Dreiser's writing on the city and is the source of the permanence of their city sketches and fiction. For example, Norris' "A Hotel Bedroom," with its coldly enumerative description of the contents of a bare, antiseptic room, captures the anonymity and impersonality of much city life. Crane and Dreiser wrote in the same spirit despite their greatly differing styles. Their intent was to render a basic truth of city life graphically and therefore symbolically—the struggle for warmth and shelter in a hostile world in "The Men in the Storm," the sullen, dispassionate weak-mindedness of the derelicts in "Curious Shifts of the Poor." In the best of their writing about the city, Norris, Crane, and Dreiser found not two worlds but one. That is, they discovered in the poor and degraded of the city qualities of human nature and experience characteristic of all life. Their work thus plays a role in one of the most important developments in modern literary history: the writer's almost unconscious shift from the natural to the man-made and from the country to the city for the concrete particulars of a generalized vision of experience. The withdrawal by Norris, Crane, and Dreiser from an overt social commentary such as Howells' and Flower's is not the rejection of social conscience that it appears to be. It is inseparable from an imaginative wisdom which senses that social justice is subsumed under universal meaning.

Jacob Riis
How the Other Half Lives

INTRODUCTION

LONG AGO it was said that "one half of the world does not know how the other half lives." That was true then. It did not know because it did not care. The half that was on top cared little for the struggles, and less for the fate of those who were underneath, so long as it was able to hold them there and keep its own seat. There came a time when the discomfort and crowding below were so great, and the consequent upheavals so violent, that it was no longer an easy thing to do, and then the upper half fell to inquiring what was the matter. Information on the subject has been accumulating rapidly since, and the whole world has had its hands full answering for its old ignorance.

In New York, the youngest of the world's great cities, that time came later than elsewhere, because the crowding had not been so great. There were those who believed that it would never come; but their hopes were vain. Greed and reckless selfishness wrought like results here as in the cities of older lands. "When the great riot occurred in 1863," so reads the testimony of the Secretary of the Prison Association of New York before a legislative committee appointed to investigate causes of the increase of crime in the State twenty-five years ago, "every hiding-place and nursery of crime discovered itself by immediate and active participation in the operations of the mob. Those very places and domiciles, and all that are like them, are to-day

How the Other Half Lives (New York, 1890), pp. 1–20. Text from this edition. I have omitted a number of diagrams of tenement housing which accompany the text.

nurseries of crime, and of the vices and disorderly courses which lead to crime. By far the largest part—eighty per cent. at least—of crimes against property and against the person are perpetrated by individuals who have either lost connection with home life, or never had any, or whose *homes had ceased to be sufficiently separate, decent, and desirable to afford what are regarded as ordinary wholesome influences of home and family*. . . . The younger criminals seem to come almost exclusively from the worst tenement house districts, that is, when traced back to the very places where they had their homes in the city here." Of one thing New York made sure at that early stage of the inquiry: the boundary line of the Other Half lies through the tenements.

It is ten years and over, now, since that line divided New York's population evenly. To-day three-fourths of its people live in the tenements, and the nineteenth century drift of the population to the cities is sending ever-increasing multitudes to crowd them. The fifteen thousand tenant houses that were the despair of the sanitarian in the past generation have swelled into thirty-seven thousand, and more than twelve hundred thousand persons call them home. The one way out he saw—rapid transit to the suburbs—has brought no relief. We know now that there is no way out; that the "system" that was the evil offspring of public neglect and private greed has come to stay, a storm-centre forever of our civilization. Nothing is left but to make the best of a bad bargain.

What the tenements are and how they grew to what they are, we shall see hereafter. The story is dark enough, drawn from the plain public records, to send a chill to any heart. If it shall appear that the sufferings and the sins of the "other half," and the evil they breed, are but as a just punishment upon the community that gave it no other choice, it will be because that is the truth. The boundary line lies there because, while the forces for good on one side vastly outweigh the bad—it were not well otherwise—in the tenements all the influences make for evil; because they are the hot-beds of the epidemics that carry death to rich and poor alike; the nurseries of pauperism and crime that fill our jails and police courts; that throw off a scum of forty thousand human wrecks to the island asylums and workhouses year by year; that turned out in the last eight years a round half million beggars to prey upon our charities; that maintain a standing army of ten thousand tramps with all that that implies; because, above all, they touch the family life with deadly moral contagion. This is their worst crime, inseparable from the system. That we have to own it the child of our own wrong does not excuse it, even though it gives it claim upon our utmost patience and tenderest charity.

What are you going to do about it? is the question of to-day. It was asked once of our city in taunting defiance by a band of political cutthroats, the legitimate outgrowth of life on the tenement-house level. Law and order found the answer then and prevailed. With our enormously swelling population held in this galling bondage, will that answer always be given? It will depend on how fully the situation that prompted the challenge is grasped. Forty per cent. of the distress among the poor, said a recent official report, is due to drunkenness. But the first legislative committee ever appointed to probe this sore went deeper down and uncovered its roots. The "conclusion forced itself upon it that certain conditions and associations of human life and habitation are the prolific parents of corresponding habits and morals," and it recommended "the prevention of drunkenness by providing for every man a clean and comfortable home." Years after, a sanitary inquiry brought to light the fact that "more than one-half of the tenements with two-thirds of their population were held by owners who made the keeping of them a business, *generally a speculation*. The owner was seeking a certain percentage on his outlay, and that percentage very rarely fell below fifteen per cent., and frequently exceeded thirty. . . . The complaint was universal among the tenants that they were entirely uncared for, and that the only answer to their requests to have the place put in order by repairs and necessary improvements was that they must pay their rent or leave. The agent's instructions were simple but emphatic: 'Collect the rent in advance, or, failing, eject the occupants.' " Upon such a stock grew this upas-tree. Small wonder the fruit is bitter. The remedy that shall be an effective answer to the coming appeal for justice must proceed from the public conscience. Neither legislation nor charity can cover the ground. The greed of capital that wrought the evil must itself undo it, as far as it can now be undone. Homes must be built for the working masses by those who employ their labor; but tenements must cease to be "good property" in the old, heartless sense. "Philanthropy and five per cent." is the penance exacted.

If this is true from a purely economic point of view, what then of the outlook from the Christian standpoint? Not long ago a great meeting was held in this city, of all denominations of religious faith, to discuss the question how to lay hold of these teeming masses in the tenements with Christian influences, to which they are now too often strangers. Might not the conference have found in the warning of one Brooklyn builder, who has invested his capital on this plan and made it pay more than a money interest, a hint worth heeding: "How shall the love of God be understood by those who have been nurtured in sight only of the greed of man?"

GENESIS OF THE TENEMENT

The first tenement New York knew bore the mark of Cain from its birth, though a generation passed before the writing was deciphered. It was the "rear house," infamous ever after in our city's history. There had been tenant-houses before, but they were not built for the purpose. Nothing would probably have shocked their original owners more than the idea of their harboring a promiscuous crowd; for they were the decorous homes of the old Knickerbockers, the proud aristocracy of Manhattan in the early days.

It was the stir and bustle of trade, together with the tremendous immigration that followed upon the war of 1812 that dislodged them. In thirty-five years the city of less than a hundred thousand came to harbor half a million souls, for whom homes had to be found. Within the memory of men not yet in their prime, Washington had moved from his house on Cherry Hill as too far out of town to be easily reached. Now the old residents followed his example; but they moved in a different direction and for a different reason. Their comfortable dwellings in the once fashionable streets along the East River front fell into the hands of real-estate agents and boarding-house keepers; and here, says the report to the Legislature of 1857, when the evils engendered had excited just alarm, "in its beginning, the tenant-house became a real blessing to that class of industrious poor whose small earnings limited their expenses, and whose employment in workshops, stores, or about the warehouses and thoroughfares, render a near residence of much importance." Not for long, however. As business increased, and the city grew with rapid strides, the necessities of the poor became the opportunity of their wealthier neighbors, and the stamp was set upon the old houses, suddenly become valuable, which the best thought and effort of a later age have vainly struggled to efface. Their *large* rooms were partitioned into *several smaller ones,* without regard to light or ventilation, the rate of rent being lower in proportion to space or height from the street; and they soon became filled from cellar to garret with a class of tenantry living from hand to mouth, loose in morals, improvident in habits, degraded, and squalid as beggary itself." It was thus the dark bedroom, prolific of untold depravities, came into the world. It was destined to survive the old houses. In their new rôle, says the old report, eloquent in its indignant denunciation of "evils more destructive than wars," "they were not intended to last. Rents were fixed high enough to cover damage and abuse from this class, from whom nothing was expected, and the most was made of them while they lasted. Neatness, order, cleanliness, were never dreamed of in connection with the tenant-house system, as it spread its localities from year to year; while reckless slovenliness, discontent, privation, and ignorance were left to work out their invariable results, until the entire premises reached the level of tenant-house dilapidation, containing, but sheltering not, the miserable hordes that crowded beneath mouldering, water-rotted roofs or burrowed among the rats of clammy cellars." Yet so illogical is human greed that, at a later day, when called to account, "the proprietors frequently urged the filthy habits of the tenants as an excuse for the condition of their property, utterly losing sight of the fact that it was the tolerance of those habits which was the real evil, and that for this they themselves were alone responsible."

Still the pressure of the crowds did not abate, and in the old garden where the stolid Dutch burgher grew his tulips or early cabbages a rear house was built, generally of wood, two stories high at first. Presently it was carried up another story, and another. Where two families had lived ten moved in. The front house followed suit, if the brick walls were strong enough. The question was not always asked, judging from complaints made by a contemporary witness, that the old buildings were "often carried up to a great height without regard to the strength of the foundation walls." It was rent the owner was after; nothing was said in the contract about either the safety or the comfort of the tenants. The garden gate no longer swung on its rusty hinges. The shell-paved walk had become an alley; what the rear house had left of the garden, a "court." Plenty such are yet to be found in the Fourth Ward, with here and there one of the original rear tenements.

Worse was to follow. It was "soon perceived by estate owners and agents of property that a greater percentage of profits could be realized by the conversion of houses and blocks into barracks, and dividing their space into smaller proportions capable of containing human life within four walls. . . . Blocks were rented of real estate owners, or 'purchased on time,' or taken in charge at a percentage, and held for under-letting." With the appearance of the middleman, wholly irresponsible, and utterly reckless and unrestrained, began the era of tenement building which turned out such blocks as Gotham Court, where, in one cholera epidemic that scarcely touched the clean wards, the tenants died at the rate of one hundred and ninety-five to the thousand of population; which forced the general mortality of the city up from 1 in 41.83 in 1815, to 1 in 27.33 in 1855, a year of unusual freedom from epidemic disease, and which wrung from the early organizers of the Health Department this wail: "There are numerous examples of tenement-houses in which are lodged several hundred people that have a *pro rata* allotment of ground area scarcely equal to two square yards upon the city lot, court-yards and all in-cluded." The tenement-house population had swelled to half a million souls by that time, and on the East Side, in what is still the most densely populated district in all the world, China not excluded, it was packed at the rate of 290,000 to the square mile, a state of affairs wholly unexampled. The utmost cupidity of other lands and other days had never contrived to herd much more than half that number within the same space. The greatest crowding of Old London was at the rate of 175,816. Swine roamed the streets and gutters as their principal scavengers. The death of a child in a tenement was regis-tered at the Bureau of Vital Statistics as "plainly due to suffocation in the foul air of an unventilated apartment," and the Senators, who had come down from Albany to find out what was the matter with New York, reported that "there are annually cut off from the population by disease and death enough human beings to people a city, and enough human labor to sustain it." And yet experts had testified that, as compared with up-town, rents were from twenty-five to thirty per cent. higher in the worst slums of the lower wards, with such accom-modations as were enjoyed, for instance, by a "family with boarders" in Cedar Street, who fed hogs in the cellar that contained eight or ten loads of manure; or "one room 12 x 12 with five families living in it, comprising twenty persons of both sexes and all ages, with only two beds, without partition, screen, chair, or table." The rate of rent has been successfully maintained to the present day, though the hog at least has been eliminated.

Lest anybody flatter himself with the notion that these were evils of a day that is happily past and may safely be forgotten, let me men-tion here three very recent instances of tenement-house life that came under my notice. One was the burning of a rear house in Mott Street, from appearances one of the original tenant-houses that made their owners rich. The fire made homeless ten families, who had paid an average of $5 a month for their mean little cubby-holes. The owner himself told me that it was *fully* insured for $800, though it brought him in $600 a year rent. He evidently considered himself especially entitled to be pitied for losing such valuable property. Another was the case of a hard-working family of man and wife, young people from the old country, who took poison together in a Crosby Street tenement because they were "tired." There was no other explanation, and none was needed when I stood in the room in which they had lived. It was in the attic with sloping ceiling and a single window so far out on the roof that it seemed not to belong to the place at all. With scarcely room enough to turn around in they had been compelled to pay five dollars and a half a month in advance. There were four such rooms in that attic, and together they brought in as much as many a handsome little cottage in a pleasant part of Brooklyn. The third instance was that of a colored family of husband, wife, and baby in a wretched rear rookery in West Third Street. Their rent was eight dollars and a half for a single room on the top-story, so small that I was unable to get a photograph of it even by placing the camera outside the open door. Three short steps across either way would have measured its full extent.

There was just one excuse for the early tenement-house builders, and their successors may plead it with nearly as good right for what it is worth. "Such," says an official report, "is the lack of house-room in the city that any kind of tenement can be immediately crowded with lodgers, if there is space offered." Thousands were living in cellars. There were three hundred underground lodging-houses in the city when the Health Department was organized. Some fifteen years before that the old Baptist Church in Mulberry Street, just off Chatham Street, had been sold, and the rear half of the frame structure had been converted into tenements that with their swarming population became the scandal even of that reckless age. The wretched pile harbored no less than forty families, and the annual rate of deaths to the population was officially stated to be 75 in 1,000. These tenements were an extreme type of very many, for the big barracks had by this time spread east and west and far up the island into the sparsely settled wards. Whether or not the title was clear to the land upon which they were built was of less account than that the rents were collected. If there were damages to pay, the tenant had to foot them. Cases were "very frequent when property was in litigation, and two or three different parties were collecting rents." Of course under such circumstances "no repairs were ever made."

The climax had been reached. The situation was summed up by the Society for the Improvement of the Condition of the Poor in these words: "Crazy old buildings, crowded rear tenements in filthy yards, dark, damp basements, leaking garrets, shops, outhouses, and stables converted into dwellings, though scarcely fit to shelter brutes, are habitations of thousands of our fellow-beings in this wealthy, Christian city." "The city," says its historian, Mrs. Martha Lamb, commenting on the era of aqueduct building between 1835 and 1845, "was a general asylum for vagrants." Young vagabonds, the natural offspring of such "home" conditions, overran the streets. Juvenile crime increased fearfully year by year. The Children's Aid Society and kindred philanthropic organizations were yet unborn, but in the city directory was to be found the address of the "American Society for the Promotion of Education in Africa."

THE AWAKENING

The dread of advancing cholera, with the guilty knowledge of the harvest field that awaited the plague in New York's slums, pricked the conscience of the community into action soon after the close of the war. A citizens' movement resulted in the organization of a Board of Health and the adoption of the "Tenement-House Act" of 1867, the first step toward remedial legislation. A thorough canvass of the tenements had been begun already in the previous year; but the cholera first, and next a scourge of small-pox, delayed the work, while emphasizing the need of it, so that it was 1869 before it got fairly under way and began to tell. The dark bedroom fell under the ban first. In that year the Board ordered the cutting of more than forty-six thousand windows in interior rooms, chiefly for ventilation—for little or no light was to be had from the dark hallways. Air-shafts were unknown. The saw had a job all that summer; by early fall nearly all the orders had been carried out. Not without opposition; obstacles were thrown in the way of the officials on the one side by the owners of the tenements, who saw in every order to repair or clean up only an item of added expense to diminish their income from the rent; on the other side by the tenants themselves, who had sunk, after a generation of unavailing protest, to the level of their surroundings, and were at last content to remain there. The tenements had bred their Nemesis, a proletariat ready and able to avenge the wrongs of their crowds. Already it taxed the city heavily for the support of its jails and charities. The basis of opposition, curiously enough, was the same at both extremes; owner and tenant alike considered official interference an infringement of personal rights, and a hardship. It took long years of weary labor to make good the claim of the sunlight to such corners of the dens as it could reach at all. Not until five years after did the department succeed at last in ousting the "cave-dwellers" and closing some five hundred and fifty cellars south of Houston Street, many of them below tide-water, that had been used as living apartments. In many instances the police had to drag the tenants out by force.

The work went on; but the need of it only grew with the effort. The Sanitarians were following up an evil that grew faster than they went; like a fire, it could only be headed off, not chased, with success. Official reports, read in the churches in 1879, characterized the younger criminals as victims of low social conditions of life and unhealthy, overcrowded lodgings, brought up in "an atmosphere of actual darkness, moral and physical." This after the saw had been busy in the dark corners ten years! "If we could see the air breathed by these poor creatures in their tenements," said a well-known physician, "it would show itself to be fouler than the mud of the gutters." Little improvement was apparent despite all that had been done. "The new tenements, that have been recently built, have been usually as badly planned as the old, with dark and unhealthy rooms, often over wet cellars, where extreme overcrowding is permitted," was the verdict of one authority. These are the houses that today perpetuate the worst traditions of the past, and they are counted by thousands. The Five Points had been cleansed, as far as the immediate neighborhood was concerned, but the Mulberry Street Bend was fast outdoing it in foulness not a stone's throw away, and new centres of corruption were continually springing up and getting the upper hand whenever vigilance was relaxed for ever so short a time. It is one of the curses of the tenement-house system that the worst houses exercise a levelling influence upon all the rest, just as one bad boy in a schoolroom will spoil the whole class. It is one of the ways the evil that was "the result of forgetfulness of the poor," as the Council of Hygiene mildly put it, has of avenging itself.

The determined effort to head it off by laying a strong hand upon the tenement builders that has been the chief business of the Health Board of recent years, dates from this period. The era of the air-shaft has not solved the problem of housing the poor, but it has made good use of limited opportunities. Over the new houses sanitary law exercises full control. But the old remain. They cannot be summarily torn down, though in extreme cases the authorities can order them cleared. The outrageous overcrowding, too, remains. It is characteristic of the tenements. Poverty, their badge and typical condition, invites —compels it. All efforts to abate it result only in temporary relief. As long as they exist it will exist with them. And the tenements will exist in New York forever.

To-day, what is a tenement? The law defines it as a house "occupied by three or more families, living independently and doing their cooking on the premises; or by more than two families on a floor, so living and cooking and having a common right in the halls, stairways, yards, etc." That is the legal meaning, and includes flats and apartment-houses, with which we have nothing to do. In its narrower sense the typical tenement was thus described when last arraigned before the bar of public justice: "It is generally a brick building from four to six stories high on the street, frequently with a store on the first floor which, when used for the sale of liquor, has a side opening for the benefit of the inmates and to evade the Sunday law; four families occupy each floor, and a set of rooms consists of one or two dark closets, used as bedrooms, with a living room twelve feet by ten. The staircase is too often a dark well in the centre of the house, and no direct through ventilation is possible, each family being separated from the

other by partitions. Frequently the rear of the lot is occupied by another building of three stories high with two families on a floor." The
picture is nearly as true to-day as ten years ago, and will be for a long
time to come. The dim light admitted by the air-shaft shines upon
greater crowds than ever. Tenements are still "good property," and
the poverty of the poor man his destruction. A barrack down town
where he *has to live* because he is poor brings in a third more rent
than a decent flat house in Harlem. The statement once made a sensation that between seventy and eighty children had been found in
one tenement. It no longer excites even passing attention, when the
sanitary police report counting 101 adults and 91 children in a Crosby
Street house, one of twins, built together. The children in the other,
if I am not mistaken, numbered 89, a total of 180 for two tenements!
Or when a midnight inspection in Mulberry Street unearths a hundred and fifty "lodgers" sleeping on filthy floors in two buildings. Spite
of brown-stone trimmings, plate-glass and mosaic vestibule floors, the
water does not rise in summer to the second story, while the beer
flows unchecked to the all-night picnics on the roof. The saloon with
the side-door and the landlord divide the prosperity of the place between them, and the tenant, in sullen submission, foots the bills.

Where are the tenements of to-day? Say rather: where are they
not? In fifty years they have crept up from the Fourth Ward slums
and the Five Points the whole length of the island, and have polluted
the Annexed District to the Westchester line. Crowding all the
lower wards, wherever business leaves a foot of ground unclaimed;
strung along both rivers, like ball and chain tied to the foot of every
street, and filling up Harlem with their restless, pent-up multitudes,
they hold within their clutch the wealth and business of New York,
hold them at their mercy in the day of mob-rule and wrath. The bullet-
proof shutters, the stacks of hand-grenades, and the Gatling guns of
the Sub-Treasury are tacit admissions of the fact and of the quality of
the mercy expected. The tenements to-day are New York, harboring
three-fourths of its population. When another generation shall have
doubled the census of our city, and to that vast army of workers, held
captive by poverty, the very name of home shall be as a bitter mock-
ery, what will the harvest be?

William Dean Howells
An East-Side Ramble

THE NEW YORKERS, following the custom of Europe, often fence themselves about with a great deal of ceremony in social matters, even such small social matters as making calls.

Some ladies have days when they receive calls; others have no specified day, and then you take your chance of being turned from the door without seeing them, or if you find them, of finding them reluctant and preoccupied. A friend of mine says he has often felt as if he had been admitted through the error of the man or the maid who opened the door to him at such houses, and who returned, after carrying up his name, to say, with a frightened air, that the lady would be down in a moment.

But when there are days there is never any misgiving about letting you in. The door is whisked open before you have had time to ring, sometimes by a servant who has the effect of not belonging to the house, but hired for the afternoon. Then you leave your card on a platter of some sort in the hall to attest the fact of your visit, and at the simpler houses find your way into the drawing-room unannounced, though the English custom of shouting your name before you is very common and is always observed where there is any pretense to fashion. Certain ladies receive once a week throughout the season; others receive on some day each week of December or January or February, as the case may be. When there is this limit to a month, the reception insensibly takes on the character of an afternoon tea, and, in fact, it varies from that only in being a little less crowded. There is tea or chocolate or mild punch and a table spread with pastries and sweets, which hardly any one touches. A young lady dedicates herself to the service of each urn and offers you the beverage that flows from it. There is a great air of gayety, a very excited chatter of female voices, a constant flutter of greeting and leave-taking and a general sense of amiable emptiness and bewildered kindness when you come away. The genius of these little affairs is supposed to be informality,

Impressions and Experiences (New York, 1896), pp. 127–49. Text from this edition.

but at some houses where you enjoy such informalities you find two men in livery on the steps outside, a third opens the door for you, a fourth takes your hat and stick, a fifth receives your overcoat and a sixth catches at your name and miscalls it into the drawing room.

I.

But I must not give too exclusive an impression of ceremony in the New-Yorkers. I made some calls about Christmas-time last year in a quarter of the city where the informalities are real and where the hospitalities, such as they were, I thought as sincere as in the houses where the informalities are more apparent. The sort of calls I made were rather fashionable some years ago, but are so no longer. It was a fad to make them, and the fad, like all really nice fads, came from England, and perhaps it has now died out here because it has died out there. At any rate, it seems certain that there is now less interest, less curiosity, concerning the home life of the poor than there was then among the comfortable people. I do not say there is less sympathy— there must be still a good deal of sympathy—but I should say there was less hope with the well-to-do of bettering the condition of the ill-to-do; some philosophers even warn us against indulging a feeling of commiseration, lest it should encourage the poor to attempt themselves to better their condition.

Yet there are no signs of rebellion on the part of the poor, whom I found as tame and peaceful, apparently, when I went the rounds of their unceremonious at-homes as the most anxious philosopher could desire. My calls were by no means of the nature of a perquisition, but they left very little unknown to me, I fancy, of the way the poor live, so frank and simple is their life. They included some tenements of the American quarter, near the point of the island, on the West Side, and a rather greater number on the East Side, in the heart of the district abandoned chiefly to the Russian Jews, though there are no doubt other nationalities to be found there. It is said to be more densely populated than any other area in the world, or at least in Christendom, for within a square mile there are more than three hundred and fifty thousand men, women and children. One can imagine from this fact alone how they are housed and what their chances of the comforts and decencies of life may be. But I must not hurry to the region of these homes before I have first tried to show the interiors of that quarter called American, where I found the Americans represented, as they are so often, by Irish people. The friend who went with me on my calls led me across the usual surface tracks, under the usual elevated tracks, and suddenly dodged before me into an alleyway about two feet wide. This crept under houses fronting on the squalid street we had left and gave into a sort of court some ten or twelve feet wide by thirty or forty feet long. The buildings surrounding it were low and very old. One of them was a stable, which contributed its stench to the odors that rose from the reeking pavement and from the closets filling an end of the court, with a corner left beside them for the hydrant that supplied the water of the whole inclosure. It is from this court that the inmates of the tenements have their sole chance of sun and air. What the place must be in summer I had not the heart to think, and on the wintry day of my visit I could not feel the fury of the skies which my guide said would have been evident to me if I had seen it in August. I could better fancy this when I climbed the rickety stairs within one of the houses and found myself in a typical New York tenement. Then I almost choked at the thought of what a hot day, what a hot night, must be in such a place, with the two small windows inhaling the putrid breath of the court and transmitting it, twice fouled by the passage through the living-room, to the black hole in the rear, where the whole family lay on the heap of rags that passed for a bed.

We had our choice which door to knock at on the narrow landing, a yard wide at most, which opened into such tenements to the right and left, as many stories up as the stairs mounted. We stood at once in the presence of the hostess; there was no ceremony of sending in our cards here, or having our names called to her. In one case we found her over the washtub, with her three weeks' babe bundled in a chair beside it. A table, with a half-eaten loaf, that formed her break-fast, on it, helped, with the cooking-stove, to crowd the place past any possibility of sitting down, if there had been chairs to sit in; so we stood, as people do at an afternoon tea. At sight of us the woman be-gan to cry and complain that her man had been drunk and idle for a month and did nothing for her; though in these times he might have been sober and idle and done as little. Some good soul was paying the rent for her, which was half as great as would have hired a de-cent flat in a good part of the town; but how her food came or the coal for her stove remained a mystery which we did not try to solve. She wiped her tears at the exhibition of a small coin, which she had perhaps dimly foreseen through them from the moment they began to flow. It was wrong, perhaps, to give her money, but it was not very wrong, perhaps, for the money was not very much, and if it pauper-ized her it could not have been said that she was wholly unpauper-ized before she took it. These are very difficult cases, but all life is a hopeless tangle, and the right is something that does not show itself at once, especially in economical affairs.

In another tenement we found a family as gay and hopeful as this was dismal and desperate. An Irish lady with a stylish fringe of red

hair decorating her forehead, welcomed us with excuses for the state
of the apartment, which in the next breath she proved herself very
proud of, for she said that if people were not comfortable in their
houses it was because they were slovenly and untidy. I could not
see that she was neater than her neighbor on the landing below. She
had a florid taste in pictures, and half a dozen large colored prints
went far to hide the walls, which, she said, the landlord had lately had
whitewashed, though to eyes less fond than hers they showed a livid
blue. The whitewashing was the sole repairs which had been put
upon her tenement since she came into it, but she seemed to think it
quite enough; and her man, who sat at leisure near the stove, in the
three days' beard which seems inseparable from idle poverty, was
quite boastful of its advantages. He said that he had lived in that court
for thirty years and there was no such air anywhere else in this world.
I could readily believe him, being there to smell it and coming away
with the taste of it in my mouth. Like other necessaries of life, it must
have been rather scanty in that happy home, especially at night, when
the dark fell outside and a double dark thickened in the small bin
which stood open to our gaze at the end of the room. The whitewash
seemed not to have penetrated to this lair, where a frowzy mattress
showed itself on a rickety bedstead. The beds in these sleeping-holes
were never made up; they were rounded into a heap and seemed
commonly of a coarse brown sacking. They had always a horrible
fascination for me. I fancied them astir with a certain life which, if
there had been a consensus of it to that effect, might have walked off
with them.

All the tenements here were of this size and shape—a room with
windows opening upon the court and at the rear the small black bin
or pen for the bed. The room was perhaps twelve feet square and the
bin was six, and for such a dwelling the tenant pays six dollars a month.
If he fails to pay it he is evicted, and some thirty thousand evictions
have taken place in the past year. But an eviction is by no means the
dreadful hardship the reader would perhaps imagine it. To be sure,
it means putting the tenant on the sidewalk with his poor household
gear in any weather and at any hour; but if it is very cold or very wet
weather, the evicted family is seldom suffered to pass the night there.
The wretched neighbors gather about and take them in, and their life
begins again on the old terms; or the charities come to their aid, and
they are dispersed into the different refuges until the father or mother
can find another hole for them to crawl into. Still, natural as it all is, I
should think it must surprise an Irishman, who supposed he had left
eviction behind him in his native land, to find it so rife in the country
of his adoption.

II.

My friend asked me if I would like to go into any other tenements, but I thought that if what I had seen was typical, I had seen enough in that quarter. The truth is, I had not yet accustomed myself to going in upon people in that way, though they seemed accustomed to being gone in upon without any ceremony but the robust "Good-morning!" my companion gave them by way of accounting for our presence, and I wanted a little interval to prepare myself for further forays. The people seemed quite ready to be questioned, and answered us as persons in authority. They may have taken us for detectives, or agents of benevolent societies, or journalists in search of copy. In any case, they had nothing to lose and they might have something to gain; so they received us kindly and made us as much at home among them as they knew how. It may have been that in some instances they supposed that we were members of the Board of Health and were their natural allies against their landlords.

I had not realized before how much this noble institution can befriend the poor, so potently sustained as it is in the discharge of its duties by the popular sentiment in a land where popular sentiment is so often so weak. It has full power, in the public interest, to order repairs and betterments necessary for the general health in any domicile, rich or poor, in the city, and no man's pleasure or profit may hinder it. In cases of contagion or infection, it may isolate the neighborhood or vacate the premises, or, in certain desperate conditions, destroy them. As there are always pestilences of some sort preying upon the poor (as if their poverty were not enough), my companion could point out a typhus quarter, which the Board had shut up and which we must not approach. Such minor plagues as smallpox, scarlet-fever, and diphtheria are quickly discovered and made known, and the places that they have infested are closed till they can be thoroughly purified. Any tenant believing his premises to be in an unwholesome or dangerous state may call in the Board, and from its decision the landlord has no appeal. He must make the changes the Board ordains, and he must make them at his own cost, though no doubt, when the tenant can pay, he contrives somehow to make him pay in the end. The landlord, especially if he battens on the poorer sort of tenants, is always in fear of the Board, and the tenant is in love with it, for he knows that, in a community otherwise delivered over to the pursuit of pelf or pleasure, it stands his ready friend, whose mandate private interest obeys as it obeys no other. It seems to have more honor than any other institution among us, and, amid the most frightful corruption of every kind, to remain incorruptible. Very likely the landlord may sometimes think that it abuses its power, but the tenant never thinks so, and the public seems always to agree with the tenant. The press, which is so keen to scent out paternalism in municipal or national affairs, has not yet perceived any odor of it in the Board of Health, and stands its constant friend, though it embodies in the most distinctive form the principle that, in a civilized community, the collective interest is supreme. Even if such an extension of its powers were not in the order of evolution, it would not be so illogical for the Board of Health to command the abatement of poverty when the diseases that flow from poverty cannot be otherwise abated. I should not like to prophesy that it will ever do so, but stranger things have happened through the necessity that knows no law, not even the law of demand and supply—the demand of Moloch and the supply of Misery.

III.

I do not know whether the Hebrew quarter, when I began to make my calls there, seemed any worse than the American quarter or not. But I noticed presently a curious subjective effect in myself, which I offer for the reader's speculation.

There is something in a very little experience of such places that blunts the perception, so that they do not seem so dreadful as they are; and I should feel as if I were exaggerating if I recorded my first impression of their loathsomeness. I soon came to look upon the conditions as normal, not for me, indeed, or for the kind of people I mostly consort with, but for the inmates of the dens and lairs about me. Perhaps this was partly their fault; they were uncomplaining, if not patient, in circumstances where I believe a single week's sojourn, with no more hope of a better lot than they could have, would make anarchists of the best people in the city. Perhaps the poor people themselves are not so thoroughly persuaded that there is anything very unjust in their fate, as the compassionate think. They at least do not know the better fortune of others, and they have the habit of passively enduring their own. I found them usually cheerful in the Hebrew quarter, and they had so much courage as enabled them to keep themselves noticeably clean in an environment where I am afraid their betters would scarcely have had heart to wash their faces and comb their hair. There was even a decent tidiness in their dress, which I did not find very ragged, though it often seemed unseasonable and insufficient. But here again, as in many other phases of life, I was struck by men's heroic superiority to their fate, if their fate is hard; and I felt anew that if prosperous and comfortable people were as good in proportion to their fortune as these people were they would be as the angels of light, which, I am afraid they now but faintly resemble.

One of the places we visited was a court somewhat like that we had already seen in the American quarter, but rather smaller and with more the effect of a pit, since the walls around it were so much higher. There was the same row of closets at one side and the hydrant next them, but here the hydrant was bound up in rags to keep it from freezing, apparently, and the wretched place was by no means so foul under foot. To be sure, there was no stable to contribute its filth, but we learned that a suitable stench was not wanting from a bakery in one of the basements, which a man in good clothes and a large watch-chain told us rose from it in suffocating fumes at a certain hour, when the baker was doing some unimaginable thing to the bread. This man seemed to be the employer of labor in one of the rooms above, and he said that when the smell began they could hardly breathe. He caught promptly at the notion of the Board of Health, and I dare say that the baker will be duly abated. None of the other people complained, but that was perhaps because they had only their Yiddish to complain in, and knew that it would be wasted on us. They seemed neither curious nor suspicious concerning us; they let us go everywhere, as if they had no thought of hindering us. One of the tenements we entered had just been vacated; but there was a little girl of ten there, with some much smaller children, amusing them in the empty space. Through a public-spirited boy, who had taken charge of us from the beginning and had a justly humorous sense of the situation, we learned that this little maid was not the sister but the servant of the others, for even in these low levels society makes its distinctions. I dare say that the servant was not suffered to eat with the others when they had anything to eat, and that when they had nothing her inferiority was somehow brought home to her. She may have been made to wait and famish after the others had hungered some time. She was a cheerful and friendly creature and her small brood were kept tidy like herself.

The basement under this vacant tenement we found inhabited, and though it was a most preposterous place for people to live, it was not as dirty as one would think. To be sure, it was not very light and all the dirt may not have been visible. One of the smiling women who were there made their excuses, "Poor people; cannot keep very nice," and laughed as if she had said a good thing. There was nothing in the room but a table and a few chairs and a stove, without fire, but they were all contentedly there together in the dark, which hardly let them see one another's faces. My companion struck a match and held it to the cavernous mouth of an inner cellar half as large as the room we were in, where it winked and paled so soon that I had only a glimpse of the bed, with the rounded heap of bedding on it; but out of this hole, as if she had been a rat, scared from it by the light, a young girl came, rubbing her eyes and vaguely smiling, and vanished up-stairs somewhere.

IV.

I found no shape or size of tenement but this. There was always the one room, where the inmates lived by day, and the one den, where they slept by night, apparently all in the same bed, though probably the children were strewn about the floor. If the tenement were high up the living-room had more light and air than if it were low down; but the sleeping-hole never had any light or air of its own. My calls were made on one of the mild days which fell before last Christmas, and so I suppose I saw these places at their best; but what they must be when the summer is seven times heated without, as it often is in New York, or when the arctic cold has pierced these hapless abodes and the inmates huddle together for their animal heat, the reader must imagine for himself. The Irish-Americans had flaming stoves, even on that soft day, but in the Hebrew tenements I found no fire. They were doubtless the better for this, and it is one of the comical anomalies of the whole affair that they are singularly healthy. The death rate among them is one of the lowest in the city, though whether for their final advantage it might not better be the highest, is one of the things one must not ask one's self. In their presence I should not dare to ask it, even in my deepest thought. They are then so like other human beings and really so little different from the best, except in their environment, that I had to get away from this before I could regard them as wild beasts.

I suppose there are and have been worse conditions of life, but if I stopped short of savage life I found it hard to imagine them. I did not exaggerate to myself the squalor that I saw, and I do not exaggerate it to the reader. As I have said, I was so far from sentimentalizing it that I almost immediately reconciled myself to it, as far as its victims were concerned. Still, it was squalor of a kind which, it seemed to me, it could not be possible to outrival anywhere in the life one commonly calls civilized. It is true that the Indians who formerly inhabited this island were no more comfortably lodged in their wigwams of bark and skins than these poor New-Yorkers in their tenements. But the wild men pay no rent, and if they are crowded together upon terms that equally forbid decency and comfort in their shelter, they have the freedom of the forest and the prairie about them; they have the illimitable sky and the whole light of day and the four winds to breathe when they issue into the open air. The New York tenement dwellers, even when they leave their lairs, are still pent in their high-walled streets, and inhale a thousand stenches of their own and others' making. The street, except in snow and rain, is always better than their horrible houses, and it is doubtless because they pass so much of their time in the street that the death rate is so low among them. Perhaps their domiciles can be best likened for darkness and discomfort to the dugouts or sod huts of the settlers on the great plains. But these are only temporary shelters, while the tenement dwellers have no hope of better housing; they have neither the prospect of a happier fortune through their own energy as the settlers have, nor any chance from the humane efforts and teachings of missionaries, like the savages. With the tenement dwellers it is from generation to generation, if not for the individual, then for the class, since no one expects that there will not always be tenement dwellers in New York as long as our present economical conditions endure.

V

When I first set out on my calls I provided myself with some small silver, which I thought I might fitly give, at least to the children, and in some of the first places I did this. But presently I began to fancy an unseemliness in it, as if it were an indignity added to the hardship of their lot, and to feel that unless I gave all my worldly wealth to them I was in a manner mocking their misery. I could not give everything, for then I should have had to come upon charity myself, and so I mostly kept my little coins in my pocket; but when we mounted into the court again from that cellar apartment and found an old, old woman there, wrinkled and yellow, with twinkling eyes and a toothless smile, waiting to see us, as if she were as curious in her way as we were in ours, I was tempted. She said in her Yiddish, which the humorous boy interpreted, that she was eighty years old, and she looked a hundred, while she babbled unintelligibly but very cheerfully on. I gave her a piece of twenty-five cents and she burst into a blessing, that I should not have thought could be bought for money. We did not stay to hear it out, but the boy did, and he followed to report it to me, with a gleeful interest in its beneficent exaggerations. If it is fulfilled I shall live to be a man of many and prosperous years, and I shall die possessed of wealth that will endow a great many colleges and found a score of libraries. I do not know whether the boy envied me or not, but I wish I could have left that benediction to him, for I took a great liking to him, his shrewd smile, his gay eyes, his promise of a Hebrew nose, and his whole wise little visage. He said that he went to school and studied reading, writing, geography and everything. All the children we spoke to said that they went to school, and they were quick and intelligent. They could mostly speak English, while most of their elders knew only Yiddish.

The sound of this was around us on the street we issued into, and which seemed from end to end a vast bazaar, where there was a great deal of selling, whether there was much buying or not. The place is humorously called the pig-market by the Christians, because everything in the world but pork is to be found there. To me its activity was a sorrowfully amusing satire upon the business ideal of our plutocratic civilization. These people were desperately poor, yet they preyed upon one another in their commerce, as if they could be enriched by selling dear or buying cheap. So far as I could see they would only impoverish each other more and more, but they trafficked as eagerly as if there were wealth in every bargain. The sidewalks and the roadways were thronged with peddlers and purchasers, and everywhere I saw splendid types of that old Hebrew world which had the sense if not the knowledge of God when all the rest of us lay sunk in heathen darkness. There were women with oval faces and olive tints, and clear, dark eyes, relucent as evening pools, and men with long beards of jetty black or silvery white, and the noble profiles of their race. I said to myself that it was among such throngs that Christ walked, it was from such people that he chose his Disciples and his friends; but I looked in vain for him in Hester street. Probably he was at that moment in Fifth Avenue.

VI.

After all, I was loath to come away. I should have liked to stay and live awhile with such as they, if the terms of their life had been possible, for there were phases of it that were very attractive. That constant meeting and that neighborly intimacy were superficially at least of a very pleasant effect, and though the whole place seemed abandoned to mere trade, it may have been a necessity of the case, for I am told that many of these Hebrews have another ideal, and think and vote in the hope that the land of their refuge shall yet some day keep its word to the world, so that men shall be equally free in it to the pursuit of happiness. I suppose they are mostly fugitives from the Russian persecution, and that from the cradle their days must have been full of fear and care, and from the time they could toil that they must have toiled at whatever their hands found to do. Yet they had not the look of a degraded people; they were quiet and orderly, and I saw none of the drunkenness or the truculence of an Irish or low American neighborhood among them. There were no policemen in sight, and the quiet behavior that struck me so much seemed not to have been enforced. Very likely they may have moods different from that I saw, but I only tell of what I saw, and I am by no means ready yet to preach poverty as a saving grace. Though they seemed so patient and even cheerful in some cases, I do not think it is well for human beings to live whole families together in one room with a kennel out of it, where modesty may survive, but decency is impossible. Neither do I think they can be the better men and women for being insufficiently clothed and fed, though so many of us appear none the better for being housed in palaces and clad in purple and fine linen and faring sumptuously every day.

I have tried to report simply and honestly what I saw of the life of our poorest people that day. One might say it was not so bad as it is painted, but I think it is quite as bad as it appeared; and I could not see that in itself or in its conditions it held the promise or the hope of anything better. If it is tolerable, it must endure; if it is intolerable, still it must endure. Here and there one will release himself from it, and doubtless numbers are alway doing this, as in the days of slavery there were always fugitives; but for the great mass the captivity remains. Upon the present terms of leaving the poor to be housed by private landlords, whose interest it is to get the greatest return of money for the money invested, the very poorest must always be housed as they are now. Nothing but public control in some form or other can secure them a shelter fit for human beings.

Benjamin Orange Flower
A Pilgrimage and a Vision

PERHAPS there is no more effective method of awakening the sleeping consciences of our people to a realization of the essential immorality and injustice of present social conditions, than by presenting some striking contrasts, such as may be witnessed by any one living

Arena, VII (March, 1893), 422–32. Republished in *Civilization's Inferno: Studies in the Social Cellar* (Boston, 1893), pp. 193–221. Text from *Civilization's Inferno*.

in our great cities, but which are usually overlooked in an age of fierce competition and ceaseless battle for gold. It is my purpose to give us simply as possible the story of an afternoon's pilgrimage recently taken through two commonwealths within the borders of Boston.

It was a cold, clear, crisp January afternoon. I left my office at one o'clock. Passing in front of the massive library building and the magnificent New Old South Church, one of the most imposing temples in our city, dedicated to the worship of the humble Son of Man, I turned down Boylston Street. On my left was the unpretentious Second Unitarian Church; on my right, across Copley Square, stood the showy and somewhat pretentious Back Bay Museum; almost directly in front rose that magnificent model of church architecture, Trinity, the pride of New England, and a church whose pewholders are worth many millions of dollars. On reaching Clarendon Street I turned toward the heart of the Back Bay, and in a few minutes I had passed the Commonwealth Avenue Baptist Church, whose heaven-piercing spire is ornamented with angels holding golden trumpets to their mouths, presumably proclaiming "Peace on earth and good will to men." The human eye loves the beautiful; and yielding to the natural temptation, I swept the broad avenue from the Public Garden to the Back Bay Park. Through the leafless trees I saw on either side a wall of splendid palaces. No cottages or hovels offended the eye of wealth. Here dwell scores of men who, without seriously feeling the expense, could transform the slums of Boston by erecting model apartment houses after the manner employed so wisely by George Peabody in London; while in so doing they would lessen crime, raise the average morality, and make life, for thousands of their fellow-men, mean something far more than a mere hopeless and savage struggle on the animal plane. Slowly moving toward the Public Garden, I passed more than one home where live wealth's favored sons, who, without making a perceptible inroad upon their accumulations, could give to our Commonwealth a great industrial home, equipped and ready to receive and transform the children of the slums, who are orphans or worse than orphans, and who are now, month by month, being swept with irresistible power into the vortex of crime destined to curse the society of to-morrow and generations yet unborn—children who are cursed at birth and by environment, but who would, nevertheless, become useful members of society, if placed in an institution where they would feel the elevating influence of love and the refinement of culture, and where they would be taught to completely master at least two trades, while their minds and souls were being trained by intellectual and moral culture.

With these thoughts in mind I slowly approached Arlington Street. Among the carriages which passed me, my attention was particularly attracted to one bearing a coat-of-arms, and whose driver was in full livery. The very horses seemed to feel that they were aristocratic animals, as with sleek coats and arched necks they pranced by. Within this carriage sat two ladies, but I saw no marks of content on their faces; rather, a worn, wearied, anxious, and dissatisfied expression. They were evidently surrounded by the luxury which wealth gives, and they probably spend their summers abroad, mingling with the fashionable devotees of the decaying aristocracies of the Old World; for the arms emblazoned on the carriage spoke of an attempt to ape foreign custom and a contempt for republican simplicity. Wealth apparently gave them what gold could bestow, but it evidently had not given the priceless pearl of life, the serenity of soul which comes alone from living for others. This led me to study the faces I passed in this commonwealth of the rich. The wrinkles of care and anxiety, the shadow of apprehension, the unutterable soul-craving, which haunts eyes that are unsatisfied—these marked many faces. Some, it is true, wore the light, joyous expressions which so well become youth, and now and then I met a person upon whose silver brow peace seemed to rest content. Jealousy, sensualism, and unsatisfied desire were visible on many countenances; and I could not help feeling that the conditions which enabled colossal fortune to rise by the side of starvation and increasing misery had robbed a vast majority of the children of wealth of the only thing which makes life worth living. Indeed, such must be the case. The divine in man cannot blossom or life yield its richest treasures while gold is society's god. So long as the first question asked is, "How rich is he?"; so long as the standard is gold instead of character; so long as men feel and believe that money is the greatest thing in the world, the deepest and finest toned chords in the harp of life will give forth no melody; the supreme gift of life, that peace which comes only as the result of sinking self for others, will be exiled from the human heart; while that priceless essence of divinity in man, *the soul,* will wither, shrivel, and become as something dead.

I went through the avenue, down Arlington Street, and ascended Beacon Hill almost to its golden-crested dome. I had passed uninterrupted rows of palaces. I had found no hovel or cottage, and I had seen no sign of want except in the soul-hunger which peered forth from many eyes. The residents of many of the palaces I had passed give fashionable balls and banquets each winter, at which the champagne drank, alone, would keep scores of starving mortals in comparative comfort through the pitiless winter months. I remembered that only a few weeks before I had seen carried away the *débris* of one of these fashionable parties. For this special occasion fifteen cases of champagne had been ordered, over thirteen cases of which had been consumed by the guests before half-past five in the morning, at which hour the festivities had come to an end. I wondered then, and I wondered as I walked past the home of the gentleman who gave the ball, how much of the divine in the nature of those champagne-imbibers vanished that cold winter night, for the soul withers much as does a weed-choked flower when the animal eclipses the spiritual in our being.

Leaving Beacon Street, I turned down the slope of the hill leading toward the populous and plebeian quarter of the West End. It was not long before the scenes of fashionable wealth disappeared; and it was curious to see along some streets how the old-time wealth, which once made these quarters the most fashionable and select part of the city, seemed to be struggling against the ever-increasing waves of poverty. A few blocks farther, and I had entered another world, the commonwealth of want. Here scenes of abject misery and sickening depravity among the young and old are often witnessed; although here, also, amid vice, penury, and woe, every now and then there blossoms forth a royal soul, evincing such heroism and true nobility as to give one hope for all mankind. It was in this part of the city, a short time since, that the following tragic incident occurred: A little fatherless waif sold newspapers, the money for which went largely to supply a drunken mother with rum. Amost nightly the little fellow ascended to his home in the garret, only to receive abuse, and not unfrequently a brutal beating from his partially intoxicated parent. One night he returned without as much money as the woman expected. She had been drinking a great deal that day, and at once began abusing the boy. As she talked, rage rose in her liquor-inflamed brain; finally she seized him, saying she would throw him out of the window. The little fellow pleaded, and fought for his life, but she pushed him through the glass; he struggled with all his strength, and managed to get back in the room but the glass had cut him most horribly and the sight of blood only served to inflame the mother, who now threw the bleeding child on the floor, and sprang upon him. At this moment neighbors broke in. The boy almost bled to death before medical assistance could be summoned. The police who interrogated him, when they arrested the mother, could by no method of questioning force the child to say anything that would criminate her. She, however, was taken to jail on the testimony of spectators. A friend who is spending his life in the slums of the West End gave me the details of this incident, and added: "I visited the little fellow at the hospital a few days ago. He was bearing up bravely, and in conversation would not allow a word to be said against his mother. 'It is drink that is to blame,' he insisted."

The case of this little boy reminds me of another tragedy enacted in the slums of the North End, a few months ago. A poor father having lost his wife, was overtaken by chronic invalidism. His little savings were soon exhausted. He had two small children, and driven to despair when he contemplated the probable fate of his children, he finally decided that all should leave the world together. He killed his children and then cut his own throat. He left behind a pathetic letter setting forth the struggle he had undergone and the reasons which led to the tragic deeds. These incidents are representative of tragedies occurring so frequently that they have long since dulled our sensibilities. We read of them to-day and forget them by to-morrow. And yet until we feel in our own souls something of the agony of heart experienced by these victims of despair, we will not appreciate the appalling wrongs to be righted by justice and love. And perhaps it may be well to pause here long enough to note some characteristic tragedies which portray the causes leading to the death of representatives in different groups among those who struggle upon the verge of the abyss only at last to fall before remorseless social conditions which enable the few to monopolize the land, control the public highways and fatten upon class laws or special privileges.

Some time ago the details of a most heart-rending tragedy crept into the papers. It occurred about the time that an eminent American Divine declared to a young man, who endeavored to interest him in the suffering poor, "That one must go to the Old World to find involuntary poverty." Since then the condition of our very poor in the great cities has grown steadily more and more deplorable. I give the details of this case as reported by the Chicago dailies at the time of its occurrence:

Martin Arndt, a tailor, aged 53, was found dead in the park near the Douglas Monument early yesterday morning. A bullet-hole near the left temple and a small single-barrelled pistol in his right hand indicated the cause. The body was removed to No. 1318 State St., where he lived. His wife did not know how to account for the suicide. Her husband had left home early Thursday morning as usual, taking his lunch with him, to go to work. About ten A.M., however, the mail carrier handed her a letter, which contained an explanation. It had been written and posted Thursday evening. This was the substance:

Dear Anne: I spoke to the book-keeper, Mr. Priddart, at Clement & Sayers', and requested him to give me half of a cent more for each coat, but he replied that he couldn't do it. He allowed me to take one lot at half a cent more. But immediately afterwards Mr. Raahe (the foreman) came and told me he had something nice to tell me: "Mr. Priddart had engaged another man, who would press the coats for one cent, and as soon as you have that lot of coats done you can stop work." I told him when a man wanted a trifle more for his work, he got discharged; that I thought it was rather mean. I looked all over for another place, but could not find one. I don't know what I shall do now, and I have made up my mind not to return to you again. I looked over the constitution of the Harigari, and find that if a brother commits suicide his wife and children receive the regular benefit—$500; and from the Druids you will have no difficulty in getting the money to bury me. You will be better off than if I live. Therefore it is my intention to end this miserable life, and I have picked out the Douglas Monument as the place to die. There you will find my corpse. I beg you to forgive me. I can't do otherwise. I hope my folks (brothers and sisters in Germany) will not hear anything about it. If you marry again do not let your man mistreat Hugo (his son). I commit this deed with my full senses, although I know well what a disgrace I put on you and the family. I cannot do otherwise. Sooner or later it would have happened. That is all I have to say.   M. ARNDT.

It seems that Arndt had worked only a short time for Clement & Sayers,—this being his second week. The coats referred to were of linen, and a man can press half-a-dozen in an hour. Last week, by working ten hours a day, he made $4.80. It was his habit to ride from 1318 State Street to 416 Milwaukee Avenue in the morning at a cost of ten cents, and to walk home at night,—a distance of five miles. Had he ridden both ways, the $4.80 would have been reduced to $3.60. He was a temperate man, but hard work had reduced him to almost skin and bones. Having been dismissed, and there being few chances for employment nowadays, he made up his mind to go where bread and butter are not needed. That he was determined to end his life is evidenced by two wounds,—one in the body below the heart, and another in the head. He must have fired first at his heart. Missing it and not dying, he deliberately loaded the pistol a second time and fired into his brain, and this accomplished his purpose.

Here are the details of another suicide due to present social conditions; which further impresses the contemplative mind with the difference between the altruism of Jesus and the motive power which to-day animates a nation boasting that it is Christian, while it permits such frightful tragedies to pass with little or no protest from the shepherds or the flocks who represent the Nazarine. A few months ago the body of a half-starved girl was found in the lake at Chicago. It was the corpse of Mamie Jennings—beautiful, ill-starred Mamie Jennings—one of an army which poverty is to-day hounding to death in a land which boasts of unexampled prosperity. Here is the story condensed from the daily papers. Mamie Jennings was the daughter of a once prosperous gentleman, who through successive misfortunes came at last to want, and died in utter destitution. Mamie was a beautiful girl over twenty years of age. Her mother was a confirmed invalid. In the great overflowing city, crowded with the unemployed, the poor girl found the struggle for bread, raiment and shelter for her mother and herself a frightful battle. There was, however, much innate heroism in the fiber of her being, and she faced fate bravely as ever strong men faced the cannon. At last her health broke down, but she could not afford to be sick; a starving mother's face was constantly before her eyes. One who investigated the case after her death wrote thus graphically of her struggle:

> Almost unable to stand from weakness, she bent over a washtub all that day, and when she returned home in the evening she cried herself to sleep. At five o'clock in the morning she arose, and without any breakfast—for there was only enough in the house for one—she started off to work. She was unable to walk down town, and she took the last nickel in the house to pay her fare. When she reached the Troy she was sick. "I don't believe I'll be able to work to-day," she said to the cashier. There were dark circles under her eyes and she trembled from the cold. The cashier told her to go home and return Friday. After leaving the place, about seven o'clock, nothing was seen of her until her body was found in the lake.

The same writer thus concludes his pen-picture of this every-day tragedy, which has become so common as merely to call for short notices in the papers:—

> There are hundreds of thousands in this land of boasted plenty and misery, who are condemned, through no fault of their own, to the same life of grinding toil and hopeless penury that Mamie Jennings lived; and the marvel is, not that this poor, crushed, suffering, starving girl determined to end it all with one plunge, and welcome oblivion or the unknown, rather than endure it longer, but that so few of the miserable do likewise.

I have paused in my pilgrimage long enough to briefly refer to some grim, everyday tragedies which are typical, in order if possible, to impress the reader with the real significance of the awful happenings so common to-day as to excite little comment.

From the West End I passed to what is known as the slums of the North End, and was joined by a friend whose life is spent in saving the sinking, much as the heroic life-savers spend theirs on the ocean's treacherous shores. In the slums of the North End we catch a glimpse of the social nadir of Boston. Within ten minutes' walk from the historic Old North Church, and within an hour's stroll from the palaces of Beacon Hill, we encounter poverty so terrible, that its existence in the heart of a Christian centre of wealth and culture, brands our civilization with shame, and puts a blister on Religion's brow—all the more because so much of it is uninvited poverty.

The casual observer who traverses the streets of the North End, little imagines the horrible squalor all around him, for the reason that almost all the dilapidated buildings are hidden from view by brick fronts. The worst features of the North End slums are unsuspected by our people who have not passed up the scores of alleyways, through the narrow corridors, or down through the cellar-like passages which line the streets, into the courtyards of the democracy of night. Those who have thus penetrated into the real heart of the slums are appalled. Frequently the buildings are brick, facing the street; but passing through the alley-way we find great, dilapidated wooden houses in the rear, which swarm with human beings. If the passers-by could see what the brick walls which front Hanover and other streets of the North End hide from view, I believe a sense of self-respect, if no higher motive, would be voiced in an agitation so determined as to lead to radical changes. But from all appearance, we must wait for some terrible contagion, arising from these plague spots, to strike down thousands of the children of the rich, before justice will be heard.

The first family visited presented a very pitiful spectacle; and as it typifies a class far larger than our popular economists would have easy-going people believe, I will give the facts somewhat in detail. The father is an industrious Italian, who has succeeded for the past few years in securing employment most of the time. He and his wife were very frugal. They feared the approach of a rainy day when sickness or decrepitude might bring them from the brink of starvation into the depths. Hence every penny possible was saved. They had three children, the oldest eight. The mother worked out, making what she could. The little eight-year-old child kept the home, and tended her young brother and sister. By self-denial and strict economy this little family had saved one hundred dollars, when a blow fell upon them. The overwork and constant strain endured by the wife and mother expressed itself in a stroke of paralysis, the whole of one side of the body being rendered lifeless. The husband, who seems a very kind-hearted man, was compelled to leave his work to care for his wife. He summoned doctors. Of course the source of income ceased; meantime, rent, doctor's bills, fuel, and food day by day ate up the careful savings of several years. The wife rallied a little, and the afflicted husband sought work. His place had been filled by another; and then followed a weary search for something, *anything* to do; but in the winter there are many seeking work and he found it impossible to obtain employment at any price. During this time all their savings had disappeared; they had no money for coal or food. At this juncture a young lady, who had become interested in the sufferers, visited my friend in the North End with money to gladden some hearts during the Christmas season. Together they visited this family. The day was bitter cold; but in the wretched den, which these unfortunates call home, the messengers of love found the invalid wife and hungry children with no fire and no food. The young lady purchased coal and provisions, and in other ways brightened Christmas for these poor children of an adverse fate. I saw the family a week later; they still enjoyed the warmth and food provided by this noble-hearted young woman. The rent paid by this family is nine dollars a month; the father can as yet get no work; the rooms, two in number, look out upon a small and filthy court. The surroundings are squalid; stifling odors on every hand. In the house the most abject poverty is everywhere visible. Here a father, mother, and three little children are on the very brink of the abyss, through no fault of their own. In spite of industry and pinching frugality they are facing starvation, and even work is denied. This family, as I have observed, is a fair type of numbers of families in Boston's vortex of want.

Is it right that millions of dollars of acquired wealth should every year be lavished in wanton luxuries, which enervate manhood and undermine the virility of civilization, while God's children in the social cellar are starving? Is it right that we build churches costing from five hundred thousand to five million dollars each, while our brothers are seeking work to save their loved ones, and finding none? *This is one of the most solemn questions which confronts our present civilization.* If Christianity meant half what Jesus intended it should mean, this state of things could not endure for a single day.

In another tenement we found, on the fourth floor, an old woman living in a solitary room only five feet wide. This was her home— dining-room, sleeping-room, and kitchen, scarcely more than a closet. This poor woman pays seventy-five cents a week rent. She is nearing the grave; and I felt, on studying her face, so deeply wrinkled by a life of anxious care and years of suffering and privation, that here death would surely be a messenger of relief.

Descending a few steps into a sombre cellar, we found the abode of a family of six. Two dark, damp rooms or burrows constituted the home of this family. They were very cold, as there was no vestige of fire in the room. The air also was heavy with vile odors. Here were several little children being raised amid filth, in an atmosphere reeking with moral impurity and crime. They will form a part of the civilization of to-morrow.

In this neighborhood we visited a widow with two little children; her husband was lost at sea, and she supports the family by her needle.

It is useless to add that life is one long, dreary, and well-nigh hopeless nightmare to her, as it is to scores of widow women in the slums. The sea is almost as cruel as man, and hundreds of poor women who live in the squalor of our sea-ports wait weary years for loved ones who come no more.

Off a vile-smelling court we found a family of three children. The mother was up town sewing. The world of these little ones is bounded for the most part by the four walls of two small rooms. Here, amid the plainest furniture and in plenty of dirt, from morning till night the little girl watches her little brothers. They are Portuguese, but attend the Bethel Mission. "Can you not sing us a song?" said my friend. After some persuasion, the little girl and the oldest boy sang, "My Country, 'Tis of Thee, Sweet Land of Liberty!" I involuntarily started. What grim satire was I hearing! Little dwarfed lives, starving in poverty and wretchedness, in the filth of the slums, singing, "Sweet Land of Liberty!" I was glad that they did not comprehend the meaning of the song, for it would have made life more bitter.

We visited many more places where poverty was what I term uninvited; but these, being typical, will enable us to catch a glimpse of the commonwealth of the unfortunates at the social nadir. I have not the space to show another phase of this problem or to cite cases to illustrate how this life breaks down the moral nature; how a life in dens unfit for brutes, brutalizes God's children. We hear much about the vice and crime and the drunkenness of the slums; to me it is a marvel that there is not more. When I see the lavish waste of wealth for wines and luxuries at the social zenith, while abject poverty abounds within cannon range of the scene of revelry, I sometimes almost lose faith in man. But when I visit the slums and see virtue and probity under such a terrible strain, and with everything pressing viceward, I have my faith in humanity restored. That there is intemperance, crime, and immorality there, no one denies. This trinity of the night holds high carnival at the social nadir; but that, in spite of environment and the brutalizing influence everywhere present, virtue, industry, and self-respect still live, is to me a continual source of wonder, and testifies most eloquently to the innate spark of divinity in the human soul. I returned from my pilgrimage heart-sickened and depressed. The squalor, the filth, the vile odors, the hungry souls, the haunting eyes, the pinched faces of starved youth and helpless age, produced a sense of weariness and oppression difficult to describe. I soon fell into a painful reverie. How is it, I asked, that the commonwealth of the prosperous is so selfishly short-sighted? Do not these millionaires see in the loved ones around them something more priceless than the gold they worship? Do they not see that at their very doors are cesspools of disease, where death-breeding germs will some day subtly steal upward and permeate the air of their exclusive realm, until their own loved fragile flowers will wither and fall, leaving their homes strangely desolate? Can they not understand the profound wisdom of the passages in the Scriptures which teach us that "No man liveth unto himself," and "That it is more blessed to give than to receive"? Can they not feel that only as we elevate, purify, and ennoble other homes, do we glorify and protect our own hearthstones, and that sooner or later retribution will overtake the selfish soul?

Then I must have fallen asleep, for before me stood an angel with face sad, yet wonderfully sweet, and the angel said, "Look!" And I saw the slums of our city, and from a hundred homes I beheld something almost impalpable emanating—something which resembled smoke, which assumed a thousand fantastic and gruesome forms, as in great clouds it slowly floated over the city. Then I heard a great cry. The sobbing of a mighty city was audible. Death was everywhere present. I beheld thousands of our people fleeing to the depots; but scarcely had they left the city when the wires flashed, quick, sharp, and unsympathetic, the fateful news that all cities and towns were quarantined against Boston. I saw that numbers fleeing died on the way, and others, finding all places barred against them, returned to die at home. The plague, impalpable but terrible, seemed omnipresent. The city was draped in black. "The innocent and noble are dying," I said. "Say rather, 'They are being promoted' "; but I saw a tear glisten in the angel's eyes, and I said, "Was all this waste of life necessary?" And the angel said, "Even so, for man had hardened his heart against his brother man. He had closed his ears against the cry of the poor for justice. He had sowed to the wind, and is now reaping the whirlwind. Sorrow," continued the angel, and the voice was rich in melody, "makes man thoughtful. In the midnight of grief he hears the voice of justice, which is the voice of the Most High. Look once more!" Now I beheld a scene of marvellous beauty opening before my view. Great buildings, each covering a square and from six to eight stories high, rose on every hand. Each was built in the form of a hollow square, and within the enclosures I saw borders of flowers fringing playgrounds, where were fountains and many happy children. The music of their laughter chimed melodiously with the splashing of the water. Here and there I noticed large temple-like buildings, and I said, "What are these?" The angel replied, "We will enter one." At the threshold (for in my dream I moved as thought travels) I was impressed by the immensity and simplicity of the structure. We entered and descended to the basement. I beheld great swimming-pools and an immense gymnasium; above were large eating-halls, where plain food was served at reasonable prices; beyond the eating-halls were commodious reading-rooms, free to all the people. We ascended a broad stairway to the next floor. Here I saw a large hall, in which a clear-voiced orator was describing the wonders of other lands and ages, and by the aid of a magnificent stereopticon was entertaining and instructing an immense audience. This also was free. In another hall an artist was entertaining a large congregation by giving an effective charcoal talk. Beyond was a free night school. "These quarters are the habitation of the poor, once the slums of Boston," said the angel; "but" she continued, "let us look further," and now I beheld a broad, green expanse dotted with beautiful houses and some large buildings. "This," explained the angel, "is the home of orphan children. Here within each cottage may be found twenty little ones. In the large buildings a wonderful schooling is being given. Each child is made master of a trade, while his soul is being developed by love, by music, and by ethical teaching. The intellect is also schooled. To the children this is heaven, for love meets them on every hand. "This," said the angel, "which you see is only the first step; it is the lifeboat sent out to save a few who are sinking; it is an earnest of the awakening of the divine in man. Beyond and above this, Progress, Fraternity, and Justice are leading the people. All special privileges and class laws have been abolished. Through the broad land societies of human brotherhood have been formed pledged to love all God's children, to drown the hoarse roar of hate with the music of love; to overcome evil by good; to drive out the darkness by the light." The angel vanished. I awoke.

Stephen Crane

An Experiment in Misery

TWO MEN STOOD regarding a tramp.

"I wonder how he feels," said one, reflectively. "I suppose he is

New York Press, April 22, 1894. Text from *The New York City Sketches of Stephen Crane*, ed. R. W. Stallman and E. R. Hagemann (New York, 1966), pp. 33–43.

homeless, friendless, and has, at the most, only a few cents in his pocket. And if this is so, I wonder how he feels."

The other being the elder, spoke with an air of authoritative wisdom. "You can tell nothing of it unless you are in that condition yourself. It is idle to speculate about it from this distance."

"I suppose so," said the younger man, and then he added as from an inspiration: "I think I'll try it. Rags and tatters, you know, a couple of dimes, and hungry, too, if possible. Perhaps I could discover his point of view or something near it."

"Well, you might," said the other, and from those words begins this veracious narrative of an experiment in misery.

The youth went to the studio of an artist friend, who, from his store, rigged him out in an aged suit and a brown derby hat that had been made long years before. And then the youth went forth to try to eat as the tramp may eat, and sleep as the wanderers sleep. It was late at night, and a fine rain was swirling softly down, covering the pavements with a bluish luster. He began a weary trudge toward the downtown places, where beds can be hired for coppers. By the time he had reached City Hall Park he was so completely plastered with yells of "bum" and "hobo," and with various unholy epithets that small boys had applied to him at intervals that he was in a state of profound dejection, and looked searchingly for an outcast of high degree that the two might share miseries. But the lights threw a quivering glare over rows and circles of deserted benches that glistened damply, showing patches of wet sod behind them. It seemed that their usual freights of sorry humanity had fled on this night to better things. There were only squads of well dressed Brooklyn people, who swarmed toward the Bridge.

The young man loitered about for a time, and then went shuffling off down Park row. In the sudden descent in style of the dress of the crowd he felt relief. He began to see others whose tatters matched his tatters. In Chatham square there were aimless men strewn in front of saloons and lodging houses. He aligned himself with these men, and turned slowly to occupy himself with the pageantry of the street.

The mists of the cold and damp night made an intensely blue haze, through which the gaslights in the windows of stores and saloons shone with a golden radiance. The street cars rumbled softly, as if going upon carpet stretched in the aisle made by the pillars of the elevated road. Two interminable processions of people went along the wet pavements, spattered with black mud that made each shoe leave a scar-like impression. The high buildings lurked a-back, shrouded in shadows. Down a side street there were mystic curtains of purple and black, on which lamps dully glittered like embroidered flowers.

A saloon stood with a voracious air on a corner. A sign leaning against the front of the doorpost announced: "Free hot soup tonight." The swing doors snapping to and fro like ravenous lips, made gratified smacks, as if the saloon were gorging itself with plump men.

Caught by the delectable sign, the young man allowed himself to be swallowed. A bartender placed a schooner of dark and portentous beer on the bar. Its monumental form up-reared until the froth a-top was above the crown of the young man's brown derby.

"Soup over there, gents," said the bartender, affably. A little yellow man in rags and the youth grasped their schooners and went with speed toward a lunch counter, where a man with oily but imposing whiskers ladled genially from a kettle until he had furnished his two mendicants with a soup that was steaming hot and in which there were little floating suggestions of chicken. The young man, sipping his broth, felt the cordiality expressed by the warmth of the mixture, and he beamed at the man with oily but imposing whiskers, who was presiding like a priest behind an altar. "Have some more, gents?" he inquired of the two sorry figures before him. The little yellow man accepted with a swift gesture, but the youth shook his head and went out, following a man whose wondrous seediness promised that he would have a knowledge of cheap lodging houses.

On the sidewalk he accosted the seedy man. "Say, do you know a cheap place t' sleep?"

The other hesitated for a time, gazing sideways. Finally he nodded in the direction of up the street. "I sleep up there," he said, "when I've got th' price."

"How much?"

"Ten cents."

The young man shook his head dolefully. "That's too rich for me."

At that moment there approached the two a reeling man in strange garments. His head was a fuddle of bushy hair and whiskers from which his eyes peered with a guilty slant. In a close scrutiny it was possible to distinguish the cruel lines of a mouth, which looked as if its lips had just closed with satisfaction over some tender and piteous morsel. He appeared like an assassin steeped in crime performed awkwardly.

But at this time his voice was tuned to the coaxing key of an affectionate puppy. He looked at the men with wheedling eyes and began to sing a little melody for charity.

"Say, gents, can't yeh give a poor feller a couple of cents t' git a bed. Now, yeh know how a respecter'ble gentlem'n feels when he's down on his luck an' I—"

The seedy man, staring with imperturbable countenance at a train which clattered overhead, interrupted in an expressionless voice: "Ah, go t' h——!"

But the youth spoke to the prayerful assassin in tones of astonishment and inquiry. "Say, you must be crazy! Why don't yeh strike somebody that looks as if they had money?"

The assassin, tottering about on his uncertain legs, and at intervals brushing imaginary cobwebs from before his nose, entered into a long explanation of the psychology of the situation. It was so profound that it was unintelligible.

When he had exhausted the subject the young man said to him: "Let's see th' five cents."

The assassin wore an expression of drunken woe at this sentence, filled with suspicion of him. With a deeply pained air he began to fumble in his clothing, his red hands trembling. Presently he announced in a voice of bitter grief, as if he had been betrayed: "There's on'y four."

"Four," said the young man thoughtfully. "Well, look-a-here, I'm a stranger here, an' if ye'll steer me to your cheap joint I'll find the other three."

The assassin's countenance became instantly radiant with joy. His whiskers quivered with the wealth of his alleged emotions. He seized the young man's hand in a transport of delight and friendliness.

"B'gawd," he cried, "if ye'll do that, b'gawd, I'd say yeh was a damned good feller, I would, an' I'd remember yeh all m' life, I would, b'gawd, an' if I ever got a chance I'd return th' compliment" —he spoke with drunken dignity—"b'gawd, I'd treat yeh white, I would, an' I'd allus remember yeh——"

The young man drew back, looking at the assassin coldly. "Oh, that's all right," he said. "You show me th' joint—that's all you've got t' do."

The assassin, gesticulating gratitude, led the young man along a dark street. Finally he stopped before a little dusty door. He raised his hand impressively. "Look-a-here," he said, and there was a thrill of deep and ancient wisdom upon his face, "I've brought yeh here, an' that's my part, ain't it? If th' place don't suit yeh yeh needn't git mad at me, need yeh? There won't be no bad feelin', will there?"

"No," said the young man.

The assassin waved his arm tragically and led the march up the steep stairway. On the way the young man furnished the assassin with three pennies. At the top a man with benevolent spectacles looked at them through a hole in the board. He collected their money, wrote some names on a register, and speedily was leading the two men along a gloom shrouded corridor.

Shortly after the beginning of this journey the young man felt his liver turn white, for from the dark and secret places of the building there suddenly came to his nostrils strange and unspeakable odors that assailed him like malignant diseases with wings. They seemed to be from human bodies closely packed in dens; the exhalations from a hundred pairs of reeking lips; the fumes from a thousand bygone debauches; the expression of a thousand present miseries.

A man, naked save for a little snuff colored undershirt, was parading sleepily along the corridor. He rubbed his eyes, and, giving vent to a prodigious yawn, demanded to be told the time.

"Half past one."

The man yawned again. He opened a door, and for a moment his form was outlined against a black, opaque interior. To this door came the three men, and as it was again opened the unholy odors rushed out like released fiends, so that the young man was obliged to struggle as against an overpowering wind.

It was some time before the youth's eyes were good in the intense gloom within, but the man with benevolent spectacles led him skillfully, pausing but a moment to deposit the limp assassin upon a cot. He took the youth to a cot that lay tranquilly by the window, and, showing him a tall locker for clothes that stood near the head with the ominous air of a tombstone, left him.

The youth sat on his cot and peered about him. There was a gas jet in a distant part of the room that burned a small flickering orange hued flame. It caused vast masses of tumbled shadows in all parts of the place, save where, immediately about it, there was a little gray haze. As the young man's eyes became used to the darkness he could see upon the cots that thickly littered the floor the forms of men sprawled out, lying in deathlike silence or heaving and snoring with tremendous effort, like stabbed fish.

The youth locked his derby and his shoes in the mummy case near him and then lay down with his old and familiar coat around his shoulders. A blanket he handled gingerly, drawing it over part of the coat. The cot was leather covered and cold as melting snow. The youth was obliged to shiver for some time on this affair, which was like a slab. Presently, however, his chill gave him peace, and during this period of leisure from it he turned his head to stare at his friend, the assassin, whom he could dimly discern where he lay sprawled on a cot in the abandon of a man filled with drink. He was snoring with incredible vigor. His wet hair and beard dimly glistened and his inflamed nose shone with subdued luster like a red light in a fog.

Within reach of the youth's hand was one who lay with yellow breast and shoulders bare to the cold drafts. One arm hung over the side of the cot and the fingers lay full length upon the wet cement floor of the room. Beneath the inky brows could be seen the eyes of the man exposed by the partly opened lids. To the youth it seemed that he and this corpse-like being were exchanging a prolonged stare and that the other threatened with his eyes. He drew back, watching this neighbor from the shadows of his blanket edge. The man did not move once through the night, but lay in this stillness as of death, like a body stretched out, expectant of the surgeon's knife.

And all through the room could be seen the tawny hues of naked flesh, limbs thrust into the darkness, projecting beyond the cots; upreared knees; arms hanging, long and thin, over the cot edges. For the most part they were statuesque, carven, dead. With the curious lockers standing all about like tombstones there was a strange effect of a graveyard, where bodies were merely flung.

Yet occasionally could be seen limbs wildly tossing in fantastic nightmare gestures, accompanied by guttural cries, grunts, oaths. And there was one fellow off in a gloomy corner, who in his dreams was oppressed by some frightful calamity, for of a sudden he began to utter long wails that went almost like yells from a hound, echoing wailfully and weird through this chill place of tombstones, where men lay like the dead.

The sound, in its high piercing beginnings that dwindled to final melancholy moans, expressed a red and grim tragedy of the unfathomable possibilities of the man's dreams. But to the youth these were not merely the shrieks of a vision pierced man. They were an utterance of the meaning of the room and its occupants. It was to him the protest of the wretch who feels the touch of the imperturbably granite wheels and who then cries with an impersonal eloquence, with a strength not from him, giving voice to the wail of a whole section, a class, a people. This, weaving into the young man's brain and mingling with his views of these vast and somber shadows that like mighty black fingers curled around the naked bodies, made the young man so that he did not sleep, but lay carving biographies for these men from his meager experience. At times the fellow in the corner howled in a writhing agony of his imaginations.

Finally a long lance point of gray light shot through the dusty panes of the window. Without, the young man could see roofs drearily white in the dawning. The point of light yellowed and grew brighter, until the golden rays of the morning sun came in bravely and strong. They touched with radiant color the form of a small, fat man, who snored in stuttering fashion. His round and shiny bald head glowed suddenly with the valor of a decoration. He sat up, blinked at the sun, swore fretfully and pulled his blanket over the ornamental splendors of his head.

The youth contentedly watched this rout of the mystic shadows before the bright spears of the sun and presently he slumbered. When he awoke he heard the voice of the assassin raised in valiant curses. Putting up his head he perceived his comrade seated on the side of the cot engaged in scratching his neck with long finger nails that rasped like files.

"Hully Jee dis is a new breed. They've got can openers on their feet," he continued in a violent tirade.

The young man hastily unlocked his closet and took out his clothes. As he sat on the side of the cot, lacing his shoes, he glanced about and saw that daylight had made the room comparatively common-place and uninteresting. The men, whose faces seemed stolid, serene or absent, were engaged in dressing, while a great crackle of bantering conversation arose.

A few were parading in unconcerned nakedness. Here and there were men of brawn, whose skins shone clear and ruddy. They took splendid poses, standing massively, like chiefs. When they had dressed in their ungainly garments there was an extraordinary change. They then showed bumps and deficiencies of all kinds.

There were others who exhibited many deformities. Shoulders were slanting, bumped, pulled this way and pulled that way. And notable among these latter men was the little fat man who had refused to allow his head to be glorified. His pudgy form, builded like a pear, bustled to and fro, while he swore in fishwife fashion. It appeared that some article of his apparel had vanished.

The young man, attired speedily, went to his friend, the assassin. At first the latter looked dazed at the sight of the youth. This face seemed to be appealing to him through the cloud wastes of his memory. He scratched his neck and reflected. At last he grinned, a broad smile gradually spreading until his countenance was a round illumination. "Hello, Willie," he cried, cheerily.

"Hello," said the young man. "Are yeh ready t' fly?"

"Sure." The assassin tied his shoe carefully with some twine and came ambling.

When he reached the street the young man experienced no sudden relief from unholy atmospheres. He had forgotten all about them, and had been breathing naturally and with no sensation of discomfort or distress.

He was thinking of these things as he walked along the street, when he was suddenly startled by feeling the assassin's hand, trembling with excitement, clutching his arm, and when the assassin spoke, his voice went into quavers from a supreme agitation.

"I'll be hully, bloomin' blowed, if there wasn't a feller with a nightshirt on up there in that joint!"

The youth was bewildered for a moment, but presently he turned to smile indulgently at the assassin's humor.

"Oh, you're a d— liar," he merely said.

Whereupon the assassin began to gesture extravagantly and take oath by strange gods. He frantically placed himself at the mercy of remarkable fates if his tale were not true. "Yes, he did! I cross m' heart thousan' times!" he protested, and at the time his eyes were large with amazement, his mouth wrinkled in unnatural glee. "Yessir! A nightshirt! A hully white nightshirt!"

"You lie!"

"Nosir! I hope ter die b'fore I kin git anudder ball if there wasn't a jay wid a hully, bloomin' white nightshirt!"

His face was filled with the infinite wonder of it. "A hully white nightshirt," he continually repeated.

The young man saw the dark entrance to a basement restaurant. There was a sign which read, "No mystery about our hash," and there were other age stained and world battered legends which told him that the place was within his means. He stopped before it and spoke to the assassin. "I guess I'll git somethin' t' eat."

At this the assassin, for some reason, appeared to be quite embarrassed. He gazed at the seductive front of the eating place for a moment. Then he started slowly up the street. "Well, goodby, Willie," he said, bravely.

For an instant the youth studied the departing figure. Then he called out, "Hol' on a minnet." As they came together he spoke in a certain fierce way, as if he feared that the other could think him to be weak. "Look-a-here, if yeh wanta git some breakfas' I'll lend yeh three cents t' do it with. But say, look-a-here, you've gota git out an' hustle. I ain't goin' t' support yeh, or I'll go broke b'fore night. I ain't no millionaire."

"I take me oath, Willie," said the assassin, earnestly, "th' on'y thing I really needs is a ball. Me t'roat feels like a fryin' pan. But as I can't git a ball, why, th' next bes' thing is breakfast, an' if yeh do that fer me, b'gawd, I'd say yeh was th' whitest lad I ever see."

They spent a few moments in dexterous exchanges of phrases, in which they each protested that the other was, as the assassin had originally said, a "respecter'ble gentlem'n." And they concluded with mutual assurances that they were the souls of intelligence and virtue. Then they went into the restaurant.

There was a long counter, dimly lighted from hidden sources. Two or three men in soiled white aprons rushed here and there.

The youth bought a bowl of coffee for two cents and a roll for one cent. The assassin purchased the same. The bowls were webbed with brown seams, and the tin spoons wore an air of having emerged from the first pyramid. Upon them were black, moss like encrustations of age, and they were bent and scarred from the attacks of long forgotten teeth. But over their repast the wanderers waxed warm and mellow. The assassin grew affable as the hot mixture went soothingly down his parched throat, and the young man felt courage flow in his veins.

Memories began to throng in on the assassin, and he brought forth long tales, intricate, incoherent, delivered with a chattering swiftness as from an old woman. "—great job out'n Orange. Boss keep yeh hustlin', though, all time. I was there three days, and then I went an' ask'im t' lend me a dollar. 'G-g-go ter the devil,' he ses, an' I lose me job."

—"South no good. Damn niggers work for twenty-five an' thirty cents a day. Run white man out. Good grub, though. Easy livin'."

—"Yas; useter work little in Toledo, raftin' logs. Make two or three dollars er day in the spring. Lived high. Cold as ice, though, in the winter"—

"I was raised in northern N'York. O-o-o-oh, yeh jest oughto live there. No beer ner whisky, though, way off in the woods. But all th' good hot grub yeh can eat. B'gawd, I hung around there long as I could till th' ol' man fired me. 'Git t'hell outa here, yeh wuthless skunk, git t'hell outa here an' go die,' he ses. 'You're a fine father,' I ses, 'you are,' an' I quit 'im."

As they were passing from the dim eating place they encountered an old man who was trying to steal forth with a tiny package of food, but a tall man with an indomitable mustache stood dragon fashion, barring the way of escape. They heard the old man raise a plaintive protest. "Ah, you always want to know what I take out, and you never see that I usually bring a package in here from my place of business."

As the wanderers trudged slowly along Park row, the assassin began to expand and grow blithe. "B'gawd, we've been livin' like kings," he said, smacking appreciative lips.

"Look out or we'll have t' pay fer it t' night," said the youth, with gloomy warning.

But the assassin refused to turn his gaze toward the future. He went with a limping step, into which he injected a suggestion of lamblike gambols. His mouth was wreathed in a red grin.

In the City Hall Park the two wanderers sat down in the little circle of benches sanctified by traditions of their class. They huddled in their old garments, slumbrously conscious of the march of the hours which for them had no meaning.

The people of the street hurrying hither and thither made a blend of black figures, changing, yet frieze like. They walked in their good clothes as upon important missions, giving no gaze to the two wanderers seated upon the benches. They expressed to the young man his infinite distance from all that he valued. Social position, comfort, the pleasures of living, were unconquerable kingdoms. He felt a sudden awe.

And in the background a multitude of buildings, of pitiless hues and sternly high, were to him emblematic of a nation forcing its regal head into the clouds, throwing no downward glances; in the sublimity of its aspirations ignoring the wretches who may flounder at its feet. The roar of the city in his ear was to him the confusion of strange tongues, babbling heedlessly; it was the clink of coin, the voice of the city's hopes which were to him no hopes.

He confessed himself an outcast, and his eyes from under the lowered rim of his hat began to glance guiltily, wearing the criminal expression that comes with certain convictions.

"Well," said the friend, "did you discover his point of view?"

"I don't know that I did," replied the young man; "but at any rate I think mine own has undergone a considerable alteration."

Frank Norris
A Hotel Bedroom

THE WALLS were whitewashed and bare of pictures or ornaments, and the floor was covered with a dull turkey-red carpet. The furniture was a set, all the pieces having a family resemblance to each other. The bed stood against the right-hand wall, a huge double bed with the name of the hotel on the corners of its spread and pillow cases. In the exact middle of the room underneath the gas fixtures was the centre table, and on it a pitcher of ice water and a porcelain match safe, with ribbed sides, in the form of a truncated cone. Precisely opposite the bed stood the bureau, near to the bureau was the door of the closet, and next to this in the corner was the washstand with

San Francisco *Wave*, XVI (March 13, 1897), 7. Text from *The Complete Edition of Frank Norris* (Garden City, N. Y., 1928), X, 80. Reprinted by permission of Frank C. Preston.

its new cake of soap and its three clean, glossy towels. To the left
of the door was the electric bell and the directions for using it; and
on the door itself a card as to the hours for meals, the rules of the
hotel, and the extract from the code regulating the liabilities of inn-
keepers. The room was clean, aggressively, defiantly clean, and there
was a smell of soap in the air.

It was bare of any personality; of the hundreds who had lived and
suffered and perhaps died there, not a trace or suggestion remained.
Their different characters had not left the least impress upon its air
and appearance. Only a few hairpins were scattered on the bottom
of one of the drawers and two forgotten medicine bottles still remained
upon the top shelf of the closet.

Stephen Crane

The Men in the Storm

AT ABOUT THREE O'CLOCK of the February afternoon, the blizzard
began to swirl great clouds of snow along the streets, sweeping it
down from the roofs and up from the pavements until the faces of
pedestrians tingled and burned as from a thousand needle-prickings.
Those on the walks huddled their necks closely in the collars of their
coats and went along stooping like a race of aged people. The drivers
of vehicles hurried their horses furiously on their way. They were
made more cruel by the exposure of their positions, aloft on high
seats. The street cars, bound up-town, went slowly, the horses slipping and straining in the spongy brown mass that lay between the
rails. The drivers, muffled to the eyes, stood erect and facing the
wind, models of grim philosophy. Overhead the trains rumbled and
roared, and the dark structure of the elevated railroad, stretching over
the avenue, dripped little streams and drops of water upon the mud
and snow beneath it.

All the clatter of the street was softened by the masses that lay

Arena, X (October, 1894), 662–67. Text from this publication.

Crane is describing the blizzard of February, 1894, which came at the
end of a severe winter made worse by an economic depression.

upon the cobbles until, even to one who looked from a window, it became important music, a melody of life made necessary to the ear by the dreariness of the pitiless beat and sweep of the storm. Occasionally one could see black figures of men busily shovelling the white drifts from the walks. The sounds from their labor created new recollections of rural experiences which every man manages to have in a measure. Later, the immense windows of the shops became aglow with light, throwing great beams of orange and yellow upon the pavement. They were infinitely cheerful, yet in a way they accented the force and discomfort of the storm, and gave a meaning to the pace of the people and the vehicles, scores of pedestrians and drivers, wretched with cold faces, necks and feet, speeding for scores of unknown doors and entrances, scattering to an infinite variety of shelters, to places which the imagination made warm with the familiar colors of home.

There was an absolute expression of hot dinners in the pace of the people. If one dared to speculate upon the destination of those who came trooping, he lost himself in a maze of social calculations; he might fling a handful of sand and attempt to follow the flight of each particular grain. But as to the suggestion of hot dinners, he was in firm lines of thought, for it was upon every hurrying face. It is a matter of tradition; it is from the tales of childhood. It comes forth with every storm.

However, in a certain part of a dark West-side street, there was a collection of men to whom these things were as if they were not. In this street was located a charitable house where for five cents the homeless of the city could get a bed at night and, in the morning, coffee and bread.

During the afternoon of the storm, the whirling snows acted as drivers, as men with whips, and at half-past three, the walk before the closed doors of the house was covered with wanderers of the street, waiting. For some distance on either side of the place they could be seen lurking in doorways and behind projecting parts of buildings, gathering in close bunches in an effort to get warm. A covered wagon drawn up near the curb sheltered a dozen of them. Under the stairs that led to the elevated railway station, there were six or eight, their hands stuffed deep in their pockets, their shoulders stooped, jiggling their feet. Others always could be seen coming, a strange procession, some slouching along with the characteristic hopeless gait of professional strays, some coming with hesitating steps wearing the air of men to whom this sort of thing was new.

It was an afternoon of incredible length. The snow, blowing in twisting clouds, sought out the men in their meagre hiding-places and skilfully beat in among them, drenching their persons with showers of fine, stinging flakes. They crowded together, muttering, and fumbling in their pockets to get their red, inflamed wrists covered by the cloth.

Newcomers usually halted at one of the groups and addressed a question, perhaps much as a matter of form, "Is it open yet?"

Those who had been waiting inclined to take the questioner seriously and become contemptuous. "No; do yeh think we'd be standin' here?"

The gathering swelled in numbers steadily and persistently. One could always see them coming, trudging slowly through the storm.

Finally, the little snow plains in the street began to assume a leaden hue from the shadows of evening. The buildings upreared gloomily save where various windows became brilliant figures of light that made shimmers and splashes of yellow on the snow. A street lamp on the curb struggled to illuminate, but it was reduced to impotent blindness by the swift gusts of sleet crusting its panes.

In this half-darkness, the men began to come from their shelter places and mass in front of the doors of charity. They were of all types, but the nationalities were mostly American, German and Irish. Many were strong, healthy, clear-skinned fellows with that stamp of countenance which is not frequently seen upon seekers after charity. There were men of undoubted patience, industry and temperance, who in time of ill-fortune, do not habitually turn to rail at the state of society, snarling at the arrogance of the rich and bemoaning the cowardice of the poor, but who at these times are apt to wear a sudden and singular meekness, as if they saw the world's progress marching from them and were trying to perceive where they had failed, what they had lacked, to be thus vanquished in the race. Then there were others of the shifting, Bowery lodging-house element who were used to paying ten cents for a place to sleep, but who now came here because it was cheaper.

But they were all mixed in one mass so thoroughly that one could not have discerned the different elements but for the fact that the laboring men, for the most part, remained silent and impassive in the blizzard, their eyes fixed on the windows of the house, statues of patience.

The sidewalk soon became completely blocked by the bodies of the men. They pressed close to one another like sheep in a winter's gale, keeping one another warm by the heat of their bodies. The snow came down upon this compressed group of men until, directly from above, it might have appeared like a heap of snow-covered merchandise, if it were not for the fact that the crowd swayed gently with a unanimous, rhythmical motion. It was wonderful to see how the snow lay upon the heads and shoulders of these men, in little ridges an inch thick perhaps in places, the flakes steadily adding drop and drop, precisely as they fall upon the unresisting grass of the fields. The feet of the men were all wet and cold and the wish to warm them accounted for the slow, gentle, rhythmical motion. Occasionally some man whose ears or nose tingled acutely from the cold winds would wriggle down until his head was protected by the shoulders of his companions.

There was a continuous murmuring discussion as to the probability of the doors being speedily opened. They persistently lifted their eyes toward the windows. One could hear little combats of opinion.

"There's a light in th' winder!"

"Naw; it's a reflection f'm across th' way."

"Well, didn't I see 'em lite it?"

"You did?"

"I did!"

"Well, then, that settles it!"

As the time approached when they expected to be allowed to enter, the men crowded to the doors in an unspeakable crush, jamming and wedging in a way that it seemed would crack bones. They surged heavily against the building in a powerful wave of pushing shoulders. Once a rumor flitted among all the tossing heads.

"They can't open th' doors! Th' fellers er smack up ag'in 'em."

Then a dull roar of rage came from the men on the outskirts; but all the time they strained and pushed until it appeared to be impossible for those that they cried out against to do anything but be crushed to pulp.

"Ah, git away f'm th' door!"

"Git outa that!"

"Throw 'em out!"

"Kill 'em!"

"Say, fellers, now, what th' 'ell? Give 'em a chanct t' open th' door!"

"Yeh damned pigs, give 'em a chanct t' open th' door!"

Men in the outskirts of the crowd occasionally yelled when a boot-heel of one of frantic trampling feet crushed on their freezing extremities.

"Git off me feet, yeh clumsy tarrier!"

"Say, don't stand on me feet! Walk on th' ground!"

A man near the doors suddenly shouted: "O-o-oh! Le' me out—le' me out!" And another, a man of infinite valor, once twisted his head so as to half face those who were pushing behind him. "Quit yer shovin', yeh"—and he delivered a volley of the most powerful and singular invective straight into the faces of the men behind him. It was as if he was hammering the noses of them with curses of triple brass. His face, red with rage, could be seen; upon it, an expression of sublime disregard of consequences. But nobody cared to reply to his imprecations; it was too cold. Many of them snickered and all continued to push.

In occasional pauses of the crowd's movement the men had opportunity to make jokes; usually grim things, and no doubt very uncouth. Nevertheless, they are notable—one does not expect to find the quality of humor in a heap of old clothes under a snowdrift.

The winds seemed to grow fiercer as time wore on. Some of the gusts of snow that came down on the close collection of heads cut like knives and needles, and the men huddled, and swore, not like dark assassins, but in a sort of an American fashion, grimly and desperately, it is true, but yet with a wondrous under-effect, indefinable and mystic, as if there was some kind of humor in this catastrophe, in this situation in a night of snow-laden winds.

Once the window of the huge dry-goods shop across the street furnished material for a few moments of forgetfulness. In the brilliantly-lighted space appeared the figure of a man. He was rather stout and very well clothed. His whiskers were fashioned charmingly after those of the Prince of Wales. He stood in an attitude of magnificent reflection. He slowly stroked his moustache with a certain grandeur of manner, and looked down at the snow-encrusted mob. From below, there was denoted a supreme complacence in him. It seemed that the sight operated inversely, and enabled him to more clearly regard his own environment, delightful relatively.

One of the mob chanced to turn his head and perceive the figure in the window. "Hello, lookit 'is whiskers," he said genially.

Many of the men turned then, and a shout went up. They called to him in all strange keys. They addressed him in every manner, from familiar and cordial greetings to carefully-worded advice concerning changes in his personal appearance. The man presently fled, and the mob chuckled ferociously like ogres who had just devoured something.

They turned then to serious business. Often they addressed the stolid front of the house.

"Oh, let us in fer Gawd's sake!"

"Let us in or we'll all drop dead!"

"Say, what's th' use o' keepin' all us poor Indians out in th' cold?"

And always some one was saying, "Keep off me feet."

The crushing of the crowd grew terrific toward the last. The men, in keen pain from the blasts, began almost to fight. With the pitiless whirl of snow upon them, the battle for shelter was going to the strong. It became known that the basement door at the foot of a little steep flight of stairs was the one to be opened, and they jostled and heaved in this direction like laboring fiends. One could hear them panting and groaning in their fierce exertion.

Usually some one in the front ranks was protesting to those in the rear: "O—o—ow! Oh, say, now, fellers, let up, will yeh? Do yeh wanta kill somebody?"

A policeman arrived and went into the midst of them, scolding and berating, occasionally threatening, but using no force but that of his hands and shoulders against these men who were only struggling to get in out of the storm. His decisive tones rang out sharply: "Stop that pushin' back there! Come, boys, don't push! Stop that! Here, you, quit yer shovin'! Cheese that!"

When the door below was opened, a thick stream of men forced a way down the stairs, which were of an extraordinary narrowness and seemed only wide enough for one at a time. Yet they somehow went down almost three abreast. It was a difficult and painful operation. The crowd was like a turbulent water forcing itself through one tiny outlet. The men in the rear, excited by the success of the others, made frantic exertions, for it seemed that this large band would more than fill the quarters and that many would be left upon the pavements. It would be disastrous to be of the last, and accordingly men with the snow biting their faces, writhed and twisted with their might. One expected that from the tremendous pressure, the narrow passage to the basement door would be so choked and clogged with human limbs and bodies that movement would be impossible. Once indeed the crowd was forced to stop, and a cry went along that a man had been injured at the foot of the stairs. But presently the slow movement began again, and the policeman fought at the top of the flight to ease the pressure on those who were going down.

A reddish light from a window fell upon the faces of the men when they, in turn, arrived at the last three steps and were about to enter. One could then note a change of expresion that had come over their features. As they thus stood upon the threshold of their hopes, they looked suddenly content and complacent. The fire had passed from their eyes and the snarl had vanished from their lips. The very force of the crowd in the rear, which had previously vexed them, was regarded from another point of view, for it now made it inevitable that they should go through the little doors into the place that was cheery and warm with light.

The tossing crowd on the sidewalk grew smaller and smaller. The snow beat with merciless persistence upon the bowed heads of those who waited. The wind drove it up from the pavements in frantic forms of winding white, and it seethed in circles about the huddled forms, passing in, one by one, three by three, out of the storm.

Theodore Dreiser
Curious Shifts of the Poor

AT THE HOUR when Broadway assumes its most interesting aspect, a peculiar individual takes his stand at the corner of Twenty-sixth street. It is the hour when the theatres are just beginning to receive their patrons. Fire signs, announcing the night's amusements, blaze on every hand. Cabs and carriages, their lamps gleaming like yellow eyes, patter by. Couples and parties of three and four are freely mingled in the common crowd which passes by in a thick stream, laughing and jesting. On Fifth avenue are loungers, a few wealthy strollers, a gentleman in evening dress with a lady at his side, some clubmen, passing from one smoking room to another. Across the way the great hotels, the Hoffman House and the Fifth Avenue, show a hundred gleaming windows, their cafés and billiard rooms filled with a pleasure-loving throng. All about, the night has a feeling of pleasure and exhilaration, the curious enthusiasm of a great city, bent upon finding joy in a thousand different ways.

In the midst of this lightsome atmosphere a short, stocky-built soldier, in a great cape-overcoat and soft felt hat, takes his stand at the corner. For a while he is alone, gazing like any idler upon an ever-fascinating scene. A policeman passes, saluting him as Captain, in a friendly way. An urchin, who has seen him there before, stops and gazes. To all others he is nothing out of the ordinary save in dress, a stranger, whistling for his own amusement.

As the first half hour wanes, certain characters appear. Here and there in the passing crowd one may see now and then a loiterer, edging interestedly near. A slouchy figure crosses the opposite corner and glances furtively in his direction. Another comes down Fifth avenue to the corner of Twenty-sixth street, takes a general survey and hobbles off again. Two or three noticeable Bowery types edge along the Fifth avenue side of Madison Square, but do not venture over.

Demorest's, XXXVI (November, 1899), 22–26. Text from this publication.

Dreiser later worked each of these vignettes into his account of Hurstwood's decline in the final chapters of *Sister Carrie.*

The soldier in his cape-overcoat walks a line of ten feet at his corner, to and fro, whistling.

As nine o'clock approaches, some of the hubbub of the earlier hour passes. On Broadway the crowd is neither so thick nor so gay. There are fewer cabs passing. The atmosphere of the hotels is not so youthful. The air, too, is colder. On every hand move curious figures, watchers and peepers without an imaginary circle, which they are afraid to enter—dozens in all. Presently, with the arrival of a keener sense of cold, one figure comes forward. It crosses Broadway from out the shadow of Twenty-sixth street, and, in a halting, circuitous way, arrives close to the waiting figure. There is something shamefaced, a diffident air about the movement, as if the intention were to conceal any idea of stopping until the very last moment. Then, suddenly, close to the soldier comes the halt. The Captain looks in recognition, but there is no especial greeting. The newcomer nods slightly, and murmurs something, like one who waits for gifts. The other simply motions toward the edge of the walk.

"Stand over there."

The spell is broken. Even while the soldier resumes his short, solemn walk, other figures shuffle forward. They do not so much as greet the leader, but join the one, shuffling and hitching and scraping their feet.

"Cold, isn't it?"

"I don't like winter."

"Looks as though it might snow."

The motley company has increased to ten. One or two know each other and converse. Others stand off a few feet, not wishing to be in the crowd, and yet not counted out. They are peevish, crusty, silent, eying nothing in particular, and moving their feet. The soldier, counting sufficient to begin, comes forward.

"Beds, eh, all of you?"

There is a general shuffle and murmur of approval.

"Well, line up here. I'll see what I can do. I haven't a cent myself."

They fall into a sort of broken, ragged line. One sees now some of the chief characteristics by contrast. There is a wooden leg in the line. Hats are all drooping, a collection that would ill become a second-hand Hester street basement collection. Trousers are all warped and frayed at the bottom, and coats worn and faded. In the glare of the street lights, some of the faces look dry and chalky. Others are red with blotches, and puffed in the cheeks and under the eyes. One or two are raw-boned and remind one of railroad hands. A few spectators come near, drawn by the seemingly conferring group, then more and more, and quickly there is a pushing, gaping crowd. Someone in the line begins to talk.

"Silence!" exclaims the Captain. "Now, then, gentlemen, these men are without beds. They have got to have some place to sleep to-night. They can't lie out in the street. I need twelve cents to put one to bed. Who will give it to me?"

No reply.

"Well, we'll have to wait here, boys, until someone does. Twelve cents isn't so very much for one man."

"Here is fifteen," exclaims a young man, who is peering forward with strained eyes. "It's all I can afford."

"All right; now I have fifteen. Step out of the line," and seizing the one at the end of the line nearest him by the shoulder, the Captain marches him off a little way and stands him up alone.

Coming back, he resumes his place before the little line and begins again.

"I have three cents here. These men must be put to bed somehow. There are," counting, "one, two, three, four, five, six, seven, eight, nine, ten, eleven, twelve men. Nine cents more will put the next man to bed, give him a good, comfortable bed for the night. I go right along and look after that myself. Who will give me nine cents?"

One of the watchers, this time a middle-aged man, hands in a five-cent piece.

"Good. Now I have eight cents. Four more will give this man a bed. Come, gentlemen, we are going very slow this evening. You all have good beds. How about these?"

"Here you are," remarked a bystander, putting a coin into his hand.

"That," says the Captain, looking at the coin, "pays for two beds for two men and leaves five for the next one. Who will give seven cents more?"

On the one hand the little line of those whose beds are secure is growing, but on the other the bedless waxes long. Silently the queer drift of poverty washes in, and they take their places at the foot of the line unnoticed. Ever and anon the Captain counts and announces the number remaining. Its growth neither dismays nor interests him. He does not even speak of it. His concern is wholly over the next man, and the securing of twelve cents. Strangers, gazing out of mere curiosity, find their sympathies enlisted, and pay into the hands of the Captain dimes and quarters, as he states in a short, brusque, unaffected way, the predicament of the men.

In the line of men whose beds are secure, a relaxed air is apparent. The strain of uncertainty being removed, there is moderate good feeling, and some leaning toward sociability. Those nearest one another begin to talk. Politics, religion, the state of the government, some news-paper sensations, and the more notorious facts of the world find mouth-pieces and auditors here. Vague and rambling are the discussions. Cracked and husky voices pronounce forcibly on odd things. There are squints and leers and dull ox-like stares from those who are too dull or too weary to converse.

Standing tells. In the course of time the earliest arrivals become weary and uneasy. There is a constant shifting from one foot to the other, a leaning out and looking back to see how many more must be provided for before the company can march away. Comments are made and crude wishes for the urging forward of things.

"Huh! There's a lot back there yet."

"Yes, must be over a hundred to-night."

"Look at the guy in the cab."

"Captain's a great fellow, ain't he?"

A cab has stopped. Some gentleman in evening dress reaches out a bill to the Captain, who takes it with simple thanks, and turns away to his line. There is a general craning of necks as the jewel in the broad white shirt-front sparkles and the cab moves off. Even the crowd gapes in awe.

"That fixes up nine men for the night," says the Captain, counting out as many of the line near him. "Line up over there. Now, then, there are only seven. I need twelve cents."

Money comes slow. In the course of time the crowd thins out to a meagre handful. Fifth avenue, save for an occasional cab or foot-passenger, is bare. Broadway is thinly peopled with pedestrians. Only now and then a stranger passing notices the small group, hands out a coin and goes away, unheeding.

The Captain is stolid and determined. He talks on, very slowly, ut-tering the fewest words, and with a certain assurance, as though he could not fail.

"Come, I can't stay out here all night. These men are getting tired and cold. Someone give me four cents."

There comes a time when he says nothing at all. Money is handed him, and for each twelve cents he singles out a man and puts him in the other line. Then he walks up and down as before, looking at the ground.

The theatres let out. Fire signs disappear. A clock strikes eleven. Another half hour, and he is down to the last two men.

A lady in opera cape and rustling silk skirt comes down Fifth avenue, supported by her escort. The latter glances at the line and comes over. There is a bill in his fingers.

"Here you are," he says.

"Thanks," says the Captain. "Now we have some for to-morrow night."

The last two are lined up. The soldier walks along, studying his line and counting.

"One hundred and thirty-seven," he exclaims, when he reaches the head.

"Now, boys, line up there. Steady now, we'll be off in a minute."

He places himself at the head and calls out, "Forward, march!" and away they go.

Across Fifth avenue, through Madison Square, by the winding path, east on Twenty-third street, and down Third avenue trudges the long, serpentine company.

Below Tenth street is a lodging house, and here the queer, ragamuffin line brings up, while the Captain enters in to arrange. In a few minutes the deal is consummated, and the line marches slowly in, each being provided with a key as the Captain looks on. When the last one has disappeared up the dingy stairway, he comes out, muffles his great coat closer in the cold air, pulls down his slouch brim, and tramps, a solitary, silent figure, into the night.

Such is the Captain's idea of his duty to his fellow man. He is a strange man, with a strange bias. Utter confidence in Providence, perfectly sure that he deals direct with God, he takes this means of fulfilling his own destiny.

Outside the door of what was once a row of red brick family dwellings, in Fifteenth street, but what is now a mission or convent house of the Sisters of Mercy, hangs a plain wooden contribution box, on which is painted the statement that every noon a meal is given free to all those who apply and ask for aid. This simple announcement is modest in the extreme, covering, as it does, a charity so broad. Unless one were looking up this matter in particular, he could stand at Sixth avenue and Fifteenth street for days, around the noon hour, and never notice that, out of the vast crowd that surges along that busy thoroughfare, there turned out, every few seconds, some weatherbeaten, heavy-footed specimen of humanity, gaunt in countenance, and dilapidated in the matter of clothes. The fact is true, however, and the colder the day the more apparent it becomes. Space and lack of culinary room compels an arrangement which permits of only twenty-five or thirty eating at one time, so that a line has to be formed outside, and an orderly entrance effected.

One such line formed on a January day last year. It was peculiarly cold. Already, at eleven in the morning, several shambled forward out of Sixth avenue, their thin clothes flapping and fluttering in the wind, and leaned up against the iron fence. One came up from the west out of Seventh avenue and stopped close to the door, nearer than all the others. Those who had been waiting before him, but farther away, now drew near, and by a certain stolidity of demeanor, no words being spoken, indicated that they were first. The newcomer looked sullenly along the line and then moved out, taking his place at the foot. When order had been restored, the animal feeling of opposition relaxed.

"Must be pretty near noon," ventured one.

"It is," said another; "I've been waitin' nearly an hour."

"Gee, but it's cold."

The line was growing rapidly. Those at the head evidently congratulated themselves upon not having long to wait. There was much jerking of heads and looking down the line.

"It don't matter much how near you get to the front, so long as you're in the first twenty-five. You all go in together," commented one of the first twenty-five.

"This here Single Tax is the thing. There ain't goin' to be no order till it comes," said another, discussing that broader topic.

At last the door opened and the motherly Sister looked out. Slowly the line moved up, and one by one thirty men passed in. Then she interposed a stout arm and the line halted with six men on the steps. In this position they waited. After a while one of the earliest to go in came out, and then another. Every time one came out the line moved up. And this continued until two o'clock, when the last hungry dependent crossed the threshold, and the door was closed.

It was a winter evening. Already at four o'clock, the sombre hue of night was thickening the air. A heavy snow was falling—a fine, picking, whipping snow, borne forward by a swift wind in long, thin lines. The street was bedded with it, six inches of cold, soft carpet, churned brown by the crush of teams and the feet of men. Along the Bowery, men slouched through it with collars up and hats pulled over their ears.

Before a dirty four-story building gathered a crowd of men. It began with the approach of two or three, who hung about the closed wooden doors, and beat their feet to keep them warm. They made no effort to go in, but shifted ruefully about, digging their hands deep in their pockets, and leering at the crowd and the increasing lamps. There were old men with grizzled beards and sunken eyes; men who were comparatively young, but shrunken by disease; men who were middle-aged.

With the growth of the crowd about the door came a murmur. It was not conversation, but a running comment directed at anyone in general. It contained oaths and slang phrases.

"I wisht they'd hurry up."

"Look at the copper watchin'."

"Maybe it ain't winter, nuther."

"I wisht I was with Otis."

Now a sharper lash of wind cut down, and they huddled closer. There was no anger, no threatening words. It was all sullen endurance, unlightened by either wit or good fellowship.

A carriage went jingling by with some reclining figure in it. One of the members nearest the door saw it.

"Look at the bloke ridin'."

"He ain't so cold."

"Eh! Eh! Eh!" yelled another, the carriage having long since passed out of hearing.

Little by little the night crept on. Along the walk a crowd turned out on its way home. Still the men hung around the door, unwavering.

"Ain't they ever goin' to open up?" queried a hoarse voice suggestively.

This seemed to renew general interest in the closed door, and many gazed in that direction. They looked at it as dumb brutes look, as dogs paw and whine and study the knob. They shifted and blinked and muttered, now a curse, now a comment. Still they waited, and still the snow whirled and cut them.

A glimmer appeared through the transom overhead, where some-one was lighting the gas. It sent a thrill of possibility through the watcher. On the old hats and peaked shoulders snow was piling. It gathered in little heaps and curves, and no one brushed it off. In the center of the crowd the warmth and steam melted it, and water trickled off hat-rims and down noses which the owners could not reach to scratch. On the outer rim the piles remained unmelted. Those who could not get in the center lowered their heads to the weather and bent their forms.

At last the bars grated inside and the crowd pricked up its ears. There was someone who called, "Slow up there now!" and then the door opened. It was push and jam for a minute, with grim, beast si-lence to prove its quality, and then the crowd lessened. It melted in-ward like logs floating, and disappeared. There were wet hats and shoulders, a cold, shrunken, disgruntled mass, pouring in between bleak walls. It was just six o'clock, and there was supper in every hur-rying pedestrian's face.

"Do you sell anything to eat here?" questioned one of the grizzled old carpet-slippers who opened the door.

"No; nothin' but beds."

The waiting throng had been housed.

For nearly a quarter of a century Fleischman, the caterer, has given a loaf of bread to anyone who will come for it to the rear door of his restaurant, on the corner of Broadway and Ninth street, at midnight. Every night, during twenty-three years, about three hundred men have formed in line, and, at the appointed time, marched past the doorway, picked their loaf from a great box placed just outside, and vanished again into the night. From the beginning to the present time there has been little change in the character or number of these men. There are two or three figures that have grown familiar to those who have seen this little procession pass year after year. Two of them have missed scarcely a night in fifteen years. There are about forty, more or less, regular callers. The remainder of the line is formed of strangers every night.

The line is not allowed to form before eleven o'clock. At this hour, perhaps a single figure shambles around the corner and halts on the edge of the sidewalk. Other figures appear and fall in behind. They come almost entirely one at a time. Haste is seldom manifest in their approach. Figures appear from every direction, limping slowly, slouching stupidly, or standing with assumed or real indifference, until the end of the line is reached, when they take their places and wait.

Most of those in the line are over thirty. There is seldom one under twenty. A low murmur of conversation is heard, but for the most part the men stand in stupid, unbroken silence. Here and there are two or three talkative ones, and if you pass close enough you will hear every topic of the times discussed or referred to, except those which are supposed to interest the poor. Wretchedness, poverty, hunger and distress are never mentioned. The possibilities of a match between prize-ring favorites, the day's evidence in the latest murder trial, the chance of war in Africa, the latest improvements in automobiles, the prosperity or depression of some other portion of the world, or the mistakes of the Government, from Washington to the campaign in Manila. These, or others like them, are the topics of whatever conversation is held. It is for the most part a rambling, disconnected conversation.

"Wait until Dreyfus gets out of prison," said one to his little black-eyed neighbor one night, "and you'll see them guys fallin' on his neck."

"Maybe they will and maybe they won't," the other muttered. "You needn't think, just because you see dagoes selling violets on Broadway, that the spring is here."

The passing of a Broadway car awakens a vague idea of progress, and some one remarks: "They'll have them things running by liquid air before we know it."

"I've driv mule cars by here myself," replies another.

A few moments before twelve a great box of bread is pushed outside the door, and exactly on the hour a portly round-faced German takes his position by it, and calls "Ready." The whole line at once, like a well-drilled company of regulars, moves swiftly, in good marching time, diagonally across the sidewalk to the inner edge and pushes, with only the noise of tramping feet, past the box. Each man reaches for a loaf, and, breaking line, wanders off by himself. Most of them do not even glance at their bread, but put it indifferently under their coats or in their pockets.

In the great sea of men here are these little eddies of driftwood, a hundred nightly in Madison Square, 300 outside a bakery at midnight, crowds without the lodging-houses in stormy weather, and all this day after day. These are the poor in body and in spirit. The lack of houses and lands and fine clothing is nothing. Many have these and are equally wretched. The cause of misery lies elsewhere. The attitude of pity which the world thinks proper to hold toward poverty is misplaced—a result of the failure to see and to realize. Poverty of worldly goods is not in itself pitiful. A sickly body, an ignorant mind, a narrow spirit, brutal impulses and perverted appetites are the pitiful things. The adding of material riches to one thus afflicted would not remove him from out the pitiful. On the other hand, there are so-called poor people in every community among its ornaments. There is no pity for them, but rather love and honor. They are rich in wisdom and influence.

The individuals composing this driftwood are no more miserable than others. Most of them would be far more uncomfortable if compelled to lead respectable lives. They cannot be benefited by money. There may be a class of poor for whom a little money judiciously expended would result in good, but these are the lifeless flotsam and jetsam of society without vitality to ever revive. Few among them would survive a month if they should come suddenly into the possession of a fortune.

Their parade before us should not appeal to our pity, but should awaken us to what we are—for society is no better than its poorest type. They expose what is present, though better concealed, everywhere. They are the few skeletons of the sunlight—types of these with which society's closests are full. Civilization, in spite of its rapid progress, is still in profound ignorance of the things essential to a healthy, happy and prosperous life. Ignorance and error are everywhere manifest in the miseries and sufferings of men. Wealth may create an illusion, or modify a ghastly appearance of ignorance and error, but it cannot change the effect. The result is as real in the mansions of Fifth avenue as in the midnight throng outside a baker's door.

The livid-faced dyspeptic who rides from his club to his apartments and pauses on the way to hand his dollar to the Captain should awaken the same pity as the shivering applicant for a free bed whom his dollar aids—pity for the ignorance and error that cause the distress of the world.

Part Six

THE SOCIAL CRISIS

Pictures from Hell

Explanations and Solutions

Social Reality

299

Ward McAllister, *Society as I Have Found It*
John Jay Chapman, *Society*

The "Gay Nineties" were gay primarily for the very wealthy. The decade began with an agricultural depression well underway, and in 1893 a major financial panic affected the entire country. During the severe winter of 1893–94 approximately twenty percent of the labor force was unemployed, and by the following summer the prevalence of tramps became a national concern. Violent strikes occurred at Carnegie's Homestead works in 1892 and at Pullman's great Chicago factory in 1894. Westerners in particular felt that the traditional political parties no longer represented their interests, and the People's Party (or Populists) arose as one of the most significant third parties in American political history. It was only in 1898, with bumper crops in America and good markets elsewhere, with the discovery of gold in Alaska, and with the euphoria of the swift and total victory over Spain, that there was a lessening of the widespread belief that the country was in the midst of a major social and political crisis.

The most perceptive minds of the decade, however, realized that low wheat prices or unemployment were outward signs of a far deeper social malaise. To such writers as Hamlin Garland or Stephen Crane, whose backgrounds were rural or middle-class, a visit to a steel mill or a coal mine was equivalent to a journey to hell. Extreme variations in temperature and light and the ear-shattering clamour of machinery suggested to them a Satanic underworld in which man was a tortured prisoner. Garland and Crane, and William Wyckoff, in his account of his experience as a day laborer, stressed above all that life as a miner or mill hand, a farmer or laborer, was primarily a daily grind of mind-numbing, body-wearying physical drudgery. The realization that most work in America was essentially machine-like led Garland to comment ironically, "Upon such toil rests the splendor of American civilization," and Wyckoff to state more directly, "From work like ours there seems to have been eliminated every element which constitutes the nobility of labor." When Edwin Markham's "The Man with the Hoe" was published in early 1899, it caught the public imagination and became the most celebrated American poem of the decade. Markham concisely and powerfully stated the great truth of modern working-class life which other writers had only obliquely represented —that unremitting physical labor brutalizes and eventually kills the spirit of man. Social and political reforms could of course alleviate this condition to some degree, as they eventually did. But the insight that man in an industrial society can be turned into a machine was so sharpened in focus and intensity during the 1890's that it remained one of the principal motifs of modern American literature.

The immediate effect of the depression of the mid-1890's, however, was to stimulate a search for immediate solutions. The popularity of Charles Sheldon's *In His Steps* testified to the appeal of the traditional belief that if every man acted as a Christian toward his fellow man, Christianity would exist as a social reality. The average factory worker or farmer might respond to this appeal on Sunday, but on Monday he usually required a more tangible remedy. In particular, he responded to the idea that his condition could be attributed to a single all-powerful force whose removal or defeat would result in a better society for the working man. To some this force was the Gold Standard, to others it was the Trust, and to still others it was Capitalism. The emotional appeal in all instances was to the image of an Enemy. It was the appeal of a People's Crusade against the Evil of Special Privilege and Intrenched Wealth, and its rhetoric was that of militant Christianity, with William Jennings Bryan's Cross of Gold speech less an extreme than a moderate example.

Even though the Western farmer and Eastern mechanic heard the same drum, they responded to different lyrics, and there were some writers who played an entirely different tune. Finley Peter Dunne's caricature of a Populist convention revealed the city man's belief that the Populists were ignorant hayseeds, a belief which helped carry the East for McKinley in 1896. And Thomas Bailey Aldrich's distrust of immigration represented both a New England Brahmin and a Western prejudice. It was William Graham Sumner who best stated the opposition to both Eastern and Western reform movements. A confirmed Social Darwinist, Sumner's argument that to attempt "to make the world over" was to tamper dangerously with both natural law and democracy was the expressed position of the Republican Party and the emotional attitude of a large number of Americans who had been bred for generations on a rhetoric of self-help and individualism. The return of prosperity in 1898 appeared to confirm Sumner and the Republicans; it was to be many years before the distinction between "natural" and "social" was generally accepted.

The social crisis of the 1890's had characteristics other than those concerning working conditions or economic depression. To William Dean Howells, one of the deplorable characteristics of modern American life was the growth of an inflexible class system, a way of life which he associated with Europe and the past. His Utopian satire of class assumptions was matched by George Ade's burlesque of class perogatives and by Ward McAllister's unwitting confirmation of the vacuous power of upper-class biases. The most penetrating analysis of the changing nature of American society, however, was that of George Jay Chapman. Without denying obvious class difference, he found an underlying intellectual conformity and dishonesty in all American life, and he attributed this quality to the pervasiveness of business ethics in every phase of American experience. Chapman thus discovered and defined Babbittry some twenty-five years before Sinclair Lewis gave the idea wide currency.

None of the social crises of the 1890's were solved. Rather, the major effect of the widespread absorption in social problems was to clear the air of old and harmful ideas. Despite the economic recovery of 1898, by the close of the decade most thinking men could no longer maintain that work was inherently Godly, that rich and poor were alike in their opportunities and goals, that America was classless, and that Americans spoke their minds fearlessly. If nothing else was gained, at least the old myths were beginning to crumble.

Hamlin Garland
Homestead and Its Perilous Trades

A COLD, THIN October rain was falling as I took the little ferry-boat and crossed the Monongahela River to see Homestead and its iron-mills. The town, infamously historic already, sprawled over the irregu-

McClure's, III (June, 1894), 3–20. Text from this publication.

Garland was visiting Homestead in October, 1893, approximately a year after the end of the Homestead strike. Called by the Amalgamated Association of Iron and Steel Workers in protest against a lowering of wages, the

lar hillside, circled by the cold gray river. On the flats close to the water's edge there were masses of great sheds, out of which grim smoke-stacks rose with a desolate effect, like the black stumps of a burned forest of great trees. Above them dense clouds of sticky smoke rolled heavily away.

Higher up the tenement-houses stood in dingy rows, alternating with vacant lots. Higher still stood some Queen Anne cottages, toward which slender sidewalks climbed like goat paths.

The streets of the town were horrible; the buildings were poor; the sidewalks were sunken, swaying, and full of holes, and the crossings were sharp-edged stones set like rocks in a river bed. Everywhere the yellow mud of the street lay kneaded into a sticky mass, through which groups of pale, lean men slouched in faded garments, grimy with the soot and grease of the mills.

The town was as squalid and unlovely as could well be imagined, and the people were mainly of the discouraged and sullen type to be found everywhere where labor passes into the brutalizing stage of severity. It had the disorganized and incoherent effect of a town which has feeble public spirit. Big industries at differing eras have produced squads of squalid tenement-houses far from the central portion of the town, each plant bringing its gangs of foreign laborers in raw masses to camp down like an army around its shops.

Such towns are sown thickly over the hill-lands of Pennsylvania, but this was my first descent into one of them. They are American only in the sense in which they represent the American idea of business.

The Carnegie mills stood down near the river at some distance from the ferry landing, and thither I took my way through the sticky yellow mud and the gray falling rain. I had secured for my guide a young man whose life had been passed in Homestead and who was quite familiar with the mills and workmen. I do not think he over-stated the hardships of the workmen, whose duties he thoroughly understood. He spoke frankly and without undue prejudice of the management and the work.

We entered the yard through the fence which was aggrandized into a stockade during the riots of a year ago. We were in the yard of the "finished beams." On every side lay thousands of tons of iron. There came toward us a group of men pushing a cart laden with girders for building. They were lean men, pale and grimy. The rain was falling upon them. They wore a look of stoical indifference, though one or two of the younger fellows were scuffling as they pushed behind the car.

---

strike had lasted for almost five months. With the aid of Pinkerton agents and scabs, Carnegie and his chief manager, Henry Clay Frick, were able to reopen the plant, and the union admitted defeat in November, 1892.

Farther on was heard the crashing thunder of falling iron plates, the hoarse coughing of great engines, and the hissing of steam. Suddenly through the gloom I caught sight of the mighty up-soaring of saffron and sapphire flame, which marked the draught of the furnace of the Bessemer steel plant far down toward the water. It was a magnificent contrast to the dusky purple of the great smoky roofs below.

The great building which we entered first was a beam mill, "one of the finest in the world," my guide said. It was an immense shed, open at the sides, and filled with a mixed and intricate mass of huge machinery. On every side tumultuous action seemed to make every inch of ground dangerous. Savage little engines went rattling about among the piles of great beams. Dimly on my left were huge engines, moving with thunderous pounding.

"Come to the starting point," said my guide. I followed him timidly far up toward the other end, my eyes fixed on the beautiful glow of a red-hot bloom of metal swung high in the air. It lighted the interior with a glorious light.

I was looking at this beautiful light when my guide pulled me suddenly behind some shelter. The furious scream of a saw broke forth, the monstrous exaggeration of a circular wood-saw—a saw that melted its way through a beam of solid iron with deafening outcry, producing a gigantic glowing wheel of spattering sparks of golden fire. While it lasted all else was hid from sight.

"That's the saw which cuts the beams of iron into lengths as ordered," my guide said, and we hurried past.

Everywhere in this pandemoniac shed was the thunder of reversing engines, the crash of falling iron, the rumbling growl of rollers, the howl of horrible saws, the deafening hiss of escaping steam, the wild vague shouts of workmen.

"Here are the ingots of steel, just as they come from the Bessemer converting mill," said my guide, pointing toward the mouth of the shed where some huge hunks of iron lay. "And there are the 'soaking pits,' or upright furnaces, where they are heated for rolling. They are perpendicular furnaces, or pits, you see."

We moved toward the mouths of the pits, where a group of men stood with long shovels and bars in their hands. They were touched with orange light, which rose out of the pits. The pits looked like wells or cisterns of white-hot metal. The men signalled a boy, and the huge covers, which hung on wheels, were moved to allow them to peer in at the metal. They threw up their elbows before their eyes, to shield their faces from the heat, while they studied the ingots within.

"It takes grit to stand there in July and August," said my guide. "Don't it, Joe?" he said to one of the men whom he knew. The man nodded, but was too busy to do more.

"I'd as soon go to hell at once," I replied. He laughed.

"But that isn't all. Those pits have to have their bottoms made after every 'heat,' and they can't wait for 'em to cool. The men stand by and work over them when it's hot enough to burn your boot-soles. Still it beats the old horizontal furnace."

A huge crane swung round and dipped into one of the pits and rose again, bringing one of the ingots, which was heated to proper point for rolling. Its glow made the eye recoil, and threw into steel-blue relief the gray outside rain. It was about six feet long and twenty inches square.

The crane swung round and laid it upon a roadway of steel travellers that carried it up to the waiting jaws of the rollers. High up above it stood the chief "roller," with his hand upon a lever, and as the glowing mass ambled forward, his eyes gauged it, and his hand controlled it.

Like a bar of soap through a wringer it went, and as it passed it lowered and lengthened, exploding at the end into flaming scales of fire.

"The power of two thousand five hundred horses is in that engine," said my guide. "The actual squeezing power exerted is of course several thousand tons."

Back the bar came with the same jar and tumult, a little longer and a little thinner; back and forth, until it grew into a long band of pink and rose purple. A swift and dangerous dragon that engine, whose touch was deadly. Thence the bar passed to the monstrous saw whose ear-splitting howl rose at intervals as it cut the beams into fixed lengths. From this the pieces passed into a low flat oven flaming fiercely; there to be kept hot while waiting their turn in the next process.

They passed finally to the "finishing rollers," where they took the completed form of building beams. A vast carrier which moved sidewise with rumbling roar conveyed them across the intervening space. A man rode this carrier like a mahout his elephant, occupying a small platform high on the pyramidal mass of machinery.

Up at the pits again I stood to watch the "heaters" at their task. The crane and the travellers handled these huge pieces of iron deftly and surely, and moulded them into shape, as a girl might handle a cake of dough. Machinery has certainly come in here to lessen the horrors of the iron-worker's life, to diminish the number of deaths by exploding metal or by the leap of curling or breaking beams.

I watched the men as they stirred the deeps beneath. I could not help admiring the swift and splendid action of their bodies. They had the silence and certainty one admires in the tiger's action. I dared not move for fear of flying metal, the swift swing of a crane, or the

sudden lurch of a great carrier. The men could not look out for me.
They worked with a sort of desperate attention and alertness.

"That looks like hard work," I said to one of them to whom my companion introduced me. He was breathing hard from his work.

"Hard! I guess it's hard. I lost forty pounds the first three months
I came into this business. It sweats the life out of a man. I often drink
two buckets of water during twelve hours; the sweat drips through
my sleeves, and runs down my legs and fills my shoes."

"But that isn't the worst of it," said my guide; "it's a dog's life. Now,
those men work twelve hours, and sleep and eat out ten more. You
can see a man don't have much time for anything else. You can't see
your friends, or do anything but work. That's why I got out of it. I
used to come home so exhausted, staggering like a man with a 'jag.'
It ain't any place for a sick man—is it, Joe?"

Joe was a tall young fellow, evidently an assistant at the furnace.
He smiled. "It's all the work I want, and I'm no chicken—feel that
arm."

I felt his arm. It was like a billet of steel. His abdomen was like a
sheet of boiler iron. The hair was singed from his hands and arms by
the heat of the furnace.

"The tools I handle weigh one hundred and fifty pounds, and four
o'clock in August they weigh about a ton."

"When do you eat?"

"I have a bucket of 'grub'; I eat when I can. We have no let-up
for eating. This job I'm on now isn't so bad as it might be, for we're
running easy; but when we're running full, it's all I can stand."

One of the men made a motion, and the ponderous cover moved a
little to one side, and the bottom-makers ran long bars down into the
pit and worked desperately, manipulating the ganister which lined
the sides. The vivid light seemed to edge them with flame.

"Yes, sir; that is a terrible job in summer," repeated my companion.
"When the whole mill is hot, and you're panting for breath, it takes
nerve to walk up to that soaking pit or a furnace door."

"Oh, well, when you get ready to go home, your carriage comes for
you, I suppose," I said to Joe.

He looked at me with a look that was not humorous. "I pattered
down here in the mud, and crawled through a hole in the
fence. That's the way I'll crawl home to-morrow morning at six. That's
the way we all do."

He turned suddenly and pointed at a pale, stoop-shouldered man
in grimy clothes. "There's one of the best-paid men in the mill. See
any kid gloves on him? He'd look gay in a carriage at six o'clock in
the morning, wouldn't he?"

I watched the man as he climbed to his perch on the great carrier that handled the beams, passing them from the rough roller to the finishing roller. As he took his place a transformation took place in him. He became alert, watchful, and deft. He was a man heavily marked by labor.

We went on into the boiler-plate mills, still noisier, still more grandiose in effect. The rosy slabs of iron were taken from the white-hot furnaces by a crane (on which a man sat and swung, moving with it, guiding it) quite as in the beam mill. They were dropped upon a similar set of travellers, but as they passed through the rollers a man flung a shovelful of salt upon them, and each slab gave off a terrific exploding roar, like a hundred guns sounding together. As they passed to and fro, they grew thinner in form and richer in tone. The water which sprayed them ran about, fled and returned in dark spatters, like flocks of frightened spiders. The sheet warped and twisted, and shot forward with a menacing action which made me shiver.

Everywhere in this enormous building were pits like the mouth of hell, and fierce ovens giving off a glare of heat, and burning wood and iron, giving off horrible stenches of gases. Thunder upon thunder, clang upon clang, glare upon glare! Torches flamed far up in the dark spaces above. Engines moved to and fro, and steam sissed and threatened.

Everywhere were grimy men with sallow and lean faces. The work was of the inhuman sort that hardens and coarsens.

"How long do you work?" I asked of a young man who stood at the furnace near me.

"Twelve hours," he replied. "The night set go on at six at night and come off at six in the morning. I go on at six and off at six."

"For how much pay?"

"Two dollars and a quarter."

"How much do those men get shovelling there in the rain?"

"One dollar and forty cents." (A cut has since taken place.)

"What proportion of the men get that pay?"

"Two-thirds of the whole plant, nearly two thousand. There are thirty-five hundred men in the mills. They get all prices, of course, from a dollar and forty cents up to the tonnage men, who get five and ten dollars per day when the mills run smooth."

"I suppose not many men make ten dollars per day."

"Well, hardly." He smiled. "Of course the 'rollers' and the 'heaters' get the most, but there are only two 'rollers' to each mill, and three 'heaters,' and they are responsible for their product. The most of the men get under two dollars per day."

"And it is twelve hours' work without stop?"

"You bet! And then again you see we only get this pay part of the time. The mills are liable to be shut down part of the year. They shut down part of the night sometimes, and of course we're docked. Then, again, the tendency of the proprietors is to cut down the tonnage men; that is, the 'rollers' and 'heaters' are now paid by the ton, but they'll some day be paid by the day, like the rest of us."

"You bet they will," said my guide, who seemed quite familiar with the facts.

"Of course, you understand the tonnage men are responsible for their product. You see the improvement of machinery helps them, but it don't help the common laborer much. It wouldn't help the tonnage men if the company could fill their places cheaper. They don't pay them by the ton because they want to, but because they have to. But the tonnage men 'll get it next year."

"That's right," said the man at the furnace door, as he seized his shovel to "line" the furnace.

The helper wheeled in a load of sand and gravel before the furnace door. He signalled a boy, the heavy iron door rose, the "heater" seized one of the long shovels, the helper lifted it with his own shovel and placed it in the mouth of the furnace and swiftly heaped it with sand. The "heater" ran the shovel in and turned it over on a thin place in the lining, and smoothed the sand out with desperate haste. The helper lifted the now red-hot shovel to the next door. The cover rose, and the process repeated. In each oven the beams reposed like potatoes in an oven.

By the time the helper had a moment to spare he was wet with sweat. As he stood near me I noticed his grimy and sooty shirt, which lay close to his lean chest.

"One of the worst features about this thing is the sudden change of temperature. Now, that man's reeking with sweat, and this cold wind blowing upon him," I said to my guide. "It's always too hot or too cold."

I was shivering with the chill, and it seemed to be almost certain sickness to stand thus exposed to the wind which swept through.

When these beams were "done" to a white heat, a massive carrier, with nippers like huge tongs, moved with a sidewise rush before one of the oven doors. A shout to the boy high against the wall, and the cover again rose, the carrier thrust its two hands in and hauled out the glowing beam, and from thence swung it upon the roadway of travellers, whence it galloped like a live thing into the jaws of the rollers.

We passed on into the older mills, where cruder methods are still in use. Man seems closer to the hot iron here. Everywhere dim figures with grappling hooks worked silently and desperately, guiding, measuring, controlling, moving masses of white-hot metal. High up the superintending foremen, by whistle or shout, arrested the movement of the machinery and the gnome-like figures beneath.

Here were made the steel rails for street railways. The process was the same in essence. Each crude mass of metal was heated in oven-like furnaces tended by dim figures of bare-armed men, thence drawn by cranes and swung upon a roadway and thrust into the rollers. Then it ran back and forth, back and forth, lengthening into a swift and terrible serpent of red. One that I saw had split at the end, and its resemblance to a serpent was startling as it shot toward us in sinuous thrust.

Upon such toil rests the splendor of American civilization.

The converting mill was the most gorgeous and dangerous of all. Here the crude product is turned into steel by the Bessemer process. It also was a huge shed-like building open on two sides. In the centre stood supports for two immense pear-shaped pots, which swung on pivots ten or twelve feet from the floor. Over each pot was a huge chimney. Out of each pot roared alternately a ferocious geyser of saffron and sapphire flame, streaked with deeper yellow. From it a light streamed—a light that flung violet shadows everywhere and made the gray outside rain a beautiful blue.

A fountain of sparks arose, gorgeous as ten thousand rockets, and fell with a beautiful curve, like the petals of some enormous flower. Overhead the beams were glowing orange in a base of purple. The men were yellow where the light struck them, violet in shadow. Wild shouts resounded amid the rumbling of an overhead train, and the squeal of a swift little engine, darting in and out laden with the completed castings. The pot began to burn with a whiter flame. Its fluttering, humming roar silenced all else.

"It is nearly ready to pour," said my companion; "the carbon is nearly burnt away."

"Why does it burn so ferociously?"

"Through the pivot a blast of oxygen is delivered with an enormous pressure. This unites with the silicon and carbon and carries it away to the surface. He'd better pour now, or the metal will burn."

Underneath the other pot men were shovelling away slag in the rain of falling sparks. They worked with desperate haste. To their wrists dangled disks of leather to protect their hands from heat. It was impossible to see what manner of men they were. They resembled human beings only in form.

A shout was heard, and a tall crane swung a gigantic ladle under the converting vessel, which then mysteriously up-ended, exploding like a cannon a prodigious discharge of star-like pieces of white-hot slag. The "blowers" on their high platform across the shed sheltered themselves behind a wall.

I drew back into the rain. "They call this the death-trap," shouted my companion, smiling at my timid action.

Down came the vessel, until out of it streamed the smooth flow of terribly beautiful molten metal. As it ran nearly empty and the ladle swung away, the dripping slag fell to the ground exploding, leaping viciously, and the scene became gorgeous beyond belief, with orange and red and green flame.

Into this steam and smoke and shower of sparks the workmen leapt, and were dimly seen preparing for another blast, prying off crusted slag, spraying the ladle, and guiding the cranes.

Meanwhile, high up above them in the tumult, an engine backed up with a load of crude molten iron, discharged into the converter, and the soaring saffron and orange and sapphire flames began again.

"Yes, the men call this the death-trap," repeated my guide, as we stood in the edge of the building; "they wipe a man out here every little while."

"In what way does death come?" I asked.

"Oh, all kinds of ways. Sometimes a chain breaks, and a ladle tips over, and the iron explodes—like that." He pointed at the newly emptied retort, out of which the drippings fell into the water which lay beneath like pools of green gold. As it fell, each drop exploded in a dull report.

"Sometimes the slag falls on the workmen from that roadway up there. Of course, if everything is working all smooth and a man watches out, why, all right! But you take it after they've been on duty twelve hours without sleep, and running like hell, everybody tired and loggy, and it's a different story."

My guide went on:

"You take it back in the beam mill—you saw how the men have to scatter when the carriers or the cranes move—well, sometimes they don't get out of the way; the men who should give warning don't do it quick enough."

"What do those men get who are shovelling slag up there?"

"Fourteen cents an hour. If they worked eight hours, like a carpenter, they'd get one dollar and twelve cents."

"So a man works in peril of his life for fourteen cents an hour," I remarked.

"That's what he does. It ain't the only business he does it in, though."

"No," put in a young villager, who was looking on like ourselves. "A man'll do most anything to live."

"Just as everywhere, the man who does the hardest work gets the poorest pay," I said, remembering Shelley's discovery.

We moved away, back toward the great plate mill. The lifting crane fascinated me. A man perched upon it like a monkey on the limb of a tree; and the creature raised, swung, lowered, shot out, opened its monstrous beak, seized the slab of iron, retreated, lifted, swung and dropped it upon the carriers. It was like a living thing, some strange creature unabashed by heat or heavy weights. To get in its way meant death. To guide it for twelve hours without accident exhausts a workman like running an engine on an express-train.

We stood to watch the making of rails. And as the rosy serpent grew slenderer and swifter it seemed to take on life. It curved lightly, unaccountably, and shot with menacing mouth past groups of workmen.

"Sometimes they break," said my guide, "and then they sweep things." And his words pictured the swing of a red-hot scythe.

"The wonder to me is, you don't all die of exposure and the changes of heat and cold."

My guide looked serious. "You don't notice any old men here." He swept his hand about the building. "It shortens life, just like mining; there is no question about that. That, of course, doesn't enter into the usual statement. But the long hours, the strain, and the sudden changes of temperature use a man up. He quits before he gets fifty. I can see lots of fellows here who are failing. They'll lay down in a few years. I went all over that, and I finally came to the decision that I'd peddle groceries rather than kill myself at this business."

"Well, what is the compensation? I mean, why do men keep on?"

"Oh, the common hands do it because they need a job, I suppose, and fellows like Joe expect to be one of the high-paid men."

"How much would that be per year?"

"Oh, three thousand or possibly four thousand a year."

"Does that pay for what it takes out of you?"

"No, I don't think it does," he confessed. "Still, a man has got to go into something."

As night fell the scene became still more grandiose and frightful. I hardly dared move without direction. The rosy ingots, looking like stumps of trees reduced to coals of living fire, rose from their pits of flame and dropped upon the tables, and galloped head on against the rollers, sending off flakes of rosy scale. As they went through, the giant engine thundered on, reversing with a sound like a nearby cannon; and everywhere the jarring clang of great beams fell upon the ear. Wherever the saw was set at work, great wheels of fire rose out of the obscure murk of lower shadow.

"I'm glad I don't have to work here for a living," said the young man of the village, who stood near me looking on.

"Oh, this is nothing," said my guide. "You should see it when they're running full in summer. Then it gets *hot* here. Then you should see 'em when they reline the furnaces and converting vessels. Imagine getting into that Bessemer pot in July, hot enough to pop corn; when you had to work like the devil and then jump out to breathe."

"I wouldn't do it," said the young villager; "I'd break into jail first." He had an outside job. He could afford to talk that way.

"Oh, no, you wouldn't; you'd do it. We all submit to such things, out of habit, I guess. There are lots of other jobs as bad. A man could stand work like this six hours a day. That's all a man ought to do at such work. They could do it, too; they wouldn't make so much, but the hands would live longer."

"They probably don't care whether the hands live or die," I said, "provided they do every ounce they can while they do live."

"I guess that's right," said the other young fellow with a wink. "Mill-owners don't run their mills for the benefit of the men."

"How do you stand on the late strike?" I asked another man.

"It's all foolishness; you can't do anything that way. The tonnage men brought it on; they could afford to strike, but we couldn't. The men working for less than two dollars can't afford to strike."

"'While capital wastes, labor starves,'" I ventured to quote.

"That's the idea; we can't hurt Carnegie by six months' starving. It's *our* ribs that'll show through our shirts."

"Then the strikes do not originate among the men of lowest pay?"

"No; a man working for fourteen cents an hour hasn't got any surplus for a strike." He seemed to voice the general opinion.

A roar as of a hundred lions, a thunder as of cannons, flames that made the electric light look like a twinkling blue star, jarring clang of falling iron, burst of spluttering flakes of fire, scream of terrible saws, shifting of mighty trucks with hiss of steam! This was the scene upon which I looked back; this tumult I was leaving. I saw men prodding in the deep soaking pits where the ingots glowed in white-hot chambers. I saw other men in the hot yellow glare from the furnaces. I saw men measuring the serpentine rosy beams. I saw them send the saw flying into them. I saw boys perched high in cages, their shrill voices sounding wild and animal-like in the midst of the uproar: a place into which men went like men going into war for the sake of wives and children, urged on by necessity, blinded and dulled by custom and habit; an inhuman place to spend four-fifths of one's waking hours. I crawled dismally back to my boarding-place, in the deep darkness, the chill, and the falling rain. The farther I got from those thundering beams and screaming saws, the deeper I drew my breath. Oh, the peace and sweetness of the dim hills across the river!

I ate breakfast the next morning with two of the men I had seen the evening before. There was little of grace or leisurely courtesy in their actions. Their hearts were good, but their manners were those of

ceaseless toilers. They resembled a Western threshing crew in all
but their pallor.

"The worst part of the whole business is this," said one of them, as
I was about saying good-by. "It brutalizes a man. You can't help it.
You start in to be a man, but you become more and more a machine,
and pleasures are few and far between. It's like any severe labor. It
drags you down mentally and morally, just as it does physically. I
wouldn't mind it so much if it weren't for the long hours. Many a
trade would be all right if the hours could be shortened. Twelve
hours is too long."

Again I boarded the little ferry and crossed the Monongahela on
my way to the East. Out of those grim chimneys the belching smoke
rose, defiling the cool, sweet air. Through this greenish-purple cloud
the sun, red and large, glowed like an ingot of steel rising from a pit,
filling the smoke with flushes of beautiful orange and rose amid the
blue. The river was azure and burning gold, and the sun threw the
most glorious shadows behind the smoke. Beyond lay the serene hills,
a deeper purple.

Under the glory of gold and purple I heard the grinding howl of
the iron-saws, and the throbbing, ferocious roar of the furnaces. The
ferry-boat left a wake of blue that shone like the neck of a dove; and
over the hills swept a fresh, moist wind. In the midst of God's bright
morning, beside the beautiful river, the town and its industries lay
like a cancer on the breast of a human body.

Stephen Crane
In the Depths of a Coal Mine

THE "BREAKERS" squatted upon the hillsides and in the valley like
enormous preying monsters, eating of the sunshine, the grass, the

McClure's, III (August, 1894), 195–209. Text from this publication.

The mine was near Scranton. Crane was accompanied by his artist friend
Corwin Knapp Linson, who illustrated the article for its appearance in
McClure's.

green leaves. The smoke from their nostrils had ravaged the air of coolness and fragrance. All that remained of vegetation looked dark, miserable, half-strangled. Along the summit line of the mountain a few unhappy trees were etched upon the clouds. Overhead stretched a sky of imperial blue, incredibly far away from the sombre land.

We approached the colliery over paths of coal dust that wound among the switches. A "breaker" loomed above us, a huge and towering frame of blackened wood. It ended in a little curious peak, and upon its sides there was a profusion of windows appearing at strange and unexpected points. Through occasional doors one could see the flash of whirring machinery. Men with wondrously blackened faces and garments came forth from it. The sole glitter upon their persons was at their hats, where the little tin lamps were carried. They went stolidly along, some swinging lunchpails carelessly; but the marks upon them of their forbidding and mystic calling fascinated our new eyes until they passed from sight. They were symbols of a grim, strange war that was being waged in the sunless depths of the earth.

Around a huge central building clustered other and lower ones, sheds, engine-houses, machine-shops, offices. Railroad tracks extended in web-like ways. Upon them stood files of begrimed coal cars. Other huge structures similar to the one near us, upreared their uncouth heads upon the hills of the surrounding country. From each a mighty hill of culm extended. Upon these tremendous heaps of waste from the mines, mules and cars appeared like toys. Down in the valley, upon the railroads, long trains crawled painfully southward, where a low-hanging gray cloud, with a few projecting spires and chimneys, indicated a town.

Car after car came from a shed beneath which lay hidden the mouth of the shaft. They were dragged, creaking, up an inclined cable road to the top of the "breaker."

At the top of the "breaker," laborers were dumping the coal into chutes. The huge lumps slid slowly on their journey down through the building, from which they were to emerge in classified fragments. Great teeth on revolving cylinders caught them and chewed them. At places there were grates that bid each size go into its proper chute. The dust lay inches deep on every motionless thing, and clouds of it made the air dark as from a violent tempest. A mighty gnashing sound filled the ears. With terrible appetite this huge and hideous monster sat imperturbably munching coal, grinding its mammoth jaws with unearthly and monotonous uproar.

In a large room sat the little slate-pickers. The floor slanted at an angle of forty-five degrees, and the coal, having been masticated by the great teeth, was streaming sluggishly in long iron troughs. The boys sat straddling these troughs, and as the mass moved slowly, they grabbed deftly at the pieces of slate therein. There were five or six of them, one above another, over each trough. The coal is expected to be fairly pure after it passes the final boy. The howling machinery was above them. High up, dim figures moved about in the dust clouds.

These little men were a terrifically dirty band. They resembled the New York gamins in some ways, but they laughed more, and when they laughed their faces were a wonder and a terror. They had an air of supreme independence, and seemed proud of their kind of villainy. They swore long oaths with skill.

Through their ragged shirts we could get occasional glimpses of shoulders black as stoves. They looked precisely like imps as they scrambled to get a view of us. Work ceased while they tried to ascertain if we were willing to give away any tobacco. The man who perhaps believes that he controls them came and harangued the crowd. He talked to the air.

The slate-pickers all through this region are yet at the spanking period. One continually wonders about their mothers, and if there are any schoolhouses. But as for them, they are not concerned. When they get time off, they go out on the culm heap and play baseball, or fight with boys from other "breakers" or among themselves, according to the opportunities. And before them always is the hope of one day getting to be door boys down in the mines; and, later, mule-boys; and yet later, laborers and helpers. Finally, when they have grown to be great big men, they may become miners, real miners, and go down and get "squeezed," or perhaps escape to a shattered old man's estate with a mere "miner's asthma." They are very ambitious.

Meanwhile they live in a place of infernal dins. The crash and thunder of the machinery is like the roar of an immense cataract. The room shrieks and blares and bellows. Clouds of dust blur the air until the windows shine pallidly afar off. All the structure is a-tremble from the heavy sweep and circle of the ponderous mechanism. Down in the midst of it sit these tiny urchins, where they earn fifty-five cents a day each. They breathe this atmosphere until their lungs grow heavy and sick with it. They have this clamor in their ears until it is wonderful that they have any hoodlum valor remaining. But they are uncowed; they continue to swagger. And at the top of the "breaker" laborers can always be seen dumping the roaring coal down the wide, voracious maw of the creature.

Over in front of a little tool-house a man smoking a pipe sat on a bench. "Yes," he said, "I'll take yeh down if yeh like." He led us by little cinder paths to the shed over the shaft of the mine. A gigantic fan-wheel near by was twirling swiftly. It created cool air for the miners, who on the lowest vein of this mine were some eleven hundred and fifty feet below the surface. As we stood silently waiting for the elevator we had opportunity to gaze at the mouth of the shaft. The walls were of granite blocks, slimy, moss-grown, dripping with water. Below was a curtain of ink-like blackness. It was like the opening of an old well, sinister from tales of crimes.

The black, greasy cables began to run swiftly. We stood staring at them and wondering. Then of a sudden the elevator appeared and stopped with a crash. It was a plain wooden platform. Upon two sides iron bars ran up to support a stout metal roof. The men upon it, as it came into view, were like apparitions from the center of the earth.

A moment later we marched aboard, armed with little lights, feeble and gasping in the daylight. There was an instant's creak of machinery, and then the landscape, that had been framed for us by the door-posts of the shed, disappeared in a flash. We were dropping with extraordinary swiftness straight into the earth. It was a plunge, a fall. The flames of the little lamps fluttered and flew and struggled like tied birds to release themselves from the wicks. "Hang on," bawled our guide above the tumult.

The dead black walls slid swiftly by. They were a swirling dark chaos on which the mind tried vainly to locate some coherent thing, some intelligible spot. One could only hold fast to the iron bars and listen to the roar of this implacable descent. When the faculty of balance is lost, the mind becomes a confusion. The will fought a great battle to comprehend something during this fall, but one might as well have been tumbling among the stars. The only thing was to await revelation.

It was a journey that held a threat of endlessness.

Then suddenly the dropping platform slackened its speed. It began to descend slowly and with caution. At last, with a crash and a jar, it stopped. Before us stretched an inscrutable darkness, a soundless place of tangible loneliness. Into the nostrils came a subtly strong odor of powder-smoke, oil, wet earth. The alarmed lungs began to lengthen their respirations.

Our guide strode abruptly into the gloom. His lamp flared shades of yellow and orange upon the walls of a tunnel that led away from the foot of the shaft. Little points of coal caught the light and shone like diamonds. Before us there was always the curtain of an impenetrable night. We walked on with no sound save the crunch of our feet upon the coal-dust of the floor. The sense of an abiding danger in the roof was always upon our foreheads. It expressed to us all the unmeasured, deadly tons above us, as if the roof were a superlative might that regarded with the supreme calmness of almighty power the little men at its mercy. Sometimes we were obliged to bend low to avoid it. Always our hands rebelled vaguely from touching it, refusing to affront this gigantic mass.

All at once, far ahead, shone a little flame, blurred and difficult of location. It was a tiny, indefinite thing, like a wisp-light. We seemed to be looking at it through a great fog. Presently there were two of them. They began to move to and fro and dance before us.

After a time we came upon two men crouching where the roof of the passage came near to meeting the floor. If the picture could have been brought to where it would have had the opposition and the contrast of the glorious summer-time earth, it would have been a grim and ghastly thing. The garments of the men were no more sable than their faces, and when they turned their heads to regard our tramping party, their eyeballs and teeth shone white as bleached bones. It was like the grinning of two skulls there in the shadows. The tiny lamps in their hats made a trembling light that left weirdly shrouded the movements of their limbs and bodies. We might have been confronting terrible spectres.

But they said, "Hello, Jim," to our conductor. Their mouths expanded in smiles—wide and startling smiles.

In a moment they turned again to their work. When the lights of our party reinforced their two lamps, we could see that one was busily drilling into the coal with a long thin bar. The low roof ominously pressed his shoulders as he bent at his toil. The other knelt behind him on the loose lumps of coal.

He who worked at the drill engaged in conversation with our guide. He looked back over his shoulder, continuing to poke away. "When are yeh goin' t' measure this up, Jim?" he demanded. "Do yeh wanta git me killed?"

"Well, I'd measure it up t'-day, on'y I ain't got me tape," replied the other.

"Well, when will yeh? Yeh wanta hurry up," said the miner. "I don't wanta git killed."

"Oh, I'll be down on Monday."

"Humph!"

They engaged in a sort of an altercation in which they made jests.

"You'll be carried out o' there feet first before long."

"Will I?"

Yet one had to look closely to understand that they were not about to spring at each other's throats. The vague illumination created all the effect of the snarling of two wolves.

We came upon other little low-roofed chambers, each containing two men, a "miner," who makes the blasts, and his "laborer," who loads the coal upon the cars and assists the miner generally. And at each place there was this same effect of strangely satanic smiles and eyeballs wild and glittering in the pale glow of the lamps.

Sometimes the scenes in their weird strength were absolutely infernal. Once, when we were traversing a silent tunnel in another mine, we came suddenly upon a wide place where some miners were lying down in a group. As they upreared to gaze at us, it resembled a resurrection. They slowly uprose with ghoul-like movements, mysterious figures robed in enormous shadows. The swift flashes of the steel-gleaming eyes were upon our faces.

At another time, when my companion, struggling against difficulties, was trying to get a sketch of the mule, "Molly Maguire," a large group of miners gathered about us intent upon the pencil of the artist. "Molly," indifferent to the demands of art, changed her position after a moment and calmly settled into a new one. The men all laughed, and this laugh created the most astonishing and supernatural effect. In an instant the gloom was filled with luminous smiles. Shining forth all about us were eyes glittering as with cold blue flame. "Whoa, Molly," the men began to shout. Five or six of them clutched "Molly" by her tail, her head, her legs. They were going to hold her motionless until the portrait was finished. "He's a good feller," they had said of the artist, and it would be a small thing to hold a mule for him. Upon the roof were vague dancing reflections of red and yellow.

From this tunnel of our first mine we went with our guide to the foot of the main shaft. Here we were in the most important passage of a mine, the main gangway. The wonder of these avenues is the noise —the crash and clatter of machinery as the elevator speeds upward with the loaded cars and drops thunderingly with the empty ones. The place resounds with the shouts of mule-boys, and there can always be heard the noise of approaching coal-cars, beginning in mild rumbles and then swelling down upon one in a tempest of sound. In the air is the slow painful throb of the pumps working at the water which collects in the depths. There is booming and banging and crashing, until one wonders why the tremendous walls are not wrenched by the force of this uproar. And up and down the tunnel there is a riot of lights, little orange points flickering and flashing. Miners stride in swift and sombre procession. But the meaning of it all is in the deep bass rattle of a blast in some hidden part of the mine. It is war. It is the most savage part of all in the endless battle between man and nature. These miners are grimly in the van. They have carried the war into places where nature has the strength of a million giants. Sometimes their enemy becomes exasperated and snuffs out ten, twenty, thirty lives. Usually she remains calm, and takes one at a time with method and precision. She need not hurry. She possesses eternity. After a blast, the smoke, faintly luminous, silvery, floats silently through the adjacent tunnels.

In our first mine we speedily lost all ideas of time, direction, distance. The whole thing was an extraordinary, black puzzle. We were impelled to admire the guide because he knew all the tangled passages. He led us through little tunnels three and four feet wide and with roofs that sometimes made us crawl. At other times we were in avenues twenty feet wide, where double rows of tracks extended. There were stretches of great darkness, majestic silences. The three hundred miners were distributed into all sorts of crevices and corners of the labyrinth, toiling in this city of endless night. At different points one could hear the roar of traffic about the foot of the main shaft, to which flowed all the commerce of the place.

We were made aware of distances later by our guide, who would occasionally stop to tell us our position by naming a point of the familiar geography of the surface. "Do you remember that rolling-mill yeh passed coming up? Well, you're right under it." "You're under th' depot now." The length of these distances struck us with amazement when we reached the surface. Near Scranton one can really proceed for miles, in the black streets of the mines.

Over in a wide and lightless room we found the mule-stables. There we discovered a number of these animals standing with an air of calmness and self-possession that was somehow amazing to find in a mine. A little dark urchin came and belabored his mule "China" until he stood broadside to us that we might admire his innumerable fine qualities. The stable was like a dungeon. The mules were arranged in solemn rows. They turned their heads toward our lamps. The glare made their eyes shine wondrously like lenses. They resembled enormous rats.

About the room stood bales of hay and straw. The commonplace air worn by the long-eared slaves made it all infinitely usual. One had to wait to see the tragedy of it. It was not until we had grown familiar with the life and the traditions of the mines that we were capable of understanding the story told by these beasts standing in calm array, with spread legs.

It is a common affair for mules to be imprisoned for years in the limitless night of the mines. Our acquaintance, "China," had been four years buried. Upon the surface there had been the march of the seasons; the white splendor of snows had changed again and again to the glories of green springs. Four times had the earth been ablaze with the decorations of brilliant autumns. But "China" and his friends had remained in these dungeons from which daylight, if one could get a view up a shaft, would appear a tiny circle, a silver star aglow in a sable sky.

Usually when brought to the surface, the mules tremble at the earth radiant in the sunshine. Later, they go almost mad with fantastic joy. The full splendor of the heavens, the grass, the trees, the breezes, breaks upon them suddenly. They caper and career with extravagant mulish glee. A miner told me of a mule that had spent some delirious months upon the surface after years of labor in the mines. Finally the time came when he was to be taken back. But the memory of a black existence was upon him; he knew that gaping mouth that threatened to swallow him. No cudgellings could induce him. The men held conventions and discussed plans to budge that mule. The celebrated quality of obstinacy in him won him liberty to gambol clumsily about on the surface.

After being long in the mines, the mules are apt to duck and dodge at the close glare of lamps, but some of them have been known to have piteous fears of being left in the dead darkness. We met a boy who said that sometimes the only way he could get his team to move was to run ahead of them with the light. Afraid of the darkness, they would follow.

To those who have known the sunlight there may come the fragrant dream of a lost paradise. Perhaps this is what they brood over as they stand solemnly flapping their ears. Perhaps they despair and thirst for this bloomland that lies in an unknown direction and at impossible distances.

In wet mines, gruesome fungi grow upon the wooden props that support the uncertain-looking ceiling. The walls are dripping and dank. Upon them, too, frequently grows a moss-like fungus, white as a druid's beard, that thrives in these deep dens, but shrivels and dies at contact with the sunlight.

Great and mystically dreadful is the earth from a mine's depth. Man is in the implacable grasp of nature. It has only to tighten slightly, and he is crushed like a bug. His loudest shriek of agony would be as impotent as his final moan to bring help from that fair land that lies, like Heaven, over his head. There is an insidious, silent enemy in the gas. If the huge fanwheel on the top of the earth should stop for a brief period, there is certain death. If a man escape the gas, the floods, the "squeezes" of falling rock, the cars shooting through little tunnels, the precarious elevators, the hundred perils, there usually comes to him an attack of "miner's asthma" that slowly racks and shakes him into the grave. Meanwhile he gets three dollars per day, and his laborer one dollar and a quarter.

In the chamber at the foot of the shaft, as we were departing, a group of the men were resting. They lay about in careless poses. When we climbed aboard the elevator, we had a moment in which to turn and regard them. Then suddenly the study in black faces and crimson and orange lights vanished. We were on our swift way to the surface. Far above us in the engine-room, the engineer sat with his hand on a lever and his eye on the little model of the shaft wherein a miniature elevator was making the ascent even as our elevator was making it. Down one of those tremendous holes, one thinks naturally of the engineer.

Of a sudden the fleeting walls became flecked with light. It increased to a downpour of sunbeams. The high sun was afloat in a splendor of spotless blue. The distant hills were arrayed in purple and stood like monarchs: A glory of gold was upon the near-by earth. The cool fresh air was wine.

Of that sinister struggle far below there came no sound, no suggestion save the loaded cars that emerged one after another in eternal procession and went creaking up the incline that their contents might be fed into the mouth of the "breaker," imperturbably cruel and insatiate, black emblem of greed, and of the gods of this labor.

Walter A. Wyckoff
A Day-Laborer at West Point

*   *   *

I HAVE SET for myself to-day the task of describing the past week of actual service in the ranks of the industrial army. My pen runs wide of the subject, and I have to force it to the retrospect. There were five working-days of nine hours and a quarter each, less the "called time" eaten out by the rain. Never was there clearer proof of the pure relativity of time measured by an artificial standard. Hours had no meaning; there were simply ages of physical torture, and short intervals when the physical reaction was an ecstasy.

We were called at six on Tuesday morning; and at twenty min-

Scribner's, XXII (September, 1897), 282–95. Republished in *The Workers: An Experiment in Reality: The East* (New York, 1897), pp. 37–47, 60–67. Text from *The Workers*.

The period involved in the sketch is late July, 1891. Although there was an agricultural depression in the West, labor was still "dear" in the East.

utes to seven we had breakfasted, and were ready to start for the
works, each with his dinner folded in a piece of newspaper. Passing
from our side street to the road which leads to the Post, we were at
once merged in a throng of workingmen moving in our direction.

I was suddenly aware of a novel impression of individuality. Gangs
of workingmen, as I recalled them, were uniform effects in earth-
stained jeans and rugged countenances, rough with a varying growth
of stubborn beard. To have distinguished among them would have
seemed like distinguishing among a crowd of Chinese. Now individuality began to appear in its vital separateness, and to awaken the
sense of infinite individual sensation, from which we instinctively
shrink as we do from the thought of unbroken continuity of consciousness.

But my eyes were growing sensitive to other differences, certainly
to the broad distinction between skilled and unskilled workmen. Many
orders of labor were represented—masons and carpenters and brick-
layers and plasterers, besides unskilled laborers. An evident superiority in intelligence, accompanied by a certain indefinable superiority
in dress, was the general mark of skilled labor. And then the class of
unskilled workers was noticeably heterogeneous in composition, while
many of the other class were plainly of American birth.

It is a mile from Highland Falls to West Point, and we moved briskly.
There was little conversation among the men. Most of them had taken
off their coats, and with these over their arms and their dinner-pails in
hand, they walked in silence, with their eyes on the road. The morning was sultry and overhung with heavy clouds, full of the promise of
rain. A forest lines much of the road, and from the overhanging
boughs fell great drops of dew, dotting the surface of soft dust. The
wayside weeds and bushes were gray with a coating of dust, and
seemed to cry out in the still, hot air for the suspended rain.

The old Academic building stood near to the Mess Hall at the southern end of the Post. In process of removal one wing had been blown
up by dynamite, I was told, and now its site lay deep in heaps of
débris. It was here that one gang of laborers was employed, and it was
with them that the boss had instantly given me a job upon my application on the previous morning.

There were about sixty men in the company. Most of them stood
grouped among the ruins, ready to begin work on the hour. I had but
to follow their example. I hung my coat, with my dinner in one
pocket, on a neighboring fence, and brought a shovel from the tool-
house, and joined the other men. We stood silent, like a company at
attention. The teamsters drove up with their carts, and the bosses
counted them. In another moment the head boss, who had been

keeping his eye on his watch, shut the case with a sharp metallic click, and shouted "Turn out!" in stentorian tones.

The effect was magical. The scene changed on the instant from one of quiet to one of noisy activity. Men were loosening the ruined mass with their picks, and urging their crow-bars between the blocks of stone, and shovelling the finer refuse into the carts, and loading the coarser fragments with their hands. The gang-boss, mounted upon a section of wall, began to direct the work before him. A cart had been driven among the ruins, and he called three of us to load it with the jagged masonry that lay heaped about it. It was too coarse to be handled with shovels, and we went at it with our hands. They were soon bleeding from contact with the sharp edges of rock; but the dust acted as a styptic and helped vastly in the hardening process. When the cart was loaded, another took its place, and then a third and a fourth.

In a harsh, resonant voice the boss was shouting his orders over our heads, to the farthermost portion of the works. His short, thickset, muscular figure seemed rooted to the masonry on which he stood. The mingled shrewdness and brute strength of his hard face marked him as a product of natural selection for the place that he filled. His restless gray eyes were everywhere at once, and his whole personality was tense with a compelling physical energy. If the work slackened in any portion of the ruins, his voice took on a vibrant quality as he raised it to the shout of "Now, boys, at it there!" and then a lash of stinging oaths. You could feel a quickening of muscular force among the men, like the show of eager industry in a section of a school-room that has fallen suddenly under the master's questioning eye.

In the dust which rose from the débris I picked up a mass of heavy plaster, and, before detecting my mistake, I tossed it into the cart. But the boss had seen the action, and instantly noticed the error, and now all his attention was directed upon me. In short, incisive sentences, ringing with malediction, he cursed me for an ignoramus and threatened me with discharge. I could feel the amused side-glances of the men, and could hear their muffled laughter.

At last all the carts were loaded and driven away, and until their return, some of us were set at assorting the débris—throwing the splintered laths and bricks and fragments of stone and plaster into separate heaps. The work compelled a stooping posture, and the pain of lacerated fingers was as nothing compared with the agony of muscles cramped and forced to unaccustomed use.

A business-like young fellow, with the air of a clerk, now began to move among the men, and they showed the keenest interest in his approach. I heard them speak of him as the "timekeeper," but I had no knowledge of such a functionary, and I wondered whether he had any business with me. He hailed me with a brisk "What is your number?" I looked at him in surprise. "He's a new hand," shouted the boss from his elevation. "What's your name?" asked the timekeeper, as he turned a page in his book. I told him, and when he had written it he drew from his pocket a brass disk, upon which was stamped the number six, and this he told me to wear, suspended by its string, and to show it to him as often as he made his rounds.

The cartmen had reappeared and received their loads, and had again driven off, in long procession, in the direction of Highland Falls. We went back to the varied torture of assorting. But the pain was not purely physical. The work was too mechanical to require close attention, and yet too exhausting to admit of mental effort. I did not know how to prevent my mind from preying upon itself.

At last I hit upon a plan which appealed to me. I simply went back in imagination to the familiar country-seat, and followed the morning through a likely course. We met at breakfast, and complained of the discomfort of the sultry day as we discussed our plans, and then we walked over the lawn to the pier. Two cruising sloops, that had waited in the hope of a freshening breeze, now weighed anchor, and under main-sail and top-sail and jib drifted slowly out of the harbor. We watched them in idle curiosity, wondering at the distinctness with which the conversation of the yachtsmen came back to us across the oily placidity of still water, until they seemed almost half way to the spindle, and then we agreed upon a morning ride. We telephoned to the stables, and before we were ready the horses stood restless under the *porte-cochère*. Step by step I followed our progress along the road that skirts the inlet, and across the crumbling bridge on the turnpike, and under the great, drooping elms which line the village-street in Fairfield, and up the long ascent of the Greenfield Hill to the old church, and then home by the "back road." The dogs came running at us from the stables with short, sharp barks of welcome as we cantered past, and we called to them by name. As we turned by the reservoir, we could see a groom running down the path in order to reach the house before us. Hot from the ride, we passed through the dim mystery of the hall and billiard-room and den, and out upon the veranda, where a breath of air was stirring, and the fountain played softly in its bed of vines and flowers. Louis had returned from market. Our letters lay in order on the settle, and near them, neatly folded, were the morning papers. And now Louis's approach was heralded by the tinkling of ice against the glass of bumpers of cooling drinks, and his bow was accompanied with a polite reminder that luncheon would be served in half an hour.

I had been working with all my strength. Now I looked up at the boss in some hope of a sign of the noon hour. There was none. Painfully I went back to the work. Again I tried to find diversion in this new device. Slowly, with double the needed time for each event, I followed the morning through another imaginary series. Now I was sure that the boss had made a mistake and had lost track of the time, and was working us far into the afternoon. The clouds had thickened, and the growing darkness I was certain was the coming night. Great drops of rain began to fall, but the men paid them no heed. Soon the drops quickened to a shower, and still the men worked on. The moisture from within and without had made us wringing wet when the boss ordered us to quit. We bolted for our coats and dinner-pails, and then huddled in the shelter of the still-standing walls of the ruin. Through one of the great doorways I caught sight of the tower of a neighboring building with a clock in it. It was twenty minutes to nine! In all that eternity since we began to load the first cart, we had been working one hour and forty minutes, and had each earned about twenty-nine cents.

The rain cost us an hour of working-time, and then we went back, and found some relief from the earlier discomfort in the saturation which had thoroughly settled the dust.

In another hour, with no freshening of the air, the clouds faded out of the sky. The sun shone full upon us, and there arose from the heaps of ruin a mist heavy with the smell of damp plaster. But I had my "second wind" at last, and I worked now with the feeling of some reserve of physical strength. It was with surprise that I heard the loud voice of the head boss in a shout of "Time's up!" and almost before I knew what had happened the men were seated on the ground, in the shadows of the walls, eating their dinners.

I opened mine with much curiosity. There were two huge sandwiches, with slices of corned beef between the bread, and a bit of cheese and a piece of apple-pie, very damp and oozing. Among the other men, with my aching back pressed against the wall, I sat and ate my dinner, lingering over the last crumbs like a child with some rare dainty.

At the end of the forty-five minutes allowed to us at noon, there came again, from the head boss, the order to "Turn out." In a moment the scene of the morning was renewed. There was the same alternation between loading the carts and assorting the débris.

We had been but a few minutes at work when the cadets went marching past, on their way to mess. Familiar as most of the men were with the sight, they seized eagerly upon the diversion that it offered. The boss relaxed his vigilance. The work visibly slackened, as we lent ourselves to the fascination of individual motion merged into perfect harmony of collective movement. Conspicuous in the rear was the awkward squad, very hot in its effort to walk erect, and keep its shoulders back and its little fingers on the seams of its trousers. The men laughed merrily at the comical contrast between such grotesquely strenuous efforts at conformity and the ease and strength and grace of the unison which preceded it.

No rain came to give us breathing-space in the afternoon. Hour by hour the relentless work went on. The sun had soon absorbed the last drop of the morning rain, and now the ruins lay burning hot under our feet. The air quivered in the heat reflected from the stone and plaster about us; the fine lime-dust choked our breathing as we shovelled the refuse into the carts. You could hear the muttered oaths of the men, as they swore softly in many tongues at the boss, and cursed him for a brute. But ceaselessly the work went on. We worked as though possessed by a curious numbness that kept us half-unconscious of the straining effort, which had become mechanical, until we were brought to by some spasm of strained muscles.

*   *   *

I shall be on the road again to-morrow morning, and I shall go as penniless as I came, but somewhat richer in experience. I have been through nearly a week of labor, and have survived it, and have honestly earned my living as a working-man. In the future I shall have the added confidence which comes of knowing that, if work offers, I shall probably be able to perform it. But this is not the only cause of my increased light-heartedness. I am frankly glad to get away from the job on the old Academic building. This is a selfish feeling, and is not without the cowardice of all selfishness. I hope for a job of another kind, for a time at least, because I wish to see some hopefuller side of the lot of common labor. When we draw too near to the hand of Fate, and begin to feel as though there were a wrong in the nature of things, it is best, perhaps, to change our point of view—if we can. This may account for some of the drifting restlessness among working-men of my class.

The salient features of our condition are plain enough. We are unskilled laborers. We are grown men, and are without a trade. In the labor market we stand ready to sell to the highest bidder our mere muscular strength for so many hours each day. We are thus in the lowest grade of labor. We are here, and not higher in the scale, by reason of a variety of causes. Some of us were thrown upon our own resources in childhood, and have earned our living ever since, and by the line of least resistance we have simply grown to be unskilled workmen. Opportunities came to some of us of learning useful trades, and we neglected them, and now we have no developed skill to aid us in earning a living, and we must take the work that offers.

Some of us were bred to farm labor, and almost from our earliest recollection we worked in the fields, until, tiring of country life, we determined to try some other; and we have turned to this work as being within our powers, and as affording us a change. Still others among us, like Wilson, really learned a trade; but the market offers no further demand for the peculiar skill we possess, and so we are forced back upon skilless labor. And selling our muscular strength in the open market for what it will bring, we sell it under peculiar conditions. It is all the capital that we have. We have no reserve means of subsistence, and cannot, therefore, stand off for a "reserve price." We sell under the necessity of satisfying imminent hunger. Broadly speaking, we must sell our labor or starve; and as hunger is a matter of a few hours, and we have no other way of meeting this need, we must sell at once for what the market offers for our labor. And for some of us there is other pressure, unspeakable, immeasurable pressure, in the needs of wife and children.

The contractor buys our labor as he buys other commodities, like brick and iron and stone, which enter into the construction of the new building. But he buys of us under certain restrictions to us both. The law of supply and demand does not apply to our labor with the same freedom as to other merchandize. We are human beings, and some of us have social ties, which bricks and iron have not, and we do not, therefore, move to favorable markets with the same ease and certainty as these. Besides, we are ignorant men, and behind what we have to sell is no trained intelligence, nor a knowledge of prices and of the best means of reaching the best markets. And then we are poor men, who must sell when we find a purchaser, for no "reserve price" is possible to us.

The law of supply and demand meets with these restrictions and others. If it applied with perfect freedom to our commodity, we should infallibly be where is the greatest demand for our labor; and with perfect acquaintance with the markets we should always sell in the dearest. But the benefits of perfect freedom of supply and demand would not be ours alone. If we sold in the dearest markets, the employer would as certainly buy in the cheapest. He has capital in the form of the means of subsistence, and can stand off for a "reserve price," and could force us to sell at last in the pinch of hunger, and in competition with starving men.

As matters are, our wages might rise, in an increased demand for labor, far above their present point; but even under pressure of decreasing demand, and with scores of needy men eager to take our places, our wages, if we had employment at all, would not fall far below their present level. So much has civilization done for us. It does not insure to us a chance to earn a living, but it does measurably insure to us that what we earn by day's labor, such as this, will at least be a living.

As unskilled laborers we are unorganized men. We are members of no union. We must deal individually with our employer, under all the disadvantages which encumber our position in the market as compared with his.

But his position is not an enviable one. He is a competitor in a freer market than ours. He has secured his contract as the lowest bidder, under a keener competition than we know, and in every dime that he must add to wages in order to attract labor, and in every dollar paid to an inefficient workman, and in every unforeseen difficulty or delay in the work, he sees a scaling from the margin of profit, which is already, perhaps, the narrowest that will attract capital into the field of production. The results of our labor are worth nothing to him as finished product until given sections of the work are completed. In the meantime he must advance to us our wages out of capital which is a product of past labor, his own and ours as workingmen, and of other capital. And this he must continue to do, even if his margin of profit should wholly disappear, and even if ultimate loss should be the net result of the expenditure of his labor and capital. In every case, before any other commodity has been paid for, we have insured to us the price for which we have sold our labor.

Our employer is buying labor in a dear market. One dollar and sixty cents for a day of nine hours and a quarter is a high rate for unskilled workmen. And the demand continues, for I notice that the boss accepts every man who applies for a job. The contractor is paying high for labor, and he will certainly get from us as much work as he can at the price. The gang-boss is secured for this purpose, and thoroughly does he know his business. He has sole command of us. He never saw us before, and he will discharge us all when the débris is cleared away and the site made ready for the constructive labors of the skilled workmen. In the meantime he must get from us, if he can, the utmost of physical labor which we, individually and collectively, are capable of. If he should drive some of us to exhaustion, and we should not be able to continue at work, he would not be the loser, for the market would soon supply him with others to take our places.

We are ignorant men, and we have a slender hold of economic principles, but so much we clearly see: that we have sold our labor where we could sell it dearest, and our employer has bought it where he could buy it cheapest. He has paid high for it, but not from philanthropic motives, and he will get at the price, he must get, all the labor that he can; and, by a strong instinct which possesses us, we shall part with as little as we can. And there you have, in its rudimentary form, the bear and the bull sides of the market.

You tell us that our interests are identical with those of our employer. That may be true on some ground unknown to us, but we live from hand to mouth, and we think from day to day, and we have no power to "reach a hand through time, to catch the far-off interest of tears." From work like ours there seems to us to have been eliminated every element which constitutes the nobility of labor. We feel no personal pride in its progress, and no community of interest with our employer. He plainly shares this lack of unity of interest; for he takes for granted that we are dishonest men, and that we will cheat him if we can; and so he watches us through every moment, and forces us to realize that not for an hour would he intrust his interests to our hands. There is for us in our work none of the joy of responsibility, none of the sense of achievement, only the dull monotony of grinding toil, with the longing for the signal to quit work, and for our wages at the end of the week.

We expect the ready retort that we get what we deserve, that no field of labor was closed to us, and that we are where we are because we are fit, or have fitted ourselves, for nothing better. Unskilled labor must be done, and, in the natural play of productive activity, it must inevitably be done by those who are excluded from the higher forms of labor by incapacity, or inefficiency, or misfortune, or lack of ambition. And being what we are, the dregs of the labor market, and having no certainty of permanent employment, and no organization among ourselves, by means of which we can deal with our employer and he with us by some other than an individual hold upon each other, we must expect to work under the watchful eye of a gang-boss, and not only be directed in our labor, but be driven, like the wage-slaves that we are, through our tasks.

•   •   •

Hamlin Garland
Under the Lion's Paw

> "Along this main-travelled road trailed an endless line of prairie-
> schooners, coming into sight at the east, and passing out of sight
> over the swell to the west. We children used to wonder where they
> were going and why they went."

IT WAS THE LAST of autumn and first day of winter coming together.
All day long the ploughmen on their prairie farms had moved to and
fro on their wide level field through the falling snow, which melted
as it fell, wetting them to the skin—all day, notwithstanding the frequent squalls of snow, the dripping, desolate clouds, and the muck
of the furrows, black and tenacious as tar.

Under their dripping harness the horses swung to and fro silently,
with that marvellous uncomplaining patience which marks the horse.
All day the wild geese, honking wildly, as they sprawled sidewise
down the wind, seemed to be fleeing from an enemy behind, and
with neck outthrust and wings extended, sailed down the wind, soon
lost to sight.

Yet the ploughman behind his plough, though the snow lay on his
ragged great-coat, and the cold clinging mud rose on his heavy
boots, fettering him like gyves, whistled in the very beard of the
gale. As day passed, the snow, ceasing to melt, lay along the ploughed
land, and lodged in the depth of the stubble, till on each slow round
the last furrow stood out black and shining as jet between the
ploughed land and the gray stubble.

When night began to fall, and the geese, flying low, began to alight
invisibly in the near cornfield, Stephen Council was still at work "finishing a land." He rode on his sulky-plough when going with
the wind, but walked when facing it. Sitting bent and cold but cheery
under his slouch hat, he talked encouragingly to his four-in-hand.

"Come round there, boys!—round agin! We got t' finish this land.

Harper's Weekly, XXXIII (September 7, 1889), 726–27. Republished in
Main-Travelled Roads (Boston, 1891), pp. 217–40. Text from Main-
Travelled Roads.

Come in there, Dan! *Stiddy*, Kate!—stiddy! None o' y'r tantrums, Kittie. It's purty tuff, but got a be did. *Tchk! tchk!* Step along, Pete! Don't let Kate git y'r single-tree on the wheel. *Once* more!"

They seemed to know what he meant, and that this was the last round, for they worked with greater vigor than before.

"Once more, boys, an' sez I oats an' a nice warm stall, an' sleep f'r all."

By the time the last furrow was turned on the land it was too dark to see the house, and the snow changing to rain again. The tired and hungry man could see the light from the kitchen shining through the leafless hedge, and lifting a great shout, he yelled, "Sup*per* f'r a half a dozen!"

It was nearly eight o'clock by the time he had finished his chores and started for supper. He was picking his way carefully through the mud, when the tall form of a man loomed up before him with a premonitory cough.

"Waddy ye want?" was the rather startled question of the farmer.

"Well, ye see," began the stranger, in a deprecating tone, "we'd like t' git in f'r the night. We've tried every house f'r the last two miles, but they hadn't any room f'r us. My wife's jest about sick, 'n' the children are cold and hungry—"

"Oh, y' want a stay all night, eh?"

"Yes, sir; it 'ud be a great accom—"

"Waal, I don't make it a practice t' turn anybuddy away hungry, not on sech nights as this. Drive right in. We ain't got much, but sech as it is—"

But the stranger had disappeared. And soon his steaming, weary team, with drooping heads and swinging single-trees, moved past the well to the block beside the path. Council stood at the side of the "schooner" and helped the children out—two little half-sleeping children—and then a small woman with a babe in her arms.

"There ye go!" he shouted, jovially, to the children. "*Now* we're all right. Run right along to the house there, an' tell Mam' Council you wants sumpthin' t' eat. Right this way, Mis'—keep right off t' the right there. I'll go an' git a lantern. Come," he said to the dazed and silent group at his side.

"Mother," he shouted, as he neared the fragrant and warmly-lighted kitchen, "here are some wayfarers an' folks who need sumpthin' t' eat an' a place t' snooze." He ended by pushing them all in.

Mrs. Council, a large, jolly, rather coarse-looking woman, took the children in her arms. "Come right in, you little rabbits. 'Most asleep, hay? Now here's a drink o' milk f'r each o' ye. I'll have s'm tea in a minute. Take off y'r things and set up t' the fire."

While she set the children to drinking milk, Council got out his lantern and went out to the barn to help the stranger about his team, where his loud, hearty voice could be heard as it came and went between the hay-mow and the stalls.

The woman came to light as a small, timid, and discouraged-looking woman, but still pretty, in a thin and sorrowful way.

"Land sakes! And you've travelled all the way from Clear Lake t'-day in this mud! Waal! waal! No wonder you're all tired out. Don't wait f'r the men, Mis'—" She hesitated, waiting for the name.

"Haskins."

"Mis' Haskins, set right up to the table an' take a good swig o' tea, whilst I make y' s'm toast. It's green tea, an' it's good. I tell Council as I git older I don't seem t' enjoy Young Hyson n'r Gunpowder. I want the reel green tea, jest as it comes off'n the vines. Seems t' have more heart in it some way. Don't s'pose it has. Council says it's all in m' eye."

Going on in this easy way, she soon had the children filled with bread and milk and the woman thoroughly at home, eating some toast and sweet-melon pickles, and sipping the tea.

"See the little rats!" she laughed at the children. "They're full as they can stick now, and they went to go to bed. Now don't git up, Mis' Haskins; set right where you are an' let me look after 'em. I know all about young ones, though I am all alone now. Jane went an' married last fall. But, as I tell Council, it's lucky we keep our health. Set right there, Mis' Haskins; I won't have you stir a finger."

It was an unmeasured pleasure to sit there in the warm, homely kitchen, the jovial chatter of the housewife driving out and holding at bay the growl of the impotent, cheated wind.

The little woman's eyes filled with tears which fell down upon the sleeping baby in her arms. The world was not so desolate and cold and hopeless, after all.

"Now I hope Council won't stop out there and talk politics all night. He's the greatest man to talk politics an' read the *Tribune*. How old is it?"

She broke off and peered down at the face of the babe.

"Two months 'n' five days," said the mother, with a mother's exactness.

"Ye don't say! I want t' know! The dear little pudzy-wudzy!" she went on, stirring it up in the neighborhood of the ribs with her fat forefinger.

"Pooty tough on 'oo to go gallivant'n' 'cross lots this way."

"Yes, that's so; a man can't lift a mountain," said Council, entering the door. "Sarah, this is Mr. Haskins from Kansas. He's been eat up 'n' drove out by grasshoppers."

"Glad t' see yeh! Pa, empty that wash-basin 'n' give him a chance t' wash."

Haskins was a tall man, with a thin, gloomy face. His hair was a reddish brown, like his coat, and seemed equally faded by the wind and sun. And his sallow face, though hard and set, was pathetic some-how. You would have felt that he had suffered much by the line of his mouth showing under his thin, yellow mustache.

"Hain't Ike got home yet, Sairy?"

"Hain't seen 'im."

"W-a-a-l, set right up, Mr. Haskins; wade right into what we've got; 'tain't much, but we manage to live on it—she gits fat on it," laughed Council, pointing his thumb at his wife.

After supper, while the women put the children to bed, Haskins and Council talked on, seated near the huge cooking-stove, the steam rising from their wet clothing. In the Western fashion, Council told as much of his own life as he drew from his guest. He asked but few questions; but by and by the story of Haskins's struggles and defeat came out. The story was a terrible one, but he told it quietly, seated with his elbows on his knees, gazing most of the time at the hearth.

"I didn't like the looks of the country, anyhow," Haskins said, partly rising and glancing at his wife. "I was ust t' northern Ingyannie, where we have lots a timber 'n' lots o' rain, 'n' I didn't like the looks o' that dry prairie. What galled me the worst was goin' s' far away acrosst so much fine land layin' all through here vacant."

"And the 'hoppers eat ye four years hand running, did they?"

"Eat! They wiped us out. They chawed everything that was green. They jest set around waitin' f'r us to die t' eat us too. My God! I ust t' dream of 'em sitt'n' 'round on the bedpost, six feet long, workin' their jaws. They eet the fork-handles. They got worse 'n' worse till they jest rolled on one another, piled up like snow in winter. Well, it ain't no use; if I was t' talk all winter I couldn't tell nawthin'. But all the while I couldn't help thinkin' of all that land back here that nobuddy was usin', that I ought a had 'stead o' bein' out there in that cussed country."

"Waal, why didn't ye stop an' settle here?" asked Ike, who had come in and was eating his supper.

"Fer the simple reason that you fellers wantid ten 'r fifteen dollars an acre fer the bare land, and I hadn't no money fer that kind o' thing."

"Yes, I do my own work," Mrs. Council was heard to say in the pause which followed. "I'm a-gettin' purty heavy t' be on m' laigs all day, but we can't afford t' hire, so I keep rackin' around somehow, like a foundered horse. S' lame—I tell Council he can't tell how lame

I am f'r I'm jest as lame in one laig as t'other." And the good soul
laughed at the joke on herself as she took a handful of flour
and dusted the biscuit-board to keep the dough from sticking.

"Well, I hain't *never* been very strong," said Mrs. Haskins. "Our
folks was Canadians an' small-boned, and then since my last child I
hain't got up again fairly. I don't like t' complain—Tim has about all
he can bear now—but they was days this week when I jest wanted to
lay right down an' die."

"Waal, now, I'll tell ye," said Council from his side of the stove, si-
lencing everybody with his good-natured roar, "I'd go down and *see*
Butler, *anyway*, if I was you. I guess he'd let you have his place purty
cheap; the farm's all run down. He's ben anxious t' let t' somebuddy
next year. It 'ud be a good chance fer you. Anyway, you go to bed,
and sleep like a babe. I've got some ploughin' t' do anyhow, an' we'll
see if somethin' can't be done about your case. Ike, you go out an'
see if the horses is all right, an' I'll show the folks t' bed."

When the tired husband and wife were lying under the generous quilts of the spare bed, Haskins listened a moment to the wind
in the eaves, and then said, with a slow and solemn tone:

"There are people in this world who are good enough t' be angels,
an' only haff t' die to *be* angels."

II.

Jim Butler was one of those men called in the west "land poor."
Early in the history of Rock River he had come into the town and
started in the grocery business in a small way, occupying a small building in a mean part of the town. At this period of his life he earned
all he got, and was up early and late, sorting beans, working over butter, and carting his goods to and from the station. But a change came
over him at the end of the second year, when he sold a lot of land
for four times what he paid for it. From that time forward he believed
in land speculation as the surest way of getting rich. Every cent he
could save or spare from his trade he put into land at forced sale, or
mortgages on land, which were "just as good as the wheat," he was
accustomed to say.

Farm after farm fell into his hands, until he was recognized as one
of the leading land-owners of the county. His mortgages were scattered all over Cedar County, and as they slowly but surely fell in he
sought usually to retain the former owner as tenant.

He was not ready to foreclose; indeed, he had the name of being
one of the "easiest" men in the town. He let the debtor off again and
again, extending the time whenever possible.

"I don't want y'r land," he said. "All I'm after is the int'rest on my money—that's all. Now if y' want 'o stay on the farm, why, I'll give y' a good chance. I can't have the land layin' vacant." And in many cases the owner remained as tenant.

In the mean time he had sold his store; he couldn't spend time in it; he was mainly occupied now with sitting around town on rainy days, smoking and "gassin' with the boys," or in riding to and from his farms. In fishing time he fished a good deal. Doc Grimes, Ben Ashley, and Cal Cheatham were his cronies on these fishing excursions or hunting trips in the time of chickens or partridges. In winter they went to northern Wisconsin to shoot deer.

In spite of all these signs of easy life, Butler persisted in saying he "hadn't money enough to pay taxes on his land," and was careful to convey the impression that he was poor in spite of his twenty farms. At one time he was said to be worth fifty thousand dollars, but land had been a little slow of sale of late, so that he was not worth so much. A fine farm, known as the Higley place, had fallen into his hands in the usual way the previous year, and he had not been able to find a tenant for it. Poor Higley, after working himself nearly to death on it, in the attempt to lift the mortgage, had gone off to Dakota, leaving the farm and his curse to Butler.

This was the farm which Council advised Haskins to apply for; and the next day Council hitched up his team and drove down town to see Butler.

"You jest lem *me* do the talkin'," he said. "We'll find him wearin' out his pants on some salt-barrel somewe'rs; and if he thought you *wanted* a place, he'd sock it to you hot and heavy. You jest keep quiet; I'll fix 'im."

Butler was seated in Ben Ashley's store, telling "fish yarns," when Council sauntered in casually.

"Hello, But; lyin' agin, hay?"

"Hello, Steve! how goes it?"

"Oh, so-so. Too dang much rain these days. I thought it was goin' t' freeze f'r good last night. Tight squeak if I git m' ploughin' done. How's farmin' with *you* these days?"

"Bad. Ploughin' ain't half done."

"It 'ud be a religious idee f'r you t' go out an' take a hand y'rself."

"I don't haff to," said Butler, with a wink.

"Got anybody on the Higley place?"

"No. Know of anybody?"

"Waal, no; not eggsackly. I've got a relation back t' Michigan who's ben hot an' cold on the idee o' comin' West f'r some time. *Might* come if he could get a good lay-out. What do you talk on the farm?"

"Well, I d' know. I'll rent it on shares or I'll rent it money rent."

"Waal, how much money, say?"

"Well, say ten per cent on the price—two-fifty."

"Waal, that ain't bad. Wait on 'im till 'e thrashes?"

Haskins listened eagerly to his important question, but Council was coolly eating a dried apple which he had speared out of a barrel with his knife. Butler studied him carefully.

"Well, knocks me out of twenty-five dollars interest."

"My relation 'll need all he's got t' git his crops in," said Council, in the same indifferent way.

"Well, all right; *say* wait," concluded Butler.

"All right; this is the man. Haskins, this is Mr. Butler—no relation to Ben—the hardest working man in Cedar county."

On the way home Haskins said: "I ain't much better off. I'd like that farm; it's a good farm, but it's all run down, an' so'm I. I could make a good farm of it if I had half a show. But I can't stock it n'r seed it."

"Waal, now, don't you worry," roared Council in his ear. "We'll pull y' through somehow till next harvest. He's agreed t' hire it ploughed, an' you can earn a hundred dollars ploughin an' y' c'n git the seed o' me, an' pay me back when y' can."

Haskins was silent with emotion, but at last he said, "I ain't got nothin' t' live on."

"Now don't you worry 'bout that. You jest make your headquarters at ol' Steve Council's. Mother'll take a pile o' comfort in havin' y'r wife an children 'round. Y' see Jane's married off lately, an' Ike's away a good 'eal, so we'll be darn glad t' have ye stop with us this winter. Nex' spring we'll see if y' can't git a start agin;" and he chirruped to the team, which sprang forward with the rumbling, clattering wagon.

"Say, looky here, Council, you can't do this. I never saw—" shouted Haskins in his neighbor's ear.

Council moved about uneasily in his seat, and stopped his stammering gratitude by saying: "Hold on, now; don't make such a fuss over a little thing. When I see a man down, an' things all on top of 'm, I jest like t' kick em off an' help 'm up. That's the kind of religion I got, an' it's about the *only* kind."

They rode the rest of the way home in silence. And when the red light of the lamp shone out into the darkness of the cold and windy night, and he thought of this refuge for his children and wife, Haskins could have put his arm around the neck of his burly companion and squeezed him like a lover; but he contented himself with saying: "Steve Council, you'll git y'r pay f'r this some day."

"Don't want any pay. My religion ain't run on such business principles."

The wind was growing colder, and the ground was covered with a white frost, as they turned into the gate of the Council farm, and the children came rushing out, shouting "Papa's come!" They hardly looked like the same children who had sat at the table the night before. Their torpidity under the influence of sunshine and Mother Council had given way to a sort of spasmodic cheerfulness, as insects in winter revive when laid on the earth.

III.

Haskins worked like a fiend, and his wife, like the heroic woman that she was, bore also uncomplainingly the most terrible burdens. They rose early and toiled without intermission till the darkness fell on the plain, then tumbled into bed, every bone and muscle aching with fatigue, to rise with the sun next morning to the same round of the same ferocity of labor.

The eldest boy, now nine years old, drove a team all through the spring, ploughing and seeding, milked the cows, and did chores innumerable, in most ways taking the place of a man; an infinitely pathetic but common figure—this boy—on the American farm, where there is no law against child labor. To see him in his coarse clothing, his huge boots, and his ragged cap, as he staggered with a pail of water from the well, or trudged in the cold and cheerless dawn out into the frosty field behind his team, gave the city-bred visitor a sharp pang of sympathetic pain. Yet Haskins loved his boy, and would have saved him from this if he could, but he could not.

By June the first year the result of such Herculean toil began to show on the farm. The yard was cleaned up and sown to grass, the garden ploughed and planted, and the house mended. Council had given them four of his cows.

"Take 'em an' run 'em on shares. I don't want a milk s' many. Ike's away s' much now, Sat'd'ys an' Sund'ys, I can't stand the bother anyhow."

Other men, seeing the confidence of Council in the new-comer, had sold him tools on time; and as he was really an able farmer, he soon had round him many evidences of his care and thrift. At the advice of Council he had taken the farm for three years, with the privilege of re-renting or buying at the end of the term.

"It's a good bargain, an' y' want 'o nail it," said Council. "If you have any kind ov a crop, you can pay y'r debts, an' keep seed an' bread."

The new hope which now sprang up in the heart of Haskins and his wife grew great almost as a pain by the time the wide field of wheat began to wave and rustle and swirl in the winds of July. Day after day he would snatch a few moments after supper to go and look at it.

"Have ye seen the wheat t'-day, Nettie?" he asked one night as he rose from supper.

"No, Tim, I ain't had time."

"Well, take time now. Le's go look at it."

She threw an old hat on her head—Tommy's hat—and looking almost pretty in her thin sad way, went out with her husband to the hedge.

"Ain't it grand, Nettie? Just look at it."

It was grand. Level, russet here and there, heavy-headed, wide as a lake, and full of multitudinous whispers and gleams of wealth, it stretched away before the gazers like the fabled field of the cloth of gold.

"Oh, I think—I *hope* we'll have a good crop, Tim; and oh, how good the people have been to us!"

"Yes; I don't know where we'd be t'-day if it hadn't ben f'r Council and his wife."

"They're the best people in the world," said the little woman, with a great sob of gratitude.

"We'll be in the field on Monday, sure," said Haskins, gripping the rail on the fence as if already at the work of the harvest.

The harvest came, bounteous, glorious, but the winds came and blew it into tangles, and the rain matted it here and there close to the ground, increasing the work of gathering it threefold.

Oh, how they toiled in those glorious days! Clothing dripping with sweat, arms aching, filled with briers, fingers raw and bleeding, backs broken with the weight of heavy bundles, Haskins and his man toiled on. Tommy drove the harvester while his father and a hired man bound on the machine. In this way they cut ten acres every day, and almost every night after supper, when the hand went to bed, Haskins returned to the field, shocking the bound grain in the light of the moon. Many a night he worked till his anxious wife came out to call him in to rest and lunch.

At the same time she cooked for the men, took care of the children, washed and ironed, milked the cows at night, made the butter, and sometimes fed the horses and watered them while her husband kept at the shocking. No slave in the Roman galleys could have toiled so frightfully and lived, for this man thought himself a free man, and that he was working for his wife and babes.

When he sank into his bed with a deep groan of relief, too tired to change his grimy, dripping clothing, he felt that he was getting nearer and nearer to a home of his own, and pushing the wolf of want a little farther from his door.

There is no despair so deep as the despair of a homeless man or woman. To roam the roads of the country or the streets of the city, to feel there is no rood of ground on which the feet can rest, to halt weary and hungry outside lighted windows and hear laughter and song within—these are the hungers and rebellions that drive men to crime and women to shame.

It was the memory of this homelessness, and the fear of its coming again, that spurred Timothy Haskins and Nettie, his wife, to such ferocious labor during that first year.

IV.

" 'M, yes; 'm, yes; first-rate," said Butler, as his eye took in the neat garden, the pigpen, and the well-filled barn-yard. "You're git'n' quite a stock around yer. Done well, eh?"

Haskins was showing Butler around the place. He had not seen it for a year, having spent the year in Washington and Boston with Ashley, his brother-in-law, who had been elected to Congress.

"Yes, I've laid out a good deal of money during the last three years. I've paid out three hundred dollars f'r fencin'."

"Um—h'm! I see, I see," said Butler, while Haskins went on.

"The kitchen there cost two hundred; the barn ain't cost much in money, but I've put a lot o' time on it. I've dug a new well, and I—"

"Yes, yes. I see! You've done well. Stalk worth a thousand dollars," said Butler, picking his teeth with a straw.

"About that," said Haskins, modestly. "We begin to feel 's if we wuz git'n' a home f'r ourselves; but we've worked hard. I tell ye we begin to feel it, Mr. Butler, and we're goin' t' begin t' ease up purty soon. We've been kind o' plannin' a trip back t' *her* folks after the fall ploughin's done."

"*Eggs*-actly!" said Butler, who was evidently thinking of something else. "I suppose you've kine o' kalklated on stayin' here three years more?"

"Well, yes. Fact is, I think I c'n buy the farm this fall, if you'll give me a reasonable show."

"Um—m! What do you call a reasonable show?"

"Waal; say a quarter down and three years' time."

Butler looked at the huge stacks of wheat which filled the yard, over which the chickens were fluttering and crawling, catching grasshoppers, and out of which the crickets were singing innumerably. He smiled in a peculiar way as he said, "Oh, I won't be hard on yer. But what did you expect to pay f'r the place?"

"Why, about what you offered it for before, two thousand five hundred, or *possibly* the three thousand dollars," he added quickly, as he saw the owner shake his head.

"This farm is worth five thousand and five hundred dollars," said Butler, in a careless but decided voice.

"*What!*" almost shrieked the astounded Haskins. "What's that? Five thousand? Why, that's double what you offered it for three years ago."

"Of course; and it's worth it. It was all run down then; now it's in good shape. You've laid out fifteen hundred dollars in improvements, according to your own story."

"But *you* had nothin' t' do about that. It's my work an' my money."

"You bet it was; but it's my land."

"But what's to pay me for all my—?"

"Ain't you had the use of 'em?" replied Butler, smiling calmly into his face.

Haskins was like a man struck on the head with a sand-bag; he couldn't think; he stammered as he tried to say: "But—I never 'd git the use— You'd rob me. More'n that: you agreed—you promised that I could buy or rent at the end of three years at—"

"That's all right. But I didn't say I'd let you carry off the improvements, nor that I'd go on renting the farm at two-fifty. The land is doubled in value, it don't matter how; it don't enter into the question; an' now you can pay me five hundred dollars a year rent, or take it on your own terms at fifty-five hundred, or—git out."

He was turning away when Haskins, the sweat pouring from his face, fronted him, saying again:

"But *you've* done nothing to make it so. You hain't added a cent. I put it all there myself, expectin' to buy. I worked an' sweat to improve it. I was workin' f'r myself an' babes—"

"Well, why didn't you buy when I offered to sell? What y' kickin' about?"

"I'm kickin' about payin' you twice f'r my own things—my own fences, my own kitchen, my own garden."

Butler laughed. "You're too green t' eat, young feller. *Your* improvements! The law will sing another tune."

"But I trusted your word."

"Never trust anybody, my friend. Besides, I didn't promise not to do this thing. Why, man, don't look at me like that. Don't take me for a thief. It's the law. The reg'lar thing. Everybody does it."

"I don't care if they do. It's stealin' jest the same. You take three thousand dollars of my money. The work o' my hands and my wife's." He broke down at this point. He was not a strong man mentally. He could face hardship, ceaseless toil, but he could not face the cold and sneering face of Butler.

"But I don't take it," said Butler, coolly. "All you've got to do is to go on jest as you've been a-doin', or give me a thousand dollars down, and a mortgage at ten per cent on the rest."

Haskins sat down blindly on a bundle of oats near by, and with staring eyes and drooping head went over the situation. He was under the lion's paw. He felt a horrible numbness in his heart and limbs. He was hid in a mist, and there was no path out.

Butler walked about, looking at the huge stacks of grain, and pulling now and again a few handfuls out, shelling the heads in his hands and blowing the chaff away. He hummed a little tune as he did so. He had an accommodating air of waiting.

Haskins was in the midst of the terrible toil of the last year. He was walking again in the rain and the mud behind his plough, he felt the dust and dirt of the threshing. The ferocious husking time, with its cutting wind and biting, clinging snows, lay hard upon him. Then he thought of his wife, how she had cheerfully cooked and baked, without holiday and without rest.

"Well, what do you think of it?" inquired the cool, mocking, insinuating voice of Butler.

"I think you're a thief and a liar!" shouted Haskins, leaping up. "A black-hearted houn'!" Butler's smile maddened him; with a sudden leap he caught a fork in his hands, and whirled it in the air. "You'll never rob another man, damn ye!" he grated through his teeth, a look of pitiless ferocity in his accusing eyes.

Butler shrank and quivered, expecting the blow; stood, held hypnotized by the eyes of the man he had a moment before despised— a man transformed into an avenging demon. But in the deadly hush between the lift of the weapon and its fall there came a gush of faint, childish laughter, and then across the range of his vision, far away and dim, he saw the sun-bright head of his baby girl, as, with the pretty tottering run of a two-year-old, she moved across the grass of the door-yard. His hands relaxed; the fork fell to the ground; his head lowered.

"Make out y'r deed an' morgige, an' git off'n my land, an' don't ye never cross my line agin; if y' do, I'll kill ye."

Butler backed away from the man in wild haste, and climbing into his buggy with trembling limbs, drove off down the road, leaving Haskins seated dumbly on the sunny pile of sheaves, his head sunk into his hands.

Edwin Markham

The Man with the Hoe

Written after seeing Millet's

World-Famous Painting

> *God made man in His own image,*
> *in the image of God made He him.*—Genesis.

> Bowed by the weight of centuries he leans
> Upon his hoe and gazes on the ground,
> The emptiness of ages in his face,
> And on his back the burden of the world.
> Who made him dead to rapture and despair,
> A thing that grieves not and that never hopes,
> Stolid and stunned, a brother to the ox?
> Who loosened and let down this brutal jaw?
> Whose was the hand that slanted back this brow?
> Whose breath blew out the light within this brain?
> Is this the Thing the Lord God made and gave
> To have dominion over sea and land;
> To trace the stars and search the heavens for power;
> To feel the passion of Eternity?
> Is this the Dream He dreamed who shaped the suns
> And pillared the blue firmament with light?
> Down all the stretch of Hell to its last gulf
> There is no shape more terrible than this—
> More tongued with censure of the world's blind greed—
> More filled with signs and portents for the soul—
> More fraught with menace to the universe.

San Francisco *Examiner*, January 15, 1899. Republished in *The Man with the Hoe* (New York, 1899), pp. 15–18. Text from *The Man with the Hoe.*

Markham had first seen a reproduction of Jean Francois Millet's "The Man with the Hoe" in 1886 and later saw the original at a San Francisco exhibition.

What gulfs between him and the seraphim!
Slave of the wheel of labor, what to him
Are Plato and the swing of Pleiades?
What the long reaches of the peaks of song,
The rift of dawn, the reddening of the rose?
Through this dread shape the suffering ages look;
Time's tragedy is in that aching stoop;
Through this dread shape humanity betrayed,
Plundered, profaned and disinherited,
Cries protest to the Judges of the World,
A protest that is also prophecy.

O masters, lords and rulers in all lands,
Is this the handiwork you give to God,
This monstrous thing distorted and soul-quenched?
How will you ever straighten up this shape;
Touch it again with immortality;
Give back the upward looking and the light;
Rebuild in it the music and the dream;
Make right the immemorial infamies,
Perfidious wrongs, immedicable woes?

O masters, lords and rulers in all lands,
How will the Future reckon with this Man?
How answer his brute question in that hour
When whirlwinds of rebellion shake the world?
How will it be with kingdoms and with kings—
With those who shaped him to the thing he is—
When this dumb Terror shall reply to God,
After the silence of the centuries?

Charles M. Sheldon
In His Steps
Chapter I

> "For hereunto were ye called; because Christ also suffered for
> you, leaving you an example, that ye should follow his steps."

IT WAS Friday morning and the Rev. Henry Maxwell was trying to
finish his Sunday morning sermon. He had been interrupted several
times and was growing nervous as the morning wore away and the sermon grew very slowly towards a satisfactory finish.

"Mary," he called to his wife, as he went up stairs after the last
interruption, "if any one comes after this, I wish you would say that I
am very busy and cannot come down unless it is something very important."

"Yes, Henry. But I am going over to visit the Kindergarten and you
will have the house all to yourself."

The minister went up into his study and shut the door. In a few
minutes he heard his wife go out.

He settled himself at his desk with a sigh of relief and began to
write. His text was from First Peter, ii: 21.

"For hereunto were ye called; because Christ also suffered for
you, leaving you an example, that ye should follow his steps."

He had emphasized in the first part of his sermon the Atonement
as a personal sacrifice, calling attention to the fact of Jesus' suffering
in various ways, in his life as well as in his death. He had gone on to
emphasize the Atonement from the side of example, giving illustrations from the life and teaching of Jesus, to show how faith in the
Christ helped to save men because of the pattern or character he displayed for their imitation. He was now on the third and last point, the
necessity of following Jesus in his sacrifice and example.

He had just put down, "3: Steps; What are they?" And was about
to enumerate them in logical order when the bell rang sharply. It

In His Steps: "What Would Jesus Do?" (Chicago, 1897), pp. 5–25. Text
from this edition.

was one of those clock-work bells and always went off as a clock might go if it tried to strike twelve all at once.

Henry Maxwell sat at his desk and frowned a little. He made no movement to answer the bell. Very soon it rang again. Then he rose and walked over to one of his windows which commanded a view of the front door.

A man was standing on the steps. He was a young man very shabbily dressed.

"Looks like a tramp," said the minister. "I suppose I'll have to go down, and—"

He did not finish the sentence, but he went down stairs and opened the front door.

There was a moment's pause as the two men stood facing each other; then the shabby-looking young man said,

"I'm out of a job, sir, and thought maybe you might put me in the way of getting something."

"I don't know of anything. Jobs are scarce," replied the minister beginning to shut the door slowly.

"I didn't know but you might perhaps be able to give me a line to the city railway or superintendent of the shops or something," continued the young man, shifting his faded hat from one hand to the other nervously.

"It would be of no use. You will have to excuse me. I am very busy this morning. I hope you will find something. Sorry I can't give you something to do here. But I keep only a horse and a cow and do the work myself."

The Rev. Henry Maxwell closed the door and heard the man walk down the steps. As he went up into his study he saw from his hall window that the man was going slowly down the street, still holding his hat between his hands. There was something in the figure so dejected, homeless and forsaken, that the minister hesitated a moment as he stood looking at it. Then he turned to his desk, and with a sigh began the writing where he had left off.

He had no more interruptions and when his wife came in two hours later, the sermon was finished, the loose leaves gathered up and neatly tied together and laid on his Bible, all ready for the Sunday morning service.

"A queer thing happened at the Kindergarten this morning, Henry," said his wife while they were eating dinner. "You know I went over with Mrs. Brown to visit the school, and just after the games, while the children were at the tables, the door opened and a young man came in, holding a dirty hat in both hands. He sat down near the door and never said a word. Only looked at the children. He was evidently a tramp, and Miss Wren and her assistant, Miss Kyle, were a little frightened at first, but he sat there very quietly and after a few minutes he went out."

"Perhaps he was tired and wanted to rest somewhere. The same man called here, I think. Did you say he looked like a tramp?"

"Yes, very dusty, shabby and generally tramp-like. Not more than thirty or thirty-three years old, I should say."

"The same man," said the Rev. Henry Maxwell thoughtfully.

"Did you finish your sermon, Henry?" his wife asked after a pause.

"Yes, all done. It has been a very busy week with me. The two sermons cost me a good deal of labor."

"They will be appreciated by a large audience to-morrow, I hope," replied his wife smiling. "What are you going to preach about in the morning?"

"Following Christ. I take up the Atonement under the heads of Sacrifice and Example, and then show the steps needed to follow his sacrifice and example."

"I am sure it is a good sermon. I hope it won't rain Sunday. We have had so many rainy days lately."

"Yes, the audiences have been quite small for some time. People will not come out to church in a storm." The Rev. Henry Maxwell sighed as he said it. He was thinking of the careful, laborious efforts he had made in preparing sermons for large audiences that failed to appear.

But Sunday morning dawned on the town of Raymond one of those perfect days that sometimes come after long periods of wind and rain and mud. The air was clear and bracing, the sky was free from all threatening signs, and every one in Henry Maxwell's parish prepared to go to church. When the service opened at eleven o'clock, the large building was filled with an audience of the best-dressed, most comfortable looking people in Raymond.

The First Church of Raymond believed in having the best music that money could buy and its quartette choir this morning was a great source of pleasure to the congregation. The anthem was inspiring. All the music was in keeping with the subject of the sermon. And the anthem was an elaborate adaptation to the most modern music, of the hymn,

> Jesus, I my cross have taken,
> All to leave and follow thee.

Just before the sermon, the soprano sang a solo, the well known hymn,

> Where He leads me I will follow,
> I'll go with Him, with Him all the way.

Rachel Winslow looked very beautiful that morning as she stood up behind the screen of carved oak which was significantly marked with the emblems of the cross and the crown. Her voice was even more beautiful than her face, and that meant a great deal. There was a general rustle of expectation over the audience as she rose. Henry Maxwell settled himself contentedly behind the pulpit. Rachel Winslow's singing always helped him. He generally arranged for a song before the sermon. It made possible a certain inspiration of feeling that he knew made his delivery more impressive.

People said to themselves they had never heard such singing even in the First Church. It is certain that if it had not been a church service, her solo would have been vigorously applauded. It even seemed to Henry Maxwell when she sat down that something like an attempted clapping of hands or a striking of feet on the floor swept through the church. He was startled by it. As he rose, however, and laid his sermon on the open Bible, he said to himself he had been deceived. Of course it could not occur. In a few moments he was absorbed in his sermon and everything else was forgotten in the pleasure of the delivery.

No one had ever accused Henry Maxwell of being a dull preacher. On the contrary he had often been charged with being sensational. Not in what he said so much as in his way of saying it. But the First Church people liked that. It gave their preacher and their parish a pleasant distinction that was agreeable.

It was also true that the pastor of the First Church loved to preach. He seldom exchanged. He was eager to be in his own pulpit when Sunday came. There was an exhilarating half-hour for him as he stood facing a church full of people and knew that he had a hearing. He was peculiarly sensitive to variations in the attendance. He never preached well before a small audience. The weather also affected him decidedly. He was at his best before just such an audience as faced him now, on just such a morning. He felt a glow of satisfaction as he went on. The church was the first in the city. It had the best choir. It had a membership composed of the leading people, representatives of the wealth, society and intelligence of Raymond. He was going abroad on a three months' vacation in the summer, and the circumstances of his pastorate, his influence and his position as pastor of the first church in the city—

It is not certain that the Rev. Henry Maxwell knew just how he could carry on all that thought in connection with his sermon, but as he drew near the end of it he knew that he had at some point in his delivery had all these feelings. They had entered into the very substance of his thought, it might have been all in a few seconds of time; but he had been conscious of defining his position and his emotions as well as if he had held a soliloquy, and his delivery partook of the thrill of deep personal satisfaction.

The sermon was interesting. It was full of striking sentences. They would have commanded attention printed. Spoken with the passion of a dramatic utterance that had the good taste never to offend with a suspicion of ranting or declamation, they were very effective. If the Rev. Henry Maxwell that morning felt satisfied with the conditions of his pastorate, the parish of First Church also had a similar feeling as it congratulated itself on the presence in the pulpit of this scholarly, refined, somewhat striking face and figure, preaching with such animation and freedom from all vulgar, noisy, or disagreeable mannerism.

Suddenly, into the midst of this perfect accord and concord between preacher and audience, there came a very remarkable interruption. It would be difficult to indicate the extent of the shock which this interruption measured. It was so unexpected, so entirely contrary to any thought of any person present that it offered no room for argument, or, for the time being, of resistance.

The sermon had come to a close. The Rev. Henry Maxwell had turned the half of the big Bible over upon his manuscript and was about to sit down, as the quartette prepared to rise and sing the closing selection,

> All for Jesus, All for Jesus,
> All my being's ransomed powers,

when the entire congregation was startled by the sound of a man's voice. It came from the rear of the church, from one of the seats under the gallery. The next moment the figure of a man came out of the shadow there and walked down the middle aisle.

Before the startled congregation realized what was being done, the man had reached the open space in front of the pulpit and had turned about, facing the people.

"I've been wondering since I came in here—" they were the words he used under the gallery, and he repeated them, "if it would be just the thing to say a word at the close of this service. I'm not drunk and I'm not crazy, and I'm perfectly harmless; but if I die, as there is every likelihood I shall in a few days, I want the satisfaction of thinking that I said my say in a place like this, before just this sort of a crowd."

Henry Maxwell had not taken his seat and he now remained standing, leaning on his pulpit, looking down at the stranger. It was the man who had come to his house Friday morning, the same dusty, worn, shabby-looking young man. He held his faded hat in his two hands. It seemed to be a favorite gesture. He had not been shaved and his

hair was rough and tangled. It was doubtful if any one like this had
ever confronted the First Church within the sanctuary. It was toler-
ably familiar with this sort of humanity out on the street, around
the Railroad shops, wandering up and down the avenue, but it
had never dreamed of such an incident as this so near.

There was nothing offensive in the man's manner or tone. He was
not excited and he spoke in a low but distinct voice. Henry Maxwell
was conscious, even as he stood there smitten into dumb astonishment at the event, that somehow the man's action reminded him of
a person he had once seen walking and talking in his sleep.

No one in the church made any motion to stop the stranger or in
any way interrupt him. Perhaps the first shock of his sudden appearance deepened into genuine perplexity concerning what was best to
do. However that may be, he went on as if he had no thought of interruption and no thought of the unusual element he had introduced
into the decorum of the First Church service. And all the while he
was speaking, Henry Maxwell leaned over the pulpit, his face growing more white and sad every moment. But he made no movement
to stop him and the people sat smitten into breathless silence. One
other face, that of Rachel Winslow, from the choir seats, stared white
and intent down at the shabby figure with the faded hat. Her face
was striking at any time. Under the pressure of the present unheard-of
incident, it was as personally distinct as if it had been framed in fire.

"I'm not an ordinary tramp, though I don't know of any teaching
of Jesus that makes one kind of a tramp less worth saving than another. Do you?" He put the question as naturally as if the whole congregation had been a small private Bible class. He paused just a
moment and coughed painfully. Then he went on.

"I lost my job ten months ago. I am a printer by trade. The new
linotype machines are beautiful specimens of invention, but I know
six men who have killed themselves inside of the year just on account
of those machines. Of course I don't blame the newspapers for getting the machines. Meanwhile, what can a man do? I know I never
learned but the one trade and that's all I can do. I've tramped all
over the country trying to find something. There are a good many
others like me. I'm not complaining, am I? Just stating facts. But I was
wondering, as I sat there under the gallery, if what you call following
Jesus is the same thing as what he taught. What did he mean when he
said, 'Follow me'? The minister said," here the man turned about and
looked up at the pulpit, "that it was necessary for the disciple of Jesus
to follow his steps, and he said the steps were, obedience, faith, love,
and imitation. But I did not hear him tell just what he meant that
to mean, especially the last step. What do Christians mean by following the steps of Jesus? I've tramped through this city for three

days trying to find a job and in all that time I've not had a word
of sympathy or comfort except from your minister here, who said he
was sorry for me and hoped I would find a job somewhere. I suppose
it is because you get so imposed on by the professional tramp that
you have lost your interest in the other sort. I'm not blaming anybody,
am I? Just stating facts? Of course I understand you can't all go out
of your way to hunt up jobs for people like me. I'm not asking you to,
but what I feel puzzled about is, what is meant by following Jesus?
Do you mean that you are suffering and denying yourselves and trying
to save lost suffering humanity just as I understood Jesus did? What
do you mean by it? I see the ragged edge of things a good deal. I
understand there are more than five hundred men in this city
in my case. Most of them have families. My wife died four months
ago. I'm glad she is out of trouble. My little girl is staying with a
printer's family until I find a job. Somehow I get puzzled when I
see so many Christians living in luxury and singing, 'Jesus, I my
cross have taken, all to leave and follow thee,' and remember how my
wife died in a tenement in New York city, gasping for air and asking God to take the little girl too. Of course I don't expect you people can prevent every one from dying of starvation, lack of proper
nourishment and tenement air, but what does following Jesus
mean? I understand that Christian people own a good many of the
tenements. A member of a church was the owner of the one where
my wife died, and I have wondered if following Jesus all the way
was true in his case. I heard some people singing at a church prayer
meeting the other night,

> All for Jesus, all for Jesus;
> All my being's ransomed powers;
> All my thoughts and all my doings,
> All my days and all my hours,

and I kept wondering as I sat on the steps outside just what they
meant by it. It seems to me there's an awful lot of trouble in the
world that somehow wouldn't exist if all the people who sing such
songs went and lived them out. I suppose I don't understand. But
what would Jesus do? Is that what you mean by following his steps?
It seems to me sometimes as if the people in the city churches had
good clothes and nice houses to live in, and money to spend for
luxuries, and could go away on summer vacations and all that,
while the people outside of the churches, thousands of them, I mean,
die in tenements and walk the streets for jobs, and never have a piano
or a picture in the house, and grow up in misery and drunkenness
and sin—" the man gave a queer lurch over in the direction of the
communion table and laid one grimy hand on it. His hat fell upon

the carpet at his feet. A stir went through the congregation. Dr. West half rose from his feet, but as yet the silence was unbroken by any voice or movement worth mentioning in the audience. The man passed his other hand across his eyes, and then, without any warning, fell heavily forward on his face, full length, up the aisle.

Henry Maxwell spoke, "We will consider the service dismissed." He was down the pulpit stairs and kneeling by the prostrate form before any one else. The audience instantly rose and the aisle was crowded. Dr. West pronounced the man alive. He had fainted away. "Some heart trouble," the doctor also muttered as he helped carry him into the pastor's study.

Henry Maxwell and a group of his church members remained some time in the study. The man lay on the couch there and breathed heavily. When the question of what to do with him came up, the minister insisted upon taking him to his house. He lived near by and had an extra room. Rachel Winslow said, "Mother has no company at present. I am sure we would be glad to give him a place with us." She looked strangely agitated. No one noticed it particularly. They were all excited over the strange event, the strangest that First Church people could remember. But the minister insisted on taking charge of the man and when a carriage came, the unconscious but living form was carried to his house and with the entrance of that humanity into the minister's spare room a new chapter in Henry Maxwell's life began, and yet no one, himself least of all, dreamed of the remarkable change it was destined to make in all his after definition of Christian discipleship.

The event created a great sensation in the First Church parish. People talked of nothing else for a week. It was the general impression that the man had wandered into the church in a condition of mental disturbance caused by his troubles, and that all the time he was talking he was in a strange delirium of fever and really ignorant of his surroundings. That was the most charitable construction to put upon his action; it was the general agreement also that there was a singular absence of anything bitter or complaining in what the man had said. He had throughout spoken in a mild apologetic tone, almost as if he were one of the congregation seeking for light on a very difficult subject.

The third day after his removal to the minister's house there was a marked change in his condition. The doctor spoke of it and offered no hope. Saturday morning he still lingered, although he had rapidly failed as the week drew near to its close. Sunday morning just before the clock struck one, he rallied and asked if his child had come. The minister had sent for her at once as soon as he had been able to secure her address from some letters found in the man's pocket. He had been conscious and able to talk coherently only a few moments since his attack. "The child is coming. She will be here," Henry Maxwell said as he sat there, his face showing marks of the strain of the week's vigil. For he had insisted on sitting up nearly every night.

"I shall never see her in this world," the man whispered. Then he uttered with great difficulty the words, "You have been good to me. Somehow I feel as if it was what Jesus would do." After a few moments he turned his head slightly, and before Henry Maxwell could realize the fact, the doctor said, "He is gone."

The Sunday morning that dawned on the city of Raymond was exactly like the Sunday of the week before. Henry Maxwell entered his pulpit to face one of the largest congregations that had ever crowded First Church. He was haggard and looked as if he had just risen from a long illness. His wife was at home with the little girl who had come on the morning train an hour after her father died. He lay in that spare room, his troubles over, and Henry Maxwell could see the face as he opened the Bible and arranged his different notices on the side of the desk as he had been in the habit of doing for ten years.

The service that morning contained a new element. No one could remember when the minister had preached in the morning without notes. As a matter of fact he had done so occasionally when he first entered the ministry, but for a long time he had carefully written out every word of his morning sermon, and nearly always his evening discourse as well. It cannot be said that his sermon this morning was very striking or impressive. He talked with considerable hesitation. It was evident that some great idea struggled in his thought for utterance but it was not expressed in the theme he had chosen for his preaching. It was near the close of his sermon that he began to gather a certain strength that had been painfully lacking at the beginning. He closed the Bible and stepping out at the side of the desk, he faced his people, and began to talk to them about the remarkable scene of the week before.

"Our brother," somehow the words sounded a little strange coming from Henry Maxwell's lips, "passed away this morning. I have not yet had time to learn all his history. He had one sister living in Chicago. I have written her and have not yet received an answer. His little girl is with us and will remain for the time."

He paused and looked over the house. He thought he had never seen so many earnest faces during the entire pastorate. He was not able yet to tell his people his experiences, the crisis through which he was even now moving. But something of his feeling passed from him to them, and it did not seem to him that he was acting under a careless impulse at all to go on and break to them, this morning, something of the message he bore in his heart. So he went on.

"The appearance and words of this stranger in the church last Sunday made a very powerful impression on me. I am not able to conceal from you or myself the fact that what he said, followed as it has been by his death in my house, has compelled me to ask as I never asked before, 'What does following Jesus mean?' I am not in a position yet to utter any condemnation of this people, or, to a certain extent, of myself, either in our Christlike relations to this man or the number he represents in the world. But all that does not prevent me from feeling that much that the man said was so vitally true that we must face it in an attempt to answer it or else stand condemned as Christian disciples. A good deal that was said here last Sunday was in the nature of a challenge to Christianity as it is seen and felt in our churches. I have felt this with increasing emphasis every day since. And I do not know that any time is more appropriate than the present for me to propose a plan or a purpose which has been forming in my mind as a satisfactory reply to much that was said here last Sunday."

Again Henry Maxwell paused and looked into the faces of his people. There were some strong, earnest men and women in the First Church. The minister could see Edward Norman, Editor of the Raymond "Daily News." He had been a member of First Church for ten years. No man was more honored in the community. There was Alexander Powers, Superintendent of the Railroad shops. There was Donald Marsh, President of Lincoln College, situated in the suburbs of Raymond. There was Milton Wright, one of the great merchants of Raymond, having in his employ at least one hundred men in various shops. There was Dr. West who, although still comparatively young, was quoted as authority in special surgical cases. There was young Jasper Chase, the author, who had written one successful book and was said to be at work on a new novel. There was Miss Virginia Page, the heiress, who through the recent death of her father had inherited a million at least, and was gifted with unusual attractions of person and intellect. And not least of all, Rachel Winslow from her seat in the choir glowed with her peculiar beauty of light this morning because she was so intensely interested in the whole scene.

There was some reason perhaps, in view of such material in the First Church, for Henry Maxwell's feeling of satisfaction whenever he considered his parish as he had the previous Sunday. There was a large number of strong individual characters who claimed membership there. But as he noted their faces this morning, Henry Maxwell was simply wondering how many of them would respond to the strange proposition he was about to make. He continued slowly, taking time to choose his words carefully and giving the people an impression they had never felt before, even when he was at his best, with his most dramatic delivery.

"What I am going to propose now is something which ought not to appear unusual or at all impossible of execution. Yet I am aware that it will be so regarded by a large number, perhaps, of the members of the church. But in order that we may have a thorough understanding of what we are considering, I will put my proposition very plainly, perhaps bluntly. I want volunteers from the First Church who will pledge themselves earnestly and honestly for an entire year not to do anything without first asking the question, 'What would Jesus do?' And after asking that question, each one will follow Jesus as exactly as he knows how, no matter what the results may be. I will of course include myself in this company of volunteers, and shall take for granted that my church here will not be surprised at my future conduct as based upon this standard of action, and will not oppose whatever is done if they think Christ would do it. Have I made my meaning clear? At the close of the service here I want all those members of the church who are willing to join such a company to remain, and we will talk over the details of the plan. Our motto will be, 'What would Jesus do?' Our aim will be to act just as he would if he were in our places, regardless of immediate results. In other words, we propose to follow Jesus' steps as closely and as literally as we believe he taught his disciples to do. And those who volunteer to do this will pledge themselves for an entire year, beginning with to-day, so to act."

Henry Maxwell paused again and looked over his church. It is not easy to describe the sensation that such a simple proposition apparently made. Men glanced at one another in astonishment. It was not like Henry Maxwell to define Christian discipleship in this way. There was evident confusion of thought over his proposition. It was understood well enough, but there was apparently a great difference of opinion as to the application of Jesus' teaching and example.

Henry Maxwell calmly closed the service with a brief prayer. The organist began his postlude immediately after the benediction and the people began to go out. There was a great deal of conversation. Animated groups stood all over the church discussing the minister's proposition. It was evidently provoking great discussion. After several minutes Henry Maxwell asked all who expected to remain, to pass into the lecture room on the side. He himself was detained at the front of the church talking with several persons there, and when he finally turned around, the church was empty. He walked over to the lecture room entrance and went in. He was almost startled to see the people who were there. He had not made up his mind about any of his members, but he had hardly expected that so many were ready to enter into such a literal testing of their discipleship as now awaited them. There were perhaps fifty members present. Among them were Rachel Winslow and Virginia Page, Mr. Norman, President Marsh, Alexander Powers the Railroad Superintendent, Milton Wright, Dr. West, and Jasper Chase.

The pastor closed the door of the lecture room and stood before the little group. His face was pale and his lips trembled with emotion. It was to him a genuine crisis in his own life and that of his parish. No man can tell until he is moved by the Divine Spirit what he may do, or how he may change the current of a lifetime of fixed habits of thought and speech and action. Henry Maxwell did not, as we have said, yet know himself all that he was passing through, but he was conscious of a great upheaval in his definitions of Christian discipleship and he was moved with a depth of feeling he could not measure, as he looked into the faces of these men and women on this occasion.

It seemed to him that the most fitting word to be spoken first was that of prayer. He asked them all to pray with him. And almost with the first syllable he uttered there was a distinct presence of the Spirit felt by them all. As the prayer went on, this presence grew in power. They all felt it. The room was filled with it as plainly as if it had been visible. When the prayer closed there was a silence that lasted several moments. All the heads were bowed. Henry Maxwell's face was wet with tears. If an audible voice from heaven had sanctioned their pledge to follow the Master's steps, not one person present could have felt more certain of the divine blessing. And so the most serious movement ever started in the First Church of Raymond was begun.

"We all understand," said Henry Maxwell, speaking very quietly, "what we have undertaken to do. We pledge ourselves to do everything in our daily lives after asking the question, 'What would Jesus do?' regardless of what may be the result to us. Some time I shall be able to tell you what a marvelous change has come over my life within a week's time. I cannot now. But the experience I have been through since last Sunday has left me so dissatisfied with my previous definition of discipleship that I have been compelled to take this action. I did not dare begin it alone. I know that I am being led by the hand of divine love in all this. The same divine impulse must have led you also. Do we understand fully what we have undertaken?"

"I want to ask a question," said Rachel Winslow.

Every one turned towards her. Her face glowed with a beauty that no loveliness could ever create.

"I am a little in doubt as to the source of our knowledge concerning what Jesus would do. Who is to decide for me just what he would do in my case? It is a different age. There are many perplexing questions in our civilization that are not mentioned in the teaching of Jesus. How am I going to tell what he would do?"

"There is no way that I know of," replied Mr. Maxwell, "except as we study Jesus through the medium of the Holy Spirit. You remember what Christ said speaking to his disciples about the Holy Spirit:

"'Howbeit, when He, the Spirit of Truth is come, He shall guide you into all the truth: for He shall not speak from Himself; but what things soever He shall hear, these shall He speak: and He shall declare unto you the things that are to come. He shall glorify me: for He shall take of mine and shall declare it unto you. All things whatsoever the Father hath are mine: therefore said I that He taketh of mine and shall declare it unto you.'

"There is no other test that I know of. We shall all have to decide what Jesus would do after going to that source of knowledge."

"What if others say of us when we do certain things, that Jesus would not do so?" asked the Superintendent of railroads.

"We cannot prevent that. But we must be absolutely honest with ourselves. The standard of Christian action cannot vary in most of our acts."

"And yet what one church member thinks Jesus would do, another refuses to accept as his possible course of action. What is to render our conduct uniformly Christlike? Will it be possible to reach the same conclusions always in all cases?" asked President Marsh.

Henry Maxwell was silent some time. Then he answered:

"No. I don't know that we can expect that. But when it comes to a genuine, honest, enlightened following of Jesus' steps, I cannot believe there will be any confusion either in our own minds or in the judgment of others. We must be free from fanaticism on one hand and too much caution on the other. If Jesus' example is the example for the world, it certainly must be feasible to follow it. But we need to remember this great fact. After we have asked the Spirit to tell us what Jesus would do and have received an answer to it, we are to act regardless of the results to ourselves. Is that understood?"

All the faces in the room were raised toward the minister in solemn assent. There was no misunderstanding the proposition. Henry Maxwell's face quivered again as he noted the President of the Endeavor Society, with several members, seated back of the older men and women.

They remained a little longer talking over details and asking questions, and agreed to report to one another every week at a regular meeting the result of their experiences in following Jesus in this way. Henry Maxwell prayed again. And again, as before, the Spirit made Himself manifest. Every head remained bowed a long time. They went away finally in silence. There was a feeling that prevented speech. Henry Maxwell shook hands with them all as they went out. Then he went to his own study room back of the pulpit and kneeled down. He remained there alone nearly half an hour. When he went home, he went into the room where the dead body lay. As he looked at the face, he cried in his heart again for strength and wisdom. But not even yet did he realize that a movement had been begun which would lead to the most remarkable series of events that the city of Raymond had ever known.

Populist Party Platform

ASSEMBLED UPON the 116th anniversary of the Declaration of Independence, the People's Party of America, in their first national convention, invoking upon their action the blessing of Almighty God, put forth in the name and on behalf of the people of this country, the following preamble and declaration of principles:

PREAMBLE

The conditions which surround us best justify our co-operation; we meet in the midst of a nation brought to the verge of moral, politi-

Republished from *Documents of American History,* ed. Henry Steele Commager, 6th ed. (New York, 1958), II, 143–46. Text from this edition.

The platform was officially adopted by the People's Party on July 4, 1892, during its presidential nominating convention at Omaha. Much of the preamble was written by Ignatius Donnelly, a radical novelist, and had already appeared in the February, 1892, platform of the party.

cal, and material ruin. Corruption dominates the ballot-box, the Legislatures, the Congress, and touches even the ermine of the bench.
The people are demoralized; most of the States have been compelled
to isolate the voters at the polling places to prevent universal intimidation and bribery. The newspapers are largely subsidized or muz-
zled, public opinion silenced, business prostrated, homes covered
with mortgages, labor impoverished, and the land concentrating
in the hands of capitalists. The urban workmen are denied the right
to organize for self-protection, imported pauperized labor beats down
their wages, a hireling standing army, unrecognized by our laws, is
established to shoot them down, and they are rapidly degenerating
into European conditions. The fruits of the toil of millions are boldly
stolen to build up colossal fortunes for a few, unprecedented in the
history of mankind; and the possessors of these, in turn, despise the
Republic and endanger liberty. From the same prolific womb of
governmental injustice we breed the two great classes—tramps and
millionaires.

The national power to create money is appropriated to enrich
bond-holders; a vast public debt payable in legal-tender currency
has been funded into gold-bearing bonds, thereby adding millions
to the burdens of the people.

Silver, which has been accepted as coin since the dawn of history,
has been demonetized to add to the purchasing power of gold by
decreasing the value of all forms of property as well as human labor,
and the supply of currency is purposely abridged to fatten usurers,
bankrupt enterprise, and enslave industry. A vast conspiracy against
mankind has been organized on two continents, and it is rapidly taking possession of the world. If not met and overthrown at once it
forebodes terrible social convulsions, the destruction of civilization,
or the establishment of an absolute despotism.

We have witnessed for more than a quarter of a century the struggles of the two great political parties for power and plunder, while
grievous wrongs have been inflicted upon the suffering people. We
charge that the controlling influences dominating both these parties
have permitted the existing dreadful conditions to develop without
serious effort to prevent or restrain them. Neither do they now promise us any substantial reform. They have agreed together to ignore, in
the coming campaign, every issue but one. They propose to drown the
outcries of a plundered people with the uproar of a sham battle over
the tariff, so that capitalists, corporations, national banks, rings, trusts,
watered stock, the demonetization of silver and the oppressions of
the usurers may all be lost sight of. They propose to sacrifice our
homes, lives, and children on the altar of mammon; to destroy the

multitude in order to secure corruption funds from the millionaires.

Assembled on the anniversary of the birthday of the nation, and filled with the spirit of the grand general and chief who established our independence, we seek to restore the government of the Republic to the hands of the "plain people," with which class it originated. We assert our purposes to be identical with the purposes of the National Constitution; to form a more perfect union and establish justice, insure domestic tranquillity, provide for the common defence, promote the general welfare, and secure the blessings of liberty for ourselves and our posterity.

We declare that this Republic can only endure as a free government while built upon the love of the people for each other and for the nation; that it cannot be pinned together by bayonets; that the Civil War is over, and that every passion and resentment which grew out of it must die with it, and that we must be in fact, as we are in name, one united brotherhood of free men.

Our country finds itself confronted by conditions for which there is no precedent in the history of the world; our annual agricultural productions amount to billions of dollars in value, which must, within a few weeks or months, be exchanged for billions of dollars' worth of commodities consumed in their production; the existing currency supply is wholly inadequate to make this exchange; the results are falling prices, the formation of combines and rings, the impoverishment of the producing class. We pledge ourselves that if given power we will labor to correct these evils by wise and reasonable legislation, in accordance with the terms of our platform.

We believe that the power of government—in other words, of the people—should be expanded (as in the case of the postal service) as rapidly and as far as the good sense of an intelligent people and the teachings of experience shall justify, to the end that oppression, injustice, and poverty shall eventually cease in the land.

While our sympathies as a party of reform are naturally upon the side of every proposition which will tend to make men intelligent, virtuous, and temperate, we nevertheless regard these questions, important as they are, as secondary to the great issues now pressing for solution, and upon which not only our individual prosperity but the very existence of free institutions depend; and we ask all men to first help us to determine whether we are to have a republic to administer before we differ as to the conditions upon which it is to be administered, believing that the forces of reform this day organized will never cease to move forward until every wrong is righted and equal rights and equal privileges securely established for all the men and women of this country.

PLATFORM

We declare, therefore—

First.—That the union of the labor forces of the United States this day consummated shall be permanent and perpetual; may its spirit enter into all hearts for the salvation of the Republic and the uplifting of mankind.

Second.—Wealth belongs to him who creates it, and every dollar taken from industry without an equivalent is robbery. "If any will not work, neither shall he eat." The interests of rural and civil labor are the same; their enemies are identical.

Third.—We believe that the time has come when the railroad corporations will either own the people or the people must own the railroads; and should the government enter upon the work of owning and managing all railroads, we should favor an amendment to the constitution by which all persons engaged in the government service shall be placed under a civil-service regulation of the most rigid character, so as to prevent the increase of the power of the national administration by the use of such additional government employes.

FINANCE.—We demand a national currency, safe, sound, and flexible issued by the general government only, a full legal tender for all debts, public and private, and that without the use of banking corporations; a just, equitable, and efficient means of distribution direct to the people, at a tax not to exceed 2 per cent, per annum, to be provided as set forth in the sub-treasury plan of the Farmers' Alliance, or a better system; also by payments in discharge of its obligations for public improvements.

1. We demand free and unlimited coinage of silver and gold at the present legal ratio of 16 to 1.
2. We demand that the amount of circulating medium be speedily increased to not less than $50 per capita.
3. We demand a graduated income tax.
4. We believe that the money of the country should be kept as much as possible in the hands of the people, and hence we demand that all State and national revenues shall be limited to the necessary expenses of the government, economically and honestly administered.
5. We demand that postal savings banks be established by the government for the safe deposit of the earnings of the people and to facilitate exchange.

TRANSPORTATION.—Transportation being a means of exchange and a public necessity, the government should own and operate the railroads in the interest of the people. The telegraph and telephone, like the post-office system, being a necessity for the transmission of news, should be owned and operated by the government in the interest of the people.

LAND.—The land, including all the natural sources of wealth, is the heritage of the people, and should not be monopolized for speculative purposes, and alien ownership of land should be prohibited. All land now held by railroads and other corporations in excess of their actual needs, and all lands now owned by aliens should be reclaimed by the government and held for actual settlers only.

EXPRESSION OF SENTIMENTS

Your Committee on Platform and Resolutions beg leave unanimously to report the following:

Whereas, Other questions have been presented for our consideration, we hereby submit the following, not as a part of the Platform of the People's Party, but as resolutions expressive of the sentiment of this Convention.

1. RESOLVED, That we demand a free ballot and a fair count in all elections, and pledge ourselves to secure it to every legal voter without Federal intervention, through the adoption by the States of the unperverted Australian or secret ballot system.

2. RESOLVED, That the revenue derived from a graduated income tax should be applied to the reduction of the burden of taxation now levied upon the domestic industries of this country.

3. RESOLVED, That we pledge our support to fair and liberal pensions to ex-Union soldiers and sailors.

4. RESOLVED, That we condemn the fallacy of protecting American labor under the present system, which opens our ports to the pauper and criminal classes of the world and crowds out our wage-earners; and we denounce the present ineffective laws against contract labor, and demand the further restriction of undesirable emigration.

5. RESOLVED, That we cordially sympathize with the efforts of organized workingmen to shorten the hours of labor, and demand a rigid enforcement of the existing eight-hour law on Government work, and ask that a penalty clause be added to the said law.

6. RESOLVED, That we regard the maintenance of a large standing army of mercenaries, known as the Pinkerton system, as a menace to our liberties, and we demand its abolition; and we condemn the recent invasion of the Territory of Wyoming by the hired assassins of plutocracy, assisted by Federal officers.

7. RESOLVED, That we commend to the favorable consideration of

the people and the reform press the legislative system known as the initiative and referendum.

8. Resolved, That we favor a constitutional provision limiting the office of President and Vice-President to one term, and providing for the election of Senators of the United States by a direct vote of the people.

9. Resolved, That we oppose any subsidy or national aid to any private corporation for any purpose.

10. Resolved, That this convention sympathizes with the Knights of Labor and their righteous contest with the tyrannical combine of clothing manufacturers of Rochester, and declare it to be a duty of all who hate tyranny and oppression to refuse to purchase the goods made by the said manufacturers, or to patronize any merchants who sell such goods.

James B. Weaver
Trusts

A Trust is defined to be a combination of many competing concerns under one management. The object is to increase profits through reduction of cost, limitation of product and increase of the price to the consumer. The term is now applied, and very properly, to all kinds of combinations in trade which relate to prices, and without regard to whether all or only part of the objects named are had in view.

Combinations which we now call trusts have existed in this country for a considerable period, but they have only attracted general attention for about ten years. We have in our possession copies of the agreements of the Standard Oil and Sugar Trusts. The former is dated January 2, 1882, and the latter August 6, 1887.

Trusts vary somewhat in their forms of organization. This is caused by the character of the property involved and the variety of objects

A Call to Action (Des Moines, Iowa, 1892), pp. 387–94. Text from this edition.

Weaver, the Populist candidate for president, published A Call to Action as a campaign document.

to be attained. The great trusts of the country consist of an association or consolidation of a number of associations engaged in the same line of business—each company in the trust being first separately incorporated. The stock of these companies is then turned over to a board of trustees who issue back trust certificates in payment for the stock transferred. The trust selects its own board of directors and henceforth has complete control of the entire business and can regulate prices, limit or stimulate production as they may deem best for the parties concerned in the venture. The trust itself is not necessarily incorporated. Many of the strongest, such as the "Standard Oil Trust," the "Sugar Trust," and "The American Cotton Seed Oil Trust" and others are not. They are the invisible agents of associated artificial intangible beings. They are difficult to find, still harder to restrain and so far as present experience has gone they are practically a law unto themselves.

The power of these institutions has grown to be almost incalculable. Trustees of the Standard Oil Trust have issued certificates to the amount of $90,000,000, and each certificate is worth to-day $165 in the market, which makes their real capital at least $148,500,000, to say nothing of the added strength of their recent European associations. They have paid quarterly dividends since their organization in 1882. The profits amount to $20,000,000 per year. The Trust is managed by a Board of Trustees all of whom reside in New York. The combine really began in 1869, but the present agreement dates no further back than January, 1882. The only record kept of the meetings of these Trustees is a note stating that the minutes of the previous meeting were read and approved. The minutes themselves are then destroyed. These facts were brought to light by an investigation before the New York Senate February, 1888. Col. George Bliss and Gen. Roger A. Pryor acted as council for the people and a great many things were brought out concerning the Standard, and a multitude of other combines, which had not before been well understood. John D. Rockefeller, Charles Pratt, Henry M. Rogers, H. M. Flagler, Benjamin Brewster, J. N. Archibald, William Rockefeller and W. H. Tilford are the trustees and they personally own a majority of the stock. Seven hundred other persons own the remainder. This trust holds the stock of forty-two corporations, extending into thirteen States. The Cotton Seed Oil Trust holds the stock of eighty-five corporations extending into fifteen States.

Trust combinations now dominate the following products and divisions of trade: Kerosene Oil, Cotton Seed Oil, Sugar, Oat meal, Starch, White Corn Meal, Straw Paper, Pearled Barley, Coal, Straw Board, Lumber, Castor Oil, Cement, Linseed Oil, Lard, School Slate, Oil Cloth, Salt, Cattle, Meat Products, Gas, Street Railways, Whisky, Paints, Rubber, Steel, Steel Rails, Steel and Iron Beams, Cars, Nails, Wrought Iron Pipes, Iron Nuts, Stoves, Lead, Copper, Envelopes, Wall Paper, Paper Bags, Paving Pitch, Cordage, Coke, Reaping, Binding and Mowing Machines, Threshing Machines, Plows, Glass, Water Works, Warehouses, Sand Stone, Granite, Upholsterers' Felt, Lead Pencils, Watches and Watch Cases, Clothes Wringers, Carpets, Undertakers' Goods and Coffins, Planes, Breweries, Milling, Flour, Silver Plate, Plated Ware and a vast variety of other lines of trade.

The Standard Oil and its complement, the American Cotton Oil Trust, were the advance guard of the vast army of like associations which have overrun and now occupy every section of the country and nearly all departments of trade. The Standard has developed into an international combine and has brought the world under its yoke. In 1890 the largest German and Dutch petroleum houses fell under the control of the Standard Oil Company, and the oil importing companies of Bremen, Hamburg and Stettin were united by the Standard into a German-American Petroleum Company, with its seat at Bremen. In 1891 the Paris Rothschilds, who control the Russian oil fields, effected a combination with the Standard Oil Trust, which makes the combine world wide; and so far as this important article of consumption is concerned, it places all mankind at their mercy. Our information concerning this international oil trust is derived from the report concerning the Petroleum Monopoly of Europe by Consul-General Edwards, of Berlin, made to the Secretary of State, June 25, 1891, and published in Consular Reports No. 131.

Now that the Petroleum Combine has accomplished the conquest of the world, what is to hinder every other branch of business from accomplishing the same end? The Standard has led the way and demonstrated the feasibility of such gigantic enterprises and others will doubtless be quick to follow. Already, indeed, the Anthracite coal barons have followed their example so far as this country is concerned, and the "Big Four," who control the meat products of this country, have reached out and subsidized the ship room and other facilities for international trade in that line. We hear also well authenticated rumors that other combinations, looking to the complete control of every branch of mercantile business, are already in existence and making what they regard as very satisfactory progress.

The Sugar Trust, which now fixes the price of 3,000,000,000 pounds of sugar annually consumed in the United States, is managed upon substantially the same plan as the Standard Oil Trust, and so, in fact, are all of the great combines. They rule the whole realm of commerce with a rod of iron and levy tribute upon the country amounting to hundreds of millions of dollars annually—an imposition which the people would not think for a moment of submitting to if exacted by their Government.

Are Trusts Legal?

It is clear that trusts are contrary to public policy and hence in conflict with the Common law. They are monopolies organized to destroy competition and restrain trade. Enlightened public policy favors competition in the present condition of organized society. It was held in 1880, Central Ohio Salt Company *vs.* Guthrie, 35 Ohio St., 666, that a trust was illegal and void. The Pennsylvania courts held the same way against the Coal Trust of that State. Morris Coal Company *vs.* Vorday, 68 Pa. St., 173.

In 1869 a coal company in New York had contracted to buy coal from several firms upon condition that they would not sell coal to other persons in that locality. The party buying the coal did not pay for it, whereupon suit was brought to collect. The court refused to enforce the bargain, holding that the contract was illegal. Arnot *vs.* Pittison Coal Company, 68 N. Y., 558. The same rule was upheld by the courts at Louisiana in 1859. In Illinois a Grain Dealer's Combine was held to be illegal. The question arose in a suit brought to compel a proper division of the profits. The court refused to enforce the agreement. See Croft *vs.* McConoughy, 79 Ill., 346. The same character of decisions will be found in perhaps a majority of the States. Indeed, since the days when Coke was Lord Chief Justice of England, more than a century and a half ago, the courts in both England and America have held such combinations to be illegal and void. See "Case of the Monopolies," 11 Coke, 84.

It is contended by those interested in Trusts that they tend to cheapen production and diminish the price of the article to the consumer. It is conceded that these results may follow temporarily and even permanently in some instances. But it is not the rule. When such effects ensue they are merely incidental to the controlling object of the association. Trusts are speculative in their purposes and formed to make money. Once they secure control of a given line of business they are masters of the situation and can dictate to the two great classes with which they deal—the producer of the raw material and the consumer of the finished product. They limit the price of the raw material so as to impoverish the producer, drive him to a single market, reduce the price of every class of labor connected with the trade, throw out of employment large numbers of persons who had before been engaged in a meritorious calling and finally, prompted by insatiable avarice, they increase the price to the consumer and thus complete the circle of their depredations. Diminished prices is the bribe which they throw into the market to propitiate the public. They will take it back when it suits them to do so.

The Trust is organized commerce with the Golden Rule excluded and the trustees exempted from the restraints of conscience.

They argue that competition means war and is therefore destructive. The Trust is eminently docile and hence seeks to destroy competition in order that we may have peace. But the peace which they give us is like that which exists after the leopard has devoured the kid. This professed desire for peace is a false pretense. They dread the war of competition because the people share in the spoils. When rid of that they always turn their guns upon the masses and depredate without limit or mercy. The main weapons of the trust are threats, intimidation, bribery, fraud, wreck and pillage. Take one well authenticated instance in the history of the Oat Meal Trust as an example. In 1887 this Trust decided that part of their mills should stand idle. They were accordingly closed. This resulted in the discharge of a large number of laborers who had to suffer in consequence. The mills which were continued in operation would produce seven million barrels of meal during the year. Shortly after shutting down the Trust advanced the price of meal one dollar per barrel and the public was forced to stand the assessment. The mills were more profitable when idle than when in operation.

The Sugar Trust has it within its power to levy a tribute of $30,000,000 upon the people of the United States by simply advancing the price of sugar one cent per pound for one year.

If popular tumult breaks out and legislation in restraint of these depredations is threatened, they can advance prices, extort campaign expenses and corruption funds from the people and force the disgruntled multitude to furnish the sinews of war for their own destruction. They not only have the power to do these things, but it is their known mode of warfare and they actually practice it from year to year.

The most distressing feature of this war of the Trusts is the fact that they control the articles which the plain people consume in their daily life. It cuts off their accumulations and deprives them of the staff upon which they fain would lean in their old age.

THE REMEDY

For nearly three hundred years the Anglo-Saxon race has been trying to arrest the encroachments of monopoly and yet the evil has flourished and gained in strength from age to age. The courts have come to the aid of enlightened sentiment, pronounced all such combinations contrary to public policy, illegal and their contracts void; and still they have continued to thrive. Thus far repressive and prohibitory legislation have proved unavailing. Experience has shown that when men, for the sake of gain, will openly violate the moral law and infringe upon the plain rights of their neighbors, they will not be restrained by ordinary prohibitory measures. It is the application of force to the situation and force must be met with force. The States should pass stringent penal statutes which will visit personal responsibility upon all agents and representatives of the trust who aid or assist in the transaction of its business within the State. The General Government, through its power to lay and collect taxes, should place an excise or internal revenue tax of from 25 to 40 per cent on all manufacturing plants, goods, wares or merchandise of whatever kind and wherever found when owned by or controlled in the interest of such combines or associations, and this tax should be a first lien upon such property until the tax is paid. The details of such a bill would not be difficult to frame. Such a law would destroy the Trust root and branch. Whenever the American people really try to overthrow these institutions they will be able to do so and to further postpone action is a crime.

WHAT OF THE FUTURE?

One of the main charges against Charles the First, was that he had fostered and created monopolies. His head went to the block. Nearly every great struggle of the English race has been caused by the unjust exactions of tribute—against the extortions of greed. Our own war for Independence was a war against taxes. Our late internal struggle was for the freedom of labor and the right of the laborer to possess and enjoy his own. That struggle is still on and it is now thundering at our gates with renewed energy. It will not down, though the Trust heap Ossa upon Pelion. The people will rise and overturn the despoilers though they shake the earth by the displacement.

These vast struggles are great teachers and the world is learning rapidly. We are coming to know that great combinations reduce the cost of production and soon the world will grasp the idea that the people can combine and protect themselves. In this combine, in this co-operation of all, there will be no discrimination and the bounties of Heaven will be open alike to the weak and the powerful. We welcome the conflict. There is no time to lose nor can the battle begin too soon.

Henry Vincent
Start of the Commonweal

HAVING A PROPER UNDERSTANDING of the objects and aims of the Commonweal as set forth by the leader of the movement, the reader is now invited to observe the start of the Coxey force on its great journey to the Capitol of the Nation: At noon on Easter Sunday, and a little in advance of the advertised time, the Commonweal marched out of Massillon. A large crowd of people had assembled to witness its departure, and as the army moved through the public square of the city of its birth, there were in its ranks, by actual count, just 122 people on foot, horseback and in wagons. At the head of the column was the official standard of the army, carried by an aid, and the American flag, in the hands of Jasper Johnson, a brawny negro, of Buchanan, W. Va., who is one of Coxey's earliest recruits from that place.

Carl Browne, marshal, came next mounted on a magnificent white horse, clad in high top boots, corduroy trowsers, buckskin jacket, a fur overcoat and a huge sombrero. Supporting him was "Doc" Kirkland, of Pittsburg, with two aids. Behind these was President Coxey, seated in his phaeton, to which was attached a beautiful pair of spirited horses driven by a negro coachman. Mrs. Coxey, her little son and Miss Jones drove with the army to its first stopping place, at Reedurban, four miles distant. The day was cold and raw, and the grotesque, not to say pitiable, appearance of the nondescript gathering gave strong grounds for the humorous and half sarcastic accounts sent out by the newspaper men and the associated press of the first breaking of camp and the beginning of the long march to Washington. At 2 P.M. Reedurban was reached and a halt was made for luncheon. This first halt was one of the most critical points in the whole march. As already stated the weather was extremely disagreeable, snowing

The Story of the Commonweal (Chicago, 1894), pp. 56–81. Text from this edition.

Jacob Coxey, a successful businessman of Massillon, Ohio, had organized his "army" as a "living petition" to Congress for the enactment of free silver and public works legislation. It left Massillon on Easter Day, 1894, amid much national publicity, and arrived in Washington on May 1.

most of the time, accompanied by a piercing wind which chilled to the marrow the best clad men in the army. Many of them, however, had no overcoats, so that their sufferings during that first half day's march were indeed severe and well calculated to test their courage and powers of endurance. Despite these trying and disheartening conditions, there were no desertions worth mentioning, and at 4 P.M. the army reached Canton, stronger in numbers than when it left Massillon. Here its reception was no less enthusiastic in character than that accorded at Reedurban. By this time the newspapers had already heralded far and wide. that attachment proceedings had been begun by certain of Mr. Coxey's creditors for the sole purpose of disarranging his plans and of staying the progress of the Commonweal movement. Citizens of Canton, justly indignant at this proposed treatment, had appointed a committee to prepare an address to the country calling for funds to aid Mr. Coxey in the same manner the people had been given the opportunity a short time before to contribute to the financial relief of Ohio's distinguished chief executive.

The scenes attendant upon the entrance of the Commonweal into Canton were, to say the least, impressive. Fully twenty thousand people gathered in the street and greeted its approach with hearty cheers, in which it was observed that the squad of special police, which had been hastily organized to preserve order, joined as warmly as did the citizens in general. Marshal Browne on his milk-white steed at the head of the column, formed the picturesque figure he has so often been described as making. Behind him came the rank and file, marching two abreast, bearing their banners, and with happy faces and proud and independent bearing they looked much more the embodiment of American manhood than is often seen in anti-election processions in the cities. To be sure there were in that body of men characters well worthy the pencil of any sketch artist. Old and young, ragged and well clothed, hungry and well fed, the clean and the dirty were all there, but all seemed cheerful and determined of purpose.

Camp was pitched in a vacant woodlot adjoining the city workhouse and at the outset some trouble was had with an individual who owned the adjacent premises, and who, misled by reports as to the character of the army, bitterly protested against its too intimate proximity. He was soon taken, however, with the prevailing fever of friendly enthusiasm and his open hostility soon turned into the heartiest co-operation and support. That night speeches were made by both Coxey and Browne, and were listened to by large and attentive crowds. President Coxey stated in his utterances that up to that hour the movement had fully come up to his full expectations and that as a peace army it had already demonstrated it needed no police surveillance. Turning to his own followers he said: "You have here a sample of the people's thoughtful sympathy, shown in the wagonloads of bread, meat and provisions with which they have so liberally provided us. And as they read of this movement and its progress toward their localities there will be no lack of sustenance to enable the army to continue its march to Washington."

The night at Canton was bitterly cold, and the big tent not being large enough to hold all the men, quite a number were lodged in the city hall. Camp was broken the following morning at 10 o'clock, and the march to Louisville, a distance of twelve miles, was made in less than three hours, the army arriving with nearly one hundred more men than it had on reaching Canton.

At Louisville an incident occurred which not only was a vindication of the character of the men composing the Commonweal, but also established the claims made that it was purely a peace organization. It appears that a resident of the town had missed a valuable watch, and very naturally its disappearance was charged to the Commonwealers. Marshal Browne promptly had the body of men drawn up in line and every man was thoroughly searched. It is hardly necessary to say that no watch was discovered, while the additional fact was brought out that in all that body of men there were no weapons of any kind, beyond a few harmless jackknives.

The start from Canton, however, had been delayed for two hours on account of the receipt, by associated press dispatches, of Senator Stewart's letter to Mr. Coxey, who immediately prepared his reply and gave it to the public through the same channels. The senator's letter, which attracted much attention at the time, is as follows:

UNITED STATES SENATE, March 24, 1894.

GENERAL J. S. COXEY, Massillon, Ohio:

Dear Sir:—The preservation of life, liberty and the pursuit of happiness was intrusted to the people under the Constitution of the United States. A free ballot was the means by which the sovereign people could retain the rights acquired by the patriots who gained the independence and established the government of the United States. There was a time when the ballot placed the control of the government in Washingtons, Jeffersons, Jacksons and Lincolns. Such use of the ballot sent terror and dismay to tyrants, despots, and plundering oligarchies throughout the world. The enemies of justice and human rights predicted that the success of the ballot was temporary; that man was not capable of self-government. The destruction of ancient republics and the repeated failures of the people to govern themselves was cited in proof of their contention that despotism, oppression and slavery were the fate of the human race. There have been no Washingtons, Jeffersons, Jacksons or Lincolns elected President of the United States in the two decades. A soulless despot of alien origin is monarch of the commercial world. His name is money. His servants are administrative and legislative bodies. The army you are collecting used the ballot to put the army, the navy, and the treasury department under the control of banks and bondholders and place in the halls of Congress representatives to do the bidding of the money-changers.

The ides of November are approaching. An opportunity for the people to strike for liberty will again be presented. The old parties, which have surrendered the rights of the people to the rule of concentrated capital, will ask for a renewal of their lease of power at the ballot box. Every movement of the people to obtain relief outside of the forms of law will be denounced as anarchy. The purse strings of the nation are held by Congress under the dictation of the administration, and the President is commander in chief of the army and navy of the United States. The attempt of a starving multitude to march to Washington will furnish an excuse for using the power of the governments of the states, and of the United States to put down anarchy and insurrection. The vigor with which the laws will be executed against starving people will be an argument in the next election for continuing in power concentrated capital as necessary for the maintenance of law and order. The sufferings of the people are the result of electing the men to office who do the bidding of the money powers, which by legislation and administration have destroyed more than one-half the metallic money of the world and cornered the other half. Twenty years of uninterrupted rule of banks and bondholders have concentrated the wealth of the world in the hands of the few, and enabled them to seize the telegraph, the press, and nearly every other avenue through which the people can obtain information of the cunning devices by which the parasites absorb what the masses produce. There is but one battlefield where the forces of liberty and equality can meet and overthrow the enemy of human rights. There is no law now on the statute books authorizing the President of the United States to march an army against the people at the ballot box. Every attempt to place the ballot under the control of federal authority has thus far been successfully resisted. Let your army be reinforced by the millions of the unemployed and by the wealth producers of the nation, and be thoroughly mobilized for the battle in November, when a victory for the rights of man against the despotism of banks and bonds is possible.

Abandon the folly of marching an unarmed multitude of starving laborers against the modern appliances of war under the control of a soulless money trust. Such folly will augment the power of the oppressor and endanger the safety of the ballot itself. Disorder is all that is required to insure the supremacy of the armed forces of the money powers at the polls. The Constitution of the United States is our charter of liberty. It has been subverted by an oligarchy of concentrated wealth. False agents of the people have betrayed their trust and brought misery and want when abundance and prosperity seemed assured. Traitors to human rights have usurped the power of the government through the machinery of party and the arts of demagogues. Hurl them from power. Trust no man who has once deceived you. Let the government of the United States be administered for and not against the people. Use the ballot to protect liberty, justice and equal rights, and not to elevate to power the agents of banks and bonds to perpetuate the rule of an oligarchy of wealth.

Yours very truly,

WILLIAM M. STEWART.

To this letter Mr. Coxey replied briefly as follows: "DEAR SIR: I have seen your letter in the newspapers addressed 'General Coxey.' Allow me to inform you that I am not a general. I am simply the president of the J. S. Coxey Good Roads Association of the United States and ex-officio of the Commonweal of Christ. I am not heading an army, no matter how much a subsidized press, at the dictation of a money power, tries to make this appear, and all the epithets hurled at us as being anarchists or a mob get more weight from ill-advised admissions by our friends than all else besides. The warfare of the silver men against gold and bonds under your leadership in the United States Senate was magnificent. The morning dispatches state that even the President of the United States is engaged in a deal with Wall street to veto the Bland seigniorage bill in the sole interest of gold. So the die is cast. We shall march on peaceably and depend upon the outpouring of a peaceful public to defend us from Pinkerton's policemen, military, soldiers of petty party politicians. This is a non-partisan movement and he who is not with us is against us; there is not room for neutral ground, and that a house divided against itself cannot stand is as true today as when originally uttered and used in the dark days of the Civil war by Abraham Lincoln, the father of the legal tender. Following in his footsteps we seek to dethrone gold, as our forefathers did King George in 1776, and once more have legal tender money such as would be if the two Coxey bills are passed. Now we have followed your leadership, advocating the bill for unlimited coinage of silver as money, and if we are to judge of the silver men by you, looked upon as you are as their mouthpiece, your attitude in slighting this movement as folly places you and the silver men you represent in an unenviable position as the ally of our common enemy—gold. Thus the rubicon has been crossed by the silver forces and we cannot falter. The fiat must now go forth—demonetization of gold as well as silver. Yours,   J. S. COXEY."

The band camped for the night at Louisville, and on the following morning set out for Alliance, facing a driving snowstorm and trudging along almost impassable roads, but, despite these conditions, made the journey of nearly fourteen miles in about three hours. The reception here was a most cordial one. A local committee, headed by D. W. Smith, a leading business man, had secured the fair grounds for a camping place and provided an abundance of provisions. Fully three thousand people assembled to see the men enter the city, and later in the afternoon gathered in the opera house to listen to speeches made by Browne and Coxey, whose utterances were frequently loudly cheered. In the evening Marshal Browne spoke in the same hall, and a collection to aid the movement netted nearly fifty dollars.

William Jennings Bryan
Cross of Gold Speech

MR. CHAIRMAN and Gentlemen of the Convention: I would be presumptuous, indeed, to present myself against the distinguished gentlemen to whom you have listened if this were a mere measuring of abilities; but this is not a contest between persons. The humblest citizen in all the land, when clad in the armor of a righteous cause, is stronger than all the hosts of error. I come to speak to you in defense of a cause as holy as the cause of liberty—the cause of humanity.

When this debate is concluded, a motion will be made to lay upon the table the resolution offered in commendation of the administra-

The First Battle: A Story of the Campaign of 1896 (Chicago, 1896), pp. 199–206. Text from this edition.

Bryan made his famous speech on July 8, 1896, during the Democratic National Convention at Chicago. The specific issue to which he was speaking was the platform of the party, a platform which carried a free silver plank. Senator Hill of New York was a leader of the gold Democrats.

tion, and also the resolution offered in condemnation of the administration. We object to bringing this question down to the level of
persons. The individual is but an atom; he is born, he acts, he dies;
but principles are eternal; and this has been a contest over a principle.

Never before in the history of this country has there been witnessed
such a contest as that through which we have just passed. Never before in the history of American politics has a great issue been fought
out as this issue has been, by the voters of a great party. On the fourth
of March, 1895, a few Democrats, most of them members of Congress, issued an address to the Democrats of the nation, asserting that
the money question was the paramount issue of the hour; declaring
that a majority of the Democratic party had the right to control the
action of the party on this paramount issue; and concluding with the
request that the believers in the free coinage of silver in the Democratic party should organize, take charge of, and control the policy of
the Democratic party. Three months later, at Memphis, an organization was perfected, and the silver Democrats went forth openly and
courageously proclaiming their belief, and declaring that, if successful, they would crystallize into a platform the declaration which they
had made. Then began the conflict. With a zeal approaching the zeal
which inspired the crusaders who followed Peter the Hermit, our silver Democrats went forth from victory unto victory until they are
now assembled, not to discuss, not to debate, but to enter up the judgment already rendered by the plain people of this country. In this
contest brother has been arrayed against brother, father against son.
The warmest ties of love, acquaintance and association have been disregarded; old leaders have been cast aside when they have refused
to give expression to the sentiments of those whom they would lead,
and new leaders have sprung up to give direction to this cause of
truth. Thus has the contest been waged, and we have assembled here
under as binding and solemn instructions as were ever imposed upon
representatives of the people.

We do not come as individuals. As individuals we might have been
glad to compliment the gentleman from New York (Senator Hill), but
we know that the people for whom we speak would never be willing
to put him in a position where he could thwart the will of the Democratic party. I say it was not a question of persons; it was a question
of principle, and it is not with gladness, my friends, that we find ourselves brought into conflict with those who are now arrayed on the
other side.

The gentleman who preceded me (ex-Governor Russell) spoke of
the State of Massachusetts; let me assure him that not one present in
all this convention entertains the least hostility to the people of the
State of Massachusetts, but we stand here representing people who

are the equals, before the law, of the greatest citizens in the State of Massachusetts. When you (turning to the gold delegates) come before us and tell us that we are about to disturb your business interests, we reply that you have disturbed our business interests by your course.

We say to you that you have made the definition of a business man too limited in its application. The man who is employed for wages is as much a business man as his employer; the attorney in a country town is as much a business man as the corporation counsel in a great metropolis; the merchant at the cross-roads store is as much a business man as the merchant of New York; the farmer who goes forth in the morning and toils all day—who begins in the spring and toils all summer—and who by the application of brain and muscle to the natural resources of the country creates wealth, is as much a business man as the man who goes upon the board of trade and bets upon the price of grain; the miners who go down a thousand feet into the earth, or climb two thousand feet upon the cliffs, and bring forth from their hiding places the precious metals to be poured into the channels of trade are as much business men as the few financial magnates who, in a back room, corner the money of the world. We come to speak for this broader class of business men.

Ah, my friends, we say not one word against those who live upon the Atlantic coast, but the hardy pioneers who have braved all the dangers of the wilderness, who have made the desert to blossom as the rose—the pioneers away out there (pointing to the West), who rear their children near to Nature's heart, where they can mingle their voices with the voices of the birds—out there where they have erected schoolhouses for the education of their young, churches where they praise their Creator, and cemeteries where rest the ashes of their dead—these people, we say, are as deserving of the consideration of our party as any people in this country. It is for these that we speak. We do not come as aggressors. Our war is not a war of conquest; we are fighting in the defense of our homes, our families, and posterity. We have petitioned, and our petitions have been scorned; we have entreated, and our entreaties have been disregarded; we have begged, and they have mocked when our calamity came. We beg no longer; we entreat no more; we petition no more. We defy them.

The gentleman from Wisconsin has said that he fears a Robespierre. My friends, in this land of the free you need not fear that a tyrant will spring up from among the people. What we need is an Andrew Jackson to stand, as Jackson stood, against the encroachments of organized wealth.

They tell us that this platform was made to catch votes. We reply to them that changing conditions make new issues; that the principles upon which Democracy rests are as everlasting as the hills, but that they must be applied to new conditions as they arise. Conditions have arisen, and we are here to meet those conditions. They tell us that the income tax ought not to be brought in here; that it is a new idea. They criticise us for our criticism of the Supreme Court of the United States. My friends, we have not criticised; we have simply called attention to what you already know. If you want criticisms, read the dissenting opinions of the court. There you will find criticisms. They say that we passed an unconstitutional law; we deny it. The income tax law was not unconstitutional when it was passed; it was not unconstitutional when it went before the Supreme Court for the first time; it did not become unconstitutional until one of the judges changed his mind, and we cannot be expected to know when a judge will change his mind. The income tax is just. It simply intends to put the burdens of government justly upon the backs of the people. I am in favor of an income tax. When I find a man who is not willing to bear his share of the burdens of the government which protects him, I find a man who is unworthy to enjoy the blessings of a government like ours.

They say that we are opposing national bank currency; it is true. If you will read what Thomas Benton said, you will find he said that, in searching history, he could find but one parallel to Andrew Jackson; that was Cicero, who destroyed the conspiracy of Cataline and saved Rome. Benton said that Cicero only did for Rome what Jackson did for us when he destroyed the bank conspiracy and saved America. We say in our platform that we believe that the right to coin and issue money is a function of government. We believe it. We believe that it is a part of sovereignty, and can no more with safety be delegated to private individuals than we could afford to delegate to private individuals the power to make penal statutes or levy taxes. Mr. Jefferson, who was once regarded as good Democratic authority, seems to have differed in opinion from the gentleman who has addressed us on the part of the minority. Those who are opposed to this proposition tell us that the issue of paper money is a function of the bank, and that the Government ought to go out of the banking business. I stand with Jefferson rather than with them, and tell them, as he did, that the issue of money is a function of government, and that the banks ought to go out of the governing business.

They complain about the plank which declares against life tenure in office. They have tried to strain it to mean that which it does not mean. What we oppose by that plank is the life tenure which is being built up in Washington, and which excludes from participation in official benefits the humbler members of society.

Let me call your attention to two or three important things. The gentleman from New York says that he will propose an amendment to the platform providing that the proposed change in our monetary system shall not affect contracts already made. Let me remind you that there is no intention of affecting those contracts which according to present laws are made payable in gold; but if he means to say that we cannot change our monetary system without protecting those who have loaned money before the change was made, I desire to ask him where, in law or in morals, he can find justification for not protecting the debtors when the act of 1873 was passed, if he now insists that we must protect the creditors.

He says he will also propose an amendment which will provide for the suspension of free coinage if we fail to maintain the parity within a year. We reply that when we advocate a policy which we believe will be successful, we are not compelled to raise a doubt as to our own sincerity by suggesting what we shall do if we fail. I ask him, if he would apply his logic to us, why he does not apply it to himself. He says he wants this country to try to secure an international agreement. Why does he not tell us what he is going to do if he fails to secure an international agreement? There is more reason for him to do that than there is for us to provide against the failure to maintain the parity. Our opponents have tried for twenty years to secure an international agreement, and those are waiting for it most patiently who do not want it at all.

And now, my friends, let me come to the paramount issue. If they ask us why it is that we say more on the money question than we say upon the tariff question, I reply that, if protection has slain its thousands, the gold standard has slain its tens of thousands. If they ask us why we do not embody in our platform all the things that we believe in, we reply that when we have restored the money of the Constitution all other necessary reforms will be possible; but that until this is done there is no other reform that can be accomplished.

Why is it that within three months such a change has come over the country? Three months ago, when it was confidently asserted that those who believe in the gold standard would frame our platform and nominate our candidates, even the advocates of the gold standard did not think that we could elect a president. And they had good reason for their doubt, because there is scarcely a State here today asking for the gold standard which is not in the absolute control of the Republican party. But note the change. Mr. McKinley was nominated at St. Louis upon a platform which declared for the maintenance of the gold standard until it can be changed into bimetallism by international agreement. Mr. McKinley was the most popular man among the Republicans, and three months ago everybody in the Re-

publican party prophesied his election. How is it today? Why, the man
who was once pleased to think that he looked like Napoleon—that
man shudders today when he remembers that he was nominated on
the anniversary of the battle of Waterloo. Not only that, but as he lis-
tens he can hear with ever-increasing distinctness the sound of the
waves as they beat upon the lonely shores of St. Helena.

Why this change? Ah, my friends, is not the reason for the change
evident to any one who will look at the matter? No private character,
however pure, no personal popularity, however great, can protect
from the avenging wrath of an indignant people a man who will declare that he is in favor of fastening the gold standard upon this country, or who is willing to surrender the right of self-government and
place the legislative control of our affairs in the hands of foreign po-
tentates and powers.

We go forth confident that we shall win. Why? Because upon the
paramount issue of this campaign there is not a spot of ground upon
which the enemy will dare to challenge battle. If they tell us that the
gold standard is a good thing, we shall point to their platform and
tell them that their platform pledges the party to get rid of the gold
standard and substitute bimetallism. If the gold standard is a good
thing, why try to get rid of it? I call your attention to the fact that
some of the very people who are in this convention today and who
tell us that we ought to declare in favor of international bimetallism
—thereby declaring that the gold standard is wrong and that the principle of bimetallism is better—these very people four months ago were
open and avowed advocates of the gold standard, and were then telling us that we would not legislate two metals together, even with the
aid of all the world. If the gold standard is a good thing, we ought to
declare in favor of its retention and not in favor of abandoning it; and
if the gold standard is a bad thing why should we wait until other nations are willing to help us to let go? Here is the line of battle, and we
care not upon which issue they force the fight; we are prepared to meet
them on either issue or on both. If they tell us that the gold standard is
the standard of civilization, we reply to them that this, the most enlightened of all the nations of the earth, has never declared for a gold
standard and that both the great parties this year are declaring against
it. If the gold standard is the standard of civilization, why, my friends,
should we not have it? If they come to meet us on that issue we can
present the history of our nation. More than that; we can tell them
that they will search the pages of history in vain to find a single instance where the common people of any land have ever declared
themselves in favor of the gold standard. They can find where the

holders of fixed investments have declared for a gold standard, but not where the masses have.

Mr. Carlisle said in 1878 that this was a struggle between "the idle holders of idle capital" and "the struggling masses, who produce the wealth and pay the taxes of the country;" and, my friends, the question we are to decide is: Upon which side will the Democratic party fight; upon the side of "the idle holders of idle capital" or upon the side of "the struggling masses"? That is the question which the party must answer first, and then it must be answered by each individual hereafter. The sympathies of the Democratic party, as shown by the platform, are on the side of the struggling masses who have ever been the foundation of the Democratic party. There are two ideas of government. There are those who believe that, if you will only legislate to make the well-to-do prosperous, their prosperity will leak through on those below. The Democratic idea, however, has been that if you legislate to make the masses prosperous, their prosperity will find its way up through every class which rests upon them.

You come to us and tell us that the great cities are in favor of the gold standard; we reply that the great cities rest upon our broad and fertile prairies. Burn down your cities and leave our farms, and your cities will spring up again as if by magic; but destroy our farms and the grass will grow in the streets of every city in the country.

My friends, we declare that this nation is able to legislate for its own people on every question, without waiting for the aid or consent of any other nation on earth; and upon that issue we expect to carry every State in the Union. I shall not slander the inhabitants of the fair State of Massachusetts nor the inhabitants of the State of New York by saying that, when they are confronted with the proposition, they will declare that this nation is not able to attend to its own business. It is the issue of 1776 over again. Our ancestors, when but three millions in number, had the courage to declare their political independence of every other nation; shall we, their descendants, when we have grown to seventy millions, declare that we are less independent than our forefathers? No, my friends, that will never be the verdict of our people. Therefore, we care not upon what lines the battle is fought. If they say bimetallism is good, but that we cannot have it until other nations help us, we reply that, instead of having a gold standard because England has, we will restore bimetallism, and then let England have bimetallism because the United States has it. If they dare to come out in the open field and defend the gold standard as a good thing, we will fight them to the uttermost. Having behind us the producing masses of this nation and the world, supported by the commercial interests, the laboring interests, and the toilers everywhere, we will answer their demand for a gold standard by saying to them: You shall not press down upon the brow of labor this crown of thorns, you shall not crucify mankind upon a cross of gold.

Edward Bellamy
The Strikers

PRESENTLY, as we were crossing Boston Common, absorbed in conversation, a shadow fell athwart the way, and looking up, I saw towering above us a sculptured group of heroic size.

"Who are these?" I exclaimed.

"You ought to know if any one," said the doctor. "They are contemporaries of yours who were making a good deal of disturbance in your day."

But, indeed, it had only been as an involuntary expression of surprise that I had questioned what the figures stood for.

Let me tell you, readers of the twentieth century, what I saw up there on the pedestal, and you will recognize the world-famous group. Shoulder to shoulder, as if rallied to resist assault, were three figures of men in the garb of the laboring class of my time. They were bare-headed, and their coarse-textured shirts, rolled above the elbow and open at the breast, showed the sinewy arms and chest. Before them, on the ground, lay a pair of shovels and a pickaxe. The central figure, with the right hand extended, palm outward, was pointing to the discarded tools. The arms of the other two were folded on their breasts. The faces were coarse and hard in outline and bristled with unkempt beards. Their expression was one of dogged defiance, and their gaze was fixed with such scowling intensity upon the void space before them that I involuntarily glanced behind me to see what they

Equality (New York, 1897), pp. 206–211. Text from this edition.

Like Bellamy's *Looking Backward*, *Equality* is a Utopian novel set in the year 2000. Its protagonist, Julian West, is a young Bostonian of 1887, who awakens from a deep sleep to find himself in the Boston of 2000. Dr. Leete is his principal guide in this world of the future.

were looking at. There were two women also in the group, as coarse of dress and features as the men. One was kneeling before the figure on the right, holding up to him with one arm an emaciated, half-clad infant, while with the other she indicated the implements at his feet with an imploring gesture. The second of the women was plucking by the sleeve the man on the left as if to draw him back, while with the other hand she covered her eyes. But the men heeded the woman not at all, or seemed, in their bitter wrath, to know that they were there.

"Why," I exclaimed, "these are strikers!"

"Yes," said the doctor, "this is The Strikers, Huntington's masterpiece, considered the greatest group of statuary in the city and one of the greatest in the country."

"Those people are alive!" I said.

"That is expert testimony," replied the doctor. "It is a pity Huntington died too soon to hear it. He would have been pleased."

Now, I, in common with the wealthy and cultured class generally, of my day, had always held strikers in contempt and abhorrence, as blundering, dangerous marplots, as ignorant of their own best interests as they were reckless of other people's, and generally as pestilent fellows, whose demonstrations, so long as they were not violent, could not unfortunately be repressed by force, but ought always to be condemned, and promptly put down with an iron hand the moment there was an excuse for police interference. There was more or less tolerance among the well-to-do, for social reformers, who, by book or voice, advocated even very radical economic changes so long as they observed the conventionalities of speech, but for the striker there were few apologists. Of course, the capitalists emptied on him the vials of their wrath and contempt, and even people who thought they sympathized with the working class shook their heads at the mention of strikes, regarding them as calculated rather to hinder than help the emancipation of labor. Bred as I was in these prejudices, it may not seem strange that I was taken aback at finding such unpromising subjects selected for the highest place in the city.

"There is no doubt as to the excellence of the artist's work," I said, "but what was there about the strikers that has made you pick them out of our generation as objects of veneration?"

"We see in them," replied the doctor, "the pioneers in the revolt against private capitalism which brought in the present civilization. We honor them as those who, like Winkelried, 'made way for liberty, and died.' We revere in them the protomartyrs of co-operative industry and economic equality."

"But I can assure you, doctor, that these fellows, at least in my day, had not the slightest idea of revolting against private capitalism as a system. They were very ignorant and quite incapable of grasping so large a conception. They had no notion of getting along without capitalists. All they imagined as possible or desirable was a little better treatment by their employers, a few cents more an hour, a few minutes less working time a day, or maybe merely the discharge of an unpopular foreman. The most they aimed at was some petty improvement in their condition, to attain which they did not hesitate to throw the whole industrial machine into disorder."

"All which we moderns know quite well," replied the doctor. "Look at those faces. Has the sculptor idealized them? Are they the faces of philosophers? Do they not bear out your statement that the strikers, like the working-men generally, were, as a rule, ignorant, narrow-minded men, with no grasp of large questions, and incapable of so great an idea as the overthrow of an immemorial economic order? It is quite true that until some years after you fell asleep they did not realize that their quarrel was with private capitalism and not with individual capitalists. In this slowness of awakening to the full meaning of their revolt they were precisely on a par with the pioneers of all the great liberty revolutions. The minutemen at Concord and Lexington, in 1775, did not realize that they were pointing their guns at the monarchical idea. As little did the third estate of France, when it entered the Convention in 1789, realize that its road lay over the ruins of the throne. As little did the pioneers of English freedom, when they began to resist the will of Charles I, foresee that they would be compelled, before they got through, to take his head. In none of these instances, however, has posterity considered that the limited foresight of the pioneers as to the full consequences of their action lessened the world's debt to the crude initiative, without which the fuller triumph would never have come. The logic of the strike meant the overthrow of the irresponsible conduct of industry, whether the strikers knew it or not, and we can not rejoice in the consequences of that overthrow without honoring them in a way which very likely, as you intimate, would surprise them, could they know of it, as much as it does you. Let me try to give you the modern point of view as to the part played by their originals." We sat down upon one of the benches before the statue, and the doctor went on:

"My dear Julian, who was it, pray, that first roused the world of your day to the fact that there was an industrial question, and by their pathetic demonstrations of passive resistance to wrong for fifty years kept the public attention fixed on that question till it was settled? Was it your statesmen, perchance your economists, your scholars, or any other of your so-called wise men? No. It was just those despised, ridiculed, cursed, and hooted fellows up there on that pedestal who with their perpetual strikes would not let the world rest till their

wrong, which was also the whole world's wrong, was righted. Once
more had God chosen the foolish things of this world to confound the
wise, the weak things to confound the mighty.

"In order to realize how powerfully these strikes operated to impress upon the people the intolerable wickedness and folly of private
capitalism, you must remember that events are what teach men, that
deeds have a far more potent educating influence than any amount
of doctrine, and especially so in an age like yours, when the masses
had almost no culture or ability to reason. There were not lacking in
the revolutionary period many cultured men and women, who, with
voice and pen, espoused the workers' cause, and showed them the
way out; but their words might well have availed little but for the
tremendous emphasis with which they were confirmed by the men
up there, who starved to prove them true. Those rough-looking fellows, who probably could not have constructed a grammatical sentence, by their combined efforts, were demonstrating the necessity
of a radically new industrial system by a more convincing argument
than any rhetorician's skill could frame. When men take their lives
in their hands to resist oppression, as those men did, other men are
compelled to give heed to them. We have inscribed on the pedestal
yonder, where you see the lettering, the words, which the action
of the group above seems to voice:

" 'We can bear no more. It is better to starve than live on the terms
you give us. Our lives, the lives of our wives and of our children, we
set against your gains. If you put your foot upon our neck, we will
bite your heel!'

"This was the cry," pursued the doctor, "of men made desperate
by oppression, to whom existence through suffering had become of
no value. It was the same cry that in varied form but in one sense has
been the watchword of every revolution that has marked an advance
of the race—'Give us liberty, or give us death!' and never did it ring
out with a cause so adequate, or wake the world to an issue so
mighty, as in the mouths of these first rebels against the folly and the
tyranny of private capital.

"In your age, I know, Julian," the doctor went on in a gentler tone,
"it was customary to associate valor with the clang of arms and the
pomp and circumstance of war. But the echo of the fife and drum
comes very faintly up to us, and moves us not at all. The soldier has
had his day, and passed away forever with the ideal of manhood which he illustrated. But that group yonder stands for a type of
self-devotion that appeals to us profoundly. Those men risked their
lives when they flung down the tools of their trade, as truly as any
soldiers going into battle, and took odds as desperate, and not only

for themselves, but for their families, which no grateful country would care for in case of casualty to them. The soldier went forth cheered with music, and supported by the enthusiasm of the country, but these others were covered with ignominy and public contempt, and their failures and defeats were hailed with general acclamation. And yet they sought not the lives of others, but only that they might barely live; and though they had first thought of the welfare of themselves, and those nearest them, yet not the less were they fighting the fight of humanity and posterity in striking in the only way they could, and while yet no one else dared strike at all, against the economic system that had the world by the throat, and would never relax its grip by dint of soft words, or anything less than disabling blows. The clergy, the economists and the pedagogues, having left these ignorant men to seek as they might the solution of the social problem, while they themselves sat at ease and denied that there was any problem, were very voluble in their criticisms of the mistakes of the workingmen, as if it were possible to make any mistake in seeking a way out of the social chaos, which could be so fatuous or so criminal as the mistake of not trying to seek any. No doubt, Julian, I have put finer words in the mouths of those men up there than their originals might have even understood, but if the meaning was not in their words it was in their deeds. And it is for what they did, not for what they said, that we honor them as protomartyrs of the industrial republic of to-day, and bring our children, that they may kiss in gratitude the rough-shod feet of those who made the way for us."

My experiences since I waked up in this year 2000 might be said to have consisted of a succession of instantaneous mental readjustments of a revolutionary character, in which what had formerly seemed evil to me had become good, and what had seemed wisdom had become foolishness. Had this conversation about the strikers taken place anywhere else, the entirely new impression I had received of the part played by them in the great social revolution of which I shared the benefit would simply have been one more of these readjustments, and the process entirely a mental one. But the presence of this wondrous group, the lifelikeness of the figures growing on my gaze as I listened to the doctor's words, imparted a peculiar personal quality—if I may use the term—to the revulsion of feeling that I experienced. Moved by an irresistible impulse, I rose to my feet, and, removing my hat, saluted the grim forms whose living originals I had joined my contemporaries in reviling.

The doctor smiled gravely.

"Do you know, my boy," he said, "it is not often that the whirligig of Time brings round his revenges in quite so dramatic a way as this?"

Finley Peter Dunne
On a Populist Convention

"KEEP YE'ER EYE on th' Pops, Jawn. They're gr-reat people an' a gr-reat pa-arty. What is their principles? Anny ol' thing that th' other pa-arties has rijected. Some iv thim is in favor iv coinin' money out iv baled hay an' dhried apples at a ratio iv sixteen to wan, an' some is in favor iv coinin' on'y th' apples. Thim are th' inflationists. Others want th' gover'mint to divide up the rivinues equally among all la-ads that's too sthrong to wurruk. Th' Pops is again th' banks an' again the supreme court an' again havin' gas that can be blowed out be th' human lungs. A sthrong section is devoted to th' principal iv separatin' Mark Hanna fr'm his money.

"A ma-an be th' name iv Cassidy, that thravels f'r a liquor-house, was in to see me this mornin'; an' he come fr'm Saint Looey. He said it beat all he iver see or heerd tell of. Whin th' con-vintion come to ordher, th' chairman says, 'La-ads, we'll open proceedin's be havin' th' Hon'rable Rube Spike, fr'm th' imperyal Territ'ry iv Okalahoma, cough up his famous song, "Pa-pa Cleveland's Teeth are filled with Goold."' 'Mr. Chairman,' says a delegate fr'm New Mexico, risin' an' wavin' his boots in th' air, 'if th' skate fr'm Okalahoma is allowed f'r to belch anny in this here assimblage, th' diligates fr'm th' imperyal Territ'ry iv New Mexico'll lave th' hall. We have,' he says, 'in our mist th' Hon'rable Lafayette Hadley, whose notes,' he says, 'falls as sweetly on th' ear,' he says, 'as th' plunk iv hivin's rain in a bar'l,' he says. 'If annywan has a hemorrhage iv anthems in this hall, it'll be Lafe Hadley, th' Guthrie batsoon,' he says. 'Ye shall not,' he says, 'press down upon our bleedin' brows,' he says, 'this cross iv thorns,' he says. 'Ye shall not crucify th' diligates fr'm th' imperyal Territ'ry iv New Mexico on this cross iv a Mississippi nigger an' Crow Injun fr'm Okalahoma,' he says. Thereupon, says me frind Cassidy, th' New Mexico diligation left th' hall, pursued be th' diligation from Okalahoma.

"Th' chairman knowed his business. 'In ordher,' he says, 'that there

Mr. Dooley in Peace and in War (Boston, 1898), pp. 197–201. Text from this edition.

may be no disordher,' he says, 'I will call upon th' imperyal States,' he says, 'an Territ'ries,' he says, 'beginnin' with th' imperyal State iv Alabama,' he says, 'to each sind wan singer to th' platform,' he says, 'f'r to wring our hear-rts with melodies,' he says. 'Meantime,' says he, 'pathrites who have diff'rences iv opinyon on anny questions can pro-cure ex-helves be applyin' to th' sergeant-at-arms,' he says. 'Now,' he says, 'if th' gintleman fr'm th' imperyal State of Mizzoury'll hand me up a cheek full iv his eatin' tobacco,' he says, 'we'll listen to Will-yum G. Rannycaboo, th' boy melodjun iv th' imperyal State iv Ala-bama,' he says, 'who'll discoorse his well-known ballad, 'Th' Supreme Court is Full iv Standard Ile,' he says.

"Whin th' singin' had con-cluded, so me frind Cassidy says, th' chair announced that speakin' would be in ordher, an' th' con-vintion rose as wan man. Afther ordher had been enforced be th' sergeant-at-arms movin' round, an' lammin' diligates with a hoe, a tall man was seen standin' on a chair. F'r some moments th' chairman was onable to call his name, but he fin'lly found a place to spill; an' in a clear voice he says, 'F'r what purpose does th' gintleman fr'm the imperyal State iv Texas arise?' 'I arise,' says th' ma-an, 'f'r th' purpose iv warnin' this con-vintion that we have a goold-bug in our mist,' he says. Cries iv 'Throw him out!' 'Search him!' 'Hang him!' arose. 'In wandhrin' through th' hall, I just seen a man with a coat on,' he says. Great ex-citement ensood, says me frind Cassidy; an' th' thremblin' victim was brought down th' aisle. 'What have ye to say f'r ye'ersilf?' demands th' chairman in thundhrin' tones. 'On'y this,' says th' goold-bug. 'I wan-dhered in here, lookin' f'r frinds,' he says. 'I am not a goold-bug,' he says. 'I wear me coat,' he says, 'because I have no shirt,' he says. 'Gin-tlemen,' says th' chairman, 'a mistake has been made,' he says. 'This here person, who bears th' appearance iv a plutocrat, is all right un-derneath,' he says. 'He's a diligate to th' silver convintion,' he says. 'Go in peace,' he says.

"Be this time 'twas gr-rowin' late, an' th' convintion adjourned. 'Be-fure ye lave,' says th' chairman, 'I have to announce that on account iv th' chairman of the comity havin' been imprisoned in a foldin'-bed an' th' sicrity havin' mistook th' fire extinguisher f'r a shower bath, they'll be no meetin' iv th' comity on rules till to-morrow night. Durin' th' interval,' he says, 'th' convintion'll continue ketch-as-ketch can,' he says."

"Well," said Mr. McKenna, "to think of taking this here country out of the hands of William C. Whitney and Grover Cleveland and J. Pierpont Morgan and Ickleheimer Thalmann, and putting it in the hands of such men. What do you think about it?"

"I think," said Mr. Dooley, "that Cassidy lied."

William Graham Sumner
The Absurd Effort
to Make the World Over

It will not probably be denied that the burden of proof is on those who affirm that our social condition is utterly diseased and in need of radical regeneration. My task at present, therefore, is entirely negative and critical; to examine the allegations of fact and the doctrines which are put forward to prove the correctness of the diagnosis and to warrant the use of the remedies proposed.

The propositions put forward by social reformers nowadays are chiefly of two kinds. There are assertions in historical form, chiefly in regard to the comparison of existing with earlier social states, which are plainly based on defective historical knowledge, or at most on current stock historical dicta which are uncritical and incorrect. Writers very often assert that something never existed before because they do not know that it ever existed before, or that something is worse than ever before because they are not possessed of detailed information about what has existed before. The other class of propositions consists of dogmatic statements, which, whether true or not, are unverifiable. This class of propositions is the pest and bane of current economic and social discussion. Upon a more or less superficial view of some phenomenon a suggestion arises which is embodied in a philosophical proposition and promulgated as a truth. From the form and nature of such propositions they can always be brought under the head of "ethics." This word at least gives them an air of elevated sentiment and purpose, which is the only warrant they possess. It is impossible to test or verify them by any investigation or logical process whatsoever. It is therefore very difficult for any one who feels a high responsibility for historical statements, and who absolutely rejects any statement which is unverifiable, to find a common platform for discussion, or to join issue satisfactorily in taking the negative.

When any one asserts that the class of skilled and unskilled manual

Forum, XVII (March, 1894), 92–102. Text from this publication.

laborers of the United States are worse off now in respect to diet, clothing, lodgings, furniture, fuel, and lights; in respect to the age at which they can marry; the number of children they can provide for; the start in life which they can give to their children; and their chances of accumulating capital,—than they ever have been at any former time, he makes a reckless assertion for which no facts have been offered in proof. Upon an appeal to facts, the contrary of this assertion would be clearly established. It suffices, therefore, to challenge those who are responsible for the assertion to make it good.

If it is said that the employed class are under much more stringent discipline than they were thirty years ago or earlier, it is true. It is not true that there has been any qualitative change in this respect within thirty years, but it is true that a movement which began at the first settlement of the country has been advancing with constant acceleration, and has become a noticeable feature within our time. This movement is the advance in the industrial organization. The first settlement was made by agriculturists, and for a long time there was scarcely any organization. There were scattered farmers, each working for himself, and some small towns with only rudimentary commerce and handicrafts. As the country has filled up, the arts and professions have been differentiated and the industrial organization has been advancing. This fact and its significance has hardly been noticed at all; but the stage of the industrial organization existing at any time, and the rate of advance in its development, are the absolutely controlling social facts. Nine-tenths of the socialistic and semisocialistic, and sentimental or ethical, suggestions by which we are overwhelmed come from failure to understand the phenomena of the industrial organization and its expansion. It controls us all because we are all in it. It creates the conditions of our existence, sets the limits of our social activity, regulates the bonds of our social relations, determines our conceptions of good and evil, suggests our life philosophy, moulds our inherited political institutions, and reforms the oldest and toughest customs, like marriage and property. I repeat that the turmoil of heterogeneous and antagonistic social whims and speculations in which we live is due to the failure to understand what the industrial organization is, and its all-pervading control over human life, while the traditions of our schools of philosophy lead us always to approach the industrial organization, not from the side of objective study, but from that of philosophical doctrine. Hence it is that we find that the method of measuring what we see happening by what are called ethical standards, and of proposing to attack the phenomena by methods thence deduced, is so popular.

The advance of a new country from the very simplest social coordination up to the highest organization is a most interesting and instructive chance to study the development of the organization. It has of course been attended all the way along by stricter subordination and higher discipline. All organization implies restriction of liberty. The gain of power is won by narrowing individual range. The methods of business in colonial days were loose and slack to an inconceivable degree. The movement of industry has been all the time toward promptitude, punctuality, and reliability. It has been attended all the way by lamentations about the good old times; about the decline of small industries; about the lost spirit of comradeship between employer and employee; about the narrowing of the interests of the workman; about his conversion into a machine or into a "ware"; and about industrial war. These lamentations have all had reference to unquestionable phenomena attendant on advancing organization. In all occupations the same movement is discernible,—in the learned professions, in schools, in trade, commerce, and transportation. It is to go on faster than ever, now that the continent is filled up by the first superficial layer of population over its whole extent, and the intensification of industry has begun. The great inventions both make the intension of the organization possible, and make it inevitable, with all its consequences, whatever they may be. I must expect to be told here, according to the current fashions of thinking, that we ought to control the development of the organization. The first instinct of the modern man is to get a law passed to forbid or prevent what, in his wisdom, he disapproves. A thing which is inevitable, however, is one which we cannot control. We have to make up our minds to it, adjust ourselves to it, and sit down to live with it. Its inevitableness may be disputed, in which case we must re-examine it; but if our analysis is correct, when we reach what is inevitable we reach the end, and our regulations must apply to ourselves, not to the social facts.

Now the intensification of the social organization is what gives us greater social power. It is to it that we owe our increased comfort and abundance. We are none of us ready to sacrifice this. On the contrary, we want more of it. We would not return to the colonial simplicity and the colonial exiguity if we could. If not, then we must pay the price. Our life is bounded on every side by conditions. We can have this, if we will agree to submit to that. In the case of industrial power and product the great condition is combination of force under discipline and strict co-ordination. Hence the wild language about wage-slavery and capitalistic tyranny.

In any state of society no great achievements can be produced without great force. Formerly great force was attainable only by slavery aggregating the power of great numbers of men. Roman civilization was built on this. Ours has been built on steam. It is to be built on electricity. Then we are all forced into an organization around these natural forces and adapted to the methods of their application; and although we indulge in rhetoric about political liberty, nevertheless we find ourselves bound tight in a new set of conditions, which control the modes of our existence and determine the directions in which alone economic and social liberty can go.

If it is said that there are some persons in our time who have become rapidly and in a great degree rich, it is true; if it is said that large aggregations of wealth in the control of individuals is a social danger, it is not true.

The movement of the industrial organization which has just been described has brought out a great demand for men capable of managing great enterprises. Such have been called "captains of industry." The analogy with military leaders suggested by this name is not misleading. The great leaders in the development of the industrial organization need those talents of executive and administrative skill, power to command, courage, and fortitude, which were formerly called for in military affairs and scarcely anywhere else. The industrial army is also as dependent on its captains as a military body is on its generals. One of the worst features of the existing system is that the employees have a constant risk in their employer. If he is not competent to manage the business with success, they suffer with him. Capital also is dependent on the skill of the captain of industry for the certainty and magnitude of its profits. Under these circumstances there has been a great demand for men having requisite ability for this function. As the organization has advanced, with more impersonal bonds of coherence and wider scope of operations, the value of this functionary has rapidly increased. The possession of the requisite ability is a natural monopoly. Consequently, all the conditions have concurred to give to those who possessed this monopoly excessive and constantly advancing rates of remuneration.

Another social function of the first importance in an intense organization is the solution of those crises in the operation of it which are called the conjuncture of the market. It is through the market that the lines of relation run which preserve the system in harmonious and rhythmical operation. The conjuncture is the momentary sharper misadjustment of supply and demand which indicates that a redistribution of productive effort is called for. The industrial organization needs to be insured against these conjunctures, which, if neglected, produce a crisis and catastrophe; and it needs that they shall be anticipated and guarded against as far as skill and foresight can do it. The rewards of this function for the bankers and capitalists who perform it are very great. The captains of industry and the capitalists who operate on the conjuncture, therefore, if they are successful, win, in these days, great fortunes in a short time. There are no earnings which are more legitimate or for which greater services are rendered to the whole industrial body. The popular notions about this matter really assume that all the wealth accumulated by these classes of persons would be here just the same if they had not existed. They are supposed to have appropriated it out of the common stock. This is so far from being true that, on the contrary, their own wealth would not be but for themselves; and, besides that, millions more, many-fold greater than their own, scattered in the hands of thousands, would not exist but for them.

Within the last two years I have travelled from end to end of the German Empire several times on all kinds of trains. I reached the conviction, looking at the matter from the passenger's standpoint, that, if the Germans could find a Vanderbilt, and put their railroads in his hands for twenty-five years, letting him reorganize the system and make twenty-five million dollars out of it for himself in that period, they would make an excellent bargain.

But it is repeated until it has become a commonplace which people are afraid to question, that there is some social danger in the possession of large amounts of wealth by individuals. I ask, why? I heard a lecture two years ago by a man who holds perhaps the first chair of political economy in the world. He said, among other things, that there was great danger in our day from great accumulations; that this danger ought to be met by taxation, and he referred to the fortunes of the Rothschilds and to the great fortunes made in America, to prove his point. He omitted, however, to state in what the danger consisted, or to specify what harm has ever been done by the Rothschild fortunes or by the great fortunes accumulated in America. It seemed to me that the assertions he was making, and the measures he was recommending, *ex cathedra*, were very serious to be thrown out so recklessly. It is hardly to be expected that novelists, popular magazinists, amateur economists, and politicians will be more responsible. It would be easy, however, to show what good is done by accumulations of capital in a few hands,—that is, under close and direct management, permitting prompt and accurate application; also to tell what harm is done by loose and unfounded denunciations of any social component or any social group. In the recent debates on the income tax, the assumption that great accumulations of wealth are socially harmful and ought to be broken down by taxation was treated as an axiom, and we had direct proof how dangerous it is to fit out the average politician with such unverified and unverifiable dogmas, as his warrant for his modes of handling the direful tool of taxation.

Great figures are set out as to the magnitude of certain fortunes and the proportionate amount of the national wealth held by a fraction of the population, and eloquent exclamation points are set against them. If the figures were beyond criticism, what would they prove? Where is the rich man who is oppressing anybody? If there was one, the newspapers would ring with it. The facts about the accumulation of wealth do not constitute a plutocracy, as I will show below. Wealth, in itself considered, is only power, like steam, or electricity, or knowledge. The question of its good or ill turns on the question how it will be used. To prove any harm in aggregations of wealth it must be shown that great wealth is, as a rule, in the ordinary course of social affairs, put to a mischievous use. This cannot be shown beyond the very slightest degree, if at all.

Therefore, all the allegations of general mischief, social corruption, wrong, and evil in our society must be referred back to those who make them, for particulars and specifications. As they are offered to us we cannot allow them to stand, because we discern in them faulty observation of facts, or incorrect interpretation of facts, or a construction of facts according to some philosophy, or misunderstanding of phenomena and their relations, or incorrect inferences, or crooked deductions.

Assuming, however, that the charges against the existing "capitalistic"—that is, industrial—order of things are established, it is proposed to remedy the ill by reconstructing the industrial system on the principles of democracy. Once more we must untangle the snarl of half ideas and muddled facts.

Democracy is, of course, a word to conjure with. We have a democratic-republican political system, and we like it so well that we are prone to take any new step which can be recommended as "democratic," or which will round out some "principle" of democracy to a fuller fulfilment. Everything connected with this domain of political thought is crusted over with false historical traditions, cheap philosophy, and undefined terms, but it is useless to try to criticise it. The whole drift of the world for five hundred years has been toward democracy. That drift, produced by great discoveries and inventions, and by the discovery of a new continent, has raised the middle class out of the servile class. In alliance with the crown they crushed the feudal classes. They made the crown absolute in order to do it. Then they turned against the crown, and, with the aid of the handicraftsmen and peasants, conquered it. Now the next conflict which must inevitably come is that between the middle capitalist class and the proletariat, as the word has come to be used. If a certain construction is put on this conflict, it may be called that between democracy and plutocracy, for it seems that industrialism must be developed into plutocracy by the conflict itself. That is the conflict which stands before civilized society to-day. All the signs of the times indicate its commencement, and it is big with fate to mankind and to civilization.

Although we cannot criticise democracy profitably, it may be said of it, with reference to our present subject, that up to this time democracy never has done anything, either in politics, social affairs, or industry, to prove its power to bless mankind. If we confine our attention to the United States, there are three difficulties with regard to its alleged achievements, and they all have the most serious bearing on the proposed democratization of industry.

1. The time during which democracy has been tried in the United States is too short to warrant any inferences. A century or two is a very short time in the life of political institutions, and if the circumstances change rapidly during the period the experiment is vitiated.

2. The greatest question of all about American democracy is whether it is a cause or a consequence. It is popularly assumed to be a cause, and we ascribe to its beneficent action all the political vitality, all the easiness of social relations, all the industrial activity and enterprise which we experience, and which we value and enjoy. I submit, however, that, on a more thorough examination of the matter, we shall find that democracy is a consequence. There are economic and sociological causes for our political vitality and vigor, for the ease and elasticity of our social relations, and for our industrial power and success. Those causes have also produced democracy, given it success, and have made its faults and errors innocuous. Indeed, in any true philosophy, it must be held that in the economic forces which control the material prosperity of a population lie the real causes of its political institutions, its social class-adjustments, its industrial prosperity, its moral code, and its world-philosophy. If democracy and the industrial system are both products of the economic conditions which exist, it is plainly absurd to set democracy to defeat those conditions in the control of industry. If, however, it is not true that democracy is a consequence, and I am well aware that very few people believe it, then we must go back to the view that democracy is a cause. That being so, it is difficult to see how democracy, which has had a clear field here in America, is not responsible for the ills which Mr. Bellamy and his comrades in opinion see in our present social state, and it is difficult to see the grounds of asking us to entrust it also with industry. The first and chief proof of success of political measures and systems is

that, under them, society advances in health and vigor, and that industry develops without causing social disease. If this has not been the
case in America, American democracy has not succeeded. Neither
is it easy to see how the masses, if they have undertaken to rule, can
escape the responsibilities of ruling, especially so far as the consequences affect themselves. If, then, they have brought all this distress
upon themselves under the present system, what becomes of the argument for extending the system to a direct and complete control of
industry?

3. It is by no means certain that democracy in the United States
has not, up to this time, been living on a capital inherited from aristocracy and industrialism. We have no pure democracy. Our democracy is limited at every turn by institutions which were developed
in England in connection with industrialism and aristocracy, and these
institutions are of the essence of our system. While our people are
passionately democratic in temper, and will not tolerate a doctrine
that one man is not as good as another, they have common sense
enough to know that he is not; and it seems that they love and cling
to the conservative institutions quite as strongly as they do to the democratic philosophy. They are, therefore, ruled by men who talk the
philosophy and govern by the institutions. Now it is open to Mr. Bellamy to say that the reason why democracy in America seems to be
open to the charge made in the last paragraph, of responsibility for all
the ill which he now finds in our society, is because it has been infected
with industrialism (capitalism); but, in that case, he must widen the
scope of his proposition and undertake to purify democracy before
turning industry over to it. The Socialists generally seem to think that
they make their undertakings easier when they widen their
scope, and make them easiest when they propose to remake everything; but in truth social tasks increase in difficulty in an enormous
ratio as they are widened in scope.

The question, therefore, arises, if it is proposed to reorganize the
social system on the principles of American democracy, whether the
institutions of industrialism are to be retained. If so, all the virus of
capitalism will be retained. It is forgotten, in many schemes of social
reformation in which it is proposed to mix what we like with what
we do not like, in order to extirpate the latter, that each must undergo
a reaction from the other, and that what we like may be extirpated
by what we do not like. We may find that instead of democratizing
capitalism we have capitalized democracy,—that is, have brought
in plutocracy. Plutocracy is a political system in which the ruling force
is wealth. The denunciations of capital which we hear from all the reformers is the most eloquent proof that the greatest power in the

world to-day is capital. They know that it is, and confess it most when they deny it most strenuously. At present the power of capital is social and industrial, and only in a small degree political. So far as capital is political, it is on account of political abuses, such as tariffs and special legislation on the one hand, and legislative strikes on the other. These conditions exist in the democracy to which it is proposed to transfer the industries. What does that mean except bringing all the power of capital once for all into the political arena, and precipitating the conflict of democracy and plutocracy at once? Can any one imagine that the masterfulness, the overbearing disposition, the greed of gain, and the ruthlessness in methods, which are the faults of the master of industry at his worst, would cease when he was a functionary of the State, which had relieved him of risk and endowed him with authority? Can any one imagine that politicians would no longer be corruptly fond of money, intriguing, and crafty, when they were charged, not only with patronage and government contracts, but also with factories, stores, ships, and railroads? Could we expect anything except that, when the politician and the master of industry were joined in one, we should have the vices of both unchecked by the restraints of either? In any socialistic state there will be one set of positions which will offer chances of wealth beyond the wildest dreams of avarice, viz. on the governing committees. Then there will be rich men whose wealth will indeed be a menace to social interests, and instead of industrial peace there will be such war as no one has dreamed of yet: the war between the political ins and outs,—that is, between those who are on the committee and those who want to get on it.

We must not drop the subject of democracy without one word more. The Greeks already had occasion to notice a most serious distinction between two principles of democracy which lie at its roots. Plutarch says that Solon got the archonship in part by promising equality, which some understood of esteem and dignity, others of measure and number. There is one democratic principle which means that each man should be esteemed for his merit and worth, for just what he is, without regard to birth, wealth, rank, or other adventitious circumstances. The other principle is that each one of us ought to be equal to all the others in what he gets and enjoys. The first principle is only partially realizable, but, so far as it goes, it is elevating and socially progressive and profitable. The second is not capable of an intelligible statement. The first is a principle of industrialism. It proceeds from and is intelligible only in a society built on the industrial virtues, free endeavor, security of property, and repression of the baser vices; that is, in a society whose industrial system is built on labor and exchange. The other is only a rule of division for robbers who have to divide plunder, or monks who have to divide gifts. If, therefore, we want to democratize industry in the sense of the first principle, we need only perfect what we have now, expecially on its political side. If we try to democratize it in the sense of the other principle, we corrupt politics at one stroke; we enter upon an industrial enterprise which will waste capital and bring us all to poverty; and we set loose greed and envy as ruling social passions.

If this poor old world is as bad as they say, one more reflection may check the zeal of the headlong reformer. It is at any rate a tough old world. It has taken its trend and curvature and all its twists and tangles from a long course of formation. All its wry and crooked gnarls and knobs are therefore stiff and stubborn. If we puny men by our arts can do anything at all to straighten them, it will only be by modifying the tendencies of some of the forces at work, so that, after a sufficient time, their action may be changed a little, and slowly the lines of movement may be modified. This effort, however, can at most be only slight, and it will take a long time. In the mean time spontaneous forces will be at work, compared with which our efforts are like those of a man trying to deflect a river; and these forces will have changed the whole problem before our interferences have time to make themselves felt. The great stream of time and earthly things will sweep on just the same in spite of us. It bears with it now all the errors and follies of the past, the wreckage of all the philosophies, the fragments of all the civilizations, the wisdom of all the abandoned ethical systems, the débris of all the institutions, and the penalties of all the mistakes. It is only in imagination that we stand by and look at it, and criticise it, and plan to change it. Every one of us is a child of his age and cannot get out of it. He is in the stream and is swept along with it. All his sciences and philosophy come to him out of it. Therefore the tide will not be changed by us. It will swallow up both us and our experiments. It will absorb the efforts at change and take them into itself as new but trivial components, and the great movement of tradition and work will go on unchanged by our fads and schemes. The things which will change it are the great discoveries and inventions, the new reactions inside the social organism, and the changes in the earth itself on account of changes in the cosmical forces. These causes will make of it just what, in fidelity to them, it ought to be. The men will be carried along with it and be made by it. The utmost they can do by their cleverness will be to note and record their course as they are carried along, which is what we do now; and is that which leads us to the vain fancy that we can make or guide the movement. That is why it is the greatest folly of which a man can be capable, to sit down with a slate and pencil to plan out a new social world.

Thomas Bailey Aldrich
Unguarded Gates

Wide open and unguarded stand our gates,
Named of the four winds, North, South, East, and West;
Portals that lead to an enchanted land
Of cities, forests, fields of living gold,
Vast prairies, lordly summits touched with snow,
Majestic rivers sweeping proudly past
The Arab's date-palm and the Norseman's pine—
A realm wherein are fruits of every zone,
Airs of all climes, for lo! throughout the year
The red rose blossoms somewhere—a rich land,
A later Eden planted in the wilds,
With not an inch of earth within its bound
But if a slave's foot press it sets him free.
Here, it is written, Toil shall have its wage,
And Honor honor, and the humblest man
Stand level with the highest in the law.
Of such a land have men in dungeons dreamed,
And with the vision brightening in their eyes
Gone smiling to the fagot and the sword.

Wide open and unguarded stand our gates,
And through them presses a wild motley throng—
Men from the Volga and the Tartar steppes,
Featureless figures of the Hoang-Ho,
Malayan, Scythian, Teuton, Kelt, and Slav,
Flying the Old World's poverty and scorn;
These bringing with them unknown gods and rites,
Those, tiger passions, here to stretch their claws.
In street and alley what strange tongues are loud,
Accents of menace alien to our air,
Voices that once the Tower of Babel knew!

Atlantic Monthly, LXX (July, 1892), 57. Republished in *Unguarded Gates and Other Poems* (Boston, 1895), pp. 15–17. Text from *Unguarded Gates.*

> *O Liberty, white Goddess! is it well*
> *To leave the gates unguarded? On thy breast*
> *Fold Sorrow's children, soothe the hurts of fate,*
> *Lift the down-trodden, but with hand of steel*
> *Stay those who to thy sacred portals come*
> *To waste the gifts of freedom. Have a care*
> *Lest from thy brow the clustered stars be torn*
> *And trampled in the dust. For so of old*
> *The thronging Goth and Vandal trampled Rome,*
> *And where the temples of the Cæsars stood*
> *The lean wolf unmolested made her lair.*

William Dean Howells
A Traveler from Altruria

* * *

The Altrurian himself seemed most struck with the head waiter, who showed us to our places, and while we were waiting for our supper I found a chance to explain that he was a divinity student from one of the fresh-water colleges, and was serving here during his summer vacation. This seemed to interest my friend so much that I went on to tell him that many of the waitresses, whom he saw standing there subject to the order of the guests, were country school-mistresses in the winter.

"Ah, that is as it should be," he said; "that is the kind of thing I expected to meet with in America."

"Yes," I responded, in my flattered national vanity, "if America means anything at all it means the honor of work and the recognition of

Cosmopolitan, XIV (November, 1892), 52–58. Republished in *A Traveler from Altruria* (New York, 1894), pp. 9–17, 20–22. Text from *A Traveler from Altruria.*

The American narrator of Howells' novel is host to a visitor from Altruria, a Utopian country. The Altrurian has just arrived at a New England resort hotel.

personal worth everywhere. I hope you are going to make a long stay with us. We like to have travelers visit us who can interpret the spirit of our institutions as well as read their letter. As a rule, Europeans never quite get our point of view. Now a great many of these waitresses are ladies, in the true sense of the word: self-respectful, intelligent, refined, and fit to grace——"

I was interrupted by the noise my friend made in suddenly pushing back his chair and getting to his feet. "What's the matter?" I asked. "You're not ill, I hope?"

But he did not hear me. He had run half down the dining-hall toward the slender young girl who was bringing us our supper. I had ordered rather generously, for my friend had owned to a good appetite, and I was hungry myself with waiting for him, so that the tray the girl carried was piled up with heavy dishes. To my dismay I saw, rather than heard at that distance, the Altrurian enter into a polite controversy with her, and then, as if overcoming all her scruples by sheer strength of will, possess himself of the tray and make off with it toward our table. The poor child followed him, blushing to her hair; the head waiter stood looking helplessly on; the guests, who at that late hour were fortunately few, were simply aghast at the scandal; the Altrurian alone seemed to think his conduct the most natural thing in the world. He put the tray on the side table near us, and in spite of our waitress's protests insisted upon arranging the little bird-bath dishes before our plates. Then at last he sat down, and the girl, flushed and tremulous, left the room, as I could not help suspecting, to have a good cry in the kitchen. She did not come back, and the head waiter, who was perhaps afraid to send another in her place, looked after our few wants himself. He kept a sharp eye on my friend, as if he were not quite sure he was safe, but the Altrurian resumed the conversation with all that lightness of spirits which I noticed in him after he helped the porter with the baggage. I did not think it the moment to take him to task for what he had just done; I was not even sure that it was the part of a host to do so at all, and between the one doubt and the other I left the burden of the talk to him.

"What a charming young creature!" he began. "I never saw anything prettier than the way she had of refusing my help, absolutely without coquetry or affectation of any kind. She is, as you said, a perfect lady, and she graces her work, as I am sure she would grace any exigency of life. She quite realizes my ideal of an American girl, and I see now what the spirit of your country must be from such an expression of it." I wished to tell him that while a country school-teacher who waits at table in a summer hotel is very much to be respected in her sphere, she is not regarded with that high honor which some other women command among us; but I did not find this very easy, after what I had said of our esteem for labor; and while I was thinking how I could hedge, my friend went on. "I liked England greatly, and I liked the English, but I could not like the theory of their civilization, or the aristocratic structure of their society. It seemed to me iniquitous, for we believe that inequality and iniquity are the same in the last analysis."

At this I found myself able to say: "Yes, there is something terrible, something shocking, in the frank brutality with which Englishmen affirm the essential inequality of men. The affirmation of the essential equality of men was the first point of departure with us when we separated from them."

"I know," said the Altrurian. "How grandly it is expressed in your glorious Declaration."

"Ah, you have read our Declaration of Independence then?"

"Every Altrurian has read that," answered my friend.

"Well," I went on smoothly, and I hoped to render what I was going to say the means of enlightening him without offense concerning the little mistake he had just made with the waitress; "of course we don't take that in its closest literality."

"I don't understand you," he said.

"Why, you know it was rather the political than the social traditions of England that we broke with, in the revolution."

"How is that?" he returned. "Didn't you break with monarchy and nobility, and ranks and classes?"

"Yes, we broke with all those things."

"But I found them a part of the social as well as the political structure in England. You have no kings or nobles here. Have you any ranks or classes?"

"Well, not exactly in the English sense. Our ranks and classes, such as we have, are what I may call voluntary."

"Oh, I understand. I suppose that from time to time certain ones among you feel the need of serving, and ask leave of the commonwealth to subordinate themselves to the rest of the state, and perform all the lowlier offices in it. Such persons must be held in peculiar honor. Is it something like that?"

"Well, no, I can't say it's quite like that. In fact, I think I'd better let you trust to your own observation of our life."

"But I'm sure," said the Altrurian, with a simplicity so fine that it was a long time before I could believe it quite real, "that I shall approach it so much more intelligently with a little instruction from you. You say that your social divisions are voluntary. But do I understand that those who serve among you do not wish to do so?"

"Well, I don't suppose they would serve if they could help it," I replied.

"Surely," said the Altrurian, with a look of horror, "you don't mean that they are slaves."

"Oh, no! oh, no!" I said; "the war put an end to that. We are all free, now, black and white."

"But if they do not wish to serve, and are not held in peculiar honor for serving——"

"I see that my word 'voluntary' has misled you," I put in. "It isn't the word exactly. The divisions among us are rather a process of natural selection. You will see, as you get better acquainted with the workings of our institutions, that there are no arbitrary distinctions here, but the fitness of the work for the man and the man for the work determines the social rank that each one holds."

"Ah, that is fine!" cried the Altrurian with a glow of enthusiasm. "Then I suppose that these intelligent young people who teach school in winter and serve at table in the summer are in a sort of provisional state, waiting for the process of natural selection to determine whether they shall finally be teachers or waiters."

"Yes, it might be stated in some such terms," I assented, though I was not altogether easy in my mind. It seemed to me that I was not quite candid with this most candid spirit. I added, "You know we are a sort of fatalists here in America. We are great believers in the doctrine that it will all come out right in the end."

"Ah, I don't wonder at that," said the Altrurian, "if the process of natural selection works so perfectly among you as you say. But I am afraid I don't understand this matter of your domestic service yet. I believe you said that all honest work is honored in America. Then no social slight attaches to service, I suppose?"

"Well, I can't say that, exactly. The fact is, a certain social slight does attach to service, and that is one reason why I don't quite like to have students wait at table. It won't be pleasant for them to remember it in after life, and it won't be pleasant for their children to remember it."

"Then the slight would descend?"

"I think it would. One wouldn't like to think one's father or mother had been at service."

The Altrurian said nothing for a moment. Then he remarked, "So it seems that while all honest work is honored among you, there are some kinds of honest work that are not honored so much as others."

"Yes."

"Why?"

"Because some occupations are more degrading than others."

"But why?" he persisted, as I thought, a little unreasonably.

"Really," I said, "I think I must leave you to imagine."

"I am afraid I can't," he said sadly. "Then, if domestic service is degrading in your eyes, and people are not willingly servants among you, may I ask why any are servants?"

"It is a question of bread and butter. They are obliged to be."

"That is, they are forced to do work that is hateful and disgraceful to them because they cannot live without?"

"Excuse me," I said, not at all liking this sort of pursuit, and feeling it fair to turn even upon a guest who kept it up. "Isn't it so with you in Altruria?"

"It was so once," he admitted, "but not now. In fact, it is like a waking dream to find one's self in the presence of conditions here that we outlived so long ago."

There was an unconscious superiority in this speech that nettled me, and stung me to retort: "We do not expect to outlive them. We regard them as final, and as indestructibly based in human nature itself."

*   *   *

"But I don't see yet," said the Altrurian, "just why domestic service is degrading in a country where all kinds of work are honored."

"Well, my dear fellow, I have done my best to explain. As I intimated before, we distinguish; and in the different kinds of labor we distinguish against domestic service. I dare say it is partly because of the loss of independence which it involves. People naturally despise a dependant."

"Why?" asked the Altrurian, with that innocence of his which I was beginning to find rather trying.

"Why?" I retorted. "Because it implies weakness."

"And is weakness considered despicable among you?" he pursued.

"In every community it is despised practically, if not theoretically," I tried to explain. "The great thing that America has done is to offer the race an opportunity: the opportunity for any man to rise above the rest, and to take the highest place, if he is able." I had always been proud of this fact, and I thought I had put it very well, but the Altrurian did not seem much impressed by it.

He said: "I do not see how it differs from any country of the past in that. But perhaps you mean that to rise carries with it an obligation to those below. 'If any is first among you, let him be your servant.' Is it something like that?"

"Well, it is not quite like that," I answered, remembering how very little our self-made men as a class had done for others. "Every one is expected to look out for himself here. I fancy that there would be very little rising if men were expected to rise for the sake of others, in America. How is it with you in Altruria?" I demanded, hoping to get out of a certain discomfort I felt, in that way. "Do your risen men generally devote themselves to the good of the community after they get to the top?"

"There is no rising among us," he said, with what seemed a perception of the harsh spirit of my question; and he paused a moment before he asked in his turn, "How do men rise among you?"

"That would be rather a long story," I replied. "But putting it in the rough, I should say that they rose by their talents, their shrewdness, their ability to seize an advantage and turn it to their own account."

"And is that considered noble?"

"It is considered smart. It is considered at the worst far better than a dead level of equality. Are all men equal in Altruria? Are they all alike gifted or beautiful, or short or tall?"

"No, they are only equal in duties and in rights. But, as you say just now, that is a very long story. Are they equal in nothing here?"

"They are equal in opportunities."

"Ah!" breathed the Altrurian, "I am glad to hear that."

I began to feel a little uneasy, and I was not quite sure that this last assertion of mine would hold water.

* * *

George Ade
The Fable of the Copper and
the Jovial Undergrads

ONE NIGHT three Well-Bred Young Men, who were entertained at the Best Houses wherever they went, started out to Wreck a College town.

They licked two Hackmen, set fire to an Awning, pulled down many Signs, and sent a Brick through the Front Window of a Tailor Shop. All the Residents of the Town went into their Houses and locked the Doors; Terror brooded over the Community.

Chicago Record, August 30, 1899. Republished in *Fables in Slang* (Chicago, 1899), pp. 105–109. Text from *Fables in Slang*.

A Copper heard the Racket, and saw Women and Children fleeing to Places of Safety, so he gripped his Club and ran Ponderously, overtaking the three Well-Bred Young Men in a dark part of the Street, where they were Engaged in tearing down a Fence.

He could not see them Distinctly, and he made the Mistake of assuming that they were Drunken Ruffians from the Iron Foundry. So he spoke harshly, and told them to Leave Off breaking the Man's Fence. His Tone and Manner irritated the University Men, who were not accustomed to Rudeness from Menials.

One Student, who wore a Sweater, and whose people butt into the Society Column with Sickening Regularity, started to Tackle Low; he had Bushy Hair and a Thick Neck, and his strong Specialty was to swing on Policemen and Cabbies.

At this, his Companion, whose Great Grandmother had been one of the eight thousand Close Relatives of John Randolph, asked him not to Kill the Policeman. He said the Fellow had made a Mistake, that was all; they were not Muckers; they were Nice Boys, intent on preserving the Traditions of dear old *Alma Mater*.

The Copper could hardly Believe it until they led him to a Street Lamp, and showed him their Engraved Cards and Junior Society Badges; then he Realized that they were All Right. The third Well-Bred Young Man, whose Male Parent got his Coin by wrecking a Building Association in Chicago, then announced that they were Gentlemen, and could Pay for everything they broke. Thus it will be seen that they were Rollicking College Boys and not Common Rowdies.

The Copper, perceiving that he had come very near getting Gay with our First Families, Apologized for Cutting In. The Well-Bred Young Men forgave him, and then took his Club away from him, just to Demonstrate that there were no Hard Feelings. On the way back to the Seat of Learning they captured a Night Watchman, and put him down a Man-Hole.

MORAL: *Always select the Right Sort of Parents before you start in to be Rough.*

Ward McAllister
Society as I Have Found It
Chapter XVIII

I WOULD now make some suggestions as to the proper way of introducing a young girl into New York society, particularly if she is not well supported by an old family connection. It is cruel to take a girl to a ball where she knows no one,

> And to subject her to
> The fashionable stare of twenty score
> Of well-bred persons, called the world.

Had I charged a fee for every consultation with anxious mothers on this subject, I would be a rich man. I well remember a near relative of mine once writing me from Paris, as follows: "I consign my wife and daughter to your care. They will spend the winter in New York; at once give them a ball at Delmonico's, and draw on me for the outlay." I replied, "My dear fellow, how many people do you know in this city whom you could invite to a ball? The funds you send me will be used, but not in giving a ball." The girl being a beauty, all the rest was easy enough. I gave her theatre party after theatre party, followed by charming little suppers, asked to them the *jeunesse dorée* of the day; took her repeatedly to the opera, and saw that she was there always surrounded by admirers; incessantly talked of her fascinations; assured my young friends that she was endowed with a fortune equal to the mines of Ophir, that she danced like a dream, and possessed all the graces, a sunbeam across one's path; then saw to it that she had a prominent place in every cotillion, and a fitting partner; showed her whom to smile upon, and on whom to frown; gave her the *entrée* to all the nice houses; criticised severely her toilet until it became perfect; daily met her on the Avenue with the most charming man in town, who by one pretext or another I turned over to her; made her the constant subject of conversation; insisted upon it that she was to

Society as I Have Found It (New York, 1890), pp. 239–52. Text from this edition.

be the belle of the coming winter; advised her parents that she should have her first season at Bar Harbor, where she could learn to flirt to her heart's content, and vie with other girls. Her second summer, when she was older, I suggested her passing at Newport, where she should have a pair of ponies, a pretty trap, with a well-gotten-up groom, and Worth to dress her. Here I hinted that much must depend on her father's purse, as to her wardrobe. As a friend of mine once said to me, "Your pace is charming, but can you keep it up?" I also advised keeping the young girl well in hand and not letting her give offense to the powers that be; to see to it that she was not the first to arrive and the last to leave a ball, and further, that nothing was more winning in a girl than a pleasant bow and a gracious smile given to either young or old. The fashion now for women is to hold themselves erect. The modern manner of shaking hands I do not like, but yet it is adopted. Being interested in the girl's success, I further impressed upon her the importance of making herself agreeable to older people, remembering that much of her enjoyment would be derived from them. If asked to dance a cotillion, let it be conditional that no bouquet be sent her; to be cautious how she refused the first offers of marriage made her, as they were generally the best.

A word, just here, to the newly married. It works well to have the man more in love with you than you are with him. My advice to all young married women is to keep up flirting with their husbands as much after marriage as before; to make themselves as attractive to their husbands after their marriage as they were when they captivated them; not to neglect their toilet, but rather improve it; to be as coquettish and coy after they are bound together as before, when no ties held them. The more they are appreciated by the world, the more will their husbands value them. In fashionable life, conspicuous jealousy is a mistake. A woman is bound to take and hold a high social position. In this way she advances and strengthens her husband. How many women we see who have benefited their husbands, and secured for them these advantages.

A young girl should be treated like a bride when she makes her *début* into society. Her relatives should rally around her and give her entertainments to welcome her into the world which she is to adorn. It is in excessive bad taste for such relatives to in any way refer to the cost of these dinners, balls, etc. Every one in society knows how to estimate such things. Again, at such dinners, it is not in good taste to load your table with *bonbonnières* and other articles intended to be taken away by your guests. This reminds me of a dear old lady, who, when I dined with her, always insisted on my putting in my dress coat pocket a large hothouse peach, which never reached home in a perfect state.

The launching of a beautiful young girl into society is one thing; it is another to place her family on a good, sound social footing. You can launch them into the social sea, but can they float? "Manners maketh man," is an old proverb. These they certainly must possess. There is no society in the world as generous as New York society is; "friend, parent, neighbor, all it will embrace," but once embraced they must have the power of sustaining themselves. The best quality for them to possess is modesty in asserting their claims; letting people seek them rather than attempting to rush too quickly to the front. The Prince of Wales, on a charming American young woman expressing her surprise at the cordial reception given her by London society, replied, "My dear lady, there are certain people who are bound to come to the front and stay there; you are one of them." It requires not only money, but brains, and, above all, infinite tact; possessing the three, your success is assured. If taken by the hand by a person in society you are at once led into the charmed circle, and then your own correct perceptions of what should or should not be done must do the rest. As a philosophical friend once said to me, "A gentleman can always walk, but he cannot afford to have a shabby equipage." Another philosopher soliloquized as follows: "The first evidence of wealth is your equipage." By the way, his definition of aristocracy in America was, the possession of hereditary wealth.

If you want to be fashionable, be always in the company of fashionable people. As an old beau suggested to me, If you see a fossil of a man, shabbily dressed, relying solely on his pedigree, dating back to time immemorial, who has the aspirations of a duke and the fortunes of a footman, do not cut him; it is better to cross the street and avoid meeting him. It is well to be in with the nobs who are born to their position, but the support of the swells is more advantageous, for society is sustained and carried on by the swells, the nobs looking quietly on and accepting the position, feeling they are there by divine right; but they do not make fashionable society, or carry it on. A nob can be a swell if he chooses, i.e. if he will spend the money; but for his social existence this is unnecessary. A nob is like a poet,— *nascitur non fit;* not so a swell,—he creates himself.

The value of a pleasant manner it is impossible to estimate. It is like sunshine, it gladdens; you feel it and are at once attracted to the person without knowing why. When you entertain, do it in an easy, natural way, as if it was an everyday occurrence, not the event of your life; but do it well. Learn how to do it; never be ashamed to learn. The American people have a *greater* power of "catching hold," and adapting themselves to new surroundings than any other people in the world. A distinguished diplomatist once said to me, "The best wife for a Diplomat is an American; for take her to any quarter of the globe and she adapts herself to the place and people."

If women should cultivate pleasant manners, should not men do the same? Are not manners as important to men as to women? The word "gentleman" may have its derivation from gentle descent, but my understanding of a gentleman has always been that he is a person free from arrogance, and anything like self-assertion; considerate of the feelings of others; so satisfied and secure in his own position, that he is always unpretentious, feeling he could not do an ungentlemanly act; as courteous and kind in manner to his inferiors as to his equals. The best bred men I have ever met have always been the least pretentious. Natural and simple in manner, modest in apparel, never wearing anything too *voyant*, or conspicuous; but always so well dressed that you could never discover what made them so,—the good, quiet taste of the whole producing the result.

Here, all men are more or less in business. We hardly have a class who are not. They are, of necessity, daily brought in contact with all sorts and conditions of men, and in self-defense oftentimes have to acquire and adopt an abrupt, a brusque manner of address, which, as a rule, they generally leave in their offices when they quit them. If they do not, they certainly should. When such rough manners become by practice a second nature, they unfit one to go into society. It pays well for young and old to cultivate politeness and courtesy. Nothing is gained by trying roughly to elbow yourself into society, and push your way through into the inner circle; for when such a one has reached it, he will find its atmosphere uncongenial and be only too glad to escape from it.

A short time ago, a handsome, well-dressed Englishman, well up in all matters pertaining to society, went with me to my tailor to see me try on a dress coat. I was struck with his criticisms. Standing before a glass, he said, "You must never be able to see the tails of your dress coat; if you do, discard the coat." Again, he advised one's always wearing a hat that was the fashion, losing sight of the becoming, but always following the fashion. "At a glance," he said, "I can tell a man from the provinces, simply by his hat." If you are stout, never wear a white waistcoat, or a conspicuous watch-chain. Never call attention by them to what you should try to conceal. In going to the opera, if you go to an opera box with ladies, you should wear white or light French gray gloves. Otherwise, gloves are not worn. A *boutonnière* of white hyacinths or white pinks on dress coats is much worn, both to balls and the opera. My English friend was very much struck with the fact that American women all sat on the left side of the carriage, the opposite side from what they do in England. "Ladies," he said, "should always sit behind their coachman, but the desire to see and be seen prompts them here to take the other side. In this city some half a dozen ladies show their knowledge of conventionalities and take the proper seat."

I think the great secret of life is to be contented with the position to which it has pleased God to call you. Living myself in a modest, though comfortable little house in Twenty-first Street in this city, a Wall Street banker honored me with a visit, and exclaimed against my surroundings.

"What!" said he, "are you contented to live in this modest little house? Why, man, this will never do! The first thing you must have is a fine house. I will see that you get it. All that you have to do is to let me buy ten thousand shares of stock for you at the opening of the Board; by three I can sell it, and I will then send you a check for the profit of the transaction, which will not be less than ten thousand dollars! Do it for you? Of course I will, with pleasure. You will run no risk; if there is a loss I will bear it."

I thanked my friend, assured him I was wholly and absolutely contented, and must respectfully decline his offer. A similar offer was made to me by my old friend, Commodore Vanderbilt, in his house in Washington Place. I was a great admirer of this grand old man, and he was very fond of me. He had taken me over his stables, and was then showing me his parlors and statuary, and kept all the time calling me "his boy." I turned to him and said, "Commodore, you will be as great a railroad king, as you were once an ocean king, and as you call me your boy, why don't you make my fortune?" He thought a moment, and then said, slapping me on the back, "Mc, sell everything you have and put it in Harlem stock; it is now twenty-four; you will make more money than you will know how to take care of." If I had followed his advice, I would now have been indeed a millionaire.

One word more here about the Commodore. He then turned to me and said, "Mc, look at that bust,"—a bust of himself, by Powers. "What do you think Powers said of that head?"

"What did he say?" I replied.

"He said, 'It is a finer head than Webster's!'"

John Jay Chapman
Society

*   *   *

For the sake of analysis it is convenient now to separate and again not to separate the influences of business proper from the influences of dishonesty, but in real life they are one thing. Dishonesty is a mere result of excessive devotion to money-making. The general and somewhat indefinite body of rules which are considered "honest" change from time to time. I call a thing dishonest when it offends my instinct. The next man may call it honest. The question is settled by society at large. "What can a man do and remain in his club?" That gives the practical standards of a community. The devotion of the individual to his bank account gives the reason why the financier and his agent, the boss, could always find councilmen, legislators, judges, lawyers, to be their jackals, or to put the equation with the other end first, it is the reason why the legislators could always combine to blackmail the capitalist: this political corruption is a mere spur and offshoot of our business corruption. We know more about it, because politics cannot be carried on wholly in the dark. Business can. The main facts are known. Companies organize subsidiary companies to which they vote the money of the larger company—cheating their stockholders. The railroad men get up small roads and sell them to the great roads which they control—cheating their stockholders. The purchasing agents of many great enterprises cheat the companies as a matter of course, not by a recognized system of commissions—like French cooks—but by stealth. So in trade, you cannot sell goods to the retailers, unless you corrupt the proper person. It is all politics. All our politics is business and our business is politics.

There is something you want to do, and the "practical man" is the man who knows the ropes, knows who is the proper person to be "seen." The slang word gives a picture of the times—to "see" a man means to bribe him.

New York *Times*, February 20 and 27, 1898. Republished in *Causes and Consequences* (New York, 1898), pp. 52–61, 66–71. Text from *Causes and Consequences*.

But let no one think that dishonesty or anything else begins at the top. These big business men were once little business men.

To cut rates, to have a different price for each customer, to substitute one article for another, are the prevailing policies of the seller. To give uncollectible notes, to claim rebates, to make assignments and compromises, to use one shift or another in order to get possession of goods and pay less than the contract price, are the prevailing aims of the buyer.

It is unquestionably possible for an incorruptible man to succeed in business. But his scruples are an embarrassment. Not everybody wants such a man. He insists on reducing every reckoning to pounds sterling, while the rest of the world is figuring in maravedis. He must make up in ability what he lacks in moral obliquity.

He will no doubt find his nook in time. Honesty is the greatest luxury in the world, and the American looks with awe on the man who can afford it, or insists upon having it. It is right that he should pay for it.

The long and short of the matter is that the sudden creation of wealth in the United States has been too much for our people. We are personally dishonest. The people of the United States are notably and peculiarly dishonest in financial matters.

The effect of this on government is but one of the forms in which the ruling passion is manifest. "What is there in it for me?" is the state of mind in which our people have been existing. Out of this come the popular philosophy, the social life, the architecture, the letters, the temper of the age; all tinged with the passion.

Let us look at the popular philosophy of the day. An almost ludicrous disbelief that any one can be really disinterested is met at once. Any one who takes an intelligent interest in public affairs becomes a "reformer." He is liked, if it can be reasonably inferred that he is advancing his own interests. Otherwise he is incomprehensible. He is respected, because it is impossible not to respect him, but he is regarded as a mistaken fellow, a man who interferes with things that are not his business, a meddler.

The unspoken religion of all sensible men inculcates thrift as the first virtue. Business thunders at the young man, "Thou shalt have none other gods but me." Nor is it a weak threat, for business, when it speaks, means business. The young doctor in the small town who advocates reform loses practice for two reasons: first, because it is imagined that he is not a serious man, not a good doctor, if he gives time to things outside his profession; second, because the carriage-maker does not agree with him and regards it as a moral duty to

punish him. The newsdealer in the Arcade at Rector Street lost custom because it was discovered that he was a Bryan man. The bankers
would not buy papers of him. Since the days of David, the great luxury
of the powerful has been to be free from the annoyance of other persons' opinions. The professional classes in any community are parasites
on the moneyed classes; they attend the distribution. They cannot
strike the hand that feeds them. In a country where economic laws
tend to throw the money into the hands of a certain type of men, the
morality of those men is bound to affect society very seriously.

The world-famous "timidity" of Americans in matters of opinion, is
the outward and visible sign of a mental preoccupation. Tocqueville
thought it was due to their democratic form of government. It is not
due to democracy, but to commercial conditions. In Tocqueville's day
it arose out of the slavery question, solely because that question affected trade.

In describing the social life of Boston, Josiah Quincy says of George
Ticknor's hospitality: "There seemed to be a cosmopolitan spacious-
ness about his very vestibule. He received company with great ease,
and a simple supper was always served to his evening visitors. Prescott,
Everett, Webster, Hillard, and other noted Bostonians well mixed
with the pick of such strangers as happened to be in the city, furnished
a social entertainment of the first quality. Politics, at least American
politics, were never mentioned."

It was at such "entertainments" as this that the foreign publicists
received their impressions as to the extinction of free speech in
America. Politics could not be mentioned; but this was not due to our
democratic form of government, but to the fact that Beacon Street was
trading with South Carolina. "Politics" meant slavery, and Beacon
Street could not afford to have values disturbed—not even at a dinner party.

We have seen that our more recent misgovernment has not been
due to democracy, and we now see that the most striking weakness
of our social life is not and never has been due to democracy.

Let us take an example: A party of men meet in a club, and the
subject of free trade is launched. Each of these men has been occupied
all day in an avocation where silence is golden. Shall he be the one
to speak first? Who knows but what some phase of the discussion may
touch his pocket? But the matter is deeper. Free speech is a habit. It
cannot be expected from such men, because a particular subject is
free from danger. Let the subject be dress reform, and the traders will
be equally politic.

This pressure of self-interest which prevents a man from speaking
his mind comes on top of that familiar moral terrorism of any majority,

even a majority of two persons against one, which is one of the ultimate phenomena of human intercourse.

It is difficult to speak out a sentiment that your table companions disapprove of. Even Don Quixote was afraid to confess that it was he who had set the convicts at liberty, because he heard the barber and curate denounce the thing as an outrage. Now the weight of this normal social pressure in any particular case will depend on how closely the individuals composing the majority resemble each other. But men, lighted by the same passion, pursuing one object under the similar conditions, of necessity grow alike. By a process of natural selection, the self-seekers of Europe have for sixty years been poured into the hopper of our great mill. The Suabian and the Pole each drops his costume, his language, and his traditions as he goes in. They come out American business men; and in the second generation they resemble each other more closely in ideals, in aims, and in modes of thought than two brothers who had been bred to different trades in Europe.

The uniformity of occupation, the uniformity of law, the absence of institutions, like the church, the army, family pride, in fact, the uniformity of the present and the sudden evaporation of all the past, have ground the men to a standard.

America turns out only one kind of man. Listen to the conversation of any two men in a street car. They are talking about the price of something—building material, advertising, bonds, cigars.

We have, then, two distinct kinds of pressure, each at its maximum, both due to commerce: the pressure of fear that any unpopular sentiment a man utters will show in his bank account; the pressure of a unified majority who are alike in their opinions, have no private opinions, nor patience with the private opinions of others. Of these two pressures, the latter is by far the more important.

It cannot be denied that the catchwords of democracy have been used to intensify this tyranny. If the individual must submit when outvoted in politics, he ought to submit when outvoted in ethics, in opinion, or in sentiment. Private opinion is a thing to be stamped out, like private law. A prejudice is aroused by the very fact that a man thinks for himself; he is dangerous; he is anarchistic.

But this misapplication of a dogma is not the cause but the cloak of oppression. It is like the theory of the divine right of Kings—a thing invoked by conservatism to keep itself in control, a shibboleth muttered by men whose cause will not bear argument.

We must never expect to find in a dogma the explanation of the system which it props up. That explanation must be sought for in history. The dogma records but does not explain a supremacy. Therefore, when we hear some one appeal to democratic principle for a justification in suppressing the individual, we have to reflect how firmly must this custom be established, upon what a strong basis of interest must it rest, that it has power so to pervert the ideas of democracy. A distrust of the individual running into something like hatred may be seen reflected in the press of the United States. The main point is that Americans have by business training been growing more alike every day, and have seized upon any and every authority to aid them in disciplining a recusant.

We have then a social life in which caution and formalism prevail, and can see why it is that the gathering at the club was a dull affair.

*   *   *

Mere financial dishonesty is of very little importance in the history of civilization. Who cares whether Cæsar stole or Cæsar Borgia cheated? Their intellects stayed clear. The real evil that follows in the wake of a commercial dishonesty so general as ours is the intellectual dishonesty it generates. One need not mind stealing, but one must cry out at people whose minds are so befuddled that they do not know theft when they see it. Robert Walpole bought votes. He deceived others, but he did not deceive himself.

We have seen that the retailer in the small town could not afford to think clearly upon the political situation. But this was a mere instance, a sample of his mental attitude. He dare not face any question. He must shuffle, qualify, and defer. Here at last we have the great characteristic which covers our continent like a climate—intellectual dishonesty. This state of mind does not merely prevent a man having positive opinions. The American is incapable of taking a real interest in anything. The lack of passion in the American—noticeable in his books and in himself—comes from the same habitual mental distraction; for passion is concentration. Hence also the flippancy, superficiality, and easy humor for which we are noted. Nothing except the dollar is believed to be worthy the attention of a serious man. People are even ashamed of their tastes. Until recently, we thought it effeminate for a man to play on the piano. When a man takes a living interest in anything, we call him a "crank." There is an element of self-sacrifice in any honest intellectual work which we detect at once and score with contumely.

It was not solely commercial interest that made the biographers of Lincoln so thrifty to extend and veneer their book. It was that they themselves did not, could not, take an interest in the truth about him. The second-rate quality of all our letters and verse is due to the same cause. The intellectual integrity is undermined. The literary man is concerned for what "will go," like the reformer who is half politician.

The attention of every one in the United States is on some one else's opinion, not on truth.

The matter resolves itself at last into Pilate's question: What is truth? We do not know, and shall never know. But it seems to involve a certain focussing and concentration of the attention that brings all the life within us into harmony. When this happens to us, we discover that truth is the only thing we had ever really cared about in the world. The thing seems to be the same thing, no matter which avenue we reach it by. At whatever point we are touched, we respond. A quartet, a cathedral, a sonnet, an exhibition of juggling, anything well done— we are at the mercy of it. But as the whole of us responds to it, so it takes a whole man to do it. Whatever cracks men up and obliterates parts of them, makes them powerless to give out this vibration. This is about all we know of individualism and the integrity of the individual. The sum of all the philosophies in the history of the world can be packed back into it. All the tyrannies and abuses in the world are only bad because they injure this integrity. We desire truth. It is the only thing we desire. To have it, we must develop the individual. And there are practical ways and means of doing this. We see that all our abuses are only odious because they injure some individual man's spirit. We can trace the corruption of politics into business, and find private selfishness at the bottom of it. We can see this spread out into a network of invisible influence, in the form of intellectual dishonesty blighting the minds of our people. We can look still closer and see just why and how the temperament of the private man is expressed.

We study this first in social life; for social life is the source and fountain of all things. The touchstone for any civilization is what one man says to another man in the street. Everything else that happens there bears a traceable relation to the tone of his voice. The press reflects it, the pulpit echoes it, the literature reproduces it, the architecture embodies it.

The rays of force which start in material prosperity pass through the focus of social life, and extend out into literature, art, architecture, religion, philosophy. All these things are but the sparks thrown off the gestures and gaits, the records of the social life of some civilization. That is the reason why it has been useful to pause over a club-house and study its inmates. The ball-room, the dinner-table, would have been equally instructive. The deference to reigning convention is the same everywhere. The instinct of self-concealment, the policy of classing like with like, leads to the herding of the young with the young only, the sporting with the sporting only, the rich with the rich only, which is the bane of our society. The suffocation is mitigated here and there by the influence of ambitious and educated women. They are doing their best to stem the tide which they can neither con-

trol nor understand. The stratification of our society, and its crystalliza-
tion into social groups, is little short of miraculous, considering
the lightning changes of scene. The *nouveaux riches* of one decade
are the old *noblesse* of the next decade, and yet any particular set, at
any particular time, has its exclusions, its code of hats and coats and
small talk, which are more rigid than those of London.

The only place in the country where society is not dull is Washington, because in Washington politics have always forced the social
elements to mix; because in Washington, some embers of the old
ante-bellum society survived; because the place has no commerce, and
because the foreign diplomats have been a constant factor, educating
the Americans in social matters. But Washington is not the centre of
American civilization. The controlling force in American life is not in
its politics, but in commerce. New York is the head and heart of the
United States. Chicago is America. And the elements of this life must
be sought, as always, in the small towns. Find the social factors which
are common to New York, to Poughkeepsie, and to Newport, and you
have the keynote to the country. We began with a city club. But it
would have made no difference what gathering we entered—a drawing-room at Newport, a labor union in Fifteenth Street—we should
have found the same phenomena,—formalism, suppression of the individual, intellectual dishonesty.

* * *

Part Seven

VARIETIES OF ESCAPE

James Whitcomb Riley, *The Old Swimmin'-Hole*
Richard Hovey, *Vagabondia*
Henry Adams to John Hay, November 16, 1890
Lafcadio Hearn, *Bon-Odori*
Henry Adams, *Prayer to the Virgin of Chartres*

While some writers journeyed to the slums, mines, and mills of modern America and discovered that an urban, industrial society was hell, others ventured to a lost world of simplicity, freedom, and beauty. James Whitcomb Riley and Richard Hovey found that world in memories of a rural youth and in the "open road" of an artist's life. The simple directness of these forms of escape insured a wide popularity for the literary modes of nostalgia and mild Bohemianism despite the fatuousness of much of the writing. A more significant though still traditional form of escape was that in which the writer sought the distant in both time and place as relief from the near-at-hand. Henry Adams and Lafcadio Hearn discovered in Samoa and Japan a simple and uncorrupted world of the past, a world whose beauty and nobility they symbolized in the pure sensuousness and grace of a dance. Adams went on to make the comparison between past and present explicit in his "Prayer to the Virgin of Chartres" and in *The Education of Henry Adams*: the modern man who has worshipped at the silent (and false) shrine of the Dynamo returns repentant to the simple majesty of the Lady.

"Escape" is perhaps an unsatisfactory term for the physical and emotional journeys of Hearn and Adams, because of the depth of their antagonism toward modern life. For the evocativeness and power of their responses to Japan and the Virgin express as vital a critical re-action to American life as do graphic and indignant accounts of slum life or of the interior of a steel mill.

James Whitcomb Riley
The Old Swimmin'-Hole

Oh! the old swimmin'-hole! whare the crick so still and deep
Looked like a baby-river that was laying half asleep,
And the gurgle of the worter round the drift just below
Sounded like the laugh of something we onc't ust to know
Before we could remember anything but the eyes
Of the angels lookin' out as we left Paradise;
But the merry days of youth is beyond our controle,
And it's hard to part ferever with the old swimmin'-hole.

Oh! the old swimmin'-hole! In the happy days of yore,
When I ust to lean above it on the old sickamore,
Oh! it showed me a face in its warm sunny tide
That gazed back at me so gay and glorified,
It made me love myself, as I leaped to caress

Indianapolis *Journal*, June 17, 1882. Republished in *"The Old Swimmin'-Hole" and 'Leven More Poems* (Indianapolis, 1883). Text from *Neghborly Poems* (Indianapolis, 1891), pp. 1–2.

Riley's "The Old Swimmin'-Hole" was republished many times during the 1890's and was one of the most popular poems of the decade. I have selected it for inclusion despite its initial publication in 1882 because it expresses more directly than any other poem by Riley the nostalgia for a rural boyhood which was the principal source of his immense popularity during the 1890's.

My shadder smilin' up at me with such tenderness.
But them days is past and gone, and old Time's tuck his toll
From the old man come back to the old swimmin'-hole.

Oh! the old swimmin'-hole! In the long, lazy days
When the hum-drum of school made so many run-a-ways,
How plesant was the jurney down the old dusty lane,
Whare the tracks of our bare feet was all printed so plane
You could tell by the dent of the heel and the sole
They was lots o' fun on hands at the old swimmin'-hole.
But the lost joys is past! Let your tears in sorrow roll
Like the rain that ust to dapple up the old swimmin'-hole.

Thare the bullrushes growed, and the cattails so tall,
And the sunshine and shadder fell over it all;
And it mottled the worter with amber and gold
Tel the glad lillies rocked in the ripples that rolled;
And the snake-feeder's four gauzy wings fluttered by
Like the ghost of a daisy dropped out of the sky,
Or a wownded apple-blossom in the breeze's controle
As it cut acrost some orchurd to'rds the old swimmin'-hole.

Oh! the old swimmin'-hole! When I last saw the place,
The scenes was all changed, like the change in my face;
The bridge of the railroad now crosses the spot
Whare the old divin'-log lays sunk and fergot.
And I stray down the banks whare the trees ust to be—
But never again will theyr shade shelter me!
And I wish in my sorrow I could strip to the soul,
And dive off in my grave like the old swimmin'-hole.

Richard Hovey
Vagabondia

> Off with the fetters
> That chafe and restrain!
> Off with the chain!
> Here Art and Letters,
> Music and wine,
> And Myrtle and Wanda,
> The winsome witches,
> Blithely combine.
> Here are true riches,
> Here is Golconda,
> Here are the Indies,
> Here we are free—
> Free as the wind is,
> Free as the sea,
> Free!
>
> Houp-la!
>
> What have we
> To do with the way
> Of the Pharisee?
> We go or we stay
> At our own sweet will;
> We think as we say,
> And we say or keep still
> At our own sweet will,
> At our own sweet will.
>
> Here we are free
> To be good or bad,
> Sane or mad,

Bliss Carman and Richard Hovey, *Songs from Vagabondia* (Boston, 1894), pp. 1–5. Text from this edition.

Merry or grim
As the mood may be,—
Free as the whim
Of a spook on a spree,—
Free to be oddities,
Not mere commodities,
Stupid and salable,
Wholly available,
Ranged upon shelves;
Each with his puny form
In the same uniform,
Cramped and disabled;
We are not labelled,
We are ourselves.

Here is the real,
Here the ideal;
Laughable hardship
Met and forgot,
Glory of bardship—
World's bloom and world's blot;
The shock and the jostle,
The mock and the push,
But hearts like the throstle
A-joy in the bush;
Wits that would merrily
Laugh away wrong,
Throats that would verily
Melt Hell in Song.

What though the dimes be
Elusive as rhymes be,
And Bessie, with finger
Uplifted, is warning
That breakfast next morning
(A subject she's scorning)
Is mighty uncertain!

What care we? Linger
A moment to kiss—
No time's amiss
To a vagabond's ardor—
Then finish the larder
And pull down the curtain.

Unless ere the kiss come,
Black Richard or Bliss come,
Or Tom with a flagon,
Or Karl with a jag on—
Then up and after
The joy of the night
With the hounds of laughter
To follow the flight
Of the fox-foot hours
That double and run
Through brakes and bowers
Of folly and fun.

With the comrade heart
For a moment's play,
And the comrade heart
For a heavier day,
And the comrade heart
Forever and aye.

For the joy of wine
Is not for long;
And the joy of song
Is a dream of shine;
But the comrade heart
Shall outlast art
And a woman's love
The fame thereof.

But wine for a sign
Of the love we bring!
And song for an oath
That Love is king!
And both, and both
For his worshipping!

Then up and away
Till the break of day,
With a heart that's merry,
And a Tom-and-Jerry,
And a derry-down-derry—
What's that you say,
You highly respectable
Buyers and sellers?

We should be decenter?
Not as we please inter
Custom, frugality,
Use and morality
In the delectable
Depths of wine-cellars?

Midnights of revel,
And noondays of song!
Is it so wrong?
Go to the Devil!

I tell you that we,
While you are smirking
And lying and shirking
Life's duty of duties,
Honest sincerity,
We are in verity
Free!
Free to rejoice
In blisses and beauties!
Free as the voice
Of the wind as it passes!
Free as the bird
In the weft of the grasses!
Free as the word
Of the sun to the sea—
Free!

Henry Adams to John Hay,
November 16, 1890

Vaiale [*Samoa*].

BY THIS TIME I had expected to be in Tahiti, but we have found more in Samoa than we expected. . . .

*   *   *

The curse of money has touched here, but is not yet deep, though mountain forests, covered with dense and almost impenetrable vegetation, are held at ten dollars an acre, and the poor chiefs, whose only possession is a cocoa-nut grove, have mortgaged it to the eyes. By the Berlin treaty, the whites are not permitted to buy more land from natives, but the whites already claim under one title or another, more land than exists in the whole group of islands. If the sugar cultivation is introduced, the people are lost. Nothing can stand against the frantic barbarism of the sugar-planter. As yet, the only plantations are cocoa-nut, and these are not so mischievous, especially as they are badly managed by German companies which spend more money than the Copra brings. Yet the social changes are steady, and another generation will leave behind it the finest part of the old Samoan world. The young chiefs are inferior to the old ones. Gun-powder and missionaries have destroyed the life of the nobles. In former times a great chief went into battle with no thought of the common warrior. He passed through a herd of them, and none presumed to attack him. Chiefs fought only with chiefs. The idea of being killed by a common man was sacrilege. The introduction of fire-arms has changed all

Henry Adams and His Friends: A Collection of His Unpublished Letters, comp. Harold Dean Cater (Boston, 1947). Copyright, 1947 by Harold Dean Cater. Republished in *The Selected Letters of Henry Adams,* ed. Newton Arvin (New York, 1951), pp. 129, 131–39. Text from this edition. Reprinted by permission of Houghton Mifflin Company.

Adams and his artist friend John La Farge were on an extended tour of the South Seas. At the time Samoa was a joint protectorate of Great Britain, Germany, and the United States.

this, and now, as one of the chiefs said with a voice of horror, any hunchback, behind a tree, can kill the greatest chief in Samoa.

Since I wrote to you last, I have made a journey along the coast as far as Savaii, the westernmost and largest island of the group. We were an imposing party. The Consul General Sewall, whose guests we are, was the head of it, and Sewall is extremely popular among the Malietoa and Mata-afa chiefs who consider him to have saved their lives and liberties. Their expressions of gratitude to him and to the United States are unbounded, and they certainly showed that they felt it, for in their strongholds we were received like kings. Our escort was Seumano-tafa, the chief of Apia, Malietoa's right-hand man. You may remember that, in the great hurricane at Apia, Seumano took his boat through the surf, and saved many lives. For this act, our government sent him some costly presents, among others a beautiful boat, perfectly fitted out for oars and sails. On our *malanga*, or boat-excursion, we went with Seu in his boat, and our own boat followed with our baggage and stores. We carried on Seu's boat the Samoan flag; on our own, the American; and our entire party, including servants and crews, was more than twenty men. We were absent some ten days, with fine weather, and visited the most interesting parts of the islands. I felt as though I had got back to Homer's time, and were cruising about on the Aegean with Ajax. Of all the classic spots I ever imagined, the little island of Manono was the most ideal. Ithaca was, even in the reign of Ulysses, absolutely modern by the side of it. As the *mise-en-scène* of an opera, it would be perfection. If I could note music, I would compose an opera, on the musical motives of the Samoan dances and boat-songs, gutturals, grunts and all. You may bet your biggest margin it would be a tremendous success, if the police would only keep their hands off. The ballet alone would put New York on its head with excitement. You would rush for the next steamer if you could realize the beauty of some parts of the Siva. There are figures stupid and grotesque as you please; but there are others which would make you gasp with delight, and movements which I do not exaggerate in calling unsurpassable. Then, if I could close the spectacle with the climax of the *pai-pai*, I should just clean out the bottom dollar of W. W. Astor. The *pai-pai* is a figure taboo by the missionaries, as indeed the Lancers and Virginia Reel are; but it is still danced in the late hours of the night, though we have seen it only once. Two or three women are the dancers, and they should be the best, especially in figure. They dance at first with the same movements, as far as I could see, that they use in many other figures, and as I did not know what they were dancing I paid no special attention. Presently I noticed that the chief dancer's waist-cloth seemed getting loose. This is their only dress, and it is nothing but a strip of cotton or *tapa* about eighteen inches wide, wrapped round the waist, with the end or corner tucked inside to hold it. Of course it constantly works loose, but the natives are so well used to it that they always tighten it, and I never yet have seen either man, woman or child let it fall by accident. In the *pai-pai*, the women let their *lava-lavas*, as they are called, or *siapas*, seem about to fall. The dancer pretends to tighten it, but only opens it so as to show a little more thigh, and fastens it again so low as to show a little more hip. Always turning about and moving with the chorus, she repeats this process again and again, showing more legs and hips every time, until the *siapa* barely hangs on her, and would fall except that she holds it. At last it falls; she turns once or twice more, in full view; then snatches up the *siapa* and runs away.

You must imagine these dances in a native house, lighted by the ruddy flame of a palm-leaf fire in the centre, and filled, except where the dancing is done, by old-gold men and women applauding, laughing, smoking, and smelling of cocoa-nut oil. You are sitting or lying, with your back against an outer-post. Behind you, outside, the moon is lighting a swarm of children, or women, who are also looking eagerly at the dancers. The night air is soft, and the palms rustle above the house. Your legs are cramped by long sitting cross-legged; your back aches; your eyes droop with fatigue; your head aches with the noise; you would give a fortune to be allowed to go to bed, but you can't till the dance is over and the house is cleared. You are a little feverish, for this thing has gone on, day and night, for a week, and it is more exhausting than a Pan-American railway jaunt. You are weary of travel and tired of the South Seas. You want to be at home, in your own bed, with clean sheets and a pillow, and quiet. Well! I give you my word, founded on experience, that, with all this, when you see the *pai-pai*, you are glad you came.

Of course the Siva, and especially the figure of the *pai-pai*—beautiful thighs—is made to display the form and not the face. To the Samoan, nine tenths of beauty consists in form; the other tenth in feature, coloring and such details. The Samoan Siva, like the Japanese bath, is evidently connected with natural selection; the young men and young women learn there to know who are the finest marriageable articles. Probably the girl who could make the best show in the *pai-pai* would rise in value to the village by the difference of two or three fine mats and a dozen pigs. In such a case the *pai-pai*, danced by a chief's daughter or *taupo*, does not prove license but virtue. The audience is far less moved by it than a French audience is by a good ballet. Any European suddenly taken to such a show would assume that the girl was licentious, and if he were a Frenchman he would probably ask for her. The chief would be scandalised at European want of decency. He keeps his *taupo* as carefully watched and guarded as though he were a Spaniard. The girl herself knows her own value and is not likely to throw herself away. She has no passions, though she is good-natured enough, and might perhaps elope with a handsome young fellow who made long siege of her. The Frenchman would be politely given some middle-aged woman, more or less repulsive in person, and the mother of several illegitimate children, who would have to be his only consolation for losing the object of his desire. The natives would fully appreciate the joke, and probably nickname the victim by some word preserving its memory.

I have not changed my ideas on the point of morality here. As elsewhere, vice follows vice. We have not sought it, and consequently have not found it. Thus far, no one, either man or woman, has made so much as a suggestion, by word or sign, of any licentious idea. My boatmen probably have license enough, but, as the German Consul warned me, I have none. I might as well be living in a nursery for all the vice that is shown to me, and if I did see it, I should only be amused at its simplicity beside the elaborated viciousness of Paris or even of Naples. I never have lived in so unself-conscious a place. Yesterday La Farge and I snorted with laughter because our boy Charley, a half-caste who acts as our interpreter, informed us that "a girl had just been caught running away with a man." On cross-examination, La Farge drew out the further facts that the pair were literally running, in full sight of half the town, along the main road by the seashore, when they might have dodged into a trackless forest within fifty yards; that the girl was then in a neighboring house getting a scolding from her mother; and that after the scolding she would get a beating. La Farge was so much delighted that he wanted to start off at once to see the girl, with a view, I think, to some possible picture to be called "The Elopement," but he was hard at work painting a sketch of Fang-alo sliding down the waterfall, for Clarence King's satisfaction no doubt, and he could not leave his sketch.

Apropos to cataracts of girls, they are common as any other cataracts here. Any waterfall with a ten-foot pool at its base, and a suitable drop, is sure to be used both by girls and boys, and by men as well. The difficulty is that the coast is mostly flat; the waterfalls are far off, and few of them are suited to the purpose. The only one near Apia is fully five miles away, in the hills, far from any village; and one must make up a party of girls from here, and devote a day to a regular picnic, in order to see the show. For King's sake I did this last week. My friend Fatuleia, Seumano's wife, the chiefess of Apia, took charge of the affair, and summoned half a dozen of the belles of Apia:— Fanua, the *taupo*; Otaota, whose photograph I must have sent you, a pretty girl standing before the grave-monument of a chief; Fang-alo, whose photograph you also have; Nelly, a pretty missionary girl; and two or three others. We rode two hours through the forest, and clambered down a ravine to the spot, a deep valley, with cliffs overgrown with verdure, and topped by high trees far above us. To my surprise I found that the waterfall was little more than a brook, as far as the water had to do with it, though the fall was steep enough; full twenty feet into a deep pool. For this reason the place is called the Sliding Rock, for the water has smoothed the hard stone, and covered it with a slippery grass or fine slimy growth. The girls sit in the running water, and slide or coast down, with a plunge of ten or twelve feet below. They go like a shot, and the sight is very pretty. La Farge and I were immensely amused by it, and so were the girls, who went in as though they were naiads. They wore whatever suited their ideas of propriety, from a waist-cloth to a nightgown dress; but the variety rather added to the effect, and the water took charge of the proprieties.

The most curious part of our experience here is to find that the natives are so totally different from what I imagined, and yet so like what I ought to have expected. They are a finer race than I supposed, and seem uncontaminated by outside influence. They have not suffered from diseases introduced from abroad. They have their own diseases—elephantiasis is the worst, but skin-troubles and sores are common, and eyes are apt to be affected by blemish—but they are otherwise strong and would shame any white race I ever saw, for the uniform vigor of their bodies. One never sees a tall man who is thin or feeble. Their standard of beauty varies between six feet, and six-feet-six, in height, but is always broad and muscular in proportion. The women are very nearly as strong as the men. Often in walking behind them I puzzle myself to decide from their backs whether they are men or women, and I am never sure. La Farge detects a certain widening towards the hips which I am too little trained to see; and no wonder, for I have taken enough measurements of typical specimens to be certain that a girl of my height, or say five-feet-six, will have a waist measuring at least thirty-three-and-a-half inches, and hips measuring not more than forty-two. Her upper-arm will be 14½ inches in circumference; her wrist, eight; the calf of her leg at least sixteen; her ankle near eleven; and yet her foot is but 10½ inches long, and both foot and hands are well shaped. These are masculine proportions, and the men assure me that the women have nearly the strength of men. Childbirth is an easy affair of twenty-four hours. Every motion and gesture is free and masculine. They go into battle with the men, and, as one of the most famous fighting chiefs, Pa-tu, my neighbor, told me of his own daughter who fell in battle by his side, "she was killed fighting like a man."

Now comes the quality which to me is most curious. Here are these superb men and women—creatures of this soft climate and voluptuous nature, living under a tropical sun, and skies of divine purple and blue—who ought, on my notions, to be chock-full of languid longings and passionate emotions, but they are pure Greek fauns. Their intellectual existence is made up of concrete facts. As La Farge says, they have no thoughts. They are not in the least voluptuous; they have no longings and very brief passions; they live a matter-of-fact existence that would scare a New England spinster. Even their dances—proper or improper—always represent facts, and never even attempt to reproduce an emotion. The dancers play at ball, or at bathing, or at cocoa-nut gathering, or hammer, or row, or represent cats, birds or devils, but never an abstraction. They do not know how to be voluptuous. Old Samasoni, the American pilot here for many years, and twice married to high-class native women, tells us that the worst dance he ever saw here was a literal reproduction of the marriage ceremony, and that the man went through the entire form, which is long and highly peculiar, and ended with the consummation—openly, before the whole village, delighted with the fun—but that neither actors nor spectators showed a sign of emotion or passion, but went through it as practically as though it had been a cricket-match. Their only idea was that it was funny—as, in a sense, it certainly was; that is, it was not nice. Sentiment or sentimentality is unknown to them. They are astonishingly kind to their children, and their children are very well-behaved; but there is no sentiment, only good-nature, about it. They are the happiest, easiest, smilingest people I ever saw, and the most delightfully archaic. They fight bravely, but are not morally brave. They have the virtues of healthy children—and the weaknesses of Agamemnon and Ulysses.

I could babble on indefinitely about them and their ways, but I think you care less about the Archaic than King or I do, and I might only bore you. For myself, I am not bored. I go to bed soon after nine o'clock, and sleep well till half past five. I eat bananas, mangoes, oranges, pineapples and mummy-apples by the peck. I smoke like a lobster. I write, or study water-color drawing all day. The rainy season has begun. Our gay colors and warm lights have washed out into a uniform grey and faint violet. Expeditions are too risky, for one is sure to be drenched, and the rain falls here solid. But we are well, cheerful and dread moving. I ought to take more exercise, but I don't, and time slides as though it were Fang-alo on the Sliding Rock.

* * *

Lafcadio Hearn
Bon-Odori

I.

OVER THE MOUNTAINS to Izumo, the land of the Kamiyo, the land of the Ancient Gods. A journey of four days by kuruma, with strong runners, from the Pacific to the Sea of Japan; for we have taken the longest and least frequented route.

Through valleys most of this long route lies, valleys always open to higher valleys, while the road ascends, valleys between mountains with rice-fields ascending their slopes by successions of diked terraces which look like enormous green flights of steps. Above them are shadowing sombre forests of cedar and pine; and above these wooded summits loom indigo shapes of farther hills overtopped by peaked silhouettes of vapory gray. The air is lukewarm and windless; and distances are gauzed by delicate mists; and in this tenderest of blue skies, this Japanese sky which always seems to me loftier than any other sky which I ever saw, there are only, day after day, some few filmy, spectral, diaphanous white wandering things; like ghosts of clouds, riding on the wind.

But sometimes, as the road ascends, the rice-fields disappear a while: fields of barley and of indigo, and of rye and of cotton, fringe the route for a little space; and then it plunges into forest shadows. Above all else, the forests of cedar sometimes bordering the way are astonishments; never outside of the tropics did I see any growths comparable for density and perpendicularity with these. Every trunk is straight and bare as a pillar: the whole front presents the spectacle of an immeasurable massing of pallid columns towering up into a cloud of sombre foliage so dense that one can distinguish nothing overhead but branchings lost in shadow. And the profundities beyond the rare gaps in the palisade of blanched trunks are night-black, as in Doré's pictures of fir woods.

New Orleans *Times-Democrat*, March 6, 1892. Republished in *Glimpses of Unfamiliar Japan* (Boston, 1894), I, 120–24, 128–38. Text from *Glimpses of Unfamiliar Japan*.

No more great towns; only thatched villages nestling in the folds of the hills, each with its Buddhist temple, lifting a tilted roof of blue-gray tiles above the congregation of thatched homesteads, and its miya, or Shintō shrine, with a torii before it like a great ideograph shaped in stone or wood. But Buddhism still dominates; every hilltop has its tera; and the statues of Buddhas or of Bodhisattvas appear by the roadside, as we travel on, with the regularity of mile-stones. Often a village tera is so large that the cottages of the rustic folk about it seem like little out-houses; and the traveler wonders how so costly an edifice of prayer can be supported by a community so humble. And everywhere the signs of the gentle faith appear: its ideographs and symbols are chiseled upon the faces of the rocks; its icons smile upon you from every shadowy recess by the way; even the very landscape betimes would seem to have been moulded by the soul of it, where hills rise softly as a prayer. And the summits of some are domed like the head of Shaka, and the dark bossy frondage that clothes them might seem the clustering of his curls.

But gradually, with the passing of the days, as we journey into the loftier west, I see fewer and fewer tera. Such Buddhist temples as we pass appear small and poor; and the wayside images become rarer and rarer. But the symbols of Shintō are more numerous, and the structure of its miya larger and loftier. And the torii are visible everywhere, and tower higher, before the approaches to villages, before the entrances of courts guarded by strangely grotesque lions and foxes of stone, and before stairways of old mossed rock, upsloping, between dense growths of ancient cedar and pine, to shrines that moulder in the twilight of holy groves.

At one little village I see, just beyond the torii leading to a great Shintō temple, a particularly odd small shrine, and feel impelled by curiosity to examine it. Leaning against its closed doors are many short gnarled sticks in a row, miniature clubs. Irreverently removing these, and opening the little doors, Akira bids me look within. I see only a mask,—the mask of a goblin, a Tengu, grotesque beyond description, with an enormous nose,—so grotesque that I feel remorse for having looked at it.

The sticks are votive offerings. By dedicating one to the shrine, it is believed that the Tengu may be induced to drive one's enemies away. Goblin-shaped though they appear in all Japanese paintings and carvings of them, the Tengu-Sama are divinities, lesser divinities, lords of the art of fencing and the use of all weapons.

And other changes gradually become manifest. Akira complains that he can no longer understand the language of the people. We are traversing regions of dialects. The houses are also architecturally different from those of the country-folk of the north-east; their

high thatched roofs are curiously decorated with bundles of straw
fastened to a pole of bamboo parallel with the roof-ridge, and elevated
about a foot above it. The complexion of the peasantry is darker than
in the northeast; and I see no more of those charming rosy faces one
observes among the women of the Tōkyō districts. And the peasants
wear different hats, hats pointed like the straw roofs of those little
wayside temples curiously enough called *an* (which means a straw
hat).

The weather is more than warm, rendering clothing oppressive;
and as we pass through the little villages along the road, I see much
healthy cleanly nudity: pretty naked children; brown men and boys
with only a soft narrow white cloth about their loins, asleep on the
matted floors, all the paper screens of the houses having been removed
to admit the breeze. The men seem to be lightly and supply built; but
I see no saliency of muscles; the lines of the figure are always smooth.
Before almost every dwelling, indigo, spread out upon little mats of
rice straw, may be seen drying in the sun.

The country-folk gaze wonderingly at the foreigner. At various
places where we halt, old men approach to touch my clothes, apologizing with humble bows and winning smiles for their very natural
curiosity, and asking my interpreter all sorts of odd questions. Gentler
and kindlier faces I never beheld; and they reflect the souls behind
them; never yet have I heard a voice raised in anger, nor observed an
unkindly act.

And each day, as we travel, the country becomes more beautiful,
—beautiful with that fantasticality of landscape only to be found in
volcanic lands. But for the dark forests of cedar and pine, and this far
faint dreamy sky, and the soft whiteness of the light, there are moments of our journey when I could fancy myself again in the West
Indies, ascending some winding way over the mornes of Dominica
or of Martinique. And, indeed, I find myself sometimes looking against
the horizon glow for shapes of palms and ceibas. But the brighter
green of the valleys and of the mountain-slopes beneath the woods
is not the green of young cane, but of rice-fields—thousands upon
thousands of tiny rice-fields no larger than cottage gardens, separated
from each other by narrow serpentine dikes.

*   *   *

IV.

At last, from the verge of an enormous ridge, the roadway suddenly
slopes down into a vista of high peaked roofs of thatch and green-
mossed eaves—into a village like a colored print out of old Hiroshige's

picture-books, a village with all its tints and colors precisely like the tints and colors of the landscape in which it lies. This is Kami-Ichi, in the land of Hōki.

We halt before a quiet, dingy little inn, whose host, a very aged man, comes forth to salute me; while a silent, gentle crowd of villagers, mostly children and women, gather about the kuruma to see the stranger, to wonder at him, even to touch his clothes with timid smiling curiosity. One glance at the face of the old innkeeper decides me to accept his invitation. I must remain here until to-morrow: my runners are too wearied to go farther to-night.

Weather-worn as the little inn seemed without, it is delightful within. Its polished stairway and balconies are speckless, reflecting like mirror-surfaces the bare feet of the maid-servants; its luminous rooms are fresh and sweet-smelling as when their soft mattings were first laid down. The carven pillars of the alcove (*toko*) in my chamber, leaves and flowers chiseled in some black rich wood, are wonders; and the kakemono or scroll-picture hanging there is an idyl, Hotei, God of Happiness, drifting in a bark down some shadowy stream into evening mysteries of vapory purple. Far as this hamlet is from all art-centres, there is no object visible in the house which does not reveal the Japanese sense of beauty in form. The old gold-flowered lacquer-ware, the astonishing box in which sweetmeats (*kwashi*) are kept, the diaphanous porcelain wine-cups dashed with a single tiny gold figure of a leaping shrimp, the tea-cup holders which are curled lotus-leaves of bronze, even the iron kettle with its figurings of dragons and clouds, and the brazen hibachi whose handles are heads of Buddhist lions, delight the eye and surprise the fancy. Indeed, wherever to-day in Japan one sees something totally uninteresting in porcelain or metal, something commonplace and ugly, one may be almost sure that detestable something has been shaped under foreign influence. But here I am in ancient Japan; probably no European eyes ever looked upon these things before.

A window shaped like a heart peeps out upon the garden, a wonderful little garden with a tiny pond and miniature bridges and dwarf trees, like the landscape of a teacup; also some shapely stones of course, and some graceful stone-lanterns, or tōrō, such as are placed in the courts of temples. And beyond these, through the warm dusk, I see lights, colored lights, the lanterns of the Bonku, suspended before each home to welcome the coming of beloved ghosts; for by the antique calendar, according to which in this antique place the reckoning of time is still made, this is the first night of the Festival of the Dead.

As in all the other little country villages where I have been stopping, I find the people here kind to me with a kindness and a courtesy unimaginable, indescribable, unknown in any other country, and even in Japan itself only in the interior. Their simple politeness is not an art; their goodness is absolutely unconscious goodness; both come straight from the heart. And before I have been two hours among these people, their treatment of me, coupled with the sense of my utter inability to repay such kindness, causes a wicked wish to come into my mind. I wish these charming folk would do me some unexpected wrong, something surprisingly evil, something atrociously unkind, so that I should not be obliged to regret them, which I feel sure I must begin to do as soon as I go away.

While the aged landlord conducts me to the bath, where he insists upon washing me himself as if I were a child, the wife prepares for us a charming little repast of rice, eggs, vegetables, and sweetmeats. She is painfully in doubt about her ability to please me, even after I have eaten enough for two men, and apologizes too much for not being able to offer me more.

"There is no fish," she says, "for to-day is the first day of the Bonku, the Festival of the Dead; being the thirteenth day of the month. On the thirteenth, fourteenth, and fifteenth of the month nobody may eat fish. But on the morning of the sixteenth day, the fishermen go out to catch fish; and everybody who has both parents living may eat of it. But if one has lost one's father or mother then one must not eat fish, even upon the sixteenth day."

While the good soul is thus explaining I become aware of a strange remote sound from without, a sound I recognize through memory of tropical dances, a measured clapping of hands. But this clapping is very soft and at long intervals. And at still longer intervals there comes to us a heavy muffled booming, the tap of a great drum, a temple drum.

"Oh! we must go to see it," cries Akira; "it is the Bon-odori, the Dance of the Festival of the Dead. And you will see the Bon-odori danced here as it is never danced in cities—the Bon-odori of ancient days. For customs have not changed here; but in the cities all is changed."

So I hasten out, wearing only, like the people about me, one of those light wide-sleeved summer robes—yukata—which are furnished to male guests at all Japanese hotels; but the air is so warm that even thus lightly clad, I find myself slightly perspiring. And the night is divine,—still, clear, vaster than nights of Europe, with a big white moon flinging down queer shadows of tilted eaves and horned gables and delightful silhouettes of robed Japanese. A little boy, the grandson of our host, leads the way with a crimson paper lantern; and the sonorous echoing of geta, the koro-koro of wooden sandals, fills all the street, for many are going whither we are going, to see the dance.

A little while we proceed along the main street; then, traversing a narrow passage between two houses, we find ourselves in a great open space flooded by moonlight. This is the dancing-place; but the dance has ceased for a time. Looking about me, I perceive that we are in the court of an ancient Buddhist temple. The temple building itself remains intact, a low long peaked silhouette against the star-light; but it is void and dark and unhallowed now; it has been turned, they tell me, into a schoolhouse. The priests are gone; the great bell is gone; the Buddhas and the Bodhisattvas have vanished, all save one,—a broken-handed Jizō of stone, smiling with eyelids closed, under the moon.

In the centre of the court is a framework of bamboo supporting a great drum; and about it benches have been arranged, benches from the schoolhouse, on which villagers are resting. There is a hum of voices, voices of people speaking very low, as if expecting something solemn; and cries of children betimes, and soft laughter of girls. And far behind the court, beyond a low hedge of sombre evergreen shrubs, I see soft white lights and a host of tall gray shapes throwing long shadows; and I know that the lights are the *white* lanterns of the dead (those hung in cemeteries only), and that the gray shapes are shapes of tombs.

Suddenly a girl rises from her seat, and taps the huge drum once. It is the signal for the Dance of Souls.

V.

Out of the shadow of the temple a processional line of dancers files into the moonlight and as suddenly halts,—all young women or girls, clad in their choicest attire; the tallest leads; her comrades follow in order of stature; little maids of ten or twelve years compose the end of the procession. Figures lightly poised as birds,—figures that somehow recall the dreams of shapes circling about certain antique vases; those charming Japanese robes, close-clinging about the knees, might seem, but for the great fantastic drooping sleeves, and the curious broad girdles confining them, designed after the drawing of some Greek or Etruscan artist. And, at another tap of the drum, there begins a performance impossible to picture in words, something unimaginable, phantasmal,—a dance, an astonishment.

All together glide the right foot forward one pace, without lifting the sandal from the ground, and extend both hands to the right, with a strange floating motion and a smiling, mysterious obeisance. Then the right foot is drawn back, with a repetition of the waving of hands and the mysterious bow. Then all advance the left foot and repeat the previous movements, half-turning to the left. Then all take two gliding paces forward, with a single simultaneous soft clap of the hands, and the first performance is reiterated, alternately to right and left; all the sandaled feet gliding together, all the supple hands waving together, all the pliant bodies bowing and swaying together. And so slowly, weirdly, the processional movement changes into a great round, circling about the moonlit court and around the voiceless crowd of spectators.

And always the white hands sinuously wave together, as if weaving spells, alternately without and within the round, now with palms upward, now with palms downward; and all the elfish sleeves hover duskily together, with a shadowing as of wings; and all the feet poise together with such a rhythm of complex motion, that, in watching it, one feels a sensation of hypnotism—as while striving to watch a flowing and shimmering of water.

And this soporous allurement is intensified by a dead hush. No one speaks, not even a spectator. And, in the long intervals between the soft clapping of hands, one hears only the shrilling of the crickets in the trees, and the *shu-shu* of sandals, lightly stirring the dust. Unto what, I ask myself, may this be likened? Unto nothing; yet it suggests some fancy of somnambulism,—dreamers, who dream themselves flying, dreaming upon their feet.

And there comes to me the thought that I am looking at something immemorially old, something belonging to the unrecorded beginnings of this Oriental life, perhaps to the crepuscular Kamiyo itself, to the magical Age of the Gods; a symbolism of motion whereof the meaning has been forgotten for innumerable years. Yet more and more unreal the spectacle appears, with its silent smilings, with its silent bowings, as if obeisance to watchers invisible; and I find myself wondering whether, were I to utter but a whisper, all would not vanish forever, save the gray mouldering court and the desolate temple, and the broken statue of Jizō, smiling always the same mysterious smile I see upon the faces of the dancers.

Under the wheeling moon, in the midst of the round, I feel as one within the circle of a charm. And verily this is enchantment; I am bewitched, bewitched by the ghostly weaving of hands, by the rhythmic gliding of feet, above all by the flitting of the marvelous sleeves—apparitional, soundless, velvety as a flitting of great tropical bats. No; nothing I ever dreamed of could be likened to this. And with the consciousness of the ancient hakaba behind me, and the weird invitation of its lanterns, and the ghostly beliefs of the hour and the place, there creeps upon me a nameless, tingling sense of being haunted. But no! these gracious, silent, waving, weaving shapes are not of the Shadowy Folk, for whose coming the white fires were kindled: a strain of song, full of sweet, clear quavering, like the call of a bird, gushes from some girlish mouth, and fifty soft voices join the chant:—

Sorota soroimashita odorikoga sorota,
Soroikite, kita hare yukata.

"Uniform to view [*as ears of young rice ripening in the field*] all clad alike in summer festal robes, the company of dancers have assembled."

Again only the shrilling of the crickets, the *shu-shu* of feet, the gentle clapping; and the wavering hovering measure proceeds in silence, with mesmeric lentor,—with a strange grace, which, by its very naïveté, seems old as the encircling hills.

Those who sleep the sleep of centuries out there, under the gray stones where the white lanterns are, and their fathers, and the fathers of their fathers' fathers, and the unknown generations behind them, buried in cemeteries of which the place has been forgotten for a thousand years, doubtless looked upon a scene like this. Nay! the dust stirred by those young feet was human life, and so smiled and so sang under this self-same moon, "with woven paces, and with waving hands."

Suddenly a deep male chant breaks the hush. Two giants have joined the round, and now lead it, two superb young mountain peasants nearly nude, towering head and shoulders above the whole of the assembly. Their kimono are rolled about their waists like girdles, leaving their bronzed limbs and torsos naked to the warm air; they wear nothing else save their immense straw hats, and white tabi, donned expressly for the festival. Never before among these people saw I such men, such thews; but their smiling beardless faces are comely and kindly as those of Japanese boys. They seem brothers, so like in frame, in movement, in the timbre of their voices, as they intone the same song:—

No demo yama demo ko wa umiokeyo,
Sen ryō kura yori ko ga takara.

"Whether brought forth upon the mountain or in the field, it matters nothing: more than a treasure of one thousand ryō, a baby precious is."

And Jizō, the lover of children's ghosts, smiles across the silence.

Souls close to nature's Soul are these; artless and touching their thought, like the worship of that Kishibojin to whom wives pray. And after the silence, the sweet thin voices of the women answer:—

Oomu otoko ni sowa sanu oya wa,
Oyade gozaranu ko no kataki.

"The parents who will not allow their girl to be united with her lover; they are not the parents, but the enemies of their child."

And song follows song; and the round ever becomes larger; and the hours pass unfelt, unheard, while the moon wheels slowly down the blue steeps of the night.

A deep low boom rolls suddenly across the court, the rich tone of some temple bell telling the twelfth hour. Instantly the witchcraft ends, like the wonder of some dream broken by a sound; the chanting ceases; the round dissolves in an outburst of happy laughter, and chatting, and softly-voweled callings of flower-names which are names of girls, and farewell cries of "*Sayōnara!*" as dancers and spectators alike betake themselves homeward, with a great *koro-koro* of getas.

And I, moving with the throng, in the bewildered manner of one suddenly roused from sleep, know myself ungrateful. These silvery-laughing folk who now toddle along beside me upon their noisy little clogs, stepping very fast to get a peep at my foreign face, these but a moment ago were visions of archaic grace, illusions of necromancy, delightful phantoms; and I feel a vague resentment against them for thus materializing into simple country-girls.

VI.

Lying down to rest, I ask myself the reason of the singular emotion inspired by that simple peasant-chorus. Utterly impossible to recall the air, with its fantastic intervals and fractional tones;—as well attempt to fix in memory the purlings of a bird; but the indefinable charm of it lingers with me still.

Melodies of Europe awaken within us feelings we can utter, sensations familiar as mother-speech, inherited from all the generations behind us. But how explain the emotion evoked by a primitive chant totally unlike anything in Western melody,—impossible even to write in those tones which are the ideographs of our music-tongue?

And the emotion itself—what is it? I know not; yet I feel it to be something infinitely more old than I,—something not of only one place or time, but vibrant to all common joy or pain of being, under the universal sun. Then I wonder if the secret does not lie in some untaught spontaneous harmony of that chant with Nature's most ancient song, in some unconscious kinship to the music of solitudes,—all trillings of summer life that blend to make the great sweet Cry of the Land.

Henry Adams
Prayer to the Virgin of Chartres

Gracious Lady:—

Simple as when I asked your aid before;
*   Humble as when I prayed for grace in vain*
Seven hundred years ago; weak, weary, sore
*   In heart and hope, I ask your help again.*

You, who remember all, remember me;
*   An English scholar of a Norman name,*
I was a thousand who then crossed the sea
*   To wrangle in the Paris schools for fame.*

When your Byzantine portal was still young
*   I prayed there with my master Abailard;*
When Ave Maris Stella was first sung,
*   I helped to sing it here with Saint Bernard.*

When Blanche set up your gorgeous Rose of France
*   I stood among the servants of the Queen;*
And when Saint Louis made his penitence,
*   I followed barefoot where the King had been.*

For centuries I brought you all my cares,
*   And vexed you with the murmurs of a child;*
You heard the tedious burden of my prayers;
*   You could not grant them, but at least you smiled.*

Letters to a Niece and Prayer to the Virgin of Chartres (Boston, 1920),
pp. 125–34. Text from this edition. Reprinted by permission of Houghton
Mifflin Company.

Although not published until 1920, Adams' poem was written in late
1900 or early 1901.

If then I left you, it was not my crime,
Or if a crime, it was not mine alone.
All children wander with the truant Time.
Pardon me too! You pardoned once your Son!

For He said to you:—"Wist ye not that I
Must be about my Father's business?" So,
Seeking his Father he pursued his way
Straight to the Cross towards which we all must go.

So I too wandered off among the host
That racked the earth to find the father's clue.
I did not find the Father, but I lost
What now I value more, the mother,—You!

I thought the fault was yours that foiled my search;
I turned and broke your image on its throne,
Cast down my idol, and resumed my march
To claim the father's empire for my own.

Crossing the hostile sea, our greedy band
Saw rising hills and forests in the blue;
Our father's kingdom in the promised land!
—We seized it, and dethroned the father too.

And now we are the Father, with our brood,
Ruling the Infinite, not Three but One;
We made our world and saw that it was good;
Ourselves we worship, and we have no son.

Yet we have Gods, for even our strong nerve
Falters before the Energy we own.
Which shall be master? Which of us shall serve?
Which wears the fetters? Which shall bear the crown?

Brave though we be, we dread to face the Sphinx,
Or answer the old riddle she still asks.
Strong as we are, our reckless courage shrinks
To look beyond the piece-work of our tasks.

But when we must, we pray, as in the past
Before the Cross on which your Son was nailed.
Listen, dear lady! You shall hear the last
Of the strange prayers Humanity has wailed.

Prayer to the Dynamo

Mysterious Power! Gentle Friend!
   Despotic Master! Tireless Force!
You and We are near the End.
Either You or We must bend
   To bear the martyrs' Cross.

We know ourselves, what we can bear
   As men; our strength and weakness too;
Down to the fraction of a hair;
And know that we, with all our care
   And knowledge, know not you.

You come in silence, Primal Force,
   We know not whence, or when, or why;
You stay a moment in your course
To play; and, lo! you leap across
   To Alpha Centauri!

We know not whether you are kind,
   Or cruel in your fiercer mood;
But be you Matter, be you Mind,
We think we know that you are blind,
   And we alone are good.

We know that prayer is thrown away,
   For you are only force and light;
A shifting current; night and day;
We know this well, and yet we pray,
   For prayer is infinite,

Like you! Within the finite sphere
   That bounds the impotence of thought,
We search an outlet everywhere
But only find that we are here
   And that you are—are not!

What are we then? the lords of space?
   The master-mind whose tasks you do?
Jockey who rides you in the race?
Or are we atoms whirled apace,
   Shaped and controlled by you?

Still silence! Still no end in sight!
   No sound in answer to our cry!
Then, by the God we now hold tight,
Though we destroy soul, life and light,
   Answer you shall—or die!

We are no beggars! What care we
   For hopes or terrors, love or hate?
What for the universe? We see
Only our certain destiny
   And the last word of Fate.

Seize, then, the Atom! rack his joints!
   Tear out of him his secret spring!
Grind him to nothing!—though he points
To us, and his life-blood anoints
   Me—the dead Atom-King!

A curious prayer, dear lady! is it not?
   Strangely unlike the prayers I prayed to you!
Stranger because you find me at this spot,
   Here, at your feet, asking your help anew.

Strangest of all, that I have ceased to strive,
   Ceased even care what new coin fate shall strike.
In truth it does not matter. Fate will give
   Some answer; and all answers are alike.

So, while we slowly rack and torture death
   And wait for what the final void will show,
Waiting I feel the energy of faith
   Not in the future science, but in you!

The man who solves the Infinite, and needs
   The force of solar systems for his play,
Will not need me, nor greatly care what deeds
   Made me illustrious in the dawn of day.

He will send me, dethroned, to claim my rights,
   Fossil survival of an age of stone,
Among the cave-men and the troglodytes
   Who carved the mammoth on the mammoth's bone.

He will forget my thought, my acts, my fame,
  As we forget the shadows of the dusk,
Or catalogue the echo of a name
  As we the scratches on the mammoth's tusk.

But when, like me, he too has trod the track
  Which leads him up to power above control,
He too will have no choice but wander back
  And sink in helpless hopelessness of soul,

Before your majesty of grace and love,
  The purity, the beauty and the faith;
The depth of tenderness beneath; above,
  The glory of the life and of the death.

When your Byzantine portal still was young,
  I came here with my master Abailard;
When Ave Maris Stella was first sung,
  I joined to sing it here with Saint Bernard.

When Blanche set up your glorious Rose of France,
  In scholar's robes I waited on the Queen;
When good Saint Louis did his penitence,
  My prayer was deep like his: my faith as keen.

What loftier prize seven hundred years shall bring,
  What deadlier struggles for a larger air,
What immortality our strength shall wring
  From Time and Space, we may—or may not—care;

But years, or ages, or eternity,
  Will find me still in thought before your throne,
Pondering the mystery of Maternity,
  Soul within Soul,—Mother and Child in One!

Help me to see! not with my mimic sight—
  With yours! which carried radiance, like the sun,
Giving the rays you saw with—light in light—
  Tying all suns and stars and worlds in one.

Help me to know! not with my mocking art—
  With you, who knew yourself unbound by laws;
Gave God your strength, your life, your sight, your heart,
  And took from him the Thought that Is—the Cause.

Help me to feel! not with my insect sense,—
    With yours that felt all life alive in you;
Infinite heart beating at your expense;
    Infinite passion breathing the breath you drew!

Help me to bear! not my own baby load,
    But yours; who bore the failure of the light,
The strength, the knowledge and the thought of God,—
    The futile folly of the Infinite!

Part Eight

THE WAR AS CATALYST

The Spanish-American War—the "splendid little war," as John Hay described it in a letter to Theodore Roosevelt—began about six weeks after the sinking of the *Maine* in Havana Harbor on February 15, 1898, and ended in early August. Its principal military actions were the destruction of the Spanish Pacific fleet at Manila on May 1 and the successful invasion of Cuba in June. Though the war itself was brief, with few major battles and few casualties, it excited much public interest throughout the second half of the decade. The Cuban insurrection began in 1895, and by 1896 a group of Congressional

445

War Hawks and the most popular New York newspapers were clamoring for American intervention. After this long period of heightened expectation, the outbreak of war was greeted with enthusiasm by most Americans. But as evidence of mismanagement and corruption came to light and as the question of our responsibility toward our annexed or conquered possessions became an issue, there was a reversal of sentiment by many political leaders and by almost the entire literary community.

The proximity of Cuba and the extent of public interest in the war encouraged a flood of war journalism before, during, and after the conflict. Much of this writing shares certain significant characteristics. In Richard Harding Davis' "The Death of Rodriguez," Theodore Roosevelt's "Raising the Regiment," and Stephen Crane's "War Memories," ideological justification for the war is reduced to an unassailable minimum: men fight for freedom, for national honor, or because it is their job. The focus of each writer is on himself as an observer of or participant in a significant action. Various themes emerge from this involvement: Davis' admiration of courage in the face of certain death, Roosevelt's amalgam of a Western frontier spirit and Eastern sportsmanship into a Boy's Book of American Manliness, and Crane's ironic bewilderment upon discovering that death is both horrible and trivial and that war is a "business." But the literary form itself is consistently that of first-hand chronicle, a form which results in the aggrandizement of the writer's literary personality and in a distinctive narrative style. The modern vogue of the writer as a coolly aloof participant in a violent or emotional action is in part rooted in war journalism of the 1890's and in the archetypal figure of the war correspondent as exemplified by Richard Harding Davis. And the concomitant prose style of detached involvement (what Hemingway was to call irony and pity) has its most significant precursor in Stephen Crane.

The Cuban campaign was over in a few weeks and the heroes of Centreville in George Ade's fable returned home to discover that though the war itself was tame, its heroic reputation could be exploited in the States. The war, in short, could be what others thought it was, and this discovery led to its almost immediate use as the starting point for a debate on the nature of American life. To Elbert Hubbard, whose "Message to Garcia" was one of the most widely-read documents of the decade, and to Roosevelt, in his "Strenuous Life" speech, the war demonstrated the continuing ability of Americans to react courageously and unquestioningly to the call of duty and honor. Both writers, however, were interested less in the celebration of past glories than in the application of these national virtues to contemporary spheres of activity—to business life and to our commitments overseas. The lesson they drew from the apparent reluctance of many Americans to make this application was that of the perniciousness of a national spirit which seeks to question rather than to do, or to pursue a life of slothful ease rather than one of honorable combat.

Much of the debate over the war's relationship to American life inevitably focused on the principal consequence of the war—our emergence as an imperialist power. The issue was clearly divided between those who viewed our expansionist activities as a duty-bound extension of our heritage of freedom and those who saw these activities as a betrayal of that heritage. A favorite polemic technique of anti-imperialists was to offer an ironic list of the blessings of our civilization which we could expect to bestow on the benighted natives of our new possessions. Although this kind of irony was directed primarily against territorial expansion, it also contained a critique of the "blessings" themselves, as in Ernest Crosby's "We've made a pretty mess at home/ Let's make a mess abroad." Thus, the debate occasioned by the war's aftermath sharpened the national awareness of two major cultural assumptions of the 1890's: that an ethic of Anglo-Saxon, Western manliness was an adequate alternative to the effete, closed world of an industrial society, and that we must nevertheless confront and solve the social dilemmas presented by that society. It was a token of Roosevelt's centrality at the close of the decade that his commitment to a strenuous life included both expansionism and reform, and that he pursued a life of "virile" endeavor within the Eastern establishment. Beneath the directness of Roosevelt's themes and style lay many of the complexities and paradoxes of a troubled yet buoyant time.

Richard Harding Davis
The Death of Rodriguez

ADOLFO RODRIGUEZ was the only son of a Cuban farmer, who lives nine miles outside of Santa Clara, beyond the hills that surround that city to the north.

When the revolution broke out young Rodriguez joined the insurgents, leaving his father and mother and two sisters at the farm. He was taken, in December of 1896, by a force of the Guardia Civile, the corps d'élite of the Spanish army, and defended himself when they tried to capture him, wounding three of them with his machete.

He was tried by a military court for bearing arms against the government, and sentenced to be shot by a fusillade some morning, before sunrise.

Previous to execution, he was confined in the military prison of Santa Clara, with thirty other insurgents, all of whom were sentenced to be shot, one after the other, on mornings following the execution of Rodriguez.

His execution took place the morning of the 19th of January, at a place a half-mile distant from the city, on the great plain that stretches from the forts out to the hills, beyond which Rodriguez had lived for nineteen years. At the time of his death he was twenty years old.

I witnessed his execution, and what follows is an account of the way he went to death. The young man's friends could not be present, for it was impossible for them to show themselves in that crowd and that place with wisdom or without distress, and I like to think that, although Rodriguez could not know it, there was one person present when he died who felt keenly for him, and who was a sympathetic though unwilling spectator.

There had been a full moon the night preceding the execution, and when the squad of soldiers marched out from town it was still shining brightly through the mists, although it was past five o'clock. It

New York *Journal*, February 2, 1897. Republished in *Cuba in War-Time* (New York, 1897), pp. 59–73. Text from *Cuba in War-Time*.

Davis arrived in Cuba in early January, 1897, as a reporter for Hearst's New York *Journal*.

lighted a plain two miles in extent broken by ridges and gullies and covered with thick, high grass and with bunches of cactus and palmetto. In the hollow of the ridges the mist lay like broad lakes of water, and on one side of the plain stood the walls of the old town. On the other rose hills covered with royal palms, that showed white in the moonlight, like hundreds of marble columns. A line of tiny camp fires that the sentries had built during the night stretched between the forts at regular intervals and burned brightly.

But as the light grew stronger, and the moonlight faded, these were stamped out, and when the soldiers came in force the moon was a white ball in the sky, without radiance, the fires had sunk to ashes, and the sun had not yet risen.

So, even when the men were formed into three sides of a hollow square, they were scarcely able to distinguish one another in the uncertain light of the morning.

There were about three hundred soldiers in the formation. They belonged to the Volunteers, and they deployed upon the plain with their band in front, playing a jaunty quickstep, while their officers galloped from one side to the other through the grass, seeking out a suitable place for the execution, while the band outside the line still played merrily.

A few men and boys, who had been dragged out of their beds by the music, moved about the ridges, behind the soldiers, half-clothed, unshaven, sleepy-eyed, yawning and stretching themselves nervously and shivering in the cool, damp air of the morning.

Either owing to discipline or on account of the nature of their errand or because the men were still but half awake, there was no talking in the ranks, and the soldiers stood motionless, leaning on their rifles, with their backs turned to the town, looking out across the plain to the hills.

The men in the crowd behind them were also grimly silent. They knew that whatever they might say would be twisted into a word of sympathy for the condemned man or a protest against the government. So no one spoke; even the officers gave their orders in gruff whispers, and the men in the crowd did not mix together, but looked suspiciously at one another and kept apart.

As the light increased a mass of people came hurrying from the town with two black figures leading them, and the soldiers drew up at attention, and part of the double line fell back and left an opening in the square.

With us a condemned man walks only the short distance from his cell to the scaffold or the electric chair, shielded from sight by the prison walls; and it often occurs even then that the short journey is too much for his strength and courage.

But the merciful Spaniards on this morning made the prisoner walk for over a half-mile across the broken surface of the fields. I expected to find the man, no matter what his strength at other times might be, stumbling and faltering on this cruel journey, but as he came nearer I saw that he led all the others, that the priests on either side of him were taking two steps to his one, and that they were tripping on their gowns and stumbling over the hollows, in their efforts to keep pace with him as he walked, erect and soldierly, at a quick step in advance of them.

He had a handsome, gentle face of the peasant type, a light, pointed beard, great wistful eyes and a mass of curly black hair. He was shockingly young for such a sacrifice, and looked more like a Neapolitan than a Cuban. You could imagine him sitting on the quay at Naples or Genoa, lolling in the sun and showing his white teeth when he laughed. He wore a new scapula around his neck, hanging outside his linen blouse.

It seems a petty thing to have been pleased with at such a time, but I confess to have felt a thrill of satisfaction when I saw, as the Cuban passed me, that he held a cigarette between his lips, not arrogantly nor with bravado, but with the nonchalance of a man who meets his punishment fearlessly, and who will let his enemies see that they can kill but can not frighten him.

It was very quickly finished, with rough, and, but for one frightful blunder, with merciful swiftness. The crowd fell back when it came to the square, and the condemned man, the priests and the firing squad of six young volunteers passed in and the line closed behind them.

The officer who had held the cord that bound the Cuban's arms behind him and passed across his breast, let it fall on the grass and drew his sword, and Rodriguez dropped his cigarette from his lips and bent and kissed the cross which the priest held up before him.

The elder of the priests moved to one side and prayed rapidly in a loud whisper, while the other, a younger man, walked away behind the firing squad and covered his face with his hands and turned his back. They had both spent the last twelve hours with Rodriguez in the chapel of the prison.

The Cuban walked to where the officer directed him to stand, and turned his back to the square and faced the hills and the road across them which led to his father's farm.

As the officer gave the first command he straightened himself as far as the cords would allow, and held up his head and fixed his eyes immovably on the morning light which had just begun to show above the hills.

He made a picture of such pathetic helplessness, but of such courage and dignity, that he reminded me on the instant of that statue of Nathan Hale, which stands in the City Hall Park, above the roar of Broadway, and teaches a lesson daily to the hurrying crowds of moneymakers who pass beneath.

The Cuban's arms were bound, as are those of the statue, and he stood firmly, with his weight resting on his heels like a soldier on parade, and with his face held up fearlessly, as is that of the statue. But there was this difference, that Rodriguez, while probably as willing to give six lives for his country as was the American rebel, being only a peasant, did not think to say so, and he will not, in consequence, live in bronze during the lives of many men, but will be remembered only as one of thirty Cubans, one of whom was shot at Santa Clara on each succeeding day at sunrise.

The officer had given the order, the men had raised their pieces, and the condemned man had heard the clicks of the triggers as they were pulled back, and he had not moved. And then happened one of the most cruelly refined, though unintentional, acts of torture that one can very well imagine. As the officer slowly raised his sword, preparatory to giving the signal, one of the mounted officers rode up to him and pointed out silently what I had already observed with some satisfaction, that the firing squad were so placed that when they fired they would shoot several of the soldiers stationed on the extreme end of the square.

Their captain motioned his men to lower their pieces, and then walked across the grass and laid his hand on the shoulder of the waiting prisoner.

It is not pleasant to think what that shock must have been. The man had steeled himself to receive a volley of bullets in his back. He believed that in the next instant he would be in another world; he had heard the command given, had heard the click of the Mausers as the locks caught—and then, at that supreme moment, a human hand had been laid upon his shoulder and a voice spoke in his ear.

You would expect that any man who had been snatched back to life in such a fashion would start and tremble at the reprieve, or would break down altogether, but this boy turned his head steadily, and followed with his eyes the direction of the officer's sword, then nodded his head gravely, and, with his shoulders squared, took up a new position, straightened his back again, and once more held himself erect.

As an exhibition of self-control this should surely rank above feats of heroism performed in battle, where there are thousands of comrades to give inspiration. This man was alone, in the sight of the hills he knew, with only enemies about him, with no source to draw on for strength but that which lay within himself.

The officer of the firing squad, mortified by his blunder, hastily whipped up his sword, the men once more leveled their rifles, the sword rose, dropped, and the men fired. At the report the Cuban's head snapped back almost between his shoulders, but his body fell slowly, as though some one had pushed him gently forward from behind and he had stumbled.

He sank on his side in the wet grass without a struggle or sound, and did not move again.

It was difficult to believe that he meant to lie there, that it could be ended so without a word, that the man in the linen suit would not get up on his feet and continue to walk on over the hills, as he apparently had started to do, to his home; that there was not a mistake somewhere, or that at least some one would be sorry or say something or run to pick him up.

But, fortunately, he did not need help, and the priests returned— the younger one, with the tears running down his face—and donned their vestments and read a brief requiem for his soul, while the squad stood uncovered, and the men in hollow square shook their accoutrements into place, and shifted their pieces and got ready for the order to march, and the band began again with the same quickstep which the fusillade had interrupted.

The figure still lay on the grass untouched, and no one seemed to remember that it had walked there of itself, or noticed that the cigarette still burned, a tiny ring of living fire, at the place where the figure had first stood.

The figure was a thing of the past, and the squad shook itself like a great snake, and then broke into little pieces and started off jauntily, stumbling in the high grass and striving to keep step to the music.

The officers led it past the figure in the linen suit, and so close to it that the file closers had to part with the column to avoid treading on it. Each soldier as he passed turned and looked down on it, some craning their necks curiously, others giving a careless glance, and some without any interest at all, as they would have looked at a house by the roadside or a passing cart or a hole in the road.

One young soldier caught his foot in a trailing vine, and fell forward just opposite to it. He grew very red when his comrades giggled at him for his awkwardness. The crowd of sleepy spectators fell in on either side of the band. They had forgotten it, too, and the priests put their vestments back in the bag and wrapped their heavy cloaks about them, and hurried off after the others.

Every one seemed to have forgotten it except two men, who came slowly toward it from the town, driving a bullock cart that bore an unplaned coffin, each with a cigarette between his lips, and with his throat wrapped in a shawl to keep out the morning mists.

At that moment the sun, which had shown some promise of its coming in the glow above the hills, shot up suddenly from behind them in all the splendor of the tropics, a fierce, red disc of heat, and filled the air with warmth and light.

The bayonets of the retreating column flashed in it, and at the sight of it a rooster in a farmyard near by crowed vigorously and a dozen bugles answered the challenge with the brisk, cheery notes of the reveille, and from all parts of the city the church bells jangled out the call for early mass, and the whole world of Santa Clara seemed to stir and stretch itself and to wake to welcome the day just begun.

But as I fell in at the rear of the procession and looked back the figure of the young Cuban, who was no longer a part of the world of Santa Clara, was asleep in the wet grass, with his motionless arms still tightly bound behind him, with the scapula twisted awry across his face and the blood from his breast sinking into the soil he had tried to free.

Theodore Roosevelt
Raising the Regiment

DURING THE YEAR preceding the outbreak of the Spanish War I was Assistant Secretary of the Navy. While my party was in opposition, I had preached, with all the fervor and zeal I possessed, our duty to intervene in Cuba, and to take this opportunity of driving the Spaniard from the Western World. Now that my party had come to power, I felt it incumbent on me, by word and deed, to do all I could to secure the carrying out of the policy in which I so heartily believed; and from the beginning I had determined that, if a war came, somehow or other, I was going to the front.

Meanwhile, there was any amount of work at hand in getting ready the navy, and to this I devoted myself.

Naturally, when one is intensely interested in a certain cause, the

The Rough Riders (New York, 1899), pp. 1–7, 9–12, 14–19. Text from this edition.

In a famous mock review of *The Rough Riders*, Mr. Dooley (Finley Peter Dunne) suggested that the book should have been entitled "Alone in Cuba."

tendency is to associate particularly with those who take the same
view. A large number of my friends felt very differently from the way
I felt, and looked upon the possibility of war with sincere horror.
But I found plenty of sympathizers, especially in the navy, the army,
and the Senate Committee on Foreign Affairs. Commodore Dewey,
Captain Evans, Captain Brownson, Captain Davis—with these and
the various other naval officers on duty at Washington I used to hold
long consultations, during which we went over and over, not only
every question of naval administration, but specifically everything
necessary to do in order to put the navy in trim to strike quick and
hard if, as we believed would be the case, we went to war with Spain.
Sending an ample quantity of ammunition to the Asiàtic squadron
and providing it with coal; getting the battle-ships and the armored
cruisers on the Atlantic into one squadron, both to train them in
manœuvring together, and to have them ready to sail against either
the Cuban or the Spanish coasts; gathering the torpedo-boats into a
flotilla for practice; securing ample target exercise, so conducted as
to raise the standard of our marksmanship; gathering in the small
ships from European and South American waters; settling on the number and kind of craft needed as auxiliary cruisers—every one of these
points was threshed over in conversations with officers who were
present in Washington, or in correspondence with officers who, like
Captain Mahan, were absent.

As for the Senators, of course Senator Lodge and I felt precisely
alike; for to fight in such a cause and with such an enemy was merely
to carry out the doctrines we had both of us preached for many years.
Senator Davis, Senator Proctor, Senator Foraker, Senator Chandler,
Senator Morgan, Senator Frye, and a number of others also took just
the right ground; and I saw a great deal of them, as well as of many
members of the House, particularly those from the West, where the
feeling for war was strongest.

Naval officers came and went, and Senators were only in the city
while the Senate was in session; but there was one friend who was
steadily in Washington. This was an army surgeon, Dr. Leonard Wood.
I only met him after I entered the navy department, but we soon
found that we had kindred tastes and kindred principles. He had
served in General Miles's inconceivably harassing campaigns against
the Apaches, where he had displayed such courage that he won that
most coveted of distinctions—the Medal of Honor; such extraordinary
physical strength and endurance that he grew to be recognized as one
of the two or three white men who could stand fatigue and hardship
as well as an Apache; and such judgment that toward the close of the
campaigns he was given, though a surgeon, the actual command of
more than one expedition against the bands of renegade Indians. Like

so many of the gallant fighters with whom it was later my good fortune to serve, he combined, in a very high degree, the qualities of entire manliness with entire uprightness and cleanliness of character. It was a pleasure to deal with a man of high ideals, who scorned everything mean and base, and who also possessed those robust and hardy qualities of body and mind, for the lack of which no merely negative virtue can ever atone. He was by nature a soldier of the highest type, and, like most natural soldiers, he was, of course, born with a keen longing for adventure; and, though an excellent doctor, what he really desired was the chance to lead men in some kind of hazard. To every possibility of such adventure he paid quick attention. For instance, he had a great desire to get me to go with him on an expedition into the Klondike in mid-winter, at the time when it was thought that a relief party would have to be sent there to help the starving miners.

In the summer he and I took long walks together through the beautiful broken country surrounding Washington. In winter we sometimes varied these walks by kicking a foot-ball in an empty lot, or, on the rare occasions when there was enough snow, by trying a couple of sets of skis or snow-skates, which had been sent me from Canada.

But always on our way out to and back from these walks and sport, there was one topic to which, in our talking, we returned, and that was the possible war with Spain. We both felt very strongly that such a war would be as righteous as it would be advantageous to the honor and the interests of the nation; and after the blowing up of the Maine, we felt that it was inevitable. We then at once began to try to see that we had our share in it. The President and my own chief, Secretary Long, were very firm against my going, but they said that if I was bent upon going they would help me. Wood was the medical adviser of both the President and the Secretary of War, and could count upon their friendship. So we started with the odds in our favor.

At first we had great difficulty in knowing exactly what to try for. We could go on the staff of any one of several Generals, but we much preferred to go in the line. Wood hoped he might get a commission in his native State of Massachusetts; but in Massachusetts, as in every other State, it proved there were ten men who wanted to go to the war for every chance to go. Then we thought we might get positions as field-officers under an old friend of mine, Colonel—now General—Francis V. Greene, of New York, the Colonel of the Seventy-first; but again there were no vacancies.

Our doubts were resolved when Congress authorized the raising of three cavalry regiments from among the wild riders and riflemen of the Rockies and the Great Plains. During Wood's service in the Southwest he had commanded not only regulars and Indian scouts, but also white frontiersmen. In the Northwest I had spent much of my time,

for many years, either on my ranch or in long hunting trips, and had
lived and worked for months together with the cow-boy and the
mountain hunter, faring in every way precisely as they did.

Secretary Alger offered me the command of one of these regiments.
If I had taken it, being entirely inexperienced in military work, I
should not have known how to get it equipped most rapidly, for I
should have spent valuable weeks in learning its needs, with the result
that I should have missed the Santiago campaign, and might not even
have had the consolation prize of going to Porto Rico. Fortunately,
I was wise enough to tell the Secretary that while I believed I could
learn to command the regiment in a month, yet that it was just this
very month which I could not afford to spare, and that therefore I
would be quite content to go as Lieutenant-Colonel, if he would make
Wood Colonel.

This was entirely satisfactory to both the President and Secretary,
and, accordingly, Wood and I were speedily commissioned as Colonel
and Lieutenant-Colonel of the First United States Volunteer Cavalry.
This was the official title of the regiment, but for some reason or other
the public promptly christened us the "Rough Riders." At first we
fought against the use of the term, but to no purpose; and when finally
the Generals of Division and Brigade began to write in formal com-
munications about our regiment as the "Rough Riders," we adopted
the term ourselves.

*   *   *

It was impossible to take any of the numerous companies which
were proffered to us from the various States. The only organized bodies
we were at liberty to accept were those from the four Territories. But
owing to the fact that the number of men originally allotted to us, 780,
was speedily raised to 1,000, we were given a chance to accept quite
a number of eager volunteers who did not come from the Territories,
but who possessed precisely the same temper that distinguished our
Southwestern recruits, and whose presence materially benefited the
regiment.

We drew recruits from Harvard, Yale, Princeton, and many another
college; from clubs like the Somerset, of Boston, and Knickerbocker,
of New York; and from among the men who belonged neither to club
nor to college, but in whose veins the blood stirred with the same impulse which once sent the Vikings over sea. Four of the policemen who
had served under me, while I was President of the New York Police
Board, insisted on coming—two of them to die, the other two to return unhurt after honorable and dangerous service. It seemed to me
that almost every friend I had in every State had some one acquaintance who was bound to go with the Rough Riders, and for whom I
had to make a place. Thomas Nelson Page, General Fitzhugh Lee, Con-

gressman Odell of New York, Senator Morgan; for each of these, and
for many others, I eventually consented to accept some one or two
recruits, of course only after a most rigid examination into their physical capacity, and after they had shown that they knew how to ride
and shoot. I may add that in no case was I disappointed in the men
thus taken.

Harvard being my own college, I had such a swarm of applications
from it that I could not take one in ten. What particularly pleased me
not only in the Harvard but the Yale and Princeton men, and, indeed,
in these recruits from the older States generally, was that they did
not ask for commissions. With hardly an exception they entered upon
their duties as troopers in the spirit which they held to the end, merely
endeavoring to show that no work could be too hard, too disagreeable, or too dangerous for them to perform, and neither asking nor receiving any reward in the way of promotion or consideration. The
Harvard contingent was practically raised by Guy Murchie, of Maine.
He saw all the fighting and did his duty with the utmost gallantry, and
then left the service as he had entered it, a trooper, entirely satisfied
to have done his duty—and no man did it better. So it was with Dud-
ley Dean, perhaps the best quarterback who ever played on a Harvard Eleven; and so with Bob Wrenn, a quarterback whose feats ri-
valled those of Dean's, and who, in addition, was the champion tennis
player of America, and had, on two different years, saved this cham-
pionship from going to an Englishman. So it was with Yale men like
Waller, the high jumper, and Garrison and Girard; and with Princeton men like Devereux and Channing, the foot-ball players; with Lar-
ned, the tennis player; with Craig Wadsworth, the steeple-chase rider;
with Joe Stevens, the crack polo player; with Hamilton Fish, the ex-
captain of the Columbia crew, and with scores of others whose names
are quite as worthy of mention as any of those I have given. Indeed,
they all sought entry into the ranks of the Rough Riders as eagerly
as if it meant something widely different from hard work, rough fare,
and the possibility of death; and the reason why they turned out to
be such good soldiers lay largely in the fact that they were men who
had thoroughly counted the cost before entering, and who went into
the regiment because they believed that this offered their best chance
for seeing hard and dangerous service. Mason Mitchell, of New York,
who had been a chief of scouts in the Riel Rebellion, travelled all the
way to San Antonio to enlist; and others came there from distances as
great.

* * *

These men formed but a small fraction of the whole. They went
down to San Antonio, where the regiment was to gather and where
Wood preceded me, while I spent a week in Washington hurrying

up the different bureaus and telegraphing my various railroad friends,
so as to insure our getting the carbines, saddles, and uniforms that we
needed from the various armories and storehouses. Then I went down
to San Antonio myself, where I found the men from New Mexico,
Arizona, and Oklahoma already gathered, while those from Indian
Territory came in soon after my arrival.

These were the men who made up the bulk of the regiment, and
gave it its peculiar character. They came from the Four Territories
which yet remained within the boundaries of the United States; that
is, from the lands that have been most recently won over to white
civilization, and in which the conditions of life are nearest those that
obtained on the frontier when there still was a frontier. They were a
splendid set of men, these Southwesterners—tall and sinewy, with
resolute, weather-beaten faces, and eyes that looked a man straight
in the face without flinching. They included in their ranks men of
every occupation; but the three types were those of the cow-boy, the
hunter, and the mining prospector—the man who wandered hither and
thither, killing game for a living, and spending his life in the quest
for metal wealth.

In all the world there could be no better material for soldiers
than that afforded by these grim hunters of the mountains, these wild
rough riders of the plains. They were accustomed to handling wild
and savage horses; they were accustomed to following the chase
with the rifle, both for sport and as a means of livelihood. Varied
though their occupations had been, almost all had, at one time or another, herded cattle and hunted big game. They were hardened to life
in the open, and to shifting for themselves under adverse circumstances. They were used, for all their lawless freedom, to the rough
discipline of the round-up and the mining company. Some of them
came from the small frontier towns; but most were from the wilderness,
having left their lonely hunters' cabins and shifting cow-camps to seek
new and more stirring adventures beyond the sea.

They had their natural leaders—the men who had shown they could
master other men, and could more than hold their own in the eager
driving life of the new settlements.

The Captains and Lieutenants were sometimes men who had cam-
paigned in the regular army against Apache, Ute, and Cheyenne,
and who, on completing their term of service, had shown their energy
be settling in the new communities and growing up to be men of mark.
In other cases they were sheriffs, marshals, deputy-sheriffs and deputy-
marshals—men who had fought Indians, and still more often had
waged relentless war upon the bands of white desperadoes. There was
Bucky O'Neill, of Arizona, Captain of Troop A, the Mayor of Prescott, a famous sheriff throughout the West for his feats of victorious

warfare against the Apache, no less than against the white road-agents and man-killers. His father had fought in Meagher's Brigade in the Civil War; and he was himself a born soldier, a born leader of men. He was a wild, reckless fellow, soft spoken, and of dauntless courage and boundless ambition; he was stanchly loyal to his friends, and cared for his men in every way. There was Captain Llewellen, of New Mexico, a good citizen, a political leader, and one of the most noted peace-officers of the country; he had been shot four times in pitched fights with red marauders and white outlaws. There was Lieutenant Ballard, who had broken up the Black Jack gang of ill-omened notoriety, and his Captain, Curry, another New Mexican sheriff of fame. The officers from the Indian Territory had almost all served as marshals and deputy-marshals; and in the Indian Territory, service as a deputy-marshal meant capacity to fight stand-up battles with the gangs of outlaws.

Three of our higher officers had been in the regular army. One was Major Alexander Brodie, from Arizona, afterward Lieutenant-Colonel, who had lived for twenty years in the Territory, and had become a thorough Westerner without sinking the West Pointer—a soldier by taste as well as training, whose men worshipped him and would follow him anywhere, as they would Bucky O'Neill or any other of their favorites. Brodie was running a big mining business; but when the Maine was blown up, he abandoned everything and telegraphed right and left to bid his friends get ready for the fight he saw impending.

Then there was Micah Jenkins, the Captain of Troop K, a gentle and courteous South Carolinian, on whom danger acted like wine. In action he was a perfect game-cock, and he won his majority for gallantry in battle.

Finally, there was Allyn Capron, who was, on the whole, the best soldier in the regiment. In fact, I think he was the ideal of what an American regular army officer should be. He was the fifth in descent from father to son who had served in the army of the United States, and in body and mind alike he was fitted to play his part to perfection. Tall and lithe, a remarkable boxer and walker, a first-class rider and shot, with yellow hair and piercing blue eyes, he looked what he was, the archetype of the fighting man. He had under him one of the two companies from the Indian Territory; and he so soon impressed himself upon the wild spirit of his followers, that he got them ahead in discipline faster than any other troop in the regiment, while at the same time taking care of their bodily wants. His ceaseless effort was so to train them, care for them, and inspire them as to bring their fighting efficiency to the highest possible pitch. He required instant obedience, and tolerated not the slightest evasion of duty; but his mastery of his art was so thorough and his performance of his own

duty so rigid that he won at once not merely their admiration, but
that soldierly affection so readily given by the man in the ranks to
the superior who cares for his men and leads them fearlessly in battle.

All—Easterners and Westerners, Northerners and Southerners, officers and men, cow-boys and college graduates, wherever they came
from, and whatever their social position—possessed in common the
traits of hardihood and a thirst for adventure. They were to a man
born adventurers, in the old sense of the word.

*   *   *

Stephen Crane
War Memories

WE WILL PROCEED to July 1st. On that morning I marched with
my kit—having everything essential save a tooth-brush—the entire
army put me to shame, since there must have been at least fifteen
thousand tooth-brushes in the invading force—I marched with my
kit on the road to Santiago. It was a fine morning and everybody—
the doomed and the immunes—how could we tell one from the other
—everybody was in the highest spirits. We were enveloped in forest,
but we could hear, from ahead, everybody peppering away at everybody. It was like the roll of many drums. This was Lawton over at
El Caney. I reflected with complacency that Lawton's division did
not concern me in a professional way. That was the affair of another
man. My business was with Kent's division and Wheeler's division.
We came to El Poso—a hill at nice artillery range from the Spanish
defences. Here Grimes's battery was shooting a duel with one of the
enemy's batteries. Scovel had established a little camp in the rear of
the guns and a servant had made coffee. I invited Whigham to have

Anglo-Saxon Review, III (December, 1899), 16–38. Republished in *Wounds
in the Rain* (New York, 1900), pp. 270–82, 290–92. Text from *Wounds
in the Rain*.

Crane had landed in Cuba on June 7 with the first American invasion
forces. The battles described are those of San Juan Hill and El Caney.

coffee, and the servant added some hard biscuit and tinned tongue. I noted that Whigham was staring fixedly over my shoulder, and that he waved away the tinned tongue with some bitterness. It was a horse, a dead horse. Then a mule, which had been shot through the nose, wandered up and looked at Whigham. We ran away.

On top of the hill one had a fine view of the Spanish lines. We stared across almost a mile of jungle to ash-coloured trenches on the military crest of the ridge. A goodly distance back of this position were white buildings, all flying great red-cross flags. The jungle beneath us rattled with firing and the Spanish trenches crackled out regular volleys, but all this time there was nothing to indicate a tangible enemy. In truth, there was a man in a Panama hat strolling to and fro behind one of the Spanish trenches, gesticulating at times with a walking stick. A man in a Panama hat, walking with a stick! That was the strangest sight of my life—that symbol, that quaint figure of Mars. The battle, the thunderous row, was his possession. He was the master. He mystified us all with his infernal Panama hat and his wretched walking-stick. From near his feet came volleys and from near his side came roaring shells, but he stood there alone, visible, the one tangible thing. He was a Colossus, and he was half as high as a pin, this being. Always somebody would be saying: "Who *can* that fellow be?"

Later, the American guns shelled the trenches and a blockhouse near them, and Mars had vanished. It could not have been death. Once cannot kill Mars. But there was one other figure, which arose to symbolic dignity. The balloon of our signal corps had swung over the tops of the jungle's trees toward the Spanish trenches. Whereat the balloon and the man in the Panama hat and with a walking stick—whereat these two waged tremendous battle.

Suddenly the conflict became a human thing. A little group of blue figures appeared on the green of the terrible hillside. It was some of our infantry. The attaché of a great empire was at my shoulder, and he turned to me and spoke with incredulity and scorn. "Why, they're trying to take the position," he cried, and I admitted meekly that I thought they were. "But they can't do it, you know," he protested vehemently. "It's impossible." And—good fellow that he was—he began to grieve and wail over a useless sacrifice of gallant men. "It's plucky, you know! By Gawd, it's plucky! But *they can't do it!*" He was profoundly moved; his voice was quite broken. "It will simply be a hell of a slaughter with no good coming out of it."

The trail was already crowded with stretcher-bearers and with wounded men who could walk. One had to stem a tide of mute agony. But I don't know that it was mute agony. I only know that it was mute. It was something in which the silence or, more likely, the reticence was an appalling and inexplicable fact. One's senses seemed to demand that these men should cry out. But you could really find wounded men who exhibited all the signs of a pleased and contented mood. When thinking of it now it seems strange beyond words. But at the time—I don't know—it did not attract one's wonder. A man with a hole in his arm or his shoulder, or even in the leg below the knee, was often whimsical, comic. "Well, this ain't exactly what I enlisted for, boys. If I'd been told about this in Tampa, I'd have resigned from th' army. Oh, yes, you can get the same thing if you keep on going. But I think the Spaniards may run out of ammunition in the course of a week or ten days." Then suddenly one would be confronted by the awful majesty of a man shot in the face. Particularly I remember one. He had a great dragoon moustache, and the blood streamed down his face to meet this moustache even as a torrent goes to meet the jammed log, and then swarmed out to the tips and fell in big slow drops. He looked steadily into my eyes; I was ashamed to return his glance. You understand? It is very curious—all that.

The two lines of battle were royally whacking away at each other, and there was no rest or peace in all that region. The modern bullet is a far-flying bird. It rakes the air with its hot spitting song at distances which, as a usual thing, place the whole landscape in the danger-zone. There was no direction from which they did not come. A chart of their courses over one's head would have resembled a spider's web. My friend Jimmie, the photographer, mounted to the firing line with me and we gallivanted as much as we dared. The "sense of the meeting" was curious. Most of the men seemed to have no idea of a grand historic performance, but they were grimly satisfied with themselves. "Well, begawd, we done it." Then they wanted to know about other parts of the line. "How are things looking, old man? Everything all right?" "Yes, everything is all right if you can hold this ridge." "Aw, hell," said the men, "we'll hold the ridge. Don't you worry about that, son."

It was Jimmie's first action, and, as we cautiously were making our way to the right of our lines, the crash of the Spanish fire became uproarious, and the air simply whistled. I heard a quavering voice near my shoulder, and, turning, I beheld Jimmie—Jimmie—with a face bloodless, white as paper. He looked at me with eyes opened extremely wide. "Say," he said, "this is pretty hot, ain't it?" I was delighted. I knew exactly what he meant. He wanted to have the situation defined. If I had told him that this was the occasion of some mere idle desultory firing and recommended that he wait until the real battle began, I think he would have gone in a bee-line for the rear. But I told him the truth. "Yes, Jimmie," I replied earnestly, "You can take it from me that this is patent, double-extra-what-for." And immediately he nodded. "All right." If this was a big action, then he was willing to pay in his fright as a rational price for the privilege of being present. But if this was only a penny affray, he considered the price exorbitant, and he would go away. He accepted my assurance with simple faith, and deported himself with kindly dignity as one moving amid great things. His face was still as pale as paper, but that counted for nothing. The main point was his perfect willingness to be frightened for reasons. I wonder where is Jimmie? I lent him the Jamaica polo-pony one day and it ran away with him and flung him off in the middle of a ford. He appeared to me afterward and made bitter speech concerning this horse which I had assured him was a gentle and pious animal. Then I never saw Jimmie again.

Then came the night of the first of July. A group of correspondents limped back to El Poso. It had been a day so long that the morning seemed as remote as a morning in the previous year. But I have forgotten to tell you about Reuben McNab. Many years ago, I went to school at a place called Claverack, in New York State, where there was a semi-military institution. Contemporaneous with me, as a student, was Reuben McNab, a long, lank boy, freckled, sandy-haired— an extraordinary boy in no way, and yet, I wager, a boy clearly marked in every recollection. Perhaps there is a good deal in that name. Reuben McNab. You can't fling that name carelessly over your shoulder and lose it. It follows you like the haunting memory of a sin. At any rate, Reuben McNab was identified intimately in my thought with the sunny irresponsible days at Claverack, when all the earth was a green field and all the sky was a rainless blue. Then I looked down into a miserable huddle at Bloody Bend, a huddle of hurt men, dying men, dead men. And there I saw Reuben McNab, a corporal in the 71st New York Volunteers, and with a hole through his lung. Also, several holes through his clothing. "Well, they got me," he said in greeting. Usually they said that. There were no long speeches. "Well, they got me." That was sufficient. The duty of the upright, unhurt, man is then difficult. I doubt if many of us learned how to speak to our own wounded. In the first place, one had to play that the wound was nothing; oh, a mere nothing; a casual interference with movement, perhaps, but nothing more; oh, really nothing more. In the second place, one had to show a comrade's appreciation of this sad plight. As a result I think most of us bungled and stammered in the presence of our wounded friends. That's curious, eh? "Well, they got me," said Reuben McNab. I had looked upon five hundred wounded men with stolidity, or with a conscious indifference which filled me with amazement. But the apparition of Reuben McNab, the schoolmate, lying there in the mud, with a hole through his lung, awed me into stutterings, set me trembling with a sense of terrible intimacy with this war which theretofore I could have believed was a dream—

almost. Twenty shot men rolled their eyes and looked at me. Only one man paid no heed. He was dying; he had no time. The bullets hummed low over them all. Death, having already struck, still insisted upon raising a venomous crest. "If you're goin' by the hospital, step in and see me," said Reuben McNab. That was all.

At the correspondents' camp, at El Poso, there was hot coffee. It was very good. I have a vague sense of being very selfish over my blanket and rubber coat. I have a vague sense of spasmodic firing during my sleep; it rained, and then I awoke to hear that steady drumming of an infantry fire—something which was never to cease, it seemed. They were at it again. The trail from El Poso to the positions along San Juan ridge had become an exciting thoroughfare. Shots from large-bore rifles dropped in from almost every side. At this time the safest place was the extreme front. I remember in particular the one outcry I heard. A private in the 71st, without his rifle, had gone to a stream for some water, and was returning, being but a little in rear of me. Suddenly I heard this cry—"Oh, my God, come quick"— and I was conscious then to having heard the hateful zip of a close shot. He lay on the ground, wriggling. He was hit in the hip. Two men came quickly. Presently everybody seemed to be getting knocked down. They went over like men of wet felt, quietly, calmly, with no more complaint than so many automatons. It was only that lad—"Oh, my God, come quick." Otherwise, men seemed to consider that their hurts were not worthy of particular attention. A number of people got killed very courteously, tacitly absolving the rest of us from any care in the matter. A man fell; he turned blue; his face took on an expression of deep sorrow; and then his immediate friends worried about him, if he had friends. This was July 1. I crave the permission to leap back again to that date.

On the morning of July 2, I sat on San Juan hill and watched Lawton's division come up. I was absolutely sheltered, but still where I could look into the faces of men who were trotting up under fire. There wasn't a high heroic face among them. They were all men intent on business. That was all. It may seem to you that I am trying to make everything a squalor. That would be wrong. I feel that things were often sublime. But they were *differently* sublime. They were not of our shallow and preposterous fictions. They stood out in a simple, majestic commonplace. It was the behaviour of men on the street. It was the behaviour of men. In one way, each man was just pegging along at the heels of the man before him, who was pegging along at the heels of still another man, who was pegging along at the heels of still another man who— It was that in the flat and obvious way. In another way it was pageantry, the pageantry of the accomplishment of naked duty. One cannot speak of it—the spectacle of the common man serenely doing his work, his appointed work. It is the one thing in the universe which makes one fling expression to the winds and be satisfied to simply feel. Thus they moved at San Juan—the soldiers of the United States Regular Army. One pays them the tribute of the toast of silence.

Lying near one of the enemy's trenches was a red-headed Spanish corpse. I wonder how many hundreds were cognisant of this red-headed Spanish corpse? It arose to the dignity of a landmark. There were many corpses but only one with a red head. This red-head. He was always there. Each time I approached that part of the field I prayed that I might find that he had been buried. But he was always there—red-headed. His strong simple countenance was a malignant sneer at the system which was forever killing the credulous peasants in a sort of black night of politics, where the peasants merely followed whatever somebody had told them was lofty and good. But, nevertheless, the red-headed Spaniard was dead. He was irrevocably dead. And to what purpose? The honour of Spain? Surely the honour of Spain could have existed without the violent death of this poor red-headed peasant? Ah well, he was buried when the heavy firing ceased and men had time for such small things as funerals. The trench was turned over on top of him. It was a fine, honourable, soldierly fate—to be buried in a trench, the trench of the fight and the death. Sleep well, red-headed peasant. You came to another hemisphere to fight because—because you were told to, I suppose. Well, there you are, buried in your trench on San Juan hill. That is the end of it, your life has been taken—that is a flat, frank fact. And foreigners buried you expeditiously while speaking a strange tongue. Sleep well, red-headed mystery.

* * *

Pushing through the throng in the plaza we came in sight of the door of the church, and here was a strange scene. The church had been turned into a hospital for Spanish wounded who had fallen into American hands. The interior of the church was too cave-like in its gloom for the eyes of the operating surgeons, so they had had the altar table carried to the doorway, where there was a bright light. Framed then in the black archway was the altar table with the figure of a man upon it. He was naked save for a breech-clout and so close, so clear was the ecclesiastic suggestion, that one's mind leaped to a phantasy that this thin, pale figure had just been torn down from a cross. The flash of the impression was like light, and for this instant it illumined all the dark recesses of one's remotest idea of sacrilege, ghastly and wanton. I bring this to you merely as an effect, an effect of mental light and shade, if you like; something done in thought sim-

ilar to that which the French impressionists do in colour; something
meaningless and at the same time overwhelming, crushing, monstrous.
"Poor devil; I wonder if he'll pull through," said Leighton. An American surgeon and his assistants were intent over the prone figure. They
wore white aprons. Something small and silvery flashed in the surgeon's
hand. An assistant held the merciful sponge close to the man's nostrils,
but he was writhing and moaning in some horrible dream of this
artificial sleep. As the surgeon's instrument played, I fancied that
the man dreamed that he was being gored by a bull. In his pleading,
delirious babble occurred constantly the name of the Virgin, the Holy
Mother. "Good morning," said the surgeon. He changed his knife to
his left hand and gave me a wet palm. The tips of his fingers were
wrinkled, shrunken, like those of a boy who has been in swimming
too long. Now, in front of the door, there were three American sentries, and it was their business to—to do what? To keep this Spanish crowd from swarming over the operating table! It was perforce a
public clinic. They would not be denied. The weaker women and the
children jostled according to their might in the rear, while the stronger
people, gaping in the front rank, cried out impatiently when the pushing disturbed their long stares. One burned with a sudden gift of
public oratory. One wanted to say: "Oh, go away, go away, go away.
Leave the man decently alone with his pain, you gogglers. This is not
the national sport."

But within the church there was an audience of another kind. This
was of the other wounded men awaiting their turn. They lay on their
brown blankets in rows along the stone floor. Their eyes, too, were
fastened upon the operating-table, but—that was different. Meek-
eyed little yellow men lying on the floor awaiting their turns.

*   *   *

George Ade
The Fable of the Unintentional
Heroes of Centreville

In CENTREVILLE there lived two husky Young Fellows named Bill and Schuyler—commonly abbreviated to Schuy. They did not find any nourishing Excitement in a Grain Elevator, so they Enlisted to Free Cuba.

The Government gave each of them a Slouch Hat and a prehistoric Firearm. They tied Red Handkerchiefs around their Necks and started for the Front, each with his Head out of the Car Window. They gave the Sioux Yell to everybody along the Track between Centreville and Tampa.

While in Camp they played Double Pedie, smoked Corn-Cob Pipes, and cussed the Rations. They referred to the President of these United States as "Mac," and spoke of the beloved Secretary of War as "Old Alger."

After more or less Delay they went aboard a Boat, and were landed in Cuba, where they began to Shoot at everything that looked Foreign. The hot Rain drenched them, and the tropical Sun steamed them; they had Mud on their clothes, and had to sleep out. When they were unusually Tired and Hungry, they would sing Coon Songs and Roast the War Department.

At last they were ordered Home. On the way back they didn't think of Anything except their two Lady Friends, who worked in the Centreville Steam Laundry.

They rode into Town with a Machete under each Arm, and their Pockets full of Mauser Cartridges.

The first Thing they saw when they alighted from the Train was a Brass Band. It began to play, "See the Conquering Hero Comes."

Then eight Little Girls in White began to strew Flowers in their Pathway.

The Artillery company ripped out a Salute.

Chicago *Record*, August 30, 1899. Republished in *Fables in Slang* (Chicago, 1899), pp. 47–52. Text from *Fables in Slang*.

Cap Gibbs, who won his Title by owning the first Steam Thrash-
ing Machine ever seen in the County, confronted them with a Red,
White, and Blue Sash around him. He Barked in a loud Voice—it
was something about Old Glory.

Afterward the Daughters of the Revolution took them in Tow, and
escorted them to Pythian Hall, where they were given Fried Chicken,
Veal Loaf, Deviled Eggs, Crullers, Preserved Watermelon, Cottage
Cheese, Sweet Pickles, Grape Jelly, Soda Biscuit, Stuffed Mangoes,
Lemonade, Hickory-Nut Cake, Cookies, Cinnamon Roll, Lemon Pie,
Ham, Macaroons, New York Ice Cream, Apple Butter, Charlotte Russe,
Peppermint Wafers, and Coffee.

While they were Feeding, the Sons of Veterans Quartet stood on
the Rostrum with their Heads together, and sang:

> Ten-ting to-night! Ten-ting to-night,
> Ten-ting on the old-ah Campground!

At the first opportunity Bill motioned to Schuyler, and led him into
the Anteroom, where they kept the Regalia, the Kindling Wood, and
the Mop.

"Say, Schuy, what the Sam Hill does this mean?" he asked; "are we
Heroes?"

"That's what Everybody says."

"Do you Believe it?"

"No matter what I Believe; I'm goin' to let 'em have their own
Way. I may want to Run for Supervisor some Day.

MORAL: *If it is your Play to be a Hero, don't Renig.*

Elbert Hubbard
A Message to Garcia

IN ALL THIS Cuban business there is one man stands out on the horizon of my memory like Mars at perihelion.

Philistine, VIII (March, 1899), 109–16. Republished in *A Message to
Garcia* (East Aurora, N. Y., 1899). Text from *A Message to Garcia*.

The "fellow by the name of Rowan" was Lt. Andrew S. Rowan. As
Stewart Holbrook noted in his *Lost Men of American History* (1946),

When war broke out between Spain & the United States, it was very necessary to communicate quickly with the leader of the Insurgents. Garcia was somewhere in the mountain fastnesses of Cuba— no one knew where. No mail nor telegraph message could reach him. The President must secure his co-operation, and quickly.

What to do!

Some one said to the President, "There's a fellow by the name of Rowan will find Garcia for you, if anybody can."

Rowan was sent for and given a letter to be delivered to Garcia. How "the fellow by the name of Rowan" took the letter, sealed it up in an oil-skin pouch, strapped it over his heart, in four days landed by night off the coast of Cuba from an open boat, disappeared into the jungle & in three weeks came out on the other side of the Island, having traversed a hostile country on foot, and delivered his letter to Garcia, are things I have no special desire now to tell in detail.

The point I wish to make is this: McKinley gave Rowan a letter to be delivered to Garcia; Rowan took the letter & did not ask, "Where is he at?" By the Eternal! there is a man whose form should be cast in deathless bronze and the statue placed in every college of the land. It is not book-learning young men need, nor instruction about this and that, but a stiffening of the vertebrae which will cause them to be loyal to a trust, to act promptly, concentrate their energies: do the thing—"Carry a message to Garcia!"

General Garcia is dead now, but there are other Garcias.

No man, who has endeavored to carry out an enterprise where many hands were needed, but has been well nigh appalled at times by the imbecility of the average man—the inability or unwillingness to concentrate on a thing and do it.

Slip-shod assistance, foolish inattention, dowdy indifference, & half-hearted work seem the rule; and no man succeeds, unless by hook or crook, or threat, he forces or bribes other men to assist him; or mayhap, God in His goodness performs a miracle, & sends him an Angel of Light for an assistant. You, reader, put this matter to a test: You are sitting now in your office—six clerks are within call. Summon any one and make this request: "Please look in the encyclopedia and make a brief memorandum for me concerning the life of Correggio."

Will the clerk quietly say, "Yes sir," and go do the task?

Hubbard got most of his facts wrong. McKinley had nothing to do with Rowan's mission; Rowan sought out the Cuban insurgent leader Garcia before (not after) the outbreak of war; and Rowan's task was not to carry a message but to determine the strength of the rebel forces. Soon after the initial appearance of "A Message to Garcia," the New York Central Railroad ordered a half-million copies for distribution to its employees and other working men.

On your life he will not. He will look at you out of a fishy eye and ask one or more of the following questions:

Who was he?

Which encyclopedia?

Where is the encyclopedia?

Was I hired for that?

Don't you mean Bismarck?

What's the matter with Charlie doing it?

Is he dead?

Is there any hurry?

Shan't I bring you the book and let you look it up yourself?

What do you want to know for?

And I will lay you ten to one that after you have answered the questions, and explained how to find the information, and why you want it, the clerk will go off and get one of the other clerks to help him try to find Garcia—and then come back and tell you there is no such man. Of course I may lose my bet, but according to the Law of Averages, I will not.

Now if you are wise you will not bother to explain to your "assistant" that Correggio is indexed under the C's, not in the K's, but you will smile sweetly and say, "Never mind," and go look it up yourself.

And this incapacity for independent action, this moral stupidity, this infirmity of the will, this unwillingness to cheerfully catch hold and lift, are the things that put pure Socialism so far into the future. If men will not act for themselves, what will they do when the benefit of their effort is for all?

A first-mate with knotted club seems necessary; and the dread of getting "the bounce" Saturday night, holds many a worker to his place.

Advertise for a stenographer, and nine out of ten who apply, can neither spell nor punctuate—and do not think it necessary to.

Can such a one write a letter to Garcia?

"You see that book-keeper," said the foreman to me in a large factory.

"Yes, what about him?"

"Well, he's a fine accountant, but if I'd send him up town on an errand, he might accomplish the errand all right, and on the other hand, might stop at four saloons on the way, and when he got to Main Street, would forget what he had been sent for."

Can such a man be entrusted to carry a message to Garcia?

We have recently been hearing much maudlin sympathy expressed for the "down-trodden denizen of the sweatshop" and the "homeless wanderer searching for honest employment," & with it all often go many hard words for the men in power.

Nothing is said about the employer who grows old before his time in a vain attempt to get frowsy ne'er-do-wells to do intelligent work; and his long, patient striving with "help" that does nothing but loaf when his back is turned. In every store and factory there is a constant weeding-out process going on. The employer is constantly sending away "help" that have shown their incapacity to further the interests of the business, and others are being taken on. No matter how good times are, this sorting continues, only if times are hard and work is scarce, the sorting is done finer—but out and forever out, the incompetent and unworthy go. It is the survival of the fittest. Self-interest prompts every employer to keep the best—those who can carry a message to Garcia.

I know one man of really brilliant parts who has not the ability to manage a business of his own, and yet who is absolutely worthless to any one else, because he carries with him constantly the insane suspicion that his employer is oppressing, or intending to oppress him. He cannot give orders; and he will not receive them. Should a message be given him to take to Garcia, his answer would probably be, "Take it yourself, and be damned!"

To-night this man walks the streets looking for work, the wind whistling through his thread-bare coat. No one who knows him dare employ him, for he is a regular fire-brand of discontent. He is impervious to reason, and the only thing that can impress him is the toe of a thick-soled No. 9 boot.

Of course I know that one so morally deformed is no less to be pitied than a physical cripple; but in our pitying, let us drop a tear, too, for the men who are striving to carry on a great enterprise, whose working hours are not limited by the whistle, and whose hair is fast turning white through the struggle to hold in line dowdy indifference, slip-shod imbecility, and the heartless ingratitude, which, but for their enterprise, would be both hungry & homeless.

Have I put the matter too strongly? Possibly I have; but when all the world has gone a-slumming I wish to speak a word of sympathy for the man who succeeds—the man who, against great odds, has directed the efforts of others, and having succeeded, finds there's nothing in it: nothing but bare board and clothes.

I have carried a dinner pail & worked for day's wages, and I have also been an employer of labor, and I know there is something to be said on both sides. There is no excellence, per se, in poverty; rags are no recommendation; & all employers are not rapacious and high-handed, any more than all poor men are virtuous.

My heart goes out to the man who does his work when the "boss" is away, as well as when he is at home. And the man, who, when given a letter for Garcia, quietly takes the missive, without asking any idiotic questions, and with no lurking intention of chucking it into the nearest

sewer, or of doing aught else but deliver it, never gets "laid off," nor
has to go on a strike for higher wages. Civilization is one long anxious
search for just such individuals. Anything such a man asks shall be
granted; his kind is so rare that no employer can afford to let him go.
He is wanted in every city, town and village—in every office, shop,
store and factory. The world cries out for such: he is needed, &
needed badly—the man who can carry a message to Garcia.

Theodore Roosevelt
The Strenuous Life

IN SPEAKING TO YOU, men of the greatest city of the West, men of
the State which gave to the country Lincoln and Grant, men who pre-
eminently and distinctly embody all that is most American in the American character, I wish to preach, not the doctrine of ignoble ease,
but the doctrine of the strenuous life, the life of toil and effort, of
labor and strife; to preach that highest form of success which comes,
not to the man who desires mere easy peace, but to the man who
does not shrink from danger, from hardship, or from bitter toil, and
who out of these wins the splendid ultimate triumph.

A life of slothful ease, a life of that peace which springs merely from
lack either of desire or of power to strive after great things, is as little
worthy of a nation as of an individual. I ask only that what every
self-respecting American demands from himself and from his sons
shall be demanded of the American nation as a whole. Who among
you would teach your boys that ease, that peace, is to be the first consideration in their eyes—to be the ultimate goal after which they
strive? You men of Chicago have made this city great, you men of Illinois have done your share, and more than your share, in making
America great, because you neither preach nor practise such a doctrine. You work yourselves, and you bring up your sons to work. If
you are rich and are worth your salt, you will teach your sons that

Given as an address before the Hamilton Club of Chicago on April 10, 1899.
Published in The Strenuous Life: Essays and Addresses (New York, 1900),
pp. 1–10, 15–21. Text from The Strenuous Life.

though they may have leisure, it is not to be spent in idleness; for wisely used leisure merely means that those who possess it, being free from the necessity of working for their livelihood, are all the more bound to carry on some kind of non-remunerative work in science, in letters, in art, in exploration, in historical research—work of the type we most need in this country, the successful carrying out of which reflects most honor upon the nation. We do not admire the man of timid peace. We admire the man who embodies victorious effort; the man who never wrongs his neighbor, who is prompt to help a friend, but who has those virile qualities necessary to win in the stern strife of actual life. It is hard to fail, but it is worse never to have tried to succeed. In this life we get nothing save by effort. Freedom from effort in the present merely means that there has been stored up effort in the past. A man can be freed from the necessity of work only by the fact that he or his fathers before him have worked to good purpose. If the freedom thus purchased is used aright, and the man still does actual work, though of a different kind, whether as a writer or a general, whether in the field of politics or in the field of exploration and adventure, he shows he deserves his good fortune. But if he treats this period of freedom from the need of actual labor as a period, not of preparation, but of mere enjoyment, even though perhaps not of vicious enjoyment, he shows that he is simply a cumberer of the earth's surface, and he surely unfits himself to hold his own with his fellows if the need to do so should again arise. A mere life of ease is not in the end a very satisfactory life, and, above all, it is a life which ultimately unfits those who follow it for serious work in the world.

In the last analysis a healthy state can exist only when the men and women who make it up lead clean, vigorous, healthy lives; when the children are so trained that they shall endeavor, not to shirk difficulties, but to overcome them; not to seek ease, but to know how to wrest triumph from toil and risk. The man must be glad to do a man's work, to dare and endure and to labor; to keep himself, and to keep those dependent upon him. The woman must be the housewife, the helpmeet of the homemaker, the wise and fearless mother of many healthy children. In one of Daudet's powerful and melancholy books he speaks of "the fear of maternity, the haunting terror of the young wife of the present day." When such words can be truthfully written of a nation, that nation is rotten to the heart's core. When men fear work or fear righteous war, when women fear motherhood, they tremble on the brink of doom; and well it is that they should vanish from the earth, where they are fit subjects for the scorn of all men and women who are themselves strong and brave and high-minded.

As it is with the individual, so it is with the nation. It is a base untruth to say that happy is the nation that has no history. Thrice happy

is the nation that has a glorious history. Far better it is to dare mighty
things, to win glorious triumphs, even though checkered by failure,
than to take rank with those poor spirits who neither enjoy much nor
suffer much, because they live in the gray twilight that knows not
victory nor defeat. If in 1861 the men who loved the Union had believed that peace was the end of all things, and war and strife the
worst of all things, and had acted up to their belief, we would have
saved hundreds of thousands of lives, we would have saved hundreds
of millions of dollars. Moreover, besides saving all the blood and treasure we then lavished, we would have prevented the heartbreak of
many women, the dissolution of many homes, and we would have
spared the country those months of gloom and shame when it seemed
as if our armies marched only to defeat. We could have avoided all
this suffering simply by shrinking from strife. And if we had thus
avoided it, we would have shown that we were weaklings, and that
we were unfit to stand among the great nations of the earth. Thank
God for the iron in the blood of our fathers, the men who upheld the
wisdom of Lincoln, and bore sword or rifle in the armies of Grant! Let
us, the children of the men who proved themselves equal to the
mighty days, let us, the children of the men who carried the great
Civil War to a triumphant conclusion, praise the God of our fathers
that the ignoble counsels of peace were rejected; that the suffering
and loss, the blackness of sorrow and despair, were unflinchingly
faced, and the years of strife endured; for in the end the slave was
freed, the Union restored, and the mighty American republic placed
once more as a helmeted queen among nations.

We of this generation do not have to face a task such as that our
fathers faced, but we have our tasks, and woe to us if we fail to perform them! We cannot, if we would, play the part of China, and be
content to rot by inches in ignoble ease within our borders, taking no
interest in what goes on beyond them, sunk in a scrambling commercialism; heedless of the higher life, the life of aspiration, of toil and
risk, busying ourselves only with the wants of our bodies for the day,
until suddenly we should find, beyond a shadow of question, what
China has already found, that in this world the nation that has trained
itself to a career of unwarlike and isolated ease is bound, in the end,
to go down before other nations which have not lost the manly and
adventurous qualities. If we are to be a really great people, we must
strive in good faith to play a great part in the world. We cannot avoid
meeting great issues. All that we can determine for ourselves is whether
we shall meet them well or ill. In 1898 we could not help being
brought face to face with the problem of war with Spain. All we could
decide was whether we should shrink like cowards from the contest,
or enter into it as beseemed a brave and high-spirited people; and,

once in, whether failure or success should crown our banners. So it is now. We cannot avoid the responsibilities that confront us in Hawaii, Cuba, Porto Rico, and the Philippines. All we can decide is whether we shall meet them in a way that will redound to the national credit, or whether we shall make of our dealings with these new problems a dark and shameful page in our history. To refuse to deal with them at all merely amounts to dealing with them badly. We have a given problem to solve. If we undertake the solution, there is, of course, always danger that we may not solve it aright; but to refuse to undertake the solution simply renders it certain that we cannot possibly solve it aright. The timid man, the lazy man, the man who distrusts his country, the over-civilized man, who has lost the great fighting, masterful virtues, the ignorant man, and the man of dull mind, whose soul is incapable of feeling the mighty lift that thrills "stern men with empires in their brains"—all these, of course, shrink from seeing the nation undertake its new duties; shrink from seeing us build a navy and an army adequate to our needs; shrink from seeing us do our share of the world's work, by bringing order out of chaos in the great, fair tropic islands from which the valor of our soldiers and sailors has driven the Spanish flag. These are the men who fear the strenuous life, who fear the only national life which is really worth leading. They believe in that cloistered life which saps the hardy virtues in a nation, as it saps them in the individual; or else they are wedded to that base spirit of gain and greed which recognizes in commercialism the be-all and end-all of national life, instead of realizing that, though an indispensable element, it is, after all, but one of the many elements that go to make up true national greatness. No country can long endure if its foundations are not laid deep in the material prosperity which comes from thrift, from business energy and enterprise, from hard, unsparing effort in the fields of industrial activity; but neither was any nation ever yet truly great if it relied upon material prosperity alone. All honor must be paid to the architects of our material prosperity, to the great captains of industry who have built our factories and our railroads, to the strong men who toil for wealth with brain or hand; for great is the debt of the nation to these and their kind. But our debt is yet greater to the men whose highest type is to be found in a statesman like Lincoln, a soldier like Grant. They showed by their lives that they recognized the law of work, the law of strife, they toiled to win a competence for themselves and those dependent upon them; but they recognized that there were yet other and even loftier duties—duties to the nation and duties to the race.

We cannot sit huddled within our own borders and avow ourselves merely an assemblage of well-to-do hucksters who care nothing for what happens beyond. Such a policy would defeat even its own end;

for as the nations grow to have ever wider and wider interests, and are brought into closer and closer contact, if we are to hold our own in the struggle for naval and commercial supremacy, we must build up our power without our own borders. We must build the isthmian canal, and we must grasp the points of vantage which will enable us to have our say in deciding the destiny of the oceans of the East and the West.

So much for the commercial side. From the standpoint of international honor the argument is even stronger. The guns that thundered off Manila and Santiago left us echoes of glory, but they also left us a legacy of duty. If we drove out a medieval tyranny only to make room for savage anarchy, we had better not have begun the task at all. It is worse than idle to say that we have no duty to perform, and can leave to their fates the islands we have conquered. Such a course would be the course of infamy. It would be followed at once by utter chaos in the wretched islands themselves. Some stronger, manlier power would have to step in and do the work, and we would have shown ourselves weaklings, unable to carry to successful completion the labors that great and high-spirited nations are eager to undertake.

The work must be done; we cannot escape our responsibility; and if we are worth our salt, we shall be glad of the chance to do the work —glad of the chance to show ourselves equal to one of the great tasks set modern civilization. But let us not deceive ourselves as to the importance of the task. Let us not be misled by vainglory into underestimating the strain it will put on our powers. Above all, let us, as we value our own self-respect, face the responsibilities with proper seriousness, courage, and high resolve. We must demand the highest order of integrity and ability in our public men who are to grapple with these new problems. We must hold to a rigid accountability those public servants who show unfaithfulness to the interests of the nation or inability to rise to the high level of the new demands upon our strength and our resources.

*   *   *

The army and the navy are the sword and the shield which this nation must carry if she is to do her duty among the nations of the earth—if she is not to stand merely as the China of the western hemisphere. Our proper conduct toward the tropic islands we have wrested from Spain is merely the form which our duty has taken at the moment. Of course we are bound to handle the affairs of our own household well. We must see that there is civic honesty, civic cleanliness, civic good sense in our home administration of city, State, and nation. We must strive for honesty in office, for honesty toward the creditors of the nation and of the individual; for the widest freedom of individual initiative where possible, and for the wisest control of individual initiative where it is hostile to the welfare of the many. But because we set our own household in order we are not thereby excused from playing our part in the great affairs of the world. A man's first duty is to his own home, but he is not thereby excused from doing his duty to the State; for if he fails in this second duty it is under the penalty of ceasing to be a freeman. In the same way, while a nation's first duty is within its own borders, it is not thereby absolved from facing its duties in the world as a whole; and if it refuses to do so, it merely forfeits its right to struggle for a place among the peoples that shape the destiny of mankind.

In the West Indies and the Philippines alike we are confronted by most difficult problems. It is cowardly to shrink from solving them in the proper way; for solved they must be, if not by us, then by some stronger and more manful race. If we are too weak, too selfish, or too foolish to solve them, some bolder and abler people must undertake the solution. Personally, I am far too firm a believer in the greatness of my country and the power of my countrymen to admit for one moment that we shall ever be driven to the ignoble alternative.

The problems are different for the different islands. Porto Rico is not large enough to stand alone. We must govern it wisely and well, primarily in the interest of its own people. Cuba is, in my judgment, entitled ultimately to settle for itself whether it shall be an independent state or an integral portion of the mightiest of republics. But until order and stable liberty are secured, we must remain in the island to insure them, and infinite tact, judgment, moderation, and courage must be shown by our military and civil representatives in keeping the island pacified, in relentlessly stamping out brigandage, in protecting all alike, and yet in showing proper recognition to the men who have fought for Cuban liberty. The Philippines offer a yet graver problem. Their population includes half-caste and native Christians, warlike Moslems, and wild pagans. Many of their people are utterly unfit for self-government, and show no signs of becoming fit. Others may in time become fit but at present can only take part in self-government under a wise supervision, at once firm and beneficent. We have driven Spanish tyranny from the islands. If we now let it be replaced by savage anarchy, our work has been for harm and not for good. I have scant patience with those who fear to undertake the task of governing the Philippines, and who openly avow that they do fear to undertake it, or that they shrink from it because of the expense and trouble; but I have even scanter patience with those who make a pretense of humanitarianism to hide and cover their timidity, and who cant about "liberty" and the "consent of the governed," in order to excuse themselves for their unwillingness to play the part of men.

Their doctrines, if carried out, would make it incumbent upon us to leave the Apaches of Arizona to work out their own salvation, and to decline to interfere in a single Indian reservation. Their doctrines condemn your forefathers and mine for ever having settled in these United States.

England's rule in India and Egypt has been of great benefit to England, for it has trained up generations of men accustomed to look at the larger and loftier side of public life. It has been of even greater benefit to India and Egypt. And finally, and most of all, it has advanced the cause of civilization. So, if we do our duty aright in the Philippines, we will add to that national renown which is the highest and finest part of national life, will greatly benefit the people of the Philippine Islands, and, above all, we will play our part well in the great work of uplifting mankind. But to do this work, keep ever in mind that we must show in a very high degree the qualities of courage, of honesty, and of good judgment. Resistance must be stamped out. The first and all-important work to be done is to establish the supremacy of our flag. We must put down armed resistance before we can accomplish anything else, and there should be no parleying, no faltering, in dealing with our foe. As for those in our own country who encourage the foe, we can afford contemptuously to disregard them; but it must be remembered that their utterances are not saved from being treasonable merely by the fact that they are despicable.

When once we have put down armed resistance, when once our rule is acknowledged, then an even more difficult task will begin, for then we must see to it that the islands are administered with absolute honesty and with good judgment. If we let the public service of the islands be turned into the prey of the spoils politician, we shall have begun to tread the path which Spain trod to her own destruction. We must send out there only good and able men, chosen for their fitness, and not because of their partizan service, and these men must not only administer impartial justice to the natives and serve their own government with honesty and fidelity, but must show the utmost tact and firmness, remembering that, with such people as those with whom we are to deal, weakness is the greatest of crimes, and that next to weakness comes lack of consideration for their principles and prejudices.

I preach to you, then, my countrymen, that our country calls not for the life of ease but for the life of strenuous endeavor. The twentieth century looms before us big with the fate of many nations. If we stand idly by, if we seek merely swollen, slothful ease and ignoble peace, if we shrink from the hard contests where men must win at hazard of their lives and at the risk of all they hold dear, then the bolder and stronger peoples will pass us by, and will win for themselves the domination of the world. Let us therefore boldly face the life of strife, resolute to do our duty well and manfully; resolute to uphold righteousness by deed and by word; resolute to be both honest and brave, to serve high ideals, yet to use practical methods. Above all, let us shrink from no strife, moral or physical, within or without the nation, provided we are certain that the strife is justified, for it is only through strife, through hard and dangerous endeavor, that we shall ultimately win the goal of true national greatness.

Finley Peter Dunne
Expansion

"WHILE WE PLANT what Hogan calls th' starry banner iv Freedom in th' Ph'lippeens," said Mr. Dooley, "an' give th' sacred blessin' iv liberty to the poor, downtrodden people iv thim unfortunate isles,—dam thim!—we'll larn thim a lesson."

"Sure," said Mr. Hennessy, sadly, "we have a thing or two to larn oursilves."

"But it isn't f'r thim to larn us," said Mr. Dooley. " 'Tis not f'r thim wretched an' degraded crathers, without a mind or a shirt iv their own, f'r to give lessons in politeness an' liberty to a nation that mannyfacthers more dhressed beef than anny other imperyal nation in th' wurruld. We say to thim: 'Naygurs,' we say, 'poor, dissolute, uncovered wretches,' says we, 'whin th' crool hand iv Spain forged man'cles f'r ye'er limbs, as Hogan says, who was it crossed th' say an' shtruck off th' comealongs? We did,—by dad, we did. An' now, ye mis'rable, childish-minded apes, we propose f'r to larn ye th' uses iv liberty. In ivry city in this unfair land we will erect school-houses an' packin' houses an' houses iv correction; an' we'll larn ye our language, because 'tis aisier to larn ye ours than to larn oursilves yours. An' we'll give ye clothes, if ye pay f'r thim; an', if ye don't, ye can go without. An', whin ye're hungry, ye can go to th' morgue—we mane th' resth-

Mr. Dooley in the Hearts of His Countrymen (Boston, 1899), pp. 3–7. Text from this edition.

General Emilio Aguinaldo was the leader of the Philippine insurgents.

rant—an' ate a good square meal iv ar-rmy beef. An' we'll sind th' gr-reat Gin'ral Eagan over f'r to larn ye etiquette, an' Andhrew Carnegie to larn ye pathriteism with blow-holes into it, an' Gin'ral Alger to larn ye to hould onto a job; an', whin ye've become edycated an' have all th' blessin's iv civilization that we don't want, that'll count ye one. We can't give ye anny votes, because we haven't more thin enough to go round now; but we'll threat ye th' way a father shud threat his childher if we have to break ivry bone in ye'er bodies. So come to our ar-rms,' says we.

"But, glory be, 'tis more like a rasslin' match than a father's embrace. Up gets this little monkey iv an' Aggynaldoo, an' says he, 'Not for us,' he says. 'We thank ye kindly; but we believe,' he says, 'in pathronizin' home industhries,' he says. 'An',' he says, 'I have on hand,' he says, 'an' f'r sale,' he says, 'a very superyor brand iv home-made liberty, like ye'er mother used to make,' he says. ' 'Tis a long way fr'm ye'er plant to here,' he says, 'an' be th' time a cargo iv liberty,' he says, 'got out here an' was handled be th' middlemen,' he says, 'it might spoil,' he says. 'We don't want anny col' storage or embalmed liberty,' he says. 'What we want an' what th' ol' reliable house iv Aggynaldoo,' he says, 'supplies to th' thrade,' he says, 'is fr-esh liberty r-right off th' far-rm,' he says. 'I can't do annything with ye'er proposition,' he says. 'I can't give up,' he says, 'th' rights f'r which f'r five years I've fought an' bled ivry wan I cud reach,' he says. 'Onless,' he says, 'ye'd feel like buyin' out th' whole business,' he says. 'I'm a pathrite,' he says; 'but I'm no bigot,' he says.

"An' there it stands, Hinnissy, with th' indulgent parent kneelin' on th' stomach iv his adopted child, while a dillygation fr'm Boston bastes him with an umbrella. There it stands, an' how will it come out I dinnaw. I'm not much iv an expansionist mesilf. F'r th' las' tin years I've been thryin' to decide whether 'twud be good policy an' thrue to me thraditions to make this here bar two or three feet longer, an' manny's th' night I've laid awake tryin' to puzzle it out. But I don't know what to do with th' Ph'lippeens anny more thin I did las' summer, befure I heerd tell iv thim. We can't give thim to anny wan without makin' th' wan that gets thim feel th' way Doherty felt to Clancy whin Clancy med a frindly call an' give Doherty's childher th' measles. We can't sell thim, we can't ate thim, an' we can't throw thim into th' alley whin no wan is lookin'. An' 'twud be a disgrace f'r to lave befure we've pounded these frindless an' ongrateful people into insinsibility. So I suppose, Hinnissy, we'll have to stay an' do th' best we can an' lave Andhrew Carnegie secede fr'm th' Union. They's wan consolation; an' that is, if th' American people can govern thimsilves, they can govern annything that walks."

"An' what 'd ye do with Aggy—what-d'ye-call-him?" asked Mr. Hennessy.

"Well," Mr. Dooley replied, with brightening eyes, "I know what they'd do with him in this ward. They'd give that pathrite what he asks, an' thin they'd throw him down an' take it away fr'm him."

Platform of the American
Anti-Imperialist League

WE HOLD THAT the policy known as imperialism is hostile to liberty and tends toward militarism, an evil from which it has been our glory to be free. We regret that it has become necessary in the land of Washington and Lincoln to reaffirm that all men, of whatever race or color, are entitled to life, liberty, and the pursuit of happiness. We maintain that governments derive their just powers from the consent of the governed. We insist that the subjugation of any people is "criminal aggression" and open disloyalty to the distinctive principles of our Government.

We earnestly condemn the policy of the present National Administration in the Philippines. It seeks to extinguish the spirit of 1776 in those islands. We deplore the sacrifice of our soldiers and sailors, whose bravery deserves admiration even in an unjust war. We denounce the slaughter of the Filipinos as a needless horror. We protest against the extension of American sovereignty by Spanish methods.

We demand the immediate cessation of the war against liberty, begun by Spain and continued by us. We urge that Congress be promptly convened to announce to the Filipinos our purpose to concede to them the independence for which they have so long fought and which of right is theirs.

The United States have always protested against the doctrine of

Republished in *Documents of American History,* ed. Henry Steele Commager, 6th ed. (New York, 1958), II, 192–93. Text from this edition.

The platform was adopted on October 18, 1899, at the Anti-Imperialist Congress in Chicago.

international law which permits the subjugation of the weak by the strong. A self-governing state cannot accept sovereignty over an unwilling people. The United States cannot act upon the ancient heresy that might makes right.

Imperialists assume that with the destruction of self-government in the Philippines by American hands, all opposition here will cease. This is a grievous error. Much as we abhor the war of "criminal aggression" in the Philippines, greatly as we regret that the blood of the Filipinos is on American hands, we more deeply resent the betrayal of American institutions at home. The real firing line is not in the suburbs of Manila. The foe is of our own household. The attempt of 1861 was to divide the country. That of 1899 is to destroy its fundamental principles and noblest ideals.

Whether the ruthless slaughter of the Filipinos shall end next month or next year is but an incident in a contest that must go on until the Declaration of Independence and the Constitution of the United States are rescued from the hands of their betrayers. Those who dispute about standards of value while the Republic is undermined will be listened to as little as those who would wrangle about the small economies of the household while the house is on fire. The training of a great people for a century, the aspiration for liberty of a vast immigration are forces that will hurl aside those who in the delirium of conquest seek to destroy the character of our institutions.

We deny that the obligation of all citizens to support their Government in times of grave National peril applies to the present situation. If an Administration may with impunity ignore the issues upon which it was chosen, deliberately create a condition of war anywhere on the face of the globe, debauch the civil service for spoils to promote the adventure, organize a truth-suppressing censorship and demand of all citizens a suspension of judgement and their unanimous support while it chooses to continue the fighting, representative government itself is imperiled.

We propose to contribute to the defeat of any person or party that stands for the forcible subjugation of any people. We shall oppose for reëlection all who in the White House or in Congress betray American liberty in pursuit of un-American gains. We still hope that both of our great political parties will support and defend the Declaration of Independence in the closing campaign of the century.

We hold, with Abraham Lincoln, that "no man is good enough to govern another man without that man's consent. When the white man governs himself, that is self-government, but when he governs himself and also governs another man, that is more than self-government— that is despotism." "Our reliance is in the love of liberty which God has planted in us. Our defense is in the spirit which prizes liberty as the heritage of all men in all lands. Those who deny freedom to others deserve it not for themselves, and under a just God cannot long retain it."

We cordially invite the coöperation of all men and women who remain loyal to the Declaration of Independence and the Constitution of the United States.

William Vaughn Moody
On a Soldier Fallen in the Philippines

Streets of the roaring town,
Hush for him, hush, be still!
He comes, who was stricken down
Doing the word of our will.
Hush! Let him have his state,
Give him his soldier's crown.
The grists of trade can wait
Their grinding at the mill,
But he cannot wait for his honor, now the trumpet has been blown.
Wreathe pride now for his granite brow, lay love on his breast of stone.

Toll! Let the great bells toll
Till the clashing air is dim.
Did we wrong this parted soul?
We will make it up to him.
Toll! Let him never guess
What work we set him to.
Laurel, laurel, yes;
He did what we bade him do.
Praise, and never a whispered hint but the fight he fought was good;
Never a word that the blood on his sword was his country's own heart's-
    blood.

Atlantic Monthly, LXXXVII (February, 1901), 288. Republished in *Poems* (Boston, 1901), pp. 24–25. Text from *Poems.*

A flag for the soldier's bier
Who dies that his land may live;
O, banners, banners here,
That he doubt not nor misgive!
That he heed not from the tomb
The evil days draw near
When the nation, robed in gloom,
With its faithless past shall strive.
Let him never dream that his bullet's scream went wide of its island
*   mark,*
Home to the heart of his darling land where she stumbled and sinned
*   in the dark.*

Ernest Crosby

The Real "White Man's Burden"
With apologies to Rudyard Kipling

Take up the White Man's burden.
*   Send forth your sturdy kin,*
And load them down with Bibles
*   And cannon-balls and gin.*
Throw in a few diseases
*   To spread the tropic climes,*
For there the healthy niggers
*   Are quite behind the times.*

And don't forget the factories.
*   On those benighted shores*
They have no cheerful iron mills,
*   Nor eke department stores.*
They never work twelve hours a day,
*   And live in strange content,*

Swords and Plowshares (New York, 1902), pp. 33–35. Text from this
edition.

Altho they never have to pay
    A single sou of rent.

Take up the White Man's burden,
    And teach the Philippines
What interest and taxes are
    And what a mortgage means.
Give them electrocution chairs,
    And prisons, too, galore,
And if they seem inclined to kick,
    Then spill their heathen gore.

They need our labor question, too,
    And politics and fraud—
We've made a pretty mess at home,
    Let's make a mess abroad.
And let use ever humbly pray
    The Lord of Hosts may deign
To stir our feeble memories
    Lest we forget—the Maine.

Take up the White Man's burden.
    To you who thus succeed
In civilizing savage hordes,
    They owe a debt, indeed;
Concessions, pensions, salaries,
    And privilege and right—
With outstretched hands you raised to bless
    Grab everything in sight.

Take up the White Man's burden.
    And if you write in verse,
Flatter your nation's vices
    And strive to make them worse.
Then learn that if with pious words
    You ornament each phrase,
In a world of canting hypocrites
    This kind of business pays.

Part Nine

THE SENSE OF
THE TRAGIC

Ambrose Bierce, *One of the Missing*
Sarah Orne Jewett, *Poor Joanna*
Stephen Crane, *The Open Boat*
Theodore Dreiser, *Nigger Jeff*

The stories which conclude this collection are major works by four of the best writers to emerge during the 1890's. Stephen Crane's "The Open Boat" is often considered his most finished work of fiction, while Ambrose Bierce's "One of the Missing" and Sarah Orne Jewett's "Poor Joanna" are from the writers' best single volumes—*Tales of Soldiers and Civilians* and *The Country of the Pointed Firs*. Theodore Dreiser's "Nigger Jeff" is not as well known as his novels *Sister Carrie* and *An American Tragedy,* but it contains many of the same themes. The stories are strikingly different in form and technique, ranging from the contrived tensions of Bierce's tale to Miss Jewett's relaxed, indirect narrative, from Crane's tendency toward allegory to Dreiser's "realism" of incident and detail. But despite these and other differences, the stories contain a significant common element—their author's sense of the tragic nature of experience.

This belief that the great realities of life are often those of pain, suffering, and death does not appear as a dominant theme in the work of the major writers of the 1870's and 80's—Mark Twain, Henry James, and William Dean Howells. Although the "new" writers of the 1890's were less skilled than their predecessors in many aspects of fiction, they reasserted a sense of tragedy in life. Of course, each writer expressed his own distinctive vision. Bierce and Crane saw a tragic fatality, whether cruelly grotesque or coldly indifferent in its effect, present in all life; their work is appropriately "cosmic" in its allusions to "Powers" and to gods of Nature. For Jewett and Dreiser, life's pain and suffering have their roots in the actualities of a moment—the decay and death of an area and its values, or the surge of sex in a youth on a spring morning.

In all of these stories, the principal tragic figures are neither heroic nor noble in any conventional or traditional senses of these terms. But whether the doomed figure is a cocky private, a farmer's daughter, a ship's oiler, or an ignorant Negro, he is rendered significant by his human capacity to feel pain and to die. It is Dreiser who above all makes explicit this new vision of the tragic by the device of an initiation story involving a reporter (that is, a kind of artist) and a Negro made brute-like by fear. For the reporter Davies comes to realize the "tragedy" of Jeff's fate and will try to "get it all in" his story.

The writers of the 1890's were coming increasingly to probe the common and the low for the tragic nature of life, as so many writers have done in our own time. But they discovered not only the pain and violence at the heart of life but also a compensating community of spirit at this center—a sense of oneness in travail which was expressed as Crane's "subtle brotherhood of men," Jewett's warmhearted women of Dunnet Landing, and Dreiser's theme of the indestructibility of family love and loyalty. In the 1890's the tragic sense of life took new and unusual forms, but it still contained that profound ambivalence of response to human nature and experience which has always characterized the tragic vision.

Ambrose Bierce
One of the Missing

JEROME SEARING, a private soldier of General Sherman's army, then confronting the enemy at and about Kenesaw Mountain, Georgia, turned his back upon a small group of officers, with whom he had been talking in low tones, stepped across a light line of earthworks, and disappeared in a forest. None of the men in line behind the works had said a word to him, nor had he so much as nodded to them in passing, but all who saw understood that this brave man had been intrusted with some perilous duty. Jerome Searing, though a private, did not serve in the ranks; he was detailed for service at division headquarters, being borne upon the rolls as an orderly. "Orderly" is a word covering a multitude of duties. An orderly may be a messenger, a clerk, an officer's servant—anything. He may perform services for which no provision is made in orders and army regulations. Their nature may depend upon his aptitude, upon favor, upon accident. Private Searing, an incomparable marksman, young—it is surprising how young we all were in those days—hardy, intelligent, and insensible to fear, was a scout. The general commanding his division was not content to obey orders blindly without knowing what was in his front, even when his command was not on detached service, but formed a fraction of the line of the army; nor was he satisfied to receive his knowledge of his *vis-a-vis* through the customary channels; he wanted to know more than he was apprised of by the corps commander and the collisions of pickets and skirmishers. Hence Jerome Searing—with his extraordinary daring, his woodcraft, his sharp eyes and truthful tongue. On this occasion his instructions were simple: to get as near the enemy's lines as possible and learn all that he could.

In a few moments he had arrived at the picket line, the men on duty there lying in groups of from two to four behind little banks of earth scooped out of the slight depression in which they lay, their rifles protruding from the green boughs with which they had masked their

San Francisco *Examiner*, March 11, 1888. Republished in *Tales of Soldiers and Civilians* (San Francisco, 1891), pp. 69–91. Text from *Tales of Soldiers and Civilians*.

small defenses. The forest extended without a break toward the front, so solemn and silent that only by an effort of the imagination could it be conceived as populous with armed men, alert and vigilant—a forest formidable with possibilities of battle. Pausing a moment in one of these rifle pits to apprise the men of his intention, Searing crept stealthily forward on his hands and knees and was soon lost to view in a dense thicket of underbrush.

"That is the last of him," said one of the men; "I wish I had his rifle; those fellows will hurt some of us with it."

Searing crept on, taking advantage of every accident of ground and growth to give himself better cover. His eyes penetrated everywhere, his ears took note of every sound. He stilled his breathing, and at the cracking of a twig beneath his knee stopped his progress and hugged the earth. It was slow work but not tedious; the danger made it exciting, but by no physical signs was the excitement manifest. His pulse was as regular, his nerves were as steady, as if he were trying to trap a sparrow.

"It seems a long time," he thought, "but I cannot have come very far; I am still alive."

He smiled at his own method of estimating distance, and crept forward. A moment later he suddenly flattened himself upon the earth and lay motionless, minute after minute. Through a narrow opening in the bushes he had caught sight of a small mound of yellow clay— one of the enemy's rifle pits. After some little time he cautiously raised his head, inch by inch, then his body upon his hands, spread out on each side of him, all the while intently regarding the hillock of clay. In another moment he was upon his feet, rifle in hand, striding rapidly forward with little attempt at concealment. He had rightly interpreted the signs, whatever they were; the enemy was gone.

To assure himself beyond a doubt before going back to report upon so important a matter, Searing pushed forward across the line of abandoned pits, running from cover to cover in the more open forest, his eyes vigilant to discover possible stragglers. He came to the edge of a plantation—one of those forlorn, deserted homesteads of the last years of the war, upgrown with brambles, ugly with broken fences, and desolate with vacant buildings having blank apertures in place of doors and windows. After a keen reconnoissance from the safe seclusion of a clump of young pines, Searing ran lightly across a field and through an orchard to a small structure which stood apart from the other farm buildings, on a slight elevation, which he thought would enable him to overlook a large scope of country in the direction that he supposed the enemy to have taken in withdrawing. This building, which had originally consisted of a single room, elevated upon four posts about ten feet high, was now little more than a roof; the floor had fallen away, the joists and planks loosely piled on the ground below or resting on end at various angles, not wholly torn from their fastenings above. The supporting posts were themselves no longer vertical. It looked as if the whole edifice would go down at the touch of a finger. Concealing himself in the debris of joists and flooring, Searing looked across the open ground between his point of view and a spur of Kenesaw Mountain, a half mile away. A road leading up and across this spur was crowded with troops—the rear guard of the retiring enemy, their gun barrels gleaming in the morning sunlight.

Searing had now learned all that he could hope to know. It was his duty to return to his own command with all possible speed and report his discovery. But the gray column of infantry toiling up the mountain road was singularly tempting. His rifle—an ordinary "Springfield," but fitted with a globe sight and hair trigger—would easily send its ounce and a quarter of lead hissing into their midst. That would probably not affect the duration and result of the war, but it is the business of a soldier to kill. It is also his pleasure if he is a good soldier. Searing cocked his rifle and "set" the trigger.

But it was decreed from the beginning of time that Private Searing was not to murder anybody that bright summer morning, nor was the Confederate retreat to be announced by him. For countless ages events had been so matching themselves together in that wondrous mosaic to some parts of which, dimly discernible, we give the name of history, that the acts which he had in will would have marred the harmony of the pattern.

Some twenty-five years previously the Power charged with the execution of the work according to the design had provided against that mischance by causing the birth of a certain male child in a little village at the foot of the Carpathian Mountains, had carefully reared it, supervised its education, directed its desires into a military channel, and in due time made it an officer of artillery. By the concurrence of an infinite number of favoring influences and their preponderance over an infinite number of opposing ones, this officer of artillery had been made to commit a breach of discipline and fly from his native country to avoid punishment. He had been directed to New Orleans (instead of New York) where a recruiting officer awaited him on the wharf. He was enlisted and promoted, and things were so ordered that he now commanded a Confederate battery some three miles along the line from where Jerome Searing, the Federal scout, stood cocking his rifle. Nothing had been neglected—at every step in the progress of both these men's lives, and in the lives of their ancestors and contemporaries, and of the lives of the contemporaries of their ancestors—the right thing had been done to bring about the desired result. Had anything in all this vast concatenation been overlooked, Private Searing might have fired on the retreating Confederates that morning, and would perhaps have missed. As it fell out, a captain of artillery, having nothing better to do while awaiting his turn to pull out and be off, amused himself by sighting a field piece obliquely to his right at what he took to be some Federal officers on the crest of a hill, and discharged it. The shot flew high of its mark.

As Jerome Searing drew back the hammer of his rifle, and, with his eyes upon the distant Confederates, considered where he could plant his shot with the best hope of making a widow or an orphan or a childless mother—perhaps all three, for Private Searing, although he had repeatedly refused promotion, was not without a certain kind of ambition—he heard a rushing sound in the air, like that made by the wings of a great bird swooping down upon its prey. More quickly than he could apprehend the gradation, it increased to a hoarse and horrible roar, as the missile that made it sprang at him out of the sky, striking with a deafening impact one of the posts supporting the confusion of timbers above him, smashing it into matchwood, and bringing down the crazy edifice with a loud clatter, in clouds of blinding dust!

Lieutenant Adrian Searing, in command of the picket guard on that part of the line through which his brother Jerome had passed on his mission, sat with attentive ears in his breastwork behind the line. Not the faintest sound escaped him; the cry of a bird, the barking of a squirrel, the noise of the wind among the pines—all were anxiously noted by his overstrained sense. Suddenly, directly in front of his line, he heard a faint, confused rumble, like the clatter of a falling building translated by distance. At the same moment an officer approached him on foot from the rear and saluted.

"Lieutenant," said the aide, "the colonel directs you to move forward your line and feel the enemy if you find him. If not, continue the advance until directed to halt. There is reason to think that the enemy has retreated."

The lieutenant nodded and said nothing; the other officer retired. In a moment the men, apprised of their duty by the non-commissioned officers in low tones, had deployed from their rifle pits and were moving forward in skirmishing order, with set teeth and beating hearts. The lieutenant mechanically looked at his watch. Six o'clock and eighteen minutes.

When Jerome Searing recovered consciousness, he did not at once understand what had occurred. It was, indeed, some time before he opened his eyes. For a while he believed that he had died and been buried, and he tried to recall some portions of the burial service. He thought that his wife was kneeling upon his grave, adding her weight to that of the earth upon his breast. The two of them, widow and earth, had crushed his coffin. Unless the children should persuade her to go home, he would not much longer be able to breathe. He felt a sense of wrong. "I cannot speak to her," he thought; "the dead have no voice; and if I open my eyes I shall get them full of earth."

He opened his eyes—a great expanse of blue sky, rising from a fringe of the tops of trees. In the foreground, shutting out some of the trees, a high, dun mound, angular in outline and crossed by an intricate, patternless system of straight lines; in the center a bright ring of metal—the whole an immeasurable distance away—a distance so inconceivably great that it fatigued him, and he closed his eyes. The moment that he did so he was conscious of an insufferable light. A sound was in his ears like the low, rhythmic thunder of a distant sea breaking in successive waves upon the beach, and out of this noise, seeming a part of it, or possibly coming from beyond it, and intermingled with its ceaseless undertone, came the articulate words: "Jerome Searing, you are caught like a rat in a trap—in a trap, trap, trap."

Suddenly there fell a great silence, a black darkness, an infinite tranquillity, and Jerome Searing, perfectly conscious of his rathood, and well assured of the trap that he was in, remembered all, and, nowise alarmed, again opened his eyes to reconnoitre, to note the strength of his enemy, to plan his defense.

He was caught in a reclining posture, his back firmly supported by a solid beam. Another lay across his breast, but he had been able to shrink a little away from it so that it no longer oppressed him, though it was immovable. A brace joining it at an angle had wedged him against a pile of boards on his left, fastening the arm on that side. His legs, slightly parted and straight along the ground, were covered upward to the knees with a mass of débris which towered above his narrow horizon. His head was as rigidly fixed as in a vice; he could move his eyes, his chin—no more. Only his right arm was partly free. "You must help us out of this," he said to it. But he could not get it from under the heavy timber athwart his chest, nor move it outward more than six inches at the elbow.

Searing was not seriously injured, nor did he suffer pain. A smart rap on the head from a flying fragment of the splintered post, incurred simultaneously with the frightfully sudden shock to the nervous system, had momentarily dazed him. His term of unconsciousness, including the period of recovery, during which he had had the strange fancies, had probably not exceeded a few seconds, for the dust of the wreck had not wholly cleared away as he began an intelligent survey of the situation.

With his partly free right hand he now tried to get hold of the beam which lay across, but not quite against, his breast. In no way could he do so. He was unable to depress the shoulder so as to push the elbow beyond that edge of the timber which was nearest his knees; failing in that, he could not raise the forearm and hand to grasp the beam. The brace that made an angle with it downward and backward prevented him from doing anything in that direction, and between it and his body the space was not half as wide as the length of his forearm. Obviously he could not get his hand under the beam nor over it; he could not, in fact, touch it at all. Having demonstrated his inability, he desisted, and began to think if he could reach any of the débris piled upon his legs.

In surveying the mass with a view to determining that point, his attention was arrested by what seemed to be a ring of shining metal immediately in front of his eyes. It appeared to him at first to surround some perfectly black substance, and it was somewhat more than a half inch in diameter. It suddenly occurred to his mind that the blackness was simply shadow, and that the ring was in fact the muzzle of his rifle protruding from the pile of débris. He was not long in satisfying himself that this was so—if it was a satisfaction. By closing either eye he could look a little way along the barrel—to the point where it was hidden by the rubbish that held it. He could see the one side, with the corresponding eye, at apparently the same angle as the other side with the other eye. Looking with the right eye, the weapon seemed to be directed at a point to the left of his head, and *vice versa*. He was unable to see the upper surface of the barrel, but could see the under surface of the stock at a slight angle. The piece was, in fact, aimed at the exact center of his forehead.

In the perception of this circumstance, in the recollection that just previously to the mischance of which this uncomfortable situation was the result, he had cocked the gun and set the trigger so that a touch would discharge it. Private Searing was affected with a feeling of uneasiness. But that was as far as possible from fear; he was a brave man, somewhat familiar with the aspect of rifles from that point of view, and of cannon, too; and now he recalled, with something like amusement, an incident of his experience at the storming of Missionary Ridge, where, walking up to one of the enemy's embrasures from which he had seen a heavy gun throw charge after charge of grape among the assailants, he thought for a moment that the piece had been withdrawn; he could see nothing in the opening but a brazen circle. What that was he had understood just in time to step aside as it pitched another peck of iron down that swarming slope. To face firearms is one of the commonest incidents in a soldier's life—firearms, too, with malevolent eyes blazing behind them. That is what a soldier is for. Still, Private Searing did not altogether relish the situation, and turned away his eyes.

After groping, aimless, with his right hand for a time, he made an ineffectual attempt to release his left. Then he tried to disengage his head, the fixity of which was the more annoying from his ignorance of what held it. Next he tried to free his feet, but while exerting the powerful muscles of his legs for that purpose it occurred to him that a disturbance of the rubbish which held them might discharge the rifle; how it could have endured what had already befallen it he could not understand, although memory assisted him with various instances in point. One in particular he recalled, in which, in a moment of mental abstraction, he had clubbed his rifle and beaten out another gentleman's brains, observing afterward that the weapon which he had been diligently swinging by the muzzle was loaded, capped, and at full cock—knowledge of which circumstance would doubtless have cheered his antagonist to longer endurance. He had always smiled in recalling that blunder of his "green and salad days" as a soldier, but now he did not smile. He turned his eyes again to the muzzle of the gun, and for a moment fancied that it had moved; it seemed somewhat nearer.

Again he looked away. The tops of the distant trees beyond the bounds of the plantation interested him; he had not before observed how light and feathery they seemed, nor how darkly blue the sky was, even among their branches, where they somewhat paled it with their green; above him it appeared almost black. "It will be uncomfortably hot here," he thought, "as the day advances. I wonder which way I am looking."

Judging by such shadows as he could see, he decided that his face was due north; he would at least not have the sun in his eyes, and north—well, that was toward his wife and children.

"Bah!" he exclaimed aloud, "what have they to do with it?"

He closed his eyes. "As I can't get out, I may as well go to sleep. The rebels are gone, and some of our fellows are sure to stray out here foraging. They'll find me."

But he did not sleep. Gradually he became sensible of a pain in his forehead—a dull ache, hardly perceptible at first, but growing more and more uncomfortable. He opened his eyes and it was gone—closed them and it returned. "The devil!" he said, irrelevantly, and stared again at the sky. He heard the singing of birds, the strange metallic note of the meadow lark, suggesting the clash of vibrant blades. He fell into pleasant memories of his childhood, played again with his brother and sister, raced across the fields, shouting to alarm the sedentary larks, entered the somber forest beyond, and with timid steps

followed the faint path to Ghost Rock, standing at last with audible
heart throbs before the Dead Man's Cave and seeking to penetrate
its awful mystery. For the first time he observed that the opening of
the haunted cavern was encircled by a ring of metal. Then all else
vanished and left him gazing into the barrel of his rifle as before. But
whereas before it had seemed nearer, it now seemed an inconceivable
distance away, and all the more sinister for that. He cried out, and,
startled by something in his own voice—the note of fear—lied to himself in denial: "If I don't sing out I may stay here till I die."

He now made no further attempt to evade the menacing stare
of the gun barrel. If he turned away his eyes an instant it was to look
for assistance (although he could not see the ground on either side
the ruin), and he permitted them to return, obedient to the imperative
fascination. If he closed them, it was from weariness, and instantly the
poignant pain in his forehead—the prophecy and menace of the bullet
—forced him to reopen them.

The tension of nerve and brain was too severe; nature came to his
relief with intervals of unconsciousness. Reviving from one of these,
he became sensible of a sharp, smarting pain in his right hand, and
when he worked his fingers together, or rubbed his palm with them,
he could feel that they were wet and slippery. He could not see the
hand, but he knew the sensation; it was running blood. In his delirium
he had beaten it against the jagged fragments of the wreck, had
clutched it full of splinters. He resolved that he would meet his fate
more manly. He was a plain, common soldier, had no religion and not
much philosophy; he could not die like a hero, with great and wise
last words, even if there were someone to hear them, but he could
die "game," and he would. But if he could only know when to expect
the shot!

Some rats which had probably inhabited the shed came sneaking
and scampering about. One of them mounted the pile of débris that
held the rifle; another followed, and another. Searing regarded them
at first with indifference, then with friendly interest; then, as the
thought flashed into his bewildered mind that they might touch the
trigger of his rifle, he screamed at them to go away. "It is no business
of yours," he cried.

The creatures left; they would return later, attack his face, gnaw
away his nose, cut his throat—he knew that, but he hoped by that
time to be dead.

Nothing could now unfix his gaze from the little ring of metal with
its black interior. The pain in his forehead was fierce and constant. He
felt it gradually penetrating the brain more and more deeply, until at
last its progress was arrested by the wood at the back of his head. It
grew momentarily more insufferable; he began wantonly beating his

lacerated hand against the splinters again to counteract that horrible
ache. It seemed to throb with a slow, regular, recurrence each pulsation sharper than the preceding, and sometimes he cried out, thinking
he felt the fatal bullet. No thoughts of home, of wife and children, of
country, of glory. The whole record of memory was effaced. The world
had passed away—not a vestige remained. Here in this confusion of
timbers and boards is the sole universe. Here is immortality in
time—each pain an everlasting life. The throbs tick off eternities.

Jerome Searing, the man of courage, the formidable enemy, the
strong, resolute warrior, was as pale as a ghost. His jaw was fallen; his
eyes protruded; he trembled in every fiber; a cold sweat bathed his
entire body; he screamed with fear. He was not insane—he was terrified.

In groping about with his torn and bleeding hand he seized at
last a strip of board, and, pulling, felt it give way. It lay parallel with
his body, and by bending his elbow as much as the contracted space
would permit, he could draw it a few inches at a time. Finally it was
altogether loosened from the wreckage covering his legs; he could lift
it clear of the ground its whole length. A great hope came into his
mind: perhaps he could work it upward, that is to say backward, far
enough to lift the end and push aside the rifle; or, if that were too
tightly wedged, so hold the strip of board as to deflect the bullet. With
this object he passed it backward inch by inch, hardly daring to breathe
lest that act somehow defeat his intent, and more than ever unable to
remove his eyes from the rifle, which might perhaps now hasten to
improve its waning opportunity. Something at least had been gained;
in the occupation of his mind in this attempt at self-defense he was less
sensible of the pain in his head and had ceased to scream. But he was
still dreadfully frightened and his teeth rattled like castanets.

The strip of board ceased to move to the suasion of his hand. He
tugged at it with all his strength, changed the direction of its length
all he could, but it had met some extended obstruction behind him,
and the end in front was still too far away to clear the pile of débris
and reach the muzzle of the gun. It extended, indeed, nearly as far
as the trigger guard, which, uncovered by the rubbish, he could imperfectly see with his right eye. He tried to break the strip with his
hand, but had no leverage. Perceiving his defeat, all his terror returned, augmented tenfold. The black aperture of the rifle appeared to
threaten a sharper and more imminent death in punishment of his
rebellion. The track of the bullet through his head ached with an in-
tenser anguish. He began to tremble again.

Suddenly he became composed. His tremor subsided. He clinched
his teeth and drew down his eyebrows. He had not exhausted his means
of defense; a new design had shaped itself in his mind—another plan

of battle. Raising the front end of the strip of board, he carefully
pushed it forward through the wreckage at the side of the rifle
until it pressed against the trigger guard. Then he moved the end
slowly outward until he could feel that it had cleared it, then, closing
his eyes, thrust it against the trigger with all his strength! There was
no explosion; the rifle had been discharged as it dropped from his
hand when the building fell. But Jerome Searing was dead.

A line of Federal skirmishers swept across the plantation toward the
mountain. They passed on both sides of the wrecked building, observing nothing. At a short distance in their rear came their commander, Lieutenant Adrian Searing. He casts his eyes curiously upon
the ruin and sees a dead body half buried in boards and timbers. It
is so covered with dust that its clothing is Confederate gray. Its face
is yellowish white; the cheeks are fallen in, the temples sunken, too,
with sharp ridges about them, making the forehead forbiddingly
narrow; the upper lip, slightly lifted, shows the white teeth, rigidly
clinched. The hair is heavy with moisture, the face as wet as the dewy
grass all about. From his point of view the officer does not observe the
rifle; the man was apparently killed by the fall of the building.

"Dead a week," said the officer curtly, moving on mechanically
pulling out his watch as if to verify his estimate of time. Six o'clock and
forty minutes.

Sarah Orne Jewett
Poor Joanna

ONE EVENING my ears caught a mysterious allusion which Mrs. Todd
made to Shell-heap Island. It was a chilly night of cold northeasterly
rain, and I made a fire for the first time in the Franklin stove in my

Atlantic Monthly, LXXVIII (July, 1896), 78–88. Republished in *The
Country of the Pointed Firs* (Boston, 1896), pp. 98–126. Text from *The
Country of the Pointed Firs*.

The narrator of "Poor Joanna" is a summer visitor to Dunnet Landing
who has taken a room in Mrs. Todd's house. Mrs. Todd, an amateur
herbalist, prepares syrups and medicines for the local population.

room, and begged my two housemates to come in and keep me company. The weather had convinced Mrs. Todd that it was time to make a supply of cough-drops, and she had been bringing forth herbs from dark and dry hiding-places, until now the pungent dust and odor of them had resolved themselves into one mighty flavor of spearmint that came from a simmering caldron of syrup in the kitchen. She called it done, and well done, and had ostentatiously left it to cool, and taken her knitting-work because Mrs. Fosdick was busy with hers. They sat in the two rocking-chairs, the small woman and the large one, but now and then I could see that Mrs. Todd's thoughts remained with the cough-drops. The time of gathering herbs was nearly over, but the time of syrups and cordials had begun.

The heat of the open fire made us a little drowsy, but something in the way Mrs. Todd spoke of Shell-heap Island waked my interest. I waited to see if she would say any more, and then took a roundabout way back to the subject by saying what was first in my mind: that I wished the Green Island family were there to spend the evening with us,—Mrs. Todd's mother and her brother William.

Mrs. Todd smiled, and drummed on the arm of the rocking-chair. "Might scare William to death," she warned me; and Mrs. Fosdick mentioned her intention of going out to Green Island to stay two or three days, if this wind didn't make too much sea.

"Where is Shell-heap Island?" I ventured to ask, seizing the opportunity.

"Bears nor'east somewheres about three miles from Green Island; right off-shore, I should call it about eight miles out," said Mrs. Todd. "You never was there, dear; 't is off the thoroughfares, and a very bad place to land at best."

"I should think 't was," agreed Mrs. Fosdick, smoothing down her black silk apron. "'T is a place worth visitin' when you once get there. Some o' the old folks was kind o' fearful about it. 'T was 'counted a great place in old Indian times; you can pick up their stone tools 'most any time if you hunt about. There's a beautiful spring o' water, too. Yes, I remember when they used to tell queer stories about Shell-heap Island. Some said 't was a great bangeing-place for the Indians, and an old chief resided there once that ruled the winds; and others said they'd always heard that once the Indians come down from up country an' left a captive there without any bo't, an' 't was too far to swim across to Black Island, so called, an' he lived there till he perished."

"I've heard say he walked the island after that, and sharp-sighted folks could see him an' lose him like one o' them citizens Cap'n Little-page was acquainted with up to the north pole," announced Mrs. Todd grimly. "Anyway, there was Indians,—you can see their shell-heap that named the island; and I've heard myself that 't was one o' their cannibal places, but I never could believe it. There never was no cannibals on the coast o' Maine. All the Indians o' these regions are tame-looking folks."

"Sakes alive, yes!" exclaimed Mrs. Fosdick. "Ought to see them painted savages I've seen when I was young out in the South Sea Islands! That was the time for folks to travel, 'way back in the old whalin' days!"

"Whalin' must have been dull for a lady, hardly ever makin' a lively port, and not takin' in any mixed cargoes," said Mrs. Todd. "I never desired to go a whalin' v'y'ge myself."

"I used to return feelin' very slack an' behind the times, 't is true," explained Mrs. Fosdick, "but 't was excitin', an' we always done extra well, and felt rich when we did get ashore. I liked the variety. There, how times have changed; how few seafarin' families there are left! What a lot o' queer folks there used to be about here, anyway, when we was young, Almiry. Everybody's just like everybody else, now; nobody to laugh about, and nobody to cry about."

It seemed to me that there were peculiarities of character in the region of Dunnet Landing yet, but I did not like to interrupt.

"Yes," said Mrs. Todd after a moment of meditation, "there was certain a good many curiosities of human natur' in this neighborhood years ago. There was more energy then, and in some the energy took a singular turn. In these days the young folks is all copy-cats, 'fraid to death they won't be all just alike; as for the old folks, they pray for the advantage o' bein' a little different."

"I ain't heard of a copy-cat this great many years," said Mrs. Fosdick laughing; "'t was a favorite term o' my grandmother's. No, I wa'n't thinking o' those things, but of them strange straying creatur's that used to rove the country. You don't see them now, or the ones that used to hive away in their own houses with some strange notion or other."

I thought again of Captain Littlepage, but my companions were not reminded of his name; and there was brother William at Green Island, whom we all three knew.

"I was talking o' poor Joanna the other day. I had n't thought of her for a great while," said Mrs. Fosdick abruptly. "Mis' Brayton an' I recalled her as we sat together sewing. She was one o' your peculiar persons, wa'n't she? Speaking of such persons," she turned to explain to me, "there was a sort of a nun or hermit person lived out there for years all alone on Shell-heap Island. Miss Joanna Todd, her name was,—a cousin o' Almiry's late husband."

I expressed my interest, but as I glanced at Mrs. Todd I saw that she was confused by sudden affectionate feeling and unmistakable desire for reticence.

"I never want to hear Joanna laughed about," she said anxiously.

"Nor I," answered Mrs. Fosdick reassuringly. "She was crossed in love,—that was all the matter to begin with; but as I look back, I can see that Joanna was one doomed from the first to fall into a melancholy. She retired from the world for good an' all, though she was a well-off woman. All she wanted was to get away from folks; she thought she wasn't fit to live with anybody, and wanted to be free. Shell-heap Island come to her from her father, and first thing folks knew she'd gone off out there to live, and left word she didn't want no company. 'T was a bad place to get to, unless the wind an' tide were just right; 't was hard work to make a landing."

"What time of year was this?" I asked.

"Very late in the summer," said Mrs. Fosdick. "No, I never could laugh at Joanna, as some did. She set everything by the young man, an' they were going to marry in about a month, when he got bewitched with a girl 'way up the bay, and married her, and went off to Massachusetts. He wasn't well thought of,—there were those who thought Joanna's money was what had tempted him; but she'd given him her whole heart, an' she wa'n't so young as she had been. All her hopes were built on marryin', an' havin' a real home and somebody to look to; she acted just like a bird when its nest is spoilt. The day after she heard the news she was in dreadful woe, but the next she came to herself very quiet, and took the horse and wagon, and drove fourteen miles to the lawyer's, and signed a paper givin' her half of the farm to her brother. They never had got along very well together, but he didn't want to sign it, till she acted so distressed that he gave in. Edward Todd's wife was a good woman, who felt very bad indeed, and used every argument with Joanna; but Joanna took a poor old boat that had been her father's and lo'ded in a few things, and off she put all alone, with a good land breeze, right out to sea. Edward Todd ran down to the beach, an' stood there cryin' like a boy to see her go, but she was out o' hearin'. She never stepped foot on the mainland again long as she lived."

"How large an island is it? How did she manage in winter?" I asked.

"Perhaps thirty acres, rocks and all," answered Mrs. Todd, taking up the story gravely. "There can't be much of it that the salt spray don't fly over in storms. No, 't is a dreadful small place to make a world of; it has a different look from any of the other islands, but there's a sheltered cove on the south side, with mud-flats across one end of it at low water where there's excellent clams, and the big shell-heap keeps some o' the wind off a little house her father took the trouble

to build when he was a young man. They said there was an old house
built o' logs there before that, with a kind of natural cellar in the
rock under it. He used to stay out there days to a time, and anchor
a little sloop he had, and dig clams to fill it, and sail up to Portland.
They said the dealers always gave him an extra price, the clams were
so noted. Joanna used to go out and stay with him. They were
always great companions, so she knew just what 't was out there. There
was a few sheep that belonged to her brother an' her, but she bar-
gained for him to come and get them on the edge o' cold weather. Yes,
she desired him to come for the sheep; an' his wife thought perhaps
Joanna 'd return, but he said no, an' lo'ded the bo't with warm things
an' what he thought she'd need through the winter. He come home
with the sheep an' left the other things by the house, but she never
so much as looked out o' the window. She done it for a penance.
She must have wanted to see Edward by that time."

Mrs. Fosdick was fidgeting with eagerness to speak.

"Some thought the first cold snap would set her ashore, but she
always remained," concluded Mrs. Todd soberly.

"Talk about the men not having any curiosity!" exclaimed Mrs.
Fosdick scornfully. "Why, the waters round Shell-heap Island were
white with sails all that fall. 'T was never called no great of a fishin'-
ground before. Many of 'em made excuse to go ashore to get water
at the spring; but at last she spoke to a bo't-load, very dignified and
calm, and said that she'd like it better if they'd make a practice of
getting water to Black Island or somewheres else and leave her alone,
except in case of accident or trouble. But there was one man who had
always set everything by her from a boy. He'd have married her if the
other had n't come about an' spoilt his chance, and he used to get
close to th island, before light, on his way out fishin', and throw a
little bundle 'way up the green slope front o' the house. His sister
told me she happened to see, the first time, what a pretty choice he
made o' useful things that a woman would feel lost without. He stood
off fishin', and could see them in the grass all day, though sometimes
she'd come out and walk right by them. There was other bo'ts near,
out after mackerel. But early next morning his present was gone. He
did n't presume too much, but once he took her a nice firkin o' things
he got up to Portland, and when spring come he landed her a hen and
chickens in a nice little coop. There was a good many old friends had
Joanna on their minds."

"Yes," said Mrs. Todd, losing her sad reserve in the growing sympathy of these reminiscences. "How everybody used to notice whether
there was smoke out of the chimney! The Black Island folks could see
her with their spy-glass, and if they'd ever missed getting some sign
o' life they'd have sent notice to her folks. But after the first year or

two Joanna was more and more forgotten as an every-day charge. Folks lived very simple in those days, you know," she continued, as Mrs. Fosdick's knitting was taking much thought at the moment. "I expect there was always plenty of driftwood thrown up, and a poor failin' patch of spruces covered all the north side of the island, so she always had something to burn. She was very fond of workin' in the garden ashore, and that first summer she began to till the little field out there, and raised a nice parcel o' potatoes. She could fish, o' course, and there was all her clams an' lobsters. You can always live well in any wild place by the sea when you'd starve to death up country, except 't was berry time. Joanna had berries out there, blackberries at least, and there was a few herbs in case she needed them. Mullein in great quantities and a plant o' wormwood I remember seeing once when I stayed there, long before she fled out to Shell-heap. Yes, I recall the wormwood, which is always a planted herb, so there must have been folks there before the Todds' day. A growin' bush makes the best gravestone; I expect that wormwood always stood for some-body's solemn monument. Catnip, too, is a very endurin' herb about an old place."

"But what I want to know is what she did for other things," interrupted Mrs. Fosdick. "Almiry, what did she do for clothin' when she needed to replenish, or risin' for her bread, or the piece-bag that no woman can live long without?"

"Or company," suggested Mrs. Todd. "Joanna was one that loved her friends. There must have been a terrible sight o' long winter evenin's that first year."

"There was her hens," suggested Mrs. Fosdick, after reviewing the melancholy situation. "She never wanted the sheep after that first season. There wa'n't no proper pasture for sheep after the June grass was past, and she ascertained the fact and couldn't bear to see them suffer; but the chickens done well. I remember sailin' by one spring afternoon, an' seein' the coops out front o' the house in the sun. How long was it before you went out with the minister? You were the first ones that ever really got ashore to see Joanna."

I had been reflecting upon a state of society which admitted such personal freedom and a voluntary hermitage. There was something mediæval in the behavior of poor Joanna Todd under a disappointment of the heart. The two women had drawn closer together, and were talking on, quite unconscious of a listener.

"Poor Joanna!" said Mrs. Todd again, and sadly shook her head as if there were things one could not speak about.

"I called her a great fool," declared Mrs. Fosdick, with spirit, "but I pitied her then, and I pity her far more now. Some other minister would have been a great help to her,—one that preached self-forgetfulness and doin' for others to cure our own ills; but Parson Dimmick was a vague person, well meanin', but very numb in his feelin's. I don't suppose at that troubled time Joanna could think of any way to mend her troubles except to run off and hide."

"Mother used to say she didn't see how Joanna lived without having nobody to do for, getting her own meals and tending her own poor self day in an' day out," said Mrs. Todd sorrowfully.

"There was the hens," repeated Mrs. Fosdick kindly. "I expect she soon came to makin' folks o' them. No, I never went to work to blame Joanna, as some did. She was full o' feeling, and her troubles hurt her more than she could bear. I see it all now as I couldn't when I was young."

"I suppose in old times they had their shut-up convents for just such folks," said Mrs. Todd, as if she and her friend had disagreed about Joanna once, and were now in happy harmony. She seemed to speak with new openness and freedom. "Oh yes, I was only too pleased when the Reverend Mr. Dimmick invited me to go out with him. He hadn't been very long in the place when Joanna left home and friends. 'T was one day that next summer after she went, and I had been married early in the spring. He felt that he ought to go out and visit her. She was a member of the church, and might wish to have him consider her spiritual state. I wa'n't so sure o' that, but I always liked Joanna, and I'd come to be her cousin by marriage. Nathan an' I had conversed about goin' out to pay her a visit, but he got his chance to sail sooner 'n he expected. He always thought everything of her, and last time he come home, knowing nothing of her change, he brought her a beautiful coral pin from a port he'd touched at somewheres up the Mediterranean. So I wrapped the little box in a nice piece of paper and put it in my pocket, and picked her a bunch of fresh lemon balm, and off we started."

Mrs. Fosdick laughed. "I remember hearin' about your trials on the v'y'ge," she said.

"Why, yes," continued Mrs. Todd in her company manner. "I picked her the balm, an' we started. Why, yes, Susan, the minister liked to have cost me my life that day. He would fasten the sheet, though I advised against it. He said the rope was rough an' cut his hand. There was a fresh breeze, an' he went on talking rather high flown, an' I felt some interested. All of a sudden there come up a gust, and he give a screech and stood right up and called for help, 'way out there to sea. I knocked him right over into the bottom o' the bo't, getting by to catch hold of the sheet an' untie it. He wasn't but a little man; I helped him right up after the squall passed, and made a handsome apology to him, but he did act kind o' offended."

"I do think they ought not to settle them landlocked folks in parishes where they're liable to be on the water," insisted Mrs. Fosdick. "Think of the families in our parish that was scattered all about the bay, and what a sight o' sails you used to see, in Mr. Dimmick's day, standing across to the mainland on a pleasant Sunday morning, filled with church-going folks, all sure to want him some time or other! You couldn't find no doctor that would stand up in the boat and screech if a flaw struck her."

"Old Dr. Bennett had a beautiful sailboat, didn't he?" responded Mrs. Todd. "And how well he used to brave the weather! Mother always said that in time o' trouble that tall white sail used to look like an angel's wing comin' over the sea to them that was in pain. Well, there's a difference in gifts. Mr. Dimmick was not without light."

" 'T was light o' the moon, then," snapped Mrs. Fosdick; "he was pompous enough, but I never could remember a single word he said. There, go on, Mis' Todd; I forget a great deal about that day you went to see poor Joanna."

"I felt she saw us coming, and knew us a great way off; yes, I seemed to feel it within me," said our friend, laying down her knitting. "I kept my seat, and took the bo't inshore without saying a word; there was a short channel that I was sure Mr. Dimmick wasn't acquainted with, and the tide was very low. She never came out to warn us off nor anything, and I thought, as I hauled the bo't up on a wave and let the Reverend Mr. Dimmick step out, that it was somethin' gained to be safe ashore. There was a little smoke out o' the chimney o' Joanna's house, and it did look sort of homelike and pleasant with wild mornin'-glory vines trained up; an' there was a plot o' flowers under the front window, portulacas and things. I believe she'd made a garden once, when she was stopping there with her father, and some things must have seeded in. It looked as if she might have gone over to the other side of the island. 'T was neat and pretty all about the house, and a lovely day in July. We walked up from the beach together very sedate, and I felt for poor Nathan's little pin to see if 't was safe in my dress pocket. All of a sudden Joanna come right to the fore door and stood there, not sayin' a word."

My companions and I had been so intent upon the subject of the conversation that we had not heard any one open the gate, but at this moment, above the noise of the rain, we heard a loud knocking. We were all startled as we sat by the fire, and Mrs. Todd rose hastily and went to answer the call, leaving her rocking-chair in violent motion. Mrs. Fosdick and I heard an anxious voice at the door speaking of a sick child, and Mrs. Todd's kind, motherly voice inviting the messenger in: then we waited in silence. There was a sound of heavy dropping of rain from the eaves, and the distant roar and undertone of the sea.

My thoughts flew back to the lonely woman on her outer island; what separation from humankind she must have felt, what terror and sadness, even in a summer storm like this!

"You send right after the doctor if she ain't better in half an hour," said Mrs. Todd to her worried customer as they parted; and I felt a warm sense of comfort in the evident resources of even so small a neighborhood, but for the poor hermit Joanna there was no neighbor on a winter night.

"How did she look?" demanded Mrs. Fosdick, without preface, as our large hostess returned to the little room with a mist about her from standing long in the wet doorway, and the sudden draught of her coming beat out the smoke and flame from the Franklin stove. "How did poor Joanna look?"

"She was the same as ever, except I thought she looked smaller," answered Mrs. Todd after thinking a moment; perhaps it was only a last considering thought about her patient. "Yes, she was just the same, and looked very nice, Joanna did. I had been married since she left home, an' she treated me like her own folks. I expected she'd look strange, with her hair turned gray in a night or somethin', but she wore a pretty gingham dress I'd often seen her wear before she went away; she must have kept it nice for best in the afternoons. She always had beautiful, quiet manners. I remember she waited till we were close to her, and then kissed me real affectionate, and inquired for Nathan before she shook hands with the minister, and then she invited us both in. 'T was the same little house her father had built him when he was a bachelor, with one livin'-room, and a little mite of a bedroom out of it where she slept, but 't was neat as a ship's cabin. There was some old chairs, an' a seat made of a long box that might have held boat tackle an' things to lock up in his fishin' days, and a good enough stove so anybody could cook and keep warm in cold weather. I went over once from home and stayed 'most a week with Joanna when we was girls, and those young happy days rose up before me. Her father was busy all day fishin' or clammin'; he was one o' the pleasantest men in the world, but Joanna's mother had the grim streak, and never knew what 't was to be happy. The first minute my eyes fell upon Joanna's face that day I saw how she had grown to look like Mis' Todd. 'T was the mother right over again."

"Oh dear me!" said Mrs. Fosdick.

"Joanna had done one thing very pretty. There was a little piece o' swamp on the island where good rushes grew plenty, and she'd gathered 'em, and braided some beautiful mats for the floor and a thick cushion for the long bunk. She'd showed a good deal of invention; you see there was a nice chance to pick up pieces o' wood and boards that drove ashore, and she'd made good use o' what she found. There wasn't no clock, but she had a few dishes on a shelf, and flowers set about in shells fixed to the walls, so it did look sort of homelike, though so lonely and poor. I couldn't keep the tears out o' my eyes, I felt so sad. I said to myself, I must get mother to come over an' see Joanna; the love in mother's heart would warm her, an' she might be able to advise."

"Oh no, Joanna was dreadful stern," said Mrs. Fosdick.

"We were all settin' down very proper, but Joanna would keep stealin' glances at me as if she was glad I come. She had but little to say; she was real polite an' gentle, and yet forbiddin'. The minister found it hard," confessed Mrs. Todd; "he got embarrassed, an' when he put on his authority and asked her if she felt to enjoy religion in her present situation, an' she replied that she must be excused from answerin', I thought I should fly. She might have made it easier for him; after all, he was the minister and had taken some trouble to come out, though 't was kind of cold an' unfeelin' the way he inquired. I thought he might have seen the little old Bible a-layin' on the shelf close by him, an' I wished he knew enough to just lay his hand on it an' read somethin' kind an' fatherly 'stead of accusin' her, an' then given poor Joanna his blessin' with the hope she might be led to comfort. He did offer prayer, but 't was all about hearin' the voice o' God out o' the whirlwind; and I thought while he was goin' on that anybody that had spent the long cold winter all alone out on Shell-heap Island knew a good deal more about those things than he did. I got so provoked I opened my eyes and stared right at him.

"She didn't take no notice, she kep' a nice respectful manner towards him, and when there come a pause she asked if he had any interest about the old Indian remains, and took down some queer stone gouges and hammers off of one of her shelves and showed them to him same 's if he was a boy. He remarked that he 'd like to walk over an' see the shell-heap; so she went right to the door and pointed him the way. I see then that she'd made her some kind o' sandal-shoes out o' the fine rushes to wear on her feet; she stepped light an' nice in 'em as shoes."

Mrs. Fosdick leaned back in her rocking-chair and gave a heavy sigh.

"I didn't move at first, but I'd held out just as long as I could," said Mrs. Todd, whose voice trembled a little. "When Joanna returned from the door, an' I could see that man's stupid back departin' among the wild rose bushes, I just ran to her an' caught her in my arms. I wasn't so big as I be now, and she was older than me, but I hugged her tight, just as if she was a child. 'Oh, Joanna dear,' I says, 'won't you come ashore an' live 'long o' me at the Landin', or go over to Green

Island to mother's when winter comes? Nobody shall trouble you, an'
mother finds it hard bein' alone. I can't bear to leave you here'—and
I burst right out crying. I'd had my own trials, young as I was, an' she
knew it. Oh, I did entreat her; yes, I entreated Joanna."

"What did she say then?" asked Mrs. Fosdick, much moved.

"She looked the same way, sad an' remote through it all," said Mrs.
Todd mournfully. "She took hold of my hand, and we sat down close
together; 't was as if she turned round an' made a child of me. 'I haven't
got no right to live with folks no more,' she said. 'You must never
ask me again, Almiry: I've done the only thing I could do, and I've
made my choice. I feel a great comfort in your kindness, but I don't
deserve it. I have committed the unpardonable sin; you don't understand,' says she humbly. 'I was in great wrath and trouble, and my
thoughts was so wicked towards God that I can't expect ever to be
forgiven. I have come to know what it is to have patience, but I have
lost my hope. You must tell those that ask how 't is with me,' she said,
'an' tell them I want to be alone.' I could n't speak; no, there wa'n't
anything I could say, she seemed so above everything common. I was
a good deal younger then than I be now, and I got Nathan's little coral
pin out o' my pocket and put it into her hand; and when she saw it
and I told her where it come from, her face did really light up for a
minute, sort of bright an' pleasant. 'Nathan an' I was always good
friends; I'm glad he don't think hard of me,' says she. 'I want you to
have it, Almiry, an' wear it for love o' both o' us,' and she handed it
back to me. 'You give my love to Nathan,—he's a dear good man,'
she said; 'an' tell your mother, if I should be sick she mustn't wish
I could get well, but I want her to be the one to come.' Then she
seemed to have said all she wanted to, as if she was done with the
world, and we sat there a few minutes longer together. It was real
sweet and quiet except for a good many birds and the sea rollin' up
on the beach; but at last she rose, an' I did too, and she kissed me and
held my hand in hers a minute, as if to say good-by; then she turned
and went right away out o' the door and disappeared.

"The minister come back pretty soon, and I told him I was all ready,
and we started down to the bo't. He had picked up some round stones
and things and was carrying them in his pocket-handkerchief; an' he
sat down amidships without making any question, and let me take the
rudder an' work the bo't, an' made no remarks for some time, until
we sort of eased it off speaking of the weather, an' subjects that arose
as we skirted Black Island, where two or three families lived belongin'
to the parish. He preached next Sabbath as usual, somethin' high
soundin' about the creation, and I couldn't help thinkin' he might
never get no further; he seemed to know no remedies, but he had a
great use of words."

Mrs. Fosdick sighed again. "Hearin' you tell about Joanna brings the time right back as if 't was yesterday," she said. "Yes, she was one o' them poor things that talked about the great sin; we don't seem to hear nothing about the unpardonable sin now, but you may say 't was not uncommon then."

"I expect that if it had been in these days, such a person would be plagued to death with idle folks," continued Mrs. Todd, after a long pause. "As it was, nobody trespassed on her; all the folks about the bay respected her an' her feelings; but as time wore on, after you left here, one after another ventured to make occasion to put somethin' ashore for her if they went that way. I know mother used to go to see her sometimes, and send William over now and then with something fresh an' nice from the farm. There is a point on the sheltered side where you can lay a boat close to shore an' land anything safe on the turf out o' reach o' the water. There were one or two others, old folks, that she would see, and now an' then she'd hail a passin' boat an' ask for somethin'; and mother got her to promise that she would make some sign to the Black Island folks if she wanted help. I never saw her myself to speak to after that day."

"I expect nowadays, if such a thing happened, she'd have gone out West to her uncle's folks or up to Massachusetts and had a change, an' come home good as new. The world's bigger an' freer than it used to be," urged Mrs. Fosdick.

"No," said her friend. " 'T is like bad eyesight, the mind of such a person: if your eyes don't see right there may be a remedy, but there's no kind of glasses to remedy the mind. No, Joanna was Joanna, and there she lays on her island where she lived and did her poor penance. She told mother the day she was dyin' that she always used to want to be fetched inshore when it come to the last; but she'd thought it over, and desired to be laid on the island, if 't was thought right. So the funeral was out there, a Saturday afternoon in September. 'T was a pretty day, and there wa'n't hardly a boat on the coast within twenty miles that didn't head for Shell-heap cram-full o' folks, an' all real respectful, same 's if she'd always stayed ashore and held her friends. Some went out o' mere curiosity, I don't doubt,—there's always such to every funeral; but most had real feelin', and went purpose to show it. She'd got most o' the wild sparrows as tame as could be, livin' out there so long among 'em, and one flew right in and lit on the coffin an' begun to sing while Mr. Dimmick was speakin'. He was put out by it, an' acted as if he didn't know whether to stop or go on. I may have been prejudiced, but I wa'n't the only one thought the poor little bird done the best of the two."

"What became o' the man that treated her so, did you ever hear?" asked Mrs. Fosdick. "I know he lived up to Massachusetts for a while.

Somebody who came from the same place told me that he was in trade there an' doin' very well, but that was years ago."

"I never heard anything more than that; he went to the war in one o' the early rigiments. No, I never heard any more of him," answered Mrs. Todd. "Joanna was another sort of person, and perhaps he showed good judgment in marryin' somebody else, if only he'd behaved straightforward and manly. He was a shifty-eyed, coaxin' sort of man, that got what he wanted out o' folks, an' only gave when he wanted to buy, made friends easy and lost 'em without knowin' the difference. She'd had a piece o' work tryin' to make him walk accordin' to her right ideas, but she'd have had too much variety ever to fall into a melancholy. Some is meant to be the Joannas in this world, an' 't was her poor lot."

Stephen Crane
The Open Boat

I

None of them knew the color of the sky. Their eyes glanced level, and were fastened upon the waves that swept toward them. These waves were of the hue of slate, save for the tops, which were of foaming white, and all of the men knew the colors of the sea. The horizon narrowed and widened, and dipped and rose, and at all times its edge was jagged with waves that seemed thrust up in points like rocks.

Many a man ought to have a bath-tub larger than the boat which here rode upon the sea. These waves were most wrongfully and barbarously abrupt and tall, and each froth-top was a problem in small boat navigation.

Scribner's, XXI (June, 1897), 728–40. Text from this publication.

Subtitled "A Tale Intended to Be After the Fact," Crane's story is based on the sinking of the filibustering steamer *Commodore* on January 1, 1897, off the Florida coast. Crane was aboard the *Commodore* in an attempt to reach Cuba and report the Cuban rebellion.

The cook squatted in the bottom and looked with both eyes at the six inches of gunwale which separated him from the ocean. His sleeves were rolled over his fat forearms, and the two flaps of his unbuttoned vest dangled as he bent to bail out the boat. Often he said: "Gawd! That was a narrow clip." As he remarked it he invariably gazed eastward over the broken sea.

The oiler, steering with one of the two oars in the boat, sometimes raised himself suddenly to keep clear of water that swirled in over the stern. It was a thin little oar and it seemed often ready to snap.

The correspondent, pulling at the other oar, watched the waves and wondered why he was there.

The injured captain, lying in the bow, was at this time buried in that profound dejection and indifference which comes, temporarily at least, to even the bravest and most enduring when, willy nilly, the firm fails, the army loses, the ship goes down. The mind of the master of a vessel is rooted deep in the timbers of her, though he command for a day or a decade, and this captain had on him the stern impression of a scene in the grays of dawn of seven turned faces, and later a stump of a top-mast with a white ball on it that slashed to and fro at the waves, went low and lower, and down. Thereafter there was something strange in his voice. Although steady, it was deep with mourning, and of a quality beyond oration or tears.

"Keep 'er a little more south, Billie," said he.

" 'A little more south,' sir," said the oiler in the stern.

A seat in this boat was not unlike a seat upon a bucking broncho, and, by the same token, a broncho is not much smaller. The craft pranced and reared, and plunged like an animal. As each wave came, and she rose for it, she seemed like a horse making at a fence outrageously high. The manner of her scramble over these walls of water is a mystic thing, and, moreover, at the top of them were ordinarily these problems in white water, the foam racing down from the summit of each wave, requiring a new leap, and a leap from the air. Then, after scornfully bumping a crest, she would slide, and race, and splash down a long incline and arrive bobbing and nodding in front of the next menace.

A singular disadvantage of the sea lies in the fact that after successfully surmounting one wave you discover that there is another behind it just as important and just as nervously anxious to do something effective in the way of swamping boats. In a ten-foot dingey one can get an idea of the resources of the sea in the line of waves that is not probable to the average experience, which is never at sea in a dingey. As each slaty wall of water approached, it shut all else from the view of the men in the boat, and it was not difficult to imagine that this particular wave was the final outburst of the ocean, the last effort of the grim water. There was a terrible grace in the move of the waves, and they came in silence, save for the snarling of the crests.

In the wan light, the faces of the men must have been gray. Their eyes must have glinted in strange ways as they gazed steadily astern. Viewed from a balcony, the whole thing would doubtlessly have been weirdly picturesque. But the men in the boat had no time to see it, and if they had had leisure there were other things to occupy their minds. The sun swung steadily up the sky, and they knew it was broad day because the color of the sea changed from slate to emerald-green, streaked with amber lights, and the foam was like tumbling snow. The process of the breaking day was unknown to them. They were aware only of this effect upon the color of the waves that rolled toward them.

In disjointed sentences the cook and the correspondent argued as to the difference between a life-saving station and a house of refuge. The cook had said: "There's a house of refuge just north of the Mosquito Inlet Light, and as soon as they see us, they'll come off in their boat and pick us up."

"As soon as who see us?" said the correspondent.

"The crew," said the cook.

"Houses of refuge don't have crews," said the correspondent. "As I understand them, they are only places where clothes and grub are stored for the benefit of shipwrecked people. They don't carry crews."

"Oh, yes, they do," said the cook.

"No, they don't," said the correspondent.

"Well, we're not there yet, anyhow," said the oiler, in the stern.

"Well," said the cook, "perhaps it's not a house of refuge that I'm thinking of as being near Mosquito Inlet Light. Perhaps it's a life-saving station."

"We're not there yet," said the oiler, in the stern.

II

As the boat bounced from the top of each wave, the wind tore through the hair of the hatless men, and as the craft plopped her stern down again the spray slashed past them. The crest of each of these waves was a hill, from the top of which the men surveyed, for a moment, a broad tumultuous expanse; shining and wind-riven. It was probably splendid. It was probably glorious, this play of the free sea, wild with lights of emerald and white and amber.

"Bully good thing it's an on-shore wind," said the cook. "If not, where would we be? Wouldn't have a show."

"That's right," said the correspondent.

The busy oiler nodded his assent.

Then the captain, in the bow, chuckled in a way that expressed humor, contempt, tragedy, all in one. "Do you think we've got much of a show, now, boys?" said he.

Whereupon the three were silent, save for a trifle of hemming and hawing. To express any particular optimism at this time they felt to be childish and stupid, but they all doubtless possessed this sense of the situation in their mind. A young man thinks doggedly at such times. On the other hand, the ethics of their condition was decidedly against any open suggestion of hopelessness. So they were silent.

"Oh, well," said the captain, soothing his children, "we'll get ashore all right."

But there was that in his tone which made them think, so the oiler quoth: "Yes! If this wind holds!"

The cook was bailing: "Yes! If we don't catch hell in the surf."

Canton flannel gulls flew near and far. Sometimes they sat down on the sea, near patches of brown sea-weed that rolled over the waves with a movement like carpets on a line in a gale. The birds sat comfortably in groups, and they were envied by some in the dingey, for the wrath of the sea was no more to them than it was to a covey of prairie chickens a thousand miles inland. Often they came very close and stared at the men with black beadlike eyes. At these times they were uncanny and sinister in their unblinking scrutiny, and the men hooted angrily at them, telling them to be gone. One came, and evidently decided to alight on the top of the captain's head. The bird flew parallel to the boat and did not circle, but made short sidelong jumps in the air in chicken-fashion. His black eyes were wistfully fixed upon the captain's head. "Ugly brute," said the oiler to the bird. "You look as if you were made with a jackknife." The cook and the correspondent swore darkly at the creature. The captain naturally wished to knock it away with the end of the heavy painter, but he did not dare do it, because anything resembling an emphatic gesture would have capsized this freighted boat, and so with his open hand, the captain gently and carefully waved the gull away. After it had been discouraged from the pursuit the captain breathed easier on account of his hair, and others breathed easier because the bird struck their minds at this time as being somehow grewsome and ominous.

In the meantime the oiler and the correspondent rowed. And also they rowed.

They sat together in the same seat, and each rowed an oar. Then the oiler took both oars; then the correspondent took both oars; then the oiler; then the correspondent. They rowed and they rowed. The very ticklish part of the business was when the time came for the reclining one in the stern to take his turn at the oars. By the very last star of truth, it is easier to steal eggs from under a hen than it was to change seats in the dingey. First the man in the stern slid his hand along the thwart and moved with care, as if he were of Sèvres. Then the man in the rowing seat slid his hand along the other thwart. It was all done with the most extraordinary care. As the two sidled past each other, the whole party kept watchful eyes on the coming wave, and the captain cried: "Look out now! Steady there!"

The brown mats of sea-weed that appeared from time to time were like islands, bits of earth. They were travelling, apparently, neither one way nor the other. They were, to all intents, stationary. They informed the men in the boat that it was making progress slowly toward the land.

The captain, rearing cautiously in the bow, after the dingey soared on a great swell, said that he had seen the light-house at Mosquito Inlet. Presently the cook remarked that he had seen it. The correspondent was at the oars, then, and for some reason he too wished to look at the lighthouse, but his back was toward the far shore and the waves were important, and for some time he could not seize an opportunity to turn his head. But at last there came a wave more gentle than the others, and when at the crest of it he swiftly scoured the western horizon.

"See it?" said the captain.

"No," said the correspondent, slowly, "I didn't see anything."

"Look again," said the captain. He pointed. "It's exactly in that direction."

At the top of another wave, the correspondent did as he was bid, and this time his eyes chanced on a small still thing on the edge of the swaying horizon. It was precisely like the point of a pin. It took an anxious eye to find a lighthouse so tiny.

"Think we'll make it, captain?"

"If this wind holds and the boat don't swamp, we can't do much else," said the captain.

The little boat, lifted by each towering sea, and splashed viciously by the crests, made progress that in the absence of sea-weed was not apparent to those in her. She seemed just a wee thing wallowing, miraculously, top-up, at the mercy of five oceans. Occasionally, a great spread of water, like white flames, swarmed into her.

"Bail her, cook," said the captain, serenely.

"All right, captain," said the cheerful cook.

III

It would be difficult to describe the subtle brotherhood of men that was here established on the seas. No one said that it was so. No one mentioned it. But it dwelt in the boat, and each man felt it warm him.

They were a captain, an oiler, a cook, and a correspondent, and they were friends, friends in a more curiously ironbound degree than may be common. The hurt captain, lying against the water-jar in the bow, spoke always in a low voice and calmly, but he could never command a more ready and swiftly obedient crew than the motley three of the dingey. It was more than a mere recognition of what was best for the common safety. There was surely in it a quality that was personal and heartfelt. And after this devotion to the commander of the boat there was this comradeship that the correspondent, for instance, who had been taught to be cynical of men, knew even at the time was the best experience of his life. But no one said that it was so. No one mentioned it.

"I wish we had a sail," remarked the captain. "We might try my overcoat on the end of an oar and give you two boys a chance to rest." So the cook and the correspondent held the mast and spread wide the overcoat. The oiler steered, and the little boat made good way with her new rig. Sometimes the oiler had to scull sharply to keep a sea from breaking into the boat, but otherwise sailing was a success.

Meanwhile the light-house had been growing slowly larger. It had now almost assumed color, and appeared like a little gray shadow on the sky. The man at the oars could not be prevented from turning his head rather often to try for a glimpse of this little gray shadow.

At last, from the top of each wave the men in the tossing boat could see land. Even as the light-house was an upright shadow on the sky, this land seemed but a long black shadow on the sea. It certainly was thinner than paper. "We must be about opposite New Smyrna," said the cook, who had coasted this shore often in schooners. "Captain, by the way, I believe they abandoned that life-saving station there about a year ago."

"Did they?" said the captain.

The wind slowly died away. The cook and the correspondent were not now obliged to slave in order to hold high the oar. But the waves continued their old impetuous swooping at the dingey, and the little craft, no longer under way, struggled woundily over them. The oiler or the correspondent took the oars again.

Shipwrecks are *apropos* of nothing. If men could only train for them and have them occur when the men had reached pink condition, there would be less drowning at sea. Of the four in the dingey none had slept any time worth mentioning for two days and two nights previous to embarking in the dingey, and in the excitement of clambering about the deck of a foundering ship they had also forgotten to eat heartily.

For these reasons, and for others, neither the oiler nor the correspondent was fond of rowing at this time. The correspondent wondered ingenuously how in the name of all that was sane could there be people who thought it amusing to row a boat. It was not an amusement; it was a diabolical punishment, and even a genius of mental aberrations could never conclude that it was anything but a horror to the muscles and a crime against the back. He mentioned to the boat in general how the amusement of rowing struck him, and the weary-faced oiler smiled in full sympathy. Previously to the foundering, by the way, the oiler had worked double-watch in the engine-room of the ship.

"Take her easy, now, boys," said the captain. "Don't spend yourselves. If we have to run a surf you'll need all your strength, because we'll sure have to swim for it. Take your time."

Slowly the land arose from the sea. From a black line it became a line of black and a line of white, trees, and sand. Finally, the captain said that he could make out a house on the shore. "That's the house of refuge, sure," said the cook. "They'll see us before long, and come out after us."

The distant light-house reared high. "The keeper ought to be able to make us out now, if he's looking through a glass," said the captain. "He'll notify the life-saving people."

"None of those other boats could have got ashore to give word of the wreck," said the oiler, in a low voice. "Else the life-boat would be out hunting us."

Slowly and beautifully the land loomed out of the sea. The wind came again. It had veered from the northeast to the southeast. Finally, a new sound struck the ears of the men in the boat. It was the low thunder of the surf on the shore. "We'll never be able to make the lighthouse now," said the captain. "Swing her head a little more north, Billie," said the captain.

" 'A little more north,' sir," said the oiler.

Whereupon the little boat turned her nose once more down the wind, and all but the oarsman watched the shore grow. Under the influence of this expansion doubt and direful apprehension was leaving the minds of the men. The management of the boat was still most absorbing, but it could not prevent a quiet cheerfulness. In an hour, perhaps, they would be ashore.

Their back-bones had become thoroughly used to balancing in the boat and they now rode this wild colt of a dingey like circus men. The correspondent thought that he had been drenched to the skin, but happening to feel in the top pocket of his coat, he found therein eight cigars. Four of them were soaked with sea-water; four were perfectly scatheless. After a search, somebody produced three dry matches, and thereupon the four waifs rode in their little boat, and with an assurance of an impending rescue shining in their eyes, puffed at the big cigars and judged well and ill of all men. Everybody took a drink of water.

IV

"Cook," remarked the captain, "there don't seem to be any signs of life about your house of refuge."

"No," replied the cook. "Funny they don't see us!"

A broad stretch of lowly coast lay before the eyes of the men. It was of low dunes topped with dark vegetation. The roar of the surf was plain, and sometimes they could see the white lip of a wave as it spun up the beach. A tiny house was blocked out black upon the sky. Southward, the slim light-house lifted its little gray length.

Tide, wind, and waves were swinging the dingey northward. "Funny they don't see us," said the men.

The surf's roar was here dulled, but its tone was, nevertheless, thunderous and mighty. As the boat swam over the great rollers, the men sat listening to this roar. "We'll swamp sure," said everybody.

It is fair to say here that there was not a life-saving station within twenty miles in either direction, but the men did not know this fact and in consequence they made dark and opprobrious remarks concerning the eyesight of the nation's life-savers. Four scowling men sat in the dingey and surpassed records in the invention of epithets.

"Funny they don't see us."

The light-heartedness of a former time had completely faded. To their sharpened minds it was easy to conjure pictures of all kinds of incompetency and blindness and, indeed, cowardice. There was the shore of the populous land, and it was bitter and bitter to them that from it came no sign.

"Well," said the captain, ultimately, "I suppose we'll have to make a try for ourselves. If we stay out here too long, we'll none of us have strength left to swim after the boat swamps."

And so the oiler, who was at the oars, turned the boat straight for the shore. There was a sudden tightening of muscles. There was some thinking.

"If we don't all get ashore—" said the captain. "If we don't all get ashore, I suppose you fellows know where to send news of my finish?"

They then briefly exchanged some addresses and admonitions. As for the reflections of the men, there was a great deal of rage in them. Perchance they might be formulated thus: "If I am going to be drowned—if I am going to be drowned—if I am going to be drowned, why, in the name of the seven mad gods who rule the sea, was I allowed to come thus far and contemplate sand and trees? Was I brought here merely to have my nose dragged away as I was about to nibble the sacred cheese of life? It is preposterous. If this old ninny-woman, Fate, cannot do better than this, she should be deprived of the management of men's fortunes. She is an old hen who knows not her intention. If she has decided to drown me, why did she not do it in the beginning and save me all this trouble. The whole affair is absurd. . . . But, no, she cannot mean to drown me. She dare not drown me. She cannot drown me. Not after all this work." Afterward the man might have had an impulse to shake his fist at the clouds: "Just you drown me, now, and then hear what I call you!"

The billows that came at this time were more formidable. They seemed always just about to break and roll over the little boat in a turmoil of foam. There was a preparatory and long growl in the speech of them. No mind unused to the sea would have concluded that the dingey could ascend these sheer heights in time. The shore was still afar. The oiler was a wily surfman. "Boys," he said, swiftly, "she won't live three minutes more and we're too far out to swim. Shall I take her to sea again, captain?"

"Yes! Go ahead!" said the captain.

This oiler, by a series of quick miracles, and fast and steady oarsmanship, turned the boat in the middle of the surf and took her safely to sea again.

There was a considerable silence as the boat bumped over the furrowed sea to deeper water. Then somebody in gloom spoke. "Well, anyhow, they must have seen us from the shore by now."

The gulls went in slanting flight up the wind toward the gray desolate east. A squall, marked by dingy clouds, and clouds brick-red, like smoke from a burning building, appeared from the southeast.

"What do you think of those life-saving people? Ain't they peaches?"

"Funny they haven't seen us."

"Maybe they think we're out here for sport! Maybe they think we're fishin'. Maybe they think we're damned fools."

It was a long afternoon. A changed tide tried to force them southward, but wind and wave said northward. Far ahead, where coastline, sea, and sky formed their mighty angle, there were little dots which seemed to indicate a city on the shore.

"St. Augustine?"

The captain shook his head. "Too near Mosquito Inlet."

And the oiler rowed, and then the correspondent rowed. Then the oiler rowed. It was a weary business. The human back can become the seat of more aches and pains than are registered in books for the composite anatomy of a regiment. It is a limited area, but it can become the theatre of innumerable muscular conflicts, tangles, wrenches, knots, and other comforts.

"Did you ever like to row, Billie?" asked the correspondent.

"No," said the oiler. "Hang it."

When one exchanged the rowing-seat for a place in the bottom of the boat, he suffered a bodily depression that caused him to be careless of everything save an obligation to wiggle one finger. There was cold sea-water swashing to and fro in the boat, and he lay in it. His head, pillowed on a thwart, was within an inch of the swirl of a wave crest, and sometimes a particularly obstreperous sea came in-board and drenched him once more. But these matters did not annoy him. It is almost certain that if the boat had capsized he would have tumbled comfortably out upon the ocean as if he felt sure that it was a great soft mattress.

"Look! There's a man on the shore!"

"Where?"

"There! See 'im? See 'im?"

"Yes, sure! He's walking along."

"Now he's stopped. Look! He's facing us!"

"He's waving at us!"

"So he is! By thunder!"

"Ah, now, we're all right! Now we're all right! There'll be a boat out here for us in half an hour."

"He's going on. He's running. He's going up to that house there."

The remote beach seemed lower than the sea, and it required a searching glance to discern the little black figure. The captain saw a floating stick and they rowed to it. A bath-towel was by some weird chance in the boat, and, tying this on the stick, the captain waved it. The oarsman did not dare turn his head, so he was obliged to ask questions.

"What's he doing now?"

"He's standing still again. He's looking, I think. . . . There he goes again. Toward the house. . . . Now he's stopped again."

"Is he waving at us?"

"No, not now! he was, though."

"Look! There comes another man!"

"He's running."

"Look at him go, would you."

"Why, he's on a bicycle. Now he's met the other man. They're both waving at us. Look!"

"There comes something up the beach."

"What the devil is that thing?"

"Why, it looks like a boat."

"Why, certainly it's a boat."

"No, it's on wheels."

"Yes, so it is. Well, that must be the life-boat. They drag them along shore on a wagon."

"That's the life-boat, sure."

"No, by——, it's—it's an omnibus."

"I tell you it's a life-boat."

"It is not! It's an omnibus. I can see it plain. See? One of these big hotel omnibuses."

"By thunder, you're right. It's an omnibus, sure as fate. What do you suppose they are doing with an omnibus? Maybe they are going around collecting the life-crew, hey?"

"That's it, likely. Look! There's a fellow waving a little black flag. He's standing on the steps of the omnibus. There come those other two fellows. Now they're all talking together. Look at the fellow with the flag. Maybe he ain't waving it."

"That ain't a flag, is it? That's his coat. Why, certainly, that's his coat."

"So it is. It's his coat. He's taken it off and is waving it around his head. But would you look at him swing it."

"Oh, say, there isn't any life-saving station there. That's just a winter resort hotel omnibus that has brought over some of the boarders to see us drown."

"What's that idiot with the coat mean? What's he signaling, anyhow?"

"It looks as if he were trying to tell us to go north. There must be a life-saving station up there."

"No! He thinks we're fishing. Just giving us a merry hand. See? Ah, there, Willie."

"Well, I wish I could make something out of those signals. What do you suppose he means?"

"He don't mean anything. He's just playing."

"Well, if he'd just signal us to try the surf again, or to go to sea and wait, or go north, or go south, or go to hell—there would be some reason in it. But look at him. He just stands there and keeps his coat revolving like a wheel. The ass!"

"There come more people."

"Now there's quite a mob. Look! Isn't that a boat?"

"Where? Oh, I see where you mean. No, that's no boat."

"That fellow is still waving his coat."

"He must think we like to see him do that. Why don't he quit it. It don't mean anything."

"I don't know. I think he is trying to make us go north. It must be that there's a life-saving station there somewhere."

"Say, he ain't tired yet. Look at 'im wave."

"Wonder how long he can keep that up. He's been revolving his coat ever since he caught sight of us. He's an idiot. Why aren't they getting men to bring a boat out. A fishing boat—one of those big yawls—could come out here all right. Why don't he do something?"

"Oh, it's all right, now."

"They'll have a boat out here for us in less than no time, now that they've seen us."

A faint yellow tone came into the sky over the low land. The shadows on the sea slowly deepened. The wind bore coldness with it, and the men began to shiver.

"Holy smoke!" said one, allowing his voice to express his impious mood, "if we keep on monkeying out here! If we've got to flounder out here all night!"

"Oh, we'll never have to stay here all night! Don't you worry. They've seen us now, and it won't be long before they'll come chasing out after us."

The shore grew dusky. The man waving a coat blended gradually into this gloom, and it swallowed in the same manner the omnibus and the group of people. The spray, when it dashed uproariously over the side, made the voyagers shrink and swear like men who were being branded.

"I'd like to catch the chump who waved the coat. I feel like soaking him one, just for luck."

"Why? What did he do?"

"Oh, nothing, but then he seemed so damned cheerful."

In the meantime the oiler rowed, and then the correspondent rowed, and then the oiler rowed. Gray-faced and bowed forward, they mechanically, turn by turn, plied the leaden oars. The form of the light-house had vanished from the southern horizon, but finally a pale star appeared, just lifting from the sea. The streaked saffron in the west passed before the all merging darkness, and the sea to the east was black. The land had vanished, and was expressed only by the low and drear thunder of the surf.

"If I am going to be drowned—if I am going to be drowned—if I am going to be drowned, why, in the name of the seven mad gods, who rule the sea, was I allowed to come thus far and contemplate sand and trees? Was I brought here merely to have my nose dragged away as I was about to nibble the sacred cheese of life?"

The patient captain, drooped over the water-jar, was sometimes obliged to speak to the oarsman.

"Keep her head up! Keep her head up!"

" 'Keep her head up,' sir." The voices were weary and low.

This was surely a quiet evening. All save the oarsman lay heavily and listlessly in the boat's bottom. As for him, his eyes were just capable of noting the tall black waves that swept forward in a most sinister silence, save for an occasional subdued growl of a crest.

The cook's head was on a thwart, and he looked without interest at the water under his nose. He was deep in other scenes. Finally he spoke. "Billie," he murmured, dreamfully, "what kind of pie do you like best?"

V

"Pie," said the oiler and the correspondent, agitatedly. "Don't talk about those things, blast you!"

"Well," said the cook, "I was just thinking about ham sandwiches, and——"

A night on the sea in an open boat is a long night. As darkness settled finally, the shine of the light, lifting from the sea in the south, changed to full gold. On the northern horizon a new light appeared, a small bluish gleam on the edge of the waters. These two lights were the furniture of the world. Otherwise there was nothing but waves.

Two men huddled in the stern, and distances were so magnificent in the dingey that the rower was enabled to keep his feet partly warmed by thrusting them under his companions. Their legs indeed extended far under the rowing-seat until they touched the feet of the captain forward. Sometimes, despite the efforts of the tired oarsman, a wave came piling into the boat, an icy wave of the night, and the chilling water soaked them anew. They would twist their bodies for a moment and groan, and sleep the dead sleep once more, while the water in the boat gurgled about them as the craft rocked.

The plan of the oiler and the correspondent was for one to row until he lost the ability, and then arouse the other from his sea-water couch in the bottom of the boat.

The oiler plied the oars until his head drooped forward, and the overpowering sleep blinded him. And he rowed yet afterward. Then he touched a man in the bottom of the boat, and called his name. "Will you spell me for a little while?" he said, meekly.

"Sure, Billie," said the correspondent, awakening and dragging himself to a sitting position. They exchanged places carefully, and the oiler, cuddling down in the sea-water at the cook's side, seemed to go to sleep instantly.

The particular violence of the sea had ceased. The waves came without snarling. The obligation of the man at the oars was to keep the boat headed so that the tilt of the rollers would not capsize her, and to preserve her from filling when the crests rushed past. The black waves were silent and hard to be seen in the darkness. Often one was almost upon the boat before the oarsman was aware.

In a low voice the correspondent addressed the captain. He was not sure that the captain was awake, although this iron man seemed to be always awake. "Captain, shall I keep her making for that light north, sir?"

The same steady voice answered him. "Yes. Keep it about two points off the port bow."

The cook had tied a life-belt around himself in order to get even the warmth which this clumsy cork contrivance could donate, and he seemed almost stove-like when a rower, whose teeth invariably chattered wildly as soon as he ceased his labor, dropped down to sleep.

The correspondent, as he rowed, looked down at the two men sleeping under foot. The cook's arm was around the oiler's shoulders, and, with their fragmentary clothing and haggard faces, they were the babes of the sea, a grotesque rendering of the old babes in the wood.

Later he must have grown stupid at his work, for suddenly there was a growling of water, and a crest came with a roar and a swash into the boat, and it was a wonder that it did not set the cook afloat in his life-belt. The cook continued to sleep, but the oiler sat up, blinking his eyes and shaking with the new cold.

"Oh, I'm awful sorry, Billie," said the correspondent, contritely.

"That's all right, old boy," said the oiler, and lay down again and was asleep.

Presently it seemed that even the captain dozed, and the correspondent thought that he was the one man afloat on all the oceans. The wind had a voice as it came over the waves, and it was sadder than the end.

There was a long, loud swishing astern of the boat, and a gleaming trail of phosphorescence, like blue flame, was furrowed on the black waters. It might have been made by a monstrous knife.

Then there came a stillness, while the correspondent breathed with the open mouth and looked at the sea.

Suddenly there was another swish and another long flash of bluish light, and this time it was alongside the boat, and might almost have been reached with an oar. The correspondent saw an enormous fin speed like a shadow through the water, hurling the crystalline spray and leaving the long glowing trail.

The correspondent looked over his shoulder at the captain. His face was hidden, and he seemed to be asleep. He looked at the babes of the sea. They certain were asleep. So, being bereft of sympathy, he leaned a little way to one side and swore softly into the sea.

But the thing did not then leave the vicinity of the boat. Ahead or

astern, on one side or the other, at intervals long or short, fled the long
sparkling streak, and there was to be heard the whiroo of the dark fin.
The speed and power of the thing was greatly to be admired. It cut
the water like a gigantic and keen projectile.

The presence of this biding thing did not affect the man with the
same horror that it would if he had been a picnicker. He simply looked
at the sea dully and swore in an undertone.

Nevertheless, it is true that he did not wish to be alone with the
thing. He wished one of his companions to awaken by chance and keep
him company with it. But the captain hung motionless over the water-
jar and the oiler and the cook in the bottom of the boat were plunged
in slumber.

VI

"If I am going to be drowned—if I am going to be drowned—if
I am going to be drowned, why, in the name of the seven mad gods,
who rule the sea, was I allowed to come thus far and contemplate
sand and trees?"

During this dismal night, it may be remarked that a man would
conclude that it was really the intention of the seven mad gods to
drown him, despite the abominable injustice of it. For it was certainly
an abominable injustice to drown a man who had worked so hard, so
hard. The man felt it would be a crime most unnatural. Other people
had drowned at sea since galleys swarmed with painted sails, but
still——

When it occurs to a man that nature does not regard him as important, and that she feels she would not maim the universe by disposing
of him, he at first wishes to throw bricks at the temple, and he hates
deeply the fact that there are no bricks and no temples. Any visible
expression of nature would surely be pelleted with his jeers.

Then, if there be no tangible thing to hoot he feels, perhaps, the
desire to confront a personification and indulge in pleas, bowed to one
knee, and with hands supplicant, saying: "Yes, but I love myself."

A high cold star on a winter's night is the word he feels that she
says to him. Thereafter he knows the pathos of his situation.

The men in the dingey had not discussed these matters, but each
had, no doubt, reflected upon them in silence and according to his
mind. There was seldom any expression upon their faces save the
general one of complete weariness. Speech was devoted to the business of the boat.

To chime the notes of his emotion, a verse mysteriously entered the
correspondent's head. He had even forgotten that he had forgotten
this verse, but it suddenly was in his mind.

A soldier of the Legion lay dying in Algiers,
There was lack of woman's nursing, there was dearth of woman's tears;
But a comrade stood beside him, and he took that comrade's hand
And he said: "I shall never see my own, my native land."

In his childhood, the correspondent had been made acquainted with the fact that a soldier of the Legion lay dying in Algiers, but he had never regarded the fact as important. Myriads of his school-fellows had informed him of the soldier's plight, but the dinning had naturally ended by making him perfectly indifferent. He had never considered it his affair that a soldier of the Legion lay dying in Algiers, nor had it appeared to him as a matter for sorrow. It was less to him than breaking of a pencil's point.

Now, however, it quaintly came to him as a human, living thing. It was no longer merely a picture of a few throes in the breast of a poet, meanwhile drinking tea and warming his feet at the grate; it was an actuality—stern, mournful, and fine.

The correspondent plainly saw the soldier. He lay on the sand with his feet out straight and still. While his pale left hand was upon his chest in an attempt to thwart the going of his life, the blood came between his fingers. In the far Algerian distance, a city of low square forms was set against a sky that was faint with the last sunset hues. The correspondent, plying the oars and dreaming of the slow and slower movements of the lips of the soldier, was moved by a profound and perfectly impersonal comprehension. He was sorry for the soldier of the Legion who lay dying in Algiers.

The thing which had followed the boat and waited had evidently grown bored at the delay. There was no longer to be heard the slash of the cut-water, and there was no longer the flame of the long trail. The light in the north still glimmered, but it was apparently no nearer to the boat. Sometimes the boom of the surf rang in the correspondent's ears, and he turned the craft seaward then and rowed harder. South-ward, someone had evidently built a watch-fire on the beach. It was too low and too far to be seen, but it made a shimmering, roseate reflection upon the bluff back of it, and this could be discerned from the boat. The wind came stronger, and sometimes a wave suddenly raged out like a mountain-cat and there was to be seen the sheen and sparkle of a broken crest.

The captain, in the bow, moved on his water-jar and sat erect. "Pretty long night," he observed to the correspondent. He looked at the shore. "Those life-saving people take their time."

"Did you see that shark playing around?"

"Yes, I saw him. He was a big fellow, all right."

"Wish I had known you were awake."

Later the correspondent spoke into the bottom of the boat.

"Billie!" There was a slow and gradual disentanglement. "Billie, will you spell me?"

"Sure," said the oiler.

As soon as the correspondent touched the cold comfortable sea-water in the bottom of the boat, and had huddled close to the cook's life-belt he was deep in sleep, despite the fact that his teeth played all the popular airs. This sleep was so good to him that it was but a moment before he heard a voice call his name in a tone that demonstrated the last stages of exhaustion. "Will you spell me?"

"Sure, Billie."

The light in the north had mysteriously vanished, but the correspondent took his course from the wide-awake captain.

Later in the night they took the boat farther out to sea, and the captain directed the cook to take one oar at the stern and keep the boat facing the seas. He was to call out if he should hear the thunder of the surf. This plan enabled the oiler and the correspondent to get respite together. "We'll give those boys a chance to get into shape again," said the captain. They curled down and, after a few preliminary chatterings and trembles, slept once more the dead sleep. Neither knew they had bequeathed to the cook the company of another shark, or perhaps the same shark.

As the boat caroused on the waves, spray occasionally bumped over the side and gave them a fresh soaking, but this had no power to break their repose. The ominous slash of the wind and the water affected them as it would have affected mummies.

"Boys," said the cook, with the notes of every reluctance in his voice, "she's drifted in pretty close. I guess one of you had better take her to sea again." The correspondent, aroused, heard the crash of the toppled crests.

As he was rowing, the captain gave him some whiskey and water, and this steadied the chills out of him. "If I ever get ashore and anybody shows me even a photograph of an oar——"

At last there was a short conversation.

"Billie. . . . Billie, will you spell me?"

"Sure," said the oiler.

VII

When the correspondent again opened his eyes, the sea and the sky were each of the gray hue of the dawning. Later, carmine and gold was painted upon the waters. The morning appeared finally, in its splendor, with a sky of pure blue, and the sunlight flamed on the tips of the waves.

On the distant dunes were set many little black cottages, and a tall white wind-mill reared above them. No man, nor dog, nor bicycle appeared on the beach. The cottages might have formed a deserted village.

The voyagers scanned the shore. A conference was held in the boat. "Well," said the captain, "if no help is coming, we might better try a run through the surf right away. If we stay out here much longer we will be too weak to do anything for ourselves at all." The others silently acquiesced in this reasoning. The boat was headed for the beach. The correspondent wondered if none ever ascended the tall wind-tower, and if then they never looked seaward. This tower was a giant, standing with its back to the plight of the ants. It represented in a degree, to the correspondent, the serenity of nature amid the struggles of the individual—nature in the wind, and nature in the vision of men. She did not seem cruel to him then, nor beneficent, nor treacherous, nor wise. But she was indifferent, flatly indifferent. It is, perhaps, plausible that a man in this situation, impressed with the unconcern of the universe, should see the innumerable flaws of his life and have them taste wickedly in his mind and wish for another chance. A distinction between right and wrong seems absurdly clear to him, then, in this new ignorance of the grave-edge, and he understands that if he were given another opportunity he would mend his conduct and his words, and be better and brighter during an introduction, or at a tea.

"Now, boys," said the captain, "she is going to swamp sure. All we can do is to work her in as far as possible, and then when she swamps, pile out and scramble for the beach. Keep cool now and don't jump until she swamps sure."

The oiler took the oars. Over his shoulders he scanned the surf. "Captain," he said, "I think I'd better bring her about, and keep her head-on to the seas and back her in."

"All right, Billie," said the captain. "Back her in." The oiler swung the boat then and, seated in the stern, the cook and the correspondent were obliged to look over their shoulders to contemplate the lonely and indifferent shore.

The monstrous inshore rollers heaved the boat high until the men were again enabled to see the white sheets of water scudding up the slanted beach. "We won't get in very close," said the captain. Each time a man could wrest his attention from the rollers, he turned his glance toward the shore, and in the expression of the eyes during this contemplation there was a singular quality. The correspondent, observing the others, knew that they were not afraid, but the full meaning of their glances was shrouded.

As for himself, he was too tired to grapple fundamentally with the fact. He tried to coerce his mind into thinking of it, but the mind was dominated at this time by the muscles, and the muscles said they did not care. It merely occurred to him that if he should drown it would be a shame.

There were no hurried words, no pallor, no plain agitation. The men simply looked at the shore. "Now, remember to get well clear of the boat when you jump," said the captain.

Seaward the crest of a roller suddenly fell with a thunderous crash, and the long white comber came roaring down upon the boat.

"Steady now," said the captain. The men were silent. They turned their eyes from the shore to the comber and waited. The boat slid up the incline, leaped at the furious top, bounced over it, and swung down the long back of the waves. Some water had been shipped and the cook bailed it out.

But the next crest crashed also. The tumbling boiling flood of white water caught the boat and whirled it almost perpendicular. Water swarmed in from all sides. The correspondent had his hands on the gunwale at this time, and when the water entered at that place he swiftly withdrew his fingers, as if he objected to wetting them.

The little boat, drunken with this weight of water, reeled and snuggled deeper into the sea.

"Bail her out, cook! Bail her out," said the captain.

"All right, captain," said the cook.

"Now, boys, the next one will do for us, sure," said the oiler. "Mind to jump clear of the boat."

The third wave moved forward, huge, furious, implacable. It fairly swallowed the dingey, and almost simultaneously the men tumbled into the sea. A piece of life-belt had lain in the bottom of the boat, and as the correspondent went overboard he held this to his chest with his left hand.

The January water was icy, and he reflected immediately that it was colder than he had expected to find it off the coast of Florida. This appeared to his dazed mind as a fact important enough to be noted at the time. The coldness of the water was sad; it was tragic. This fact was somehow mixed and confused with his opinion of his own situation that it seemed almost a proper reason for tears. The water was cold.

When he came to the surface he was conscious of little but the noisy water. Afterward he saw his companions in the sea. The oiler was ahead in the race. He was swimming strongly and rapidly. Off to the correspondent's left, the cook's great white and corked back bulged out of the water, and in the rear the captain was hanging with his one good hand to the keel of the overturned dingey.

There is a certain immovable quality to a shore, and the correspondent wondered at it amid the confusion of the sea.

It seemed also very attractive, but the correspondent knew that it was a long journey, and he paddled leisurely. The piece of life-preserver lay under him, and sometimes he whirled down the incline of a wave as if he were on a hand-sled.

But finally he arrived at a place in the sea where travel was beset with difficulty. He did not pause swimming to inquire what manner of current had caught him, but there his progress ceased. The shore was set before him like a bit of scenery on a stage, and he looked at it and understood with his eyes each detail of it.

As the cook passed, much farther to the left, the captain was calling to him, "Turn over on your back, cook! Turn over on your back and use the oar."

"All right, sir." The cook turned on his back, and, paddling with an oar, went ahead as if he were a canoe.

Presently the boat also passed to the left of the correspondent with the captain clinging with one hand to the keel. He would have appeared like a man raising himself to look over a board fence, if it were not for the extraordinary gymnastics of the boat. The correspondent marvelled that the captain could still hold to it.

They passed on, nearer to shore—the oiler, the cook, the captain—and following them went the water-jar, bouncing gayly over the seas.

The correspondent remained in the grip of this strange new enemy —a current. The shore, with its white slope of sand and its green bluff, topped with little silent cottages, was spread like a picture before him. It was very near to him then, but he was impressed as one who in a gallery looks at a scene from Brittany or Algiers.

He thought: "I am going to drown? Can it be possible? Can it be possible? Can it be possible? Perhaps an individual must consider his own death to be the final phenomenon of nature.

But later a wave perhaps whirled him out of this small deadly current, for he found suddenly that he could again make progress toward the shore. Later still, he was aware that the captain, clinging with one hand to the keel of the dingey, had his face turned away from the shore and toward him, and was calling his name. "Come to the boat! Come to the boat!"

In his struggle to reach the captain and the boat, he reflected that when one gets properly wearied, drowning must really be a comfortable arrangement, a cessation of hostilities accompanied by a large degree of relief, and he was glad of it, for the main thing in his mind for some moments had been horror of the temporary agony. He did not wish to be hurt.

Presently he saw a man running along the shore. He was undressing with most remarkable speed. Coat, trousers, shirt, everything flew magically off him.

"Come to the boat," called the captain.

"All right, captain." As the correspondent paddled, he saw the captain let himself down to bottom and leave the boat. Then the correspondent performed his one little marvel of the voyage. A large wave caught him and flung him with ease and supreme speed completely over the boat and far beyond it. It struck him even then as an event in gymnastics, and a true miracle of the sea. An overturned boat in the surf is not a plaything to a swimming man.

The correspondent arrived in water that reached only to his waist, but his condition did not enable him to stand for more than a moment. Each wave knocked him into a heap, and the under-tow pulled at him.

Then he saw the man who had been running and undressing, and undressing and running, come bounding into the water. He dragged ashore the cook, and then waded toward the captain, but the captain waved him away, and sent him to the correspondent. He was naked, naked as a tree in winter, but a halo was about his head, and he shone like a saint. He gave a strong pull, and a long drag, and a bully heave at the correspondent's hand. The correspondent, schooled in the minor formulæ, said: "Thanks, old man." But suddenly the man cried: "What's that?" He pointed a swift finger. The correspondent said: "Go."

In the shallows, face downward, lay the oiler. His forehead touched sand that was periodically, between each wave, clear of the sea.

The correspondent did not know all that transpired afterward. When he achieved safe ground he fell, striking the sand with each particular part of his body. It was as if he had dropped from a roof, but the thud was grateful to him.

It seems that instantly the beach was populated with men with blankets, clothes, and flasks, and women with coffee-pots and all the remedies sacred to their minds. The welcome of the land to the men from the sea was warm and generous, but a still and dripping shape was carried slowly up the beach, and the land's welcome for it could only be the different and sinister hospitality of the grave.

When it came night, the white waves paced to and fro in the moonlight, and the wind brought the sound of the great sea's voice to the men on shore, and they felt that they could then be interpreters.

Theodore Dreiser
Nigger Jeff

THE CITY EDITOR was waiting for his good reporter, Eugene Davies.
He had cut an item from one of the afternoon papers and laid it aside
to give to Mr. Davies. Presently the reporter appeared.

It was one o'clock of a sunny, spring afternoon. Davies wore a new
spring suit, a new hat and new shoes. In the lapel of his coat was a
small bunch of violets. He was feeling exceedingly well and good-
natured. The world seemed worth singing about.

"Read that, Davies," said the city editor, handing him the clipping.
"I'll tell you what I want you to do afterward."

The reporter stood by the editorial chair and read:

> Pleasant Valley, Mo., April 16.
> A most dastardly crime has just been reported here. Jeff Ingalls, a
> negro, this morning assaulted Ada Whittier, the nineteen-year-old
> daughter of Morgan Whittier, a well-to-do farmer, whose home is four
> miles south of this place. A posse, headed by Sheriff Mathews, has
> started in pursuit. If he is caught, it is thought he will be lynched.

The reporter raised his eyes as he finished.

"You had better go out there, Davies," said the city editor. "It
looks as if something might come of that. A lynching up here would be
a big thing."

Davies smiled. He was always pleased to be sent out of town. It
was a mark of appreciation. The city editor never sent any of the
other boys on these big stories. What a nice ride he would have.

He found Pleasant Valley to be a small town, nestling between green
slopes of low hills, with one small business corner and a rambling array of lanes. One or two merchants of St. Louis lived out here, but
otherwise it was exceedingly rural. He took note of the whiteness of
the little houses, the shimmering beauty of the little creek you had to
cross in going from the depot. At the one main corner a few men were

Ainslee's, VIII (November, 1901), 366–75. Republished in *Free and Other
Stories* (New York, 1918). Text from *Ainslee's.*

gathered about a typical village barroom. Davies headed for this as being the most apparent source of information.

In mingling with the company, he said nothing about his errand. He was very shy about mentioning that he was a newspaper man.

The whole company was craving excitement and wanted to see something come of the matter. They hadn't had such a chance to work up wrath and satisfy their animal propensities in years. It was a fine opportunity and such a righteous one.

He went away thinking that he had best find out for himself how the girl was. Accordingly he sought the old man that kept a stable in the village and procured a horse. No carriage was to be had. Davies was not an excellent rider, but he made a shift of it. The farm was not so very far away, and before long he knocked at the front door of the house, set back a hundred feet from the rough country road.

"I'm from the *Republic*," he said, with dignity. His position took very well with farmers. "How is Miss Whittier?"

"She's doing very well," said a tall, rawboned woman. "Won't you come in? She's rather feverish, but the doctor says she'll be all right."

Davies acknowledged the invitation by entering. He was anxious to see the girl, but she was sleeping, and under the influence of an opiate.

"When did this happen?" he asked.

"About eight o'clock this morning," said the woman. "She started off to go over to our next neighbor here, Mr. Edmonds, and this negro met her. I didn't know anything about it until she came crying through the gate and dropped down in here."

"Were you the first one to meet her?" asked Davies.

"Yes, I was the only one," said Mrs. Whittier. "The men had gone out in the fields."

Davies listened to more of the details, and then rose to go. He was allowed to have a look at the girl, who was rather pretty. In the yard he met a country chap who had come over to hear the news. This man imparted more information.

"They're lookin' all around south of here," said the man, speaking of the crowd supposed to be in search. "I expect they'll make short work of him if they get him."

"Where does this negro live?" asked Davies.

"Oh, right down here a little way. You follow this road to the next crossing and turn to the right. It's a little log house that sits back off the road—something like this, only it's got a lot of chips scattered about."

Davies decided to go there, but changed his mind. It was getting late. He had better return to the village, he thought.

Accordingly, he rode back and put the horse in the hands of its owner. Then he went over to the principal corner. Much the same company was still present. He wondered what these people had been doing all the time. He decided to ingratiate himself by imparting a little information.

Just then a young fellow came galloping up.

"They've got him," he shouted, excitedly, "they've got him."

A chorus of "whos" and "wheres," with sundry other queries, greeted this information as the crowd gathered about the rider.

"Why, Mathews caught him up here at his own house. Says he'll shoot the first man that dares to try to take him away. He's taking him over to Clayton."

"Which way'd he go?" exclaimed the men.

"'Cross Sellers' Lane," said the rider. "The boys think he's going to Baldwin."

"Whoopee," yelled one of the listeners. "Are you going, Sam?"

"You bet," said the latter. "Wait'll I get my horse."

Davies waited no longer. He saw the crowd would be off in a minute to catch up with the sheriff. There would be information in that quarter. He hastened after his horse.

"He's eating," said the man.

"I don't care," exclaimed Davies. "Turn him out. I'll give you a dollar more."

The man led the horse out, and the reporter mounted.

When he got back to the corner several of the men were already there. The young man who had brought the news had dashed off again.

Davies waited to see which road they would take. Then he did the riding of his life.

In an hour the company had come in sight of the sheriff, who, with two other men, was driving a wagon he had borrowed. He had a revolver in each hand and was sitting with his face toward the group, that trailed after at a respectful distance. Excited as every one was, there was no disposition to halt the progress of the law.

"He's in that wagon," Davies heard one man say. "Don't you see they've got him tied and laid down in there?"

Davies looked.

"We ought to take him away and hang him," said one of the young fellows who rode nearest the front.

"Where's old man Whittier?" asked one of the crowd, who felt that they needed a leader.

"He's out with the other crowd," was the reply.

"Somebody ought to go and tell him."

"Clark's gone," assured another, who hoped for the worst.

Davies rode among the company very much excited. He was astonished at the character of the crowd. It was largely impelled to its excited jaunt by curiosity and a desire to see what would happen.

There was not much daring in it. The men were afraid of the determined sheriff. They thought something ought to be done, but they did not feel like getting into trouble.

The sheriff, a sage, lusty, solemn man, contemplated the recent addition to these trailers with considerable feeling. He was determined to protect his man and avoid injustice. A mob should not have him if he had to shoot, and if he shot, he was going to empty both revolvers, and those of his companions. Finally, since the company thus added to did not dash upon him, he decided to scare them off. He thought he could do it since they trailed like calves.

"Stop a minute," he said to his driver.

The latter pulled up. So did the crowd behind. Then the sheriff stood over the prostrate body of the negro, who lay trembling in the jolting wagon bed and called back to the men.

"Go on away from here, you people," he said. "Go on, now. I won't have you foller after me."

"Give us the nigger," yelled one in a half-bantering, half-derisive tone of voice.

"I'll give you five minutes to go on back out of this road," returned the sheriff grimly. They were about a hundred feet apart. "If you don't, I'll clear you out."

"Give us the nigger!"

"I know you, Scott," answered the sheriff, recognizing the voice. "I'll arrest every last one of you to-morrow. Mark my word!"

The company listened in silence, the horses champing and twisting.

"We've got a right to follow," answered one of the men.

"I give you fair warning," said the sheriff, jumping from his wagon and leveling his pistols as he approached. "When I count five, I'll begin to shoot."

He was a serious and stalwart figure as he approached, and the crowd retreated.

"Get out o' this now," he yelled. "One, two——"

The company turned completely and retreated.

"We'll follow him when he gets farther on," said one of the men in explanation.

"He's got to do it," said another. "Let him get a little ahead."

The sheriff returned to his wagon and drove on. He knew that he would not be obeyed, and that safety lay in haste alone. If he could only make them lose track of him and get a good start it might be possible to get to Clayton and the strong county jail by morning.

Accordingly he whipped up his horses while keeping his grim lookout.

"He's going to Baldwin," said one of the company of which Davies was a member.

"Where is that?" asked Davies.

"Over west of here, about four miles."

The men lagged, hesitating what to do. They did not want to lose sight of him, and yet cowardice controlled them. They did not want to get into direct altercation with the law. It wasn't their place to hang the man, although he ought to be hanged and it would be a stirring and exciting thing if he were. Consequently, they desired to watch and be on hand—to get old Whittier and his son Jake if they could, who were out looking elsewhere. They wanted to see what the father and brother would do.

The quandary was solved by Dick Hewlitt, who suggested that they could get to Baldwin by going back to Pleasant Valley and taking the Sand River pike. It was a shorter cut than this. Maybe they could beat the sheriff there. Accordingly, while one or two remained to track the sheriff, the rest set off at a gallop to Pleasant Valley. It was nearly dusk when they got there and stopped for a few minutes at the corner store. Here they talked, and somehow the zest to follow departed; they were not certain now of going on. It was supper time. The fires of evening meals were marked by upcurling smoke. Evidently the sheriff had them worsted for to-night. Morg Whittier had not been found. Neither had Jake. Perhaps they had better eat. Two or three had already secretly fallen away.

They were telling the news to the one or two storekeepers, when Jake Whittier, the girl's brother, and several companions came riding up. They had been scouring the territory to the north of the town.

"The sheriff's got him," said one of the company. "He's taking him over to Baldwin in a wagon."

"Which way did he go?" asked young Jake, whose hardy figure, worn, hand-me-down clothes and rakish hat showed up picturesquely as he turned on his horse.

"'Cross Sellers' Lane. You won't get him that way. Better take the short cut."

A babble of voices was making the little corner interesting. One told how he had been caught, another that the sheriff was defiant, a third that men were tracking him, until the chief points of the drama had been spoken, if not heard.

"Come on, boys," said Jake, jerking at the reins and heading up the pike. "I'll get the damn nigger."

Instantly suppers were forgotten. The whole customary order of the evening was neglected. The company started off on another exciting jaunt, up hill and down dale, through the lovely country that lay between Baldwin and Pleasant Valley.

Davies was very weary of his saddle. He wondered when he was to write his story. The night was exceedingly beautiful. Stars were already beginning to shine. Distant lamps twinkled like yellow eyes from the cottages in the valleys on the hillsides. The air was fresh and tender. Some pea fowls were crying afar off and the east promised a golden moon.

Silently the assembled company trotted on—no more than a score in all. It was too grim a pilgrimage for joking. Young Jake, riding silently toward the front, looked as if he meant business. His friends did not like to say anything to him, seeing that he was the aggrieved. He was left alone.

After an hour's riding Baldwin came into view, lying in a sheltering cup of low hills. Its lights were twinkling softly, and there was an air of honest firesides and cheery suppers about it which appealed to Davies in his hungry state. Still, he had no thought but of carrying out his mission.

Once in the village they were greeted by calls of recognition. Everybody knew what they had come for. The local storekeepers and loungers followed the cavalcade up the street to the sheriff's house, for the riders had now fallen into a solemn walk.

"You won't get him, boys," said Seavey, the young postmaster and telegraph operator, as they passed his door. "Mathews says he's sent him to Clayton."

At the first street corner they were joined by several men who had followed the sheriff.

"He tried to give us the slip," they said, excitedly, "but he's got the nigger in the house there, down in the cellar."

"How do you know?"

"I saw him bring him in this way. I think he is, anyhow."

A block from the sheriff's little white cottage the men parleyed. They decided to go up and demand the negro.

"If he don't turn him out, we'll break in the door and take him," said Jake.

"That's right. We'll stand by you, Whittier."

A throng had gathered. The whole village was up in arms. The one street was alive and running with people. Riders pranced up and down, hallooing. A few shot off revolvers. Presently the mob gathered about the sheriff's gate, and Jake stepped forward as leader.

Their coming was not unexpected. Sheriff Mathews was ready for them with a double-barreled Winchester. He had bolted the doors and put the negro in the cellar, pending the arrival of the aid he had telegraphed for to Clayton. The latter was cowering and chattering in the darkest corner of his dungeon against the cold, damp earth, as he hearkened to the voices and the firing of the revolvers. With wide, bulging eyes, he stared into the gloom.

Jake, the son and brother, took the precautionary method of calling to the sheriff.

"Hello, Mathews!"

"Eh, eh, eh," bellowed the crowd.

Suddenly the door flew open, and appearing first in the glow of the lamp came the double barrel of a Winchester, followed by the form of the sheriff, who held his gun ready for a quick throw to the shoulder. All except Jake fell back.

"We want that nigger," said Jake, deliberately.

"He isn't here," said the sheriff.

"Then what you got that gun for?" yelled a voice.

The sheriff made no answer.

"Better give him up, Mathews," called another, who was safe in the crowd, "or we'll come in and take him."

"Lookee here, gentlemen," said the sheriff, "I said the man wasn't here. I say it again. You couldn't have him if he was and you can't come in my house. Now, if you people don't want trouble, you'd better go on away."

"He's down in the cellar," yelled another.

The sheriff waved his gun slightly.

"Why don't you let us see?" said another.

"You'd better go away from here now," cautioned the sheriff.

The crowd continued to simmer and stew, while Jake stood out before. He was very pale and determined, but lacked initiative.

"He won't shoot. Why don't you go in, boys, and get him?"

"He won't, eh?" thought the sheriff. Then he said aloud: "The first man that comes inside that gate takes the consequences."

No one ventured near the gate. It seemed as if the planned assault must come to nothing.

"You'd better go away from here," cautioned the sheriff again. "You can't come in, it'll only mean bloodshed."

There was more chattering and jesting while the sheriff stood on guard. He said no more. Nor did he allow the banter, turmoil and lust for tragedy to disturb him. Only he kept his eye on Jake, on whose movements the crowd hung.

"I'll get him," said Jake, "before morning."

The truth was that he felt the weakness of the crowd. He was, to all intents and purposes, alone, for he did not inspire confidence.

Thus the minutes passed. It became a half hour and then an hour. With the extending time pedestrians dropped out and then horsemen. Some went up the street, several back to Pleasant Valley, more galloped about until there were very few left at the gate. It was plain that organization was lost. Finally Davies smiled and came away. He was sure he had a splendid story.

He began to look for something to eat, and hunted for the telegraph operator.

He found the operator first and told him he wanted to write a story and file it. The latter said there was a table in the little post-office and telegraph station which he could use. He got very much interested in Davies, and when he asked where he could get something to eat, said he would run across the street and tell the proprietor of the only boarding-house to fix him something which he could eat as he wrote.

"You start your story," he said, "and I'll come back and see if I can get the *Republic*."

Davies sat down and started the account.

"Very obliging postmaster," he thought, but he had so often encountered pleasant and obliging people on his rounds, that he soon dropped that thought.

The food was brought and Davies wrote. By eight-thirty the *Republic* answered an often-repeated call.

"Davies at Baldwin," ticked the post master, "get ready for quite a story."

"Let 'er go," answered the operator in the *Republic*, who had been expecting this dispatch.

Davies turned over page after page as the events of the day formulated themselves in his mind. He ate a little between whiles, looking out through the small window before him, where afar off he could see a lonely light twinkling in a hillside cottage. Not infrequently he stopped work to see if anything new was happening. The operator also wandered about, waiting for an accumulation of pages upon which he could work, but making sure to catch up with the writer. The two became quite friendly.

Davies finished his dispatch with the caution that more might follow, and was told by the city editor to watch it. Then he and the postmaster sat down to talk.

About twelve o'clock the lights in all the village houses had vanished and the inhabitants had gone to bed. The man-hunters had retired, and the night was left to its own sounds and murmurs, when suddenly the faint beating of hoofs sounded out on the Sand River Pike, which led away toward Pleasant Valley, back of the post-office. The sheriff had not relaxed any of his vigilance. He was not sleeping. There was no sleep for him until the county authorities should come to his aid.

"Here they come back again," exclaimed the postmaster.

"By George, you're right," said Davies.

There was a clattering of hoofs and grunting of saddle girths as a large company of men dashed up the road and turned into the narrow street of the village.

Instantly the place was astir again. Lights appeared in doorways, and windows were thrown open. People were gazing out to see what new movement was afoot. Davies saw that there was none of the hip and hurrah business about this company such as had characterized the previous descent. There was grimness everywhere, and he began to feel that this was the beginning of the end. He ran down the street toward the sheriff's house, arriving a few moments after the crowd, which was in part dismounted.

With the clear moon shining straight overhead, it was nearly as bright as day. Davies made out several of his companions of the afternoon and Jake, the son. There were many more, though, whom he did not know, and foremost among them an old man. He was strong, iron-gray and wore a full beard. He looked very much like a blacksmith.

While he was still looking, the old man went boldly forward to the little front porch of the house and knocked at the door. Some one lifted a curtain at the window and peeped out.

"Hello, in there," the old man cried, knocking again and much louder.

"What do you want?" said a voice.

"We want that nigger."

"Well, you can't have him. I've told you people once."

"Bring him out or we'll break down the door," said the old man.

"If you do, it's at your own risk. I'll give you three minutes to get off that porch."

"We want that nigger."

"If you don't get off that porch I'll fire through the door," said the voice, solemnly. "One, two——"

The old man backed cautiously away.

"Come out, Mathews," yelled the crowd. "You've got to give him up. We ain't going back without him."

Slowly the door opened, as if the individual within was very well satisfied as to his power to handle the mob. It revealed the tall form of Sheriff Mathews, armed with his Winchester. He looked around very stolidly and then addressed the old man as one would a friend.

"You can't have him, Morgan," he said, "it's against the law."

"Law or no law," said the old man, "I want that nigger."

"I can't let you have him, Morgan. It's against the law. You oughtn't to be coming around here at this time of night acting so."

"Well, we'll take him, then," said the old man, making a move.

The sheriff leveled his gun on the instant.

"Stand back, there," he shouted, noticing a movement on the part of the crowd. "I'll blow ye into kingdom come, sure as hell."

The crowd halted at this assurance.

The sheriff lowered his weapon as if he thought the danger were over.

"You all ought to be ashamed of yourselves," he said, softly, his voice sinking to a gentle, neighborly reproof, "tryin' to upset the law this way."

"The nigger didn't upset the law, did he?" asked one, derisively.

The sheriff made no answer.

"Give us that scoundrel, Mathews, you'd better do it," said the old man. "It'll save a heap of trouble."

"I'll not argue with you, Morgan. I said you couldn't have him, and you can't. If you want bloodshed, all right. But don't blame me. I'll kill the first man that tries to make a move this way."

He shifted his gun handily and waited. The crowd stood outside his little fence murmuring.

Presently the old man retired and spoke to several leaders.

There was more murmuring, and then he came back to the dead line.

"We don't want to cause trouble, Mathews," he began, explanatively, moving his hand oratorically, "but we think you ought to see that it won't do you any good to stand out. We think that——"

Davies was watching young Jake, the son, whose peculiar attitude attracted his attention. The latter was standing poised at the edge of the crowd, evidently seeking to remain unobserved. His eyes were on the sheriff, who was hearkening to the old man. Suddenly, when the sheriff seemed for a moment mollified and unsuspecting, he made a quick run for the porch. There was an intense movement all along the line, as the life and death of the deed became apparent. Quickly the sheriff drew his gun to his shoulder. He pressed both triggers at the same time, but not before Jake reached him. The latter knocked the gun barrel upward and fell upon his man. Both shots blazed out over the heads of the crowd in red puffs, and then followed a general onslaught. Men leaped the fence by tens, and crowded upon the little cottage. They swarmed on every side of the house, and crowded about the porch and the door, where four men were scuffling with the sheriff. The latter soon gave up, vowing vengeance. Torches were brought and a rope. A wagon drove up and was backed into the yard. Then began the calls for the negro.

The negro had been crouching in his corner in the cellar, trembling for his fate ever since the first attack. He had not dozed or lost consciousness during the intervening hours, but cowered there, wondering and praying. He was terrified lest the sheriff might not get him away in time. He was afraid that every sound meant a new assault. Now, however, he had begun to have the faintest glimmerings of hope when the new murmurs of contention arose. He heard the gallop of the horses' feet, voices of the men parleying, the ominous knock on the door.

At this sound, his body quaked and his teeth chattered. He began to quiver in each separate muscle and run cold. Already he saw the men at him, beating and kicking him.

"Before God, boss, I didn't mean to," he chattered, contemplating the chimera of his brain with startling eyes. "Oh, my God! boss, no, no. Oh, no, no."

He crowded closer to the wall. Another sound greeted his ears. It was the roar of a shotgun. He fell, groveling upon the floor, his nails digging in the earth.

"Oh, my Lawd, boss," he moaned, "oh, my Lawd, boss, don't kill me. I won't do it no mo'. I didn't go to do it. I didn't." His teeth were in the wet earth.

It was but now that the men were calling each other to the search. Five jumped to the outside entrance way of the low cellar, carrying a rope. Three others followed with their torches. They descended into the dark hole and looked cautiously about.

Suddenly, in the farthest corner, they espied him. In his agony, he had worked himself into a crouching position, as if he were about to spring. His hands were still in the earth. His eyes were rolling, his mouth foaming.

"Oh, my Lawd!" he was repeating monotonously, "oh, my Lawd!"

"Here he is. Pull him out, boys," cried several together.

The negro gave one yell of horror. He quite bounded as he did so, coming down with a dead chug on the earthen floor. Reason had forsaken him. He was a groveling, foaming brute. The last gleam of intelligence was that which notified him of the set eyes of his pursuers.

Davies was standing ten feet back when they began to reappear. He noted the heads of the torches, the disheveled appearance of the men, the scuffling and pulling. Then he clapped his hands over his mouth and worked his fingers convulsively, almost unconscious of what he was doing.

"Oh, my God," he whispered, his voice losing power.

The sickening sight was that of negro Jeff, foaming at the mouth, bloodshot in the eyes, his hands working convulsively, being dragged up the cellar steps, feet foremost. They had tied a rope about his waist and feet, and had hauled him out, leaving his head to hang and drag. The black face was distorted beyond all human semblance.

"Oh, my God!" said Davies again, biting his fingers unconsciously.

The crowd gathered about, more horror-stricken than gleeful at their own work. The negro was rudely bound and thrown like a sack of wheat into the wagon bed. Father and son mounted to drive, and the crowd took their horses. Wide-eyed and brain-racked, Davies ran for his own. He was so excited, he scarcely knew what he was doing.

Slowly the gloomy cavalcade took its way up the Sand River Pike. The moon was pouring down a wash of silvery light. The shadowy trees were stirring with a cool night wind. Davies hurried after and joined the silent, tramping throng.

"Are they going to hang him?" he asked.

"That's what they got him for," answered the man nearest him.

Davies dropped again into silence and tried to recover his nerves. The gloomy company seemed a terrible thing. He drew near the wagon and looked at the negro.

The latter seemed out of his senses. He was breathing heavily and groaning. His eyes were fixed and staring, his face and hands bleeding as if they had been scratched or trampled on. He was bundled up like limp wheat.

Davies could not stand it longer. He fell back, sick at heart. It seemed a ghastly, unmerciful way to do. Still, the company moved on and he followed, past fields lit white by the moon, under dark, silent groups of trees, through which the moonlight fell in patches, up hilltops and down into valleys, until at last the little stream came into view, sparkling like a molten flood of silver in the night. After a time the road drew close to the water and made for a wagon bridge, which could be seen a little way ahead. The company rode up to this and halted. Davies dismounted with the others. The wagon was driven up to the bridge and father and son got out.

Fully a score of men gathered about, and the negro was lifted from the wagon. Davies thought he could not stand it, and went down by the waterside slightly above the bridge. He could see long beams of iron sticking out over the water, where the bridge was braced.

The men fastened a rope to a beam and then he could see that they were fixing the other end around the negro's neck.

Finally the curious company stood back.

"Have you anything to say?" a voice demanded.

The negro only lolled and groaned, slobbering at the mouth. He was out of his mind.

Then came the concerted action of four men, a lifting of a black mass in the air, and then Davies saw the limp form plunge down and pull up with a creaking sound of rope. In the weak moonlight it seemed as if the body were struggling, but he could not tell. He watched, wide-mouthed and silent, and then the body ceased moving. He heard the company depart, but that did not seem important. Only the black mass swaying in the pale light, over the shiny water of the stream seemed wonderful.

He sat down upon the bank and gazed in silence. He was not afraid. Everything was summery and beautiful. The whole cavalcade disappeared, the moon sank. The light of morning began to show as tender lavender and gray in the east. Still he sat. Then came the roseate hue of day, to which the waters of the stream responded, the white pebbles shining beautifully at the bottom. Still the body hung black and limp, and now a light breeze sprang up and stirred it visibly. At last he arose and made his way back to Pleasant Valley.

Since his duties called him to another day's work here, he idled about, getting the details of what was to be done. He talked with citizens and officials, rode out to the injured girl's home, rode to Baldwin to see the sheriff. There was singular silence and placidity in that corner. The sheriff took his defeat as he did his danger, philosophically.

It was evening again before he remembered that he had not discovered whether the body had been removed. He had not heard why the negro came back or how he was caught. The little cabin was two miles away, but he decided to walk, the night was so springlike. Before he had traveled half way, the moon arose and stretched long shadows of budding trees across his path. It was not long before he came upon the cabin, set well back from the road and surrounded with a few scattered trees. The ground between the door and the road was open, and strewn with the scattered chips of a woodpile. The roof was sagged and the windows patched in places, but, for all that, it had the glow of a home. Through the front door, which stood open, the blaze of a fire shone, its yellow light filling the interior with golden fancies.

Davies stopped at the door and knocked, but received no answer. He looked in on the battered cane chairs and aged furniture with considerable interest.

A door in the rear room opened, and a little negro girl entered, carrying a battered tin lamp, without any chimney. She had not heard his knock, and started perceptibly at the sight of his figure in the doorway. Then she raised her smoking lamp above her head in order to see better and approached.

There was something comical about her unformed figure and loose gingham dress. Her black head was strongly emphasized by little pigtails of hair done up in white twine, which stood out all over her head. Her dark skin was made apparently more so by contrast with her white teeth and the whites of her eyes.

Davies looked at her for a moment and asked, "Is this where Ingalls lives?"

The girl nodded her head. She was exceedingly subdued, and looked as if she had been crying.

"Has the body been brought here?" he asked.

"Yes, suh," she answered, with a soft negro accent.

"When did they bring it home?"

"This moanin'."

"Are you his sister?"

"Yes, suh."

"Well, can you tell me how they caught him?" asked Davies, feeling slightly ashamed to intrude thus. "What did he come back for?"

"To see us," said the girl.

"Well, did he want anything? He didn't come just to see you, did he?"

"Yes, suh," said the girl, "he come to say good-by."

Her voice wavered.

"Didn't he know he might get caught?" asked Davies.

"Yes, suh, I think he did."

She still stood very quietly holding the poor battered lamp up, and looking down.

"Well, what did he have to say?" asked Davies.

"He said he wanted tuh see motha'. He was a-goin' away."

The girl seemed to regard Davies as an official of some sort, and he knew it.

"Can I have a look at the body?" he asked.

The girl did not answer, but started as if to lead the way.

"When is the funeral?" he asked.

"To-morrow."

The girl led him through several bare sheds of rooms to the furthermost one of the line. This last seemed a sort of storage shed for odds and ends. It had several windows, but they were bare of glass, and open to the moonlight, save for a few wooden boards nailed across from the outside. Davies had been wondering all the while at the lonely and forsaken air of the place. No one seemed about but this little girl. If they had colored neighbors, none thought it worth while to call.

Now, as he stepped into this cool, dark, exposed outer room, the desolation seemed complete. The body was there in the middle of the bare room, stretched upon an ironing board, which rested on a box and a chair, and covered with a white sheet. All the corners of the room were quite dark, and only in the middle were shining splotches of moonlight.

Davies came forward, but the girl left him, carrying her lamp. She did not seem able to remain. He lifted the sheet, for he could see well enough, and looked at the stiff, black form. The face was extremely distorted, even in death, and he could see where the rope had tightened. A bar of cool moonlight lay across the face and breast. He was still looking, thinking soon to restore the covering, when a sound, half sigh, half groan, reached his ears.

He started as if a ghost had touched him. His muscles tightened.

Instantly his heart was hammering like mad in his chest. His first impression was that it came from the dead.

"Oo-o-ohh," came the sound again, this time whimpering, as if some one were crying.

He turned quickly, for now it seemed to come from the corner. Greatly disturbed, he hesitated, and then as his eyes strained he caught the shadow of something. It was in the extreme corner, huddled up, dark, almost indistinguishable crouching against the cold walls.

"Oh, oh, oh," was repeated, even more plaintively than before.

Davies began to understand. He approached lightly. Then he made out an old black mammy, doubled up and weeping. She was in the very niche of the corner, her head sunk on her knees, her tears falling, her body rocking to and fro.

Davies drew silently back. Before such grief, his intrusion seemed cold and unwarranted. The sensation of tears came to his eyes. He covered the dead, and withdrew.

Out in the moonlight, he struck a pace, but soon stopped and looked back. The whole dreary cabin, with its one golden door, where the light was, seemed a pitiful thing. He swelled with feeling and pathos as he looked. The night, the tragedy, the grief, he saw it all.

"I'll get that in," he exclaimed, feelingly, "I'll get it all in."

Biographical Glossary

ABBOTT, LYMAN (1835–1922). A Congregational clergyman of liberal views, Abbott was also a prominent journalist. He was closely associated with Henry Ward Beecher, and succeeded Beecher both as editor of the *Christian Union* (later the *Outlook*) and as minister of the Plymouth Congregational Church in Brooklyn. During the 1890's these positions made him widely influential in popular religious thought.

ADAMS, HENRY (1838–1918). The great-grandson of John Adams and the grandson of John Quincy Adams, Henry Adams pursued various careers—principally those of teacher and writer of history—all, he thought, unsuccessfully. A man of great personal force and cultivation, he believed that the grossness of late nineteenth-century American politics prohibited him from entering public life, and he turned more and more to medieval history and to autobiography as means of expressing his sense of cultural displacement. His major work in American history appeared during the 1870's and 1880's, but his most significant books—*Mont-Saint-Michel and Chartres* and *The Education of Henry Adams*—were privately printed in 1904 and 1907.

ADE, GEORGE (1866–1944). Born in Indiana, Ade was graduated from Purdue University and soon afterwards entered newspaper work. In 1890 he became a reporter for the Chicago *News* (later called the *Record*), where he established a reputation as a writer of humorous columns dealing with Chicago life, many of them in dialect. His first great success, however, came with *Fables in Slang* (1899) and *More Fables in Slang* (1900). He later also had a successful career as a playwright.

ALDRICH, THOMAS BAILEY (1836–1907). New Hampshire born, Aldrich settled in Boston and became a successful writer of children's books and sentimental verse. He succeeded Howells as editor of the *Atlantic Monthly* in 1881 and maintained the magazine as a pillar of New England Brahmin culture. After his resignation in 1890, he traveled widely but sustained his place as a commanding New England man of letters.

ALLEN, JAMES LANE (1849–1925). Raised on a Kentucky farm, Allen taught school in his native state and gradually gained a reputation as a local color poet and short story writer. He moved to New York in the early 1890's and wrote his most important and successful novels during this decade, taking up such controversial subjects as youthful sex in *Summer in Arcady* (1896) and Darwinism in *The Reign of Law* (1900) and achieving great popularity with his romances *A Kentucky Cardinal* (1894) and *The Choir Invisible* (1897).

BELLAMY, EDWARD (1850–1898). Bellamy spent most of his life in western Massachusetts, where he was born and raised. He had won a minor reputation as a short story writer interested in social problems when *Looking Backward*, the most famous Utopian romance of its time, appeared in 1888. He thereupon became active in various political and social reform movements, but his health failed and he died shortly after the publication of his second Utopian romance, *Equality* (1897).

BIERCE, AMBROSE (1842–1914?). Born in Ohio, Bierce served with distinction in the Civil War and then migrated to San Francisco. For the rest of his life Bierce was a successful journalist, principally in

San Francisco but also in Washington and London. His column for Hearst's San Francisco *Examiner,* which he began in 1887, was famous for its mordant wit. The 1890's were his most fruitful period of short story writing, but his work attracted little attention. Embittered and morose in his later years, he disappeared in Mexico under mysterious circumstances.

BRYAN, WILLIAM JENNINGS (1860–1925). Although closely identified with Nebraska, Bryan was born and raised in Illinois and did not move to Lincoln until 1887. A lawyer, he was elected to Congress in 1890 but was defeated for the Senate in 1894. He was thus a relatively obscure figure when his famous Cross of Gold speech and the control of the Democratic National Convention by Western and Southern free silver delegates gave him the presidential nomination in 1896 at the age of 36. He was closely defeated by McKinley in one of the most bitter campaigns in American political history. He remained a major figure in Democratic politics, however, and was again defeated by McKinley in 1900 and by Theodore Roosevelt in 1908.

BURROUGHS, JOHN (1837–1921). Burroughs was born and raised near Roxbury, New York, in the lower Catskills, and lived there most of his life. A great lover of the outdoors, he soon began to publish nature essays and by the mid-1870's was firmly established as a popular essayist. During the 1880's he was influenced by John Fiske, the American follower of Herbert Spencer, an influence which is best illustrated in Burroughs' *The Light of Day* (1900).

CHAPMAN, JOHN JAY (1862–1933). Born into a well-to-do New York family, Chapman was graduated from Harvard in 1885. Although he was a man of brilliant intellect and a powerful writer, his life was marred by a series of personal tragedies and serious illnesses. One of Chapman's productive periods, however, was the 1890's, when he was active in New York politics in opposition to Tammany Hall. A writer on many subjects, he was at his best in the polemic essay.

CHOPIN, KATE (1851–1904). Born Kate O'Flaherty in St. Louis, Kate Chopin was married in 1870 to Oscar Chopin and spent the following twelve years in New Orleans and the Cajun country of Louisiana. After her husband's death and her return to St. Louis, she began to write short fiction and, with the appearance of her first collection of stories, *Bayou Folk* (1894), she achieved a modest reputation as a Louisiana local color writer. Her best single work, the novel *The Awakening* (1899), was severely attacked for its "French" themes of feminine sexuality and of adultery, and she produced little afterwards.

CLEMENS, SAMUEL LANGHORNE (MARK TWAIN) (1835–1910). Mark Twain spent most of the 1890's living and traveling abroad. His work of the decade is remarkably varied, from the pot-boiling *Tom Sawyer, Detective* (1896) to the hero-worshipping *Personal Recollections of Joan of Arc* (1896) to the first and best version of *The Mysterious Stranger* (written 1898; published 1916). Plagued by financial and family difficulties for most of the decade, he was both court jester to the American public and a man of intense personal bitterness.

CRANE, STEPHEN (1871–1900). Born into a prominent New Jersey and clerical family, Crane left college after a year for a Bohemian life as a free-lance New York newspaperman. He published his first novel, *Maggie: A Girl of the Streets* (1893), at his own expense, and it was only with the great success of *The Red Badge of Courage* in late 1895 that he became self-supporting as a writer. In the meantime, he had visited the West and Mexico in early 1895 and had written and published some of his best poetry in *The Black Riders* (1895). During the final years of Crane's life he covered the Greco-Turkish and Spanish-American wars, lived extravagantly in England with Cora Taylor (the former madame of a Jacksonville bordello), and wrote incessantly. He died of tuberculosis in the Black Forest.

CROSBY, ERNEST H. (1856–1907). Crosby was from a distinguished and wealthy New York family. He was a successful New York lawyer when the influence of Tolstoy led him into active social reform. He helped found the Social Reform Club of New York and wrote two books on Tolstoy as well as considerable fiction and poetry.

DARROW, CLARENCE (1857–1938). Darrow was a small-town Ohio lawyer until 1887, when he moved to Chicago and quickly became celebrated for his defense of labor leaders and labor causes. A life-long free-thinker of the Tom Paine variety, Darrow had many interests besides law and lectured and wrote on most of them. Among his works is a novel, *Farmington* (1904). In later years, Darrow was best-known as one of the defense lawyers in the Scopes Trial.

DAVIS, RICHARD HARDING (1864–1916). From a literary Philadelphia family (his mother was the novelist Rebecca Harding Davis), Davis entered journalism after leaving college and in 1890 was managing editor of *Harper's Weekly* at the age of 26. He became famous during the 1890's as a foreign correspondent in various exotic and troubled corners of the globe. His fiction was also popular, particularly his Van Bibber stories (light tales of a New York socialite) and his romantic adventure novels. A remarkably handsome man, he is said to have served as the model for Charles Dana Gibson's illustrations of the "all-American" male.

DREISER, THEODORE (1871–1945). The son of a Catholic German immigrant, Dreiser was born in Terre Haute and raised in various Indiana towns. He was a newspaperman in Chicago, St. Louis, and Pittsburgh from 1892 to 1894, but on his move to New York in late 1894 he drifted into editorial work and then free-lance magazine writing. He turned to fiction in the summer of 1899 with a number of short stories, but the attempted suppression of his first novel, *Sister Carrie* (1900), caused him to suffer a nervous collapse, and it was to be over ten years before he published his next novel.

DUNNE, FINLEY PETER (1867–1936). Dunne was born into an Irish-American Chicago family. He entered newspaper work in the mid-1880's, and in the early 1890's began to write his "Mr. Dooley" columns for the Chicago *Post*. Although successful in Chicago, they did not gain wide recognition until 1898, when Dunne broadened their subject to include national concerns and published his first collection, *Mr. Dooley in Peace and in War*. He continued to bring out Mr. Dooley books for many years.

FIELD, EUGENE (1850–1895). Although born in St. Louis, Field was raised primarily in Massachusetts. After holding jobs in various Midwestern newspapers, he became a columnist for the Chicago *News* (later called the Chicago *Record*) in 1883 and soon became famous for his "Sharps and Flats" column, to which he contributed satiric "paragraphs," sentimental children's verse, and much miscellaneous commentary on people and events.

FISKE, JOHN (1842–1901). New England bred, Fiske was graduated from Harvard in 1863 and lived most of his life in Cambridge. He had become a disciple of Herbert Spencer while attending Harvard, and he devoted much of the next two decades to popularizing Spencer's ideas, particularly in his *Outlines of Cosmic Philosophy* (1874). During his later career he published widely in the field of American history, though he continued to be a respected writer and lecturer on philosophical and religious subjects.

FLOWER, BENJAMIN ORANGE (1858–1918). The son of a clergyman, Flower was destined for the church until his great interest in social reform led him into journalism. In 1889 in Boston he founded the *Arena*, one of the most widely-read and influential radical monthlies of the 1890's. The single tax, feminism, Populism, Socialism, temperance—these and many other issues found an outlet in its pages.

FREEMAN, MARY E. WILKINS (1852–1930). Mrs. Freeman was born in Randolph, Massachusetts, where she lived for almost fifty years and which she used as the setting for many of her best stories. She began contributing to *Harper's Monthly* in the mid-1880's, and the publication of her first two collections of stories—*A Humble Romance* (1887) and *A New England Nun* (1891)—established her as one of the best New England local color writers. Her novels were less successful than her stories, and her work declined in quality after her marriage to Dr. Charles Freeman in 1902.

GARLAND, HAMLIN (1860–1940). Garland was raised on Midwestern farms, principally in Wisconsin and Iowa, and did not make his way East to undertake a literary career until 1884. Largely self-educated, he matured slowly, but by the late 1880's was writing powerful stories of Midwestern life. Collected in *Main-Travelled Roads* (1891) and *Prairie Folks* (1893), they remain his best work. A man of wide interests and liberal sympathies, Garland engaged in many reform activities during the early 1890's, among them the single tax, Populism, and feminism. He settled in Chicago in 1894 and a few years later shifted his interests from the Midwest and reform to success as a popular Rocky Mountain romancer.

HEARN, LAFCADIO (1850–1904). Hearn had an exotic background and life. The son of an Irish father and Greek mother, he was raised largely in Ireland and England, but immigrated—penniless—to America in 1869. After some years of dismal poverty, he became a newspaperman, first in Cincinnati and then, in 1877, in New Orleans. In New Orleans he did some of his best writing, particularly in short fiction and the travel sketch. In 1890 Hearn went to Japan to write a series of travel sketches. He remained there for the rest of his life, supporting himself by teaching and writing.

HOVEY, RICHARD (1864–1900). After graduation from Dartmouth in 1885, Hovey pursued a career as poet and dramatist until his early death. Although he devoted most of his energy to a series of ambitious verse dramas on Arthurian themes, he achieved fame primarily as the co-author (with Bliss Carman) of the Bohemian *Songs from Vagabondia* (1894).

HOWELLS, WILLIAM DEAN (1837–1920). By 1890 Howells was established as the foremost American man of letters. After a decade as an editor and writer of travel books, he had blossomed into a novelist in the mid-1870's, and during the next fifteen years wrote his most significant works of fiction. His "Editor's Study" column in *Harper's Monthly* from 1886 to 1892, in which he championed the cause of literary realism, made him a center of controversy during the early 1890's. Howells had lived in Boston for most of his literary career, and his move to New York in 1888 marked both the end of New England domination of the American literary scene and Howells' own increased interest in such social problems as slums and industrial unrest.

HUBBARD, ELBERT (1856–1915). Hubbard was a successful business-man when, in 1892, he decided to become an artist and craftsman. In 1895 in East Aurora, New York (near Buffalo), he founded a com-munity devoted to the arts, in particular to fine printing and to hand-made furniture. Also in 1895 he began to publish from East Aurora the *Philistine,* a popular pseudo-Bohemian magazine. A man of great personal force, Hubbard made a financial success of his various enter-prises and ruled his community with an iron hand. He went down on the *Lusitania* on May 7, 1915.

JAMES, WILLIAM (1842–1910). Like his brother Henry, William James was educated in a miscellaneous fashion in Europe and America. He entered the Lawrence Scientific School of Harvard in 1861 and received his medical degree from Harvard in 1869. From 1872 to the end of his life he was closely associated with Harvard, first as instructor of physiology and ultimately as professor of philosophy. His famous and monumental *Principles of Psychology* appeared in 1890. By the 1890's, however, James' interests had become both philosophical and psychological, and the publication of his *The Will to Believe* (1897) was a major step in the popularization of the philosophy of pragmatism.

JEWETT, SARAH ORNE (1849–1909). Miss Jewett was born and raised in South Berwick, Maine (the Dunnet Landing of *The Country of the Pointed Firs*) and spent much of her life there. She began to contribute stories of the Maine coast to the *Atlantic Monthly* in 1869, and her first collection—*Deephaven* (1877)—established her repu-tation.

LONDON, JACK (1876–1916). London led an adventurous life. His early experiences included oyster pirating in San Francisco Bay, hoboing across the country, and gold mining in Alaska. On his return from the Klondike in the summer of 1898 he set out to become a suc-cessful short story writer. By 1900, with the publication of his first collection, *The Son of the Wolf*, he had "arrived," and for the remainder of his life was one of the most famous writers of his time.

MABIE, HAMILTON WRIGHT (1845–1916).   A graduate of Williams, Mabie practiced law for some years before turning to editing and writing. He was associated for most of his career with the *Christian Union*, a liberal Congregationalist journal, but his reputation was based primarily on a series of books on miscellaneous literary and religious topics published during the 1890's, of which *My Study Fire* (1890) and *Books and Culture* (1896) are characteristic.

MCALLISTER, WARD (1827–1895).   Born in Savannah, McAllister made a fortune as a San Francisco lawyer during the early 1850's and thereupon retired to New York, where he began his long career as a leader of Newport and New York society. By the late 1860's he was the social arbiter of New York. He is famous for having coined the phrase "the four hundred" to describe the socially acceptable number of New York families.

MARKHAM, EDWIN (1852–1940).   Markham was born in Oregon and was raised on a ranch near San Francisco. He drifted into schoolteaching and was an obscure writer of conventional verse when the great popularity of "The Man with the Hoe" catapulted him into fame in 1899. Markham moved from Oakland to New York, and though he continued to write poetry for the remainder of his life, he was never to achieve the popularity or effect of his first great success.

MOODY, WILLIAM VAUGHN (1869–1910).   From a poor Midwestern family, Moody worked his way through a B.A. and M.A. from Harvard and in 1895 became a teacher of English at the University of Chicago. His major interests were creative rather than scholarly, however, and he gained a considerable reputation with the publication of *Poems* in 1901. During the last decade of his life he devoted much of his energy to the writing of plays, both in prose and verse.

NORRIS, FRANK (1870–1902).   The son of a wealthy businessman, Norris was born in Chicago but spent the formative years of his adolescence in San Francisco. He attended the University of California from 1890 to 1894 and then spent an additional year at Harvard, where he wrote early drafts of *McTeague* (1899) and *Vandover and the Brute* (1914). In the spring of 1896 he became a staff writer for the *Wave*, a San Francisco weekly, and held this post until his move to New York in early 1898. *McTeague* was not a critical success, but *The Octopus* (1901) and *The Pit* (1903)—the first two novels in his trilogy of the Wheat—established him as one of the foremost younger American writers. He died of peritonitis following an appendicitis operation.

Riis, Jacob (1849–1914). Born in Denmark, Riis immigrated to New York in 1870. He supported himself in various ways until the late 1870's, when he began his career as a New York journalist. From 1888 to 1899, Riis was a police reporter for the New York *Evening Sun.* His experiences as a reporter led him to write a series of books exposing conditions of New York life, of which *How the Other Half Lives* (1890) was the first and the most famous.

Riley, James Whitcomb (1849–1916). Riley drifted into newspaper work after growing up in Indiana. While a reporter for the Indianapolis *Journal,* he began to write and publish dialect poems under the pseudonym Benj. F. Johnson, of Boone. These were collected in 1883, and by the late 1880's Riley was a successful popular poet.

Robinson, Edwin Arlington (1869–1935). Robinson was raised in Gardiner, Maine, the Tilbury Town of some of his best early poetry. He attended Harvard for two years but then returned to Gardiner, where he wrote the poems of his first two collections—*The Torrent and the Night Before* (1896) and *The Children of the Night* (1897) —neither of which attracted attention. In 1902 Robinson moved to New York, where he worked as a time-keeper on a subway construction project. He continued to write and publish, however, and in 1916 he gained recognition as a major poet with *The Man Against the Sky.*

Roosevelt, Theodore (1858–1919). Of old Dutch New York stock, Roosevelt was graduated from Harvard in 1880. His major interests were history and politics, and in 1882 he was elected to the New York legislature and published his first book of history. During the 1880's, Roosevelt spent much time in the Dakota Territory, where he owned a ranch. Out of his enthusiasm for the West came a number of books, of which his monumental *The Winning of the West* (1889–1896) is the most significant. He held various minor political offices during the 1880's and 90's, including that of Police Commissioner of New York during 1895 and 1896. The election of McKinley in 1896 brought him into the cabinet as Assistant Secretary of the Navy, but his first national fame resulted from the great publicity given the Rough Riders. He was elected governor of New York in 1898 and vice president in 1900.

Sheldon, Charles M. (1857–1946). Sheldon was graduated from Brown University in 1883 and from Andover Theological Seminary in 1886. In 1888 he accepted a pastorate at Topeka, Kansas, where he remained until 1919. In order to encourage attendance at Sunday evening services, Sheldon substituted stories with religious themes for sermons. One such fictional series was *In His Steps*, which was initially published in a Chicago religious journal and then, in 1897, in book form. It became one of the all-time best sellers, with some 25 million copies sold in 21 languages, but because of a faulty copyright Sheldon received little remuneration.

SUMNER, WILLIAM GRAHAM (1840–1910). From a Connecticut working-class background, Sumner was graduated from Yale in 1863. He entered the ministry, but his interests soon centered on social and political matters. In 1872 he accepted a professorship of political science at Yale, where he remained for the rest of his life. A firm proponent of Spencerian and Free Trade economic principles, Sumner wrote and lectured on these subjects with great vigor. Much of his best work of the 1880's and 1890's is in the essay form, with his major book, *Folkways* (1907), appearing late in his career.

THOMPSON, MAURICE (1844–1901). One of a number of prominent late nineteenth-century Indiana authors, Thompson practiced law until 1884, when he turned to editing and to the writing of popular nature essays and fiction. He achieved only moderate success until his *Alice of Old Vincennes* (1900) became a best-seller.

TURNER, FREDERICK JACKSON (1861–1932). Born in western Wisconsin, Turner took a B.A. and M.A. from the University of Wisconsin and a Ph.D. from Johns Hopkins in 1890. He returned to Wisconsin as an assistant professor of history and remained in Madison until 1910, when he moved to Harvard. Although he published comparatively little, Turner's ideas were extremely influential after the appearance of "The Significance of the Frontier in American History," a paper which he read at the World's Columbian Exposition in Chicago in July, 1893.

VINCENT, HENRY (?). An obscure figure, Vincent's only published work appears to be his account of Coxey's Army.

WEAVER, JAMES B. (1833–1912). Raised on an Iowa farm, Weaver practiced law in Iowa and then fought in the Civil War, emerging as a Brigadier General. In the late 1870's he became a leader in the Greenback Party, which opposed restriction of the currency, and was elected to Congress for four terms. When the Populists succeeded the Greenback Party, Weaver continued to be a major figure in the new party and was nominated its presidential candidate in the election of 1892. His *A Call to Action* was published during the campaign.

WHARTON, EDITH (1862–1937). Born Edith Newbold Jones, Mrs. Wharton was from an old and distinguished New York family. In 1885 she married Edward Wharton, a man of wealth 13 years her senior. The marriage was unsuccessful, and by the early 1890's Mrs. Wharton was beginning to write fiction. Her first collection, *The Greater Inclination*, appeared in 1899. The major phase of her career was from *The House of Mirth* (1905) to *The Age of Innocence* (1920).

WISTER, OWEN (1860–1938). Wister was born into a socially prominent Philadelphia family. He seemed destined for a career in music, but ill-health took him to Wyoming for the first time in 1885, and he continued to visit the West for over ten years. Despite having undertaken the profession of law in Philadelphia, in the early 1890's he began to write short stories of the West and collected three volumes of Western stories before *The Virginian* appeared in 1902. Wister's novel was extremely popular, and has been made into a movie four times. Wister continued to write for the rest of his long career but never returned to Western themes.

WYCKOFF, WALTER A. (1865–1908). Wyckoff was graduated from Princeton in 1888 and continued his studies at the Princeton Theological Seminary. Believing that his knowledge of American social problems was inadequate and second-hand, he set out in July, 1891, to live the life of a manual worker. For over a year and a half he worked at various jobs in different parts of the country, from Connecticut to California. On his return, he shifted his interests from theology to sociology and became an assistant professor of political economy at Princeton. His account of his experience, *The Workers* (1897–98), attracted much attention on its appearance.

Chronology

1888

November 6: Benjamin Harrison (Republican) defeats Grover Cleveland (Democrat) for the presidency.

1890

Principal Publications:
  Lafcadio Hearn, *Two Years in the French West Indies.*
  James A. Herne, *Margaret Fleming.*
  W. D. Howells, *A Hazard of New Fortunes.*
  Henry James, *The Tragic Muse.*
  William James, *The Principles of Psychology.*

July 2: Sherman Antitrust Act is passed by the Congress.

1891

Principal Publications:
  Ambrose Bierce, *Tales of Soldiers and Civilians.*
  Ignatius Donnelly, *Caesar's Column.*
  Mary Wilkins Freeman, *A New England Nun.*
  Hamlin Garland, *Main-Travelled Roads.*
  W. D. Howells, *Criticism and Fiction.*

May 4: International Copyright Act is passed by the Congress.
August 12: Death of James Russell Lowell.
September 28: Death of Herman Melville.

1892

Principal Publications:
  Edgar Saltus, *Imperial Purple.*

March 26: Death of Walt Whitman.
July 4–5: Populist Party National Convention.

July 6: Battle between strikers and Pinkerton agents at Carnegie's Homestead works.

September 7: Death of John Greenleaf Whittier.

November 8: Grover Cleveland (Democrat) defeats Benjamin Harrison (Republican) and James B. Weaver (Populist) for the presidency.

1893

Principal Publications:

Stephen Crane, *Maggie: A Girl of the Streets.*

F. Marion Crawford, *The Novel: What It Is.*

Henry B. Fuller, *The Cliff-Dwellers.*

Frederick Jackson Turner, "The Significance of the Frontier in American History."

May–October: World's Columbian Exposition, Chicago.

June 27: Wall Street collapse.

1894

Principal Publications:

Bliss Carman and Richard Hovey, *Songs from Vagabondia.*

Kate Chopin, *Bayou Folk.*

Paul L. Ford, *The Honorable Peter Stirling.*

Hamlin Garland, *Crumbling Idols.*

William H. Harvey, *Coin's Financial School.*

Lafcadio Hearn, *Glimpses of Unfamiliar Japan.*

W. D. Howells, *A Traveler from Altruria.*

Henry Demarest Lloyd, *Wealth Against Commonwealth.*

Mark Twain, *Pudd'nhead Wilson.*

March 25–May 1: "Coxey's Army" marches on Washington.

May 11: Pullman strike begins in Chicago. (General railway strike called in June; Cleveland sends U.S. troops to Chicago in July.)

October 7: Death of Oliver Wendell Holmes.

1895

Principal Publications:

Brooks Adams, *The Law of Civilization and Decay.*

Stephen Crane, *The Red Badge of Courage.*

Hamlin Garland, *Rose of Dutcher's Coolly.*

February 24: Outbreak of the Cuban revolution.

1896

Principal Publications:
  Harold Frederic, *The Damnation of Theron Ware.*
  Sarah Orne Jewett, *The Country of the Pointed Firs.*
  Theodore Roosevelt, *The Winning of the West* (1889–1896)
  Mark Twain, *Joan of Arc.*

August 12: Gold is discovered in the Klondike. (The Klondike gold
  rush occurred in the summers of 1897, 1898, and 1899.)
November 3: William McKinley (Republican) defeats William Jennings Bryan (Democrat) for the presidency.

1897

Principal Publications:
  Richard Harding Davis, *Soldiers of Fortune.*
  Henry James, *The Spoils of Poynton* and *What Maisie Knew.*
  William James, *The Will to Believe and Other Essays.*
  S. Weir Mitchell, *Hugh Wynne, Free Quaker.*
  E. A. Robinson, *The Children of the Night.*
  Charles M. Sheldon, *In His Steps.*

1898

Principal Publications:
  John Jay Chapman, *Causes and Consequences.*
  Finley Peter Dunne, *Mr. Dooley in Peace and in War.*
  Charles Major, *When Knighthood Was in Flower.*
  Edward N. Westcott, *David Harum.*
  Walter A. Wyckoff, *The Workers . . . The East* and *The Workers
    . . . The West* (1897–98).

February 15: Battleship *Maine* blows up in Havana harbor.
April 25: United States declares war against Spain.
May 1: Admiral Dewey destroys the Spanish Pacific fleet at Manila
  Bay.
June 7: First American troops land in Cuba.
July 1: Battle of El Caney and San Juan Hill, including the "charge"
  of the Rough Riders.
August 12: End of hostilities between the United States and Spain.
November 8: Theodore Roosevelt is elected governor of New York.
December 10: Treaty of Paris, formally ending the Spanish-American
        War, results in America gaining possession of Guam, Puerto

Rico, and the Philippines. Hawaii had been annexed earlier in 1898.

1899

Principal Publications:
> George Ade, *Fables in Slang*.
> Kate Chopin, *The Awakening*.
> Winston Churchill, *Richard Carvel*.
> Stephen Crane, *The Monster and Other Stories*.
> John Dewey, *The School and Society*.
> John Fiske, *A Century of Science* and *Through Nature to God*
> Paul L. Ford, *Janice Meredith*.
> Edwin Markham, *The Man with the Hoe*.
> Frank Norris, *McTeague*.
> Theodore Roosevelt, *The Rough Riders*.
> Booth Tarkington, *The Gentleman from Indiana*.
> Thorstein Veblen, *The Theory of the Leisure Class*.

February 4: Philippine rebellion against American occupation begins (to last till mid-1902).

1900

Principal Publications:
> Theodore Dreiser, *Sister Carrie*.
> Mary Johnston, *To Have and To Hold*.
> Jack London, *The Son of the Wolf*.
> William Vaughn Moody, *The Masque of Judgment*.
> Theodore Roosevelt, *The Strenuous Life*.
> Maurice Thompson, *Alice of Old Vincennes*.
> Mark Twain, *The Man That Corrupted Hadleyburg*.

June 5: Death of Stephen Crane.
November 6: William McKinley (Republican) defeats William Jennings Bryan (Democrat) for the presidency. Theodore Roosevelt is elected vice president.

Selected Bibliography

I have limited this list to works which deal either with the period in general or with specific dominant issues of the period.

AARON, DANIEL. *Men of Good Hope: A Story of American Progressives.* New York, 1951.

AHNEBRINK, LARS. *The Beginnings of Naturalism in American Fiction.* Cambridge, Mass., 1950.

BEER, THOMAS. *The Mauve Decade: American Life at the End of the Nineteenth Century.* New York, 1926.

BERTHOFF, WARNER. *The Ferment of Realism: American Literature, 1884–1919.* New York, 1965.

BREMMER, ROBERT H. *From the Depths: The Discovery of Poverty in the United States.* New York, 1956.

BROOKS, VAN WYCK. *The Confident Years: 1885–1915.* New York, 1952.

CADY, EDWIN H. "The Strenuous Life as a Theme in American Cultural History." In *New Voices in American Studies,* ed. Ray B. Browne et al. Lafayette, Ind., 1966.

CANBY, HENRY SEIDEL. *The Age of Confidence: Life in the Nineties.* New York, 1934.

DITZION, SIDNEY H. *Marriage, Morals, and Sex in America: A History of Ideas.* New York, 1953.

FALK, ROBERT P. "The Literary Criticism of the Genteel Decades, 1870–1900." In *The Development of American Literary Criticism,* ed. Floyd Stovall. Chapel Hill, N.C., 1955.

FAULKNER, HAROLD U. *Politics, Reform, and Expansion, 1890–1900.* New York, 1959.

FREIDEL, FRANK B. *The Splendid Little War.* Boston, 1958.

GINGER, RAY. *Altgeld's America: The Lincoln Ideal Versus Changing Realities.* New York, 1958.

HICKS, JOHN D. *The Populist Revolt: A History of the Farmers' Alliance and the People's Party.* Minneapolis, 1931.

HIGHAM, JOHN. "The Reorientation of American Culture in the 1890's." In *The Origins of Modern Consciousness,* ed. John Weiss. Detroit, 1965.

HOFSTADTER, RICHARD. *The Age of Reform: From Bryan to Franklin Delano Roosevelt.* New York, 1955.

——. *Social Darwinism in American Thought, 1860–1915.* Philadelphia, 1944.

KAZIN, ALFRED. *On Native Grounds: An Interpretation of Modern American Prose Literature.* New York, 1942.

KINDILIEN, CARLIN T. *American Poetry in the Eighteen Nineties.* Providence, R.I., 1956.

KNIGHT, GRANT C. *The Critical Period in American Literature.* Chapel Hill, N.C., 1951.

LYNN, KENNETH S. *The Dream of Success: A Study of the Modern American Imagination.* Boston, 1955.

MARTIN, JAY. *Harvests of Change: American Literature, 1865–1914.* Englewood Cliffs, N.J., 1967.

MARX, LEO. *The Machine in the Garden: Technology and the Pastoral Ideal in America.* New York, 1964.

PERSONS, STOW, ed. *Evolutionary Thought in America.* New Haven, 1950.

PIZER, DONALD. *Realism and Naturalism in Nineteenth-Century American Literature.* Carbondale, Ill., 1966.

PRATT, JULIUS W. *Expansionists of 1898: The Acquisition of Hawaii and the Spanish Islands.* Baltimore, 1936.

SCHLESINGER, ARTHUR M. *The Rise of the City, 1878–1898.* New York, 1933.

SMITH, HENRY NASH. *Virgin Land: The American West as Symbol and Myth.* Cambridge, Mass., 1950.

TAYLOR, GEORGE R., ed. *The Turner Thesis Concerning the Role of the Frontier in American History.* Boston, 1949.

WALCUTT, CHARLES C. *American Literary Naturalism: A Divided Stream.* Minneapolis, 1956.

WASSERSTROM, WILLIAM. *Heiress of All the Ages: Sex and Sentiment in the Genteel Tradition.* Minneapolis, 1959.

ZIFF, LARZER. *The American 1890s: Life and Times of a Lost Generation.* New York, 1966.

ABCDEFGHIJ—CO—7654321